WITHDRAWN

THE ASHGATE RESEARCH COMPANION TO BIOSOCIAL THEORIES OF CRIME

What I love about the field of Criminology is that insofar as theories are concerned, Criminology welcomes all comers with open arms, while insofar as empirical methodology is concerned, Criminology never strays from its singular devotion to a standard of excellence. This exciting new book edited by Beaver and Walsh is quintessentially Criminology. It marries innovative bio-social theory of crime with rigorous empirical science…and somehow manages to make it all very readable. Anyone who wishes to be a contemporary criminologist must make themselves familiar with the content of this new book. Any criminologist who does not read this book is by definition falling behind the times.

Terrie E. Moffitt, Duke University, USA and King's College London, UK

This is the most impressive, comprehensive, and informative review of research on biological contributions to criminology. It should be required reading for all criminologists who are interested in understanding and explaining criminal behaviour.

David P. Farrington, Cambridge University, UK

ASHGATE
RESEARCH
COMPANION

The *Ashgate Research Companions* are designed to offer scholars and graduate students a comprehensive and authoritative state-of-the-art review of current research in a particular area. The companions' editors bring together a team of respected and experienced experts to write chapters on the key issues in their speciality, providing a comprehensive reference to the field.

The Ashgate Research Companion to Biosocial Theories of Crime

Edited by

KEVIN M. BEAVER
Florida State University, USA

ANTHONY WALSH
Boise State University, USA

ASHGATE

Published by
Ashgate Publishing Limited
Wey Court East
Union Road
Farnham
Surrey GU9 7PT
England

Ashgate Publishing Company
Suite 420
101 Cherry Street
Burlington,
VT 05401-4405
USA

www.ashgate.com

British Library Cataloguing in Publication Data
The Ashgate research companion to biosocial theories of crime.
   1. Criminology. 2. Criminal behavior--Physiological
   aspects. 3. Criminal behavior--Genetic aspects. 4. Crime--
   Sociological aspects. 5. Evolutionary psychology.
   I. Biosocial theories of crime II. Beaver, Kevin M.
   III. Walsh, Anthony, 1941-
   364.2'4-dc22

Library of Congress Cataloging-in-Publication Data
The Ashgate research companion to biosocial theories of crime / [edited] by Kevin M. Beaver and Anthony Walsh.
      p. cm.
   Includes bibliographical references and index.
   ISBN 978-1-4094-0843-7 (hbk) -- ISBN 978-1-4094-0844-4 (ebook)
1. Criminology. 2. Criminal psychology. 3. Criminal behavior--Genetic aspects.
4. Environmental psychology. I. Beaver, Kevin M. II. Walsh, Anthony, 1941-

HV6025.A82 2011
364.2'5--dc22

2011015947

ISBN 9781409408437 (hbk)
ISBN 9781409408444 (ebk)

Printed and bound in Great Britain by
MPG Books Group, UK

Contents

PART VI: IMPLICATIONS OF BIOSOCIAL RESEARCH

List of Figures

List of Contributors

Todd A. Armstrong, Sam Houston State University

Kevin M. Beaver, Florida State University

Charles Beekman, The Pennsylvania State University

Denise Paquette Boots, University of Texas—Dallas

H. Harrington Cleveland, The Pennsylvania State University

Raymond E. Collins, Rutgers Alumni Association

Matt DeLisi, Iowa State University

Lisabeth Fisher DiLalla, Southern Illinois University School of Medicine

Ryan M. Ellsworth, University of Missouri

Christopher J. Ferguson, Texas A&M International University

Yu Gao, University of Pennsylvania

Sufna Gheyara, Southern Illinois University School of Medicine

Chris L. Gibson, University of Florida

Andrea Glenn, University of Pennsylvania

Ralph Groom, Saint Louis University

William F. McKibbin, University of Michigan—Flint

Kristan Moore, University of Cincinnati

David G. Mueller, Boise State University

Jamie Newsome, University of Cincinnati

Craig T. Palmer, University of Missouri

Melissa Peskin, University of Pennsylvania

Adrian Raine, University of Pennsylvania

Anna Rudo-Hutt, University of Pennsylvania

Joseph Rukus, University of Florida

Todd K. Shackelford, Oakland University

Stephen G. Tibbetts, California State University, San Bernardino

Kyle Treiber, University of Cambridge

Michael G. Vaughn, Saint Louis University

Anthony Walsh, Boise State University

Richard P. Wiebe, Fitchburg State University

John Paul Wright, University of Cincinnati

Yaling Yang, University of Pennsylvania

Yao Zheng, The Pennsylvania State University

PART I
INTRODUCTION AND
OVERVIEW OF BIOSOCIAL
CRIMINOLOGY

Biosocial Criminology

Kevin M. Beaver and Anthony Walsh

Introduction

There is virtually an endless supply of criminological theories designed to explain the various factors that ultimately lead to the development of criminal, delinquent, and antisocial behaviors. These theories are remarkably different in the factors that are identified as being salient to the etiology of criminal behavior. Some theories, for example, focus on parental socialization, some focus on neighborhood-level factors, some focus on subcultures, others focus on peer group socialization, and so on. The common theme cutting across virtually every single dominant criminological theory is that social factors are the be-all and end-all when it comes to explaining crime and other forms of antisocial behavior. If theories are to be judged on their predictive ability and their ability to organize known correlates into a coherent and unified framework, then the existing mainstream criminological theories do not have much merit. For the most part, these theories are not very good at explaining crime nor are they very good at predicting who will eventually become a criminal. To illustrate, rarely do multivariate regression models reveal that a single variable derived from a criminological theory explains more than 10–20 percent of the variance, with most explaining less than 10 percent of the variance. Even when multiple indicators of a theory or of competing theories are simultaneously entered into a regression equation, the total amount of variance explained is typically far less than 30 percent. The point is that whether theoretically informative variables are examined in isolation or cumulatively, they leave most of the variance in antisocial behaviors unexplained.

Because criminological theories and research have relatively little explanatory power, it would seem reasonable that newer criminological theories should be developed that focus on a broader swath of variables other than those typically studied by criminologists. Unfortunately, this has not historically been the case. Instead, criminologists have tended to develop new theories that integrate the same old sociological variables simply packaged in a different way. Or, worse, they have argued that the empirical studies testing these theories are not measuring the key constructs correctly or that empirical studies have other flaws that make the results not believable. The bedrock of science is falsification, whereby theories and ideas that are not supported are discarded (or at least modified) and replaced with newer theories. Criminology has tended to work in an opposite way by not falsifying any theory, but continuing to add more and more theories to the existing pool. The end result is an even larger number of criminological theories, each of which is relatively weak at explaining crime, delinquency, and antisocial behavior.

What criminology needs is somewhat of a paradigm shift, where a broader array of variables is examined, where new ideas and explanations are offered, and where existing knowledge is linked to other disciplines. Enter biosocial criminology. Biosocial criminology is an emerging interdisciplinary perspective that seeks to explain crime and antisocial behavior by recognizing the potential importance of a host of factors including genetic factors, neuropsychological factors, environmental factors, and evolutionary factors (Beaver, 2009; Walsh, 2009; Walsh & Beaver, 2009). This represents a dramatic departure from mainstream criminological theories that ignore the potential explanatory power of genetics, neuropsychology, and evolutionary psychology. This departure from mainstream criminology, however, might be exactly what is needed to advance the field and, more importantly, to develop criminological theories that are much more accurate and much more powerful explanations of antisocial behaviors.

The goal of this volume is to provide an overview to biosocial criminology and the central issues related to this perspective. We have been fortunate enough to pull together some of the leading experts on the biosocial perspective to create a well-rounded, informative, and cutting-edge book on the emerging field of biosocial criminology. The contributions to this book have been organized into six different, but interrelated themes, each of which pertains to a different aspect of biosocial criminology. In the following pages, we will provide a brief overview of each section of the book and a short introduction to each chapter.

Overview of Biosocial Criminology

Biosocial criminology is an interdisciplinary perspective that is designed to integrate information across diverse fields of study to form a unified and coherent perspective from which to study crime and criminals. Although this approach to studying crime may seem relatively obvious to those in disciplines other than criminology, in fact this is quite a revolutionary and controversial idea within the confines of criminology. For the most part, criminologists view biosocial explanations to crime and antisocial behaviors as dangerous and oppressive. Environmental theories, in contrast, are seen as progressive and humane. To understand why this sentiment exists among criminologists it is essential to reflect on their academic training. Historically, most criminologists earned their undergraduate and graduate degrees in sociology programs, where they learned the ins and outs of how social institutions affect human behaviors. At the same time, most sociology programs and most sociologists despise any mention that biology could affect human behavior. The problem, however, is that sociologists know virtually nothing about biology and genetics and thus are not in an objective position to assess its influence on behavior. Van den Berghe (1990, p. 177) captured the state of sociology accurately when he noted that "[s]ociological resistance to biological thinking is in large part *trained* incompetence, not simply garden-variety anthropocentrism. Many sociologists are not merely oblivious about biology; they are militantly and proudly ignorant." This "trained incompetence" has unfortunately trickled down to criminologists, where criminologists know virtually nothing about biology and genetics. To illustrate, a recent survey of criminologists revealed that the modal number of graduate-level biology courses taken by criminologists was zero, while the modal number of graduate-level sociology courses taken by criminologists was 10 (Cooper, Walsh, & Ellis, 2010). It takes no stretch of the imagination to consider the ramifications that this graduate-level training has on the way criminologists conduct research and teach their courses.

There is reason to be optimistic, however. During the past five years or so, an emerging number of empirical studies have been published by criminologists and within criminological journals that are devoted to exploring the biosocial origins of antisocial behaviors. These studies have relied on quantitative approaches to study the utility of biosocial criminology as opposed to more theoretical arguments that peppered the field prior to the 2000s. Part of the reason for the shift from a theoretical tradition to a more quantitative tradition has to do with the availability of data. Today there are a number of large, longitudinal samples that are available to criminologists that include genetic/biological markers as well as more traditional environmental markers. This advance in data has allowed criminologists to begin to explore virtually every measure of interest to criminologists. And, the results of these studies, which will be discussed in detail throughout the rest of this volume, have provided some strong support in favor of the biosocial perspective.

Criminologists employing the biosocial perspective are interested in examining the biological/genetic factors that are related to crime as well as the environmental factors that are related to crime. It should be noted that this approach is not a throwback to the outdated nature versus nurture debate. Instead, the biosocial perspective recognizes the exquisite complexity of human behavior and thus focuses on the various ways in which biological/genetic factors interface with environmental factors to produce differing propensities for antisocial behaviors. Seen in this way, the biosocial perspective is not about nature versus nurture, but more about nature and nurture (Rutter, 2006). Other fields of study, including psychology and psychiatry, have already embraced this interdisciplinary approach, largely because the evidence implicating both biology/genetics and the environment in the etiology of human behaviors is so overwhelming that it could be considered axiomatic. For criminologists, this type of approach to studying crime is relatively foreign. This book will explore the various ways in which a biosocial perspective can be used to study crime, criminals, and antisocial behavior.

Part I of this volume contains three chapters that are designed to provide an introduction and overview to the biosocial perspective. The chapter penned by Anna Rudo-Hutt and her colleagues provides a thorough review of the literature examining the biosocial interactions and correlates to criminal behavior. One of the themes that emerges from this chapter and that continually pops up in other chapters is that biological/genetic effects are frequently quite small or nonexistent unless they are paired to a criminogenic environment. The third chapter in this section was written by Todd Armstrong and explores the link between heart rate and criminal involvement. In this chapter, Armstrong provides a critical and exhaustive review of the various ways in which heart rate could ultimately lead to crime.

In the chapters that follow you will be taken on a journey through the biosocial perspective beginning with genetics then moving through the brain, environmental factors, evolutionary psychology, and finally you will end with a discussion of the implications of biosocial research. Our hope is that these chapters will inspire more criminologists to join the ranks of biosocial criminology and seek to unpack the biosocial underpinnings to antisocial behaviors.

Genetics and Crime

Of all the areas of biosocial criminology, the potential link between genetics and crime instills the most fear and the most backlash among mainstream criminologists. Mainstream criminologists, for example, worry that if genes are found to be implicated in the etiology of antisocial behaviors, then a new eugenics movement will be born. There are also concerns about whether genetic research would trickle into sentencing decisions, such that offenders who have genetic propensities for crimes will be locked away for long periods of time. Much of the opposition to studying genetics and crime, however, flows from ignorance. As the chapters in this volume make clear, genes are not deterministic nor are they fatalistic; they work in a probabilistic way that increase the likelihood of displaying certain forms of antisocial behaviors. If criminologists simply learned a bit about genetics, and the way that they could affect criminal behavior, then most of their fears would likely be laid to rest.

There are two main ways that biosocial criminologists explore the genetic foundations to antisocial behaviors. First, samples of kinship pairs (especially twin pairs) are analyzed to decompose phenotypic variance into three components: a heritability component, a shared environmental component, and a nonshared environmental component. Heritability captures the proportion of variance in a phenotype accounted for by genetic factors. The shared environment captures all non-genetic factors that make siblings similar to each other, while the nonshared environmental captures all non-genetic factors that make siblings different from each other. Together, heritability, the shared environment, and the nonshared environment account for 100 percent of the phenotypic variance.

These types of research designs—broadly referred to as behavioral genetic research designs—are frequently attacked by criminologists and other social scientists for a number of different reasons. Interestingly, though, behavioral genetic research designs actually provide the strongest evidence in favor of environmental effects on antisocial behaviors. In traditional criminological research designs, the effects that genes could potentially have on antisocial behaviors are assumed to be zero—that is, they are not measured and thus represent a potential confounder. Any statistically significant associations that are detected between measures of the environment and measures of antisocial behaviors therefore could be spurious. Indeed, empirical research tends to suggest that associations between family environments and criminal and delinquent outcomes are attenuated significantly and sometimes rendered spurious when genetic effects are modeled directly (Wright & Beaver, 2005). So, instead of fearing behavioral genetic research designs, criminologists should embrace these methodologies as they provide some of the most accurate ways to isolate environmental effects on a range of antisocial behaviors and personality traits.

The second main way that biosocial criminologists test for genetic effects on antisocial phenotypes is by employing molecular genetic association research designs. With this type of research design, biosocial criminologists go directly to the DNA and examine whether specific DNA markers that vary across people (known as genetic polymorphisms) are associated with variation in antisocial phenotypes. Molecular genetic association studies for crime and delinquency remain relatively in their infancy, but already there is a solid body of research linking specific polymorphisms, especially those involved in neurotransmission, to an array of antisocial outcomes (Gunter, Vaughn, & Philibert, 2010). As more and more molecular genetic studies are undertaken by biosocial criminologists, it is likely that our knowledge of the molecular genetics to crime will increase at an exponential rate.

One of the key findings to emerge from the molecular genetic research is that single polymorphisms tend to have relatively small effects on antisocial behaviors when examined in isolation. Single genes can have quite large effects, though, when they are paired with criminogenic environments. This finding, where genetic effects are amplified in the face of environmental liabilities, is known as a gene–environment interaction. Gene–environment interaction research represents one of the "hot topic" areas in the behavioral sciences and it has even gained attention among some social scientists. This area of research holds particular promise for criminology as it will help to add specificity to theory and research by indicating who is most likely to be affected by criminogenic environments.

The chapters included in this section of the volume elaborate on many of these issues and topics related to genetics and crime. Lisabeth Fisher DiLalla and Sufna Gheyara open this section by providing an overview of the genetics of criminality and delinquency. Their chapter covers the methodologies that are employed in genetic research and it also discuss the findings of the literature that has tested for a genetic basis to criminal and delinquent behavior. Chapter 5, written by John Paul Wright and his colleagues, expands on the gene–crime link by discussing the molecular genetics underpinnings to crime and delinquency. This chapter focuses on acquainting the reader with the basics to molecular genetics and then discussing the specific genes that have been found to be associated with criminal behavior. Christopher Ferguson follows up with a chapter devoted to examining the gene–

environment interactions as they relate to antisocial behavior. Ferguson's chapter takes the reader on a tour of some of the landmark studies that have found criminal behavior to be shaped, in part, by gene–environment interactions. Together, these three chapters provide a very detailed and informative introduction to the link between genetics and criminal involvement.

The Brain and Crime

The human brain weighs only about three pounds, but it represents the single most exquisitely complex entity known to man. Virtually every single action, thought, decision, and feeling travels through the neural highways housed in the brain. Information is processed across the brain through neurotransmission. During the process of neurotransmission, neurotransmitters are released from neurons where they cross the synapse and lock into other neurons. The type of neurotransmitter that locks into the neuron will dictate the resulting response. The process of neurotransmission is especially critical to normal human functioning and fluctuations in baseline levels of certain neurotransmitters, such as dopamine and serotonin, have been linked to an array of psychopathologies, including antisocial behaviors. The first chapter included in this section of the volume, written by Raymond Collins, explores the link between neurotransmitters and antisocial behavior by providing an overview of neurotransmitters and the research examining their association with various types of aggression.

Not all human brains, however, are created equally. Some brains are better able to arrive at rational decisions than others, some brains are better able to complete complex mathematical equations, and some brains are better able to control the innate impulses related to sexual arousal and aggression. These phenotypic differences have been mapped, in part, to variation in both the structure and the functioning of the human brain. Brain structure captures quantifiable aspects of the brain, such as the size, length, volume, and density of certain areas of the brain. Brain function, in contrast, captures the processes that are performed by the brain, such as how active the brain is when performing certain tasks.

Advanced neuroimaging machines are used to measure both brain structure and brain function. The earliest neuroimaging techniques, such as computed axial tomography (CAT) scans and magnetic resonance imaging (MRI), were used to assess brain structure. Relatively recent developments have led to the creation of imaging machines that are now able to examine the functioning of the brain. Functional magnetic resonance imaging (fMRI), positron emission tomography (PET), and single photon emission computed tomography (SPECT) are three of the more widely used imaging techniques that assess the functioning of the human brain. A good deal of neuroimaging studies have been undertaken to examine whether the structure and the functioning of the brain is related to different types of antisocial behaviors. The results of these studies have provided strong evidence revealing that both the structure and the functioning of the brain are implicated, to some degree, in the etiology of aggression, vio... (Wright, Tibbetts, & Daigle, 2008).

The available neuroimaging research has identified ... brain that have been the most consistently linked with antiso... limbic system and the prefrontal cortex. The limbic system is locate... the brainstem and includes a number of primitive brain structures, in... amygdala, the hippocampus, and the thalamus. The main way in which the ... system is related to antisocial behavior is by creating emotions, such as ange... and jealousy, that may ultimately facilitate the commission of a violent act. Matt DeLisi's chapter in this section of the volume provides a very thorough and detailed explanation of the limbic system and the evidence tying it to the development of antisocial behaviors.

The other area of the brain that has been implicated in crime, aggression, and antisocial behavior is the prefrontal cortex. Located directly behind the forehead, the prefrontal cortex is often referred to as the CEO of the brain and is responsible for higher-order executive functions, such as the ability to delay gratification and the ability to control impulses. Because the prefrontal cortex is interconnected with the limbic system, it is largely responsible for curtailing the emotions and impulses that are generated from the structures in the limbic system. If the limbic system is overactive or if the prefrontal cortex is underactive and unable to quell the emotions flowing from the limbic system, then this is a recipe for antisocial behavior. The chapter by Denise Boots in this section of the volume explores the various ways in which the brain, including the prefrontal cortex, is related to violence over the entire life course. This chapter should prove to be especially useful for those who are beginning to search for how neurobiological perspectives can inform the study of crime and criminals.

Even though the brain appears to be centrally involved in the development of antisocial behaviors, there has been little attempt to create criminological theories organized around the brain. One of the main exceptions is Moffitt's (1993) developmental taxonomy theory focusing on the etiology of life-course-persistent (LCP) offenders. This highly influential theory postulates that LCP offenders, who make up only about 6 percent of the population but account for more than 50 percent of all crimes, develop because of two interacting factors: neuropsychological deficits and an adverse environment. The dynamic interplay between these factors sets an individual on an LCP trajectory that is nearly impossible to derail. Moffitt's theory has accrued a significant amount of empirical support, but interestingly the criminogenic effects associated with neuropsychological deficits (and other brain structures/functions) have not been integrated into any other mainstream criminological theory. Kyle Treiber's chapter, however, represents a step in the right direction to correct this gap in the criminological literature. Treiber shows how situational action theory (SAT) is informed and guided by neurobiological factors. This type of theoretical emphasis on biology and neurobiology is needed to increase the accuracy of criminological theories (Walsh, 2002).

social criminology among
...y and genetics are studied,
...e ignored. Nothing could be
...y concerned with identifying the
etiology of antisocial behaviors as
...ctors that are important. The main
controls for the effects of genes while
...nainstream criminological research is
...id Rowe (1994) brought attention to this
...(1998) expanded on Rowe's argument. The
...ng the association between an environmental
va...   ...ion, and a child outcome, such as antisocial
behavi...   ...fied if the research design does not control for
genetic fac...   ...ally all criminological studies fail to control for
genes necessaril,   ...he effects of environmental variables are upwardly
biased. For example,   ...e a study revealed that parents who are abusive to
their children will have   ...ildren who ultimately mature into antisocial adults.
Most social scientists would interpret this finding to mean that there is a causal
connection between abusing a child and having them turn out to be antisocial. An
alternative explanation exists, however. It is quite possible, for instance, that the
genetic factors that cause a parent to be abusive are transmitted to the child, which,
in turn, causes them to turn out to be antisocial. In short, the link between abuse
and antisocial behavior is spurious owing to the confounding effects of genes.
Unfortunately, criminological research rarely considers this possibility.

Another drawback to mainstream criminological research examining the effects
of environments on crime is that most environments are influenced, at least in part,
by genetic factors. This type of gene–environment interplay is referred to as gene–
environment correlation and highlights the fact that environments are not purely
social, but rather are biosocial entities affected by genetic propensities. To illustrate,
exposure to antisocial peer groups has emerged as one of the strongest and most
consistent predictors of adolescent delinquency. Usually, measures of delinquent
peers are claimed by social learning theorists and purportedly capture the social
process by which youths learn to become delinquent. In stark contrast to this view
is the behavioral genetic research revealing that exposure to antisocial peer groups
is structured in large part by genetic factors. Selecting and choosing environments
(in this case, peer groups) is governed by each person's unique genotype. The first
chapter in this section, written by H. Harrington Cleveland and his colleagues,
expands on these issues by exploring the problems and biases with mainstream
criminological research that does not take into account genetic effects. Cleveland
et al.'s chapter is particular important to criminologists because it 1) shows the
limitations of standard criminological research and 2) offers guidance for how
these limitations can be overcome.

Another point of departure from mainstream criminological research is that biosocial research places a great deal of emphasis on nonshared environmental factors, but not much of an emphasis on shared environmental factors. Recall that nonshared environmental factors are environments that are unique to each sibling which make them different from each other, whereas shared environments are environments that are the same between siblings that make them more alike. Behavioral genetic research has consistently revealed that shared environments account for only a small percentage of variance in antisocial behaviors, typically around 10 percent or less. Nonshared environments, on the other hand, have been shown to be highly influential, usually explaining around 40 percent of the variance in measures of antisocial behaviors. These findings have been generated in thousands of studies using hundreds of thousands of kinship pairs and thus are unlikely the result of a statistical or methodological artifact.

Although behavioral genetic research based on kinship pairs is able to estimate the proportion of variance accounted for by nonshared environmental factors, these research designs reveal no information about the specific nonshared environments that are influential. Other research designs are therefore needed to uncover the specific nonshared environments related to antisocial behaviors. One group of nonshared environments that is thought to be involved in the development of antisocial tendencies is birth complications. Birth complications represent one of the first environmental factors that are encountered and very serious birth complications can cause irreversible damage to the brain. The chapter by Stephen Tibbetts examines the literature testing for associations between birth complications and criminality. Tibbetts highlights many of the key findings drawn from this body of research and also offers suggestions for areas that need to be addressed in the future.

The biosocial perspective also recognizes the saliency of environments that occur during the very first few years after birth, a time period when the human brain is undergoing significant growth that can be affected by environmental stimuli. Although criminological research also recognizes the importance of environments early in life, most of the research produced by criminologists focuses on environments that are encountered during adolescence or even adulthood. There is now a sizeable pool of evidence indicating, however, that early life environments are the ones that have the most lasting effects on children. Matt DeLisi and Michael Vaughn's chapter discusses the literature on early family environments and their connection with the development of childhood temperaments that are linked with subsequent problem behaviors.

The last chapter in this section of the volume deals with one of the hallmark issues in criminology: the link between social class and crime. Criminological theory and research consistently suggests that persons from low social class are more likely to be involved in criminal behavior when compared against those residing in high social class families. What has eluded criminologists, however, are the underlying processes that ultimately produce such criminal behavior. Anthony Walsh and David Mueller's chapter examines the connection between social class and crime by applying a biosocial perspective to it. The end result is a chapter that provides some much needed insight into how, why, and in what ways social class and crime are linked.

Evolutionary Psychology and Crime

The human genome is the DNA library of the accumulated wisdom of millions of years of natural selection. Genes that sit on the shelves of that library are there because they provided advantages to our ancestors in the pursuit of the shared goals of all life forms: survival and reproduction. Evolutionary psychology is an approach that utilizes the synthesis of natural selection and population genetics to test hypotheses regarding the functional advantages conferred by those traits. It is interested in distal "why" questions rather than proximate "how" questions of interest to geneticists and other behavioral scientists. Evolutionary psychology is even more environmentally friendly than behavior genetics because it looks for environmental causes of behavioral variation and focuses on human similarities rather than differences. Evolutionary psychologists do not deny human genetic differences distributed around adaptive means; they simply focus on central tendency rather than variation.

Evolution is succinctly defined as changes in a population's gene pool over time by selective retention and elimination of genes. The nature of any living thing is the sum of its evolutionary adaptations. An adaptation is a design feature that arose and promoted its increased frequency through an extended period of natural selection because it functioned to increase survival and/or reproductive success. These evolutionary design features may be morphological, physiological, or behavioral.

Criminologists are interested in behavior, and while few social scientists deny evolutionary thinking as it relates to morphology and physiology, many have an aversion to analyzing human behavior from a Darwinian perspective. Those with such an aversion fail to realize that it would be truly bizarre if humans alone among all animal species were independent from their evolutionary history. Behavioral analysis is at the very heart of evolutionary processes because behavior is evoked in response to environmental challenges, and natural selection passes judgment on behavior that has fitness consequences. Selection for behavioral traits is almost certainly more rapid than for physical traits because organisms play an active part in the selection of their behavior, and behavior analysis should further our understanding of evolution because the functioning of the whole organism drives evolution. After all, it is behavior that creates new variants, and then, and only then, can natural selection work its process of selective retention and elimination. When we speak of the evolution of behavior we are talking about behavioral traits and general propensities to behave in one way rather than in another, not about specific behaviors.

Two of the chapters in this section analyze the nature of rape from an evolutionary perspective. Rape is the most contentious form of behavior that evolutionary psychologists examine because many people have a tendency to confuse *natural* with *good*. Philosophers of science call this tendency the naturalistic fallacy; the mistake of confusing is with ought; that is, passing a moral judgment on an empirical fact. The first chapter in this section by William McKibbin and Todd Shackelford concentrates on women's evolved mechanisms that help them to resist rape. Their basic notion is that because rape is a traumatic experience that leads to many negative consequences for women, such as physical injury, pregnancy, and partner desertion, women may have evolved psychological mechanisms designed to motivate rape avoidance behaviors. McKibbin and Shackelford present and discuss these mechanisms in the form of their Rape Avoidance Inventory.

The second chapter by Ryan Ellsworth and Craig Palmer entitled examines the evidence for both rape and rape-avoidance adaptations. This chapter is an update of the progress made since the publication of the controversial book, *A natural history of rape* (Thornhill & Palmer, 2000). Ellsworth and Palmer emphasize the need to avoid the naturalistic fallacy and that leads one to imply that if rape may be an adaptation then it is somehow justifiable. They want their work to be seen as identifying the nature of rape and its avoidance, because they view this as an important step in preventing the occurrence of this horrible crime.

The third chapter, by Richard Wiebe, examines one of criminology's most revered concepts—self-control—from an evolutionary point of view. Wiebe notes that self-control is socially functional but that low self-control is advantageous in enabling us to quickly satisfy our desires. He then asks why high self-control developed if low self-control behaviors can satisfy desires. He then proceeds to demonstrate the evolutionary advantages to behaviors and practices associated with self-control.

Implications of Biosocial Research

Perhaps the biggest concern surrounding the biosocial perspective centers on the potential policy implications flowing from this line of research. The general view held among criminologists is that biosocial research can only lead to inhumane and oppressive policies, such as a new eugenics movement. This attack on biosocial criminology is completely unfounded for at least two reasons. First, research should not be guided by the potential policy implications that could result from it; instead, research should be guided by empirical evidence and the pursuit of the truth that is free of political correctness and ideology. Pretending that biology/genetics does not matter simply because of the fear of the policy implications will certainly not move the field closer to the truth. All that it will do is to create a false knowledge base that was mythically constructed by criminologists concerned more about policy than reality. As with any type of maladaptive outcome, ranging from autism to cancer, the only way to prevent or cure it is by accurately identifying its causes. The only way to accurately identify the causes of crime and delinquency is by exploring all potential causes, not just those that are deemed acceptable by sociological criminologists.

Second, it is quite narcissistic of sociological criminologists to think that they can forecast which types of research would lead to progressive policies versus those that would lead to oppressive policies. For example, criminologists, in general, tend to be highly liberal and opposed to the death penalty. Despite this disciplinary allegiance to oppose the death penalty, their research had no effect on the relatively recent Supreme Court decision to outlaw the death penalty for juveniles. Instead, the research that was cited in the Court's decision was largely biosocial in origin. Neuroscience research revealing that the brains of adolescents are not as fully developed as the brains of adults was the major impetus persuading the Court to abolish the death penalty for adolescents. To most criminologists, this decision was highly progressive and was a victory for the liberal approach to crime control. Paradoxically, though, it was the research produced from a biosocial perspective, not a sociological one, that scored the victory for criminologists.

The extent to which a biosocial perspective can inform public policy, however, is not yet well known and likely will not be known for some time. Contemporary biosocial research is still in its infancy and at this point we are still trying to uncover the complex ways in which environmental factors and genetics work to produce antisocial behaviors. Even so, there is emerging evidence indicating that the biosocial perspective can be quite effective for creating programs that reduce and prevent crime and delinquency. Michael Vaughn and Ralph Groom's chapter on biosocial prevention and treatment strategies explores some of the ways that biosocial research can be used to help decrease antisocial behaviors. This chapter is particularly useful for highlighting the fact that prevention and intervention programs grounded in a biosocial approach are not about forced sterilization or simply medicating offenders. As more and more research is produced by biosocial criminologists, information about how this line of inquiry can guide and inform potential intervention and prevention programs most certainly will increase.

The last chapter in the volume extends the discussion about the implications of such research. Authored by Joseph Rukus and Chris Gibson, this chapter addresses in a more general way how biosocial criminology may ultimately affect the functioning of the criminal justice system. The issues brought up in this chapter will likely become more and more salient as more and more genetic research begins to find its way into criminal cases. Deciding whether genetic research should be allowed in court, and how it can be used by the court, will likely be one of the more important legal issues that the court system will encounter in the next couple of decades.

Conclusions

The biosocial perspective is beginning to gain a significant amount of traction within the field of criminology. As the twenty-first century progresses, and we begin to learn more about the functioning of certain genes, the neurobiological basis to behaviors, and the biological foundations to personality, the biosocial perspective will become even more important. Some leaders in the field, such as Francis T. Cullen, have even argued that it is now time to abandon a purely sociological approach to crime and replace it with a biosocial approach (Cullen, 2009). We agree, and our hope is that this volume will inspire more and more criminologists to shed their allegiance to sociology and begin to explore the various ways in which biosocial criminology can contribute to a scientific understanding of crime, criminals, and antisocial behavior in general.

References

Beaver, K. M. (2009). *Biosocial criminology: A primer*. Dubuque, IA: Kendall/Hunt.

Cooper, J. A., Walsh, A., & Ellis, L. (2010). Is criminology moving toward a paradigm shift? Evidence from a survey of the American Society of Criminology. *Journal of Criminal Justice Education, 21*, 332–347.

Cullen, F. T. (2009). Foreword. In Walsh, A., & Beaver, K. M. (eds.), *Biosocial criminology: New directions in theory and research* (pp. xv–xvii). New York, NY: Routledge.

Gunter, T. D., Vaughn, M. G., & Philibert, R. A. (2010). Behavioral genetics in antisocial spectrum disorders and psychopathy: A review of the recent literature. *Behavioral Sciences and the Law, 28*, 148–173.

Harris, J. R. (1998). *The nurture assumption: Why children turn out the way they do*. New York,NY: Touchstone.

Moffitt, T. E. (1993). Adolescence-limited and life-course persistent antisocial behavior: A developmental taxonomy. *Psychological Review, 100*, 674–701.

Rowe, D. C. (1994). *The limits of family influence: Genes, experience, and behavior*. New York, NY: Guilford.

Rutter, J. (2006). *Genes and behavior: Nature-nurture interplay explained*. Malden, MA: Blackwell.

Thornhill, R., & Palmer, C. T. (2000). *A natural history of rape: Biological bases of sexual coercion*. Cambridge, MA: MIT Press.

van den Berghe, P. L. (1990). Why most sociologists don't (and won't) think evolutionarily. *Sociological Forum, 5*, 173–185.

Walsh, A. (2002). *Biosocial criminology: Introduction and integration*. Cincinnati, OH: Anderson.

Walsh, A. (2009). *Biology and criminology: The biosocial synthesis*. New York, NY: Routledge.

Walsh, A., & Beaver, K. M. (2009). *Biosocial criminology: New directions in theory and research*. New York, NY: Routledge.

Wright, J. P., & Beaver, K. M. (2005). Do parents matter in creating self-control in their children? A genetically informed test of Gottfredson and Hirschi's theory of low self-control. *Criminology, 43*, 1169–1202.

Wright, J. P., Tibbetts, S. G., & Daigle, L. E. (2008). *Criminals in the making: Criminality across the life course*. Los Angeles, CA: Sage.

Biosocial Interactions and Correlates of Crime

Anna Rudo-Hutt, Yu Gao, Andrea Glenn, Melissa Peskin,

Yaling Yang, and Adrian Raine

Introduction

Every level of analysis of biological factors – from molecular genetics, to brain structure and function, to neuropsychological performance – has found links between biology and antisocial behavior. Likewise, a number of social or environmental factors – maltreatment, socioeconomic status, education, and so on – are believed to contribute to crime and aggression. Over the past two decades, increasing interest in the interaction between biological and social factors in various behaviors and disorders has led to several fruitful lines of research. A great deal of such research has supported the interacting roles of nature and nurture in the development of criminality. This chapter will provide an overview of some of the major biosocial findings in research on crime and antisocial behavior.

Early Health Risks

Research on early health risk factors offers some of the most persuasive evidence that interactions of biological and social risk factors significantly increase risk for criminal behavior. Several pre- and peri-natal factors including minor physical anomalies, nicotine or alcohol exposure, and birth complications have been shown to predispose to crime, especially when combined with environmental risk factors.

Minor Physical Anomalies

Minor physical anomalies (MPAs) consist of fairly minor physical abnormalities such as adherent ear lobes, a single palmar crease, and a furrowed tongue. MPAs have been linked to pregnancy disorders and are viewed as biomarkers for fetal neural maldevelopment near the end of the first trimester (Firestone & Peters, 1983). Since the epidermis and the central nervous system (CNS) have shared embryological origins, MPAs are considered indicators of atypical CNS and brain development. While there may be a genetic component to MPAs, they may also be caused by environmental factors that affect the fetus, such as anoxia, bleeding, and infection (Guy, Majorski, Wallace, & Guy, 1983).

Primary Findings

A number of studies have found a relationship between elevated numbers of MPAs and increased antisocial behavior in children, adolescents, and adults (Raine, 1993). MPAs have been particularly linked to violent as opposed to nonviolent offending. For instance, Arseneault, Tremblay, Boulerice, Seguin, and Saucier (2000) showed that MPAs measured at age 14 in 170 males predicted violent but not nonviolent delinquency at age 17. The authors reported that these effects were independent of childhood physical aggression or family adversity. In another study, an increased level of MPAs was associated with recidivistic violent criminal behavior (Kandel, Brennan, Mednick, & Michelson, 1989). Kandel et al. (1989) assessed MPAs in 265 11- to 13-year-old Danish children, and found that recidivistic violent offenders had a greater number of MPAs compared with subjects with one or no violent offenses, according to police records of criminal behavior when the subjects were 20 to 22 years of age. These studies suggest that prenatal insults toward the end of the first three months of pregnancy may increase risk for violent behavior as a result of abnormal brain development.

Biosocial Interactions

Several studies have reported that MPAs interact with psychosocial factors in predisposing to crime. Mednick and Kandel (1988) assessed MPAs in 129 boys during visits to a pediatrician at age 12 and found that MPAs were related to violent crime, but not nonviolent property offenses when the subjects were 21 years old. However, when the authors examined family stability and intactness as a moderating factor, they found that MPAs only predicted later criminal involvement for those reared in unstable, nonintact homes. Brennan, Mednick and Raine (1997) reported a similar finding using a sample of 72 male offspring of parents with psychiatric diagnoses. Particularly high rates of adult violent crime were found in individuals who had both family adversity and MPAs compared to those who had only one of these risk factors. Another study, by Pine, Shaffer, Schonfeld, and

Davies (1997), examined whether MPAs interacted with environmental risk factors, such as low socioeconomic status (SES), spousal conflict, and marital disruption, in predicting later disruptive behavior disorders. Pine et al. (1997) found that individuals with both increased MPAs and environmental risk, assessed at age seven, had an elevated risk for disruptive behavior in general, and conduct disorder, in particular, at age 17. These three studies suggest that MPAs interact with adverse environmental experiences such that psychosocial factors predispose to criminal and violent behavior more strongly, and sometimes only, among individuals with high biological risk. Neurodevelopmental abnormalities such as MPAs thus appear to increase susceptibility to psychosocial risk factors for antisocial and violent behavior.

Prenatal Nicotine and Alcohol Exposure

Primary findings

A convergence of evidence from multiple sources has convincingly demonstrated that children who are exposed to maternal smoking during pregnancy have an elevated risk of later criminal behavior throughout the life-course (see Wakschlag, Pickett, Cook, Benowitz, & Leventhal, 2002, for a review). Studies have shown that maternal prenatal smoking predicts childhood externalizing behavior, conduct disorder, delinquency, and adult criminal and violent offending (Brennan, Grekin, & Mednick, 1999; Brennan, Grekin, Mortensen, & Mednick, 2002; Fergusson, Horwood, & Lynskey, 1993; Fergusson, Woodward, & Horwood, 1998; Orlebeke, Knol, & Verhulst, 1997; Rantakallio, Laara, Isohanni, & Moilanen, 1992; Wakschlag et al., 1997; Weissman, Warner, Wickramaratne, & Kandell, 1999). Three studies have also documented a dose-response relationship between the degree of maternal smoking during pregnancy and the extent of later criminal behavior in offspring (Brennan et al., 1999; Maughan, Taylor, Caspi, & Moffitt, 2004; Maughan, Taylor, Taylor, Butler, & Bynner, 2001).

Fetal alcohol exposure is also an established risk factor for antisocial behavior in children, adolescents, and adults (Fast, Conry, & Loock, 1999; Olson et al., 1997; Streissguth, Barr, Kogan, & Bookstein, 1996). Fetal Alcohol Syndrome (FAS) is characterized by a host of cognitive, behavioral, social, and physical deficits and results from heavy alcohol consumption during pregnancy. However, deficits are observed even in those who have been prenatally exposed to alcohol yet do not meet diagnostic criteria for FAS (Schonfeld, Mattson, & Riley, 2005). For example, two studies found high rates of delinquency in children and adolescents with heavy fetal alcohol exposure, even if they did not have FAS (Mattson & Riley, 2000; Roebuck, Mattson, & Riley, 1999). In addition, research has demonstrated that adolescents who were prenatally exposed to alcohol are overrepresented in the juvenile justice system (Fast et al., 1999). One study found that 3 percent of adolescents in a juvenile inpatient forensic psychiatry unit were diagnosed with FAS, and 22 percent were diagnosed with fetal alcohol effects (Fast et al., 1999). Another study reported that 61 percent of adolescents, 58 percent of adults, and 14 percent of children between the ages of six to 11 with fetal alcohol exposure had a history of trouble with the law (Streissguth et al., 1996).

Biosocial interactions

A number of studies have revealed interactions between maternal smoking during pregnancy and psychosocial risks in the prediction of later crime. Importantly, these studies had large sample sizes, assessed long-term outcomes, prospectively collected data, and controlled for potential confounds such as parental antisocial behavior, drug use, and low SES. In one study using a sample of 4,169 males born between 1959 and 1961 in Denmark, Brennan et al. (1999) found a dose-response relationship between the number of cigarettes subjects' mothers had smoked daily while pregnant, and the extent of subjects' nonviolent and violent crime at 34 years of age. Moreover, Brennan et al. (1999) reported that these effects were specific to persistent criminal behavior, rather than delinquency in adolescence. Arrest records revealed that subjects whose mothers smoked 20 cigarettes a day while pregnant had a two-fold increase in adult violent offending. However, the authors found that when maternal prenatal smoking was combined with delivery complications, there was a five-fold increase in adult violent offending; in contrast, prenatal nicotine exposure without delivery complications did not lead to increased violence in offspring. Another study, by Rasanan et al. (1999), found a two-fold increase in violent crime at age 26 in the offspring of women who smoked during pregnancy, and showed that prenatal nicotine exposure combined with being raised in a single-parent family, led to an 11.9-fold increase in recidivistic violent offending. Furthermore, prenatal nicotine exposure combined with four psychosocial risk factors (teenage pregnancy, single-parent family, unwanted pregnancy, and developmental motor delays), led to a 14.2-fold increase in recidivistic violence. As in the previous study, this study found increased risk particularly for persistent violent offending, rather than violence in general or property crime. Finally, a study by Gibson and Tibbetts (2000) documented an interaction between prenatal nicotine exposure and parental absence in predisposing to early onset of antisocial behavior and offending.

Birth Complications

Biosocial interactions

Several methodologically rigorous studies have demonstrated that obstetric complications interact with psychosocial risk factors in predicting conduct disorder, delinquency, and impulsive crime and violence in adulthood. In one study, birth complications combined with a disruptive family environment (which included such experiences as maternal separation, illegitimacy, marital discord, parental mental health problems, and paternal absence) predisposed to delinquency over and above either biological or psychosocial risk factor independently (Werner, 1987). Raine, Brennan, and Mednick (1994, 1997) also demonstrated the importance of biosocial interactions in predicting violent crime in two prospective longitudinal studies. In the first of these studies, Raine, Brennan, and Mednick (1994) investigated whether the early experience of extreme maternal rejection (e.g., unwanted pregnancy, attempts to abort the fetus, and institutional care of the infant during the first year of life) interacted with birth complications in predisposing to adult violent crime in a sample of 4,269 males born in Copenhagen, Denmark, between 1959 to 1961. Raine, Brennan, and Mednick (1994) demonstrated that birth complications significantly interacted with maternal rejection in predisposing to violent crime at 18 years of age, and that while only 4 percent of the sample experienced both birth complications and maternal rejection, this group was responsible for 18 percent of the violent offenses perpetrated by the whole sample. In a follow-up study, Raine, Brennan, and Mednick (1997) reassessed criminal violence in the same sample at age 34. The authors replicated the biosocial interaction for violent but not nonviolent crime. Moreover, they showed that the results applied specifically to serious violence, rather than violent threats, and to early-onset as opposed to late-onset violence. Obstetric complications have been shown to interact with various psychosocial risk factors (parental mental illness, poor parenting, familial adversity) in a number of studies using large samples from around the world (Arseneault, Tremblay, Boulerice, & Saucier, 2002; Brennan, Mednick, & Mednick, 1993; Hodgins, Kratzer, & McNeil, 2001; Piquero & Tibbetts, 1999).

In contrast to these findings, two studies failed to document an interaction between birth complications and environmental risk factors (Cannon et al., 2002; Laucht et al., 2000). However, these studies differed in several important ways from the studies cited above. Cannon and colleagues (2002) examined 601 individuals with schizophrenia spectrum disorders; thus, other differences in brain functioning in this sample may have obscured findings related to violence. Laucht et al. (2000) only followed a small sample of 322 children until eight years of age. Raine and colleagues (Raine, 2002a and 2002b; Scarpa & Raine, 2007) have argued that CNS insults resulting from perinatal complications may be particularly related to life-course persistent antisocial behavior, rather than child antisocial behavior. A majority of evidence thus suggests that birth complications interact with psychosocial risk factors in predisposing to violent crime.

Genetics

Compelling evidence for genetic influences on criminal behavior comes from studies using a diverse set of methodological approaches (Beaver, DeLisi, Wright, & Vaughn, 2009; Popma & Raine, 2006). Researchers attempting to determine the relative importance of genetic contributions to crime have employed twin, adoptive, and molecular genetic designs. Although studies have found heritability estimates that range from 7 to 85 percent, the majority of studies have reported heritability estimates in the 40 to 60 percent range. (Arsenault et al., 2003; Beaver et al., 2009; Jaffee et al., 2005; Jaffee, Caspi, Moffitt, & Taylor, 2004; Lyons et al., 1995;

Miles & Carey, 1997; Moffitt, 2005; Rhee & Waldman, 2002; Rowe, 1986; Slutske et al., 1997). Methodological differences between studies, such as how antisocial behavior is operationalized, sample age, age of offending onset, and gender have all likely contributed to variation in heritability estimates. For example, some researchers have operationalized antisocial behavior in terms of behavior (i.e. the violation of legal or social norms), while others have defined it as the presence of a psychiatric diagnosis such as conduct disorder, while still others have used aggression severity.

One important moderator of the magnitude of genetic and environmental influences on delinquency appears to be sample age. Research has revealed that the relative importance of genes and environment in the etiology of criminal behavior shifts across the lifespan (Goldman & Ducci, 2007). The majority of studies have reported lower heritability estimates and higher shared environmental contributions to delinquency and conduct problems in childhood compared to adolescence (Jacobson, Prescott, & Kendler, 2002; Lyons et al., 1995; Miles & Carey, 1997). This is consistent with the notion that genetic influences on delinquency tend to increase with age while shared environmental effects tend to decrease (Goldman & Ducci, 2007). Studies have also found that early and persistent delinquent behavior is more heritable than childhood-limited antisocial behavior. In addition, while some genes have been found to influence criminal behavior across the lifespan, others only have an effect during adolescence or adulthood (Goldman & Ducci, 2007).

Research has also suggested that heritability estimates differ for aggressive versus non-aggressive offending. For instance, studies have found that aggressive offending, which includes physical acts of aggression such as fighting, is more heritable than non-aggressive offending, which includes behavior such as rule-breaking and theft (Eley, Lichtenstein, & Moffitt, 2003). Conversely, shared environmental factors, such as family criminality, family poverty, and poor parenting, appear to have a greater effect on non-aggressive offending, although genetic influences have also been found to influence some of these factors (Moffitt, 2005).

Studies have implicated several candidate genes in the development of offending and antisocial behavior; however, none of these genes have been found to account for a large percentage of the phenotypic variance in crime (Goldman & Ducci, 2007). This suggests both that many genes are involved in increasing vulnerability to antisocial behavior, and that gene–environment interactions are involved in the etiology of criminal behavior. One particularly influential study documenting a gene–environment interaction in the prediction of antisocial behavior was performed by Caspi and colleagues (2002). In a large sample of male children in New Zealand, the authors examined a functional polymorphism in the gene encoding monoamine oxidase A (MAO-A; a neurotransmitter-metabolizing enzyme) and childhood maltreatment. Maltreated children with a genotype conferring high levels of MAO-A expression were less likely to develop conduct disorder in adolescence or engage in violent crime in adulthood than maltreated children with a genotype conferring low levels of MAO-A expression.

Caspi et al.'s (2002) study was one of the first to reveal that children's susceptibility to environmental risk factors may be moderated by specific genotypes. However, not all studies have revealed the same pattern of results. Nilsson et al. (2008) found that female adolescents with high expression of MAO-A were *more* likely to exhibit impulsive aggression when exposed to an unfavorable environment. Similarly, a recent study found that childhood physical abuse was associated with increased violent recidivism in individuals with the high MAO-A activity genotype (Tikkanen et al., 2010). In this study, MAO-A genotype alone had no main effect on the risk of recidivism. These studies emphasize that biological and social factors considered alone are often not able to predict criminal behavior, but must be considered within the same context.

Overall, these studies show that a commonly studied social factor such as childhood adversity may result in different patterns of antisocial behavior depending on the biological makeup of the individual. Caspi et al.'s (2002) findings may also help explain why some children who experience maltreatment do not become violent or abusive and display resilience in the face of environmental adversity, whereas others perpetuate the cycle of violence in later life. Thus, research employing a wide array of methodologies has persuasively shown that there are genetic influences on criminal and antisocial behavior.

Hormones and Neurotransmitters

At the molecular level, there have also been findings of interactions between biological and social factors, particularly in studies of hormones and neurotransmitters. These studies have generally found that the combination of biological and social variables is better able to explain antisocial behavior than either type of variable alone.

Hormones

Hormones are molecules that are released into the bloodstream and travel to act at a different location in the body. Common hormones that have been associated with antisocial behavior are cortisol and testosterone. Cortisol is a glucocorticoid hormone that is part of the body's stress reactivity network and serves to mobilize the body's resources and to provide energy in times of stress (Kudielka & Kirschbaum, 2005). Biologically-based studies have generally found cortisol levels to be reduced in antisocial children (van Goozen, Matthys, Cohen-Kettenis, Thijssen, & van Engeland, 1998), adolescents (Loney et al., 2006), and adults (Cima, Smeets, & Jelicic, 2008; Holi et al., 2006), suggesting that these individuals may be less responsive to stressors and may be less fearful of negative consequences such as potential punishment.

Testosterone is a sex hormone that is part of the hypothalamic-pituitary-gonadal (HPG) axis. It is primarily released by the testes in males and the ovaries in females. Males have several times the amount of testosterone as females. Because there are large sex differences in antisocial behavior, with the male-to-female ratio being about 4:1 for antisocial personality disorder and as large as 10:1 for violent crimes (van Honk & Schutter, 2007), it has been hypothesized that testosterone may be involved in aggressive behavior. Elevated testosterone levels have been associated with antisocial behavior and violent crime in adults (Banks & Dabbs, 1996; Dabbs, Frady, & Carr, 1987).

Only a few studies have explored whether there are interactions between hormone measurements and social factors. This may be partly due to the fact that social factors are not measured or are not analyzed in many biologically-based studies. The findings from the following studies suggest that social factors may be important in gaining a complete picture of the role of hormones as a risk factor for antisocial behavior.

Dabbs and Morris (1990) found that high testosterone was associated with higher levels of childhood and adult delinquency in participants of low socioeconomic status (SES), but this relationship was much weaker in participants with high SES. Although the mechanism of this effect is unknown, one possibility is that individuals with high SES have protective factors that help them to avoid antisocial behavior, despite their high levels of testosterone. In another study, Mazur (1995) found that a combined biosocial model involving the hormones cortisol, testosterone, and thyroxin, in combination with social factors including age, education, and income better predicted delinquent behavior than a biological or social model alone. This emphasizes the importance of including both biological and social factors in order to understand how antisocial behavior develops.

An exciting new area of hormone research has begun to explore whether social factors, in the form of a psychosocial intervention, may be able to *change* hormone responses in order to reduce antisocial behavior in those at risk. Brotman et al. (2007) conducted a 22-week family-based intervention of preschool-age children at risk for antisocial behavior, and found that relative to controls, children in the intervention condition had increased cortisol levels in anticipation of a social challenge; the experimentally-induced change in cortisol levels resembled patterns found in normally developing children at low risk for antisocial behavior. This suggests that changes in external, social factors are able to alter an individual's hormonal responding, providing direct evidence that biological and social factors interact in predisposing for antisocial behavior. Contrary to the popular belief that biological factors are fixed and cannot be changed, this study shows that socially based interventions may be effective largely because of their ability to change biological responding; this study showed that changes in cortisol accounted for 69 percent of the intervention effect on reducing childhood aggression.

Furthermore, this research group found that the intervention had a stronger effect on cortisol among families demonstrating lower warmth in the home (O'Neal et al., 2010). They conducted a follow-up study of these youth and found that among lower warmth families, the intervention-induced cortisol response was predictive of later aggression levels. This suggests that the family environment is also an important factor to consider when attempting to improve biological responding. Taken together, these studies suggest that hormones act within an environmental context to predispose to antisocial behavior, and that changes in the environment can have an impact on hormones.

Neurotransmitters

Neurotransmitters are molecules that are used to signal between neurons in the central nervous system. A neurotransmitter released from one neuron affects the functioning of adjacent neurons. Common neurotransmitters include serotonin, dopamine, and norepinephrine. Related molecules include the metabolites of neurotransmitters, such as the serotonin metabolite 5-hydroxyindoleacetic acid (5-HIAA).

Numerous studies have examined the neurotransmitter serotonin in criminal groups. In a review of the literature, Berman and Coccaro (1998) conclude that reduced serotonin activity is related to aggressive behavior, particularly in those who commit or attempt to commit crimes with significant potential for harming others, such as arson and homicide. In a meta-analysis by Moore, Scarpa, and Raine (2002), the effect size for the relationship between the serotonin metabolite 5-HIAA levels and antisocial behavior was -0.45. In addition to studies that have established a relationship between serotonin and antisocial behavior, one study found that antidepressants, which increase serotonin, reduce aggression in humans (Coccaro & Kavoussi 1997).

Biosocial interactions have also been observed in studies of serotonin as well as genes that code for it. Moffitt et al. (1997) found that violent offenders with high blood serotonin levels who came from a conflicted family background were more than three times more likely to become violent by age 21 than men with only the biological or only the social risk factor. Similarly, Marks et al. (2007) found that children with low central serotonin reactivity were increasingly likely to exhibit increased conduct problems as the magnitude of psychosocial risk increased. A molecular genetics study by Sadeh et al. (2010) found that the psychopathic traits "callous-unemotional" and "narcissicm" were associated with SES in youth with two "long" variants of the serotonin transporter gene polymorphism. This gene variant is thought to alter the serotonin system, although the exact effect on serotonin transmission in the brain is not clear. Overall, these studies suggest that alterations in serotonergic function may confer risk for antisocial behavior by heightening vulnerability to environmental stress.

Overall, these findings suggest that hormones and neurotransmitters often interact with social and environmental factors to increase the likelihood of antisocial behavior. The mechanisms by which hormones and neurotransmitters may interact with social factors to result in antisocial behavior are not well understood, so future studies will be necessary to further elucidate these relationships. Increasing our understanding of how biological and social factors interact will likely have implications for the prevention and treatment of crime.

Brain Imaging

In the last few decades, an increasing amount of research has been directed toward understanding the neurobiological etiology of criminal behavior. Recent brain imaging studies have been extremely informative in providing the empirical evidence connecting structural and functional deficiencies in several brain regions with criminal behavior. Regarding structural abnormalities associated with criminal behavior, studies have largely focused on regions involved in decision-making (e.g. prefrontal cortex) and emotion regulation (e.g. amygdala, hippocampus). For example, Woermann et al. (2000) found reduced left prefrontal gray volumes in aggressive epileptic patients compared to non-aggressive epileptic patients. Supportively, Yang et al. (2005; Yang, Raine, Colletti, Toga, & Narr, 2010) also found reduced gray matter volume and thickness in the middle frontal and orbitofrontal cortex and reduced volume and surface deformations in the amygdala in psychopaths with prior convictions (i.e., unsuccessful psychopaths) compared to psychopaths without convictions (i.e., successful psychopaths) and non-psychopathic controls. In one recent study, Yang et al. (2010) revealed reduced hippocampal and parahippocampal volumes in murderers with schizophrenia compared to schizophrenia patients and non-violent controls, which is in line with another study by Boccardi et al. (2010) showing abnormal hippocampal morphology in habitually violent offenders. Using vivo diffusion tensor magnetic resonance imaging tractography, one recent study by Craig et al. (2009) further showed impaired amygdala-orbitofrontal connections in psychopaths with convictions. These studies have provided some initial evidence for brain morphological alterations associated with criminal behavior.

In common with structural imaging studies, several functional imaging studies have presented evidence suggesting impaired brain functioning in criminal offenders in several brain regions, especially in the prefrontal and temporal cortex. For example, Raine, Buchsbaum, Stanley, Lottenberg, Abel, & Stoddard (1994) found reduced glucose metabolism in the anterior medial prefrontal, orbitofrontal and superior frontal cortex in murderers compared to normal controls during a continuous performance task. Similarly, Hirono, Mega, Dinov, Mishkin, and Cummings (2000) also found individuals convicted of impulsive violent offenses to show reduced regional cerebral blood flood activity in the left anterior temporal, bilateral dorsofrontal, and right parietal cortex compared to non-violent dementia patients. Another study by Raine, Park, Lencz et al. (2001) employed a working memory task and revealed reduced activation in the right temporal cortex in violent offenders with a history of abuse compared with controls. Recently, Lee, Chan, & Raine (2009) showed that domestic violence offenders had increased brain activity to threat stimuli in the hippocampus, orbitofrontal cortex, and other regions compared with controls. These findings have provided a foundation for understanding how brain predispositions may contribute to criminal behavior, however many of these studies have focused solely on neurobiological factors for criminal behavior while providing very little if any discussion on the importance of other contributing factors, specifically social risk factors, in their explanations of criminal outcome. Such lacking in examining both biological and social etiological variables in the brain imaging field is surprising as it has been made clear that nature (genes) and nurture (environment) are inextricably intertwined in the development of the brain. Furthermore, the impact of environmental effects on the brain is not restricted to prenatal development, but continues throughout the lifetime. Thus, one would only get a partial story by investigating biological factors outside the context of the environmental influences. Here, we will review some rare instances of empirical studies with a particular focus on incorporating brain imaging and social factors that advance our understanding of how environment interacts with brain development in predisposing to criminal behavior.

The first direct examination of potential biosocial interactions in predicting crime was conducted in 1998 by Raine, Stoddard, Bihrle, and Buchsbaum, using positron emission tomography to address the issue of how social deficits moderate the relationship between brain function and criminal behavior. In brief, they divided a sample of murderers into those with and those without psychosocial deprivation. Specifically, ratings of psychosocial deprivation in this study took into account several social risk variables including early physical and sexual abuse, neglect, extreme poverty, foster home placement, having a criminal parent, severe family conflict, and a broken home. Compared to normal controls, murderers with psychosocial deprivation showed relatively good prefrontal functioning, whereas non-deprived murderers showed significantly reduced prefrontal functioning. Specifically, a 14.2 percent reduction in functioning in the right orbitofrontal cortex was found in murderers from good homes. These results suggest that the association between biological impairment and antisocial behavior are more prominent in those lacking social risk factors for antisocial behavior. Using functional magnetic resonance imaging, Raine, Park, Lencz et al. (2001) found a similar effect of biosocial interactions by comparing violent individuals with and without a child abuse history. More specifically, they found that violent offenders who had suffered severe child abuse show reduced right hemispheric functioning, particularly in the right temporal cortex. Further analyses revealed that abused individuals who had refrained from serious violence showed relatively lower left, but higher right, activation of the temporal lobe. The results further suggest that a higher functioning right temporal region may act as a protective factor in preventing one with social risk factors to commit a criminal act.

The interaction effect found in brain imaging studies on criminals are consistent with evidence in patients with brain damage suggesting that social influences, in combination with the biological risk factor of brain impairments, can predict criminal, violent behavior. For example, Lewis, Pincus, Feldman, Jackson, and Bard (1986) have demonstrated that exposure to violence and abuse in the family is the strongest factor for violent behavior in individuals with neurological impairment. Alternatively, there is also evidence that social factors can act as protective factors to prevent individuals with brain damage from future involvement in crime. For example, Mataró et al. (2001) describe a patient in Spain who suffered a similar accident to Phineas Gage when his frontal lobe was impaled by the spike of an iron gate in 1937. However, unlike Gage who later developed antisocial behavior, this patient showed no signs of hostility, outbursts, or irritability. Mataró and colleagues suggested that such a different outcome may be due to the fact that his childhood sweetheart stood by him and married him after the accident, and his family was highly protective and caring, and gave him a job in his father's factory where he could be supervised. This finding suggests that social factors such as a nurturing family environment may be able to lower the risk that an individual with brain impairments will become criminal.

Although findings are rare, these previous studies have provided initial evidence suggesting that structural or functional brain deficits, when combined with a social risk factor, may predispose one to be engaged in criminal behavior while a social protective factor may prevent a potential criminal outcome and vice versa. However, findings to date are still a long way from elucidating the complicated interactional processes of the brain and environment as they relate to outcomes of criminal behavior. One specific goal for future studies will be to determine more specifically which brain morphological/functional factors play an important role in this biosocial interactive process of leading to criminal behavior. Another goal will be to determine whether particular social risk factors interact with particular brain predispositions to produce criminal outcomes (e.g., environmental stress may be more likely to trigger criminal behavior if a biological predisposition of amygdala deficits is present that lower the person's ability to handle stressful events). Future developmental studies with more sophisticated assessments on the environment and the brain will provide invaluable information for understanding the etiological equation of criminal behavior.

Psychophysiology

Although an extensive body of research has been built up on the psychophysiological basis of antisocial and criminal behavior (see reviews by Lorber, 2004; Patrick, 2008), relatively fewer studies have been conducted to examine the possible interaction effects with psychosocial variables. Most psychophysiological research in the biosocial studies has focused on autonomic nervous system functioning at a baseline level or in response to external stimuli using measures such as skin conductance activity and heart rate. Skin conductance is usually measured from electrodes placed on the fingers or palm of the hand and is controlled exclusively by the sympathetic nervous system. Skin conductance activity captures small fluctuations in the electrical activity of the skin, with enhanced conductivity (i.e., activity) elicited by increased sweating. Heart rate measures the number of heart beats per minute and reflects the complex interactions between sympathetic and parasympathetic nervous system activity.

With the advantages of ease of data collection (especially heart rate) and their noninvasive features, psychophysiological measures have been valuable in filling the gap between genetic risk for crime and the brain abnormalities which interact with environmental factors in predisposing some individuals to antisocial, violent, and psychopathic behavior. In this section, empirical examples of interaction effects within the area of psychophysiology and relevant theoretical perspectives will be reviewed, followed by clinical implications of these findings.

First, psychophysiological risk factors have been found to interact with psychosocial variables in predisposing certain individuals to antisocial and criminal behavior. In this line of research, psychophysiological variables are dependent variables and the moderating effects of psychosocial factors are investigated. A number of studies have found that psychophysiological factors, particularly measures of skin conductance and heart rate, show stronger relationships to antisocial behavior in those from *benign* social backgrounds that lack the classic psychosocial risk factors for crime (Raine, 2002a). For example, studies have shown that poor skin conductance conditioning (see below) is a characteristic for antisocial individuals from relatively good but not bad social backgrounds (Hemming, 1981; Raine & Venables, 1981). In a longitudinal study, low heart rate at age three years has been found to predict aggression at age 11 years in children from high but not low social classes (Raine, Venables, & Mednick, 1997). These findings, as argued by the "social push" hypothesis, suggest that psychophysiological risk factors may assume greater importance when social predispositions to crime are minimized. In contrast, social causes may be more important explanations of antisocial behavior in those exposed to adverse early home conditions (Raine, 2002a).

Reduced conditioning has been a key concept of antisocial and psychopathic behavior and considered an index of emotional deficits and a proxy for amygdala dysfunction (Blair, 2007; Patrick, 2008). Among all the psychophysiological indexes, conditionability as measured by skin conductance responses in a laboratory-based classical conditioning paradigm has been studied most extensively in biological or biosocial research. For example, in a sample of 101 15-year-old male school children in England, Raine and Venables (1981) found that when subjects were from the high social classes, antisocial individuals had poor conditionability, whereas antisocial individuals from low social classes exhibited good conditionability. In a pilot study by Mednick et al. (1977) on psychophysiological functioning of antisocial individuals who were raised in criminogenic versus noncriminogenic environments, preliminary analyses suggested that criminal sons with noncriminal fathers were poor conditioners, whereas criminal sons with criminal fathers were good conditioners. These results are consistent with Eysenck's concept of "antisocialization" (Eysenck, 1977) in which Eysenck argued that individuals from criminogenic backgrounds who have good conditionability might be socialized into antisocial habits that are not punished by their parents; in contrast, individuals with poor conditionability who are raised in criminogenic environments may not develop the antisocial tactics as well as their highly conditionable counterparts.

Alternatively, some studies have documented the "dual-hazard" effect in the psychophysiological research of antisocial behavior. In these studies, the biosocial interactions are examined with antisocial and criminal behavior as dependent variables. For example, boys with a low resting heart rate have been found more likely to be rated as aggressive by their teachers if their mother was pregnant as a teenager, if they were from a low social class family, or if they were separated from a parent before age 10. They are also more likely to become adult violent criminals if they also have a poor relationship with their parents and come from a large family (Farrington, 1997). In a recent study on a community sample of 7–13-year-olds, community violence victimization was found to be positively related to proactive aggression only in children with low heart rate, and witnessed community violence was positively related to reactive aggression only in conditions of high heart rate variability (Scarpa, Tanaka, & Haden, 2008). These findings are in line with the biosocial theories of crime which predict that negative social environments in combination with deficits in biological functioning predispose to criminal outcome (Mednick, 1977).

Other studies have focused on psychophysiological correlates as protective factors against the development of antisocial and criminal behavior. For example, in a prospective longitudinal study, 15-year-old antisocial adolescents who did not become criminals by age 29 showed higher resting heart rate levels, higher skin conductance arousal, and better skin conductance conditioning when compared to their antisocial counterparts who became adult criminals (Raine, Venables, & Williams, 1995, 1996). In another study on adolescents who had criminal fathers and thus were at higher risk for antisocial outcomes, those who desisted from crime had higher skin conductance and heart rate orienting reactivity in comparison with those who eventually became criminals (Brennan et al., 1997). Therefore, enhanced autonomic nervous system functioning, as indexed by higher levels of arousal, better conditioning, and higher orienting responses, may serve as biological protective factors that reduce the likelihood that an individual will become an adult criminal.

Some researchers have attempted to integrate biosocial findings into prevention and intervention programs. One line of research concerns directly altering one's psychophysiological functioning by manipulating environmental factors. For example, in one longitudinal study, better nutrition, more physical exercise, and cognitive stimulation from ages three to five years was shown to produce long-term psychophysiological changes six years later at age 11 years, including increased skin conductance level, more orienting, and a more aroused EEG profile (Raine, Venables, Dalais et al., 2001). This environmental enrichment was also found to reduce criminal offending at age 23 years (Raine, Mellingen, Liu, Venables, & Mednick, 2003).

In summary, psychophysiological risk factors interact with psychosocial variables in predisposing certain individuals to antisocial and criminal behavior. Meanwhile, evidence of psychophysiological protective factors against the development of antisocial behavior has emerged. Finally, prevention and intervention programs aimed at reducing antisocial behavior might benefit enormously by directly improving their psychophysiological functioning through environmental manipulations. Certain psychophysiological measures, including heart rate activity, can be recorded relatively easily (e.g., using portable equipment or taking a pulse), and as such they are especially valuable to the criminologists who are attempting to explore the biosocial etiology of crime.

Neuropsychology

Neuropsychological impairments have long been known to be associated with criminal and antisocial behavior. Many areas of functioning have been found to be impaired in criminal populations, and research has focused on overall intellectual ability (especially verbal abilities) as well as executive functioning.

Intelligence

Evidence for decreased intellectual functioning (as measured by IQ) in association with antisocial behavior has been found by many researchers. In fact, at a very broad level, estimates of the average U.S. state IQ have been found to be significantly and negatively correlated with FBI crime statistics in each state (Bartels, Ryan, Urban, & Glass, 2010). Furthermore, antisocial behavior and low IQ have been found to have a common genetic basis (Koenen, Caspi, Moffitt, Rijsdijk, & Taylor, 2006). Most research on intellectual functioning in this population, however, has highlighted a discrepancy between Verbal IQ and Performance IQ. Measures of Verbal IQ include tests which require participants to answer orally and often cover fact-based or crystallized knowledge, such as defining words or solving math problems aloud. Performance IQ tasks, in contrast, involve measures of spatial and non-verbal reasoning, such as manipulating blocks or searching for symbols on a page. Studies have found decreased Verbal IQ compared to Performance IQ in children (e.g., Loney, Frick, Ellis, & McCoy, 1998; McHale, Obrzut, and Sabers 2003), adolescents (e.g., Archwamety & Katsiyannis, 2000; Dougherty et al., 2007), and adults with antisocial behavior (e.g., Kirkpatrick et al. 2007; Vitacco, Neumann, & Wodushek, 2008). However, some studies have found no relative deficit in Verbal IQ in antisocial populations (e.g., Cadesky, Mota, & Schachar, 2000; Rispens et al., 1997), and another has found deficits in spatial, but not verbal, abilities (Raine, Yaralian, Reynolds, Venables, & Mednick, 2002). A recent meta-analysis of this Performance > Verbal discrepancy found that, while the results were statistically significant for all age groups, the effect size of reduced Verbal IQ was negligible in children and small in adults (Isen, 2010). In contrast, the effect size for the discrepancy in antisocial adolescents was closer to medium in size, and reflected a six-point difference on average between Verbal and Performance IQ in delinquent adolescents (Isen, 2010). Therefore, the deficit in Verbal compared to Performance IQ appears to characterize antisocial populations, especially during adolescence.

In addition to these age-based differences in the discrepancy between Verbal and Performance IQ measures, there appear to be some differences based on race or type of antisocial behavior. For example, Isen (2010) reported that effect sizes for Black participants were smaller than for White or mixed race samples. Additionally, in one sample, the highest rates of violent delinquency were found in those adolescents who were both high in callous-unemotional (psychopathic-like) traits and high in verbal abilities (Muñoz, Frick, Kimonis, & Aucoin, 2008). Similarly, in a group of boys with conduct disorder, those who had a biological parent with antisocial personality disorder and who had Verbal IQ scores above 100 had the highest number of conduct disorder symptoms three years later (Lahey et al., 1995). Thus, it is likely that the Performance > Verbal IQ pattern is not found in all antisocial groups.

Several hypotheses have been advanced to explain the discrepancy between verbal and non-verbal measures of ability in antisocial populations. One prominent theory is that pre-existing deficits in verbal ability lead to underachievement in school, which is, in turn, a risk factor for antisocial behavior (Moffitt, Lynam, & Silva, 1994). Others argue that antisocial behavior in childhood and adolescence often includes school refusal or gaps in education due to suspensions or incarceration, and these gaps in education are what account for deficits in Verbal IQ scores (Isen, 2010). That is, Verbal IQ tests often tap knowledge learned in school (e.g., word definitions), whereas Performance IQ tests are less reliant on education. Yet another hypothesis is that verbal deficits may lead to socialization failure (Eriksson, 2005) by affecting the development of self-control (Luria, 1980). Thus, it is unclear what underlies the relationship between Verbal IQ deficits and antisocial behavior, but researchers are continuing to probe this question.

Executive Function

In comprehensive neuropsychological batteries, executive functioning (EF) is also often found to be impaired in antisocial populations. EF is conceptualized as those cognitive processes which maintain representations of and allow the achievement of goals, and these processes are believed to be controlled largely by the prefrontal cortex (Miller & Cohen, 2001). Tasks commonly used to measure EF usually require mental flexibility, strategy formation, selective attention, and suppression of habitual responses. EF tasks are often used to identify patients with frontal lobe damage.

Thus far, research has supported the hypothesis that antisocial populations have impaired scores on tests of EF. A meta-analysis of this literature found that the effect size for EF deficits in antisocial populations was in the medium to large range, and this relationship held across all ages and all EF tests included (Morgan & Lilienfeld, 2000). More recent studies have supported these results, in adult male (Kavanagh, Rowe, Hersch, Barnett, & Reznik, 2010; Dolan & Park, 2002) as well as female offenders (Giancola, Shoal, & Mezzich, 2001), and in relation to violent (Hancock, Tapscott, & Hoaken, 2010), but not nonviolent (Barker et al. 2007; Hancock et al., 2010; Levi, Nussbaum, & Rich, 2010), offending. Although not all the evidence for EF impairment in youths with conduct problems is consistent (e.g., Nigg et al., 2004), the same deficit has generally been found in recent studies of antisocial children and adolescents (Beaver, DeLisi, Vaughn, & Wright, 2010; Hughes, Zagar, Busch, Grove, & Arbit, 2009; Raine et al., 2005; Syngelaki, Moore, Savage, Fairchild, & van Goozen, 2009).

Biosocial Interactions

A number of studies have found interactions between neuropsychological deficits and social risk factors in the prediction of antisocial behavior, especially in children and adolescents. An early study by Lewis, Lovely, Yeager, and Femina (1989) found that adult offending was better predicted using neuropsychological measures and abuse history than by juvenile offending alone. High IQ has been found to be protective in the context of environmental adversity, such that children and adolescents with high intellectual functioning do not show the typical increase in antisociality in risky environments (Masten et al., 1999; Vanderbilt-Adriance & Shaw, 2008). One feature of adverse environments that has been found to negatively impact children's intellectual functioning is neighborhood violence (Sharkey, 2010). Neighborhood violence may indeed be a significant factor in predicting antisocial behavior, as a strong relationship between exposure to violent media and poor EF has been found in children with disruptive behavior disorders (Kronenberger et al., 2005).

Parent traits have also been found to interact with neuropsychological functioning. Grekin, Brennan, and Hammen (2005) found that the relationship between parental alcohol use disorders (AUD) and offspring violent delinquency was mediated by the child's executive functioning, such that parental AUD leads to poor EF in the child, thereby increasing violence in the child. Parent diagnosis of antisocial personality disorder has also been found to interact with verbal IQ in the child. Lahey et al. (1995) found that (relatively) high IQ was only protective for conduct disorder in those children who did not have a biological parent with antisocial personality disorder. One longitudinal study of women followed from childhood into adulthood and motherhood found that the women who were aggressive as children provided poorer cognitive stimulation of their own children, who in turn had poorer verbal and abstract/visual abilities (Saltaris et al., 2004). Given the link between low IQ and crime, this study suggests one mechanism by which parents may pass on antisocial behavior may involve the poor cognitive environment provided at home.

Conclusions

In sum, there is a large body of evidence supporting the interacting roles of biological and social factors in criminal behavior. Pre- and peri-natal factors, such as prenatal exposure to nicotine and alcohol and birth complications, have been found to predict crime, particularly in the context of familial adversity and other psychosocial risk factors. Genetics research has reported heritability estimates of about 40–60 percent for crime, and specific genotypes, such as that conferring high levels of MAO-A, may be protective in adverse environments, at least for some populations. High levels of testosterone and low levels of cortisol may predispose to crime, and these hormones appear to interact with each other and with social risk factors to predict antisocial behavior. Brain imaging research has found an association between decreased prefrontal cortex function and violence, and this pattern has been reported to interact with psychosocial adversity, such that murderers from good homes are more likely to show this brain deficit. Psychophysiological studies have found a similar relationship, in which the relationship between factors such as low heart rate and aggression is found only in those from benign backgrounds. Additionally, poor neuropsychological functioning is a risk factor for antisocial behavior, but good neuropsychological functioning is protective in the context of adversity. Although more work remains in clarifying these findings, especially with respect to how they apply to different types of offending (e.g., violent versus nonviolent, premeditated versus impulsive), the discovery of biosocial interactions using such a wide variety of measures lends support to the biosocial perspective on crime.

References

Archwamety, T., & Katsiyannis, A. (2000). Academic remediation, parole violations, and recidivism rates among delinquent youths. *Remedial and Special Education, 21*(3), 161–170.

Arseneault, L., Moffitt, T. E., Caspi, A., Taylor, A., Fruhlilng, A., Rijsdijk, V., Measelle, J. R., et al. (2003). Strong genetic effects on cross-situational antisocial behaviour among 5-year-old children according to mothers, teachers, examiner-observers, and twins' self-reports. *Journal of Child Psychology and Psychiatry, 44,* 832–848.

Arseneault, L., Tremblay, R. E., Boulerice, B., & Saucier, J. F. (2002). Obstetrical complications and violent delinquency: Testing two developmental pathways. *Child Development, 73,* 496–508.

Arseneault, L., Tremblay, R. E., Boulerice, B., Seguin, J. R., & Saucier, J. F. (2000). Minor physical anomalies and family adversity as risk factors for violent delinquency in adolescence. *American Journal of Psychiatry, 157,* 917–923.

Banks, T., & Dabbs, J. M. (1996). Salivary testosterone and cortisol in a delinquent and violent urban subculture. *Journal of Social Psychology, 136,* 49–56.

Barker, E. D., Séguin, J. R., White, H. R., Bates, M. E., Lacourse, E., Carbonneau, R., & Tremblay, R. E. (2007). Developmental trajectories of male physical violence and theft: Relations to neurocognitive performance. *Archives of General Psychiatry, 64*(5), 592–599.

Bartels, J. M., Ryan, J. J., Urban, L. S., & Glass, L. A. (2010). Correlations between estimates of state IQ and FBI crime statistics. *Personality and Individual Differences, 48*(5), 579–583.

Beaver, K. M., DeLisi, M., Vaughn, M. G., & Wright, J. P. (2010). The intersection of genes and neuropsychological deficits in the prediction of adolescent delinquency and low self-control. *International Journal of Offender Therapy and Comparative Criminology, 54*(1), 22–42.

Beaver, K. M., DeLisi, M., Wright, J. P., & Vaughn, M. G. (2009). Gene environment interplay and delinquent involvement: Evidence of direct and indirect, and interactive effects. *Journal of Adolescent Research, 24*, 147–168.

Berman, M. E., & Coccaro, E. F. (1998). Neurobiologic correlates of violence: Relevance to criminal responsibility. *Behavioral Sciences & the Law, 16*, 303–318.

Blair, R. J. (2007). The amygdala and ventromedial prefrontal cortex in morality and psychopathy. *Trends in Cognitive Science, 11*, 387–392.

Boccardi, M., Ganzola, R., Rossi, R., Sabattoli, F., Laakso, M. P., Repo-Tiihonen, E., Tiihonen, J., et al. (2010). Abnormal hippocampal shape in offenders with psychopathy. *Human Brain Mapping, 31*, 438–447.

Brennan, P. A., Grekin, E. R., & Mednick, S. A. (1999). Maternal smoking during pregnancy and adult male criminal outcomes. *Archives of General Psychiatry, 56*, 215–219.

Brennan, P. A., Grekin, E. R., Mortensen, E. L., & Mednick, S. A. (2002). Relationship of maternal smoking during pregnancy with criminal arrest and hospitalization for substance abuse in male and female adult offspring. *American Journal of Psychiatry, 159*, 48–54.

Brennan, P. A., Mednick, B. R., & Mednick, S. A. (1993). Parental psychopathology, congenital factors, and violence. In S. Hodgins (Ed.), *Mental disorder and crime* (pp. 244–261). Thousand Oaks: Sage.

Brennan, P. A., Mednick, S. A., & Raine, A. (1997). Biosocial interactions and violence: A focus on perinatal factors. In A. Raine, P. A. Brennan, D. Farrington, & S. A. Mednick (Eds.), *Biosocial bases of violence* (pp. 163–174). New York: Plenum.

Brennan, P. A., Raine, A., Schulsinger, F., Kirkegaard-Sorensen, L., Knop, J., Hutchings, B., Mednick, S. A., et al. (1997). Psychophysiological protective factors for male subjects at high risk for criminal behavior. *American Journal of Psychiatry, 154*, 853–855.

Brotman, L. M., Gouley, K. K., Huang, K. Y., Kamboukos, D., Fratto, C., & Pine, D. S. (2007). Effects of a psychosocial family-based preventative intervention on cortisol response to a social challenge in preschoolers at high risk for antisocial behavior. *Archives of General Psychiatry, 64*, 1172–1179.

Cadesky, E. B., Mota, V. L., & Schachar, R. J. (2000). Beyond words: How do problem children with ADHD and/or conduct problems process nonverbal information about affect? *Journal of the American Academy of Child & Adolescent Psychiatry, 39*(9), 1160–1167.

Cannon, M., Huttenen, M. O., Tanskanen, A. J., Arseneault, L., Jones, P. B., & Murray, R. M. (2002). Perinatal and childhood risk factors for later criminality and violence in schizophrenia. *British Journal of Psychiatry, 180*, 496–501.

Caspi, A., McClay, J., Moffitt, T. E., Mill, J., Martin, J., Craig, I. W., Poulton, R., et al. (2002). Role of genotype in the cycle of violence in maltreated children. *Science, 297*, 851–854.

Cima, M., Smeets, T., & Jelicic, M. (2008). Self-reported trauma, cortisol levels, and aggression in psychopathic and non-psychopathic prison inmates. *Biological Psychiatry, 78*, 75–86.

Coccaro, E. F., & Kavoussi, R. J. (1997). Fluoxetine and impulsive aggressive behavior in personality disordered subjects. *Archives of General Psychiatry, 54,* 1081–1088.

Craig, M. C., Catani, M., Deeley, Q., Latham, R., Daly, E., Kanaan, R., Murphy, D. G., et al. (2009) Altered connections on the road of psychopathy. *Molecular Psychiatry, 14,* 946–953.

Dabbs, J. M., Frady, R. L., & Carr, T. S. (1987). Saliva testosterone and criminal violence in young adult prison inmates. *Psychosomatic Medicine, 49*(2), 174–182.

Dabbs, J. M., & Morris, R. (1990). Testosterone, social class, and antisocial behavior in a sample of 4,462 men. *Psychological Science, 1,* 209–211.

Dolan, M., & Park, I. (2002). The neuropsychology of antisocial personality disorder. *Psychological Medicine, 32*(3), 417–427.

Dougherty, D. M., Dew, R. E., Mathias, C. W., Marsh, D. M., Addicott, M. A., & Barratt, E. S. (2007). Impulsive and premeditated subtypes of aggression in conduct disorder: Differences in time estimation. *Aggressive Behavior, 33*(6), 574–582.

Eley, T. C., Lichtenstein, P., & Moffitt, T. E. (2003). A longitudinal behavioral genetic analysis of the etiology of aggressive and nonaggressive antisocial behavior. *Development and Psychopathology, 15,* 383–402.

Eriksson, Å., Hodgins, S., & Tengström, A. (2005). Verbal intelligence and offending among men with schizophrenia. *International Journal of Forensic Mental Health, 4,* 191–200.

Eysenck, H. J. (1977). *Crime and personality* (3rd ed.). St. Albans, England: Paladin.

Farrington, D. P. (1997). The relationship between low resting heart rate and violence. In A. Raine, P. A. Brennan, D. P. Farrington, & S. A. Mednick (Eds.), *Biosocial bases of violence* (pp. 89–106). New York: Plenum.

Fast, D. K., Conry, J., & Loock, C. A. (1999). Identifying Fetal Alcohol Syndrome among youth in the criminal justice system. *Journal of Developmental and Behavioral Pediatrics, 20,* 370–372.

Fergusson, D. M., Horwood, J. L., & Lynskey, M. T. (1993). Maternal smoking before and after pregnancy. *Pediatrics, 92,* 815–822.

Fergusson, D. M., Woodward, L. J., & Horwood, J. (1998). Maternal smoking during pregnancy and psychiatric adjustment in late adolescence. *Archives of General Psychiatry, 55,* 721–727.

Firestone, P., & Peters, S. (1983). Minor physical anomalies and behavior in children: A review. *Journal of Autism and Developmental Disorders, 13,* 411–425.

Giancola, P. R., Shoal, G. D., & Mezzich, A. C. (2001). Constructive thinking, executive functioning, antisocial behavior, and drug use involvement in adolescent females with a substance use disorder. *Experimental and Clinical Psychopharmacology, 9*(2), 215–227.

Gibson, C. L., Piquero, A. R., & Tibbetts, S. G. (2000). Assessing the relationship between maternal cigarette smoking during pregnancy and age at first police contact. *Justice Quarterly, 17,* 519–542.

Gibson, C. L., & Tibbetts, S. G. (1998). Interaction between maternal cigarette smoking and Apgar scores in predicting offending behavior. *Psychological Reports, 83*, 579–586.

Gibson, C. L., & Tibbetts, S. G. (2000). A biosocial interaction in predicting early onset of offending. *Psychological Reports, 86*, 509–518.

Goldman, D., & Ducci, F. (2007). The genetics of psychopathic disorders. In A. R. Felthous & H. Sa (Eds.), *International handbook on psychopathic disorders and the law: Volume 1* (pp. 149–169). West Sussex, England: John Wiley & Sons Ltd.

Grekin, E. R., Brennan, P. A., & Hammen, C. (2005). Parental alcohol use disorders and child delinquency: The mediating effects of executive functioning and chronic family stress. *Journal of Studies on Alcohol, 66*, 14–22.

Guy, J. D., Majorski, L. V., Wallace, C. J., & Guy, M. P. (1983). The incidence of minor physical anomalies in adult male schizophrenics. *Schizophrenia Bulletin, 9*, 571–582.

Hancock, M., Tapscott, J. L., & Hoaken, P. N. S. (2010). Role of executive dysfunction in predicting frequency and severity of violence. *Aggressive Behavior, 36*(5), 338–349.

Hemming, J. H. (1981). Electrodermal indices in a selected prison sample and students. *Personality and Individual Differences, 2*, 37–46.

Hirono, N., Mega, M. S., Dinov, I. D., Mishkin, F., & Cummings, J. L. (2000). Left frontaltemporal hypoperfusion is associate with aggression in patient with dementia. *Archives Neurology, 57*, 861–866.

Hodgins, S., Kratzer, L., & McNeil, T. F. (2001). Obstetric complications, parenting, and risk of criminal behavior. *Archives of General Psychiatry, 58*, 746–752.

Holi, M., Auvinen-Lintunen, L., Lindberg, N., Tani, P., & Virkkunen, M. (2006). Inverse correlation between severity of psychopathic traits and serum cortisol levels in young adult violent male offenders. *Psychopathology, 39*, 102–104.

Hughes, J. R., Zagar, R. J., Busch, K. G., Grove, W. M., & Arbit, J. (2009). Looking forward in records of youth abused as children: Risks for homicidal, violent, and delinquent offenses. *Psychological Reports, 104*(1), 77–101.

Isen, J. (2010). A meta-analytic assessment of Wechsler's P>V sign in antisocial populations. *Clinical Psychology Review, 30*, 423–435.

Jacobson, K. C., Prescott, C. A., & Kendler, K. S. (2002). Sex differences in the genetic and environmental influences on the development of antisocial behavior. *Development and Psychopathology, 14*, 395–416.

Jaffee, S. R., Caspi, A., Moffitt, T. E., Dodge, K. A., Rutter, M., Taylor, A., et al. (2005). Nature ×nurture: Genetic vulnerabilities interact with physical maltreatment to promote conduct problems. *Development and Psychopathology, 17*, 67–84.

Jaffee, S. R., Caspi, A., Moffitt, T. E., & Taylor, A. (2004). Physical maltreatment victim to antisocial child: Evidence of an environmentally-mediated process. *Journal of Abnormal Psychology, 113*, 44–55.

Kandel, E., Brennan, P. A., Mednick, S. A., & Michelson, N. M. (1989). Minor physical anomalies and recidivistic adult criminal behavior. *Acta Psychiatrica Scandinavica, 79*, 103–107.

Kandel, E., & Mednick, S. A. (1991). Perinatal complications predict violent offending. *Criminology, 29*, 519–529.

Kavanagh, L., Rowe, D., Hersch, J., Barnett, K. J., & Reznik, R. (2010). Neurocognitive deficits and psychiatric disorders in a NSW prison population. *International Journal of Law and Psychiatry, 33*(1), 20–26.

Kirkpatrick, T., Joyce, E., Milton, J., Duggan, C., Tyrer, P., & Rogers, R. D. (2007). Altered memory and affective instability in prisoners assessed for dangerous and severe personality disorder. *The British Journal of Psychiatry, 190*(49), s20–26.

Koenen, K. C., Caspi, A., Moffitt, T. E., Rijsdijk, F., & Taylor, A. (2006). Genetic influences on the overlap between low IQ and antisocial behavior in young children. *Journal of Abnormal Psychology, 115*(4), 787–797.

Kronenberger, W. G., Mathews, V. P., Dunn, D. W., Wang, Y., Wood, E. A., Giauque, A. L., Li, T.-Q., et al. (2005). Media violence exposure and executive functioning in aggressive and control adolescents. *Journal of Clinical Psychology, 61*(6), 725–737.

Kudielka, B. M., & Kirschbaum, C. (2005). Sex differences in HPA axis responses to stress: A review. *Biological Psychiatry, 69*, 113–132.

Lahey, B. B., Loeber, R., Hart, E. L., Frick, P. J., Applegate, B., Zhang, Q., Russo, M. F., et al. (1995). Four-year longitudinal study of conduct disorder in boys: Patterns and predictors of persistence. *Journal of Abnormal Psychology, 104*(1), 83–93.

Laucht, M., Esser, G., Baving, L., Gerhold, M., Hoesch, I., Ihle, W., Schmidt, M. H., et al. (2000). Behavioral sequelae of perinatal insults and early family adversity at 8 years of age. *Journal of the American Academy of Child and Adolescent Psychiatry, 39*, 1229–1237.

Lee, T. M., Chan, S. C., & Raine, A. (2009). Hyperresponsivity to threat stimuli in domestic violence offenders: A functional magnetic resonance imaging study. *Journal of Clinical Psychiatry, 70*, 36–45.

Levi, M. D., Nussbaum, D. S., & Rich, J. B. (2010). Neuropsychological and personality characteristics of predatory, irritable, and nonviolent offenders: Support for a typology of criminal human aggression. *Criminal Justice and Behavior, 37*(6), 633–655.

Lewis, D. O., Lovely, R., Yeager, C., & Femina, D. D. (1989). Toward a theory of the genesis of violence: A follow-up study of delinquents. *Journal of the American Academy of Child and Adolescent Psychiatry, 28*, 431–436.

Lewis, D. O., Pincus, J. H., Feldman, M., Jackson, L., & Bard, B. (1986). Psychiatric, neurological and psychoeducational characteristics of 15 death row inmates in the United States. *American Journal of Psychiatry, 143*, 838–845.

Loney, B. R., Butler, M. A., Lima, E. N., Counts, C. A., & Eckel, L. A. (2006). The relation between salivary cortisol, callous-unemotional traits, and conduct problems in an adolescent non-referred sample. *Journal of Child Psychology and Psychiatry, 47*(1), 30–36.

Loney, B. R., Frick, P. J., Ellis, M., & McCoy, M. G. (1998). Intelligence, callous-unemotional traits, and antisocial behavior. *Journal of Psychopathology and Behavioral Assessment, 20*(3), 231–247.

Lorber, M. F. (2004). Psychophysiology of aggression, psychopathy, and conduct problems: A meta-analysis. *Psychological Bulletin, 130,* 531–552.

Luria, A. R. (1980). *Higher cortical functions in man* (2nd ed.). New York: Basic Books.

Lyons, M. J., True, W. R., Eisen, S. A., Goldberg, J., Meyer, J. M., Faraone, S. V., et al. (1995). Differential heritability of adult and juvenile traits. *Archives of General Psychiatry, 52,* 906–915.

Marks, D. J., Miller, S. R., Schulz, K. P., Newcorn, J. H., & Halperin, J. M. (2007). The interaction of psychosocial adversity and biological risk in childhood aggression. *Psychiatry Research, 151,* 221–230.

Masten, A. S., Hubbard, J. J., Gest, S. D., Tellegen, A., Garmezy, N., & Ramirez, M. (1999). Competence in the context of adversity: Pathways to resilience and maladaptation from childhood to late adolescence. *Development and Psychopathology, 11,* 143–169.

Mataró, M., Jurado, M. A., Garcia-Sánchez, C., Barraquer, L., Costa-Jussá, F. R., & Junque, C. (2001). Long-term effects of bilateral frontal brain lesion: 60 years after injury with an iron bar. *Archives of Neurology, 58,* 1139–1142.

Mattson, S. N., & Riley, E. P. (2000). Parent ratings of behavior in children with heavy prenatal alcohol exposure and IQ-matched controls. *Alcoholism: Clinical and Experimental Research, 24,* 226–231.

Maughan, B., Taylor, C., Taylor, A., Butler, N., & Bynner, J. (2001). Pregnancy smoking and childhood conduct problems: A causal association? *Journal of Child Psychology and Psychiatry, 42,* 1021–1028.

Maughan, B., Taylor, A., Caspi, A., & Moffitt, T. E. (2004). Prenatal smoking and early childhood conduct problems. *Archives of General Psychiatry, 61,* 836–843.

Mazur, A. (1995). Biosocial models of deviant behavior among male army veterans. *Biological Psychology, 41,* 271–293.

McHale, B. G., Obrzut, J. E., & Sabers, D. L. (2003). Relationship of cognitive functioning and aggressive behavior with emotionally disabled and specific learning disabled students. *Journal of Developmental & Physical Disabilities, 15*(2), 123–140.

Mednick, S. A. (1977). A biosocial theory of the learning of law-abiding behavior. In S. A. Mednick & K. O. Christiansen (Eds.), *Biosocial bases of criminal behavior* (pp. 1–8). New York: Gardner.

Mednick, S. A., & Kandel, E. S. (1988). Congenital determinants of violence. *Bulletin of the American Academy of Psychiatry and the Law, 16,* 101–109.

Mednick, S. A., Kirkegaard-Sorensen, L., Hutchings, B., Knop, J., Rosenberg. R., & Schulsinger, F. (1977). An example of biosocial interaction research: The interplay of socioenvironmental and individual factors in the etiology of criminal behavior. In S. A. Mednick & K. O. Christiansen (Eds.), *Biosocial bases of criminal behavior* (pp. 9–24). New York: Gardner.

Miles, D. R., & Carey, G. (1997). Genetic and environmental architecture of human aggression. *Journal of Personality and Social Psychology, 72,* 207–217.

Miller, E. K., & Cohen, J. D. (2001). An integrative theory of prefrontal cortex function. *Annual Review of Neuroscience, 24*(1), 167–202.

Moffitt, T. E. (2005). The new look of behavioral genetics in developmental psychopathology: Gene-environment interplay in antisocial behavior. *Psychological Bulletin, 131*, 533–554.

Moffitt, T. E., Caspi, A., Fawcett, J. W., Brammer, G. L., Raleigh, M., Yuwiler, A., & Silva, P. A. (1997). Whole blood serotonin and family background relate to male violence. In A. Raine, P. A. Brennan, D. P. Farrington, & S. A. Mednick (Eds.), *Biosocial bases of violence*. New York: Plenum Press.

Moffitt, T. E., Lynam, D. R., & Silva, P. A. (1994). Neuropsychological tests predicting persistent male delinquency. *Criminology, 32*(2), 277–300.

Moore, T. M., Scarpa, A., & Raine, A. (2002). A meta-analysis of serotonin metabolite 5-HIAA and antisocial behavior. *Aggressive Behavior, 28*, 299–316.

Morgan, A. B., & Lilienfeld, S. O. (2000). A meta-analytic review of the relation between antisocial behavior and neuropsychological measures of executive function. *Clinical Psychology Review, 20*(1), 113–136.

Muñoz, L. C., Frick, P. J., Kimonis, E. R., & Aucoin, K. J. (2008). Verbal ability and delinquency: Testing the moderating role of psychopathic traits. *Journal of Child Psychology and Psychiatry, 49*(4), 414–421.

Nigg, J. T., Glass, J. M., Wong, M. M., Poon, E., Jester, J. M., Fitzgerald, H. E., Zucker, R. A., et al. (2004). Neuropsychological executive functioning in children at elevated risk for alcoholism: Findings in early adolescence. *Journal of Abnormal Psychology, 113*(2), 302–314.

Nilsson, K. W., Wargelius, H. L., Sjoberg, R. L., Leppert, J., & Oreland, L. (2008). The MAO-A gene, platelet MAO-B activity and psychosocial environment in adolescent female alcohol-related problem behaviour. *Drug and Alcohol Dependence, 93*, 51–62.

Olson, H. C., Streissguth, A. P., Sampson, P. D., Barr, H. M., Bookstein, F. L., & Thiede, K. W. (1997). Association of prenatal alcohol exposure with behavioral and learning problems in early adolescence. *Journal of the American Academy of Child and Adolescent Psychiatry, 36*, 1187–1194.

O'Neal, C. R., Brotman, L. M., Huang, K. Y., Gouley, K. K., Kamboukos, D., Calzada, E. J., et al. (2010). Understanding relations among early family environment, cortisol response, and child aggression via a prevention experiment. *Child Development, 81*, 290–305.

Orlebeke, J. F., Knol, D. L., & Verhulst, F. C. (1997). Increase in child behavior problems resulting from maternal smoking during pregnancy. *Archives of Environmental Health, 52*, 317–321.

Patrick, C. J. (2008). Psychophysiological correlates of aggression and violence: An integrative review. *Philosophical Transactions of the Royal Society, 363*, 2543–2555.

Pine, D. S., Shaffer, D., Schonfeld, I. S., & Davies, M. (1997). Minor physical anomalies: Modifiers of environmental risks for psychiatric impairment? *Journal of the American Academy of Child and Adolescent Psychiatry, 36*, 395–403.

Piquero, A., & Tibbetts, S. (1999). The impact of pre/perinatal disturbances and disadvantaged familial environment in predicting criminal offending. *Studies on Crime and Crime Prevention, 8*, 52–70.

Popma, A., & Raine, A. (2006). Will future forensic assessment be neurobiologic? *Child and Adolescent Psychiatric Clinics of North America, 15,* 429–444.

Raine, A. (1993). *The psychopathology of crime: Criminal behavior as a clinical disorder.* San Diego, CA: Academic Press.

Raine, A. (2002a). Biosocial studies of antisocial and violent behavior in children and adults: A review. *Journal of Abnormal Child Psychology, 30,* 311–326.

Raine, A. (2002b). Annotation: The role of prefrontal deficits, low autonomic arousal and early health factors in the development of antisocial and aggressive behavior in children. *Journal of Child Psychology and Psychiatry and Allied Disciplines, 43,* 417–434.

Raine, A., Brennan, P., & Mednick, S. A. (1994). Birth complications combined with early maternal rejection at age 1 year predispose to violent crime at age 18 years. *Archives of General Psychiatry, 51,* 984–988.

Raine, A., Brennan, P., & Mednick, S. A. (1997). Interaction between birth complications and early maternal rejection in predisposing individuals to adult violence: Specificity to serious, early-onset violence. *American Journal of Psychiatry, 154,* 1265–1271.

Raine, A., Buchsbaum, M., Stanley, J., Lottenberg, S., Abel, L., & Stoddard, J. (1994). Selective reductions in prefrontal glucose metabolism in murderers. *Biological Psychiatry, 36,* 365–373.

Raine, A., Mellingen, K., Liu, J., Venables, P. H., & Mednick, S. A. (2003). Effects of environmental enrichment at ages 3–5 years on schizotypal personality and antisocial behavior at ages 17 and 23 years. *American Journal of Psychiatry, 160,* 1627–1635.

Raine, A., Moffitt, T. E., Caspi, A., Loeber, R., Stouthamer-Loeber, M., & Lynam, D. (2005). Neurocognitive impairments in boys on the life-course persistent antisocial path. *Journal of Abnormal Psychology, 114*(1), 38–49.

Raine, A., Park, S., Lencz, T., Bihrle, S., LaCasse, L., Widom, C. S., Singh, M., et al. (2001). Reduced right hemisphere activation in severely abused violent offenders during a working memory task: An fMRI study. *Aggressive Behavior, 27,* 111–129.

Raine, A., Stoddard, J., Bihrle, S., & Buchsbaum, M. (1998) Prefrontal glucose deficits in murderers lacking psychosocial deprivation. *Neuropsychiatry, Neuropsychology, Behavioral Neurology, 11,* 1–7.

Raine, A., & Venables, P. H. (1981). Classical conditioning and socialization – A biosocial interaction? *Personality and Individual Differences, 2,* 273–283.

Raine, A., Venables, P. H., Dalais, C., Mellingen, K., Reynolds, C., & Mendrek, A. (2001). Early educational and health enrichment at age 3–5 years is associated with increased autonomic and central nervous system arousal and orienting at age 11 years: Evidence from the Mauritius Child Health Project. *Psychophysiology, 38,* 254–266.

Raine, A., Venables, P. H., & Mednick, S. A. (1997). Low resting heart rate age 3 years predisposes to aggression at age 11 years: Evidence from the Mauritius Child Health Project. *Journal of American Academy of Child and Adolescent Psychiatry, 36,* 1457–1464.

Raine, A., Venables, P. H., & Williams, M. (1995). High autonomic arousal and electrodermal orienting at age 15 years as protective factors against criminal behavior at age 29 years. *American Journal of Psychiatry, 152*, 1595–1600.

Raine, A., Venables, P. H., & Williams, M. (1996). Better autonomic conditioning and faster electrodermal half-recovery time at age 15 years as possible protective factors against crime at age 29 years. *Developmental Psychology, 32*, 624–630.

Raine, A., Yaralian, P. S., Reynolds, C., Venables, P. H., & Mednick, S. A. (2002). Spatial but not verbal cognitive deficits at age 3 years in persistently antisocial individuals. *Development and Psychopathology, 14*, 25–44.

Rantakallio, P., Laara, E., Isohanni, M., & Moilanen, I. (1992). Maternal smoking during pregnancy and delinquency of the offspring: An association without causation? *International Journal of Epidemiology, 21*, 1106–1113.

Rasanen, P., Hakko, H., Isohanni, M., Hodgins, S., Jarvelin, M. R., & Tiihonen, J. (1999). Maternal smoking during pregnancy and risk of criminal behavior among adult male offspring in the northern Finland 1996 birth cohort. *American Journal of Psychiatry, 156*, 857–862.

Rhee, S. H., & Waldman, I. D. (2002). Genetic and environmental influences on antisocial behavior: A meta-analysis of twin and adoption studies. *Psychological Bulletin, 128*, 490–529.

Rispens, J., Swaab, H., van den Oord, E. J. C. G., Cohen-Kettenis, P., van Engeland, H., & van Yperen, T. (1997). WISC profiles in child psychiatric diagnosis: Sense or nonsense? *Journal of the American Academy of Child & Adolescent Psychiatry, 36*(11), 1587–1594.

Roebuck, T. M., Mattson, S. N., & Riley, E. P. (1999). Behavioral and psychosocial profiles of alcohol-exposed children. *Alcoholism: Clinical and Experimental Research, 23*, 1070–1076.

Rowe, D. C. (1986). Genetic and environmental components of antisocial behavior: A study of 265 twin pairs. *Criminology, 24*, 513–532.

Sadeh, N., Javdani, S., Jackson, J. J., Reynolds, E. K., Potenza, M. N., Gelernter, J., Verona, E., et al. (2010). Serotonin transporter gene associations with psychopathic traits in youth vary as a function of socioeconomic resources. *Journal of Abnormal Psychology, 119*, 604–609.

Saltaris, C., Serbin, L. A., Stack, D. M., Karp, J. A., Schwartzman, A. E., & Ledingham, J. E. (2004). Nurturing cognitive competence in preschoolers: A longitudinal study of intergenerational continuity and risk. *International Journal of Behavioral Development, 28*(2), 105–115.

Scarpa, A., & Raine, A. (2007). Biosocial bases of violence. In D. J. Flannery, A. T. Vazsonyi, & I. D. Waldman (Eds.), *The Cambridge handbook of violent behavior and aggression* (pp. 151–169). Cambridge: Cambridge University Press.

Scarpa, A., Tanaka, A., & Haden, S. C. (2008). Biosocial bases of reactive and proactive aggression: The roles of community violence exposure and heart rate. *Journal of Community Psychology, 36*, 969–988.

Schonfeld, A. M., Mattson, S. N., & Riley, E. P. (2005). Moral maturity and delinquency after prenatal alcohol exposure. *Journal of Studies on Alcohol, 66*, 545–554.

Sharkey, P. (2010). The acute effect of local homicides on children's cognitive performance. *Proceedings of the National Academy of Sciences, 107*(26), 11733–11738.

Slutske, W. S., Heath, A. C., Dinwiddie, S. H., Madden, P. A., Bucholz, K. K., Dunne, M. P., Martin, N. G., et al. (1997). Modeling genetic and environmental influences in the etiology of conduct disorder: A study of 2,682 adult twin pairs. *Journal of Abnormal Psychology, 106*, 266–279.

Streissguth, A. P., Barr, H. M., Kogan, J., & Bookstein, F. L. (1996). *Understanding the occurrence of secondary disabilities in clients with fetal alcohol syndrome (FAS) and fetal alcohol effects (FAE)*. Washington, DC: Centers for Disease Control and Prevention.

Syngelaki, E. M., Moore, S. C., Savage, J. C., Fairchild, G., & van Goozen, S. H. M. (2009). Executive functioning and risky decision making in young male offenders. *Criminal Justice and Behavior. Special Issue: Biosocial criminology, 36*(11), 1213–1227.

Tikkanen, R., Ducci, F., Goldman, D., Holi, M., Lindberg, N., Tiihonen, J., & Virkunnen, M. (2010). MAOA alters the effects of heavy drinking and childhood physical abuse on risk for severe impulsive acts of violence among alcoholic violent offenders. *Alcoholism, Clinical and Experimental Research, 34*, 853–860.

Vanderbilt-Adriance, E. & Shaw, D. S. (2008). Protective factors and the development of resilience in the context of neighborhood disadvantage. *Journal of Abnormal Child Psychology, 36*, 887–901.

van Goozen, S. H. M., Matthys, W., Cohen-Kettenis, P. T., Thijssen, J. H. H., & van Engeland, H. (1998). Adrenal androgens and aggression in conduct disorder prepubertal boys and normal controls. *Biological Psychiatry, 43*, 156–158.

van Honk, J., & Schutter, D. J. L. G. (2007). Testosterone reduces conscious detection of signals serving social correction: Implications for antisocial behavior. *Psychological Science, 18*, 663–667.

Vitacco, M. J., Neumann, C. S., & Wodushek, T. (2008). Differential relationships between the dimensions of psychopathy and intelligence: Replication with adult jail inmates. *Criminal Justice and Behavior, 35*(1), 48–55.

Wakschlag, L. S., Lahey, B. B., Loeber, R., Green, S. M., Gordon, R., & Leventhal, B. L. (1997). Maternal smoking during pregnancy and the risk of conduct disorder in boys. *Archives of General Psychiatry, 54*, 670–676.

Wakschlag, L. S., Pickett, K. E., Cook, E. C., Benowitz, N. L., & Leventhal, B. L. (2002). Maternal smoking during pregnancy and severe antisocial behavior in offspring: A review. *American Journal of Public Health, 92*, 966–974.

Weissman, M. M., Warner, V., Wickramaratne, P. J., & Kandel, D. B. (1999). Maternal smoking during pregnancy and psychopathology in offspring followed to adulthood. *Journal of the American Academy of Child and Adolescent Psychiatry, 38*, 892–899.

Werner, E. E. (1987). Vulnerability and resiliency in children at risk for delinquency: A longitudinal study from birth to young adulthood. In J. D. Burchard & S. N. Burchard (Eds.), *Primary prevention of psychopathology* (pp. 16–43). Newbury Park, CA: Sage.

Woermann, F. G., Van Elst, L. T., Koepp, M. J., Free, S. L., Thompson, P. J., Trimble, M. R., & Duncan, J. S. (2000). Reduction of frontal neocortical grey matter associated with affective aggression in patients with temporal lobe epilepsy: An objective voxel by voxel analysis of automatically segmented MRI. *Journal of Neurology, Neurosurgery, & Psychiatry, 68*, 162–169.

Yang, Y., Raine, A., Lencz, T., Bihrle, S., LaCasse, L., & Colletti, P. (2005). Volume reduction in prefrontal gray matter in unsuccessful criminal psychopaths. *Biological Psychiatry, 57*, 1103–1108.

Yang, Y., Raine, A., Colletti, P., Toga, A. W., & Narr, K. L. (2010). Morphological alterations in the prefrontal cortex and the amygdala in unsuccessful psychopaths. *Journal of Abnormal Psychology, 119*, 546–554.

The Relationship between Low Resting Heart Rate and Antisocial Behavior: Correlation or Causation?

Todd A. Armstrong

Based on a meta-analysis of 45 independent effect sizes from 40 studies, Ortiz and Raine (2004) concluded "low resting heart rate appears to be the best-replicated biological correlate to date of antisocial and aggressive behavior in children and adolescents" (p. 154). Research included in the Ortiz and Raine (2004) meta-analysis and subsequent studies show that low resting heart rate is predictive of crime and antisocial behavior among adults (Farington, 1997; Raine et al., 1990, 1995; Wadsworth, 1976) and that the link between resting heart rate and antisocial behavior remains net of controls for variables from traditional criminological theories (Armstrong et al., 2009; Cauffman et al., 2005; Farrington, 1997). Recent research also indicates that low resting heart rate (LRHR) is related to serious and violent antisocial behavior (SVASB), but not to more general delinquency (Armstrong et al., 2009). In their meta-analysis, Ortiz and Raine (2004) find an average effect size of 0.44 among studies testing the relationship between low resting heart rate (LRHR) and antisocial behavior (ASB). The effect size for the subset of studies testing the relationship between low heart rate reactivity (LHRR) and antisocial behavior was in an effect size of 0.76. This suggests that particular attention to LHRR may be warranted.

Raine (2002) reviewed a number of hypotheses regarding the relationship between resting heart rate and antisocial behavior. These hypotheses were organized around two main causal mechanisms. In the first, low autonomic arousal (low resting heart rate) is a marker for psychological states which in turn lead to increased antisocial behavior. In the second, physiological characteristics cause both low resting heart rate and increased antisocial behavior.

Psychological characteristics proposed as mediators between resting heart rate and antisocial behavior include stimulation seeking and fearlessness. Stimulation seeking suggests low autonomic arousal constitutes an unpleasant psychological state, with acts of antisocial behavior, including crime and delinquency, undertaken in an effort to increase arousal levels. Low resting heart rate may also be a marker of fearlessness, which leads to increased antisocial behavior through a disregard for the negative consequences of this behavior. Physiological processes potentially mediating the relationship between resting heart rate and antisocial behavior included right hemisphere dysfunction, reduced noradrenergic functioning and increased vagal tone.

In an effort to shed light on the relationship between resting heart rate and antisocial behavior, this chapter will first discuss the physiological processes that determine heart rate with specific attention to the process that may influence heart rate reactivity. Next, the chapter will identify brain regions that may explain the relationship between heart rate and antisocial behavior. Activity in these brain regions are associated with both heart rate and antisocial behavior, as well as being linked to empathy, fear conditioning, and the experience of emotion. Subsequently the chapter will review evidence for a direct influence of heart rate on antisocial behavior net of brain activity predictive of both heart rate and antisocial behavior.

Physiological Structures and Processes Contributing to Heart Rate and Changes in Heart Rate

Heart rate is determined largely by a series of structures ranging from the prefrontal cortex to direct inputs to the heart's sino-atrial node through the autonomic nervous system (ANS). The ANS has two major divisions: the parasympathetic and sympathetic nervous systems. Broadly conceived the parasympathetic nervous system (PNS) is responsible for vegetative and restorative function, while the sympathetic nervous system (SNS) is associated with the mobilization of energy under stress or the "fight or flight" response. Regarding heart rate, increases in parasympathetic nervous system activity lead to deceleration in heart rate, while relative increases in sympathetic nervous system activity are associated with heart rate increases.

Input to the ANS is provided by cortical and subcortical structures through key areas in the brain stem. Together the cortical and subcortical structures that influence heart rate along with areas in the brain stem are referred to as the central autonomic network (CAN) (Benarroch, 1993, 1997).[1] The parasympathetic and sympathetic nervous systems influence heart rate through input to the sino-atrial node. The sino-atrial node serves as the heart's pacemaker, generating electrical

---

1   The neuroanatomical structures and interconnections identified in the CAN are demonstrated through studies of animal models and through neuroimaging studies in humans. For a review of the animal literature see Cechetto (2004) and Saper (2002). For a review of neuroimaging studies in humans see Cechetto and Shoemaker (2009).

impulses that trigger heart contraction. Parasympathetic input to the sino-atrial node is conveyed by the tenth cranial or 'vagus' nerve and originates in the dorsal motor nucleus and the nucleus ambiguous in the brain stem (Levy and Warner, 1994). Sympathetic influences originate in the rostral ventrolateral medulla and are conveyed to the sino-atrial node through stellate ganglia by way of the intermediolateral (IML) column of the spinal cord (Levy and Martin, 1979).

The CAN includes cortical, limbic, and midbrain structures. Cortical structures in the CAN include the medial prefrontal cortex, and orbitofrontal cortex. Limbic structures in the CAN include the cingulate cortex, insular cortex, amygdala and the hypothalamus; midbrain structures include the parabrachial complex, nucleus of the solitary tract (NTS), and the rostral and caudal ventrolateral medulla. In the ANS, efferent neurons carry information away from the CAN and afferent neurons carry information toward the CAN. Afferent neurons suggest that autonomic arousal (or underarousal) may have a direct influence on emotion and cognition, and by extension, behavior. Feedback from these neurons ultimately returns to the insular cortex (IC) and other higher cortical structures, where central representations of bodily states are thought to influence emotion and cognition (Craig, 2002 and 2009)

Thayer et al. (2009) provide an overview of the function of the CAN and its relationship to the ANS, with medial prefrontal cortex (MPFC) and orbtiofrontal cortex influencing autonomic output through interconnections with both the cingulate cortex and the insular cortex. These regions connect directly and indirectly (through the amygdala) with hypothalamus, periaqueductal gray matter, and the parabrachial poinine nuclei, which then influence both parasympathetic and sympathetic tone through the NTS and sympathetic tone through the rostral ventrolateral medulla (RVLM). It is important to note that the connections described by Thayer et al. (2009) represent the primary connections between structures in the CAN. There are numerous interconnections between structures in the CAN. As described by Benarroch (1993), the components of the CAN tend to be reciprocally interconnected "allowing continuous feedback interactions and integration of autonomic responses" (p. 990).

The RVLM appears to be the major contributor to pre-ganglionic sympathetic nervous system tone (Guyenet, 1990; Dampney et al., 2000). Stimulation of the RVLM causes an increase in heart rate and blood pressure (Dampney, 1994). There is also evidence that pharmacological blockade of the RVLM reduces depressor effects that normally occur during the stimulation of the prefrontal cortex or areas within the lateral hypothalamus (Cechetto and Chen, 1992). The RVLM influences sympathetic tone through projections into the intermediolateral (IML) cell column (Cabot, 1990).

The RVLM and the NTS receive projections from the central nucleus of the amygdala (CeA) (Saha, 2005). The CeA is likely a key mediatory structure in mechanisms resulting in cardiovascular changes as the result of environmental stimuli. Electrical and chemical stimulation of the CeA results in responses consistent with an increase in sympathetic nervous system activity including increases in heart rate (Saha, 2005). The NTS also receives projections from the MPFC and the IC (Verberne and Owens, 1998).

Evidence Linking CAN Function to Autonomic Function Including Heart Rate

The influence of structures in the CAN on autonomic function is supported by research based on animal models (for recent reviews see Cechetto, 2004 and Saper, 2002) and by research in humans (for recent reviews see Cechetto and Shoemaker, 2009 and Thayer et al., 2009). Animal model studies rely primarily on electrical simulation/chemical activation, pharmacological blockade, and tract tracing methods. Electrical and chemical activation studies examine the effect on autonomic arousal of the activation of brain structures in animals that are analogous to those in humans. For example, in a review of research on the role of amygdala in the control of blood pressure, Saha (2005) notes that electrical stimulation of the amygdala in the cat and rat has been found to produce increases in heart rate, arterial blood pressure and muscle blood flow (p. 451). Similarly, Verberne and Owens (1998) review studies exploring cortical modulation of the cardiovascular system including work showing electrical stimulation of the MPFC results in depressor responses. Verberne (1996) suggests depressor responses may be a function of the inhibition of the sympathetic nervous system through the influence of the MPFC on the RVLM.

Applied to the study of autonomic function pharmacological blockade studies assess changes in autonomic function consequent to the chemical blockade of structures in the CAN and the ANS. Tavares et al. (2009) explored the effect of the pharmacological blockade of areas in the MPFC on the relationship between acute restraint stress and increases in heart rate in the rat. Blockade was achieved with microinjection of an unspecified synaptic blocker (CoCl2). Blockade of the prelimbic cortext (in MPFC) resulted in increased heart rate response, while blockade of the infra limbic cortex resulted in significant reductions in heart rate response. No changes occurred with blockade of other regions in MPFC. Importantly this shows different MPFC regions have distinct effects on heart rate.

Tract tracing methods explore interconnections between neuronal structures through the injection of a traceable substance in the area of interest. In anterograde tract tracing the substance is "picked up" by the cell body of a neuron and transported forward to the synapse. Retrograde tract tracing is used to trace connections from synapse to cell body. Cechetto et al. (1983) used retrograde tract tracing with horseradish peroxidase to test the structures that feed information forward to the amygdala in cats. Injections to the medial central region of the amygdala were carried by neurons to the paraventricular and ventromedial nuclei in the hypothalamus, as well as the parabrachial nuclei, showing that afferent information from the ANS is conveyed to the amygdala through the hypothalamus and brain stem.

Taken as a group, animal studies demonstrate that structures in the CAN influence autonomic nervous system function including heart rate. These studies also demonstrate profound interconnectivity between these structures. This interconnectivity is juxtaposed with primary interconnections that serve as the major pathways by which information is conveyed among CAN and ANS structures. Some of these primary interconnections are between structures in the forebrain, including the orbitofrontal cortex (OFC) and the MPFC, and structures in the limbic system including the amygdala. There is some suggestion among animal models that prefrontal cortices exhibit an inhibitory influence on lower brain structures. Verberne and Owens (1998) find that MPFC exerts a sympathoinhibitory influence on the ANS through the RVLM. Evidence of an inhibitory influence prefrontal cortices is coupled with evidence indicating that activity in the amygdala and insular cortex is predominantly associated with increases in sympathetic nervous system (SNS) arousal including increases in heart rate (Nagai et al., 2010; Saha, 2005).

Studies based on animal models are complemented by lesion studies and neuroimaging research in humans. Neuroimaging studies relate changes in the ANS activity in response to a given stimulus to activity in the brain. Many of these studies used stimuli directly related to autonomic arousal. Other studies used stimuli related to cognitive or emotional function. Examples of stimuli directly related to ANS function include isometric hand grip exercises and the Valsalva maneuver.[2] Here I will focus on neuroimaging studies of the relationship between brain activity and autonomic function that use a cognitive or affective stimuli.

A number of neuroimaging studies link MPFC activity and autonomic function in humans (Gianaros et al. 2004; Lane et al., 2009; Wager et al., 2009a and 2009b). Lane et al. (2009) explored the relationship between brain and autonomic function during the induction of happiness, sadness, and disgust. Emotion was induced by through the viewing of emotionally laden film clips and through the recall of personal experience. HF-HRV (parasympathetic nervous system tone) had substantial overlap with emotion specific regional cerebral blood flow (rCBF) in the MPFC, indicating MPFC activity was associated with increased parasympathetic tone and a depressive effect on heart rate.[3] Paralleling these results, Critchley et al. (2000a) found decreased activity in prefrontal and medial temporal regions during an arithmetic mental stressor task was associated with increased heart rate.

Activity in the MPFC and the OFC is related to increases in heart rate during social stress (Wager et al., 2009b) and activity in the MPFC is associated with decreased HF-HRV during increasingly difficult working-memory tasks (Gianaros et al., 2004). HF-HRV indexes parasympathetic influences on heart rate and decreases

---

2   The Valsalva maneuver is an attempt to exhale against a closed airway.

3   Studies of autonomic function often use analysis of the heart rate power spectrum to measure parasympathetic activity. The high-frequency range (> 0.15 Hz) of the heart rate power spectrum is uniquely influenced by parasympathetic outflow. The low-frequency range component (< 0.15 Hz) is jointly influenced by both the parasympathetic and sympathetic nervous system activity (Saul, 1990). Given the confluence of parasympathetic and sympathetic influences on the low frequency range of the heart rate power spectrum, research using power spectral analysis often focuses on changes in parasympathetic nervous system activity as indexed by the high frequency range of the heart rate power spectrum or high frequency heart rate variability (HF-HRV).

would tend to cause increases in heart rate. Neumann et al. (2006) find activity in the right frontal (premotor) cortex is related to increased HF-HRV during a face recognition task and decreased HF-HRV during an response inhibition paradigm. A positive correlation between prefrontal cortex function and HF-HRV was also found by Lane et al. (2009) when decreases in prefrontal activation were associated with decreases in HF-HRV activity. Differences in results across studies in the relationship between given cortical areas and cardiac activity may be caused by the different stimuli used in the various experiments and may reflect the activation of particular locations with a given cortical structure.

Wager et al. (2009b) find pregenual anterior cingulate cortex (ACC) activity is correlated with heart rate under conditions of social threat (public speech preparation task). Other studies have also found ACC activity was related to positive influences on heart rate. Gianaros et al. (2004) found task difficulty in working memory tasks resulted in decreased HF-HRV that overlapped with increased rCBF in the right ACC. Critchley et al. (2003) found increased activity in dorsal ACC function during a stressful cognitive task was related to increased sympathetic nervous system influences on heart rate.[4] Right ACC function is also related to increases in mean arterial pressure during mental arithmetic stressor tasks (Critchley et al., 2005), and to increases in heart rate during the presentation of pictures of faces depicting emotion. In contrast to work showing a positive relationship between heart rate and ACC activity (or changes in autonomic function associated with increases in heart rate), Matthews et al. (2004) found activation of the left ventral ACC positively correlated with HF-HRV during a counting Stroop task presenting incongruent and congruent stimuli.

Activation of the amygdala is consistently associated with increased heart rate or changes in autonomic functioning associated with increased heart rate. The strong majority of studies finding a relationship between amygdala activity and autonomic function use some sort of affective stimuli. Increases in heart rate associated with increased amygdala activity have been found during the presentation of faces portraying negative affect (Critchley et al., 2005; Kuniecki et al., 2003). Gianaros et al. (2004) found task difficulty in working memory tasks results in decreased HF-HRV that overlapped with increased rCBF in the amygdala. Yang et al. (2007) found that in adolescents, activity in the right amygdala was associated with increased sympathetic dominance of heart rate during the viewing of angry faces. Mujica-Parodi et al. (2009) found that diminished coupling (correlation) between time series based on activity in limbic structures was associated with greater sympathetic activation of the ANS.

Activity in the insular cortex (IC) is associated with increases in heart rate during the presentation of emotional faces and increased sympathetic nervous system influences on heart rate during a stressful cognitive task (Critchley et al., 2005).

---

4   Sympathetic dominance of heart rate is indicated by the ratio of LF HRV/HF HRV. Higher values are associated with increasing sympathetic nervous system effects on heart rate. The ratio is proportional to heart rate itself, with higher values indicating increased heart rate (Bootsma et al., 1994).

Gianaros et al. (2004) found decreases in HF-HRV were associated with increased rCBF in left insula during task difficulty in working memory tasks. In contrast Lane et al. (2009) found emotion specific rCBF in the mid-insula positively correlated with HF-HRV.

Based on a review of the research Thayer et al. (2009) argue activity in the prefrontal cortices associated with ANS function commonly leads to increases in HF-HRV (increased parasympathetic tone). All else being equal, increased parasympathetic tone should be associated with decreased heart rate. Forebrain influences on parasympathetic tone are supported by research using retrograde tract tracing in rats to identify forebrain neural pathways specifically involved in the parasympathetic control of heart rate (Ter Horst and Postema, 1997). Thayer et al. (2009) argue prefrontal activity associated with parasympathetic increases may serve to support behavior inhibition. While many neuroimaging studies support the proposed relationship between forebrain function, others have found function in the MPFC and OFC is related to increases in heart rate/decreased HF-HRV (Gianaros et al., 2004; Wager et al., 2009b). One possible explanation for this pattern of results is that activity in PFC structures can serve to both increase HF-HRV to support effortful cognition or withdraw HF-HRV to support the experience of emotion.

In contrast to the influence of forebrain structures on heart rate, activity in the limbic structures including the ACC, amygdala, and insular cortex, tends to result in increased sympathetic tone, a shift towards sympathetic dominance of heart rate, and increased heart rate. Neuroimaging studies show that brain activity leading to changes in autonomic function attendant to the processing of emotional faces or passive viewing of emotional faces results tends to be concentrated in structures in the limbic system (Critchley et al., 2005; Kuniecki et al., 2003; Yang et al., 2007). Studies of the relationship between brain activity and autonomic function during tasks related to emotion processing do not tend to find activation of prefrontal cortical structures including OFC and MPFC. While activity in the ACC is related to increased heart rate/decreased HF-HRV it does not tend to be related to emotional processing/passive emotion viewing tasks (Lane et al., 2009).

The Physiology of Low Heart Rate Reactivity

Forebrain influences on heart rate bypass limbic structures in some cases (Ter Horst and Postema, 1997), but can also cause changes in heart rate by influencing the function of the limbic structures including the amygdala. Structures in the forebrain including the medial prefrontal cortex and the orbitofrontal cortex are connected with the central nucleus of the amygdala through the cingulate cortex and the insula (Saha, 2005). Forebrain structures can exert an inhibitory influence on the limbic system in part through pathways to GABAergic neurons in the amygdala (Barbas et al., 2003; Shekhar et al., 2003). Reductions in prefrontal activity lead to the activation (disinhibition) of the central nucleus of the amygdala and increases in heart rate.

Thayer et al. (2009) have identified three different pathways through which increases in activity in the central nucleus of the amygdala (CeA) can lead to increases in heart rate. Two of these pathways involve the activation of inhibitory influences on SNS activity through the NTS. In the first of these, CeA activity leads to NTS inhibition, which leads to a reduction in inhibitory influences on sympathetic activity generated by the RVLM through a reduction in caudal ventrolateral medullary (CVLM) inhibitory inputs to the RVLM. The net effect is an increase in sympathetic nervous system activity (through a decreased inhibition of the rostral ventrolateral medullary sympathoexcitatory neurons) and an increase in heart rate. In the second pathway involving inhibitory processes mediated by the NTS, inhibition of the NTS leads to a reduction of parasympathetic nervous system activity when inputs to the nucleus ambiguus and dorsal vagal motor nucleus are reduced by the inhibition of the NTS. The third pathway through which increases in activity in the central nucleus of the amygdala can lead to increased heart rate is though direct activation of the RVLM by the CeA. Direct activation leads to increased sympathoexcitatory activity.

The limbic-hypothalamus-pituitary-adrenal (LHPA) axis also influences heart rate reactivity. This influence includes an influence on the sympathetic nervous system through connections between the paraventricular nucleus (PVN) of the hypothalamus and the IML and the RVLM. Activations of the PVN lead to increases in heart rate (Kc and Dick, 2010). Neurons in the hypothalamus that are associated with sympathetic nervous system activity overlap with those regulating the hormonal cascade that occurs during the fight or flight response (Jansen et al., 1995). The hypothalamus is directly connected with the amygdala, supporting a central role for the amygdala in heart rate increases (Risold et al., 1997).

The Relationship of Structures in the CAN with Empathy, Fear Conditioning, Emotion Recognition, and SVASB

Here I argue that an important part of the LHRR/SVASB relationship is spurious with both LRHR and cognitive characteristics leading to ASB caused by a common set of structures in the CAN. Specifically the amygdala, insular cortex, and ACC are all related to heart rate and also related to the shared experience of pain and fear conditioning (Lamm et al., 2011; Sehlmeyer et al., 2009). As indicated earlier, hypo reactivity in the limbic CAN, in particular the amygdala and the ACC, also leads to lower autonomic arousal, including reduced HRR, and has been implicated in recent explanations of ASB emphasizing callous unemotional traits (Shirtcliff et al., 2009) and in explanations of psychopathy (Blair, 2005).

A key part of the proposed relationship between LHRR and ASB is the suggestion that structures in the CAN that influence HRR also influence ASB. More specifically, differential function of structures in the CAN result in both LHRR and a lack of sensitivity to negative consequences for others. CAN structures have been related to a number of phenomena that may serve to contribute to a lack of sensitivity to negative consequence for others. These include, reduced sensitivity to pain in others, fear conditioning deficits, and disrupted emotion recognition. In addition to playing a key role in autonomic arousal, limbic structures including the amygdala, the IC, and the ACC are related to emotion (Damasio, 1998; LeDoux, 2000), empathy (Decety and Jackson, 2004 and 2006; Singer and Lamm, 2009), pain perception (Apkarian et al., 2005; Davis, 2000; Price, 2000), and fear conditioning (Büchel and Dolan, 2000; Sehlmeyer et al., 2009), and, most critically, antisocial and criminal behavior (DeLisi et al., 2009; Raine and Yang, 2006).

A growing body of research finds that a common set of structures underpins both responses to the direct experience of pain and the observation of pain in another. Lamm et al. (2011) conducted two meta-analyses of studies relating observed pain to brain activity as measured by fMRI. The first was based on nine studies for which fMRI images were available. The second was coordinate-based meta-analysis of 32 studies. Areas activated both in experienced pain and observed pain included the border of the medial cingulate cortex and the ACC, the IC, and the amygdala. Activation of regions in the ACC and the AI have been found during the imagination of another in a painful situation (Jackson et al., 2006), in relation to the presentation of photos depicting body parts in painful everyday life situations (Jackson et al., 2005), in response to the observation of applied thermal stimuli (Hutchison et al., 1999), and in the observation of facial expressions of pain (Saarela et al., 2007).

Sehlmeyer et al. (2009) reviewed 46 studies using fMRI or positron emission tomography (PET) to study fear conditioning and/or extinction in healthy volunteers. The reviewed studies used fMRI and/or PET to identify the neurological correlates of fear conditioning. Fear conditioning paradigms include the presentation of a previously neutral stimulus with an aversive unconditioned stimulus. In normal individuals conditioning occurs when the previously neutral stimulus begins to elicit physiological reactions (e.g., change in skin conductance, increase in heart rate) that accompany the experience of the unconditioned stimulus. Extinction occurs when the conditioned stimulus no longer elicits this physiological reaction and is caused by the repeated presentation of the conditioned stimulus in the absence of the unconditioned stimulus. Sehlmeyer et al. (2009) found frequent activation of a network of fear condition related brain areas including the amygdala, insula, and ACC. Other areas also activated included hippocampus, thalamus, the cerebellum, and the sensory cortices. Other reviews of neuroimaging research report similar results in humans (Büchel and Dolan, 2000) as have reviews of fear conditioning research in animals (Fendt and Fanselow, 1999).

Phan et al. (2002) conducted a meta-analysis of 55 PET and fMRI activation studies of emotion. Emotion induction methods included visual, auditory, and recall. Results show that MPFC was commonly activated across a range of emotions. The amygdala was specifically recruited during fear, while the ACC was the region most commonly activated during anger. Activity in the IC was differentially associated with disgust. Critchley et al. (2005) support a link between amygdala reactivity and both the processing of emotional faces and increases in heart rate, finding activity in the amygdala and the IC was associated with both response to emotional face stimuli and heart rate acceleration. Sad and angry expressions resulted in greater heart rate increases than happy and disgusted facial expression. The central role of the amygdala in the recognition of fear in others is reviewed by Adolphs (2008). Key studies show lesions of the amygdala profoundly impair the ability to recognize fearful faces (Adolphs et al., 1995; Graham et al., 2007).

Based on the above evidence I argue that amygdala, ACC, and IC are all central to the understanding of the relationship between LRHR and SVASB. The CeA serves as a key area for the translation of the psychologically induced fear and stress into cardiovascular changes. Saha (2005) notes that there is "ample evidence that the CeA plays a critical role in the integration and coordination of cardiovascular responses to acute emotional or threatening stimuli" (p. 2005). The role of CeA in determining cardiovascular responses extends to heart rate. Simulation of the CeA results in behavioral and physiological signs of anxiety and fear including increased heart rate (Iwata et al., 1987). Beyond a relationship with ANS arousal to fear inducing stimuli, under-reactivity in the amygdala has been tied to psychopathy and callous-unemotional traits (Blair, 2005; Shirtcliff et al., 2009). Studies have found reductions in the volume of the amygdala in violent offenders (Wong et al., 2007; Tiihonen et al., 2000) and psychopaths (Yang et al., 2006). Reduced activity in the amygdala has been found in adolescents with conduct disorders (Sterzer et al., 2005), violent patients with mild retardation (Critchley et al., 2000b), and psychopaths (Birbaumer et al., 2005; Kiehl et al., 2001; Veit et al., 2002).

The IC plays a central role in cardiac function. Increases in left IC activity are associated with SNS activity and increased heart rate (Nagai et al., 2010). Afferent neurons in the SNS and PNS relay information regarding the body's physiological condition to the IC. This information is then re-represented in the anterior insular cortex (AIC) where it is available for integration in emotion and decision making (Craig, 2002, 2009). In decision making, this information can provide a predicted set of physiological reactions corresponding to different behavioral possibilities. Accordingly, a number of recent reviews have ascribed a central role for the AIC in the central representation of autonomic and visceral responses (Craig 2002, 2009; Critchley, 2005; Singer et al., 2009).

Sterzer et al. (2007) found adolescents with conduct disorder had significantly less volume in left amygdale and bilateral anterior cortex. Bilateral insular gray matter volume was also significantly correlated with empathy scores, but amygdala volume was not. Insular gray matter volume and left amygdala gray matter volume both showed a correlation with aggressive behavior, but the correlation between insular gray matter volume and aggressive behavior was stronger. Studies contrasting the fear conditioning of psychopaths and controls show that psychopaths do not experience activity in the IC and the ACC while controls do (Birbaumer et al., 2005; Veit et al., 2002).

The ACC is commonly interpreted as playing a role in the evaluation of responses (Gehring and Fencsik, 2001; Swick and Turken, 2002) (from Critchley et al., 2003). ACC lesions in humans are related to difficulties in response selection and modification (Ochsner et al., 2001; Swick and Turken, 2002). In a meta-analysis of PET studies of ACC activity, Paus et al. (1998) found task difficulty was related to ACC activation. Critchley et al. (2003) suggest that evidence regarding function in the dorsal ACC regions can be parsimoniously interpreted as indicating dorsal ACC contributes to peripheral autonomic response to meet concurrent behavioral demands. The neuroimaging studies exploring ANS reactivity to cognitive and emotional challenge show that ACC activity is consistently related with increases in heart rate or ANS changes consistent with increases in heart rate. Reduced ACC activation has been found in psychopaths (Kiehl et al., 2001; Birbaumer et al., 2005), antisocial personality disorder patients (Kumari et al., 2006; Vollum et al., 2004), conductor disorder patients (Sterzer et al., 2007), and is related to aggression and defiance among boys (Boes et al., 2008).

While strong evidence linking reduced ACC activation to both heart rate and SVASB suggests ACC is important for the explanation of the relationship between LRHR and SVASB, the nature of this relationship is at issue as ACC does not appear to be related to heart rate specific to emotion (Critchley et al., 2005; Lane et al., 2009), but is related to heart rate and ANS changes consistent with increases in heart rate during cognitive challenge and stressful tasks (Critchley et al., 2003; Critchley et al., 2005; Gianaros et al., 2004; Matthews et al., 2004; Wager et al., 2009b).

While prefrontal cortex function is related to both heart rate and SVASB, it does not appear to be central to the explanation of the relationship between SVASB and LRHR. The amygdala, IC, and ACC all play a key role in explaining heart rate. Further, these structures are related to SVASB and fear conditioning, and are identified in studies of the neural commonalities in the experience of pain in one's self and the observation of pain in another. In contrast, structures in the prefrontal cortex do not tend to be related to fear conditioning or implicated in the overlap between experienced and observed pain (Lamm et al., 2011; Sehlmeyer et al., 2009). Similarly, prefrontal cortex function is clearly related to ASB and has been linked to psychopathy (Glenn and Raine, 2008); however, as Blair (2007a, 2007b) notes it does not appear to be linked to the cognitive dispositions that are an important part of the definition of psychopathy (i.e., lack of concern for others). Further, a number of studies have found that psychopaths show increased activation in forebrain areas including dorsolateral prefrontal cortex (Glenn and Raine, 2008) and lesions of MPFC led to impulsive antisocial behavior but not the instrumental antisocial behavior that is the hallmark of the psychopath (Blair, 2007b). While cortical structures implicated in the control of heart rate, but located in the PFC, are not directly implicated in the LRHR/ASB relationship, PFC deficits are likely a part of a distinct substrate for impulsive and undercontrolled ASB. Where, consistent with the model of emotion regulation in the explanation of violence suggested by Davidson et al. (2000), structures in the PFC provide "top down" control of "bottom up" impulses.

The research reviewed above fairly clearly establishes a role for lower limbic structures including the amygdala, ACC, and IC in heart rate, empathy and the experience of emotion, and antisocial behavior. With regard to the relationship between LRHR/LHRR and SVASB the most parsimonious interpretation of this evidence is that hypo-reactivity in these lower limbic structures causes both LRHR/LHRR and SVASB. Absent strong evidence for an influence of LRHR/LHRR on SVASB that is causal rather than correlational it may be best to assume that the relationship between LRHR/LHRR and SVASB is spurious, given that this explanation has the advantage of parsimony. However, there is indeed some evidence suggesting that ANS system activity can have a causal influence on behavior. This evidence, reviewed below, suggests that while some of the relationship between LRHR/LHRR and SVASB may be caused by the shared influence of lower limbic structures on both LRHR/LHRR and SVASB, it is also possible that LRHR/LHRR does have a direct causal influence on SVASB.

Explaining the Low Resting Heart Rate/Antisocial Behavior Relationship

Beyond an association due to the shared influence of CAN structures, it is also possible that ANS under-arousal including LRHR and LHRR has a causal influence on SVASB. Causal effect of the LRHR/LHRR activity on behavior can occur through autonomic feedback to limbic and higher cortical structures. Feedback on peripheral physiological states occurs through ANS afferents that return information on autonomic function to structures in the brain stem. This information is then relayed to limbic and frontal lobe areas where it is incorporated in higher order processing and exerts an influence on decision making (Craig, 2002, 2009). Afferent influences on cognitive processes are an important part of several prominent explanations of emotion and emotional influences on cognition (Damasio, 1994, 1998; Critchley, 2005; Craig, 2002, 2009; Levenson, 2003).

The argument that the ANS has a causal influence on behavior is supported by the structure of the ANS itself. Sympathetic nervous system influences on heart rate include homeostatic feedback mechanisms and what have been characterized as "feed forward" mechanisms (Dampney et al., 2002). Feedback mechanisms include the cardiopulmonary and gastrointestinal afferents that carry information from the gastrointestinal system and the cardiopulmonary system back to the brain (Cechetto and Shoemaker, 2009). Cardiopulmonary feedback mechanisms include the baroreceptor and chemoreceptor reflexes. The baroreceptor reflex occurs when feedback from arterial baroreceptors signal changes in blood pressure. Chemoreceptors are sensitive to a decrease in oxygen in the blood.

Cardiopulmonary and gastrointestinal afferents end in the nucleus of the solitary tract (NTS). Neurons conveying feedback project from the NTS directly to the rostral ventrolateral medulla (RVLM) and indirectly to the RVLM via the caudal ventrolateral medulla (CVLM). The NTS also conveys visceral feedback to higher forebrain centers including the insular cortex and the amygdala (Cechetto and Shoemaker, 2009). Information from cardiovascular and gastrointestinal afferents is relayed to the amygdala and insular cortex through relays in the parabrachial complex and through the ventral basal thalamus (Cechetto, 1987; Cechetto and Saper, 1987; Saper, 2002; Pattinson et al., 2009; Topolovec et al., 2004). It is through feedback mechanisms to the limbic structures that ANS function may causally influence limbic and higher order processes.

Neuroimaging studies demonstrate that afferent activity is represented in anterior insular cortex (AIC). Craig (2002, 2009) identified the primate lamina I spinothalamocoritcal pathway which conveys information from fine sympathetic afferents innervating all tissues in the body. Lamina I projects to the sympathetic cell columns in the spinal cord, and to the rostral ventrolateral medulla, parabrachial nucleus, periaqueductal gray matter, and catechlomingeric cell groups. Sympathetic feedback to the mid/posterior insula is conveyed directly through lamina I projections to the posterior ventromedial nucleus in the hypothalamus and indirectly through the parabrachial nucleus to the basal part of the ventromedial nucleus. Parasympathetic feedback is conveyed to the mid/posterior insula through the basal part of the ventromedial nucleus which receives projections from the NTS and from the parabrachial nucleus. The IC is then the initial cortical destination for information on the body's physiological state.

Reduced feedback regarding LHRR (autonomic arousal) can lead to reduced concern for the impact of one's actions on another through an inability to impute these consequences or more proximally through reduced HRR (autonomic arousal). A reduced concern for the impact of one's actions on another is potentially attributable to the lack of a link between negative affect on the part of another and autonomic responses commonly paired with personal negative affect. In those with LHRR, autonomic arousal typically associated with fear and pain in the self fails to get linked with environmental cues indicating the experience of these emotions on the part of another. The lack of a link between negative affect in another and autonomic responses results consistent with fear and pain in the self, results in a decrease in the inferred consequences of one's actions (including antisocial behavior) when these actions potentially result in negative emotional consequences for others. This explanation of the LHRR/SVASB can easily be conceptualized as an application of Blair's (2005) integrated emotion system (IES) model of psychopathy. In the IES model amygdala dysfunction provides the neurological substrate for the lack of empathy and guilt that accompany the behavioral manifestations of psychopathy.[5]

The idea that physiological experiences form the underpinning of the experience of emotion is generally traced back to the work of William James (1894) and Carl Lange (1885). The James–Lange position holds that central representation of physiological states serve as an important component in the experience of emotion. This position assumes that autonomic arousal provides a key physiological substrate to the experience of emotion. More recently, Damasio (1994, 1998) has offered the "somatic marker hypothesis," arguing for a role of the central representation of bodily arousal in emotion and cognition. Somatic markers represent how we feel under general classes of conditions and influence cognition in complex and

---

5   One important difference between the model proposed here and Blair's IES model is the application of limbic dysfunction to SVASB in general and not just to patterns of SVASB that meet the definition of psychopathy. Limbic deficits are viewed on a continuum with minor deficits leading to minor changes in behavior; moderate deficits leading to moderate changes in behavior; and serous deficits leading to profound patterns of SVASB potentially meeting the definition of psychopathy.

uncertain situations. In everyday language somatic markers are described as "gut feelings."

Kreibig (2010) reviewed 134 studies relating autonomic function to emotion. Autonomic changes including increases in heart rate were correlated with a range of distinct emotions. Kreibig's review and other key studies in this area show that there is considerable variation in the autonomic correlates of different emotions. This suggests that specific emotions have unique autonomic signatures (see also Ekman et al., 1983). Similarly, many of the fMRI studies of the influence of the CAN on cardiac function that were reviewed earlier show that emotion induction and cognitive challenges result in changes in ANS function.

While suggestive, these studies do not definitively demonstrate that autonomic function has a causal influence on emotion and cognition. Other research, albeit limited, provides more direct evidence of a causal role for autonomic arousal. Levenson and colleagues explored the influence of peripheral action on autonomic arousal through the Directed Facial Action task. This task provides subjects step-by-step instruction to create faces that reflect emotion. The directed facial action task produced subjective emotional experience and autonomic changes associated with emotional experience (Ekman et al., 1983; Levenson et al., 1990). The causal influence of the directed facial action task on autonomic arousal was supported by differences in arousal across emotion type. For example, greater arousal during fear or anger versus disgust (Levenson et al., 1990).

Additional evidence for the importance of the central representation of autonomic states comes from studies of primary autonomic failure (PAF). PAF occurs as a consequence of loss of neuronal cells in the peripheral autonomic nervous system and results in an inability to regulate the bodily state through ANS activity (Mathias, 2000). Those with PAF show reduced mid-insula activity during effortful mental arithmetic and exercise (Critchley et al., 2001). PAF patients also show reduced response to threat stimuli during fear conditioning related activity in their insula and amygdala (Critchley et al., 2002).

Collectively, the research reviewed above provides reasonably convincing evidence that autonomic feedback can influence the experience of emotion and cognition. In normally functioning individuals, this feedback may facilitate the internal simulation of other's autonomic states and allow the integration of this information in decision making. In those where autonomic feedback is impaired at some stage, the internal simulation of other's autonomic states is also impaired, resulting in a less accurate understanding of the consequences of one's actions for another. Consistent with the suggestion that the ability to simulate other's autonomic states is key for the understanding of affective consequences, Levenson and Ruef (1992) found the accuracy of predictions of negative affect in another increased as the similarities in autonomic arousal increased.

Given the complex nature of the CAN it is difficult to localize the potential causes of impaired autonomic feedback, but there are three general sets of CAN/ANS structures that should be considered. The first is the set of structures that are responsible for the generation of the ANS response itself. I have argued that these are amygdala, ACC, and IC. Reduced function in these areas should lead to reduced sympathetic outflow, reduced heart rate increases, and reduced afferent feedback regarding autonomic arousal, as a consequence of lower arousal itself. This reduced afferent feedback may play an important part in explaining the link between reduced activity in these structures and increases in SVASB. It is also possible that impaired function of the sympathetic and parasympathetic nervous system afferents that return information on peripheral physiological arousal may result in reduced autonomic feedback and a reduced ability to infer affective consequences. Lastly, the central representation of autonomic feedback for emotional and cognitive processes may be impaired when brain stem and cortical structures responsible for the representation of afferent feedback function poorly.

In Sum

This chapter has a number of central points of emphasis. Perhaps the most important is the argument that investigations of the relationship between LHRR/LRHR and SVASB should consider the possibility that the relationship between LHRR/LRHR and SVASB is spurious, with both being explained by reduced lower limbic activity (amygdala, IC, ACC). Research has shown lower limbic structures are related to heart rate, fear conditioning, empathy for pain, and antisocial behavior, and has established a link between LHRR/LRHR and SVASB, but has not shown that this relationship exists after controls for lower limbic function. Beginning to tease out the direction of causality between ANS function, brain function, cognitive/ emotional dispositions, and SVASB is likely to yield substantial advances to our understanding of the biological substrates of SVASB.

Beyond arguing for attention to the possibility of spuriousness, this chapter also reviews substantial, albeit indirect, evidence for the influence of ANS feedback on emotion, cognition and by extension SVASB. Further, the review of research in support of this argument suggests that it is decreased afferent feedback to cortical structures that potentially accounts for the unique contribution of ANS activity to SVASB. If this reduced feedback is indeed causally related to SVASB, it is likely through impaired ability to understand the affective consequences of one's actions for another.

This argument, that a reduced sensitivity to consequence for others and for one's self explains part of the relationship between LRHR/LHRR and SVASB, leads to eminently testable propositions. For example, if an important part of the relationship between LRHR/LHRR and SVASB is explained by sensitivity to other/ self consequences, we should anticipate first that LRHR/LHRR will be related to a lack of empathy/concern for the consequences of one's actions for another. We should also anticipate that the relationship between LRHR/LHRR and SVASB will be mediated by variation in these same empathy/concern measures. Encouragingly, these propositions are testable with little more than a carefully considered survey and some way to measure heart rate.

A final argument, implied in the above review and made expressly here, is that deficits leading to the relationship between LRHR/LHRR and SVASB are largely deficits of structures involved in the sympathetic nervous system tone, where underarousal in the SNS is both a corollary and cause of lower concern with the negative affective consequences of one's actions for others and this leads to increased SVASB. This is not to argue that parasympathetic nervous system influences are entirely unimportant for the LRHR/LHRR and SVASB relationship, but rather that their importance is substantially diminished relative to SNS influences.

Recent models of social cognition and emotion regulation have argued that PNS plays an important role in emotion regulation and social decision making (Porges, 2001, 2007; Thayer and Lane, 2000). Porges (2001, 2007) argues that 'orienting responses' are a key feature of social engagement and that increases in parasympathetic tone support the ability to appropriately respond to social stimuli (Porges, 2001, 2007). Recalling that parasympathetic tone exerts downward pressure on heart rate, this indicates that an inability to lower heart rate through parasympathetic tone will be associated with weakened emotional and behavioral regulation. This suggests that the major function of the PNS may be the suppression of SNS in support of behavioral regulation. If this is the case PNS may still have a secondary but still important influence on the relationship between LHRR/SVASB, through the withdrawal of parasympathetic tone when the potentiation of emotion is appropriate. The argument for the primacy of the SNS in the explanation of the LHRR/SVASB relationship yields another testable proposition, that measures of SNS function should mediate more of the relationship between LHRR/SVASB than measures of PNS function. While the hardware associated with specific measures of the SNS (skin conductance) and the PNS (HF-HRV) are more expensive than the cost associated with the administration of a survey and the taking of the pulse, they are still relatively inexpensive (thousands rather than tens or hundreds of thousands).

The conceptualization of the relationship between LHRR/SVASB advanced here argues for a multidimensional criminal propensity. It is widely acknowledged that an important part of between individual differences in the tendency to engage in ASB is explained by impulsivity, or in the parlance of Gottfredson and Hirschi (1990), low self-control. Yet, impulsivity is also associated with a wide variety of acts that however ill advised are nonetheless not antisocial. And while impulsivity is clearly important in the explanation of ASB, it is when this characteristic is combined with an inability to appreciate and experience the consequences of one's actions for others that a tendency toward impulsive acts gets translated into a profound and enduring pattern of antisocial behavior across the life course.

Enduring individual differences in criminal propensities then have two primary biological substrates. One linked to frontal lobe dysfunction, and the other to impaired limbic/ANS function. In the first, frontal lobe dysfunction leads to poor impulse control and in the second they lead to a lack of empathy or guilt. Yang et al. (2005) provide indirect evidence of these distinct substrates in comparisons of unsuccessful (arrested) psychopaths, successful psychopaths (not arrested), and community controls. Successful psychopaths have higher prefrontal gray matter volume than unsuccessful psychopaths. Differences between successful psychopaths and community controls in prefrontal gray matter volume were not significant. In the context of the above criminal behavior substrates, this suggests that successful psychopaths may have the lack of guilt or empathy that is the hallmark of the psychopath, but nonetheless restrain themselves from risky SVASB due to intact frontal lobe function. The successful psychopaths do not understand the negative affective consequences of their actions, and therefore are not deterred by them, but are nonetheless able to restrain themselves from acts of SVASB that would result in their arrest. In contrast, unsuccessful psychopaths with both the emotional hallmark of psychopathy and frontal lobe dysfunction neither understand the negative affective consequences of their actions nor are they able to restrain themselves in the face of the criminal justice system consequences.

References

Adolphs, R. (2008). Fear, faces, and the human amygdala. *Current Opinion in Neurobiology, 18(2),* 166–172.

Adolphs, R., Tranel, D., Damasio, H., and Damasio, A. R. (1995). Fear and the human amygdala. *The Journal of Neuroscience, 15,* 5879–5892.

Apkarian, A. V., Bushnell, M. C., Treede, R. D., and Zubieta, J. K. (2005). Human brain mechanisms of pain perception and regulation in health and disease. *European Journal of Pain, 9,* 463–484.

Armstrong, T. A., Keller, S. W., Franklin, T., and MacMillan, S. (2009). Low resting heart rate and antisocial behavior: A brief review of evidence and preliminary results from a new test. *Criminal Justice and Behavior, 36,* 1115–1130.

Barbas, H., Saha, S., Rempel-Clower, N., and Ghashghaei, T. (2003). Serial pathways from primate prefrontal cortex to autonomic areas may influence emotional expression. *BMC Neuroscience, 4,* 25–36.

Benarroch, E. E. (1993). The central autonomic network: Functional organization, dysfunction, and perspective. *Mayo Clinic Proceedings, 68,* 988–1001.

Benarroch, E. E. (1997). The central autonomic network. In Low, P. A. (ed.), *Clinical Autonomic Disorders.* 2nd ed. Philadelphia: Lippincott-Raven, 17–23.

Birbaumer, N., Veit, R., Lotze, M., Erb, M., Hermann, C., Grodd, W., and Flor, H. (2005). Deficient fear conditioning in psychopathy: A functional magnetic resonance imaging study. *Archives of General Psychiatry, 62(7),* 799–805.

Blair, R. J. R. (2005). Applying a cognitive neuroscience perspective to the disorder of psychopathy. *Development and Psychopathology, 17,* 865–891.

Blair, R. J. R. (2007a). Dysfunctions of medial and lateral orbitofrontal cortex in psychopathy. *Annals of the New York Academy of Science, 1121,* 461–479.

Blair, R. J. R. (2007b). The amygdala and ventromedial prefrontal cortex in morality and psychopathy. *Trends in Cognitive Sciences, 11,* 387–392.

Boes, A. D., Tranel, D., Anderson, S. W., and Nopoulos, P. (2008). Right anterior cingulate cortex volume is a neuroanatomical correlate of aggression and defiance in boys. *Behavioral Neuroscience, 122,* 677–684.

Bootsma, M., Swenne, C. A., Van Bolhuis, H. H., Chang, P. C., Cats, V. M., and Bruschke, A. V. (1994). Heart rate and heart rate variability as indexes of sympathovagal balance. *American Journal of Physiology, 266*, H1565–1571.

Büchel, C. and Dolan, R. J. (2000). Classical fear conditioning in functional neuroimaging. *Current Opinion in Neurobiology, 10*, 219–223.

Cabot, J. B. (1990). Sympathetic preganglionic neurons: Cytoarchitecture, ultrastructure, and biophysical properties. In Loewy, A. D. and Spyer, K. M. (eds.), *Central Regulation of Autonomic Functions*. Oxford: Oxford University Press, 44–67.

Cauffman, E., Steinberg, L., and Piquero, A. (2005). Psychological, neuropsychological, and physiological correlates of serious antisocial behavior in adolescence: The role of self-control. *Criminology, 43(1)*, 133–175.

Cechetto, D. F. (1987). Central representation of visceral function. *Federation Proceedings, 46*, 17–23.

Cechetto, D. F. (2004). Forebrain control of healthy and diseased hearts. In Armour, J. A. and Aradell, J. L. (eds.), *Basic and Clinical Neurocardiology*. Oxford: Oxford University Press, 220–251.

Cechetto, D. F. and Chen, S. J. (1992). Hypothalamic and cortical sympathetic responses relay in the medulla of the rat. *American Journal of Physiology, 263*, R544–R552.

Cechetto, D. F., Ciriello, J., and Calaresu, F. R. (1983). Afferent connections to cardiovascular sites in the amygdala: A horseradish peroxidase study in the cat. *Journal of the Autonomic Nervous System, 8*, 97–110.

Cechetto, D. F., and Saper, C. B. (1987). Evidence for a viscerotopic sensory representation in the cortex and thalamus in the rat. *Journal of Comparative Neurology, 262(1)*, 27–45.

Cechetto, D. F., and Shoemaker, K. J. (2009). Functional neuroanatomy of autonomic regulation. *Neuroimage, 47*, 795–803.

Craig, A. D. (2002). Interoception: The sense of the physiological condition of the body. *Current Opinion in Neurobiology, 13*, 500–505.

Craig, A. D. (2009). How do you feel–now? The anterior insula and human awareness. *Nature Reviews Neuroscience, 10*, 59–70.

Critchley, H. D. (2005). Neural mechanisms of autonomic, affective and cognitive integration. *The Journal of Comparative Neurology, 493*, 154–166.

Critchley, H. D., Corfield, D. R., Chandler, M. P., Mathias, C. J., and Dolan, R. J. (2000a). Cerebral correlates of autonomic cardiovascular arousal: A functional neuroimaging investigation. *The Journal of Physiology, 523*, 259–270.

Critchley, H. D., Josephs, O., O'Doherty, J., Zanini, S., Dewar, B.-K., Mathias, C. J., Cipolotti, L., Shallice, T., and Dolan, R. J. (2003). Human cingulate cortex and autonomic cardiovascular control: Converging neuroimaging and clinical evidence. *Brain, 216*, 2139–2152.

Critchley, H. D., Mathias, C. J., and Dolan R. J. (2001). Neural correlates of first and second-order representation of bodily states. *Nature Neuroscience, 2*, 207–212.

Critchley, H. D., Mathias, C. J., and Dolan, R. J. (2002). Fear-conditioning in humans: The influence of awareness and arousal on functional neuroanatomy. *Neuron, 33*, 653–663.

Critchley, H. D., Rotshtein, P., Nagai, Y., O'Doherty, J., Mathias, C. J., and Dolan, R. J. (2005). Activity in the human brain predicting differential heart rate responses to emotional facial expressions. *NeuroImage, 24*, 751–762.

Critchley, H. D., Simmons, A., Daly, E. M., Russell, A., van Amelsvoort, T., Robertson, D. M., Glover, A., and Murphy, D. G. (2000b). Prefrontal and medial temporal correlates of repetitive violence to self and others. *Biological Psychiatry, 47*, 928–934.

Damasio, A. R. (1994). Descartes' error and the future of human life. *Scientific American, 271*, 144.

Damasio, A. R. (1998). Emotion in the perspective of an integrated nervous system. *Brain Research Reviews, 26*, 83–86.

Dampney, R. A. L. (1994). Functional organization of central pathways regulating the cardiovascular system. *Physiological Reviews, 74*, 323–364.

Dampney, R. A. L., Coleman, M. J., Fontes, M. A. P., Hirooka, Y., Horiuchi, Y.-W., Polson, J. W., Potts, P. D., and Tagawa, T. (2002). Central mechanisms underlying short and long term regulation of the cardiovascular system. *Clinical and Experimental Pharmacology and Physiology, 29*, 261–268.

Dampney, R. A. L., Tagawa, T., Horiuchi, Y.-W., Potts, P. D., Fontes, W. and Polson, J. W. (2000). What drives the tonic activity of presympathetic neurons in the rostral ventrolateral medulla? *Clinical and Experimental Pharmacology and Physiology, 27*, 1049–1053.

Davidson, R. J., Putnam, K. M., and Larson, C. L. (2000). Dysfunction in the neural circuitry of emotion regulation—a possible prelude to violence. *Science, 289*, 591–594.

Davis, K. D. (2000). The neural circuitry of pain as explored with functional MRI. *Neurological Research, 22*, 313–317.

Decety, J. and Jackson, P. L. (2004). The functional architecture of human empathy. *Behavioral and Cognitive Neuroscience Reviews, 3*, 71–100.

Decety, J. and Jackson, P. L. (2006). A social-neuroscience perspective on empathy. *Current Directions in Psychological Science, 15*, 54–58.

DeLisi, M., Umprhess, Z. R., and Vaughn, M. G. (2009). The criminology of the amygdala. *Criminal Justice and Behavior, 36*, 1241–1252.

Ekman, P., Levenson, R. W., and Friesen, W. V. (1983). Autonomic nervous system activity distinguishes among emotions. *Science, 221*, 1208–1210.

Farrington, D. (1997). The relationship between low resting heart rate and violence. In Raine, A., Brennan, P., Farrington, D., and Mednick, S. (eds.), *Biosocial Bases of Violence*. New York: Plenum, 89–106.

Fendt, M. and Fanselow, M. S. (1999). The neuroanatomical and neurochemical basis of conditioned fear. *Neuroscience and Biobehavioral Reviews, 23*, 743–760.

Gehring, W. J. and Fencsik, D. E. (2001). Functions of the medial frontal cortex in the processing of conflict and errors. *The Journal of Neuroscience, 21*, 9430–9437.

Gianaros, P., Van Der Veen, F. and Jennings, J. (2004). Regional cerebral blood flow correlates with heart period and high-frequency heart period variability during working memory tasks: implications for the cortical and subcortical regulation of cardiac autonomic activity. *Psychophysiology, 41*, 521–530.

Glenn, A. and Raine, A. (2008). The neurobiology of psychopathy. *Psychiatric Clinics of North America, 31*, 463–475.

Gottfredson, Michael R. and Hirschi, Travis (1990). *A General Theory of Crime.* Stanford, CA: Stanford University Press.

Graham, R., Devinsky, O., and LaBar, K. S. (2007). Quantifying deficits in the perception of fear and anger in morphed facial expressions after bilateral amygdala damage. *Neuropsychologia, 45*, 42–54.

Guyenet, P. G. (1990). Role of the ventral medulla oblongata in blood pressure regulation. In Lowey, A. D. and Spyer, K. M. (eds.), *Central Regulation of Autonomic Functions.* New York: Oxford University Press, 145–67.

Hutchison, W. D., Davis, K. D., Lozano, A. M., Tasker, R. R., and Dostrovsky, J. O. (1999). Pain-related neurons in the human cingulate cortex, *Nature Neuroscience, 2*, 403–405.

Iwata, J., Chida, K., and LeDoux, J. E. (1987). Cardiovascular responses elicited by stimulation of neurons in the central amygdaloid nucleus in awake but not anesthetized rats resemble conditioned emotional responses. *Brain Research, 383*, 195–214.

Jackson, P. L., Meltzoff, A. N., and Decety, J. (2005). How do we perceive the pain of others: A window into the neural processes involved in empathy. *Neuroimage, 24*, 771–779.

Jackson, P. L., Brunet, E., Meltzoff, A. N., and Decety, J. (2006). Empathy examined through the neural mechanisms involved in imagining how I feel versus how you feel pain. *Neuropsychologia, 44*, 752–761.

James, W. (1894). Physical basis of emotion. *Psychological Reviews, 1*, 516–529.

Jansen, A. S., Nguyen, X. V., Karpitskly, V., Mettenleiter, T. C., and Loewy, A. D. (1995). Central command neurons of the sympathetic nervous system: Basis of the fight-or-flight response. *Science, 270*, 644–646.

Kc, P. and Dick, T. E. (2010). Modulation of cardiorepiratory function mediated by the paraventricular nucleus. *Respiratory Physiology & Neurobiology, 174*, 55–64.

Kiehl, K. A., Smith, A. M., Hare, R. D., Mendrek, A., Forster, B. B., & Brink, J. (2001). Limbic abnormalities in affective processing by criminal psychopaths as revealed by functional magnetic resonance imaging. *Biological Psychiatry, 50*, 677–684.

Kreibig, S. D. (2010). Autonomic nervous system activity in emotion: A review. *Biological Psychology, 84*, 394–421.

Kumari, V., Aasen, I., Taylor, P., Ffytche, D., Das, M., Barkataki, I., Goswami, S., O'Connell, P., Howlett, M., Williams, S. C. R., and Sharma, T. (2006). Neural dysfunction in schizophrenia: An fMRI investigation. *Schizophrenia Research, 84*, 144–164.

Kuniecki, M., Urbanik, A., Sobiecka, B., Kozub, J., and Binder, M. (2003). Central control of heart rate changes during visual affective processing as revealed by fMRI. *Acta Neurobiologiae Experimentalis, 63,* 39–48.

Lamm, C., Decety, J., and Singer, T. (2011). Meta-analytic evidence for common and distinct neural networks associated with directly experienced pain and empathy for pain. *Neuroimage, 54,* 2491–2502.

Lane, R. D., McRae, K., Reiman, E. M., Chen, K., Ahern, G. L., and Thayer, J. F. (2009). Neural correlates of heart rate variability during emotion. *Neuroimage, 44,* 213–222.

Lange, C. G. (1885). The mechanism of the emotions. In Rand B. (ed.), *The Classical Psychologist.* Boston: Houghton Mifflin, 672–685.

LeDoux, J. E. (2000). Emotion circuits in the brain. *Annual Review of Neuroscience, 23,* 155–184.

Levenson, R. W. (2003). Blood, sweat and fears. *Annals of the New York Academy of Science, 1000,* 348–366.

Levenson, R. W., Ekman, P., and Friesen, W. V. (1990). Voluntary facial action generates emotion-specific autonomic nervous system activity. *Psychophysiology, 27,* 363–384.

Levenson, R. W., and Ruef, A. M. (1992). Empathy: A physiological substrate. *Journal of Personality and Social Psychology, 63,* 234–246.

Levy, M. N. and Martin, P. (1979). Neural control of the heart. In Berne, R. M. and Sperelakis, N. (eds.), *Handbook of Physiology, sec 2, Cardiovascular System, vol I, Heart.* Washington, D.C.: American Physiological Society, 581–620.

Levy, M. N. and Warner, M. R. (1994). Parasympathetic effects on cardiac function. In Armour, J. A. and Ardell, J. L. (eds.), *Neurocardiology.* New York: Oxford University Press, 53–76.

Mathias, C. J. (2000). Disorders of the autonomic nervous system. In Bradley, W. G., Daroff, R. B., Fenichel, G. M., et al. (eds.), *Neurology in Clinical Practice.* Woburn, MA: Butterworth-Heinemann, 2131–2165.

Matthews, S. C., Paulus, M. P., Simmons, A. N., Nelesen, R. A., and Dimsdale, J. E. (2004). Functional subdivisions within anterior cingulate cortex and their relationship to autonomic nervous system function. *NeuroImage, 22,* 1151–1156.

Mujica-Parodi, L. R., Korgaonkar, M., Ravindranath, B., Greenberg, T., Tomasi, D., Wagshul, M., Ardekani, B., Guilfoyle. D., Khan, S., Zhong, Y., Chon, K., and Malaspina, D. (2009). Limbic dysregulation is associated with lowered heart rate variability and increased trait anxiety in healthy adults. *Human Brain Mapping, 30,* 47–58.

Nagai, M., Hoshide, S., and Kario, K. (2010). The insular cortex and cardiovascular system: A new insight into the brain-heart axis. *Journal of the American Society of Hypertension, 4,* 174–182.

Neumann, S. A., Brown, S. M., Ferrell, R. E., Flory, J. D., Manuck, S. B., and Hariri, A. R. (2006). Human choline transporter gene variation is associated with corticolimbic reactivity and autonomic-cholinergic function. *Biological Psychiatry, 60,* 1155–1162.

Ochsner, K. N., Kosslyn, S. M., Cosgrove, G. R., Cassem, E. H., Price, B. H., Nierenberg, A. A., and Rauch, S. L. (2001). Deficits in visual cognition and attention following bilateral anterior cingulotomy. *Neuropsychologia, 39,* 219–230.

Ortiz, J. and Raine, A. (2004). Heart rate level and antisocial behavior in children and adolescents: A meta-analysis. *Journal of the American Academy of Child & Adolescent Psychiatry, 43(2),* 154–162.

Pattinson, K. T., Mitsis, G. D., Harvey, A. K., Jbabdi, S., Dirckx, S., Mayhew, S. D., Rogers, R. T., Tracey, I., and Wise, R.G., (2009). Determination of the human brainstem respiratory control network and its cortical connections in vivo using functional and structural imaging. *NeuroImage, 44(2),* 295–305.

Paus, T., Koski, L., Caramanos, Z., and Westbury, C. (1998). Regional differences in the effects of task difficulty and motor output on blood flow response in the human anterior cingulate cortex: A review of 107 PET activation studies. *Neuroreport, 9,* 37–84.

Phan, K. L., Wager, T., Taylor, S., and Liberzon, I. (2002). Functional neuroanatomy of emotion: A meta-analysis of emotion activation studies in PET and fMRI. *NeuroImage, 16,* 331–348.

Porges, S. W. (2001). The polyvagal theory: Phylogenetic substrates of a social nervous system. *International Journal of Psychophysiology, 42,* 123–146.

Porges, S. W. (2007). The polyvagal perspective. *Biological Psychology, 74,* 116–143.

Price, D. D. (2000). Psychological and neural mechanisms of the affective dimension of pain. *Science, 288,* 1769–1772.

Raine, A. (2002). Annotation: The role of prefrontal deficits, low autonomic arousal, and early health factors in the development of antisocial and aggressive behavior in children. *Journal of Child Psychology and Psychiatry, 43(4),* 417–434.

Raine, A., Venables, P. H., and Williams, M. (1990). Relationships between central and autonomic measures of arousal at age 15 years and criminality at age 24 years. *Archives of General Psychiatry, 47,* 1003–1007.

Raine, A., Venables, P. H., and Williams, M. (1995). High autonomic arousal and electrodermal orienting at age 15 years as protective factors against criminal behavior at age 29 years. *The American Journal of Psychiatry, 152(11),* 1595–1600.

Raine, A. and Yang, Y. (2006). Neural foundations to moral reasoning and antisocial behavior. *Social Cognitive and Affective Neuroscience, 1,* 203–213.

Risold, P. Y., Thompson, R. H., and Swanson, L. W. (1997). The structural organization of connections between hypothalamus and cerebral cortex. *Brain Research Reviews, 24,* 197–254.

Saarela, M. V., Hlushchuk, Y., Williams, A. C., Schurmann, M., Kalso, E., and Hari, R. (2007). The compassionate brain: Humans detect intensity of pain from another's face. *Cerebral Cortex, 17,* 230–237.

Saha, S. (2005). Role of the central nucleus of the amygdala in the control of blood pressure: Descending pathways to medullary cardiovascular nuclei. *Clinical and Experimental Pharmacology and Physiology, 32,* 450–456.

Saper, C. B. (2002). The central autonomic nervous system: Conscious visceral perception and autonomic pattern generation. *Annual Review of Neuroscience, 25,* 433–469.

Saul, J. P. (1990). Beat-to-beat variations of heart rate reflect modulation of cardiac autonomic outflow. *News in Physiological Sciences, 5,* 32–37.

Sehlmeyer, C., Schöning, S., Zwitserlood, P., Pfleiderer, B., Kircher, T., Volker, A., and Konrad, C. (2009). Human fear conditioning and extinction in neuroimaging: A systemic review. *PLoS ONE, 4:* e5865 doi:10.1371/journal.pone.0005865.

Shekhar, A., Sajdyk, T. J., Gehlert, D. R., and Rainnie, D. G. (2003). The amygdala, panic disorder, and cardiovascular responses. *Annals of the New York Academy of Science, 985,* 308–325.

Shirtcliff, E. A., Vitacco, M. J., Graf, A. R., Gostisha, A. J., Merz, J. L., and Zahn-Waxler, C. (2009). Neurobiology of empathy and callousness: Implications for the development of antisocial behavior. *Behavioral Sciences & the Law, 27,* 137–171.

Singer, T., Critchley, H. D., and Preuschoff, K. (2009). A common role of insula in feelings, empathy and uncertainty. *Trends in Cognitive Sciences, 13,* 334–340.

Singer, T. and Lamm, C. (2009). The social neuroscience of empathy. *Annals of the New York Academy of Science, 1156,* 81–96.

Sterzer, P., Stadler, C., Krebs, A., Kleinschmidt, A., and Putska, F. (2005). Abnormal neural responses to emotional visual stimuli in adolescents with conduct disorder. *Biological Psychiatry, 57,* 7–15.

Sterzer, P., Stadler, C., Poutska, F., and Kleinschmidt, A. (2007). A structural neural deficits in adolescents with conduct disorder and its association with lack of empathy. *Neuroimage, 37,* 335–342.

Swick, D. and Turken, A. U. (2002). Dissociation between conflict detection and error monitoring in the human anterior cingulate cortex. *Proceedings of the National Academy of Sciences, 99,* 16354–16363.

Tavares, R. F., Corrêa, F. M. A., and Resstel, L. B. M. (2009). Opposite role of infralimbic and prelimbic cortex in the tachycardiac response evoked by acute restraint stress in rats. *Journal of Neuroscience Research, 87,* 2601–2607.

Ter Horst, G. J. and Postema, F. (1997). Forebrain parasympathetic control of heart activity: Retrograde transneuronal viral labeling in rats. *American Journal of Physiology, 273,* H2926–H2930.

Thayer, J. F., Hansen, A. L., Saus-Rose, E., and Johnsen, B. H. (2009). Heart rate variability, prefrontal neural function, and cognitive performance: The neurovisceral integration perspective on selfregulation, adaptation, and health. *Annals of Behavioral Medicine, 37,* 141–153.

Thayer, J. F. and Lane, R. D. (2000). A model of neurovisceral integration in emotion regulation and dysregulation. *Journal of Affective Disorders, 61,* 201–216

Tiihonen, J., Hodgins, S., Vaurio, O., Laakso, M., Repo, E., Soininen, J., Aronen, H. J., Nieminen, P., and Savolainen, L. (2000). Amygdaloid volume loss in psychopathy. *Society for Neuroscience Abstracts, 2017.*

Topolovec, J. C., Gati, J. S., Menon, R. S., Shoemaker, J. K., and Cechetto, D. F. (2004). Human cardiovascular and gustatory brainstem sites observed by functional magnetic *resonance* imaging. *Journal of Comparative Neurology, 471*, 446–461.

Verberne, A. J. M. (1996). Medullary sympathoexcitatory neurons are inhibited by the activation of the prefrontal cortex in the rate. *American Journal of Physiology, 270*, R713–R719.

Verberne, A. J. M. and Owens, N. C. (1998). Cortical modulation of the cardiovascular system. *Progress in Neurobiology, 54*, 149–168.

Veit, R., Flor, H., Erb, M., Hermann, C., Lotze, M., Grodd, W., and Birbaumer, N. (2002). Brain circuits involved in emotional learning in antisocial behavior and social phobia in humans. *Neuroscience Letters, 328*, 233–236.

Vollum, B., Richardson, P., Stirling, J., Elliott, R., Dolan, M., Chaudhry, I., Del Ben, C., McKie, S., Anderson, I., and Deakin, B. (2004). Neurobiological substrates of antisocial and borderline personality disorder: Preliminary results of a functional fMRI study. *Criminal Behaviour and Mental Health, 14(1)*, 39–54.

Wadsworth, M. E. J. (1976). Delinquency, pulse rates, and early emotional deprivation. *British Journal of Criminology, 16(3)*, 245–256.

Wager, T. D., van Ast, V., Hughes, B., Davidson, M. L., Lindquist, M. A., and Ochsner, K. N. (2009a). Brain mediators of cardiovascular responses to social threat, part II: Prefrontal-subcortical pathways and relationship with anxiety. *NeuroImage, 47*, 836–851.

Wager, T. D., Waugh, C. E., Lindquist, M., Noll, D. C., Fredrickson, B. L., and Taylor, S. F. (2009b). Brain mediators of cardiovascular responses to social threat, part I: Reciprocal dorsal and ventral sub-regions of the medial prefrontal cortex and heart-rate reactivity. *NeuroImage, 47*, 821–835.

Wong, S. W., Masse, N., Kimmerly, D. S., Menon, R. S., and Shoemaker, J. K. (2007). Ventral medial prefrontal cortex and cardiovagal control in conscious humans. *NeuroImage, 35(2)*, 698–708.

Yang, T. T., Simmons, A. N., Matthews, S. C., Tapert, S. F., Bischoff-Grethe, A., Frank, G. K., Arce, E., and Paulus, M. P. (2007). Increased amygdala activation is related to heart rate during emotion processing in adolescent subjects. *Neuroscience Letters, 428*, 109–114.

Yang, Y., Raine, A., Lencz, T., Bihrle, S., LaCasse, L., and Colletti, P. (2005). Volume reduction in prefrontal gray matter in unsuccessful criminal psychopaths. *Biological Psychiatry, 57*, 1103–1108.

Yang, Y., Raine, A., Narr, K. L., Lencz, T., and Toga, A. W. (2006). Amygdala volume reduction in psychopaths. *Society for Research in Psychopathology* [Abstract].

PART II
GENETICS AND CRIME

The Genetics of Criminality and Delinquency

Lisabeth Fisher DiLalla and Sufna Gheyara

One of the primary goals of psychological research is to understand the causes and correlates of human behavior. Much of the literature has focused on maladaptive behavior, not only as a comparison point for normal behavior, but also as a target for preventative and treatment measures. In particular, criminal and delinquent behavior, defined as violation of laws and ordinances by adults or children, respectively, have received a large amount of attention in the field. It is important to note that many behaviors that are considered delinquent, such as breaking curfew, would not be considered criminal behavior. The substantial push amongst researchers to understand criminal and delinquent behavior is largely due to the negative consequences with which they are associated. Although all maladaptive behaviors influence the acting individual in a negative way, few have the ability to harm outside parties in the same capacity as criminal behavior. Many criminal and delinquent behaviors affect more than just the perpetrator; thus, the understanding of what causes, and in turn what may prevent, such behavior has large societal implications.

Psychological research acknowledges an individual's intra- and interpersonal environments as important components in the conceptualization of human behavior. In the external environment, factors such as interpersonal relationships and socioeconomic status are related to a variety of behaviors. Similarly, intrapersonal environmental factors such as personality disposition and temperament, which are influenced by genes, are also major contributors. However, the historic dichotomy of genes and the environment, the seemingly endless "nature versus nurture" debate, has left the discipline largely split on a fundamental theme in psychology. The field of behavioral genetics aims to bridge this gap by exploring the synergistic relation that exists between genes and the environment, understanding that they dually affect each other and, thus, individual behavior. In this way, understanding genetic underpinnings is crucial in the overall conceptualization of human behavior.

The notion that an individual's genetic makeup influences criminal behavior is supported in the literature through several types of studies, all of which utilize the different methodological models of behavioral genetics. Twin and adoption studies investigate the amount of variance in a particular trait or behavior that can be accounted for by either genes, shared environment (the environment that serves to make individuals more similar to one another), or non-shared environment (those unique experiences that serve to make individuals more dissimilar to one another). Also, familial studies investigate the degree to which a given trait or behavioral pattern exists in families. Using what we know about the various degrees to which genetic material is passed between generations, we are able to determine whether certain traits or behaviors tend to "run in families."

However, a causal relation between the environment or genes and any behavior is difficult to establish. Instead, much of the field explores correlational data for its ability to predict future behavior. In this way, the genetic makeup of an individual has predictive value in determining his or her likelihood of engaging in a given behavior. This chapter will explore the genetic underpinnings of criminal and delinquent behavior, paying close attention to the implications and utility of such findings. Research examining the role of several neurotransmitters, including serotonin and dopamine, in the manifestation of criminal and delinquent behavior will also be explored, with special attention paid to the genetic polymorphisms in receptor and transporter genes that affect their amount and activity. Finally, some important ethical considerations when examining genetic influences, including historical context, will be discussed.

Genetics and Crime

One of the earliest genetic factors implicated in the development of crime was the XYY genotype in men, a theory popular in the 1960s and 1970s (Witkin et al., 1977). Remember that the typical man has an XY genotype. Because the Y chromosome only appears in men and is associated with testosterone, it was believed that men with an extra Y chromosome would be at increased risk for exhibiting exaggerated male behaviors and for acting out aggressively. Early case studies examining men with the XYY genotype concluded that they had a higher propensity for committing crimes along with lowered understanding of the consequences of their maladaptive behavior (Price & Whatmore, 1967). However, much of this research was based on individuals who were incarcerated or hospitalized in mental institutions, and therefore results only generalized to a small portion of the population.

Current research has discredited this vulnerability, noting that the association between the XYY genotype and increased criminality and aggression disappears if other factors, such as socioeconomic status or education level, are accounted for (Ike, 2000). For example, Götz, Johnstone, and Ratcliff (1999) examined men with XYY, XXY, and XY genotypes and found that the XYY men committed more crimes than the other men. However, they noted that this relationship was mediated by low education. Similar results were found by Witkin (1976) who also compared XYY, XXY, and XY men.

Beckwith and King (1974) cautioned against the false assumption that individuals with the XYY chromosome are more likely to commit crimes, citing the erroneous targeting of these individuals for intervention strategies that were not warranted. They exposed several radical "treatments" that were utilized, including injecting men with female sex hormones, despite the fact that XYY individuals do not differ in the amount of testosterone in their bodies compared to "normal" XY men. This is a prime example of how falsely interpreted genetic findings can be quite dangerous. It is very important to remember than any genetic underpinnings of criminality, or any other trait, work synergistically with the environment, serving as risk factors. Therefore, they are in no way deterministic in nature, and should not be treated as such.

Behavioral Genetics and Criminality

Behavioral genetics utilizes two main types of methodologies, adoption and twin studies, in order to understand the environmental and genetic influences on a variety of disorders and behaviors. First, adoption studies allow for examination of both genetic and environmental influences on a given phenotype. Adoption studies rely on two types of analyses, the comparison between an adopted individual and a first-degree relative who lives in a separate environment, and the comparison between an adopted individual and a genetically unrelated individual who lives in the same environment. Observed differences between adoptees and biological relatives are largely attributed to environmental influences because the two individuals share genetic material but not environment. Conversely, observed differences between adoptees and non-biological relatives are largely attributed to genetic influences, as the shared environment between the two subjects is the same (Bazzett, 2008). It is important to keep in mind that adoption studies present unique confounds in research, as those who are adopted as well as those who are eligible to adopt may not represent a normative sampling of the population (DiLalla & Gottesman, 1989).

In order to understand how the second method, twin studies, provides valuable information, an understanding of twins is necessary. There are two types of twins, monozygotic (MZ) and dizygotic (DZ). MZ twins result from a single fertilized egg splitting soon after conception. As a result, these twins share nearly 100 percent of their genetic material. DZ twins are created when two separate eggs are fertilized at the same time, and as a result the twins share about 50 percent of their genetic material, the same as any other two siblings. Therefore, greater similarity for an observed trait in MZ versus DZ twins is thought to indicate genetic influence (Bazzett, 2008).

However, unlike other siblings, twins share very similar prenatal environments. Indeed, sharing a womb helps to rule out differences due to shared aspects of the prenatal environment, including exposure to toxins or levels of circulating hormones. Comparisons between normal siblings would have to consider differences in these aspects between pregnancies as possible contributors to differences in the observed phenotype between siblings. This is largely avoided by examining twins. However, it is important to note that there can be competition prenatally for resources in the womb, and that may lead to differences between twins as a result of the prenatal environment. In addition, the postnatal environment for twins is more similar than between other siblings. Most notably, twins experience environmental events at the same age as their co-twin. The age at which one experiences external events, for example moving to a different house, may influence the impact it has on the child. A three-year-old may not experience the same level of social disruption as would a 10-year-old, who would have to move schools and leave behind friends.

Twin studies allow for estimations of heritability, or the proportion of variation in trait expression that can be attributed to genetic influences, by using our knowledge of the genetic similarities in both types of twins. Any trait is comprised of three influences: genetic influences, shared environmental influences (environmental events that result in twins becoming more similar), and non-shared environmental influences (environmental events that result in differences between twins). Therefore, it is assumed that similarities between twins are a function of both genetic and shared environmental influences.

The degree to which twins share genetic information is established by the type of twins they are, with monozygotic twins sharing nearly 100 percent of their genetic material and dizygotic twins sharing on average 50 percent of their genetic material. However, our understanding of how they share their environments relies on an important assumption, known as the equal environments assumption (EEA). According to this theory, MZ and DZ twins share their environments to the same extent, allowing for valid comparisons between the two groups. This assumption is crucial in the study of twins (Kendler, Neale, Kessler, & Heath, 1993), but need only hold true for environments that are important influences on the behaviors under study. If this assumption was false, and MZ twins were more similar in their exposure to environmental influences, heritability would be overestimated. Some researchers have argued that MZ twins are more likely to evoke similar environments than DZ twins, thus violating the EEA and inflating heritability estimates, and consequently, underestimating environmental influences (Horowitz, Videon, Schmitz, & Davis, 2003; Richardson & Norgate, 2005). One possible explanation for this occurrence is the notion of "niche selection," proposed by Eriksson and colleagues (Eriksson, Rasmussen, & Tynelius, 2006), in which genetic similarities cause individuals to select into environments that are more similar. In this way, an increase in shared environment in MZ twins would still be a reflection of genetic similarity. Although the potential violation of the EEA is an important issue to consider, the assumption appears to be validated by current research (Bouchard, 1997; Kendler et al., 1993; Plomin & Daniels, 1987; Walker, Petrill, Spinath, & Plomin, 2004).

Genetically informed studies have shed light on the genetic and environmental influences on criminality and delinquency. Meta-analyses of research on antisocial personality and behavior suggest that 40–50 percent of the variance can be explained by genetic influences (Miles & Carey, 1997; Rhee & Waldman, 2002). However, the degree to which genes impact criminal and delinquent behavior is different, appearing to have more influence in criminal versus delinquent behaviors. A large male twin sample (over 3,000 twin pairs) analyzed by Lyons and colleagues (1995) demonstrated that genetic influences are stronger for adult criminal behavior than adolescent delinquent behavior. The influence of genes also appears to increase with age within delinquency. Burt and Neiderhiser (2009) utilized longitudinal measures of delinquency in a sample of adolescent sibling pairs with varying degrees of genetic relatedness, initially examining individuals ages 10–18 (mean age of older sibling was 14.5 years), and again three years later (mean age of older sibling was 16.2 years). They found that genetic influences on delinquency increased dramatically with age from time 1 (unstandardized coefficient = 0.59) to time 2 (unstandardized coefficient = 0.87) and the shared environmental influences decreased with age (from 0.19 at time 1 to approximately zero at time 2).

Genetic and environmental influences may also differ based on biological traits of an individual. For instance, several studies have examined whether genetic influence differs for males versus females. Tuvblad, Eley, and Lichtenstein (2005) found that genetic influences were predominant in the development of delinquent behavior in girls, whereas shared-environment was the predominant influence in boys. Jacobson, Prescott, and Kendler (2002) examined over 6,000 adult twins and found that, although genetic factors appeared to influence female antisocial behavior more in children, there was no sex difference evident in adolescents or adults. Therefore, conflicting data on the relation between sex and the degree to which genes influence antisocial behavior may reflect age differences. A recent meta-analysis done by Rhee and Waldman (2002) examined 51 adoption and twin studies and found no sex differences in the degree to which genes contribute to the variance seen in antisocial behavior. Another biological factor that might influence degree of genetic influence is timing of puberty. Specifically, Burt, McGue, DeMarte, Krueger, and Iacono (2006) examined whether timing of menarche affected heritability in a sample of approximately 700 twin girls tested at age 11 and again at about age 14. They found that there were no shared genes between conduct disorder behaviors and age at menarche. Most interestingly, they found that heritability for conduct disorder was highest for the majority of girls who reached menarche at an age that was within normal limits. However, although more girls showed conduct disorder behaviors if they reached menarche at a very young age, the heritability of this behavior for this group of girls was much lower. Similarly, heritability was low for the group of girls who reached menarche at a very late age, and this group of girls showed much less conduct disorder behavior. These results demonstrate that genetic influences on conduct disorder are significant for most girls, but that environment is a more important influence for girls who mature very early or very late. Girls who mature very early are more likely to engage in delinquent behaviors for reasons other than a genetic propensity, quite possibly because of social influences such as associating with an older peer group. Alternatively, girls who mature quite late are less likely to engage in delinquent behaviors, again for reasons other than a genetic propensity, possibly as a result of associating with younger peers. Thus, although there may be a genetic influence on conduct disorder for the majority of girls, there are subgroups for whom the environment is a more influential factor.

Both twin and adoption studies have also shed light on environmental influences in the development of criminal and delinquent behavior. One of the most researched environmental influences on delinquency is the association of an individual with delinquent peers. These affiliations are especially troubling, as they have been demonstrated to amplify genetic risk for engaging in delinquent behavior (Beaver, DeLisi, Wright, & Vaughn, 2009). A study by Simonoff and colleagues (Simonoff et al., 2004) found that adolescents with delinquent friends were 3.6 times more likely to commit any crime during adolescence and five times more likely to commit violent crimes than those with no delinquent peers. However, there may not be a strict dichotomy between environmental and genetic influences, as behavioral genetic theory suggests that many environmental factors are partially genetic in nature (Plomin, DeFries, & Loehlin, 1977). The affiliation with delinquent peers may be an example of an active gene–environment correlation, the idea that individuals seek out environments based on their genes, or an evocative gene–environment correlation, in which individuals evoke specific reactions from their environment based, in part, on their genetic makeup. Specifically, an individual with genetic risk may seek out other delinquent peers, or may be sought out by those who have the propensity to behave in a delinquent or criminal manner.

Finally, genetic influences appear to differ based on the type of crime or delinquency. Several adoption studies have noted that genetic influences appear to be strong for non-violent crimes (Bohman, Cloninger, Sigvardsson, & von Knorring, 1982; Mednick, Gabrielli, & Hutchings, 1984; Sigvardsson, Cloninger, Bohman, & von Knorring, 1982) but not for violent offenses. However, Cloninger and Gottesman (1987) found that the genetic influence on violent crime was 50 percent, lower than the 78 percent found for property crime, but nevertheless substantial. These differences may reflect power issues, as Glickson (2002) pointed out that the low base rate for violent behavior reduces the power to detect significant effects.

Molecular Genetics and Criminality

Once the heritability of a given trait or disorder is determined, the next step is identifying which specific genes are involved. A gene is a location on a chromosome and is responsible for the synthesis of a specific protein in the cell. Chromosomes are an efficient way for the cell to store DNA, providing a method of organization for the vast amount of DNA in the body. There are different forms of any gene, termed alleles, which are partly responsible for the variety of the human species. The field of molecular genetics relies on understanding how these different forms of a gene, known as polymorphisms, manifest as differences in protein structure or production, and as a result, differences in behavior and mood. The resulting proteins have a direct influence on the amount of neurotransmitters in the body. The importance that neurotransmitters play in the experiencing of mood and disorder in humans underscores the importance that genes play in our understanding of human nature.

Among the various neurotransmitter systems, those involving dopamine and serotonin currently appear to be the most likely to be related to delinquency and criminality (Regoli, Hewitt, & DeLisi, 2009). The neurotransmitter dopamine is involved in cognitive and emotional behaviors, including reward and exploration (Oak et al., 2000). It also is responsible for helping to regulate emotions that otherwise can lead to highly aggressive or violent behaviors (Burfeind & Bartusch, 2010). Buckholtz et al. (2010) noted that dopamine is related to the reward system important for impulsive and antisocial behaviors that are involved in criminal behavior, and thus various genes related to dopamine production and regulation are likely to be related to criminality, although few studies have addressed this directly.

There are a number of genes that are involved in regulating dopamine in the brain. One of the most studied is the DRD4 receptor gene, which encodes proteins that respond to dopamine in the brain and is expressed to the greatest degree in the limbic system and frontal cortices. The DRD4 gene maps to 11p15.5 and contains a 48 bp VNTR (variable number tandem repeat) in the third exon (van Tol et al., 1992) which can consist of 2 to 11 repeats, although 4 and 7 are most common (Wang et al., 2004). The presence of a 7-repeat allele (receptors are less efficient at binding dopamine, leading to dopaminergic hypofunction) versus a 4-repeat allele appears to inhibit neuronal firing (Oak et al., 2000). Thus, DRD4 has been associated with behaviors such as novelty seeking in rodents, children, and adults (Bailey et al., 2007; Kluger, Siegfried, & Ebstein, 2002; Rettew & McKee, 2005; Wang et al., 2004) as well as ADHD (Faraone, Doyle, Mick, & Biederman, 2001; Wang et al., 2004), emotional reactivity (Oniszczenko & Dragan, 2005), greater craving, arousal, and related responses to smoking cues (Hutchinson et al., 2002), and low conscientiousness (Benjamin et al., 1996; Dragan & Oniszczenko, 2007), all of which may be related to delinquency and criminality. This single polymorphism may account for 4 percent of the total variance in novelty seeking. In preschool children, DRD4 was associated with maternal reports, but not observed measures, of aggression (Schmidt et al., 2002), and DRD4 interacted with low parental sensitivity to increase the likelihood of parent-rated externalizing problem behaviors (DiLalla, Elam, & Smolen, 2009). In older adolescents, this gene appears to be related to delinquent activities. Interestingly, in a Russian sample, Dmitrieva, Chen, Greenberger, Ogunseitan, and Ding (2010) found that for boys only, those with the 7-repeat DRD4 allele were significantly more likely to engage in delinquent behaviors, but not when they had been exposed to psychological trauma. Thus, if the environment was sufficiently negative, the genetic risk did not differentiate boys in terms of delinquency.

Another dopamine gene that has been studied with respect to behaviors linked to delinquency or criminality is the DRD2 gene, a dopamine receptor gene that also has been shown to relate to nicotine's effects of brain activation and behavior (Gilbert et al., 2005, 2009), which may relate to criminal behaviors. Several studies using the National Longitudinal Study of Adolescent Health (Add Health) sample have found relations between dopamine and delinquency. Boutwell and Beaver (2008) and Guo,

Roettger, and Shih (2007) both noted that males from the Add Health sample who had a risk variant of a dopamine-related gene were more likely to show delinquent behaviors. However, Boutwell and Beaver (2008) also showed that for males only, those with two risk alleles for either DRD2 or DRD4 were less likely to engage in delinquent activities, but males with only one risk allele for either gene were more likely to be delinquent. Interestingly, DeLisi, Beaver, Wright, and Vaughn (2008) found that adolescents with high-risk DRD2 and DRD4 genotypes, which should put them at greater risk for criminality, were in fact more likely than those without the high-risk genotypes to have a later onset for criminal behaviors. This is surprising because earlier onset, rather than later onset, typically represents a more serious behavior problem. Other research has suggested that early onset criminality is the most severe and most likely to continue into adulthood, but the results from DeLisi et al. suggest that there may be a form of criminality that is related to ostensibly greater genetic risk but that begins at later rather than earlier ages.

Additionally, Guo et al. (2007, 2010) found a relation between the DAT gene, a dopamine transporter gene, and delinquency, demonstrating another effect of dopamine. Guo et al. (2007) found that for males only, having the DAT1 risk allele increased the likelihood of delinquent behaviors. This risk, however, did not interact with the DRD2 gene, meaning that having risk alleles for both genes did not multiplicatively increase the risk for delinquency. In a follow-up study, Guo et al. (2010) found that having the non-risk DAT1 allele actually appears to be protective against delinquent behaviors.

Serotonin also may be important for influencing aggressive and antisocial behaviors (Dolan, 2002; Moore, Scarpa, & Raine, 2002), delinquency (Regoli et al., 2009), and crime (Raine, 1993). Much of this work has been done in adults (Berman et al., 2009; Caspi et al., 2003; Dolan, 2002); results are less clear for young children and adolescents (Beitchman et al., 2006; Haberstick, Smolen, & Hewitt, 2006). Serotonin is important for inhibiting negative emotions that might otherwise lead to aggressive types of behaviors. A meta-analysis (Moore et al., 2002) on the serotonin metabolite 5-hydroxyindoleacetic acid (5-HIAA) showed a strong effect for lowered levels of 5-HIAA among groups who had been classified as antisocial, and this was especially true for those who were younger than 30 years old. Thus, one might expect stronger effects of low serotonin levels among adolescents as well. In fact, low serotonin levels were shown to be associated with increased aggression in six- to 16-year-old children (Davidge et al., 2004). Beitchman et al. (2006) noted that the 5-HTTLPR genotype, a serotonin transporter gene, was related to increased aggression in a select sample of aggressive five- to 15-year-olds (76 percent boys). However, one study (Schmidt et al., 2002) did not find this; thus, the relation for children is still inconclusive (Beitchman et al., 2003). It is possible that low serotonin is related to decreased inhibition and increased irritability, depression, and anxiety, and therefore is only indirectly related to aggression.

The effects of serotonin on criminality have been demonstrated in several countries. One study of Chinese men convicted of violent crimes showed that a low-activity allele (S) of the 5-HTTLPR polymorphism was related to increased violence, although it was not related to antisocial personality (Liao, Hong, Shih, &

Tsai, 2004). A series of studies of Finnish men who have committed violent offenses has shown that men with low levels of serotonin are more at risk of impulsive, violent offending (see Virkkunen, Goldman, Nielsen, & Linnoila, 1995). Specifically, men with low cerebrospinal fluid (CSF) 5-HIAA were more likely to engage in violent offending and also were more likely to recidivate. Thus, at least with adult men, low levels of serotonin appear to be related to increased violent criminality across various cultures.

Impulsivity, which may be related to delinquency, criminality, and aggressive behaviors, has been associated with mono-aminergic activity, specifically with low platelet MAO (Carrasco et al., 2000). The MAOA gene codes for the monoamine oxidase A enzyme, which deaminates several neurotransmitters including dopamine and serotonin. A polymorphism in the MAOA gene affects dopaminergic and serotonergic function. Although decreased MAO should increase dopamine and serotonin, it actually appears to lead to lower levels of these neurotransmitters, perhaps because early neonatal feedback systems compensate for an overabundance (Alia-Klein et al., 2008). The MAOA polymorphism may be particularly important for criminal behaviors (Beaver & Holtfreter, 2009). Adult studies have shown a relation between low MAOA activity and violence and gang membership (Beaver et al., 2009) and aggressive and antisocial behaviors (Alia-Klein et al., 2008; Guo et al., 2008; Rowe, 2001), although these behaviors might not be related directly to genotype (Alia-Klein et al., 2008) but rather to developmental responses to genotype at early ages. Others have found a relation between a high active MAOA allele (which leads to decreased MAOA and decreased dopamine levels in brain) and novelty seeking in an adult population (Shiraishi et al., 2006). In adult criminality, there is some evidence that lower levels of MAOA are related to increased delinquency and criminality (Guo et al., 2008). Utilizing the Add Health sample and examining serious and violent delinquency in adolescents and young adults, Guo et al. (2008) showed that a 2-repeat variant of MAOA, which was much lower in activity than other variants, was related to a significant increase both in serious (non-violent) delinquency and in violent delinquency in males. This was true to a lesser degree in females. In addition, MAOA may interact with the environment, with low-active MAOA genotypes plus provocation leading to increased aggression (Caspi et al., 2002; McDermott et al., 2009), which is described in more detail below. Thus, examination of the ways in which genes and environment interact is essential for understanding the genetics behind criminality.

Gene–Environment Interaction and Correlation

Genes and environment may work together in several different ways to affect behavior. Two specific mechanisms include gene–environment interaction, which is a genetic sensitivity to the environment, and gene–environment correlation, which includes different types of correlations between genotype and the environment and which will be described in more detail below. Both are difficult to test, but with new information about specific genes, researchers are beginning to attempt to unravel these influences. The interaction between genes and environment is complicated, but it may explain much of the variance in behaviors such as criminality. If gene–environment interaction is occurring, it means that certain genotypes respond differently to specific environments. For example, someone who is genetically prone to being highly reactive may respond to a chaotic environment in a negative way because of the intense stimulation, whereas someone else who is genetically temperamentally calm may respond to that chaotic environment quite differently. The chaotic environment therefore may be a risk factor for people with one genotype but not for individuals with a different genotype.

In addition, there may be some environmental situations in which heritability is decreased because it is impossible for genotype to be fully expressed. For instance, in an environment where education is poor and there are few resources, it can be expected that intelligence would not be as highly heritable because there is not sufficient environmental latitude to allow the full expression of intellectual ability (Turkheimer, Haley, Waldron, D'Onofrio, & Gottesman, 2003). A similar effect may occur for criminality. For instance, in the Amish environment, even if there were some adolescents with a genotype that put them at risk for delinquent behaviors, they would not engage in these behaviors because the opportunities would not exist (Legrand, Keyes, McGue, Iacono, & Krueger, 2008). Comparably, at the other extreme with a negative environment, the diathesis-stress hypothesis posits that a genetic tendency toward negative behaviors will be amplified in the presence of a negative environment because of the accumulation of genetic and environmental stressors. However, some studies have demonstrated that genetic effects on antisocial behaviors are attenuated in the presence of a negative environment that allows little room for expression of positive behaviors (Moffitt, 2005). Thus, examination of gene–environment interactions are critical in understanding the role that genotype plays in the development of delinquent and criminal behaviors.

The earliest adoption study of gene–environment interaction and criminality was conducted by Mednick and colleagues (e.g., Hutchings & Mednick, 1975; Mednick et al., 1984, 1987) utilizing a Danish adoption sample. They found significant effects of both genes (criminal biological fathers) and environment (adoptive fathers), but they noted an additive rather than a multiplicative effect of these risks on sons' criminal convictions. However, other studies have demonstrated evidence of a gene–environment interaction for criminality. For instance, Cloninger, Sigvardsson, Bohman, and von Knorring (1982) provided evidence of an interaction between genetic predispositions to criminality and low social status in a sample of adopted Swedish men. Also, Crowe (1974) noted that men who had a genetic risk (being adopted away from mothers with a criminal record) and an environmental risk (spending longer periods of time in an orphanage prior to being adopted) were significantly more likely to be incarcerated for criminal activity themselves. Similarly, adoption studies in Iowa (Cadoret & Cain, 1981) and Missouri (Cadoret, Cain, & Crowe, 1983) have suggested gene–environment interaction because adoptees with alcoholic or antisocial parents who also experienced longer periods of time in foster homes or who experienced alcoholism in their adoptive homes (although this was rare) were much more likely themselves to show antisocial behaviors in adolescence. Overall, it is difficult to study gene–environment interaction effects for criminality because adoption studies have been the primary mechanism for this type of analysis, and adoptive homes tend to have little criminality because the families are carefully selected (Cadoret, 1982; DiLalla & Gottesman, 1989). Thus, results from adoption studies must be considered in this light.

However, since the advent of molecular genetics, gene–environment interactions have been studied by examining the interaction between a specific polymorphism and a specific environmental influence. One of the first and most striking g–e interaction studies on criminal behaviors was conducted by Caspi and colleagues (Caspi et al., 2002), where they examined the interaction between the MAOA genotype and early maltreatment in 442 Caucasian males who participated in the longitudinal Dunedin Multidisciplinary Health and Development Study. They found that among those with the high-risk MAOA genotype (low activity), individuals who had also been maltreated showed a greatly increased likelihood of being convicted for violent offenses as well as an increased likelihood of having informants who knew them well report symptoms of antisocial personality disorder. However, this was not born out in a clinical sample of adolescent boys (Young et al., 2006) or in several other studies (Haberstick et al., 2005; Huizinga et al., 2006). Nonetheless, a number of studies have produced similar results to Caspi et al.'s (e.g., Foley et al., 2004; Frazzetto et al., 2007). Beaver and Holtfreter (2009) examined g–e interaction for fraudulent, rather than violent, behaviors and found evidence of an MAOA by peer delinquency interaction. Males from the Add Health sample who had the high-risk MAOA genotype and who reported engagement with delinquent peers during adolescence were significantly more likely to report using someone else's credit card or writing a bad check during young adulthood. Thus, this interaction effect may be important for various types of criminal activity, not just those involving violent or physically aggressive behaviors. Similar results were found when only African American males from the Add Health sample were examined and a composite genotype score was created by summing number of risk alleles across various genes, including dopamine genes (DRD2, DRD4, and DAT1), serotonin (5HTT), and MAOA (Beaver, Sak, Vaske, & Nilsson, 2010). Environmental stress was measured as lack of maternal attachment, lack of maternal involvement, and maternal disengagement. These researchers found that gene–environment interaction was significant for adult police contacts and antisocial behaviors, although individual genotype and environment measures did not predict these behaviors by themselves. In the same sample of young adults, Vaughn, DeLisi, Beaver, and Wright (2009) reported an interaction between the DAT1 gene and number of delinquent peers. Specifically, they found that Caucasian, but not African-American, young adults who reported having few delinquent peers, but who had more DAT1 risk alleles, were significantly more likely to report having engaged in serious as well as more violent criminal activities. However, they did not find this effect for the serotonin 5-HTT gene.

There is some evidence that gene–environment interactions are also important for delinquent behaviors. Legrand et al. (2008) found that heritability of delinquency was significantly diminished in a rural sample of boys compared to an urban sample, although the effect was less strong for girls. The authors hypothesized that there were more opportunities for delinquency in an urban environment, and therefore the full range of behaviors influenced by genotype could be expressed better than in a rural environment. This supports the diathesis-stress hypothesis of accumulation of risks in combination with genetic risk factors leading to an increase in delinquent behaviors. Interestingly, Kim-Cohen et al. (2006) examined MAOA in seven-year-old children and found a gene–environment interaction effect for psychopathology, especially for the boys. They found that boys with the high-risk MAOA allele who were maltreated in early childhood were the most likely group to display psychopathological symptoms. The fact that boys with the combination of genetic and environmental risks were significantly more likely to have pathological behaviors suggests that boys at genetic risk were much more susceptible to the environmental stressor of abuse. These data correspond with the data presented by Caspi et al. (2002) showing gene–environment interaction for adult criminal behaviors when MAOA and childhood maltreatment were examined.

Gene–environment correlations (g–e correlations) reflect environments that are correlated with one's genotype, either because of "niche-picking" whereby an individual chooses an environment that suits his or her particular genotype (active g–e correlation), because of environmental responses to an individual partly as a result of the individual's particular genotype (active or evocative g–e correlation), or because the source of the environment (the parents) is the same as the source of the genotype (passive g–e correlation). G–e correlations may be relevant for delinquent or criminal behaviors because individuals who are genetically prone to behaving in these manners might also choose environments that increase the likelihood of engaging in these behaviors. It also is possible that people in the environment respond in certain ways to those who are genetically more likely to engage in these behaviors, thus increasing the likelihood of the behaviors being shown. Finally, it is possible that parents may provide both genotypes that put children at risk for these behaviors as well as rearing environments that augment that likelihood. Thus, all three types of g–e correlation may account for delinquent and criminal behaviors.

It is difficult to test directly for g–e correlations, but one study examining the role of delinquent peer interactions has provided evidence for the presence of active g–e correlation as an influence on delinquency. Specifically, using data from the Add Health study, Beaver, Wright, and DeLisi (2008) found that for males only, those who had experienced more negative maternal environments as children and who had a genetic risk by having the 10-repeat allele of the DAT1 gene were significantly more likely to report having delinquent peers as friends. Many studies have already demonstrated a strong and reliable relation between having delinquent peers and engaging in delinquent activities. Thus, the study by Beaver et al. (2008) supports the contention that a g–e correlation exists, whereby those at genetic risk for behaving in an antisocial way are more likely to spend time with peers who also behave in this way, and these together greatly increase the likelihood of engaging in delinquent behaviors.

Ethical Considerations in Genetic Research

It is critical to understand that identifying a genetic influence on any trait, including criminality, is absolutely not a deterministic judgment and does not imply that criminality is all "in the genes." In fact, genetic influences are subject to change both by the environment and by individual free will. Genetic influences can be considered in much the same way as environmental ones; they may account for a small portion of the variance in the behavior of criminality and they may influence behavior, but they occur within an environmental context. In the same way that an abused child is not destined irrevocably to abuse his or her own children or to engage in criminal activities as an adult, so too is an adult with a particular genotype not destined to behave criminally. It is important to consider genetic effects on criminality because these influences may help us to understand some of the many causes of this behavior, and within the confines of particular environments may provide information that will help to better guide intervention and prevention efforts.

Traditionally, criminologists have been loath to explore genetic influences on criminality, primarily because of a fear that embracing "genetic determinism" (Machalek & Martin, 2010) will lead down a path to accepting a loss of free will and a belief that someone with "bad genes" cannot be helped through environmental intervention. However, as Machalek and Martin (2010) point out, it is essential to understand that genes act on individuals within their environments, both the body's physiological environment as well as the individual's familial and cultural environments. Thus, it is imperative to have a clear understanding that genes may influence behavior indirectly, but that these influences are complicated and do not influence behaviors independently of the environment.

Interestingly, as described in a treatise nicely summarized by Baschetti (2008), Darwin originally posited that both altruistic and criminal behaviors were likely to have genetic influence and to be inherited across generations. Recent research has borne this out. However, enough people have been upset by the thought that criminality might have genetic influence that a conference initially planned for 1992 in Washington, D.C., featuring some of the most prominent researchers in this area of study, was postponed for three years because so many people protested the very concept (Roush, 1995). The conference, entitled "The Meaning and Significance of Research on Genetics and Criminal Behavior," was designed to allow exploration of the biological influences on criminality. However, when it was finally held, protestation was severe. In fact, protesters disrupted the conference for a full two hours, during which time they "stormed the auditorium and seized the microphones" (Roush, 1995, p. 1809).

The protesters were concerned that the study of genetic influences on criminality would lead to racist interpretations and interventions because of the disproportionate numbers of minority individuals who tend to be arrested for criminal behaviors. According to them, if these behaviors were solely the result of "bad genes," then researchers effectively would be stating that minorities have "bad genes." However, proponents of this research countered that it is essential to understand the role that genes play in influencing all behaviors, including criminality, so that we can better inform treatment and perhaps even intervene prior to the display of these behaviors. Although the protesters caused a great deal of disruption during the conference, they played an essential role in highlighting the fears and concerns that many people have about how scientific information can be abused. Talk of genetic influence on criminality played into memories of Hitler and genocide, and this potent reminder served as a catalyst for many of the scientists present at the conference to increase awareness of how their scientific findings are interpreted by those outside their fields.

It is essential to understand the importance of gene–environment interactions and correlations and to remember that genes do not "cause" behaviors, nor do they exist in a vacuum. Just as there never will be a "gene" for criminality, there also never will be genes that affect behaviors completely independently of the individual's environment, especially for a behavior as complex as criminality. We know that there are a myriad of environmental influences that increase the likelihood that criminal behavior will be enacted, including poverty, poor educational settings, crowded environmental conditions, and aggressive environments. However, we also must acknowledge that there are individual differences in responses to these environmental stressors, and genetic makeup is one important facet to consider. Sufficient evidence has now been amassed that this is no longer a question. However, our knowledge about exactly how we get from specific genes to criminal behavior is still in its very rudimentary stages. We have much to learn, and it is unclear whether we ever will completely understand all the possible, complex, individual pathways between genes and behavior. There are very important lessons that must be learned from the protestors at the 1995 conference. We must be especially wary of anyone – politicians, scientists, dogmatists – who attempt to use scientific information to support suppositions of racism, genetic bigotry, or advocation of unequal treatment or, at the extreme, genocide. Anyone who attempts to trace behavior to genotype without regard for interpretation of that genotype within its environment is in error. It is imperative that scientists be aware of the implications of their research and attempt to discourage misinterpretation by those who do not understand genetic research. The essence of behavior genetics lies in understanding how nature and nurture work together. A behavior genetic framework has the potential to greatly increase our understanding of criminality, but we must proceed with caution and do our best to ensure that our scientific findings are interpreted in light of nature, nurture, and the complicated interactions between them.

References

Alia-Klein, N., Goldstein, R. Z., Kriplani, A., Logan, J., Tomasi, D., Williams, B., Telang, B., Shumay, E., Biegon, A., Craig, I. W., Henn, F., Wang, G.-J., Volkow, N. D., & Fowler, J. S. (2008). Brain Monoamine Oxidase A activity predicts trait aggression. *The Journal of Neuroscience*, *28*, 5099–5104. doi: 10.1523/JNEUROSCI.0925-08.2008.

Bailey, J. N., Breidenthal, S. E., Jorgensen, M. J., McCracken, J. T., & Fairbanks, L. A. (2007). The association of DRD4 and novelty seeking is found in a nonhuman primate model. *Psychiatric Genetics*, *17*, 23–27. doi: 10.1097/YPG.0b013e32801140f2.

Baschetti, R. (2008). Genetic evidence that Darwin was right about criminality: Nature, not nurture. *Medical Hypotheses*, *70*(6), 1092–102. doi: 10.1016/j.mehy.2008.01.005.

Bazzett, T. (2008). *An introduction to behavior genetics*. Sunderland, MA: Sinauer Associates.

Beaver, K. M., DeLisi, M., Wright, J. P., & Vaughn, M. G. (2009). Gene-environment interplay and delinquent involvement: Evidence of direct, indirect, and interactive effects. *Journal of Adolescent Research*, *24*, 147–168. doi: 10.1177/0743558408329952.

Beaver, K. M., & Holtfreter, K. (2009). Biosocial influences on fraudulent behaviors. *The Journal of Genetic Psychology*, *170*, 101–114. doi: 10.3200/GNTP.170.2.101-114.

Beaver, K. M., Sak, A., Vaske, J., & Nilsson, J. (2010). Genetic risk, parent–child relations, and antisocial phenotypes in a sample of African-American males. *Psychiatry Research*, *175*, 160–164. doi: 10.1016/j.psychres.2009.01.024.

Beaver, K. M., Wright, J. P., & DeLisi, M. (2008). Delinquent peer group formation: Evidence of a gene × environment correlation. *The Journal of Genetic Psychology*, *169*(3), 227–244.

Beckwith, J. & King, J. (1974). XYY syndrome – a dangerous myth. *New Scientist*, *64*, 474–476.

Beitchman, J. H., Baldassarra, L., Mik, H., De Luca, L., King, N., Bender, D., et al. (2006). Serotonin transporter polymorphisms and persistent, pervasive, childhood aggression. *American Journal of Psychiatry*, *163*, 1103–1105. doi: 10.1176/appi.ajp.163.6.1103.

Beitchman, J. H., Davidge, K. M., Kennedy, J. L., Atkinson, L., Lee, V., Shapiro, S., & Douglas, L. (2003). The serotonin transporter gene in aggressive children with and without ADHD and nonaggressive matched controls. *Annals of the NY Academy of Sciences*, *1008*, 248–251. doi: 10.1196/annals.1301.025.

Benjamin, J., Li, L., Patterson, C., Greenberg, B. D., Murphy, D. L., & Hamer, D. H. (1996). Population and familial association between D4 dopamine receptor gene and measures of novelty seeking. *Nature Genetics*, *1996*, 81–84. doi: 10.1038/ng0196-81.

Berman, M. E., & Coccaro, E. F. (1998). Neurobiologic correlates of violence: Relevance to criminal responsibility. *Behavioral Sciences and the Law*, *16*(3), 303–318. doi: 10.1002/(SICI)1099-0798(199822)16:3<303::AID-BSL309>3.0.CO;2-C.

Berman, M. E., McCloskey, M. S., Fanning, J. R., Schumacher, J. A., & Coccaro, E. F. (2009). Serotonin augmentation reduces response to attack in aggressive individuals. *Psychological Science*, *20*, 714–720. doi: 10.1111/j.1467-9280.2009.02355.x.

Bohman, M., Cloninger, R., Sigvardsson, S., & von Knorring, A. (1982). Predisposition to petty criminality in Swedish adoptees: I. Genetic and environmental heterogeneity. *Archives of General Psychiatry, 39*, 1233–1241.

Bouchard, T. J., Jr. (1997). IQ similarity in twins reared apart: Findings and responses to critics. In: Sternberg, R. J. & Grigorenko, E. L. (Eds.), *Intelligence, heredity, and environment* (pp. 126–160). New York: Cambridge University Press.

Boutwell, B. B., & Beaver, K. M. (2008). A biosocial explanation of delinquency abstention. *Criminal Behavior and Mental Health, 18*(1), 59–74. doi: 10.1002/cbm.678.

Buckholtz, J. W., Treadway, M. T., Cowan, R. L., Woodward, N. D., Benning, S. D., Li, R., Ansari, M. S., Baldwin, R. M., Schwartzman, A. N., Shelby, E. S., Smith, C. E., Cole, D., Kessler, R. M., & Zal, D. H. (2010). Mesolimbic dopamine reward system hypersensitivity in individuals with psychopathic traits. *Nature Neuroscience, 13*, 419–421. doi: 10.1038/nn.2510.

Burfeind, J., & Bartusch, D. J. (2011). *Juvenile delinquency: An integrated approach*, 2nd ed. Sudbury, MA: Jones and Bartlett Pub.

Burt, S. A., McGue, M., DeMarte, J. A., Krueger, R. F., & Iacono, W. G. (2006). Timing of menarche and the origins of conduct disorder. *Archives of General Psychiatry, 63*, 890–896. doi: 10.1001/archpsyc.63.8.890.

Burt, S. A., & Neiderhiser, J. (2009). Aggressive versus nonaggressive antisocial behavior: Distinctive etiological moderation by age. *Developmental Psychology, 45*, 1164–1176. doi: 10.1037/a0016130.

Cadoret, R. J. (1982). Genotype-environment interaction in antisocial behavior. *Psychological Medicine, 12*, 235–239. doi: 10.1017/S0033291700046559.

Cadoret, R., & Cain, C. A. (1981). Environmental and genetic factors in predicting antisocial behavior in adoptees. *Psychiatric Journal of the University of Ottawa, 6*, 220–225.

Cadoret, R. J., Cain, C. A., & Crowe, R. R. (1983). Evidence for gene-environment interaction in the development of adolescent antisocial behavior. *Behavior Genetics, 13*, 301–310. doi: 10.1007/BF01071875.

Carrasco, J. L., Diaz-Marsa, M., Hollander, E., Cesar, J., & Saiz-Ruiz, J. (2000). Decreased platelet monoamine oxidase activity in female bulimia nervosa. *European Neuropsychopharmacology, 10*, 113–117. doi: 10.1016/S0924-977X(99)00061-9.

Caspi, A., McClay, J., Moffitt, T. E., Mill, J., Martin, J., Craig, I. W., et al. (2002). Role of genotype in the cycle of violence in maltreated children. *Science, 297*, 851–854.

Caspi, A., Sugden, K., Moffitt, T. E., Taylor, A., Craig, I. W., Harrington, H. L., McClay, J., Mill, J., Martin, J., Braithwaite, A., & Poulton, R. (2003). Influence of life stress on depression: Moderation by a polymorphism in the 5-HTT gene. *Science, 301*, 386–389. doi: 10.1126/science.1083968.

Cloninger, C. R., & Gottesman, I. I. (1987). Genetic and environmental factors in antisocial behavior disorders. In: Mednick, S. A, Moffitt, T. E., & Stack, S. A. (Eds.), *The causes of crime: New biological approaches*. New York: Cambridge University Press.

Cloninger, C. R., Sigvardsson, S., Bohman, M., & von Knorring, A.-L. (1982). Predisposition to petty criminality in Swedish adoptees. II. Cross-fostering analysis of gene-environment interaction. *Archives of General Psychiatry, 39*, 1242–1247.

Crowe, R. R. (1974). An adoption study of antisocial personality. *Archives of General Psychiatry, 31*, 785–781.

Davidge, K. M., Atkinson, L., Douglas, L., Lee, V., Shapiro, S., Kennedy, J. L., & Beitchman, J.H. (2004). Association of the serotonin transporter and 5HT1D[beta] receptor genes with extreme, persistent and pervasive aggressive behaviour in children. *Psychiatric Genetics, 14*, 143–146. doi: 10.1097/00041444-200409000-00004.

DeLisi, M., Beaver, K. M., Wright, J. P., & Vaughn, M. G. (2008). The etiology of criminal onset: The enduring salience of nature *and* nurture. *Journal of Criminal Justice, 36*(3), 217–223. doi: 10.1016/j.jcrimjus.2008.04.001.

DiLalla, L. F., Elam, K. K., & Smolen, A. (2009). Genetic and gene–environment interaction effects on preschoolers' social behaviors. *Developmental Psychobiology, 51*, 451–464. doi: 10.1002/dev.20384.

DiLalla, L. F., & Gottesman, I. I. (1989). Heterogeneity of causes for delinquency and criminality: Lifespan perspectives. *Development and Psychopathology, 1*, 339–349. doi: 10.1017/S0954579400000511.

Dmitrieva, J., Chen, C., Greenberger, E., Ogunseitan, O., & Ding, Y.-C. (2010). Gender-specific expression of the DRD4 gene on adolescent delinquency, anger and thrill seeking. *Social Cognitive and Affective Neuroscience, 5*, doi: 10.1093/scan/nsq020.

Dolan, M. (2002). *Neurobiological approaches to disorders of personality.* Expert paper: NHS National Programme on Forensic Mental Health Research and Development.

Dragan, W. L., & Oniszczenko, W. (2007). An association between dopamine D4 receptor and transporter gene polymorphisms and personality traits, assessed using NEO-FFI in a Polish female population. *Personality and Individual Differences, 43*, 531–540. doi: 10.1016/j.paid.2007.01.001.

Eriksson, M., Rasmussen, F., & Tynelius, P. (2006). Genetic factors in physical activity and the equal environment assumption: The Swedish Young Male Twins Study. *Behavior Genetics, 36*(2), 238–247. doi: 10.1007/s10519-005-9018-7.

Faraone, S. V., Doyle, A. E., Mick, E., & Biederman, J. (2001). Meta-analysis of the association between the 7-repeat allele of the dopamine D4 receptor gene and attention deficit hyperactivity disorder. *American Journal of Psychiatry, 158*, 1052–1057. doi: 10.1176/appi.ajp.158.7.1052.

Foley, D. L., Eaves, L. J., Wormley, B., Silberg, J. L., Maes, H. H., Kuhn, J., & Riley, B. (2004). Childhood adversity, Monoamine Oxidase A genotype, and risk for conduct disorder. *Archives of General Psychiatry, 61*, 738–744. doi: 10.1001/archpsyc.61.7.738.

Frazzetto, G., Di Lorenzo, G., Carola, V., Proietti, L., Sokolowska, E., Siracusano, A., Gross, C., & Troisi, A. (2007). Early trauma and increased risk for physical aggression during adulthood: The moderating role of MAOA genotype. *Plos One, 2*, e486.

Gilbert, D. G., Izetelny, A., Radtke, R., Hammersley, J., Rabinovich, N. E., Jameson, T. R., & Huggenvik, J. I. (2005). Dopamine receptor (DRD2) genotype-dependent effects of nicotine on attention and distraction during rapid visual information processing. *Nicotine & Tobacco Research, 7*, 361–379. doi: 10.1080/14622200500125245.

Gilbert, D. G., Zuo, Y., Rabinovich, N. E., Riise, H., Needham, R., & Huggenvik, J. I. (2009). Neurotransmission-related genetic polymorphisms, negative affectivity traits, and gender predict tobacco abstinence symptoms across 44 days with and without nicotine patch. *Journal of Abnormal Psychology, 118*(2), 322–334. doi: 10.1037/a0015382.

Glickson, J. (2002). *The neurobiology of human behaviour.* Dordrecht: Kluwer Academic Publishers.

Götz, M., Johnstone, E., & Ratcliff, S. (1999). Criminality and antisocial behaviour in unselected men with sex chromosome abnormalities. *Psychological Medicine, 29*, 953–962. doi: 10.1017/S0033291799008594.

Guo, G., Cai, T., Guo, R., Wang, H., & Harris, K. M. (2010). The dopamine transporter gene, a spectrum of most common risky behaviors, and the legal status of the behaviors. *PLoS ONE* 5(2): e9352. doi: 10.1371/journal.pone.0009352.

Guo, G., Ou, X.-M., Roettger, M., & Shih, J. C. (2008). The VNTR 2 repeat in MAOA and delinquent behavior in adolescence and young adulthood: associations and MAOA promoter activity. *European Journal of Human Genetics, 16*, 626–634. doi: 10.1038/sj.ejhg.5201999.

Guo, G., Roettger, M. E., & Shih, J. C. (2007). Contributions of the DAT1 and DRD2 genes to serious and violent delinquency among adolescents and young adults. *Human Genetics, 121*(1), 125–136. doi: 10.1007/s00439-006-0244-8.

Haberstick, B. C., Lessem, J. M., Hopfer, C. J., Smolen, A., Ehringer, M. A., Timberlake, D., & Hewitt, J. K. (2005). MAOA genotype and antisocial behaviors in the presence of childhood and adolescent maltreatment. *American Journal of Human Genetics* (Neuropsych. Genet.), *135B*, 59–64.

Haberstick, B. C., Smolen, A., & Hewitt, J. K. (2006). Family-based association test of the 5HTTLPR and aggressive behavior in a general population sample of children. *Biological Psychiatry, 59*, 836–843. doi: 10.1016/j.biopsych.2005.10.008.

Horowitz, A. V., Videon, T. M., Schmitz, M. F., & Davis, D. (2003). Rethinking twins and environments: Possible social sources for assumed genetic influences in twin research. *Journal of Health and Social Behavior, 44*(2), 111–129. doi: 10.2307/1519802.

Huizinga, D., Haberstick, B., Smolen, A., Menard, S., Young, S., Corley, R., Stallings, M., Grotpeter, J., & Hewitt, J. (2006). Childhood maltreatment, subsequent antisocial behavior, and the role of Monoamine Oxidase A genotype. *Biological Psychiatry, 60*, 677–683. doi: 10.1016/j.biopsych.2005.12.022.

Hutchings, B., & Mednick, S. A. (1975). Registered criminality in the adoptive and biological parents of registered male criminal adoptees. In: Fieve, R. R., Rosenthal, D., & Brill, H. (Eds.), *Genetic research in psychiatry* (pp. 105–116). Baltimore: Johns Hopkins University Press.

Hutchinson, K., McGeary, J., Smolen, A., Bryan, A., & Swift, R. (2002). The DRD4 VNTR polymorphism moderates craving after alcohol consumption. *Health Psychology, 21*, 139–146. doi: 10.1037/0278-6133.21.2.139.

Ike, N. (2000). Current thinking on XYY Syndrome. *Psychiatric Annals, 30*, 91–95.

Jacobson, K., Prescott, C., & Kendler, K. (2002). Sex differences in the genetic and environmental influences on the development of antisocial behavior. *Development and Psychopathology, 14*, 395–416. doi: 10.1017/s0954579402002110.

Kendler, K. S., Neale, M. C., Kessler, R. C., & Heath, A. C. (1993). A test of the equal-environment assumption in twin studies of psychiatric illness. *Behavior Genetics, 23*(1), 21–27. doi: 10.1007/BF01067551.

Kim-Cohen, J., Caspi, A., Taylor, A., Williams, B., Newcombe, R., Craig, I. W., & Moffitt, T. E. (2006). MAOA, maltreatment, and gene–environment interaction predicting children's mental health: New evidence and a meta-analysisMAOA, maltreatment G × E interaction. *Molecular Psychiatry, 11*, 903–913. doi: 10.1038/sj.mp.4001851.

Kluger, A. N., Siegfried, Z., & Ebstein, R. P. (2002). A meta-analysis of the association between DRD4 polymorphism and novelty seeking. *Molecular Psychiatry, 7*, 712–717. doi: 10.1038/sj.mp.4001082.

Legrand, L. N., Keyes, M., McGue, M., Iacono, W. G., & Krueger, R. F. (2008). Rural environments reduce the genetic influence on adolescent substance use and rule-breaking behavior. *Psychological Medicine, 38*, 1341–1350. doi: 10.1017/S0033291707001596.

Liao, D.-L., Hong, C.-J., Shih, H.-L., & Tsai, S.-J. (2004). Possible association between serotonin transporter promoter region polymorphism and extremely violent crime in Chinese males. *Neuropsychobiology, 50*, 284–287. doi: 10.1159/000080953.

Lyons, M., True, W., Eisen, S., Goldberg, J., Meyer, J., Faraone, S., Eaves, L., & Tsuang, M. (1995). Differential heritability of adult and juvenile antisocial traits. *Archives of General Psychiatry, 52*, 906–915.

McDermott, R., Tingley, D., Cowden, J., Frazzetto, G., & Johnson, D.D.P. (2009). Monoamine oxidase A gene (MAOA) predicts behavioral aggression following provocation, *PNAS, 106*(7), 2118–2123. doi: 10.1073/pnas.0808376106.

Machalek, R., & Martin, M. W. (2010). Evolution, biology, and society: A conversation for the 21st-century sociology classroom. *Teaching Sociology, 38*, 35–45. doi: 10.1177/0092055X09354078.

Mednick, S., Gabrielli, W., & Hutchings, B. (1984). Genetic influences in criminal convictions: Evidence from an adoption cohort. *Science, 224*, 891–894. doi: 10.1126/science.6719119.

Mednick, B., Reznick, C., Hocevar, D., & Baker, R. (1987). Long-term effects of parental divorce on young adult male crime. *Journal of Youth and Adolescence, 16*, 31-45. doi: 10.1007/BF02141545.

Miles, D. R., & Carey, G. (1997). Genetic and environmental architecture of human aggression. *Journal of Personality and Social Psychology, 72*, 207–217. doi: 10.1037//0022-3514.72.1.207.

Moffitt, T. E. (2005). The new look of behavioral genetics in developmental psychopathology: Gene–environment interplay in antisocial behaviors. *Psychological Bulletin, 131*, 533–554. doi: 10.1037/0033-2909.131.4.533.

Moore, T. M., Scarpa, A., & Raine, A. (2002). A meta-analysis of serotonin metabolite 5-HIAA and antisocial behavior. *Aggressive Behavior, 28*, 299–316. doi: 10.1002/ab.90027.

Oak, J. N., Oldenhof, J., & Van Tol, H. H. M. (2000). The dopamine D_4 receptor: One decade of research. *European Journal of Pharmacology, 405*, 303–327. doi: 10.1016/S0014-2999(00)00562-8.

Oniszczenko, W., & Dragan, W. L. (2005). Association between dopamine D4 receptor exon III polymorphism and emotional reactivity as a temperamental trait. *Twin Research and Human Genetics, 8*, 633–637. doi: 10.1375/183242705774860187.

Plomin, R., & Daniels, D. (1987). Why are children in the same family so different from one another? *Behavioral and Brain Sciences, 10*(1), 1–16. doi: 10.1017/S0140525X00055941.

Plomin, R., DeFries, J., & Loehlin, J. (1977). Genotype-environment interaction and correlation in the analysis of human behavior. *Psychological Bulletin, 84*, 309–322. doi: 10.1037/0033-2909.84.2.309.

Price, W., & Whatmore, P. (1967). Behavior disorders and pattern of crime among XYY males identified at a maximum security hospital. *British Medical Journal, 1*, 533–536. doi: 10.1136/bmj.1.5539.533.

Raine, A. (1993). The psychopathology of crime: Criminal behavior as a clinical disorder. San Diego, CA: Academic Press.

Regoli, R. M., Hewitt, J. D., & DeLisi, M. (2009). *Delinquency in society*, 8th ed. Sudbury, MA: Jones and Bartlett Pub.

Rettew, D. C., & McKee, L. (2005). Temperament and its role in developmental psychopathology. *Harvard Review of Psychiatry, 13*, 14–27. doi: 10.1080/10673220590923146.

Rhee, S. H., & Waldman, I. D. (2002). Genetic and environmental influences on antisocial behavior: A meta-analysis of twin and adoption studies. *Psychological Bulletin, 128*, 490–529. doi: 10.1037//0033-2909.128.3.490.

Richardson, K., & Norgate, S. (2005). The equal environments assumption of classical twin studies may not hold. *British Journal of Educational Psychology, 75*(3), 339–350. doi: 10.1348/000709904X24690.

Roush, W. (1995). Conflict marks crime conference. *Science, 269*(5232), 1808–1809. doi: 10.1126/science.7569909.

Rowe, D. C. (2001). *Biology and crime*. Los Angeles: Roxbury.

Schmidt, L. A., Fox, N. A., Rubin, K. H., Hu, S., & Hamer, D. H. (2002). Molecular genetics of shyness and aggression in preschoolers. *Personality and Individual Differences, 33*, 227–238. doi: 10.1016/S0191-8869(01)00147-7.

Shiraishi, H., Suzuki, A., Fukasawa, T., Aoshima, T., Ujiie, Y., Ishii, G., & Otani, K. (2006). Monoamine oxidase A gene promoter polymorphism affects novelty seeking and reward dependence in healthy study participants. *Psychiatric Genetics, 16*, 55–58. doi: 10.1097/01.ypg.0000199447.62044.ef.

Sigvardsson, S., Cloninger, R., Bohman, M., & van Knorring, A. (1982). Predisposition to petty criminality in Swedish adoptees: III. Sex differences and validation of the male typology. *Archives of General Psychiatry, 39,* 1248–1253.

Simonoff, E., Elander, J., Holmshaw, J., Pickles, A., Murray, R., & Rutter, M. (2004). Predictors of antisocial personality. Continuities from childhood to adult life. *British Journal of Psychiatry, 184,* 118–127. doi: 10.1192/bjp.184.2.118.

Turkheimer, E., Haley, A., Waldron, M., D'Onofrio, B., & Gottesman, I. I. (2003). Socioeconomic status modifies heritability of IQ in young children. *Psychological Science, 14,* 623–628. doi: 10.1046/j.0956-7976.2003.psci_1475.x.

Tuvblad, C., Eley, T., & Lichtenstein, P. (2005). The development of antisocial behaviour from childhood to adolescence: A longitudinal twin study. *European Child and Adolescent Psychiatry, 14,* 216–225. doi: 10.1007/s00787-005-0458-7.

Vaughn, M. G., DeLisi, M., Beaver, K. M., & Wright, J. P. (2009). DAT1 and 5HTT are associated with pathological criminal behavior in a nationally representative sample of youth. *Criminal Justice and Behavior, 36,* 1113–1124. doi: 10.1177/0093854809342839.

Virkkunen, M., Goldman, D, Nielsen, D. A., & Linnoila, M. (1995). Low brain serotonin turnover rate (low CSF 5-HIAA) and impulsive violence. *Journal of Psychiatry Neuroscience, 20,* 271–275.

Walker, S. O., Petrill, S. A., Spinath, F. M., & Plomin, R. (2004). Nature, nurture and academic achievement: A twin study of teacher assessments of 7-year-olds. *British Journal of Educational Psychology, 74*(3), 323–342. doi: 10.1348/0007099041552387.

Wang, E., Ding, Y.-C., Flodman, J. R., Kidd, J. R., Kidd, K. K., Grady, D. L., Ryder, O. A., Spence, M. A., Swanson, J. M., & Moyzis, R. K. (2004). The genetic architecture of selection at the human dopamine receptor D4 (DRD4) gene locus. *American Journal of Human Genetics, 74,* 931–944. doi: 10.1086/420854.

Witkin, H. (1976). Criminality in XYY and XXY men: The elevated crime rate of XYY males is not related to aggression. It may be related to low intelligence. *Science, 193,* 547–555.

Witkin, H. A., Mednick, S. A., Schulsinger, F., Bakkestron, E., Christiansen, K. O., Goodenough, D. R., Hirschorn, C., Lundsteen, C., Owen, D. R., Philip, J., Rubin, D. B., & Stocking, M. (1977). Criminality, aggression, and intelligence among XYY and XXY men. In: Mednick, S. A., & Christiansen, K. O. (Eds.), *Biosocial bases of criminal behavior.* New York: Gardner Press.

Young, S. E., Smolen, A., Hewitt, J. K, Haberstick, B. C., Stallings, M. C., Corley, R. P., & Crowley, T. J. (2006). Interaction between MAO-A genotype and maltreatment in the risk for conduct disorder: Failure to confirm in adolescent patients. *American Journal of Psychiatry, 163,* 1019–1025. doi: 10.1176/appi.ajp.163.6.1019.

Molecular Genetics and Crime

John Paul Wright, Kristan Moore, and Jamie Newsome

Recent technological advances, including the mapping of the human genome, have helped to introduce neuroscience and genetics to a broad audience. Not a day goes by anymore where new insights are not made into the inner-workings of genes and their sometimes subtle, and sometimes not so subtle, influence on human conduct. These insights have informed virtually every aspect of human study, even the study of criminal behavior. The role of genes in the creation and maintenance of antisocial behavior was once subject only to logical theorizing, at best, or to open speculation, at worse. This has changed. Today, scholars have available to them direct measures of candidate genes and they have the computational power to test for associations between thousands of genes and a variety of behavioral outcomes. Still, for the most part this knowledge remains locked away in esoteric scientific journals or in specialized academic texts—materials the average criminology student may never see.

In the following pages we take the average criminologist, budding or otherwise, through some of the research on genetic influences on crime and antisocial conduct. To be certain, some of this information is complex, and it requires some background knowledge of genetics. That said, we have tried to provide the reader with sufficient background knowledge to make sense of genetic findings. As we will show, understanding the complexity that occurs when genetic factors interact with environmental stimuli taxes the best minds. Even so, the task is important. Tackling this complexity will lead to new and important insights into human behavior, and it may lead to important discoveries about how best to treat antisocial conduct.

The Human Genome

The human genome is the full set of genes that each individual possesses. It is sometimes referred to as the genotype, although genotype can also refer to a specific gene. Each human receives one set of 23 chromosomes from each parent, for a total of 46 chromosomes. All these chromosomes are housed within the nucleus of the cell. One pair of chromosomes determines the sex of the individual, while the other 22 (called autosomes) hold the genes that will eventually code for all human behavioral functions and physical appearance. Every individual thus has two copies of a given gene, called alleles. These copies may not be identical. If the gene has more than one type of sequence, it is referred to as a polymorphism. Polymorphisms can take the form of different numbers of repeating nucleotide sequences descriptively called variable nucleotide repeats (VNTRs), or they can be as minor as the difference of one nucleotide called single nucleotide polymorphisms (SNPs). If the individual has two identical copies of the polymorphism, the alleles are called homozygous, and if they are different, the alleles are called heterozygous. This will become important in later sections.

Chromosomes are coiled strands of deoxyribonucleic acid (DNA). Very briefly, DNA is a double helix (two bonded strands), each with a "backbone" of sugar and phosphates and a nucleotide "base" attached to each sugar. These strands are read in opposite directions and this is referred to as being "antiparallel." There are four bases that comprise DNA; adenine (A), thymine (T), cytosine (C), and guanine (G). Adenine always pairs with thymine and cytosine always pairs with guanine. Each DNA strand is connected by hydrogen bonds between the bases.

Two processes occur when DNA is used to create proteins. The first process, transcription, occurs inside the nucleus of the cell and turns the strands of DNA into a single strand of nucleotide based material (mRNA) capable of being read for protein creation.

Transcription decomposes the bond between the strands of DNA. RNA nucleotides are the same as DNA molecules except that thymine is replaced by uracil. Once the two strands of DNA are "unzipped," free RNA bases attach to the DNA strand being replicated. A backbone of sugar and phosphates forms, RNA polymerase breaks the bonds of the DNA and mRNA strand, and the mRNA moves outside the nucleus of the cell to undergo translation. mRNA is read in three nucleotide units called codons.

Translation, the second process, occurs in the cell cytoplasm and turns mRNA into proteins. Translation begins when a ribosome attaches to the start codon and uses another type of RNA. Translation RNA (tRNA) is a codon attached to an amino acid. tRNA reads along the strand of mRNA from the start codon to the stop codon. The amino acids bond together into a polypeptide chain. At the stop codon, another biochemical terminates the translation process and frees the polypeptide chain from the ribosome. The polypeptide chain then folds specific ways to create proteins. Microtubules transport the proteins through the cell to their intended destination within the cell.

Neurotransmission

The brain is comprised of two types of cells, neurons and glial cells. Neurons are responsible for the transmission of electrochemical messages from one region of the brain to another. Glial cells are essentially support cells for the neurons and are not directly involved in neurotransmission. Each neuron has a nucleus and other cell structures necessary for ordinary cell functions that occur within the cell body. Neurotransmission occurs when the presynaptic neuron sends an electrical impulse down the body of an axon. The impulse then forces the release of neurotransmitters from the synaptic cleft. The neurotransmitters then cross what is called "synaptic space," which is 1/600th the width of a human hair, and bind to receptors of the receiving dendrite. Receptors are specific to each neurotransmitter; dopamine, for example, can only bond with a dopamine receptor, and the number and sensitivity of receptors on each dendrite is genetically determined. Once the chemical signal has been received by the dendrite, it is converted again into an electrical impulse. The electrical impulse then travels the length of the dendrite to the terminal. For those neurotransmitters that do not bind to the postsynaptic neuron, the excess is either metabolized into another substance or is picked back up by the presynaptic neuron by cell structures called transporters to be reused in later neurotransmission.

Rhee and Waldman (2007: 87) divide genes into five classes. These five classes are precursor genes, receptor genes, transporter genes, metabolite genes, and conversion genes. Precursor genes determine the rate at which precursor amino acids are turned into neurotransmitters. Receptor genes are those that code for the proteins that make up the structure of receptors in dendrites. Similarly, transporter genes code for the proteins comprising the structure of the presynaptic transporters. Metabolite genes code for those enzymes that decompose excess neurotransmitters in the synaptic cleft. One example of a metabolic enzyme that will be discussed later in this chapter is monoamine oxidase A (MAOA). Finally, conversion genes are those responsible for synthesizing neurotransmitters from precursor amino acids because the blood brain barrier prevents the passage of large molecules into the brain. For example, the amino acid tyrosine hydroxylase undergoes two transformations before becoming dopamine, while a further synthesis turns dopamine into norepinephrine.

The Serotonergic System

Serotonin, or 5-hydroxytrytamine (5-HT) is synthesized within the brain. The 5-HT molecule is too large a substance to pass through the blood brain barrier. However, the precursor to 5-HT, the amino acid *l*-tryptophan, is not. 5-HT is synthesized when *l*-tryptophan crosses the blood brain barrier and undergoes two chemical transformations regulated by the enzyme tryptophan hydroxylase (Moore, Scarpa, & Raine, 2002; Lesch & Merschdorf, 2000). Neurons that use 5-HT for transmission are clustered in the brain stem, specifically in the caudal linear nucleus and the raphe nuclei (Jacobs & Azmitia, 1992). The ascending pathways from these regions extend through the limbic system, up to the frontal cortex, and then back and around to the other regions of the neocortex (Jacobs & Azmitia, 1992). 5-HT has been found to influence multiple physiological systems and behavioral states such as feeding, aggression, impulsivity, mood, and arousal (Lucki, 1998).

Given the locations and concentrations of neurons using 5-HT for transmission, Carver, Johnson, and Joormann (2008) have proposed that the serotonergic system is likely implicated in automatic and reflexive neurological processes. Thus, 5-HT neurotransmission would be strongly implicated in behaviors that are emotionally laden and impulsive (Carver et al., 2008). Krakowski (2003) argues that the relationship between 5-HT and aggression is not a direct causal path, but is mediated by serotonin's ability to regulate emotion and to inhibit impulsivity. Specifically, it appears that impulsive behavior triggered by a strong emotional state is more likely to result in violence (Krakowski, 2003).

Empirical Assessment of the Serotonergic System

Several methods have been developed to empirically test these hypotheses. The first, tryptophan depletion, requires depleting research participants' level of 5-HT in the brain by eliminating l-tryptophan from their diet. A number of studies have found a positive relationship between the depletion of l-tryptophan and impulsivity (Robbins & Crockett, 2010; Walderhaug et al., 2002, 2007; for a review see Young & Leyton, 2002).

A second method, the administration of a serotonin agonist, measures the resulting hormonal response of prolactin. The agonist, typically fenfluramine, causes the release of serotonin stores and prevents reuptake, which in turn causes the release of prolactin from the hypothalamus. Researchers measure the amount of prolactin released, as this is considered a proxy for serotonin functioning, and then correlate this with measures of impulsivity or aggression. Studies have found an inverse relationship between prolactin responses to agonist challenge and impulsivity/aggression, but these results are occasionally tempered by sex differences (Manuck et al., 1998; Coccaro, Kavoussi, Cooper, & Hauger, 1997; Dolan, Anderson, & Deakin, 2001).

A third method is to measure the amount of the serotonin metabolite 5-HIAA in cerebrospinal fluid. This metabolite is produced when spent 5-HT in the synaptic cleft is broken down by an enzyme such as MAOA. Moore et al. (2002) conducted a meta-analysis of 16 such studies to determine an effect size for the relationship between 5-HIAA and antisocial behavior. They found an overall inverse relationship with an effect size of -0.45, a moderately strong relationship, indicating that increased antisocial behavior may be in part a function of low serotonin levels (Moore et al., 2002).

Overall, these three methods indict hypofunctioning of the serotonin system in impulsive and aggressive behavior (Seo, Patrick, & Kennealy, 2008). But what these studies have failed to account for is the mechanisms underpinning this relationship, a relationship that molecular genetic studies are equipped to explain. Lesch and Merschdorf (2000) highlight the importance of molecular genetic studies: "(V)ariation in serotonergic gene regulation and in the activity of the respective gene products plays a critical role in synaptic (functioning), thus setting the stage for expression of complex traits and their associated behaviors throughout development and adult life" (p. 597).

As discussed in previous sections, there are five classes of candidate genes that are implicated in behavior (Rhee & Waldman, 2007). Of those five, the majority of research on serotonin has centered on precursor genes, receptor genes, and transporter genes (Noblett & Coccaro, 2005). Research is being done on those genes that impact the rate of serotonin metabolism and will be covered in the section on monoamine oxidase-A. The research on serotonin transporter genes is perhaps the largest body of work at this point.

The serotonin transporter gene is located on chromosome 17 and has two polymorphisms. The first polymorphism is a VNTR with three alleles; 9, 10, and 12 tandem repeats (Serretti, Calati, Mandelli, & De Ronchi, 2006; Cadoret et al., 2003; Beitchman et al., 2003). The second polymorphism is a transporter promoter (5-HTTLPR) with two alleles, a long form (L) with 16 repeated nucleotide sequences and a short (S) form with 14 repeated nucleotide sequences (Beitchman et al., 2006). Thus, there are three possible allele combinations of 5-HTTLPR and the homozygous short form appears to be the most uncommonly occurring combination. It is generally thought that the short form is responsible for decreased serotonergic functioning, with some estimates of the short form being half as active (Heils et al., 1996).

Those studies that have examined the 5-HT VNTR have not found significant results. Patkar et al. (2002) conducted an analysis of African-American cocaine users and controls. There study did not include enough individuals with a 9-repeat allele to be include in their analysis, leaving only 10/10, 10/12, and 12/12 repeat allele combinations to test against outcomes of aggression, impulsivity, sensation seeking, depression, and addiction drug severity (Patkar et al., 2002). No allele combination was associated on any of the outcomes, however. Beitchman et al. (2003) similarly failed to locate any individuals carrying the 9-repeat allele in a sample of aggressive children and non-aggressive controls. Their study found the 10-repeat allele to be significantly more common in the aggressive children than in the controls. A later study by Beitchman et al. (2006) combined the two polymorphisms together to determine how these genes may interact to produce aggressive behavior. The alleles were combined into low, intermediate, and high expressing levels of serotonin activity. The low expressing allele combinations had a significant effect on aggression, more than doubling the subjects' risk of aggressive behavior.

Research findings of the 5-HTTLPR polymorphism are mixed. Of the studies reviewed, two failed to find any significant effect on behavioral outcomes. Patkar et al. (2002) also included the 5-HTTLPR polymorphism in their analysis and failed to find a statistically significant relationship between any of the allele combinations on aggression or impulsivity. An analysis of impulsivity or aggression in a Spanish sample of individuals who had attempted suicide and a control group of blood donors also failed to find an association (Baca-Garcia et al., 2004).

In an analysis of a nationally representative sample conducted by Vaughn, DeLisi, Beaver, & Wright (2009), 5-HTTLPR did not show a significant effect on either the number of police contacts or on violent criminal behavior, with one exception. The short allele was found to significantly impact the number of police contacts only for Blacks who also had a low number of delinquent peers (Vaughn et al., 2009). Two more studies found evidence for the interaction of the 5-HTTLPR polymorphism with environmental characteristics. First, in a sample of German offenders, 5-HTTLPR interacted with adverse childhood environments to predict chronic aggressive and violent behavior. No main effect for 5-HTTLPR was found (Reif et al., 2007).

Second, 5-HTTLPR was found to interact with sex, with having an alcoholic parent, and with having an antisocial parent in predicting the externalizing behavior of the Iowan adoptee population (Cadoret et al., 2003). Significant main effects were found between the low expressing genotypes (SS and SL) and adolescent conduct disorder, as well as adolescent aggressivity. Interactions were also detected between grade school conduct problems, the low expressing genotypes, and sex. Sex by genotype interactions were also detected for adolescent conduct disorder and adolescent aggression. Having alcoholic parents interacted with the genotype to significantly predict attention deficit problems in preschool, as well as in predicting attention deficit problems in grade school, and in predicting adolescent aggression (Cadoret et al., 2003).

Similar to Cadoret et al., Walderhaug et al. (2007) also found sex based differences in impulsive response style during tryptophan depletion. The study called for the 83 participants to undergo either tryptophan depletion or sham depletion and to complete an assessment of impulsivity and mood while so depleted. Genotype information was also collected and analyzed. During the tryptophan depletion, women tended to become more cautious while men became more impulsive. Women who were tryptophan-depleted also reported a significant decrease in mood, especially for those with the LL and SS genotypes. No genotype effect was found on the impulsivity measures. A later replication by the same main author found continuing evidence for a sex interaction with 5-HTTLPR, but significant effects for women based on genotype were not detected (Walderhaug, Herman, Magnusson, Morgan, & Landro, 2010). The men with low expressing genotypes were also assessed as more impulsive, even when they underwent sham depletion (placebo effect). However, no interaction between genotype and intervention was detected. A second study also found a sex based differences in impulsive response style during tryptophan depletion (Walderhaug et al., 2007).

A number of studies have found significant associations between 5-HTTLPR and violence, avoidance, and aggression. Liao, Hong, Shih, and Tsai (2004) found a strong relationship between carriers of at least one S allele and violence in a sample of Chinese men. These results were replicated in a sample of German offenders (Retz, Retz-Junginger, Supprian, Thome, & Rösler, 2004). The SS genotype was overrepresented in the subgroup of violent compared to nonviolent offenders (23.6% versus 8.6% respectively), while the LL genotype was overrepresented in the nonviolent offender subgroup (33.3% versus 19.4%). The percentage of LS carriers was roughly comparable between violent (56.9%) and nonviolent (58.0%) subsamples (Retz et al., 2004). Violent heroin dependent offenders were more found to be more likely to be carriers of an S allele than non-offender controls in a sample of 202 male study participants (Gerra et al., 2004b). The proportion of heroin addicted offenders with the SS genotype (29.7%) was also significantly higher than the control group (15.8%). Overall, the Short allele appears to be linked to both an increased risk of heroin addiction and with violent behavior (Gerra et al., 2004b).

A meta-analysis was conducted by Munafò et al. (2003) to assess the effect sizes of multiple genes and their effect on avoidance, aggression, and approach personality traits. Of the 79 studies included in the meta-analysis, 22 reported data for 5-HTTLPR on two personality traits; avoidance and aggression. The overall model found that both personality traits were significantly predicted by 5-HTTLPR genotype. Additionally, when a full multivariate analysis was conducted on all of the included genes, the only association to remain significant was 5-HTTLPR on avoidance (Munafò et al., 2003).

Serotonin Receptor Polymorphisms

While 14 different serotonin receptors have been found, only three types of receptors have undergone empirical investigation for their role in behavior (Olivier & van Oorschot, 2005). These are 5-HT_{1A}, 5-HT_{1B}, and 5-HT_{2A}. 5-HT_{1A} and 5-HT_{1B} serve as autoreceptors on serotonergic neurons and signal to the neuron when to cease firing and stop release of 5-HT (Olivier & van Oorschot, 2005). The distinguishing characteristic between these two types of receptors is their location on the neuron. 5-HT_{1B} receptors are located in the synaptic terminals and the 5-HT_{1A} receptors are located on the presynaptic dendrites and cell bodies. 5-HT_{2A} is responsible for the release of prolactin and cortisol from the hypothalamus in response to agonists such as fenfluramine (Cleare & Bond, 2000). Multiple SNPs have been located for each of the genes that code for 5-HT receptors (Jensen et al., 2008).

Olivier and van Oorschot reviewed the existent literature and found that SNPs in the promoter regions of the genes are responsible for differences in the functional activity of 5-HT_{1A} and 5-HT_{1B}, but the relationship between the genes for these receptors and aggression remain unclear. New et al. (2001) found a SNP substitution of a G nucleotide for a C in the 5-HT_{1B} gene was positively associated with attempted suicide history, but did not find an association between the G allele and self-reported impulsive aggression. However, in a study conducted by Jensen et al. (2008), a tentative association between conduct disorder related outcomes and the 5-HT_{1B} gene was located. This association was capable of explaining approximately 2% of the variance in the outcome. Keltikangas-Järvinen et al. (2008) found that none of the 5-HT_{1A} genotypes were not related to three measures of childhood temperament; negative emotionality, hyperactivity, and sociability.

More specifically, Keltikangas-Järvinen et al. (2008) examined the relationship between measures of childhood temperament and adulthood hostility. While they failed to find any effect on either childhood temperament, adult temperament, or a relationship between the two by 5-HT_{1A}, the C/C genotype of the 5-HT_{2A} receptors was significantly related to female sociability in childhood. The SNP has three possible genotypes; T/T, C/T, and C/C. A later analysis revealed a moderating effect in men between hyperactivity in childhood and adult hostility by 5-HT$_{1A}$ genotype (Keltikangas-Järvinen et al., 2008).

Several polymorphisms within the 5-HT$_{2A}$ have been analyzed. The first is SNP that leads to a structural change in the 5-HT$_{2A}$ gene. This change is a result of a substitution of the amino acid histidine in the receptor protein instead of the amino acid tyrosine (Arranz et al., 1998). Burt and Mikolajewski (2008) tested the effect of this SNP on self-reported antisocial behavior, physical aggression, and non-aggressive rule breaking. The researchers found a significant association between the presence of the Tyr allele on mean levels of antisocial behavior and rule breaking, but not on aggression. Those subjects with the Tyr present had lower mean levels of antisocial behavior and rule breaking (-0.36 and -0.34 respectively) than those with Tyr absent (0.07 and 0.06 respectively). This differences accounts for 2.7% of the variance in antisocial behavior (Burt & Mikolajewski, 2008).

A number of SNPs in 5-HT$_{2A}$ were examined by Giegling, Hartmann, Möller, & Rujescu (2006). Only one promoter SNP, rs6311, was associated with anger-related traits. This SNP replaces a T nucleotide with a C nucleotide, and the C nucleotide is considered to be the "risk" allele. Of the seven State Trait Anger Expression Inventory subscales, rs6311 significantly predicted trait anger (disposition to angry traits), angry reaction (disposition to react with anger), and anger out (disposition to outwardly directed anger expressions). When the effects of rs6311 on aggression-related traits were examined, the researchers found that carriers of C allele were less inhibited to aggression (Giegling et al., 2006).

Tryptophan Hydroxylase Polymorphisms

Tryptophan hydroxylase (TPH) is the enzyme that restricts the rate at which serotonin biosynthesis takes place. This particular gene is located on chromosome 11, and the polymorphism occurs when an adenosine nucleotide is replaced by cytosine. The more frequently occurring allele is referred to as the U allele, while the less common allele is designated L (Manuck et al., 1999). Findings from two studies, Manuck et al. (1999) and New et al. (1998), are in contradiction with one another. In the sample of 251 individuals who volunteered from the community, those subjects carrying any U allele had significantly higher scores on assessments of aggression, antisocial behavior, angry temperament, and outwardly directed anger expression (Manuck et al., 1999). Oppositional results from New et al. (1998) found that males carrying LL genotype scored higher on an overall assessment of impulsivity and aggression, than did males with either the UL or UU genotypes. Another contradictory finding from New et al. occurred when the LL genotype scored higher on a subscale of irritability plus assaultiveness, while Manuck et al. found non-significant results for the same outcome.

Later studies have explored the same polymorphism and the relationship between TPH continues to be contested. For example, Staner et al. (2002) failed to find any differences in alleles between impulsive patients and normal controls, while Stoltenberg et al. (2006) reports a sex-specific association between the TPH polymorphism and a clinical assessment of impulsivity. A later article by Reuter et al. (2007) contributes to the confusion. In assessing the impact of the TPH polymorphism on executive control, Reuter et al. fail to find any sex differences, but report an allele specific increase in errors and conflict behavior during an attention network test. It appears that further research must be conducted before a conclusive statement on the role of TPH on behavior can be made.

Indirect Effects of the Serotonin System on Behavior

Research has investigated the influence serotonin has on the function of brain structures such as the amygdala. In a study conducted in 2002, Hariri et al. used fMRI to assess amygdala activation in response to fearful stimuli. The researchers found that carriers of the LL 5-HTTLPR genotype have a lower response to fearful stimuli in the right amygdala than those individuals homozygous for the short allele, indicating a genetic link between serotonin function and brain regions responsible for processing emotion. Brown and Hariri (2006) reviewed similar studies to Hariri et al. (2002) and found consistent evidence for greater amygdala activation in carriers of the short allele of the 5-HTTLPR polymorphism. Included in their analysis are the results from five independent samples in seven publications. A meta-analysis of 14 studies reported that the association between 5-HTTLPR polymorphism and amygdala activation may account for up to 10% of variance in emotional behaviors (Munafò, Brown, & Hariri, 2008).

Dopamine

Dopamine is an excitory neurotransmitter involved in the "reward systems" in the brain (Blum, Cull, Braverman, & Comings, 1996; Dagher & Robbins, 2009). Dopamine is released into the brain during participation in pleasurable activities, causing the individual to experience a sense of euphoria. Research suggests having an excess of dopamine may lead to aggressive or violent behavior (Gabel, Stadler, Bjorn, & Shindledecker, 1995; Guo, Roettger, & Shih, 2007). However, a deficiency in dopamine can also lead to behavioral or cognitive problems. Blum and colleagues (1996) claim that some individuals may suffer from reward deficiency syndrome. Reward Deficiency Syndrome (RDS) reflects a neurological state of suboptimal arousal levels. Normally rewarding behaviors, such as eating, provide less neurological stimulation to those with high RDS. Because affected individuals receive less neurological stimulation from common activities, they tend to engage in behaviors that are more impulsive, obsessive, or addictive. RDS is believed to be caused by variation in the dopaminergic system, specifically in the D2 dopamine gene.

Various genes code for the production and breakdown of dopamine. Some of these dopaminergic genes, primarily DAT1, DRD2, and DRD4, have been associated with antisocial behavior, both directly and indirectly. DAT1 is a polymorphic dopamine transporter gene which codes for a protein responsible for regulating the concentration of the neurotransmitter in the synaptic cleft (Giros & Caron, 1993). Specifically, these dopamine transporters remove excess dopamine from the synaptic cleft after neurotransmission. DRD2 and DRD4 are dopamine receptor genes. These genes determine the number of dopamine receptors that will be located on the postsynaptic neurons. The greater the number of dopamine receptors, the more likely it is that the dopamine molecules will be captured during neurotransmission. DAT1, DRD2, and DRD4 have all been found to have various polymorphisms associated with maladaptive behaviors.

Evidence for a direct effect of dopamine transporter and receptor genes on aggressive and criminal behavior has been observed. In a study of more than 2,500 youths in the National Longitudinal Study of Adolescent Health, variants of DAT1 and DRD2 were related to serious and violent delinquency (Guo et al., 2007). Specifically, males with DAT1*10R/10R or DAT1*10R/9R genotypes had higher serious and violent delinquency scores at waves one, two, and three. The analysis also revealed a relationship between the DRD2*A1/A2 genotype and serious and violent delinquency across all waves.

A more recent investigation demonstrated that the 9R/9R genotype in the VNTR of DAT1 had a protective effect against numerous delinquent behaviors (Guo, Cai, Cuo, Wang, & Harris, 2010). When compared to adolescents with the 10R/10R or 10R/9R genotypes, those with the 9R/9R genotype reported significantly lower rates of delinquency, fewer sexual partners, less frequent binge drinking episodes, consumed fewer alcoholic drinks, and less frequent illegal drug use including marijuana and cocaine. Interestingly, the protective effect was strongest at ages when the given behavior is illegal, but weakened once the youth reached an age at which the behavior was legal or widely accepted for their age group. However, this relationship is not well understood. The 9R/9R genotype of the DAT polymorphism was much higher in violent antisocial offenders (Gerra et al., 2005).

In another study, a significant relationship was observed between the DAT1*10/10 or DAT* 9/10 and the DRD2 A1/A1 and A1/A2 allele genotypes and pathological aggressive behavior (Chen et al., 2007). Finally, in a recent study conducted by Beaver, Sak, Vaske, and Nilsson (2010) the DAT1, DRD2, and DRD4 all contributed to serious and violent delinquency, the number of police contacts, and total antisocial behavior during adolescence and adulthood. Taken together, these studies suggest that genetic variants may influence behavior through adolescence and into adulthood.

Signs of aggression early in life have also been attributed to variation in dopaminergic genes. Young et al. (2002) observed 790 children as part of a longitudinal study, and found that the 9-repeat variant of the DAT1 gene increases the risk of children engaging in externalizing behaviors at four and seven years of age. Parent reports indicated that these children exhibited conduct problems that were considered aggressive, oppositional, or delinquent. Similarly, children with the 7-repeat DRD4 allele and who experienced maternal insensitivity, were significantly more likely to engage in externalizing, aggressive, and oppositional behaviors (Bakermans-Kranenberg & van Ijzendoorn, 2006).

Research has also investigated the relationship between dopaminergic genes and traits and behaviors that have been closely associated with serious and violent offending. For example, diagnoses of oppositional defiance disorder (ODD) and conduct disorder (CD) during adolescence have both been linked to criminal behavior. An association between these disorders and polymorphisms in dopaminergic genes has been observed (Gabel, Stadler, Bjorn, Shindledecker, & Bowden, 1993a, 1993b; Rowe et al., 2001). For example, Beaver and colleagues (2007) found that DRD2 and DRD4 were both related to conduct disorder and adult antisocial behavior. While the main effects of the A1 allele of DRD2 and the 7R allele of DRD4 were inconsistent, individuals possessing both of these variants were significantly more likely to have conduct disorder, lifetime conduct problems, and to engage in adult antisocial behavior.

Additionally, research among 336 Caucasian subjects, tested the association between 20 genes and their contributions to ODD and CD. Variants of DAT1, DRD2, and DRD5 explained a small portion of the variance in both disorders (Comings et al., 2000a). In a follow-up study, 22 more genes were added to the analysis for a total of 42 genes (Comings et al., 2000b). Dopaminergic genes were still significantly related to diagnoses of ODD and CD.

The role of various dopamine genes in the etiology of ADHD has been a focus of research; however, such relationships are still not fully understood. Faraone, Doyle, Mick, & Biederman (2001) conducted a meta-analysis of 22 studies examining the relationship between DRD4 and ADHD. Their results indicate a small, but significant, association exists between DRD4 and ADHD. A second meta-analysis of 36 studies found that the 5R and 7R polymorphisms of DRD4 were associated with ADHD (Li, Sham, Owen, & He, 2006). In a more recent meta-analysis, the 10-repeat allele of a VNTR polymorphism in DAT1 was found to have a small role in the risk of being diagnosed with ADHD (Yang et al., 2007). Although these analyses suggest that dopaminergic genes play a role in the etiology of ADHD, other studies have not found a significant relationship (Bakker et al., 2005; Castellanos et al., 1998; Comings et al., 2000b; Holmes et al., 2000).

Genes within the dopamine system have also been found to contribute to other maladaptive traits. DRD2 and DRD4 have been associated with a disposition toward novelty seeking (Becker, Laucht, El-Faddagh, & Schmidt, 2005; Berman, Ozkaragoz, Young, & Noble, 2002; Noble et al., 1998). One study found that two alleles of DRD2 polymorphism, 48-bp VNTR and -521 C/T, both interacted and had a significant effect on novelty seeking and persistent personality scores (Lee et al., 2003). However, neither of the alleles had an independent effect on either personality score. Another study found that DRD2 and DRD4 were significantly related to novelty seeking in boys (Noble et al., 1998). While the independent effects of these polymorphisms were significant, the combined effects provided a greater contribution to novelty seeking behaviors. Munafò, Yalcin, Willis-Owen, and Flint (2008) recently conducted a meta-analysis of 48 studies published between 1996 and 2006 to achieve a better understanding of this relationship. Their analysis showed that DRD4 was not related to novelty seeking, extraversion, or impulsivity. Further research is required for a complete understanding of the role of these genes in explaining these personality traits.

Finally, research has also examined the possibility that dopaminergic genes may be related to internalizing disorders. In a sample of 240 children, the VNTR polymorphism in the DAT1 gene was associated with generalized anxiety, major depression, obsessive-compulsive behaviors, panic disorders, separation anxiety, social phobia, specific phobia, and Tourette's syndrome (Rowe et al., 1998). Additional studies have also found a relationship between DRD2 and depression (Vaske, Beaver, Wright, Boisvert, & Makarios, 2009). For example, a study of 2,380 youths found that African American females possessing the A1 allele of DRD2 were more likely to experience depression after being involved in a violent victimization (Vaske, Makarios, Boisvert, Beaver, & Wright, 2009). These studies suggest that while variation in dopamine transporter and dopamine receptor genes may influence internalizing behaviors, these effects may vary among different demographic groups. Further research must be conducted to gain a fuller understanding of these relationships.

The available research indicates that genes responsible for regulating the dopamine system within the brain may be related to a number of criminal behaviors. This association may occur directly through their effect on aggression and delinquency. In addition to the direct effects, dopaminergic genes may be associated with these behaviors indirectly through their influence on related disorders, including ODD, CD, and ADHD. They may also be associated with maladaptive traits such as a novelty seeking and impulsivity, and externalizing and internalizing behaviors. Future research may provide a better understanding for the role these genes have in shaping behavior.

Monoamine Oxidase-A

Monoamine oxidase (MAO) is an enzyme in the brain responsible for the metabolism of neurotransmitters in the synaptic cleft after neurotransmission (Roth, Breakfield, & Castiglione, 1976). Two types of MAO exist, A and B. The MAOA gene codes for the production of the MAOA enzyme, which degrades serotonin, norepinephrine, and dopamine (Brunner, Nelen, Breakefield, Ropers, & van Oost, 1993; Ellis, 1991). Alleles for the MAOA gene are generally categorized as low or high activity alleles. Having a deficiency in the MAOA enzyme may result in an abundance of neurotransmitters in the synaptic cleft, while an overproduction of the enzyme may lead to an inefficient amount of neurotransmitters. The resulting interference in neurotransmission may result in abnormal behavior.

Some research suggests that there may be an association between MAOA and aggressive behaviors. One study of adult males found that those with the 3.5- or 4-repeat variants (i.e., high activity alleles) of the 30-bp VNTR polymorphism of the

MAOA gene scored higher on aggressiveness and impulsivity than those with the 3- and 5-repeat alleles (Manuck, Flory, Ferrell, Mann, & Muldoon, 2000). A study of children also found that the 4-repeat allele may contribute to persistent aggressive behaviors (Beitchman et al., 2003). These findings suggest that the high activity alleles may be related to aggressive behaviors in children and adults.

Other studies have found that the low activity alleles may be associated with aggression and impulsivity. Brunner and colleagues (1993) examined a large kindred that included several males with a syndrome of borderline mental retardation. These men engaged in abnormal behavior, which included impulsive aggression, arson, attempted rape, and exhibitionism. The results of this study showed that males with this syndrome experienced reduced enzymatic activity of MAOA. Similar results were found in a comparison of 104 heroin-dependent and 95 health control adult males (Gerra et al., 2004a). Among heroin-dependent males, the low activity allele of MAOA gene was associated with violent offending. The frequency of the high activity allele was significantly higher among males without a history of violence. Future research may provide a clearer understanding of this relationship.

Although the research on the direct effects of genetic variation of MAOA on aggression and criminal behavior is currently inconclusive, some studies have indicated that MAOA may influence these behaviors indirectly or through interactions with environmental stimuli. For example, one study of participants of the Dunedin Multidisciplinary Health and Development Study found an interaction between the low MAOA activity allele and maltreatment (Caspi et al., 2002). Specifically, males that had experienced maltreatment during childhood and who possessed the low activity allele of MAOA were more likely to become involved in antisocial behaviors later in life. Although this comprised just 12% of the sample, this group accounted for approximately 44% of the violent convictions for the entire sample (Caspi et al., 2002).

Some research indicates that the moderating effects of MAOA may depend on the intensity of the environmental stimuli. A study of 500 male adolescents found that those with low MAOA activity were more likely to develop conduct disorder only if they had experienced severe environmental adversity (Foley et al., 2004). However, the MAOA genotype alone did not have any effect on behavior. Similarly, Widom and Brzustowicz (2006) investigated the moderating effects of MAOA genotype on the relationship between childhood neglect and violent antisocial behavior in a sample of adolescent males and females. Their findings were very similar to those of Caspi and colleagues (2002) and Foley and colleagues (2004). Their analyses revealed no significant main effects of MAOA genotype on violent and antisocial behavior. However, the low activity allele of MAOA did interact with child abuse and neglect to increase the risk of violent and antisocial behavior. These studies suggests that variation in genotype of MAOA may not have a strong direct effect on behavior, but more likely interact with environmental experiences to explain variation in behavior.

Other studies have not supported these findings. A recent study examined the moderating effects of MAOA on maltreatment and self-reported conduct problems

(Haberstick et al., 2005). A total of 774 male participants of the National Longitudinal Study of Adolescent Health were included in the analysis. The MAOA genotype of participants did not affect conduct problems or convictions. Additionally, the interaction of the MAOA genotype and maltreatment did not explain conduct problems. MAOA genotype also was not found to moderate the relationship between violent victimization in adolescence and antisocial behaviors (Haberstick et al., 2005). Similarly, a study of 247 male adolescents found that MAOA did not have a significant main effect on conduct problems (Young et al., 2006). Young and her colleagues (2006) also examined the interaction of MAOA and four types of maltreatment in their study; neglect, verbal/psychological abuse, physical abuse, and sexual abuse. There were no significant interactions between MAOA and any of these measures of maltreatment. Other studies have also concluded that MAOA did not moderate the influence of maltreatment on maladaptive outcomes (Cicchetti, Rogosch, & Sturge-Apple, 2007).

As a result of these conflicting findings, a meta-analysis was conducted to gain a better understanding of the influence of MAOA on the relationship between maltreatment and behavioral problems (Kim-Cohen et al., 2006). Kim-Cohen and her colleagues examined five independent studies on the MAO gene and its interaction with maltreatment. The gene–environment interaction of low activity MAOA and maltreatment was found to be significant in predicting antisocial outcomes. While this is not conclusive evidence, the authors suggest that it is the most convincing evidence available at this time (Kim-Cohen et al., 2006).

Overall, the research on the MAOA gene and behavior is mixed. While some studies reveal that variants of the MAOA gene may have a direct effect on aggressive behaviors, a number of studies do not support this conclusion. Although many studies do not show that there is a direct effect of MAOA on behavioral outcomes, the available evidence does signify that MAOA may have an effect on antisocial outcomes under certain environmental conditions. In light of these findings, future research should seek to refine our understanding of these relationships.

Conclusions

Human antisocial behavior is highly complex, and involves the combined influence of social, environmental, biological, and genetic antecedents. As we have shown in this review, there is considerable empirical evidence linking the regulatory subsystems of genes to criminal conduct. Genetically caused variation in the serotonin, dopamine, and MAO-A systems appears linked to a broad array of human traits and behaviors, including impulsivity, low self-control, and criminality. These three systems are the most studied regulatory systems in the human body, but they are not the only regulatory systems. Researchers are just now examining how other neurotransmitters influence behavior and interact with environmental stimuli.

Moreover, while researchers have generally studied these systems independent of other regulatory systems, it is clear that these systems are highly interdependent. The complex network of neurotransmission involved in human conduct represents an intricate web of input from various excitory and inhibitory systems. Thus, it is not just that dysregulation in, say, the dopamine system, may influence antisocial conduct, but whether the dysregulation is sufficiently offset by other inhibitory processes. Future research will have to investigate more thoroughly this possibility.

Nonetheless, the available evidence paints a complex picture of findings relating variation in human biological functioning to criminal conduct. While many studies show a statistical link between specific alleles and criminal outcomes, others do not. We believe the inconsistent findings represent important contributions to science, and ultimately may point researchers to the exact conditions under which variation in regulatory systems influence behavior. Studies on the interaction of MAO-A and childhood maltreatment, for example, represent the scientific process of confirmation and disconfirmation. This process will continue to yield important, and more specific, insights into the complex ways that genes influence human action. For now, however, the general body of evidence strongly implicates specific genes in the etiology of delinquent and criminal conduct.

References

Arranz, M. J., Munro, J., Owens, M. J., Spurlock, G., Sham, P. C., Zhao, J., et al. (1998). Evidence for association between polymorphisms in the promoter and coding regions of the 5-HT$_{2A}$ receptor gene and response to clozapine. *Molecular Psychiatry, 3*, 61–66.

Baca-Garcia, E., Vaquero, C., Diaz-Sastre, C., García-Resa, E., Saiz-Ruiz, J., Fernández-Piqueras, J., et al. (2004). Lack of association between the serotonin transporter promoter gene polymorphism and impulsivity or aggressive behavior among suicide attempters and healthy volunteers. *Psychiatry Research, 126*, 99–106.

Bakermans-Kranenberg, M. J., & van Ijzendoorn, M. H. (2006). Gene environment of the dopamine D4 receptor (DRD4) and observed maternal insensitivity predicting externalizing behavior in preschoolers. *Developmental Psychobiology, 48*, 406–409.

Bakker, S. C., van der Meulen, E.M., Oteman, N., Schelleman, H., Pearson, P. L., Buitelaar, J. K., et al. (2005). DAT 1, DRD 4, and DRD 5 polymorphisms are not associated with ADHD in Dutch families. *American Journal of Medical Genetics Part B Neuropsychiatric Genetics, 132*, 50–52.

Beaver, K., Sak, A., Vaske, J., & Nilsson, J. (2010). Genetic risk, parent-child relations and antisocial phenotypes in a sample of African-American males. *Psychiatry Research, 175*, 160–164.

Beaver, K., Wright, J., DeLisi, M., Walsh, A., Vaughn, M., Boisvert, D., & Vaske, J. (2007). A gene x gene interaction between DRD2 and DRD4 is associated with conduct disorder and antisocial behaviors in males. *Behavioral and Brain Functions, 3.* doi: 10.1186/1744-9081-3-30.

Becker, K., Laucht, M., El-Faddagh, M., & Schmidt, M. H. (2005). The dopamine D4 receptor gene exon III polymorphism is associated with novelty seeking in 15-year-old males from a high-risk community sample. *Journal of Neural Transmission, 112,* 847–858.

Beitchman, J. H., Baldassarra, L., Mik, H., De Luca, V., King, N., Bender, D., et al. (2006). Serotonin transporter polymorphisms and persistent, pervasive childhood aggression. *The American Journal of Psychiatry, 163,* 1103–1105.

Beitchman, J. H., Davidge, K. M., Kennedy, J. L., Atkinson, L., Lee, V., Shapiro, S., et al. (2003). The serotonin transporter gene in aggressive children with and without ADHD and nonaggressive matched controls. *Annals of New York Academy of Sciences, 1008,* 248–251.

Beitchman, J. H., Mik, H. M., Ehtesham, S., Douglas, L., & Kennedy, J. L. (2004). MAOA and persistent, pervasive childhood aggression. *Molecular Psychiatry, 9,* 546–547.

Berman, S., Ozkaragoz, T., Young, R., & Noble, E. P. (2002). D2 dopamine receptor gene polymorphism discriminates two kinds of novelty seeking. *Personality and Individual Differences, 33,* 867–882.

Blum, K., Cull, J. G., Braverman, E., & Comings, D. E. (1996). Reward deficiency syndrome. *American Scientist, 84,* 132–139.

Brown, S. M., & Hariri, A. R. (2006). Neuroimaging studies of serotonin gene polymorphisms: Exploring the interplay of genes, brain, and behavior. *Cognitive, Affective & Behavioral Neuroscience, 6,* 44–52.

Brunner, H. G., Nelen, M., Breakefield, X. O., Ropers, H. H., & van Oost, B. A. (1993). Abnormal behavior associated with a point mutation in the structural gene for monoamine oxidase A. *Science, 262,* 578–580.

Burt, S. A., & Mikolajewski, A. J. (2008). Preliminary evidence that specific candidate genes are associated with adolescent-onset antisocial behavior. *Aggressive Behavior, 34,* 437–445.

Cadoret, R. J., Langbehn, D., Caspers, K., Troughton, E. P., Yucuis, R., Sandhu, H. K., & Philibert, R. (2003). Associations of the serotonin transporter polymorphism with aggressivity, attention deficit, and conduct disorder in an adoptee population. *Comprehensive Psychiatry, 44,* 88–101.

Canli, T., Ferri, J., & Duman, E. A. (2009). Genetics of emotion regulation. *Neuroscience, 164,* 43–54.

Carver, C. S., Johnson, S. L., & Joormann, J. (2008). Serotonergic function, two-mode models of self-regulation, and vulnerability to depression: What depression has in common with impulsive aggression. *Psychological Bulletin, 134,* 912–943.

Caspi, A., McClay, J., Moffitt, T. E., Mill, J., Martin, J., Craig, I. W., et al. (2002). Role of genotype in the cycle of violence in maltreated children. *Science, 297,* 851–854.

Castellanos, F. X., Lau, E., Tayebi, N., Lee, P., Long, R. E., Giedd, J. N., et al. (1998). Lack of an association between a dopamine-4 receptor polymorphism and attention-deficit/hyperactivity disorder: Genetic and brain morphometric analyses. *Molecular Psychiatry, 3*(5), 431–434.

Chen, T. J. H., Blum, K., Mathews, D., Fisher, L., Schnautz, N., Braverman, E. R., et al. (2007). Preliminary association of both the dopamine D2 receptor (DRD2) [Taq1 A1 allele] and the dopamine transporter (DAT1)[480 bp allele] genes with pathological aggressive behavior, a clinical subtype of reward deficiency syndrome (RDS) in adolescents. *Gene Ther Mol Biol, 11*, 93–112.

Cicchetti, D., Rogosch, F. A., & Sturge-Apple, M. L. (2007). Interactions of child maltreatment and serotonin transporter and monoamine oxidase A polymorphisms: Depressive symptomatology among adolescents from low socioeconomic status backgrounds. *Development and Psychopathology, 19*, 1161–1180.

Cleare, A. J., & Bond, A. J. (2000). Ipsapirone challenge in aggressive men shows an inverse correlation between 5-HT$_{1A}$ receptor function and aggression. *Psychopharmacology, 148*, 344–349.

Coccaro, E. F., Kavoussi, R. J., Cooper, T. B., & Hauger, R. L. (1997). Central serotonin activity and aggression: Inverse relationship with prolactin response to *d*-fenfluramine, but not CSF 5-HIAA concentration, in human subjects. *American Journal of Psychiatry, 154*(10), 1430–1435.

Comings, D. E., Gade-Andavolu, R., Gonzalez, N., Wu, S., Muhleman, D., Blake, H., et al. (2000a). Comparison of the role of dopamine, serotonin, and noradrenaline genes in ADHD, ODD and conduct disorder: Multivariate regression analysis of 20 genes. *Clin Genet, 57*, 178–196.

Comings, D. E., Gade-Andavolu, R., Gonzalez, N., Wu, S., Muhleman, D., Blake, H., et al. (2000b). Multivariate analysis of associations of 42 genes in ADHD, ODD and conduct disorder. *Clin Genet, 58*, 31–40.

Dagher, A., & Robbins, T. W. (2009). Personality, addiction, dopamine: Insights from Parkinson's disease. *Neuron, 61*, 502–510.

Dolan, M., Anderson, I. M., & Deakin, J. F. W. (2001). Relationship between 5-HT function and impulsivity and aggression in male offenders with personality disorders. *The British Journal of Psychiatry, 178*(4), 352–359.

Ellis, L. (1991). Monoamine oxidase and criminality: Identifying an apparent biological marker for antisocial behavior. *Journal of Research in Crime and Delinquency, 28*, 227–251.

Faraone, S. V., Doyle, A. E., Mick, E., & Biederman, J. (2001). Meta-analysis of the association between the 7-repeat allele of the dopamine D4 receptor gene and attention deficit hyperactivity disorder. *American Journal of Psychiatry, 158*(7), 1052–1057.

Foley, D. L., Eaves, L. J., Wormley, B., Silberg, J. L., Maes, H. H., Kuhn, J., et al. (2004). Childhood adversity, monoamine oxidase A genotype, and risk for conduct disorder. *Archives of General Psychiatry, 61*(7), 738–744.

Gabel, S., Stadler, J., Bjorn, J., & Shindledecker, R. (1995). Homovanillic acid and dopamine-beta-hydroxylase in male youth: Relationships with paternal substance abuse and antisocial behavior. *American Journal of Drug and Alcohol Abuse, 21*, 363–378.

Gabel, S., Stadler, J., Bjorn, J., Shindledecker, R., & Bowden, C. L. (1993a). Biodevelopmental aspects of conduct disorder in boys. *Child Psychiatry and Human Development, 24*(2), 125–141.

Gabel, S., Stadler, J., Bjorn, J., Shindledecker, R., & Bowden, C. L. (1993b). Dopamine-beta-hydroxylase in behaviorally disturbed youth: relationship between teacher and parent ratings. *Biological Psychiatry, 34*, 434–443.

Gerra, G., Garofano, L., Bosari, S., Pellegrini, C., Zaimovic, A., Moi, G., et al. (2004a). Analysis of monoamine oxiase A (MAO-A) promoter polymorphism in male heroin-dependent subjects: Behavioural and personality correlates. *Journal of Neural Transmission, 111*, 611–621.

Gerra, G., Garofano, L., Santoro, G., Bosari, S., Pellegrini, C., Zaimovic, A., et al. (2004b). Association between low-activity serotonin transporter genotype and heroin dependence: Behavioral and personality correlates. *American Journal of Medical Genetics Part B Neuropsychiatric Genetics, 126B*, 37–42.

Gerra, G., Garofano, L., Pellegrini, C., Bosari, S., Zaimovic, A., Moi, G., et al. (2005). Allelic association of a dopamine transporter gene polymorphism with antisocial behaviour in heroin-dependent patients. *Addiction Biology, 10*, 275–281.

Giegling, I., Hartmann, A. M., Möller, H., & Rujescu, D. (2006). Anger- and aggression-related traits are associated with polymorphisms in the 5-HT-2A gene. *Journal of Affective Disorders, 96*, 75–81.

Giros, B., & Caron, M. G. (1993). Molecular characterization of the dopamine transporter. *Trends in Pharmacological Sciences, 14*(2), 43–49.

Guo, G., Cai, T., Guo, R., Wang, H., & Harris, K. M. (2010). The dopamine transporter gene, a spectrum of most common risky behaviors, and the legal status of the behaviors. *PLoS ONE, 5*, e9352.

Guo, G., Roettger, M. E., & Shih, J. C. (2007). Contributions of the DAT1 and DRD2 genes to serious and violent delinquency among adolescents and young adults. *Human Genetics, 121*, 125–136.

Haberstick, B. C., Lessem, J. M., Hopfer, C. J., Smolen, A., Ehringer, M. A., Timberlake, D., et al. (2005). Monoamine oxidase A(MAOA) and antisocial behaviors in the presence of childhood and adolescent maltreatment. *American Journal of Medical Genetics Part B Neuropsychiatric Genetics, 135*(1), 59–64.

Hariri, A. R., Mattay, V. S., Tessitore, A., Kolachana, B., Fera, F., Goldman, D., et al. (2002). Serotonin transporter genetic variation and the response of the human amygdala. *Science, 297*, 400–403.

Heils, A., Teufel, A., Petri, S., Stöber, G., Riederer, P., Bengel, D., et al. (1996). Allelic variation of human serotonin transporter gene expression. *Journal of Neurochemistry, 66*, 2621–2624.

Holmes, J., Payton, A., Barrett, J. H., Hever, T., Fitzpatrick, H., Trumper, A. L., et al. (2000). A family-based and case-control association study of the dopamine D4 receptor gene and dopamine transporter gene in attention deficit hyperactivity disorder. *Molecular Psychiatry, 5*, 523–530.

Jacobs, B. L., & Azmitia, E. C. (1992). Structure and function of the brain serotonin system. *Physiological Reviews, 72*, 165–229.

Jensen, K. P., Covault, J., Conner, T. S., Tennen, H., Kranzler, H. R., & Furneaux, H. M. (2008). A common polymorphism in serotonin receptor 1B mRNA moderates regulation by miR-96 and associates with aggressive human behaviors. *Molecular Psychiatry*, 1–9.

Keltikangas-Järvinen, L., Puttonen, S., Kivimäki, M., Elovainio, M., Pulkki-Råback, L., Koivu, M., et al. (2008). Serotonin receptor genes 5HT1A and 5HT2A modify the relation between childhood temperament and adulthood hostility. *Genes, Brain and Behavior*, 7, 46–52.

Kim-Cohen, J., Caspi, A., Taylor, A., Williams, B., Newcombe, R., Craig, I. W., et al. (2006). MAOA, maltreatment, and gene–environment interaction predicting children's mental health: New evidence and a meta-analysis. *Molecular Psychiatry*, 11, 903–913.

Krakowski, M. (2003). Violence and serotonin: Influence of impulse control, affect regulation, and social functioning. *Journal of Neuropsychiatry and Clinical Neuroscience*, 15, 294–305.

Lee, H. J., Lee, H. S., Kim, Y. K., Kim, S. H., Kim, L., Lee, M. S., et al. (2003). Allelic variants interaction of dopamine receptor D4 polymorphism correlate with personality traits in young Korean female population. *American Journal of Medical Genetics*, 118(1), 76–80.

Lesch, K. P., & Merschdorf, U. (2000). Impulsivity, aggression, and serotonin: A molecular psychobiological perspective. *Behavioral Sciences and the Law*, 18, 581–604.

Li, D., Sham, P. C., Owen, M. J., & He, L. (2006). Meta-analysis shows significant association between dopamine system genes and attention deficit hyperactivity disorder (ADHD). *Human Molecular Genetics*, 15(14), 2276–2284.

Liao, D., Hong, C., Shih, H., & Tsai, S. (2004). Possible association between serotonin transporter promoter region polymorphism and extremely violent crime in Chinese males. *Neuropsychobiology*, 50, 284–287.

Lucki, I. (1998). The spectrum of behaviors influenced by serotonin. *Biological Psychiatry*, 44, 151–162.

Manuck, S. B., Flory, J. D., Ferrell, R. E., Dent, K. M., Mann, J. J., & Muldoon, M. F. (1999). Aggression and anger-related traits associated with a polymorphism of the tryptophan hydroxylase gene. *Biological Psychiatry*, 45, 603–614.

Manuck, S. B., Flory, J. D., Ferrell, R. E., Mann, J. J., & Muldoon, M. F. (2000). A regulatory polymorphism of the monoamine oxidase-A gene may be associated with variability in aggression, impulsivity, and central nervous system serotonergic responsivity. *Psychiatry Research*, 95(1), 9–23.

Manuck, S. B., Flory, J. D., McCaffery, J. M., Matthews, K. A., Mann, J. J., & Muldoon, M. F. (1998). Aggression, impulsivity, and central nervous system serotonergic responsivity in a nonpatient sample. *Neuropsychopharmacology*, 19(4), 287–299.

Moore, T. M., Scarpa, A., & Raine, A. (2002). A meta-analysis of serotonin metabolite 5-HIAA and antisocial behavior. *Aggressive Behavior*, 28, 299–316.

Munafò, M. R., Clark, T. G., Moore, L. R., Payne, E., Walton, R., & Flint, J. (2003). Genetic polymorphisms and personality in healthy adults: A systematic review and meta-analysis. *Molecular Psychiatry*, 8, 471–484.

Munafò, M. R., Brown, S. M., & Hariri, A. R. (2008). Serotonin transporter (5-HTTLPR) genotype and amygdala activation: A meta-analysis. *Biological Psychiatry, 63,* 852–857.

Munafò, M. R., Yalcin, B., Willis-Owen, S. A., & Flint, J. (2008). Association of the dopamine D4 receptor (DRD4) gene and approach-related personality traits: Meta-analysis and new data. *Biological Psychiatry, 63*(2), 197–206.

New, A. S., Gelernter, J., Yovell, Y., Trestman, R. L., Nielsen, D. A., Silverman, J., et al. (1998). Tryptophan hydroxylase genotype is associated with impulsive-aggression measures: A preliminary study. *American Journal of Medical Genetics Part B Neuropsychiatric Genetics, 81,* 13–17.

New, A. S., Gelernter, J., Goodman, M., Mitropoulou, V., Koenigsberg, H., Silverman, J., et al. (2001). Suicide, impulsive aggression, and HTR1B genotype. *Biological Psychiatry, 50,* 62–65.

Noble, E. P., Ozkaragoz, T. Z., Ritchie, T. L., Zhang, X., Belin, T. R., & Sparkes, R. S. (1998). D2 and D4 dopamine receptor polymorphisms and personality. *American Journal of Medical Genetics, 81,* 257–267.

Noblett, K. L., & Coccaro, E. F. (2005). Molecular genetics of personality. *Current Psychiatry Reports, 7,* 73–80.

Olivier, B., & van Oorschot, R. (2005). 5-HT$_{1B}$ receptors and aggression: A review. *European Journal of Pharmacology, 526,* 207–217.

Patkar, A. A., Berrettini, W. D., Hoehe, M., Thornton, C. C., Gottheil, E., Hill, K., et al. (2002). Serotonin transporter polymorphisms and measures of impulsivity, aggression, and sensation seeking among African-American cocaine-dependent individuals. *Psychiatry Research, 110,* 103–115.

Reif, A., Rösler, M., Freitag, C. M., Schneider, M., Eujen, A., Kissling, C., et al. (2007). Nature and nurture predispose to violent behavior: Serotonergic genes and adverse childhood environment. *Neuropsychopharmacology, 32,* 2375–2383.

Retz, W., Retz-Junginger, P., Supprian, T., Thome, J., & Rösler, M. (2004). Association of serotonin transporter promoter gene polymorphism with violence: Relation with personality disorders, impulsivity, and childhood ADHD psychopathology. *Behavioral Sciences and the Law, 22,* 415–425.

Reuter, M., Ott, U., Vaitl, D., & Hennig, J. (2007). Impaired executive control is associated with a variation in the promoter region of the tryptophan hydroxylase 2 gene. *Journal of Cognitive Neuroscience, 19,* 401–408.

Rhee, S. H. & Waldman, I. D. (2007). Behavior-genetics of criminality and aggression. Pp. 77–90 in D. J. Flannery, A. T. Vazsonyi and I. D. Waldman (eds.), *The Cambridge Handbook of Violent Behavior and Aggression.* Cambridge: Cambridge University Press.

Robbins, T. W., & Crockett, M. J. (2010). Role of central serotonin in impulsivity and compulsivity: Comparative studies in experimental animals and humans. Pp. 415–427 in C. Müller and B. Jacobs (eds.), *Handbook of Behavioral Neurobiology of Serotonin.* London: Academic Press.

Roth, J. A., Breakefield, X. O., & Castiglione, C. M. (1976). Monoamine oxidase and catechol-O-methyltransferase activities in cultured human skin fibroblasts. *Life Sciences, 19,* 1705–1710.

Rowe, D. C., Stever, C., Chase, D., Sherman, S., Abramowitz, A., & Waldman, I. D. (2001). Two dopamine genes related to reports of childhood retrospective inattention and conduct disorder symptoms. *Molecular Psychiatry, 6*, 429–433.

Rowe, D. C., Stever, C., Gard, J. M. C., Cleveland, H. H., Sanders, M. L., Abramowitz, A., et al. (1998). The relation of the dopamine transporter gene (DAT1) to symptoms of internalizing disorders in children. *Behavior Genetics, 28*, 215–225.

Seo, D., Patrick, C. J., & Kennealy, P. J. (2008). Role of serotonin and dopamine system interactions in the neurobiology of impulsive aggression and its comorbidity with other clinical disorders. *Aggression and Violent Behavior, 13*, 383–395.

Serretti, A., Calati, R., Mandelli, L., & De Ronchi, D. (2006). Serotonin transporter gene variants and behavior: A comprehensive review. *Current Drug Targets, 7*, 1659–1669.

Staner, L., Uyanik, G., Correa, H., Tremeau, F., Monreal, J., Crocq, M., et al. (2002). A dimensional impulsive-aggressive phenotype is associated with the A218C polymorphism of the tryptophan hydroxylase gene: A pilot study in well-characterized impulsive patients. *American Journal of Medical Genetics (Neuropsychiatric Genetics), 114*, 553–557.

Stoltenberg, S. F., Glass, J. M., Chermack, S. T., Flynn, H. A., Li, S., Weston, M. E., et al. (2006). Possible association between response inhibition and a variant in the brain-expressed tryptophan hydroxylase-2 gene. *Psychiatric Genetics, 16*, 35–38.

Stoltenberg, S. F., & Nag, P. (2010). Description and validation of a dynamical systems model of presynaptic serotonin function: Genetic variation, brain activation and impulsivity. *Behavioral Genetics, 40*, 262–279.

Vaske, J., Beaver, K. M., Wright, J. P., Boisvert, D., & Makarios, M. (2009). Moderating effects of DRD2 on depression. *Stress and Health, 25*, 453–462.

Vaske, J., Makarios, M., Boisvert, D., Beaver, K. M., & Wright, J. P. (2009). The interaction of DRD2 and violent victimization on depression: An analysis by gender and race. *Journal of Affective Disorders, 112*, 120–125.

Vaughn, M. G., DeLisi, M., Beaver, K. M., & Wright, J. P. (2009). DAT1 and 5HTT are associated with pathological criminal behavior in a nationally representative sample of youth. *Criminal Justice and Behavior, 36*, 1113–1124.

Walderhaug, E., Herman, A. I., Magnusson, A., Morgan, M. J., & Landro, N. I. (2010). The short (S) allele of the serotonin transporter polymorphism and acute tryptophan depletion both increase impulsivity in men. *Neuroscience Letters, 473*, 208–211.

Walderhaug, E., Lunde, H., Nordvik, J. E., Landro, N. I., Refsum, H., & Magnusson, A. (2002). Lowering of serotonin by rapid tryptophan depletion increases impulsiveness in normal individuals. *Psychopharmacology, 164*(4), 385–391.

Walderhaug, E., Magnusson, A., Neumeister, A., Lappalainen, J., Lunde, H., Refsum, H., et al. (2007). Interactive effects of sex and 5-HTTLPR on mood and impulsivity during tryptophan depletion in healthy people. *Biological Psychiatry, 62*, 593–599.

Widom, C. S., & Brzustowicz, L. M. (2006). MAOA and the "cycle of violence:" Childhood abuse and neglect, MAOA genotype, and risk for violent and antisocial behavior. *Biological Psychiatry, 60*(7), 684–689.

Yang, B., Chan, R. C. K., Jing, J., Li, T., Sham, P., & Chen, R. Y. L. (2007). A meta-analysis of association studies between the 10-repeat allele of a VNTR polymorphism in the 3'-UTR of dopamine transporter gene and attention deficit hyperactivity disorder. *American Journal of Medical Genetics Part B: Neuropsychiatric Genetics, 144B*, 541–550.

Young, S. N., & Leyton, M. (2002). The role of serotonin in human mood and social interaction. *Pharmacology Biochemistry and Behavior, 71*(4), 857–865.

Young, S. E., Smolen, A., Corley, R. P., Krauter, K. S., DeFries, J. C., Crowley, T. J., et al. (2002). Rapid publication dopamine transporter polymorphism associated with externalizing behavior problems in children. *American Journal of Medical Genetics (Neuropsychiatric Genetics), 114*, 144–149.

Young, S. E., Smolen, A., Hewitt, J. K., Haberstick, B. C., Stallings, M. C., Corley, R. P., et al. (2006). Interaction between MAO-A genotype and maltreatment in the risk for conduct disorder: Failure to confirm in adolescent patients. *American Journal of Psychiatry, 163*(6), 1019–1025.

Gene x Environment Interactions in Antisocial Behavior

Christopher J. Ferguson

Gene x Environment Interactions in Violent Antisocial and Criminal Behavior

The degree to which complex human behaviors such as criminal acts can be attributed to genetic and/or environmental factors has been a source of controversy through the nineteenth and twentieth centuries. Ideological positions of dogma have swung between relatively stern biological positions (e.g. Lombroso, 1876/2006; Sagan & Druyan, 1992) to relatively stern learning/socialization paradigms (American Psychological Association, 1996; Joseph, 2001). Within the field of criminology it has been observed that socialization effects tend to hold sway up through the twentieth century, with biological effects comparatively minimized in theoretical perspectives (Beaver, 2009; Wright & Miller, 1998) although this may be changing somewhat in more recent years. In my own field of psychology, which has been something of a "late comer" to criminological theory, the influence of both biology and environment is at least tacitly acknowledged. However, here too, environment heavy theories often hold sway (Pinker, 2002), and the tacit approval of biological theories may be more akin to a theoretical fig leaf for environment-heavy thinking in the field, rather than a full and rigorous embrace of evolutionary and genetic principles. Nonetheless, both fields are coming to accept that understanding criminal behavior from either a staunch environmental or biological position is increasing untenable and naïve.

However the resultant *nature/nurture compromise* may have more to do with understandable fatigue regarding the squabbling between entrenched positions rather than a sophisticated understanding of or acceptance for the ways in which biology and learning contribute to behavior and interact with one another. In some cases, individuals may tacitly acknowledge biological influences in the abstract, while expressing hostility for specific biologically based approaches grounded in evolutionary theory, behavioral genetics or neuroscience. No theory should be beyond debate, challenge or possible falsification, of course. However, at times it appears that reasonably well grounded approaches to understanding the biological contributions to violent behavior rooted in evolutionary or genetic theory are challenged with atypical ferocity, whereas beloved theories based in sociology or social learning, such as the belief that spanking leads to violent behavior (Kazdin, 2008; Straus, 2008) or the largely debunked theory that viewing violent television or video games might influence youth aggression (Bushman & Anderson, 2001) are embraced with an almost naïve lack of scrutiny (see Ferguson, 2010a; Larzelere, 2008; Pinker, 2002; Savage & Yancey, 2008 for discussions). For instance Kazdin (2008) in an essay aimed at the general populace implies that spanking children can be linked to everything from childhood aggression to adulthood cancer and heart disease. Bushman and Anderson (2001) compare media violence research effect sizes favorably to those found in smoking/lung cancer research, a comparison which has since been discredited as little more than an urban legend based on faulty statistics (Block & Crain, 2007; Ferguson, 2009) yet still is often repeated. Were similarly lofty claims made by biologically minded criminologists, behavioral geneticists or evolutionary psychologists, they would be subject to intense scrutiny and rightly so. From this it seems that, although biological theories have made some strides, the intellectual environment in the social sciences remains highly resistant to such approaches, and highly defensive of traditional learning based theories.

Although the nature/nurture compromise allows for at least tacit acknowledgment of the importance of biological contributions to violence, this relatively vague position may lead to numerous misunderstandings about the interaction between genes and environment. For instance: that contributors to behavior can be easily divided into biological and learning elements; that the contribution of genetics and environment are about equal; that all behaviors must be influenced both by genetics and environment; that "environment" is synonymous with "learning" or "socialization"; that the effects of culture can be disentangled from population genetics; that genetic influences on behavior are immutable. Related to violent crime, we may add to this the belief that acknowledgment of the role of biology in violence may make it easier for criminals to use "disease" defenses (although it has been my observation that socialization based "video games made me do it" or "my parents never took me to the zoo" defenses are more common). Allowing an abstract recognition of biology, while maintaining a concrete focus on socialization may be ideologically comforting and help maintain the nature/nurture compromise. Yet such a position may also serve to stave off careful and sophisticated discussions and examinations of biological influences on violent crime.

All Have Won and Must Have Prizes

As noted earlier, I suspect that the nature/nurture compromise too often functions as an escape from the unpleasant and unproductive nature/nurture debates, rather than as any sophisticated scientific position. Moreover in some cases it may be little more than a smoke screen for some scholars to avoid being pinned down as a "tabula rasa" nurturist (Pinker, 2002) while nonetheless remaining free to defend the socialization theories that they *really* like. In any case I don't feel that the vague nature/nurture compromise is terribly illustrative or sophisticated. It may be worth examining several misconceptions about gene/environment interactions.

First, the very use of the word "environment" is a bit sloppy. A better word would have been "non-genetic" (Ferguson, 2010b). The reason for this is that many scholars (and indeed the general public) appear to conflate "environmental" influences with learning/socialization influences. Learning and socialization are certainly one kind of environmental influence. However, anything which is non-genetic is "environment" in as pertains to behavioral genetics research. This includes head injuries, infections, nutrition, exposure to toxins, etc., in addition to learning/socialization influences. Thus in the language of behavioral genetics, when results suggest that approximately 50–55 percent of the variance in violent or antisocial behavior can be attributed to genetic influences, and 5–10 percent due to shared environmental factors (these figures are about typical, see Ferguson, 2010b; Rhee & Waldman, 2002), this really doesn't tell us much about what factors, other than genetics, are influencing behavior. The 5–10 percent of shared environmental variance refers to environment which is shared between twins in a twin pair. But, although family environment certainly can be shared, so can infections or nutritional deficiencies. The remaining 40 percent of variance which is properly termed "non-shared non-genetic" variance is essentially a category for influences of uncertain origin, but which are not shared between the individuals within a twin pair. Injuries, differences in peer associations, non-infectious diseases (such as lymphoma) would be applicable, as would free will or agency if one is inclined to think in such a direction (e.g. Bandura, 2006). Thus we must be careful in discussion of "environmental" influences, as these can include many influences aside from socialization and learning.

Second, it is worth noting that dividing variance into genetics and culture presents us with a false dichotomy. If we are to examine the effects of "culture" we must do so with an understanding that culture is not some form of extra-personal deus ex machina with deliberate goals to influence our behaviors (oftentimes presented with the implication that culture, particularly Western culture, distorts our natural pacifist, egalitarian and self-actualizing inclinations). Rather what we understand as "culture" itself is likely the product, at least in part, of complex population genetics influences in which groups of homo sapiens at least partially isolated from one another (until very recently it was very difficult for someone in Japan, for instance, to mate with someone in England) and living under different selective environmental pressures develop minor or (less often) major distinctions in behavior. For example, aggressive behavior, although nearly universal in the human cultures, may be more critical for population groups living in regions with limited resources and competing for those resources with multiple other cultural groups (i.e. cultures living in the Eurasian land mass). By contrast a population group living in an area of plentiful resources and isolated from competing population groups may not see the adaptive potential of aggressive behavior.

This misunderstanding can sometimes be seen in claims that the different cultural milieus of relatively small, comparatively isolated population groups are sufficient to argue that a particular behavior is "socialized" or "socially constructed" and somehow independent of innate biological drives. As one example, it has been observed that, although most cultures (and particularly Western cultures perhaps) focus on gender identity as a dichotomy of male/female, Navajo tribes conceived of four genders (essentially allowing for male and female intersexed individuals or pseudo-hermaphrodites). The argument seems to be that if Navajo culture conceives of gender differently from "Western" culture, than gender identity is somehow "socially constructed" and such evidence can be offered as a repudiation of the notion that gender identity is innate (McKenzie, 2010). Another commonly discussed example, related to gender identity and gender roles, are the Tchambuli people of Papua New Guinea, among whom it has been reported that females are dominant, sexually aggressive and in political control, whereas males are reportedly vain about their appearance, dependent on females and politically disempowered (Mead, 1935/2001). These examples are used to suggest that gender identity and gender roles are culturally determined rather than innate. Such arguments have obvious rhetorical appeal, yet they are premature. By focusing on small, remote tribal units, sociologists have neglected to consider that such population units are reproductively isolated, and exposed to unique selective environmental pressures. Much like subgroups of Darwin's finches (or tanagers) of the Galapagos Islands which evolved different shaped beaks to adapt to different food sources, so too can isolated populations of humans evolve different traits to adapt to their local environments. We can see quite readily that this occurs for skin, hair and eye color, body fat composition, skeletal structure, musculature, eye structure, height, etc. To think that evolutionary forces which can obviously influence the physical phenotype of human groups are impotent to influence behavior appears naïve in the extreme. In this sense we can understand culture as essentially the average or normative behavior of a specific population group of humans. This is not to say that culture has no back-influence on individual humans through learning and socialization, quite far from it. But this is to say that culture very likely arises through processes of population genetics, and a backward influence of culture on individuals through socialization then may occur (see Figure 6.1).

In regards to specific isolate cultural units such as the Navajo and Tchambuli (assuming that descriptions of these groups are accurate), it is important to understand how the *founder effect* may influence these cultural units (Hey, 2005; Hussels & Morton, 1972; McKusick, Egeland, Eldridge & Krusen, 1964). To begin with, individuals who make up a migratory group, say a tribal unit who decide to sail to an isolated island, or who decide to migrate from Asia to North America, or who decide to live in isolated areas of New Guinea, are unlikely to be genetically representative of the larger group of humans who essentially stay put. Thus, splitting human groups into those who migrate and those who do not is unlikely to be akin to random assignment. This means that the group of humans who initially found a new cultural unit are unlikely to be genetically identical to the larger population groups left behind. This initial genetic difference is then magnified over generations under different environmental pressures, particularly when population groups are reproductively isolated. This helps to explain why small bands of reproductively isolated humans may exhibit striking cultural differences in behavior when compared to the broad array of human cultures through which a flow of genetic information may continuously travel (although the Japanese and English in the earlier example may have little chance to intermarry, at least in centuries past, Japanese might mate with Chinese, who might mate with Turks or Mongols, who might mate with Russians and Czechs and Persians and Arabs, who might mate with French and Germans and Spaniards who might ultimately mate with English. Thus some flow of genetic information maintains some continuity between human populations in constant contact, whereas isolated units may drift further downstream). It is reasonable to expect, therefore, that population groups in relatively close contact, particularly where intermarrying is common, will display cultural similarities to a greater degree than cultures isolated from one another with limited intermarrying.

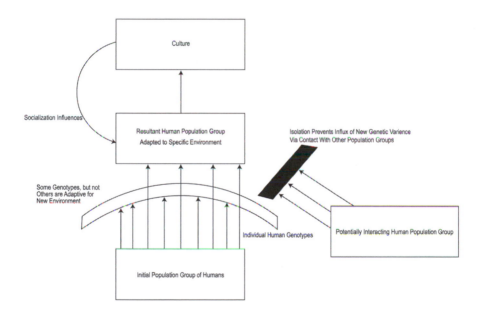

Figure 6.1 How culture arises from population genetics

This point is critical in understanding the dichotomy between "genetics" and "culture" which, despite the nature/nurture compromise, remains at the root of so many debates in the social sciences (e.g. Thornhill & Palmer, 2000 vs. Travis, 2003) with both sides staking out ideologically "pure" positions which are unnecessarily dichotomous (Smith, Borgerhoff-Mulder & Hill, 2001). To understand the way that genetic and non-genetic forces, particularly cultural forces, interact, we must see our way past the neat heuristic which carefully divides genetic and cultural influences into clear and opposing camps. I suspect that some pure social constructionists will greet the model in Figure 6.1 as something akin to heresy, and accuse me of being an apologist for evolutionary psychology.[1] However the intent of the model presented is not to suborn culture entirely under genetics, but rather to argue for a more complex weave between culture and genetics and evolution than has often been at the root of the nature/nurture compromise.

If we return to the example of gender identity, we see that many sociologist and psychologists have argued for a position in which gender identity is learned and socially constructed. At the very extreme, in some cases of genetic males born with intersex or ambiguous genitalia, these males were reassigned surgically as females in the belief that these genetic males could be socialized to adopt a female gender identity. This approach is now known to be flawed and potentially damaging to the males in question (Diamond & Sigmundson, 1997). For several decades it has become increasingly apparent that biological/genetic forces shape gender identity mainly through an area in the hypothalamus called the sexually dimorphic nucleus (Swaab & Fliers, 1985). In cases of gender identity disorder, in which genetic sex and brain identified gender identity are mismatched, the causal process appears to be androgen exposure in utero causing the brain to develop essentially into the brain of the opposite sex.[2] Thus gender identity, the sense of being male and female, and wanting to do things male and female are likely the result of genetically directed brain development, rather than learning or socialization. Environment can have an impact, less through learning influences, and more likely through accidental

---

1   I have read widely the debates on whether "evolutionary psychology" is a field which is distinct from the general application of evolutionary principles to human behavior. Nonetheless I remain a bit bemused regarding the margins between what constitutes "evolutionary psychology" and an evolutionarily informed science of human behavior that is *not* evolutionary psychology. Smith, Borgerhoff-Mulder and Hill (2001) do a most admirable job of trying to make explicit the differences which tend to focus on issues such as adaptive lag, the specificity of evolved brain modules, etc. Smith, Borgerhoff-Mulder and Hill certainly raise good points about the potential for dogmatic rigidity in evolutionary psychology. Yet I express the concern that the "I believe evolution influences behavior, but not in evolutionary psychology" position returns us to the nature/nurture fig leaf, particularly when an alternate view of "evolutionarily informed psychology" seems rather vague or absent. To whit, I am not sure I would call myself an "evolutionary psychologist", not only because I agree with some of the concerns raised by Smith, Borgerhoff-Mulder and Hill (2001), but also because I am left unsure what an evolutionary psychologist is, how one gets nominated to such a label, whether there is an application one must fill out, etc.

2   A fetus with genotype XX, and thus female, exposed to too much androgen hormones will develop a "male" hypothalamus and thus "feel" male, and a fetus with genotype XY, and thus male, exposed to too little androgen (i.e. testosterone) will have a brain that remains in the female state. Essentially fetal brains "start female" and in males the production of testosterone causes differentiation of the brain into a "male" brain. When testosterone is blocked (potentially through continued use of female hormones such as in birth control medications), feminization of the male fetus may occur.

processes that interfere with normal hormone directed masculinization of male brains, or retained feminization of female brains. Certain sex-based trends, such as heightened male aggression, and increased female investment in young are also likely the primary results of genetic and evolutionary influences rather than socialization (Ellis & Walsh, 1997; Morris, 1999; Okami & Shackelford, 2001; Pinker, 2002). It's not "correct" to say so oftentimes, but this doesn't make it any less so.

Where culture comes into play likely comes in the specific adornments, whether physical or behavioral, males and females use to advertise their gender status. Children are likely born with an innate drive to advertise their maleness or femaleness, to one degree or another (one must remember that genotypes are not invariable across individuals, so phenotypic expressions will vary), but may search out socially sanctioned avenues for doing so. For instance, in typical US culture, the wearing of miniskirts is specifically reserved for advertising femaleness. However in Scottish society males wearing miniskirts is perfectly acceptable (they call them kilts, but the difference is ornamental). No one would claim men from the land of Braveheart lack for machismo. Thus the prohibition against wearing miniskirts in one culture and the acceptance of wearing miniskirts (i.e. kilts) in another is culturally determined. Genetic Scots (of which I am one) raised in the United States seldom wear miniskirts/kilts as they have tuned in to this cultural/socialization process.

Gene x Gene Effects Unveiled

One of the exciting prospects coming out of the human genome project was the expectation that in mapping out the human genome, it might be possible to attribute complex human behaviors to specific genes or groups of genes. This expectation may have been unwilling inflamed by the great success of behavioral genetics, which regularly found that variables such as violence and antisocial behavior (Ferguson, 2010b; Rhee & Waldman, 2002), intelligence (Plomin, 1990), personality (Jang, McCrae, Angleitner, Riemann & Livesley, 1998) and mental illness (Bouchard, 2004) could be attributed in large part (often over 50 percent of the variance and sometimes much higher) to genetic factors. Occasionally certain neurological diseases such as Huntington's Disease (or Chorea) were found to be attributable to specific genetic mutations, defects or polymorphisms. However, in large part the quixotic quest to find specific genes "for" a particularly behavior such as criminal violence has been a bust.

Yet the very idea that scientists might find a "gene for violence" was always naïve. Current estimates suggest that half of all genes (the human genome has approximately 23,000; International Human Genome Sequencing Consortium, 2004) are involved in the development of the mammalian brain and nervous system (Han et al., 2009). Thus, finding direct and strong links between specific gene polymorphisms and measurable behaviors is likely to remain a difficult process given that behavior may be the product not of single gene actions, or the action of a handful of genes, but the combined interaction of hundreds or even thousands of genes in particular sequence. This misunderstanding is potentially the source of such comments as that by the American Psychological Association (APA) which, in 1996, claimed: "There is no gene for violence. Violence is a learned behavior." Although the APA pamphlet in which the comment was found acknowledged violence may interact with other inherited traits such as impulsivity and intelligence, the APA pamphlet appears to take a hard socialization view of violent behavior.

One might suppose the APA's comment is technically true if one is generous. It certainly is true that there is no *single* gene for violence. Of course at the current time at least a half dozen genetic polymorphisms have been found to play some role in the formulation of violent behavior (Ferguson & Beaver, 2009) and I suspect that number will rise over time. However the APA pamphlet attacks a "straw man" view of genetics that few serious researchers ever endorsed. There is no single gene for violence because there are *many* gene polymorphisms involved in the production of violent behavior. Fortunately the APA pamphlet in question has since been removed from the APA website. I am not knowledgeable of the circumstances under which it was removed, but I hope it was recognized that the view presented in this pamphlet was misleading to the general public and no longer scientifically tenable (if it were even back in 1996).

Much of the confusion seems to have resulted from the observation that for most complex human traits or behaviors, such as intelligence, personality or violent behavior, although the proportion of variance attributable to genetics was substantial, often more than 50 percent, the variance attributable to *single* gene polymorphisms has typically been quite modest. This is an important point to make and make clearly. Although many genes likely contribute to violent behavior there are no genes "for" violence, per se. The dystopian fear of a *Minority Report* type system in which individuals are screened prenatally for violence risk using DNA analysis is unlikely to ever become a reality. This does not speak to the impotence of genetic effects, rather to their complexity and to the complexity of gene x gene and gene x environment interactions.

The direct effects of single genes tends to be quite small, even trivial frankly, in terms of effect size (Beaver, Ratchford & Ferguson, 2009; Caspi et al., 2002; Guo, Roettger & Shih, 2007; Retz, Retz-Junginger, Supprian, Thome & Rosler, 2004; Thapar et al., 2005). This observation cautions us to avoid undue claims of genes "for violence" just as we should be skeptical of claims of single genes with powerful effects "for" any complex behavior. To expect single polymorphisms to have a major and dichotomous (violent/non-violent) impact on violent and antisocial behavior in the same manner as the extended CAG repeat pattern in the short arm of Chromosome 4 leads to Huntington's Chorea (Walker, 2007) will invariably lead to misunderstanding. Of course, the same is true for socialization and learning variables on violence, the effect size of most of which are quite modest (Ferguson, San Miguel & Hartley, 2009). Interestingly, social factors with the weakest and least consistent effects such as media violence (Ferguson et al., 2009) and spanking (Baumrind, Larzelere & Cowan, 2002), tend to attract the most dogmatic rhetoric, whereas more consistent risk factors such as peer influences (Beaver, Ratchford & Ferguson, 2009; Ferguson, San Miguel & Hartley, 2009) and self-control (Beaver, Ratchford & Ferguson, 2009; Ratchford & Beaver, 2009; Finkel, DeWall, Slotter, Oaten & Foshee, 2009) see less discussion. This may, at least in part, be due to the particularly extreme dogmas and ideologies which have developed around certain socialization based views (Grimes, Anderson & Bergen, 2008).

Thus our examination of direct single-gene effects is quite disappointing. However when one begins to examine the additive effects of multiple genes, the picture begins to change. Grigorenko and colleagues (2010) examined polymorphisms in four genes previously linked to violence (COMT, MAOA, MAOB and DβH) and found that additive effects of multiple genes accounted for a much greater percentage of the variance in violence than single genes alone. This finding shouldn't be surprising. Examining gene x gene interactions among four genes provides a much more robust picture of genetic effects on violence than single genes alone. Nonetheless even these four genes together have not brought us to the threshold of where we might like to be. The sensitivities and specificities of the various genetic models reported by Grigorenko et al. (2010) remain far below those required for the dystopian DNA test for violence some activists fear.

Gene x Environment Interactions and the Catalyst Model

Relatively few studies have examined gene x gene interactions on violent and antisocial behavior. However a fair number of studies have examined gene x environment interactions (it is reminded that we must be careful not to generally equate "environment" with socialization, although in fairness, most of these studies do examine social influences). The basic foundation for our understanding of gene x environment can be found in the diathesis-stress model of psychopathology (Zubin & Spring, 1977). Put briefly, this model proposes that abnormal behavior arises as a result of genetic predisposition combined with environmental stressors. For instance, it is well known that certain mental illnesses such as schizophrenia are highly heritable (Bouchard, 2004). Individuals are thus born with a particular predisposition for the mental illness. However, not all individuals with the genetic predisposition necessarily develop the mental illness. It seems that, in effect, genotype sets up a range of possible outcomes. However, the level of environmental stress or strain determines the specific outcome. Generally speaking, the more environmental strain, the worse the outcome. Of course, not all mental conditions see the same degree of heritability. For instance, the heritability of schizophrenia seems to be very high (about 0.80 or 80 percent of the variance; Bouchard, 2004), whereas the heritability of depression is comparatively lower (about 0.37 according to Bouchard, 2004). By this standard, the heritability of violence and antisocial traits at about 0.50–0.55 is somewhere in the middle.

Caspi and colleagues (2002) demonstrated gene x environment effects on antisocial traits in humans in a now classic study. They examined polymorphisms on the promoter region of the MAOA gene (which is involved in the production of monoamine oxidase which deanimates serotonin, norepinephrine and dopamine), particularly focusing on alleles coding for low MAOA activity. As one might suspect, given the earlier discussion of minimal direct gene effects, direct effects for polymorphisms on the MAOA gene were minimal. However, the authors noted that for individuals (all males in this study) with the low MAOA activity genotype, those who were also neglected by their parents early in life were most likely to demonstrate antisocial phenotypes. Males who did not have the low MAOA genotype were unlikely to show antisocial behavior even if they were maltreated. Males with the low MAOA genotype were also unlikely to show antisocial traits unless they also had been neglected in childhood. In the Caspi et al. sample, only 12 percent of men displayed the combination of the low MAOA genotype and exposure to childhood neglect. However these men displayed high levels of antisocial traits and accounted for 44 percent of violent convictions in the sample.

The MAOA gene may be particularly valuable in understanding why males are so much more prone to violence than females (males account for about 85 percent of violent convictions). The MAOA gene happens to be located on the X-chromosome. Males, of course, have only one X chromosome, whereas females have two (the Y chromosome in males seems to do little aside from stimulating the production of testosterone via the SRY gene). This means that if males get the low-MAOA allele on one X chromosome they do not have a second X chromosome, potentially with the high-MAOA allele to counteract it. Women, having two X chromosomes, are less likely to "come up lemons" with two low-MAOA alleles (although it certainly can happen), although they may pass the low-MAOA allele through their children.

Although there has been some controversy about the MAOA gene x environment influence on violence and antisocial traits (e.g. Haberstick et al., 2005), the evidence has generally held up over multiple studies (Kim-Cohen et al., 2006; Meyer-Lindenberg et al., 2006). Similar gene x environment effects have been found for other genes such as DAT1 and 5HTT (Reif et al., 2007; Vaughn, DeLisi, Beaver & Wright, 2009). DRD2 (DeLisi, Beaver, Wright & Vaughn, 2008) and DRD4 (Bakermans-Kranenburg & van Ijzendoorn, 2006).

Thus, speaking generally, certain genetic polymorphisms place the individual at risk for violent and antisocial outcomes. In the absence of environmental strain, the negative outcome may be less likely to come to pass. However, in the presence of significant strain in the environment, violent or antisocial phenotypes may result. To further understand how gene and environment interact in this way I refer to the Catalyst Model presented in Figure 6.2.

The Catalyst Model is essentially a diathesis-stress model, postulating that violent behavior arises through interactions between genes and environmental effects, both during development and during the time of the specific behavior. In the Catalyst Model genetic effects are considered to be a strong influence on the development of violent and antisocial phenotypes. Several environmental variables are specifically included in the Catalyst Model, namely family violence and peer delinquency as the evidence for these influences are generally consistent and strong relative to other factors. Other variables such as media violence are specifically excluded both because multivariate analyses of violence do not support the belief that media violence contributes to violent behavior (Ferguson, San Miguel & Hartley, 2009; Ybarra et al., 2008, figure 2) and because such variables are considered too distal to the organism to have sizeable impact on behavior. The catalyst model proposes that genetic polymorphisms interact with early exposure to violence, neglect or maltreatment in the family and among peers to produce personality phenotypes which are prone to antisocial and violent behavior.

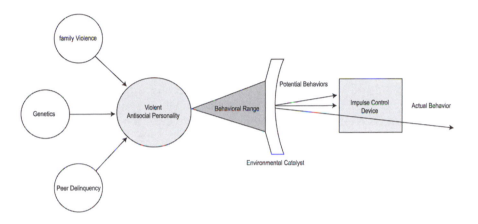

Figure 6.2 The Catalyst Model of gene x environment effects on violent behavior

This may seem to be the logical end to the model, but it is not. Although personality traits are reasonable predictors of behavior, behavior is not always consistent across all times and all situations. Thus the Catalyst Model proposes that personality traits set forth a range of potential behaviors. A proneness to violence or non-violence, if you will. Specific environmental events or catalysts will provoke narrow ranges of behavioral options in response to these stressors or catalysts. Consider, for example, a person driving on the highway. They are suddenly cut off by another, apparently rude, driver. An average person (one low in antisocial traits) might think, "In response to that I could a.) do nothing, b.) honk my horn or c.) give them the finger." In other words the personality (itself determined by gene x environment interactions) and specific environmental catalysts determine a range of potential behaviors from which the person might select. In this case an average non-antisocial person might decide to honk their horn and be done with it.

Now consider a person with a genotype prone to violence, who also has been abused as a child. He or she develops an antisocial personality, and is exposed to the same environmental catalyst. The range of behaviors this antisocial person may produce may include "In response to that I could a.) give them the finger, b.) get in front of their car and then slam on my brakes or c.) get out the .45 automatic in my glove compartment and begin firing." The range of behavioral options, while overlapping slightly at the margins, is far more extreme in response than those of an average person.

A last element of the Catalyst Model is worth noting. Namely, that the ultimate selection of the specific behavioral response is non-random, but rather depends upon the individual's impulse control and executive functioning; that is their ability to restrain more extreme impulses and positively foresee the consequences of their actions. This "impulse control device" appears to be located, in large part, in the frontal lobes of the brain, injury to which can impair impulse control and increase impulsive violence (León-Carrión & Chacartegui-Ramos, 2009; Miller, 2002; Soderstrom et al., 2002). Individuals with damage to the frontal lobes, and thus the impulse control device, may have greater difficulty restraining the most violent of their instincts. Individuals with better frontal lobe functioning may be able to hesitate before acting just long enough to select more reasonable options.

Thus the Catalyst Model helps to explain gene x environment interactions, but goes on to help explain how some violent personalities are more prone to impulsive acts than others as well as the observation that violence tends to increase during periods of strain or stress (Ferguson, San Miguel & Hartley, 2009).

Epigenesis

One process by which we may understand the interaction of genes and environment is the process of developmental epigenesis. It is well understood that the DNA of an individual is essentially immutable (aside, perhaps, from standing near the microwave for too long). However, modification of gene expression, but not underlying DNA, can occur due to experiences in the developmental process (Lickliter, 2008; Mill & Petronis, 2007). Epigenetic modifications occur through a number of processes, including DNA methylation and histone acetylation allowing for regulation of gene expression without requiring DNA mutation (Mill & Petronis, 2007). Evidence suggests that epigenetic profiles may be inherited (Levenson & Sweatt, 2005), but unlike DNA, can be dynamic and changing within individuals. Mill and Petronis (2007) discuss this issue in depth, noting that what sometimes is labeled as "environmental" effects may mask underlying genetic processes and genetic and environmental effects are more complexly intertwined than is commonly expressed in much scholarly work. Epigenetic effects may specifically account for much of the non-shared environmental variance seen in twin studies and may also explain some of the difficulties in bridging molecular and behavioral genetics outcomes. Put rather simply, certain environmental circumstances may "switch on" or "switch off" certain genes without influencing the underlying genetic profile of the individual.

In one example of potential epigenetic effects Bygren, Kaati and Edvinsson (2001) demonstrated that the grandsons of boys who ate relatively high amounts of food in a parish in Sweden during the early 1900s lived shorter lives than grandsons of boys who had eaten relatively less. This case is interesting because the estimate of food intake was based upon years in which families in this remote area experienced famines or years of relative plenty. Although these results are correlational, and causal inferences cannot be made, one possibility is that the environmental variations in "feast or famine" caused epigenetic changes in the grandfathers that were passed on through at least two generations. Experimental evidence for epigenetic effects, to date, has largely come from non-human animals. For instance, in a series of experiments, Waterland, Jirtle and colleagues (e.g. Dolinoy, Weidman, Waterland & Jirtle, 2006; Waterland & Jirtle, 2003; Waterland, Lin, Smith & Jirtle 2006) provided dietary supplementation during pregnancy in randomly assigned mice, hypothesizing that such dietary supplementation can alter the methylation of DNA. Those mice receiving dietary supplementation produce offspring displaying phenotypical differences from their mothers, whereas no such phenotypical differences were seen in control mice. These findings have potential implications for maternal diet recommendations in humans, as well as early childhood diets (Waterland, Lin, Smith & Jirtle, 2006) although more research is necessary with humans. Arai, Li, Hartley and Feig (2009) also report that exposing young female mice to enriched environments designed to enhance learning is associated with increased memory performance in their offspring. In reviewing the epigenetic literature, Jablonka and Raz (2009) find evidence for epigenetics across multiple species, with effects oftentimes extending for multiple generations beyond the first experimental manipulation.

Unfortunately, no research has examined epigenesis in relation to violent antisocial behavior as of yet. Obviously epigenesis may help us explain the mechanism by which home environment and peer environment have an influence on violent behavior. It has long been assumed that family and peer influences occur solely via socialization and learning, yet it may be possible that peers and family environment act through epigenesis to "switch on" gene alleles relevant to violent and antisocial behavior. This is an interesting and potentially fruitful avenue for future research.

References

American Psychological Association. (1996). An APA brochure on youth violence. Retrieved 2/7/07 from: www.apa.org/ppo/issues/pbviolence.html. Since removed from site.

Arai, J. A., Li, S., Hartley, D. M., & Feig, L. A. (2009). Transgenerational rescue of a genetic defect in long-term potentiation and memory formation by juvenile enrichment. *The Journal of Neuroscience, 29*(5), 1496–1502. doi:10.1523/JNEUROSCI.5057-08.2009.

Bakermans-Kranenburg, M. & van Ijzendoorn, M. (2006). Gene-environment interaction of the dopamine D4 receptor (DRD4) and observed maternal insensitivity predicting externalizing behavior in preschoolers. *Developmental Psychobiology, 48*(5), 406–409. doi:10.1002/dev.20152.

Bandura, A. (2006). Toward a psychology of human agency. *Perspectives on Psychological Science, 1*(2), 164–180. doi:10.1111/j.1745-6916.2006.00011.x.

Baumrind, D., Larzelere, R. & Cowan, P. (2002). Ordinary physical punishment: Is it harmful? Comment on Gershoff (2002). *Psychological Bulletin, 128*(4), 580–589. doi:10.1037/0033-2909.128.4.580.

Beaver, K. (2009). *Biosocial criminology: A primer.* Dubuque: Kendall/Hunt.

Beaver, K., Ratchford, M. & Ferguson, C. (2009). Evidence of genetic and environmental effects on the development of low self-control. *Criminal Justice and Behavior, 36*(11), 1158–1172. doi:10.1177/0093854809342859.

Block, J. & Crain, B. (2007). Omissions and errors in "Media violence and the American public." *American Psychologist, 62,* 252–253.

Bouchard, T. (2004). Genetic influence on human psychological traits: A survey. *Current Directions in Psychological Science, 13*(4), 148–151.

Bushman, B. & Anderson, C. (2001). Media violence and the American public. *American Psychologist, 56,* 477–489.

Bygren, L., Kaati, G. & Edvinsson, S. (2001). Longevity determined by paternal ancestors' nutrition during their slow growth period. *Acta Biotheoretica, 49*(1), 53–59.

Caspi, A., McClay, J., Moffitt, T., Mill, J., Martin, J., Craig, I., et al. (2002). Role of genotype in the cycle of violence in maltreated children. *Science, 297,* 851–854.

DeLisi, M., Beaver, K., Wright, J. & Vaughn, M. (2008). The etiology of criminal onset: The enduring salience of nature and nurture. *Journal of Criminal Justice, 36*(3), 217–223. doi:10.1016/j.jcrimjus.2008.04.001.

Diamond, M. & Sigmundson, H. (1997). Sexual reassignment at birth: Long-term review and clinical implications. *Annals of Pediatric and Adolescent Medicine, 151,* 298–304.

Dolinoy, D., Weidman, J., Waterland, R. & Jirtle, R. (2006). Maternal genistein alters coat color and protects Avy mouse offspring from obesity by modifying the fetal epigenome. *Environmental Health Perspectives, 114*(4), 567–572.

Ellis, L. & Walsh, A. (1997). Gene-based evolutionary theories in criminology. *Criminology, 35,* 229–276.

Ferguson, C. J. (2009). Is psychological research really as good as medical research? Effect size comparisons between psychology and medicine. *Review of General Psychology, 13*(2), 130–136.

Ferguson, C. J. (2010a). Blazing Angels or Resident Evil? Can violent video games be a force for good? *Review of General Psychology, 14*(2), 68–81.

Ferguson, C. J. (2010b). Genetic contributions to antisocial personality and behavior (APB): A meta-analytic review from an evolutionary perspective. *Journal of Social Psychology, 150*(2), 160–180.

Ferguson, C. J. & Beaver, K. M. (2009). Natural born killers: The genetic origins of extreme violence. *Aggression and Violent Behavior, 14*(5), 286–294.

Ferguson, C. J., San Miguel, C. & Hartley, R. D. (2009). A multivariate analysis of youth violence and aggression: The influence of family, peers, depression and media violence. *Journal of Pediatrics, 155*(6), 904–908.

Finkel, E., DeWall, C., Slotter, E., Oaten, M. & Foshee, V. (2009). Self-regulatory failure and intimate partner violence perpetration. *Journal of Personality and Social Psychology, 97*(3), 483–499. doi:10.1037/a0015433.

Grigorenko, E., DeYoung, C., Eastman, M., Getchell, M., Haeffel, G., af Klinteberg, B., et al. (2010). Aggressive behavior, related conduct problems, and variation in genes affecting dopamine turnover. *Aggressive Behavior, 36*(3), 158–176.

Grimes, T., Anderson, J. & Bergen, L. (2008). *Media violence and aggression: Science and ideology*. Thousand Oaks, CA: Sage.

Guo, G., Roettger, M. E. & Shih, J. C. (2007). Contributions of the DAT1 and DRD2 genes to serious and violence delinquency among adolescents and young adults. *Human Genetics, 121*, 125–136.

Haberstick, B., Lessem, J., Hopfer, C., Smolen, A., Ehringer, M., Tiberlake, D. & Hewitt, J. (2005). Monoamine oxidase A (MAOA) and antisocial behaviors in the presence of childhood and adolescent maltreatment. *American Journal of Molecular Genetics Part B (Neuropsychiatric Genetics), 135B*, 59–64.

Han, X., Wu, X., Chung, W., Li, T., Nekrutenko, A., Altman, N., Chen, G. & Ma, H. (2009). Transcriptome of embryonic and neonatal mouse cortex by high-throughput RNA sequencing. *Proceedings of the National Academy of Sciences, 106*, 12741–12746. doi:10.1073/pnas.0902417106.

Hey, J. (2005). On the number of new world founders: A population genetic portrait of the peopling of the Americas. *PLoS Biol, 3*(6), e193.

Hussels, I. & Morton, N. (1972). Pingelap and Mokil Atolls: Achromatopsia. *American Journal of Human Genetics, 24*(3), 304–309.

International Human Genome Sequencing Consortium (2004). Finishing the euchromatic sequence of the human genome. *Nature, 431*, 931–945. doi:10.1038/nature03001.

Jablonka, E., & Raz, G. (2009). Transgenerational epigenetic inheritance: Prevalence, mechanisms, and implications for the study of heredity and evolution. *The Quarterly Review Of Biology, 84*(2), 131–176.

Jang, K., McCrae, R., Angleitner, A., Riemann, R. & Livesley, W. (1998). Heritability of facet-level traits in a cross-cultural twin sample: Support for a hierarchical model of personality. *Journal of Personality and Social Psychology, 74*(6), 1556–1565. doi:10.1037/0022-3514.74.6.1556.

Joseph, J. (2001). Is crime in the genes? A critical review of twin and adoption studies of criminality and antisocial behavior. *Journal of Mind and Behavior, 22*(2), 179–218.

Kazdin, A. (2008). Spare the rod: Why you shouldn't hit your kids. *Slate*. Retrieved 9/13/10 from: www.slate.com/id/2200450/?from=rss.

Kim-Cohen, J., Caspi, A., Taylor, A., Williams, B., Newcombe, R., Craig, I., et al. (2006). MAOA, maltreatment, and gene-environment interaction predicting children's mental health: New evidence and a meta-analysis. *Molecular Psychiatry, 11*(10), 903–913. doi:10.1038/sj.mp.4001851.

Larzelere, R. (2008). Disciplinary spanking: The scientific evidence. *Journal of Developmental and Behavioral Pediatrics, 29*(4), 334–335. doi:10.1097/DBP.0b013e3181829f30.

León-Carrión, J. & Chacartegui-Ramos, F. (2009). Brain injuries and violent crime. *Violent crime: Clinical and social implications* (pp. 99–118). Thousand Oaks, CA: Sage Publications, Inc.

Levenson, J. M. & Sweatt, J. D. (2005). Epigenetic mechanisms in memory formation. *Nature Reviews Neuroscience, 6,* 108–118.

Lickliter, R. (2008). The growth of developmental thought: Implications for a new evolutionary psychology. *New Ideas in Psychology, 26*(3), 353–369. doi:10.1016/j.newideapsych.2007.07.015.

Lombroso, C. (1876/2006). *The criminal man.* Durham, NC: Duke University Press.

McKenzie, S. (2010). Genders and sexualities in individuation: Theoretical and clinical explorations. *The Journal of Analytical Psychology, 55*(1), 91–111. doi:10.1111/j.1468-5922.2009.01826.x.

McKusick, V. A., Egeland, J. A., Eldridge, R. & Krusen, D. E. (1964). Dwarfism in the Amish I: The Ellis-van Creveld syndrome. *Bulletin of Johns Hopkins Hospital, 115,* 306–336.

Mead, M. (1935/2001). *Sex and temperament in three primitive societies.* New York: Harper.

Meyer-Lindenberg, A., Buckholtz, J., Kolachana, B., Hariri, A., Pezawas, L., Blasi, G., et al. (2006). Neural mechanisms of genetic risk for impulsivity and violence in humans. *PNAS Proceedings of the National Academy of Sciences of the United States of America, 103*(16), 6269–6274. doi:10.1073/pnas.0511311103.

Mill, J. & Petronis, A. (2007). Molecular studies of major depressive disorder: The epigenetic perspective. *Molecular Psychiatry, 12*(9), 799–814. doi:10.1038/sj.mp.4001992.

Miller, E. (2002). Brain injury as a contributory factor in offending. *The neurobiology of criminal behavior* (pp. 137–153). Dordrecht Netherlands: Kluwer Academic Publishers.

Morris, D. (1999). *The naked ape: A zoologist's study of the human animal.* New York: Delta.

Okami, P. & Shackelford, T. (2001). Human sex differences in sexual psychology and behavior. *Annual Review of Sex Research, 12,* 186–241.

Pinker, S. (2002). *The blank slate: The modern denial of human nature.* New York: Penguin.

Plomin, R. (1990). The role of inheritance in behavior. *Science, 248,* 183. Retrieved 1/15/10 from: http://euvolution.com/articles/inheritance02.html.

Ratchford, M. & Beaver, K. (2009). Neuropsychological deficits, low self-control, and delinquent involvement: Toward a biosocial explanation of delinquency. *Criminal Justice and Behavior, 36*(2), 147–162. doi:10.1177/0093854808325967.

Reif, A., Rösler, M., Freitag, C., Schneider, M., Eujen, A., Kissling, C., et al. (2007). Nature and nurture predispose to violent behavior: Serotonergic genes and adverse childhood environment. *Neuropsychopharmacology, 32*(11), 2375–2383. doi:10.1038/sj.npp.1301359.

Retz, W., Retz-Junginger, P., Supprian, T., Thome, J. & Rosler, M. (2004). Association of serotonin transporter promoter gene polymorphism with violence: Relation with personality disorders, impulsivity and childhood ADHD psychopathology. *Behavioral Sciences and the Law, 22,* 415–425.

Rhee, S. & Waldman, I. (2002). Genetic and environmental influences on antisocial behavior: A meta-analysis of twin and adoption studies. *Psychological Bulletin, 128,* 490–529.

Sagan, C. & Druyan, A. (1992). *Shadows of forgotten ancestors: A search for who we are.* New York: Random House.

Savage, J. & Yancey, C. (2008). The effects of media violence exposure on criminal aggression: A meta-analysis. *Criminal Justice and Behavior, 35,* 1123–1136.

Smith, E., Borgerhoff-Mulder, M. & Hill, K. (2001). Controversies in the evolutionary social sciences: A guide for the perplexed. *Trends in Ecology and Evolution, 16*(3), 128–135.

Soderstrom, H., Hultin, L., Tullberg, M., Wikkelso, C., Ekholm, S. & Forsman, A. (2002). Reduced frontotemporal perfusion in psychopathic personality. *Psychiatry Research: Neuroimaging, 114*(2), 81–94. doi:10.1016/S0925-4927(02)00006-9.

Straus, M. (2008). The special issue on prevention of violence ignores the primordial violence. *Journal of Interpersonal Violence, 23*(9), 1314–1320. doi:10.1177/0886260508322266.

Swaab, D. & Fliers, E. (1985). A sexually dimorphic nucleus in the human brain. *Science, 228*(4703), 1112–1115. doi:10.1126/science.3992248.

Thapar, A., Langley, K., Fowler, T., Rice, F., Turic, D., Whittinger, N., et al. (2005). Catechol O-Methyltransferase gene variant and birth weight predict early-onset antisocial behavior in children with attention-deficit/hyperactivity disorder. *Archives of General Psychiatry, 62,* 1275–1278.

Thornhill, R. & Palmer, C. (2000). *A natural history of rape.* Cambridge, MA: MIT Press.

Travis, C. (2003). *Evolution, gender, and rape.* Cambridge, MA: MIT Press. Retrieved from PsycINFO database.

Vaughn, M., DeLisi, M., Beaver, K. & Wright, J. (2009). DAT1 and 5HTT are associated with pathological criminal behavior in a nationally representative sample of youth. *Criminal Justice and Behavior, 36*(11), 1113–1124. doi:10.1177/0093854809342839.

Walker, F. (2007). Huntington's disease. *The Lancet, 369,* 218–228.

Waterland, R. & Jirtle, R. (2003). Transposable elements: targets for early nutritional effects on epigenetic gene regulation. *Molecular and Cellular Biology, 23*(15), 5293–5300.

Waterland, R., Lin, J., Smith, C. & Jirtle, R. (2006). Post-weaning diet affects genomic imprinting at the insulin-like growth factor 2 (Igf2) locus. *Human Molecular Genetics, 15*(5), 705–716.

Wright, R. & Miller, J. (1998). Taboo until today? The coverage of biological arguments in criminology textbooks, 1961 to 1970 and 1987 to 1996. *Journal of Criminal Justice, 26*(1), 1–19. doi:10.1016/S0047-2352(97)00050-0.

Ybarra, M., Diener-West, M., Markow, D., Leaf, P., Hamburger, M. & Boxer, P. (2008). Linkages between internet and other media violence with seriously violent behavior by youth. *Pediatrics, 122*(5), 929–937.

Zubin, J. & Spring, B. (1977). Vulnerability: A new view of schizophrenia. *Journal of Abnormal Psychology, 86*(2), 103–126. doi:10.1037/0021-843X.86.2.103.

PART III
THE BRAIN AND CRIME

Neurotransmitters: Indirect Molecular Invitations to Aggression

Raymond E. Collins

Introduction

In his seminal work, *Decoding the Human Message*, Henri-Marie Laborit offers the proposition that aggression represents the very purpose of neurology and this further suggests that aggression must be an inevitable consequence of the existence of a neurological system. Laborit presents us with the premise that the preservation of existence is the primordial imperative for any organism. He further observes that, unlike plant life (which derives its source of energy directly from the sun through photosynthesis—and therefore does not require locomotion to preserve its existence), animal life has no such capacity to transform energy directly from the sun. Rather, animals need to locomote in order to forage for an energy source (Laborit, 1977). "Thus, according to Laborit, *aggression is endemic to any form of animal life*" (emphasis in original) (Pallone and Hennessey, 1996: 22).

> From the perspective of the sciences of behavior, doubtless the principle benefit has been the development of the capacity to relate behavior, attitudes, and emotional states to neurological events observable through advanced, technologically-sophisticated devices with relative scientific precision … To that extent … (criminology) can no longer afford to stand apart from the neurosciences if it intends to provide coherent accounts of human behavior, however that behavior may be inflected. (Pallone and Hennessey, 1996: 25)

Therefore, evidence from the neurosciences, heretofore either unavailable to, or ignored by, those engaged in criminological research, especially as this evidence relates to the function of the human central nervous system (CNS) and has been correlated with commission of crimes—both violent and nonviolent—can no longer be pushed aside by serious practitioners in criminal justice and criminology. Neuroscience research, however, can be daunting in its complexity and most research in the field is narrowly confined to specific areas of enquiry. No one individual may be able to grasp all facets of CNS function in detail. Nevertheless, insight into how the human neurological system functions may be garnered from the increasingly large amounts of complex research that has already appeared. Neuroscience is a very large and complex field. This chapter is a discussion of a small but increasingly important area of neuroscience as it inflects on understanding criminal behavior. This work is a look at the relevant research in neuroscience involving the relationship of neurotransmitters to crime.

One of the earliest attempts at an interdisciplinary effort to integrate the biological sciences with the study of criminology and criminal justice occurred in the 1980s. At the time, there were some in the social sciences and in criminal justice studies who clearly recognized that the neurology of the central nervous system (CNS), particularly the functions of the brain that involve cognitive and behavioral aspects, would become increasingly more important in any attempt to understand the genesis of complex human behavior including the commission of crime. This diverse group of academics, including several criminal justice/criminology practitioners, published a work entitled *The Neurotransmitter Revolution: Serotonin, Social Behavior, and the Law* (Masters and McQuire, 1994). Among the contributors to this remarkable and, at the time, innovative approach to the study of the criminal justice system was C. Ray Jeffrey (1994) whose article "The brain, the law, and the medicalization of crime" questioned whether the current criminal justice paradigm, based primarily on retribution and deterrence, was effective in reducing crime in society. "We must shift the emphasis from punishment to treatment and prevention" (Jeffrey, 1994: 174).

Knowledge in neuroscience has progressed and continues to progress at an ever accelerating rate. According to Coyle (1988) "the nearly logarithmic growth in neuroscience research" since the 1960s has yielded a major paradigm shift, producing in the process new methods for understanding the neurological functions of the brain. In addition, the proliferation of data in the field means that it is becoming much more difficult for single individuals to be able to grasp the implications of the varied and complex research findings in neuroscience as this research relates to other academic disciplines—especially as it relates to the "soft sciences" like sociology, psychology, and criminal justice or criminology.

The disciplines of criminal justice and criminology have been for the most part grounded in theory that is sociological in its conception. Until recently, for example, it has been theorized that environmental factors such as marriage appear to be the primary causes of desistance from criminal behavior, especially in early adulthood. The finding that "marriage" was one of the main factors in desistance from criminal offending at or near the onset of adulthood (Sampson and Laub, 1993) appears to have been only part of the story. There is evidence that the adolescent neurological system may play a significant role in addition to that played by the sociological effects of the institution of marriage in the desistance from offending exhibited by many offenders during early adulthood (Beaver et al., 2008; Collins, 2004: 14). This is to say that some individuals may desist from further offending behavior at the onset of adulthood even without the hypothesized benefit of the effects of marriage functioning as an institutional moderator of offending behavior. Apparently, the moderation in behavior may be just as much the result of the effects of normal adolescent neurology during the onset of adulthood. This includes the part played by neurotransmitters in the regulation of behavior including criminal behavior.

It is reasonable to suspect that there exist measurable relationships between the neurological system (CNS) and behavior, and specifically between neurotransmitter function and criminal behavior. A corollary to this view is that neurotransmission (the signaling between neurons), whether normal or pathogenic in nature, is a necessary but insufficient cause of (or inflection on) the perpetration of "criminal" behavior—that is to say, in addition, there must also be one or more environmental stimuli acting on the neurological system in order to generate behavior.

Neurotransmitters: Integral and Complex Components of the Human Neurological System

The human neurological system consists of the brain and the spinal cord. The brain is the highly organized center for the acquisition and integration of information from the environment as well as the arbiter of "appropriate" response(s) to that environment. The basic unit of the brain for information integration and response is a cellular structure called a neuron. Neurons consist of the same basic elements as other cells in higher organisms. Neurons have a nucleus which contains chromosomes and it is in the nucleus where cell transcription occurs (transcription is the process by which deoxyribonucleic acid (DNA) is replicated). The neuron also contains other organelles (in the soma or common cell body) such as mitochondria (home for mitochondrial DNA which is acquired exclusively from the mother of the organism) and the Golgi apparatus which helps in the structuring of the cell plasma membrane. The plasma membrane is not only the outer wall of the neuronal cell but functions as the site where neurological signaling occurs that enables the brain to acquire, evaluate, and act on information received from its environment. The brain consists of about 100 billion neuron cells and "[T]he regulated transmission of chemical and electrical signals through circuits formed by chains of neurons *is the basis of all behavior*. Consequently, to appreciate recent developments in psychiatry (or biosocial criminology), it is necessary to have a basic understanding of the structural and molecular properties that make such intercellular communication possible" (Barondes, 1993: 65, emphasis added).

A Word of Caution

As in most areas of scientific research, "the more we learn about intercellular communication in the nervous system, the more complicated the situation appears.

(In the 1970s researchers) smugly focused on a straight point-to-point transmission, where a presynaptically released transmitter impinged on a postsynaptic cell." What actually occurs is much more complex. Neurotransmitters were found not to act in this linear step-by-step fashion but, rather, to modulate signal transmission. For example, what may be classified as a presynaptic receptor on neuron B may also be a postsynaptic receptor on neuron A that is making an axoaxonic (axon on axon) connection with neuron B. In fact, there exists an extraordinary number of possibilities for altering any given point-to-point synaptic transmission (Cooper et al., 2003: 85–86).

Neurotransmitters are commonly referenced as "excitatory" or "inhibitory," however, in many cases each neurotransmitter may provide both functions. The function of a neurotransmitter is to "activate" one or more types of receptors which should continue the activation in a chain reaction from cell to cell (tens of thousands of times in milliseconds) until another chemical action takes place to stop the chain reaction. But it is important to understand that the effect of neurotransmission, and hence neurotransduction, on the postsynaptic cell is entirely dependent on the type of receptor involved. Glutamate, for example, is considered the most abundant "excitatory" neurotransmitter in the brain. This is not surprising when essentially all of the receptors "activated" by glutamate (GLU) express excitatory effects (promote transduction: i.e., increase the likelihood that the target cell will fire an action potential). In the case of gamma aminobutyric acid (GABA) until very recently, when anomalies in GABA function began appearing, it was believed that all of the receptors express inhibitory functions (halt action potentials and, therefore, transduction). For dopamine, both excitatory and inhibitory receptors exist. Finally, there are complex metabolic pathways in the postsynaptic cell which produce effects that may not properly be defined as either excitatory or inhibitory (von Bohlen and Dermietzel, 2002; Cooper et al., 2003; Zigmond et al., 2003).

The terms "excitatory" and "inhibitory" refer to the function of a neurotransmitter at the molecular level in promoting "transduction" (excitatory function) or in slowing or halting "transduction" (inhibitory function). These terms do not refer to the resultant behavior of an organism observed at the phenotypic level. Therefore, even though DA is associated with aggressive or violent behavior (Fogel et al., 2000: 338 citing Mattes, 1990) it is through its function as an "inhibitor" where it interferes with (metabotropically modulates) signal transduction ongoing or initiated by some other ligand (an ionotropic activity) which may likely be functioning in an "excitatory" manner. For example, DA suppresses "excitatory" signals (generally Glutamatergic in origin) between the pyramidal neurons in the prefrontal cortex— among other functions, the pyramidal neurons in the prefrontal cortex modulate cognition (Gao and Goldman-Rakic, 2003). The net effect of excitatory signals (transduction) may be a calming effect on behavior at the phenotypic level—this is also true of "inhibitory" signals which suppress signal transduction. The point to be made here is that the terms "excitatory" or "inhibitory" refer only to the effect that a ligand has (a ligand is a neurotransmitter such as glutamate (Glu) or gamma aminobutyric acid (GABA) or other molecule—NMDA or cocaine, for example) when it interacts with a receptor to promote or inhibit signal transduction. DA, then, is associated with aggressive behavior because of its "inhibitory" functions which cause dampening effects on signal transduction which, in a reaction initiated by, for example, glutamate (recall that Glu is a major "excitatory" molecule in the prefrontal cortex) may be promoting transduction signaling along a "calming" pathway (Cooper et al., 2003).

Then there is the "classic case" involving something known as "Dale's principle" where learned neuroscientists misinterpreted a restatement of the principle by John Eccles who said that a neuron releases the same transmitter at all of its processes. This was misconstrued to become "one neuron, one transmitter." However, a major conceptual change in neuroscience has been the realization that a single neuron may react with (e.g. secrete from its neuronal vesicles as well as receive at its target receptors) multiple neurotransmitters relatively contemporaneously. "It now appears that few if any neurons contain only one neurotransmitter, and in several cases three or even four transmitters have been found in a single neuron" (Deutch and Roth, 1999 cited in Zigmond et al., 2003: 221). The presence of multiple transmitters in a single neuron may indicate that "different transmitters are used by a neuron to signal different functional states to its target cell. Considerable evidence supports distinct spatial locations of receptors (such as NMDA-type glutamate receptors and certain G-protein-coupled receptors) on a neuron" (2003: 221).

Furthermore, synaptic specializations typically are presumed to be the morphological substrates of communication between two neurons. But it is now evident that nonsynaptic communication exists between neurons. Therefore, to meet the additional challenge of nonsynaptic communication, a single neuron may require more than one neurotransmitter. Because this discussion is meant only as an introduction to neurotransmitters and the roles they may potentially be ascribed in the understanding of their inflection on criminal behavior, the more complex non-linear functions of neurotransduction (referred to as neuromodulation), generally, will not be included in great detail here. The caveat issued, then, is that the observed correlation of a neurotransmitter's part in, and its apparent inflection on, any given behavior be regarded as only part of a very complex biophysiological occurrence. In the complex world of neurotransmitters, then, correlation does not necessarily indicate causation.

The Structure of Neurotransmission: Neurons, Synapses, Receptors, and Neurotransmitters

Neurons (simplified version)

The most important functions of neurons involve receiving, conducting, and storing information through various and quite complex electro-chemical processes. Neurons (nerve cells) are unique biological entities insofar as they are the primary cell structures with the ability to transmit information within a biologically grounded network that supports experience dependent mechanisms for memory storage, learning, consciousness, and response to the environment. In order to perform these tasks neurons are structurally and functionally polarized (inactive). There are three major components of neuron structural differentiation necessary to carry out these complex communication and storage functions: the cell soma (called a perikaryon in nerve cells), the axon, and the dendrite. A neuron's size, shape, and neurochemistry are important determinants of the neuron's functional role in the brain. Neurons are classified into (1) inhibitory GABAergic interneurons that are primarily localized in their signaling, although there are known to exist also many examples of GABA projection neurons; (2) the excitatory spiny stellate cells of the cerebral cortex which also signal locally; and (3) the excitatory glutamatergic efferent neurons ("efferent" neurons carry nerve signals away from the CNS while "afferent" neurons carry the signals toward the CNS (e.g. the cortical pyramidal neurons)). A single neuron may secrete only one type of neurotransmitter or it may secrete several different neurotransmitters. In addition, it is important to note that neurons form circuits which comprise the structural basis for brain function (Zigmond et al., 2003; von Bohlen and Dermietzel, 2002).

While the soma harbors the biosynthetic machinery—the nucleus, ribosomes, the endoplasmic reticulum, and the Golgi apparatus including mitochondria for energy supply—the axon is furnished with molecular and subcellular components for propagation of action potentials away from the cell body. "The axon is perhaps the most familiar functional domain of a neuron and is classically defined as the cellular process by which a neuron makes contact with a target cell to transmit information, providing a conducting structure for transmitting the action potential to a synapse, a specialized subdomain for transmission of a signal from neuron to target cell (which may be another neuron, muscle cell, etc.) most often by release of appropriate neurotransmitters" (Zigmond et al., 2003: 72). Dendrites constitute sets of branched cytoplasmic processes that extend from the cell body and result in enlargement of the soma for signal reception (von Bohlen and Dermietzel, 2002: 1). Most vertebrate neurons have multiple dendrites arising from their perikarya (soma). "Unlike axons, dendrites continuously branch and taper extensively with a reduction in caliber in daughter processes at each branching" (Zigmond et al., 2003: 75). The branched extensions of a dendrite may be contacted by the axons of many different and relatively distant neurons or they may be enervated by a single axon making multiple synaptic contacts. The dendrites are also known as receptors.

Receptors

Receptors are myriad, complex, and are essential macromolecules, along with the neuroactive substances (neurotransmitters, neuropeptides, and neurohormones, etc.), that form the molecular basis for transmission of signals throughout the CNS, and consequently, throughout the brain itself. Receptors are the macromolecules located on the surface of the neuron to which neurotransmitters bind. *Each of the neurotransmitters appears to have several different receptors* to which it may bind (e.g. serotonin has at least 13 and dopamine has five that are currently known). The neurotransmitters are generally referred to as ligands and the process by which neurotransmitters connect to the receptors is called ligand binding. The ligand binding force connecting it to its target molecule is known as its affinity for that molecular binding. This affinity concept has important implications for clinical application of therapeutic intervention in any attempts to alter unwanted behavior at the phenotypic level of an organism by medication. Affinity plays an important role in receptor binding because receptors can bind with molecules called *agonists or antagonists*. An agonist mimics the function of the neurotransmitter that it is replacing by binding with the receptor. An antagonist blocks the function of the neurotransmitter or other ligand that it is replacing when it binds to the receptor (Cooper et al., 2003; von Bohlen and Dermietzel, 2002). In many cases, receptors are named for the ligand with the highest affinity for binding with the receptor (NMDA receptors are named after a chemical that is not even produced in the brain: N-methyl-D-Aspartic acid (NMDA)). The synthetic chemical NMDA has been found useful in studying the effects of glutamate (Glu) deprivation—NMDA blocks the Glu from binding with the receptor (Watkins and Jane, 2006).

Synapses

The junction between the axon site (signal sending site) and the dendrite (signal receiving area) is referred to as the synapse. The physical separation between these two points is called the synaptic cleft. Synapses may be classified as excitatory or inhibitory depending on whether they facilitate signal transduction or retard signal transduction (transduction is defined as the transmission of a signal from the cell exterior into the cell interior). This differentiation is important to keep in mind when consideration is given to how these complex biochemical reactions may be used to understand and possibly alter human behavior, including criminally aggressive behavior. Synapses that facilitate signal transduction through a process called depolarization of the cell membrane are considered to be excitatory; those that retard signal transduction through a diametrically opposite process referred to as hyperpolarization are called inhibitory synapses (von Bohlen and Dermietzel, 2002; Barondes, 1993).

Neurotransmitters I

Neurotransmitters are part of a biochemical classification called neuroactive substances. These substances include (1) neurotransmitters such as dopamine (DA), serotonin (5HT), norepinephrine (NE), gamma-aminobutyric acid (GABA), and glutamate (Glu), among several other amino acid based molecules and (2) neuromodulaters like endorphins, gonadotropin-releasing hormone (GnRH), nitric oxide (NO), and vasopressin as well as a myriad of others (von Bohlen and Dermietzel, 2002). This review will be concerned primarily with the specific classification called neurotransmitters and, hopefully, will illuminate their relationship with criminological theory.

Neurotransmitters have been implicated in aggressive and aberrant behavior (Pallone and Hennessey, 1996; Volavka, 2002: 28–38; Raine, 1993: 81–102). In many cases, the aggressive or aberrant behavior is criminal in nature. For example, serotonin (5HT) irregularities have been linked to arson (Virkkunnen et al., 1987; Virkkunnen et al., 1994) while DA has been linked to illegal drug use—cocaine is a dopamine reuptake blocker (Kaplan and Sadock, 1999: 420)—as well as aggressive illegal behavior such as violent assaults on others (Fogel et al., 2000: 338 citing Mattes, 1990). In addition, dopamine antagonists have been found to reduce aggressiveness—specifically fighting among patients (Eichelman, 1986; Yesavage, 1984) and aggressiveness among adolescents (Molling et al., 1962) and aggressive behavior in general decreases when dopamine levels are reduced (Yudofsky et al., 1987). Furthermore, neurotransmitters have been associated with the generally reported age-related impulsive/aggressive behaviors by both males and females during adolescence (Collins, 2004). Biosynthesis of several of the neurotransmitters, including GABA, 5HT, DA, and NE, as well as other neuromodulators such as the neurohormone GnRH (gonadotropin releasing hormone which is responsible for the synthesis and release of testosterone) apparently correlates well with the widely reported and well documented phenomenon referred to as the "age-crime curve" where adolescent impulsive and aggressive behavior is linked to an increase in crime by those between 10 and 18 or 19 years of age. This aggressive behavior begins to decline from its peak activity at around the age of 18 or 19 years and continues its decline through early adulthood and later (Hirschi and Gottfredson, 1983; Glueck and Glueck, 1943; Collins, 2004).

Neurotransmitters are implicated in all behavioral functions, and they are the main biochemical messengers at the molecular level integral to interpreting and responding to outside stimuli by assessing the nature of the stimuli and, finally, in conducting signals necessary for an organism to integrate stored data (memory) necessary for response to the initial stimuli. Neurotransmitters are extremely complex in their organization and in their action on human behavior. This review shall attempt to provide a simplified understanding of the highly complex nature of the role neurotransmitters have been accorded relative to criminal behavior.

Neurotransmission's Five Steps: Synthesis, Storage, Release, Receptor Binding, and Inactivation (Simple Version)

The biosynthesis of a neurotransmitter takes place in the nerve cell (neuron). Therefore all of the chemical precursors of the neurotransmitter and the necessary enzymes that facilitate the synthesis of the neurotransmitter must be present in an active form in order for the process to occur. Storage of the neurotransmitter and its precursor, or both, is in the presynaptic nerve terminal. The release of the neurotransmitter into the synaptic cleft includes fusion of the transmitter containing vesicle with the cellular membrane which enables exocytosis (exit from the cell to synaptic and/or nonsynaptic connections) of the neurotransmitter. Released neurotransmitters (ligands) into the synaptic cleft interact (bind) with receptors on the postsynaptic (target) cell. Target receptors are membrane proteins that are coupled to intracellular proteins that transduce the signal to the cell interior where alteration of the intracellular process takes place. The receptors may be proteins that form ion channels (ionotropic receptors) that alter cell polarization or they may be metabotropic receptors utilizing the more latent onset G protein-coupled signaling generally found in transduction inhibition. Inactivation of the neurotransmission signal process occurs by (1) reuptake of the neurotransmitter into the original vesicles that released it which is aided through specific neuronal transporter proteins (e.g. 5HT/SERT and DA/DAT) on the presynaptic neuron or by (2) inactivation by enzymatic conversion (enzymatic degradation) by an enzyme such as monoamine oxidase (MAO) which, for example, degrades serotonin and dopamine, and other neurotransmitters (Zigmond et al., 2003). MAO exists in two forms: (1) MAOA which is generally nonspecific in its selection of which of the neurotransmitters it will degrade and (2) MAOB which generally degrades dopamine only (Cooper et al., 2003: 194–195; von Bohlen and Dermietzel, 2002).

Neurotransmitters II: Biogenic Amines and Amino Acids

The two major *amino acid* based neurotransmitters are glutamate and gamma-aminobutyric acid (GABA). GABA is an inhibitory amino acid (inhibits signal transduction) and glutamate is an excitatory amino aid (promotes signal transduction). These two amino acid based neurotransmitters are present in disproportionately high concentrations in the brain. "It is occasionally suggested that a simplified way to look at the brain is as a balance just between these two neurotransmitters, with all the biogenic amine … neurotransmitters simply involved in modulating that balance" (Kaplan and Sadock, 1999: 107). One of the most important features of the amino acid neurotransmitters is that the benzodiazepines, barbiturates, and several anticonvulsants act primarily through GABAergic mechanisms (as does alcohol) and that an important substance of abuse, phencyclidine (PCP) also known by the "street" name "angel dust," acts at glutamate receptors. One of the most active areas of neuroscience research involves the role of N-methyl-D-aspartate (NMDA) glutamate receptors in learning and memory (Kaplan and Sadock, 1999; Redburn and Schousboe, 1987). NMDA receptors are found primarily in the frontal cortex and are ionotropic.

The biogenic amines, DA and 5HT (among several others), are probably the best known neurotransmitters among criminologists and criminal justice practitioners. The biogenic amines are classified according to their molecular structure into indoleamines such as serotonin (5HT) which has an indole group (benzene ring fused to a five-sided nitrogen containing pyrrole ring—thus the name 5HT). The biosynthesis of serotonin is basically similar to the other biogenic amines, the catecholamines such as dopamine (DA) and norepinephrine (NE) that get their classification name from their molecular structures which also are based on a benzene ring with two hydroxyl groups (OH) attached to the benzene ring forming a catechol group—hence the name catecholamine. In both cases, indoleamines and catecholamines, the amine structure comes from the molecular makeup of the amino acid on which it is based: tryptophan for 5 Hydroxytryptamine (serotonin) and phenylalanine/tyrosine for dopamine (DA). Dopamine also serves as the precursor molecule for norepinephrine which in turn is the precursor for epinephrine (adrenaline) (Zigmond et al., 2003 citing Moore and Bloom, 1978) (also see: von Bohlen and Dermietzel, 2002; Kaplan and Sadock, 1999; Fogel et al., 2000).

Serotonin

Serotonin (5HT) is the probably first neuroactive substance to come to the attention of psychologists, sociologists, and criminologists during the 1980s. This occurred when the Gruter Institute for Law and Behavioral Research in conjunction with Dartmouth College's Rockefeller Center for the Social Sciences held a conference in November 1988 in order to confront academics in the social sciences with what Niko Tinbergen referred to as the onset of the "biological study of behavior" (Masters and McQuire, 1994: xi).

Serotonin is formed within the body but its essential precursor, tryptophan (an essential amino acid and a molecular building block for proteins without which life could not exist as we know it), is not. As a result, tryptophan must be supplied by the diet where roughly only 1 percent of dietary tryptophan is converted to serotonin. The presence in the neuron of tryptophan hydroxylase is the determinate for whether or not it is a serotonergic neuron rather than a cholinergic neuron (a neuron may be home for several neurotransmitters but is classified according to the primary neurotransmitter in the neuron). Serotonin is degraded by monoamine oxidase (MAOA) within the neuron leaving behind the metabolite 5-hydroxyindolic acid (5HIAA) of which the presence in lowered amounts in the cerebral spinal fluid (CSF) has been linked to violent recidivism and arson in males (Virkkunnen et al., 1987). In the central nervous system (CNS) serotonin (5HT) can be found in nearly every brain area. "A relatively high density of serotoninergic projections occurs in the *cerebral cortex, the hippocampus, the amygdala*" (von Bohlen and Dermietzel, 2002: 107, emphasis added) as well as in the areas involved in sight and motor movement.

Serotonin has at least seven separate types of receptors: 5HT1 through 5HT7 and each of these has several subtypes (e.g. 5HT1A, 1B, 1D, 1E, 1F, 1P, and 1S) classified by their location and function in the firing rate of serotonergic fibers. While most biogenic amines have been studied initially through their function in the Na (Sodium) and Cl (Chlorine) polarization/hyperpolarizaion ionotropic channels, more recently the 5HT1 receptors have been found to function primarily through G_i/G_0 protein-coupled metabotropic mediation which opens the potassium (K) channels or the closes the Calcium (Ca) channels—it is generally a slower and more complex process that is apparently part of the inhibition of transduction (i.e. slows or stops the excitatory signaling). The 5HT1 (serotonin) receptors are generally autoreceptors which control the autonomic nervous system as well as mediate responses to environmental stimuli involved in the expression of anxiety and the "fight or flight" response (von Bohlen and Dermietzel, 2002).

5HT7 receptors are concentrated in layers 1–3 of the cortex, as well as in neurons of the septum, the hippocampus, the thalamus, the hypothalamus, the centromedial amygdala, the periaquaductal gray area, which innervates the defense response and evaluates pain (nociception), and in the neurons of the superior collicus which controls and coordinates through visual stimuli the motor action of defense response (von Bohlen and Dermietzel, 2002: 111–112). The 5HT7 receptors are of the metabotropic G protein-coupled slow acting type.

5HT2 receptors mediate slow excitatory effects through the decrease in potassium (K) conductance of the metatropic G protein-coupled type (Zigmond et al., 2003: 269–286). They are found active in the cerebral cortex, the hippocampus, and evidence suggests that the 5HT2 receptors (in concert with 5HT1 receptors) are involved in the secretion of corticotropin-releasing factors. Corticotropin-releasing factors (CRF) are major hypothalamic neurotropic molecular responses involved in regulating the control of stress. This is especially true of the stress/anxiety associated with addiction withdrawal from opiates, cocaine, and alcohol.

5HT3 receptors are the only serotonergic receptors that function as ionotropic ligand gated ion channel (Na & Cl) quick acting receptors in contrast to the latent onset for the G protein-coupled types of serotonergic receptors 5HT1, 5HT2, 5HT4, 5HT5, 5HT6, and 5HT7. Although, recent electro-physiological observation has implicated 5HT3 type receptors in the prefrontal cortex in a slow depression of cell firing that might indicate the presence of 5HT3 receptors functioning in a metabotropic profile (Cooper et al., 2003: 295). The 5HT3 receptors are found only on neurons (unlike the other 5HT receptors which are also located on glial cells and muscle cells). This means that the only function of 5HT3 receptors is to depolarize the neuron (promote transduction through a previously hyperpolarized [closed] neuron) through the quick acting ionotropic ligand gated Na/Cl channel which causes an excitatory response in the neuron and in every neuron along a chain. The excitatory actions through the 5HT3 receptors stop when serotonin is returned to its releasing vesicles via a serotonin reuptake transporter (SERT) and by the action of monoamine oxidase (MAOA) which degrades the 5HT into the metabolites 5 hydroxyindole acetic acid (5HIAA), or 5 hydroxytrypophol, thus inhibiting the ongoing excitatory action. The primary metabolic (catabolic breakdown) action for serotonin is oxidative deamination by MAOA (von Bohlen and Dermietzel, 2002; Zigmond et al., 2003).

5HT4 receptors are metabotropic and involve only the intracellular increase of cAMP (cyclic adenosine monophosphate) which is an important secondary messenger involved in G protein-coupled inhibitory actions on adrenaline (epinephrine) which is responsible for the hyperpolarization of the neuron through the Beta-adrenoceptors. In other words, the 5HT4 receptors have as their only responsibility the inhibition of the role of adrenaline (epinephrine) when it is acting as an excitatory neurotransmitter in the brain. It should be noted that adrenaline may also function in an inhibitory role (through the alpha adrenergic receptors). 5HT5 receptors (5HT5A and B) are both metabotropic, G protein-coupled, latent onset receptors involved with adenylate cyclase cycles which regulate immune responses. The 5HT6 receptors are also metabotropic and are related to the adenylyl cyclase (same as adenylate cyclase) cycle (conversion of ATP to cAMP) which is responsible for a myriad of behavioral aspects of brain function. 5HT6 mRNA has been found in the cortex, the amygdala, the hippocampus, and the nucleus accumbens. These areas of the brain are responsible for judgment, reward, laughter, addiction, fear, and pleasure.

Because of its receptor diversity, serotonin mediates behavioral functions through many different pathways. Though serotonin has been linked to various dysfunctional, aggressive, and abnormal behaviors, some of which may be termed criminal, it must be understood that the links to such behavioral dysfunctions are complex. Serotonin is, for instance, sexually dimorphic. At least two receptors, 5HT1A and 5HT2A, differ between males and females. For example, the 5HT1A receptor shows a different expression in the mRNA of male and female rats (von Bohlen and Dermietzel, 2002 citing Zhang et al., 1999). Another example of the complexity of interaction between neurotransmitters of the same type (5HT) is illustrated by the finding that activation of the 5HT2A and 5HT2C receptors counteracts the 5HT1A regulation of NMDA (glutamate/excitatory) channels in pyramidal neurons of the prefrontal cortex (Yuen et al., 2008).

It may be instructive to recall here that the pyramidal (prefrontal cortex) neurons are responsible for cognition (Gao and Goldman-Rakic, 2003) and are "excited" into "transduction" by glutamate through NMDA receptors which are "ionotropic" quick acting ligand gated channels which "depolarize" the receptor and set in motion a chain reaction that innervates human cognition. For example, an organism starts thinking about reacting to a stimulus at the phenotypic level—e.g. you have just had the Jack of Spades come up in the "flop" of a "Texas hold 'em" game that goes very well with your two Jacks (Hearts and Diamonds) that you have as your "hole" cards that were originally dealt to you. There remain two cards to be dealt for the common use by you and the five other players at the table. They are the fourth card, aka the "turn" card and then, on a separate round of wagering, the final, fifth card, aka the "river" card. Let's say that the other two "common" cards dealt with your "third" Jack (of Spades) on the "flop" are the Ace of Spades and the ten of Spades. Dopamine will kick in here to modulate the Glu receptors that will be telling you to "bet" on the three Jacks. Glutamate will be telling you to bet fairly aggressively while dopamine will be modulating that decision through the slower metabotropic "G" protein coupled "inhibitory" response. You may make a large bet before the metabotropic DA affects the ionotropic Glu functioning NMDA receptors. But, there is more to it than DA and Glu. 5HT1A receptors are also activated by the sudden Glu depolarization of the NMDA receptors (recall that Glu/NMDA is "excitatory," aka transduction via the NA/CL ionotropic channels and the 5HT1A reaction is metabotropic through the latent onset "G" protein coupled action). The DA and 5HT1A receptors will not abruptly halt the Glu/ NMDA action but will "modulate" that action by slowing it down through partial inhibition of the NMDA receptors—receptors (dendrites) generally can, and do, handle more than one type of neurotransmitter concurrently.

In addition to the Glu/DA/5HT1A complexity of signaling it turns out that 5HT2A/C (also metabotropic) receptors "counteract" the 5HT1A receptors' attempts to "inhibit" the Glu/NMDA "excitatory" activity when these 5HT2A/C receptors are stimulated by an outside chemical (alcohol?, cocaine?) (Yuen et al., 2008). So, the "turn" card and the "river" cards are dealt and either one will be the Jack of Clubs. The question is: while your brain was being "excited" by the Glu/ NMDA stimulation in your prefrontal cortex, the human organism's seat of reason and judgment, upon seeing that you had an "unbeatable" hand of four Jacks, did the "inhibition" by modulation through metabotropic DA and 5HT1A calm you down enough after the "flop," and "turn," and "river" cards were played, so that you were able to note that if someone had a Queen and King of Spades as their "hole" cards you had just gotten a "Bad Beat" by a Royal Flush (ten, Jack, Queen, King, Ace of Spades—the highest hand in poker—better than your four Jacks). Maybe if you had enough cocaine or alcohol in your brain to kick in the 5HT2A/C receptors, you may not have seen the possibility of losing in this way.

Getting back to bland theory, it has also been reported that serotonin dysfunction has been implicated in violent and aggressive behavior (Asberg et al., 1976; Blumensohn et al., 1995; Virkkunnen, 1982; Virkkunnen et al., 1987; Vikkunnen and Linnoila, 1993; Fogel et al., 2000: 338). Ramboz et al. (1999) report that 5HT1B receptors knock out mice "when confronted with an intruder … attacked the intruder faster and more intensely than wild-type mice, suggesting an involvement of 5HT1B receptors in the modulation of violent behavior." Saudou et al. (1994) found in their research "enhanced aggressive behavior in mice lacking the 5HT1B receptor."

In a study of the effects of one of two alleles of the 5HTT (serotonin transporter) gene, Beaver et al. (2008) report that a 5HTT 484 base pair allele had a statistically significant negative effect on delinquent involvement. Serotonin transporters are responsible for the reuptake of 5HT into the presynaptic terminals as one of the mechanisms for ending signal transduction. In fact, serotonin specific reuptake inhibiters (SSRIs: Prozac, Zoloft, and Paxil) have been used to control borderline personality disorder, attention deficit/hyperactivity disorder, obsessional jealousy, self-injurious behavior, and aggression in schizophrenia (Kaplan and Sadock, 1999: 1087).

Enzymatic degradation of 5HT by MAOA is the other, and primary, mechanism for halting signal transduction by 5HT. Monoamine oxidase inhibiters (MAOIs) include: Parnate and Nardil which inhibit MAOA and selegiline, which is a MAOB specific inhibiter at doses of 20mg or less, increase biogenic amine neurotransmitter levels by inhibiting their degradation. MAOIs have been used to address post traumatic stress disorder (PTSD), social phobias, anxiety, and severe depression (Kaplan and Sadock, 1999: 1061–1062). Holmes et al. (2002) reports that dysregulation of the serotonin transporter (5HTT) has been implicated in the pathophysiology of violence and aggression. "Desensitization of 5HT(1A/1B) receptor function may contribute to reduced aggression in 5HTT KO mice" (2002:

160). This finding has been supported by the report by Naumenko et al. (2009) that the 5HTT is involved in the regulation of genetically determined fear-induced aggression in mice.

Research that has looked at other aspects of serotonin's potential involvement in antisocial behavior includes studies that reported the "low expressing" genotype variants of a 5HTTLPR polymorphism were associated with reduced reuptake activity (Lesch et al., 1996), ADHD and CD (Cadoret et al., 2003), nicotine dependence (Munafo et al., 2005), childhood aggression (Beitchman et al., 2006 and Haberstick et al., 2006), and that the short allele was more likely to be found present in violent offenders (Retz et al., 2004), and in those involved in extreme violence (Liao et al., 2004). Sysoeva et al. (2009) also report in a study designed to look at the possible modulation effect of a 5HTT polymorphism among female sport swimmers that those with the polymorphism exhibited "higher resistance to stress factors." In a discussion of research efforts in the molecular genetics of neurotransmitters, Beaver (2009) cites a report by Reif et al. (2007) that a short allele polymorphism of the 5-HTTTLPR gene when tested for a genetic interaction with the environment (G x E) "was only associated with violence for individuals exposed to a criminogenic home environment during childhood" (2009: 67). Other research that has implicated serotonin in the modulation of aggressive as well as violent behavior includes: Blumensohn et al. (1995) where violent juvenile delinquents were reported to have decreased platelet 5HT2 binding and Fogel et al. (2000: 338) who reported that lowered levels of CSF 5-HIAA have been found in interpersonally violent individuals such as arsonists and individuals adjudicated guilty of impulsive manslaughter while Lidberg and associates (1985) reported a relationship between homicide and suicide and lowered levels of CSF 5-HIAA. The evidence has clearly implicated low levels of serotonin in impulsive and violent, aggressive behavior.

"[M]ost studies report increases of serotonin with age. According to Rogers and Bloom (1985: 657), the most consistent change observed in 5-HT metabolism is an age dependent increase in 5-HIAA." It should be noted, however, that as primates become aged well into their senior years, serotonin begins to decline in the occipital cortex (Beal, 1993: 707) and this may partially explain the agitation and sometimes violent behavior exhibited by the elderly, especially those diagnosed as having Alzheimer's disease (AD).

Beaver (2009: 66) has clearly articulated the basics of serotonergic function in the CNS where he notes: "Serotonin is a neurotransmitter with inhibitory properties that modulates behaviors and serves as the body's natural brake system. When serotonin is released … neuronal activity is reduced and … aggressive tendencies and primitive impulses are dampened" (Beaver, 2009: 66 citing Clarke et al., 1999; Lidberg et al., 1985; Moore et al., 2002). In a neurologically linear world that is how it should work. Neuroactivity is more complex than that, however.

A Second Word of Caution

Beaver (2009: 68) notes that "The second enzymatic degradation polymorphism associated with antisocial phenotypes is the monoamine oxidase A (MAOA) gene … *Since the low activity alleles are not as efficient as the high activity alleles at metabolizing neurotransmitters, researchers have hypothesized that the low activity alleles are the risk alleles for the antisocial phenotypes*" (emphasis added). Beaver continues, "Studies examining the effects of MAOA on criminal behaviors have *provided inconclusive results, with some studies showing no main effect* (Caspi et al., 2002; Haberstick et al., 2005) *and others revealing that the low functioning allele is associated with low levels of aggression*" (emphasis added) (e.g. Manuck et al., 2000). There is reason for caution when testing for effects of MAOA as a predictor of antisocial behaviors.

MAOA preferentially deaminates (degrades) serotonin, norepinephrine, epinephrine, and dopamine. Dopamine is also degraded by MAOB. Serotonin serves the function of dampening excitatory behavior (primarily through its functions metabotropically: 5HT1, 5HT2, 5HT4, and 5HT5—recall that the 5HT3 receptors are ionotropic). Monoamine oxidase A (MAOA) degrades serotonin, causing it to cease its function as an inhibitory neurotransmitter. By this logic, the inefficient low level allele polymorphism of MAOA should not effectively short circuit, by enzymatic degradation, the hypothesized dampening effect that serotonin has on aggressive behavior.

It should not be surprising then if it is found that the results of testing either version of the MAOA allele (the low activity allele or the normal allele) for gene interaction(s) with environmental stimuli (G x E) are inconclusive in helping to point out the precise neurological mechanism causing the behavior. Is it the result of failure in the inhibitory action of serotonin or is it the result of failure of the enzymatic breakdown of excitatory mechanisms? Complicating the research is the fact that regardless of which allele is designated the "risk" allele, either the low level (inefficient) version or the more active (efficient) version, the polymorphism that is tested should, in theory, have some effect on the metabolism of at least four neurotransmitters: serotonin, epinephrine, norepinephrine, and dopamine. Serotonin (5HT) is, for the most part, inhibitory in its effect on neuroactivity. Epinephrine (E) may be either excitatory or inhibitory (E adrenaline alpha-adrenergic neuroactivity is inhibitory and E Beta-adrenoceptor neuroactivity is excitatory). Norepinephrine (NE) also may be either excitatory or inhibitory in its function as a neurotransmitter, while dopamine (DA) is now considered to be for the most part inhibitory (though not exclusively) in function and there is some question whether the dominant qualitative response to dopamine is excitatory or inhibitory. For example, the effects on the properties of caudate neurons by dopaminergic action ranges from excitation to inhibition with noticed variations in time of action onset. "Unambiguous pharmacological and electrophysiological analyses of the dopamine pathway thus remain to be accomplished" (Cooper et al., 2003: 228 citing Grenhoff and Johnson, 1995). Furthermore, 5HT, E, NE, and DA, through their respective sub-classifications of receptors, may all be related to some aspect of aggressive, violent, or delinquent behavior.

Even if there is found to be some effect at the behavioral level (e.g., Manuck et al.'s (2000) finding that a small number of delinquents (12 percent) were correlated with 44 percent of the convictions for violence), it is understandable why the results of such a (G x E) effect still might not be clear or "conclusive" as to the precise neurobiological mechanism involved. Manuck et al. (2000) found the defective low activity MAOA allele to be associated with "low levels of aggression." Even if Manuck et al. (2000) are correct, the following uncertainties remain: (1) the MAOA "risk" allele may not be dampening the inhibitory properties of serotonin or (2) the designated "risk" allele is effectively degrading the catecholamines E, NE, and DA and therein dampening the subsequent excitatory effects, if any, of DA, NE, and E or (3) the "risk" allele *is* dampening the inhibitory properties of serotonin but not (4) affecting the properties (inhibitory or excitatory) of the catecholamines E, NE, and DA. In other words, even if a statistically significant correlation is found between the "risk" allele, the environment, and subsequent behavior it would be difficult to determine what precise causal relationship exists between the effect and the complex neurology. What interaction between the allele and the neurology is causal?

Dopamine and the Adrenergics: Epinephrine (E) and Norepinephrine (NE)

Dopamine (DA), norepinephrine (NE), and epinephrine (E) share the same biosynthesis. Dopamine is one oxygen atom short of the molecular form for norepinephrine. Epinephrine is more complex than either DA or NE as epinephrine contains a CH_3 molecule attached to the nitrogen atom from the split NH_2 molecule shared by DA and NE molecular structures. These three neurotransmitters are referred to as catecholamines.

Dopamine receptors belong to the metabotropic class of neurotransmission and they are designated as D1 through D5. There are two functional groups of DA receptors which include the D1 and D2 groups. The D1 group consists of the D1 and D5 receptors which are linked to the adenylate cyclase cycle wherein its main function is to stimulate the formulation of cAMP by activating the stimulatory G protein, Gs. The D2 group consists of the D2, D3, and D4 receptors each of which exists in different isoforms (proteins that have the same function as other proteins but which are encoded by different genes and therefore may differ in their DNA sequence). The D2 receptor class (including D3 and D4) inhibits the formation of cAMP by activating the inhibitory G protein, Gi. A high correlation has been found between high levels of emotional detachment and low levels of D2 receptors, while the converse was found to be true of the existence of high densities of D2 receptors and strong feelings of attachment (Kaplan and Sadock, 1999; Cooper et al., 2003; von Bohlen and Dermietzel, 2002).

D1 receptors are located primarily in the forebrain where they are expressed in declining concentrations in the following order: the striatum; the amygdala; the thalamus; the mesencephalon; the hypothalamus; and the hindbrain. D1 receptors have not been located on adult dopaminergic neurons. D1 receptors are G protein-coupled and stimulate activity of adenylate cyclase as do the D5 receptors (von Bohlen and Dermietzel, 2002). D2 receptors are widely distributed throughout the brain in the following decreasing levels of concentration: the striatum; the mesencephalon; the spinal cord; the hypothalamus; and the hippocampus. These receptors appear in two isoforms which are termed D2L (long) and D2S (short) or more commonly D2A and D2B. In contrast to D1 receptors, both D2 isoforms inhibit adenylate cyclase activity (2002).

Dopamine is found in virtually all parts of the brain and it is involved in the modulation of brain functions such as cognition, learning, and anxiety related behavior. Dysfunction in the dopaminergic transmission will influence a variety of neurological and psychiatric disorders. Some dysfunctions may lead to hyperactiviy of the dopaminergic system which in turn results in an accumulation of dopamine in the synaptic cleft (this is precisely what cocaine does because cocaine has a greater affinity for dopamine receptors than does the neurotransmitter dopamine itself). This results in a blocking of the reuptake of dopamine from the synaptic cleft via the DAT (dopamine transporter). In their 2008 research on the DAT1 gene, Beaver and associates report an effect on the behavior of those individuals possessing the 10R allele of that gene. Beaver's findings correlate with the findings of previous research (Gill et al., 1997; Rowe et al., 1998, 2001; Comings et al., 2001; Guo et al., 2007). The earlier studies have reported that the 10R allele of the DAT1 gene has been implicated in a number of maladaptive disorders. What precise relationship exists between the DAT1 10R allele and the observed maladaptive behavior in terms of causative biological mechanisms responsible for the observed disorders has not yet been articulated. Nevertheless, it is clear that the DAT10R allele is associated with dysfunctional behaviors.

The D2 receptor has also been implicated in antisocial behaviors. The gene DRD2 (dopamine receptor D2) which is located on chromosome 11 has a SNP (single nucleotide polymorphism) that results in the synthesis of two alleles, one of which (A1) produces fewer receptors (Beaver et al., 2008 citing Berman and Noble, 1995; Noble et al., 1991) as well as decreased binding (Thompson et al., 1997) and reduced brain glucose metabolism (Noble et al., 1997). The D2A1 and D2A2 alleles should not be confused with the different D2A and D2B isoforms of the receptor, however. The D4 receptor has also been identified as a risk marker. A seven repeat sequence of a 48 base pair allele has been reported to be the risk identifier for several different antisocial phenotypes which include ADHD (Faraone et al., 2001), pathological gambling (Comings et al., 2001), and novelty seeking (Noble et al., 1998). Beaver et al. (2008) have questioned whether the studies by Rowe et al. (2001) and Bakermans-Kranenberg and van Hzendoorn (2006) may ultimately point to early age conduct disorder (CD) being a precursor to adolescent and adulthood criminal behaviors as a result of certain D4 receptor alleles and a posited genetic interaction with the environment (G x E).

"Generally, cholinergic and catecholaminergic mechanisms seem to be involved in the induction and enhancement of predatory aggression, whereas serotonergic and gamma-aminobutyric acid mechanisms seem to inhibit such behavior" (Kaplan and Sadock, 1999: 158). Dopamine induces aggressive behavior in rodents and humans through both excitatory and inhibitory action on the target neurons. "Apomorphine, a potent dopamine agonist, can induce fighting in rats. Dopamine antagonists tend to reduce aggression but usually at doses that also slow motor and cognitive performance" (Fogel et al., 2000: 338). Norepinephrine, like dopamine, is associated with aggressive behaviors. "Peripherally administered norepinephrine enhances shock induced fighting in rats. Alpha2-receptor agonists (Alpha2-receptors and Beta-receptors are linked to cyclic AMP [adenosine monophosphate] controlled axons which permit or inhibit passage of the catecholamines from the synaptic cleft to the cell) increase rat aggressive behavior, whereas clonidine (a catecholamine antagonist) decreases rodent aggressive behavior acutely" (Fogel et al., 2000: 338).

It should also be noted that since NE shares with DA several biosynthesis pathways, many of the age-related changes common to the DA system are reflected in the metabolism of NE. For example, NE decline was found in several human post mortem studies (Spokes, 1979; Carlsson et al., 1980; Rogers and Bloom, 1985: 654–655) and age-related decline in NE was observed in studies by Austin et al. (1978) and Ida et al. (1982) in rat hypothalamus. These age-related declines in NE, interestingly, correlate with the decline of aggressive personality traits as well as aggressive and impulsive behaviors exhibited by adolescents as they reach adulthood (Collins, 2004).

The adrenergics, NE and E, are primarily responsible for alertness and arousal. NE is released when physiological changes are activated by a stressful event. Some evidence exists that NE is also involved in the "reward" system which is primarily the domain of dopamine. The major concentrations of adrenergic receptors are found in the amygdala, the cingulated gyrus, the hippocampus, the hypothalamus, and the neocortex. Adrenergic receptors are divided into two separate classes: alpha receptors and Beta receptors. These receptors are further differentiated into alpha1, alpha2 and Beta1, Beta2 subtypes. NE is degraded by MAOA and its reuptake is through the NET (norepinephrine transporter). There is no known transporter reuptake mechanism for E which is also degraded by MAOA. "Understanding concerning the function of E-containing neurons in the brain is still very limited, but based on the distribution of E in specific brain regions, attention has been directed to their possible role in neuroendocrine mechanisms and blood pressure control" (Cooper et al., 2003: 212).

Glutamate (Glutamic Acid) (Glu)

Glutamate (Glu) is the primary excitatory neurotransmitter in the mammalian brain (taken as a complete function the neurotransmitter glutamate, its synapses, and its receptors are primarily geared toward excitatory action in the target neuron—i.e. together they promote signal transduction which, if not interdicted or otherwise modulated, causes a cascade of signaling that results in promoting, or otherwise altering, mammalian behavior). But, as recent research has reported, there are several unexpected exceptions to the heretofore commonly accepted assumption of a strictly followed glutamate/GABA paradigm as an excitatory/inhibitory neurotransmitter system in the mammalian brain. These exceptions shall be discussed after a familiarity with the properties and functions of each of the neurotransmitters GABA and glutamate has been established.

Glutamate is synthesized in the nerve terminals via (1) the Krebs cycle and (2) the glial cells from where it is transported into the nerve cells. Released glutamate is restored to the presynaptic terminals (vesicles) through reuptake. Currently, there are four known excitatory amino acid transporters (EAATs): EAAT1, EAAT2, EAAT3, and EAAT1-4. The transporters are essential to halting the excitatory signal and they lower the extracellular glutamate levels below those that can lead to excitotoxicity—which, for example, is the cause of amyotrophic lateral schlerosis (ALS or "Lou Gherig's Disease"). "There does not appear to be any significant role for enzymatic inactivation of Glu similar to that observed with GABA and the other classical [sic] neurotransmitters" (Cooper et al., 2003: 137). The receptors for glutamate are both ionotropic (13 different receptors of NMDA, AMPA, and kainite [KA]) and metabotropic (7 different receptors entitled mGluR1 through 5, 7, and 8).

One specific subtype of EAA receptor, the (ionotropic) NMDA receptor, has become a major focus of attention because of evidence that it may be involved in a wide range of both neurophysiological and pathological processes as important and diverse as memory acquisition, developmental plasticity, and epilepsy which has been associated with violent offenses such as homicide (Tebartz van Elst et al., 2000; Sumer et al., 2007) as well as with the neurotoxic effects of brain ischemia (inadequate blood supply—e.g., a blocked artery) (Cooper et al., 2003: 139). The Glu-NMDA receptor is one of the most complex examples of multiple use receptors since the demise of the "one receptor, one transmitter" only paradigm. The Glu—NMDA receptor not only binds with glutamate, but with several other ligands including (1) glysine (Gly), (2) phencyclidine (PCP), (3) a strychnine-sensitive Gly-inhibitory site, (4) a voltage-dependent Mg^{2+}-binding site, (5) an inhibitory divalent cation site which binds Zn^{2+}, and (6) a polyamine-regulatory site that facilitates NMDA receptor-mediated transmission (Cooper et al., 2003: 141). "Considerable experimental evidence indicates that the (metabotropic) mGluRs are involved in the regulation of synaptic transmission in the CNS" (2003: 145). The receptor mGluR5 is an essential factor in cocaine self-administration and may be a place to look for new treatments in addictive disorders (2003: 145).

Cocaine blocks the reuptake of dopamine because cocaine has a greater affinity for dopamine receptors through its affinity for binding to the DAT (dopamine transporter). When the DA receptor or DAT transporter is missing (as in genetic knockout experiments) the cocaine still remains addictive because a second pathway to reward exists through the 5HTT (serotonin transporter). When the mGluR5 receptor is missing (knocked out) or blocked by an antagonist such as 2-methyl-6(phenylethynyl)-pyridine, however, the reinforcement properties (reward?) involved in cocaine self-administration are noticeably absent (Chiamulera et al., 2001). These findings clearly point to glutamate as more involved as a neurotransmitter in modulating the role of dopamine in cocaine addiction.

In research that looked at the associations between sensation seeking personality scores and absolute glutamate concentrations in the ACC (anterior cingulated cortex) as well as in the hippocampal region, which was done by 3-Tesla proton magnetic resonance spectroscopy (1H-MRS), there were found to be correlations (albeit, not necessarily causal relationships) between cerebral glutamate concentrations and human behavior. Those subjects with the higher concentrations of glutamate were more likely to be among those classified as sensation seekers through the resultant scores on personality inventories (Gallinat et al., 2007).

"It is surprising that more is not known about a specific role of glutamate in aggressive behavior. The (recent research) data suggest that glutamate is important for the genesis of defensive reactions, but the contribution of glutamate to species-typical and escalated offensive aggressive behaviors awaits detailed ethopharmacological studies" (Miczek and Fish, 2006: 131). Glutamate's role may be in modifying escalated, rather than basal, levels of excitation. Therefore, its "most dramatic role in aggression may actually occur in laying down the consequences of aggression that promote its future occurrence" (2006: 131).

Gamma-aminobutyric Acid (GABA)

Gamma-aminobutyric acid is the most important and ubiquitous inhibitory neurotransmitter in the mammalian brain. GABA is synthesized from glutamate (Glu) which is the most powerful excitatory neurotransmitter in the mammalian brain. GABA is formed from glutamate by a process known as decarboxylation via the enzyme L-glutamic acid decarboxylase and pyridoxal phosphate (vitamin B6). After it has been synthesized, GABA is stored in the neuronal vesicles in the presynaptic terminals from where it is released into the synaptic cleft. GABA is removed from the synaptic cleft by (1) enzymatic degradation via GABA-T (GABA-a-oxoglutarate transaminase), and (2) reuptake via several types of transporters (GATs) (Cooper et al., 2003).

In vertebrates there are two types of receptors: GABA A which is ionotropic and GABA B which is metabotropic (there exists a third type of GABA receptor, GABA C, but it seems to be limited in scope to retinal functions). GABA A receptors are the major inhibitory neurotransmitter receptors in the brain and are the focal points of many clinically important medications. GABA is very much involved in mediating aggressive behaviors. In "killer" (genetically altered for the purpose of aggression) rats and in mice that develop aggressive behavior when placed in an environment of psychosocial isolation, GABA concentrations have been found to be significantly lower in the olfactory bulb region of the brain than in those animals that do not develop an aggressive personality after the environmental stimulus of social and psychological isolation. The use by corrections officials, for example, of isolation units variously referred to as SHUs (segregated housing units) or Ad Seg (administrative segregation), or the "hole" would probably be counter-productive in the case of someone with this neurological anomaly (lowered GABA levels in the brain), thereby actually creating worse behavior on the part of those being disciplined (through "negative reinforcement"—isolation). "[I]t appears that a lack of GABA-mediated inhibition in the olfactory bubs is one of the fundamental correlates of aggressive behavior" (Seiler and Lajtha, 1987: 21). In addition, "More and more evidence has accumulated suggesting that impairment of GABA transmission is a major pathogenetic factor in focal epilepsy" (Seiler and Lajtha, 1987 citing Ribak et al., 1979; Bakay and Harris, 1981; Lloyd et al., 1985).

A significant correlation between GABA concentrations in the brain and age-related aggressive and/or impulsive behaviors (known as the "age-crime curve") has been reported (Collins, 2004). "The dampening effect that GABA has on excitatory neurotransmission is even more important in light of the assertion by Rogers and Bloom (1985) that GABA is found in large amount in vivo prenatally and decreases from birth until age 20 when the decline in GABA levels off through middle age" (1985: 659). "From detailed determinations of GAD (L-glutamate-1-carboxylase) activity in post-mortem human brains, McGeer and McGeer (1978) came to the conclusion that there is a significant decline in GAD (a GABA metabolite) activity with age, *with a steeper decline of activity at young age*" (Seiler and Lajtha, 1987: 17, emphasis added).

Since GABA receptors are located mainly presynaptically, the binding of GABA to these receptors *inhibits the release* of neurotransmitters from the terminals. This inhibition has been observed at dopaminergic, noradrenergic, glutamatergic, and serotonergic neurons clearly indicating that GABA receptors function as *hetero-receptors* (receptors that accept binding from ligands other than their own neurotransmitter) (von Bohlen and Dermietzel, 2002). GABA, then, "modulates" (i.e. adjusts or varies) the signal transduction of many of the other neurotransmitters that function as part of the brain's messaging system, including the ones that are most closely associated with aberrant behavior (which may involve the commission of crime) as well as everyday normal brain functions.

Siever (2008) writes:

> Imbalance in glutamatergic/gabaminergic [sic] activity may contribute to hyperactivity of subcortical limbic regions. Gamma-aminobutyric acid type A (GABA[A]) receptor modulators may enhance aggression, and tiagabine, a GABA uptake inhibitor, decreases aggression, possibly by suppressing reactions to aversive stimuli. Thus, reduced activity at GABA receptors may contribute to aggression, while glutamatergic enhancement increases aggression, raising the possibility of an imbalance in the GABA/glutamatergic system in aggression. (2008: 434 citing Fish et al., 2002; Lieving et al., 2008; Lumley et al., 2004; and Hrabovszky et al., 2005)

Were it to be that the relationship between GABA and glutamate (inhibitory and excitatory neurotransmitters) would continue to remain, as first postulated, so straightforward. GABA, it appears, has all sorts of surprises in store for researchers of this inhibitory neurotransmitter. Just as neuroscientists have started to become comfortable with the almost absolute concept of GABA as the most important and primary "inhibitory neurotransmitter" in the brain, studies since the late 1990s keep popping up that point to irregularities in the accepted tenets about GABA only as the preeminent presynaptic inhibitory modulator vis-à-vis its oftentimes apparently anomalous functioning as the target of such inhibitory signaling. For example, GABA is found to play its regularly functioning role as inhibitor of the serotonergic neurons in a report by Gervasoni et al. (2000) but in a study by Lee et al. (2008) the finding is "Serotonin inhibits GABA synaptic transmission in presympathetic paraventricular nucleus neurons," an apparent about-face for GABA function.

Even more interesting is the GABA/glutamate relationship which, according to top neuropsychologists (including Siever, 2008) and neuroscientists (Kaplan and Sadock, 1999; Lee et al., 2008), is relatively straightforward: glutamate (Glu) excites (promotes neurotransduction); gamma aminobutyric acid (GABA) inhibits (arrests or prevents neurotransduction). In 1998 van den Pol and associates reported that "Glutamate *inhibits* GABA *excitatory* activity in developing neurons" (emphasis added). This is opposite to what would be the expected roles of each neurotransmitter. Furthermore, Chen and Bonham (2005) report that "Glutamate *suppresses* GABA release via *presynaptic* metatrobic glutamate receptors at baroreceptor neurones [*sic*] in rats." Presynaptic inhibition of transduction is the primary tool of GABA in its role as an inhibitory neurotransmitter and, yet, here is glutamate (heretofore considered to be exclusively excitatory) apparently using the presynaptic process (through metatrobic mGluR) to inhibit GABA. Chen and Bonham (2005) write: "In conclusion, the findings present new evidence suggesting that glutamate released at the first central baroreceptor synapses can not only regulate its own signaling, but can further shape baroreceptor signal transmission by suppressing (*inhibiting*) GABA release" (2008: 547, emphasis added). Chen and Bonham further state: "The results underscore the complexity and flexibility of mGluR (metatrobic glutamate receptor) modulation" (2005: 547). Other research reports that "Activation of metatrobic glutamate receptors *inhibits* GABAergic transmission in the rat subfornical organ" (Lee et al., 2001: 401) and "Group I metatrobic glutamate receptors *inhibit* GABA release at interneuron-Purkinje cell synapses" (Galante and Diana, 2004: 4865, emphasis added).

Review and Discussion: Neurotransmitters and Crime

It should be clear by now that the neurology of human behavior is extremely complex. There is no easy path to understanding the complexities of neurologically induced behavior—whether normal or pathological in nature—as the above exegesis on neurotransmitters as key elements of the neurological system tries to make clear. Neurotransmitters have been linked to behaviors that are considered to be within the bounds of normal, accepted behavior as well as behaviors that have been associated with impulsiveness, aggressiveness, and violence. Some of those behaviors have been seen as merely aberrant, though not illegal, and some of those behaviors have been determined to be criminal by society.

Neurotransmitters, then, are important integral components in the etiology of human behavior. They function in a very complex environment that, for the most part, is ruled by the strictures of organic chemistry and molecular biology. Neurotransmitters provide excitation of receptors in order to generate cascading signals throughout the brain (and throughout the entire human body in various motor functions, etc.) that allow behavioral responses by the human organism to both internal and external stimuli. In addition, neurotransmitters provide highly complex signals that deter or halt signaling cascades that are about to begin or are already underway. Early on, it was thought that each neurotransmitter played a specific role as either an inhibitory factor or as an excitatory factor vis-à-vis neurosignaling. As was pointed out, neurotransmission is not so simply defined. Recall our game of "Texas hold 'em" (where we considered only five neurotransmitters: DA, 5HT1A, 5HT2A/C, and Glu). Receptors may, and generally do, serve many different ligands (neurotransmitters or other chemicals such as agonists and antagonists which bind to the receptors according to the rules of affinity).

Nevertheless, some order has been detected among the roiling chemical action and reaction of neurotransmission. Serotonin is one of the earliest known neurotransmitters recognized among social scientists and psychologists to affect human behavior by inducing through complex molecular biological functions a "calming" effect on human reactions to environmental stimuli. Other neurotransmitters, it seems, appear to "agitate" the human response mechanisms toward aggressiveness or impulsiveness that sometimes culminates in violence (the adrenergics and dopamine, for example). Some neurotransmitters apparently are seen as master controllers of excitation (glutamate) or inhibition (gamma aminobutyric acid). But, too, under the extremely complex molecular interaction of the brain's signaling system glutamate and GABA appear to switch roles (when acting on each other, no less—recall Galante and Diana, 2004).

Also discussed, has been research which appears to give a practical handle to the study of these complex molecular brain signalers (Beaver et al., 2008) where it has been noted that certain DNA peculiarities may be used as "risk" markers for aberrant or otherwise inimical behavior traits. Other research has provided possible reliable behavioral risk assessment information regarding concentrations of these neurochemicals in various parts of the brain, for example, high glutamate concentrations in the ACC as a risk indicator for sensation seeking and impulsive behavior—recall, again, our "Texas" card game (Gallinat et al., 2007). There are many more examples of the potential usefulness of researching the intricate complexity of neurotransmitters and how they relate to behavior and attempts toward its practical modification as well as recognition of where well-meaning "common sense" attempts at behavior modification may go awry (Seiler and Lajtha, 1987), for example, where low levels of GABA theoretically preclude the success of "isolation" therapy (e.g. SHUs, Ad Seg, or the "hole").

Only very recently has the study of the neurology of animal behavior become of interest to those practitioners of criminology and criminal justice. There are many reasons for this, including three most likely: (1) "it is an unexceptionable proposition that paradigm shifts within any single discipline radiate outward to (as well as inward from) adjacent disciplines rather slowly, at least as those disciplines are represented … in the trappings of academic structure" (and therefore remain insulated as such specific disciplines out of irrational self-interest in protecting academic "turf") (Pallone and Hennessey, 2000: 22-1) and, (2) those who become part of the academic structure of criminology and criminal justice generally are not equipped academically to study the neurological sciences which are highly quantitative in nature and, (3) those who have made a commitment to the study of neurology and neuroscience have no reason to "step over" academically or financially from neuroscience to a "soft science" such as sociology (criminal justice).

> Hence, we have come to expect a palpable "paradigm lag" between analytic models of behavior anchored in contemporary scientific psychology (with intellectual exchange from the neurosciences) and those anchored in other social science disciplines; what remains less clear is the typical duration of such a paradigm lag and its implications for interdisciplinary communication and conceptual cross fertilization. (Collins, 2004: 14 citing Pallone and Hennessey, 2000: 22-11)

References

Asberg, M., I. Traskman, & P. Thoren (1976). 5-HIAA in the cerebrospinal fluid: A biochemical suicide predictor? *Archives of General Psychiatry* 33: 1193–1197.

Austin, J.H., E. Connole, D. Kent, & J. Collins (1978). Studies in aging of the brain. V. Reduced norepinehrine, dopamine, and cyclic AMP in rat brain with advancing age. *Age* 1: 121–124.

Bakay, R.A.E. & A.B. Harris (1981). Neurotransmitter, receptor, and biochemical changes in monkey cortical epileptic foci. *Brain Research* 206: 387–404.

Bakermans-Kranenberg, M.J. & M.H. van Hzendoorn (2006). Gene environment of the dopamine D4 receptor (DRD4) and observed maternal insensitivity predicting externalizing behavior in preschoolers. *Developmental Psychobiology* 48: 406–409.

Barondes, S.H. (1993). *Molecules and Mental Illness*. New York: Scientific American Library.

Beal, M.F. (1993). Neurochemical aspects of aging in primates. *Neurobiology of Aging* 14: 707–709.

Beaver, K.M. (2009). Molecular genetics and crime. In Walsh, A. & K.M. Beaver (Eds.) *Biosocial Criminology: New Directions in Theory and Research*. New York: Routledge, pp. 50–72.

Beaver, K.M., J.P. Wright, M. DeLisi, & M.G. Vaughn (2008). Desistance from delinquency: The marriage effect revisited and extended. *Social Science Research* 37: 736–752.

Beitchman, J.H., L. Baldassarra, H. Mik, V. De Luca, N. King, D. Bender, S. Ehtesham, & J.L. Kennedy (2006). Serotonin transporter polymorphisms and persistent, pervasive childhood aggression. *American Journal of Psychiatry* 163: 1103–1105.

Berman, S. & E.P. Noble (1995). Reduced visuospacial performance in children with the D2 dopamine receptor A1 allele. *Behavior Genetics* 25: 45–58.

Berman, S., T. Ozkaragoz, R. Young, & E.P. Noble (2002). D2 dopamine receptor gene polymorphism discriminates two kinds of novelty seeking. *Personality and Individual Differences* 33: 867–882.

Blumensohn, R., G. Ratzoni, & A. Weitzman (1995). Reduction in serotonin 5HT2 receptor binding on platelets of delinquent adolescents. *Psychopharmacology* 188(3): 354–356.

Cadoret, R.J., D. Langbehn, K. Kaspers, E.P. Troughton, R. Yucuis, H.K. Sandhu, & R. Filibert (2003). Associations of the serotonin transporter promoter polymorphism with aggressivity, attention deficit, and conduct disorder in an adoptee population. *Comprehensive Psychiatry* 44: 88–101.

Carlsson, A., R. Adolfson, S.M. Aquilonius, C.G. Gottfries, L. Oreland, L. Svennerholm, & B. Winblad (1980). Brain disorder and ergot. In *Ergot Compounds and Brain Function* 295–304. New York: Raven Press.

Caspi, A., J. McClay, T.E. Moffit, J. Mill, J. Martin, I.W. Craig, A. Taylor, & R. Poulton (2002). Role of genotype in the cycle of violence in maltreated children. *Science* 297: 851–854.

Chen, C.Y. & A.C. Bonham (2005). Glutamate suppresses GABA release via presynaptic metabotropic glutamate receptors at baroreceptor neurones [*sic*] in rats. *Journal of Physiology* 562.2: 535–551.

Chiamulera, C., M.P. Epping-Jordan, A. Zocchi, C. Marcon, C. Cottiny, S. Tacconi, M. Corsi, F. Orzi, & F. Conquet (2001). Reinforcing and locomotor stimulant effects of cocaine are absent in mGluR5 null mutant mice. *Nature Neuroscience* 4: 873–874.

Clarke, R.A., D.L. Murphy, & J.N. Constantino (1999). Serotonin and externalizing behavior in young children, *Psychiatry Research* 86: 29–40.

Collins, R.E. (2004). Onset and desistance in criminal careers: Neurobiology and the age-crime relationship. *Journal of Offender Rehabilitation* 39: 1–19.

Comings, D.E., R. Gade-Andavolu, N. Gonzalez, S. Wou, D. Muhleman, C. Chen, et al. (2001). The additive effect of neurotransmitter genes in pathological gambling. *Clinical Genetics* 60: 107–116.

Cooper, J.R., F.E. Bloom, & R.H. Roth (2003). *The Biochemical Basis of Neuropharmacology.* New York: Oxford.

Coyle, J.T. (1988). Neuroscience and psychiatry. In Talbott, J.A., R.E. Hales, & S.C. Yudolsky (Eds.). *American Psychiatric Textbook of Psychiatry.* Washington, DC: American Psychiatric Press, pp. 3–32.

Deutch, A.Y. & R.H. Roth (1999). Neurochemical systems in the central nervous system. In Charney, D.S., E.J. Nestler, & B.S. Bunney (Eds.). *Neurobiology of Mental Illness.* New York: Oxford University Press, pp. 10–25.

Eichelman, B. (1986). The biology and somatic experimental treatment of aggressive disorders. In Brodie, H.K. & P.A. Berger (Eds.). *The American Handbook of Psychiatry.*, Vol. 8. New York: Basic Books, pp. 651–678.

Faraone, S.V., A.E. Doyle, E. Mick, & J. Biederman (2001). Meta-analysis of the association between the 7-repeat allele of the dopamine D4 receptor gene and attention deficit hyperactivity disorder. *American Journal of Psychiatry* 158: 1052–1057.

Fish, E.W., J.F. Debold, & K.A. Miczek (2002). Aggressive behavior as a reinforcer in mice: Activation by allopregnanolone. *Psychopharmacology* (Berl) 163: 459–466.

Fishbein, D.H. (Ed.) (2000). *The Science, Treatment, and Prevention of Antisocial Behaviors: Application to the Criminal Justice System.* Kingston, NJ, Civic Research Institute. Pp, 22-1 to 22-13.

Fogel, B.S., R.B. Schiffer, & S.M. Rau (Eds.) (2000). *Synopsis of Neuropsychiatry.* New York: Lippincott, Williams, and Wilkins.

Galante, M. & M.A. Diana (2004). Group I metatropic receptors inhibit GABA release at interneuron-Purkinje cell synapses through endocannabinoid production. *Journal of Neuroscience* 24(20): 4865–4874.

Gallinat, J., D. Kuntz, U.E. Lang, P. Neu, N. Kassim, T. Kienast, F. Siefert, F. Schubert, & M. Bajbouj (2007). Association between cerebral glutamate and human behaviour: The sensation seeking personality trait. *Neuroimage* 34(2): 671–678.

Gao, W. & P.S. Goldman-Rakic (2003). Selective modulation of excitatory and inhibitory microcircuits by dopamine. *Proceedings of the National Academy of Sciences of the United States* 100(5): 2836–2841.

Gervasoni, D., C. Peyron, C. Rampon, B. Barbagli, G. Chouvet, N. Urbain, P. Fort, & P. Luppi (2000). Role and origin of the GABAergic innervation of dorsal raphe serotonergic neurons. *The Journal of Neuroscience* 20(11): 4217–4225.

Gill, M., G. Daly, S. Heron, Z. Hawi, & M. Fitzgerald (1997). Confirmation of association between attention deficit hyperactivity disorder and a dopamine transporter polymorphism. *Molecular Psychiatry* 2: 311–313.

Glueck, S. & E. Glueck (1943). *Criminal Careers in Retrospect.* New York: Commonwealth Fund.

Grenhoff, J. & S.W. Johnson (1995). Electrophysiological effects of dopamine receptor stimulation. In Neve, K.A. (Ed.). *The Dopamine Receptors.* Totowa: Human Press, pp. 267–304.

Guo, G., M.E. Roettger, & J.C. Shih (2007). Contributions of the DAT1 and DRD2 genes to serious and violent delinquency among adolescents and young adults. *Human Genetics* 121: 125–136.

Haberstick, B.C., A. Smolen, & J.K. Hewitt (2006). Family-based association test of the 5HTTLPR and aggressive behavior in a general population of children. *Biological Psychiatry* 59: 836–843.

Haberstick, B.C., J.M. Lessem, C.J. Hopfer, A. Smolen, M.A. Ehringer, D. Timberlake, et al. (2005). Monoamine Oxidase A (MAOA) and antisocial behavior in the presence of childhood and adolescent maltreatment. *American Journal of Medical Genetics Part B (Neuropsychiatric Genetics)* 135B: 59–64.

Hirschi, T. & M. Gottfredson (1983). Age and the explanation of crime. *American Journal of Sociology* 89: 552–584.

Holmes, A., D.L. Murphy, & J.N. Crawley (2002). Reduced aggression in mice lacking the serotonin transporter. *Psychopharmacology* 161(2): 160–167.

Hrabovszky, E., J. Halasz, W. Meelis, M.B. Kruk, Z. Liposits, & J. Haller (2005). Neurochemical characterization of hypothalamic neurons involved in attack behavior: Glutamatergic dominance and coexpression of thyrotropin releasing hormone in a subset of glutamatergic neurons. *Neuroscience* 133: 657–666.

Ida, Y., M. Tanaka, Y. Kohno, R. Nagagawa, K. Imori, A. Tsuda, Y. Hoaki, & N. Nagasaki (1982). Effects of age and stress on regional noradrenaline metabolism in rat brain. *Neurobiology of Aging* 2: 41–48.

Jeffrey, C.R. (1994). The brain, the law, and the medicalization of crime. In R. Masters and T. McQuire (Eds.). *The Neurotransmitter Revolution: Serotonin, Social Behavior, and the Law*. Carbondale: Southern Illinois University Press, pp. 161–178.

Kaplan, K.I. & B.J. Sadock (1999). *Synopsis of Psychiatry: Behavioral Science/Clinical Psychiatry*. New York: Lippincott, Williams, and Wilkins.

Laborit, H. (1977). *Decoding the Human Message*. Trans. Stephen Bodington & Alison Wilson. New York: St. Martin's.

Lee, H.S., W. Chong, S.K. Han, M.H. Lee, & P.D. Ryu (2001). Activation of metabotropic glutamate receptors inhibits GABAergic transmission in the subfornical organ. *Neuroscience* 102(2): 401–411.

Lee, K.S., T.H. Han, J.Y. Jo, G. Kang, S.Y. Lee, P.D. Ryu, J.H. Im, S.H. Jeon, & J.H. Park (2008). Serotonin inhibits GABA synaptic transmission in presympathetic paraventicular neurons. *Neuroscience Letters* 439(2): 138–142.

Lesch, K., P.D. Bengel, A. Heils, S.Z. Sabol, B.D. Greenberg, S. Petri, et al. (1996). Association of anxiety related traits with a polymorphism in the serotonin transporter gene regulatory region. *Science* 274: 1527–1531.

Liao, D.L., C.J. Hong, H.L. Shih, & S.J. Tsai (2004). Possible association between serotonin transporter region polymorphism and extremely violent crime in Chinese males. *Neuropsychology* 50: 284–287.

Lidberg, L., J.R. Tuck, M. Asberg, G.P. Scalia-Tomba, & I. Bertillson (1985). Homicide, suicide, and CSF 5-HIAA. *Acta Psychiatrica Scandinavica* 71: 230–236.

Lieving, L.M., D.R. Cherek, S.D. Lane, O.V. Tcheremissine, & S. Nouvion (2008). Effects of acute tiagabine administration on aggressive responses of adult male parolees. *Journal of Psychopharmacology* 22(2): 144–152.

Lloyd, K.D., L. Bossi, P.L. Morselli, M. Rougier, P. Loiseau, & C. Munari (1985). Biochemical evidence for dysfunction of GABA neurons in human epilepsy. In Bartholini, G., L. Bossi, K.G. Lloyd, & P.L. Morselli (Eds.). *Epilepsy and GABA Receptor Agonists: Basic and Therapeutic Research*. New York: Raven Press, pp. 43–51.

Lumley, L.A., C.L. Robinson, B.S. Slusher, K. Wozniak, M. Dawood, & J.L. Meyerhoff (2004). Reduced isolation induced aggressiveness in mice following NAALAdase inhibition. *Psychopharmacology* 171: 375–381.

McGeer, E.G. & P.L. McGeer (1978). GABA-containing neurons in schizophrenia, Huntington's chorea, and normal aging. In Hrogsgaard, L.P., J. Scheel-Kruger,

& H. Kofod (Eds.). *GABA-Neurotransmitters. Pharmacochemical, Biochemical and Pharmacological Aspects.* Copenhagen: Munksgaard, pp. 340–356.

Manuck, S.B., J.D. Flory, R.E. Ferrell, J.J. Mann, & M.F. Muldoon (2000). A regulatory polymorphism of the monoamine oxidase A gene may be associated with variability in aggression, impulsivity, and central nervous system responsivity. *Psychiatry Research* 95: 9–23.

Masters, R.D. and M.T. McQuire (Eds.) (1994). *The Neurotransmitter Revolution: Serotonin, Social Behavior, and the Law.* Carbondale: Southern Illinois University Press.

Mattes, J. (1990). Comparative effectiveness of carbamazapine and propanolol for rage outbursts. *Journal of Neuropsychiatry* 2: 159–164.

Miczek, K.A. & E.W. Fish (2006). Monoamines, GABA, glutamate, and aggression. In Nelson, R.J. (Ed.). *Biology of Aggression.* New York: Oxford University Press, pp. 114–149.

Molling, P., A. Lockner, R. Sauls, & L. Eisenberg (1962). Committed delinquent boys: The impact of perphenazine and of placebo. *Archives of General Psychiatry* 7(1): 70–76.

Moore, R.Y. & F.E. Bloom (1978). Central catecholamine neuron systems: Anatomy and physiology of the dopamine systems. *Annual Review of Neuroscience* 1: 129–169.

Moore, T.M., A. Scarpa, & A. Raine (2002). A meta-analysis of serotonin metabolite 5-HIAA and antisocial behavior. *Aggressive Behavior* 28: 299–306.

Munafo, M.R., K. Roberts, E.C. Johnstone, R.T. Walton, & P.L. Yudkin (2005). Association of serotonin transporter gene polymorphism with nicotine dependence: no evidence of an interaction with trait neuroticism. *Personality and Individual Differences* 38: 843–850.

Naumenko, V.S., R.V. Kozhemjabina, I.Z. Plusnina, & N.K. Popova (2009). Expression of serotonin transporter gene and startle response in rats with genetically determined fear-induced aggression. *Bulleton of Experimental Biology and Medicine* 147(1): 81–83.

Noble, E.P., K. Blum, T. Ritchie, A. Montgomery, & P.J. Sheridan (1991). Allelic association of the D2 dopamine receptor gene with the receptor binding characteristics in alcoholism. *Archives of General Psychiatry* 48: 648–654.

Noble, E.P., L.A. Gottshalk, J.H. Fallon, T. Ritchie, & J.C. Wu (1997). D2 polymorphism and brain regional glucose metabolism. *American Journal of Medical Genetics* 74: 762–766.

Noble, E.P., T.Z. Ozkaragoz, T.L. Ritchie, X. Zhuang, T.R. Belin, & R.S. Sparkes (1998). D2 and D4 dopamine polymorphisms and personality. *American Journal of Medical Genetics* 81: 257–267.

Pallone, N.J. and J.J. Hennessey (1996). *Tinder-Box Criminal Aggression: Neuropsychology, Demography, and Phenomenology.* New Brunswick: Transaction Publishers.

Pallone, N.J. and J.J. Hennessey (2000). Indifferent communication between social science and neuroscience—The case of "biological brain-proneness" for criminal aggression. In Raine, A. (1993). *The Psychopathology of Crime: Criminal Behavior as a Clinical Disorder.* New York: Academic Press.

Ramboz, S., F. Saudaou, D.A. Amara, C. Belsung, L. Segu, R. Misslin, M.C. Buhot, & R. Hen (1999). 5HT1B receptor knockout—behavioral consequences. *Neurosciences* 93(4): 1223–1225.

Redburn, D.A. & A. Schousboe (1987). *Neurotropic Activity of GABA During Development: Neurology and Neurobiology Volume 32.* New York: Alan R. Liss, Inc.

Reif, A., M. Rosler, C.M. Freitag, M. Schneider, A. Eujen, C. Kissling, et al. (2007). Nature and nurture predispose to violent behavior: Serotonergic genes and adverse childhood environment. *Neuropsychopharmacology* 32: 2375–2383.

Retz, W., P. Retz-Junjinger, T. Supprian, M. Rosler et al. (2004). Association of serotonin transporter promoter gene polymorphism with violence: Relation with personality disorders, impulsivity, and childhood ADHD psychopathology. *Behavioral Sciences and the Law* 22: 415–425.

Ribak, C.E., A.B. Harris, J.E. Vaughn, & E. Roberts (1979). Inhibitory GABAergic nerve terminals decrease at sites of focal epilepsy. *Science* 205: 211–240.

Rogers, J. & F.E. Bloom (1985). Neurotransmitter metabolism and function in the aging central nervous system. In Finch, C.E. and E.L. Schneider (Eds.). *Handbook of the Biology of Aging 2nd ed.* New York: Van Nostrand Rheinhold.

Rowe, D.C. (2002). *Biology and Crime.* Los Angeles: Roxbury.

Rowe, D.C., C. Stever, G. Chase, S. Sherman, A. Abramowitz, & I.D. Waldman (2001). Two dopamine genes related to reports of childhood retrospective inattention and conduct disorder symptoms. *Molecular Psychiatry* 6: 429–433.

Rowe, D.C., C. Stever, J.M.C. Gard, H.H. Cleveland, M.L. Sanders, A. Abramowitz, et al. (1998). The relation of the dopamine transporter gene (DAT1) to symptoms of internalizing disorders in children. *Behavior Genetics* 28: 215–225.

Sampson, R.J. and J.H. Laub (1993). *Crime in the Making: Pathways and Turning Points Through Life.* Cambridge, MA: Harvard University Press.

Saudou, F., D.A. Amara, A. Dierich, M. Lemaur, S. Ramboz, I. Segu, M.C. Bulock, & R. Hen (1994). Enhanced aggressive behavior in mice lacking 5HT1B receptor. *Science* 265(5180): 1875–1878.

Seiler, N. & A. Lajtha (1987). Functions of GABA in the vertebrate organism. In Redburn, D.A. and A. Schousboe (Eds.). *Neurotrophic Activity of GABA during Development. Neurology and Neurobiology Vol. 32.* New York: Alan R. Liss, Inc., pp. 1–56.

Siever, L.J. (2008). Neurobiology of aggression and violence. Reviews and overviews. *American Journal of Psychiatry* 165(4): 429–442.

Spokes, G. S. (1979). An analysis of factors influencing measurements of dopamine, noradrenaline, glutamate decarboxylase, and choline acetylase in human postmortem brain tissue. *Brain* 102: 333–346.

Sumer, M.M., L. Atik, A. Unal, U. Emre, & H.T. Atasoy (2007). Frontal lobe epilepsy is presented as ictal aggression. *Neurological Sciences* 28(1): 48–51.

Sustkova-Fiserova, M., J. Vavrova, & M. Krsiak (2009). Brain levels of GABA, glutamate and aspartate in sociable, aggressive and timid mice: An in vivo microdialysis study. *Neuro Endocrinology Letters* 30(1): 79–84.

Sysoeva, O.V., N.V. Matuchenko, M.A. Timofeeva, G.V. Portnova, M.A. Kulikova, A.G. Tonevitsky, & A.M. Ivanitsky (2009). Aggression and 5HTT polymorphism in females: Study of synchronized swimming and control groups. *International Journal of Psychophysiology* 72(3): 173–178.

Tebartz van Elst, L., F.G. Woermann, L. Lemieux, P.J. Thompson, & M.R. Trimble (2000). Affective aggression in patients with temporal lobe epilepsy: A quantitative MRI study of the amygdala. *Brain* 123(2): 234–243.

Thompson, J., M. Thomas, A. Singleton, M. Piggott, S. Lloyd, E.K. Perry, et al. (1997). D2 dopamine receptor gene (DRD2) Taq1 A polymorphism: Reduced D2 receptor binding in the human striatum with the A1 allele. *Pharmacogenetics* 7: 479–484.

van den Pol, A.N., X. Gau, P.R. Patrylo, P.K. Ghosh, & K. Obrietan (1998). Glutamate inhibits GABA excitatory activity in developing neurons. *Journal of Neuroscience* 18(24): 10749–10761.

Virkkunnen, M. (1982). Evidence for abnormal glucose tolerance test among violent offenders. *Neuropsychbiology* 8: 30–34.

Virkkunnen, M. & E. Kallilo (1987). Low blood glucose nadir in the glucose tolerance test and homicidal spouse abuse. *Aggressive Behavior* 13: 59–66.

Virkkunnen, M. & M. Linnoila (1993). Brain serotonin, type II alcoholism, and impulsive violence. *Journal in Studies on Alcohol* 54: 163–169.

Virkkunnen, M. & S. Narvanen (1987). Plasma insulin, tryptophan, and serotonin levels during the glucose tolerance test among habitually violent and impulsive offenders. *Neuropsychobiology* 17: 19–23.

Virkkunnen, M., A. Nuutila, F.K. Goodwin, & M. Linnoila (1987). Cerebrospinal fluid monoamine metabolite levels in male arsonists. *Archives of General Psychiatry* 46: 600–603.

Virkkunnen, M., R. Rawlings, R. Tokola, R.E. Poland, A. Guidotti, C. Nemeroff, G. Bissette, K. Kalogeras, S. Karononen, & M. Linnoila (1994). CSF biochemistries, glucose metabolism, and diurnal activity rhythms in alcoholic violent offenders, fire setters, and healthy volunteers. *Archives of General Psychiatry* 51: 3–20.

Volavka, J. (2002). *Neurobiology of Violence.* Washington, DC: American Psychiatric Publishing.

von Bohlen, O. & H.R. Dermietzel (2002). *Neurotransmitters and Neuromodulators: Handbook of Receptors and Biological Effects.* Weinheim: Wiley-VCH.

Watkins, J.C. & D.E. Jane (2006). The glutamate story. *British Journal of Pharmacology* (Supp. 1): 8100–8108.

Yesavage, J.A. (1984). Correlation of dangerous behavior by schizophrenics in hospital. *Journal of Psychiatric Research* 18: 225–231.

Yudofsky, S., J.M. Silver, & S.E. Schneider (1987). Pharmacologic treatment of aggression. *Psychiatric Annals* 17: 397–407.

Yuen, E.Y., Q. Jiang, P. Chen, J. Feng, & Z. Yen (2008). Activation of 5HT2A/C receptors counteracts 5HT1A regulation of N-methyl-D-aspartate receptor channels in pyramidal neurons of prefrontal cortex. *Journal of Biological Chemistry* 283: 17194–17204.

Zhang, I., W. Ma, J.L. Barker, & D.R. Rubinow (1999). Sex differences in expression of serotonin receptors (subtypes 1A and 2A) in rat brain: A possible role of testosterone. *Neuroscience* 94: 251–259.

Zigmond, M.J., F.E. Bloom, S.C. Landis, J.L. Roberts, & L.R. Squire (Eds.) (2003). *Fundamental Neuroscience*. New York: Academic Press.

The Limbic System and Crime

Matt DeLisi

Introduction

At its core, criminal behavior could be viewed as the triumph of emotion over reason. Murder is frequently borne from mundane circumstances involving interpersonal conflicts with person whom we have close emotional connections, and the primary motivators for these conflicts are anger, vengeance, lust, and other deadly sins. Other types of crimes, such as shoplifting, drug use, or drunk driving involve fleeting decisions to take what we want, and to do what we want. Freud referred to these primal drives that are able to overcome thought and reason as a component of the personality called the id. More generally, these primal, visceral emotions originate from the region of the brain known as the limbic system. The limbic system is involved in autonomic or involuntary and somatic or voluntary behavioral activities relating to emotion and emotional memory. This chapter briefly reviews the history, function, anatomy, and cortical connectivity of the limbic system with particular focus on and discussion of the amygdala which is the limbic area that is most important to the study of crime (DeLisi, Umphress, & Vaughn, 2009). In addition, linkages between the limbic system, psychopathy, homicide offending, and theoretical models of antisocial behavior are explored.

Background, Anatomy, and Cortical Connectivity

The limbic system, *limbic meaning edge, margin, or border* to the cerebral hemisphere, was purportedly discovered by and attributed to Paul Broca (of Broca's area fame) in 1878. But it was not until the 1930s and 1940s that the contemporary understanding of the limbic system and its role in memory, emotional learning, and fear conditioning was established, most famously in work by Papez (1937) and MacLean (1949, 1955). Papez was seminal in articulating the role of emotional processing in the limbic system, but focused mostly on the hippocampus. In MacLean's (1949, 1955, 1990) influential triune brain hypothesis, the limbic system was referred to as the paleomammalian component of the brain that was phylogenetically younger than the reptilian brain (which controlled the most basic instinctual behaviors involved in the survival of the species) and older than the neomammalian brain (which controlled the most evolutionarily advanced, and thus human, behaviors centering on language, cognition, and executive functioning). In reference to these two classic works, two broad points are important to understand. First, the structures of the limbic system are important for processing emotional stimuli and influencing responses in the endocrine and autonomic nervous systems. Indeed, MacLean referred to the limbic system as the "visceral brain," suggesting that it was the anatomical seat of powerful emotions. Second, the limbic system is intimately connected via the thalamus to the frontal or cortical regions where the emotional information is modulated and controlled (for an overview, see Price & Drevets, 2010).

Broadly conceived, the limbic system identifies and reacts to threatening stimuli and then transmits this information to the frontal cortices for a decision on how to respond—the self-regulation domain is known as executive functioning. The limbic system projects emotionally-laden impulses that the frontal cortices must dampen and control (Hariri, Bookheimer, & Mazziotta, 2000). For most of us, the impulses projected from the limbic system are the things we wish we could do in an ideal world without consequences. For most of us, our frontal cortices and the executive functions therein stifle the limbic suggestions. But for others, there is insufficient cortical control of the limbic messages. This can occur from heightened limbic responses to emotionally-charged, provocative stimulation, reduced cortical control, or both. Indeed, brain imaging research has discovered structural, functioning, or circuit differences in the limbic systems of diverse antisocial samples including psychopaths (Birbaumer et al., 2005; Kiehl et al., 2001), murderers (Raine, Buschbaum, & LaCasse, 1997), persons with antisocial personality disorder (Schneider et al., 2000), and domestic violence perpetrators (George et al., 2004; Lee, Chan, & Raine, 2008), and even college students with psychopathic personality traits (Gordon, Baird, & End, 2004).

The brain is endlessly divisible and specific brain regions can vary depending on the author's focus (for a detailed overview, see Clark, Boutros, & Mendez, 2008). The classic limbic structures are the hippocampus, amygdala, septum, cingulate gyrus, hypothalamus, and thalamus (a generic representation appears in Figure 8.1). The hippocampus is involved in memory, learning, and emotion. It is also responsible for the regulation of responsiveness to stress, and is particularly affected by acute stressors such as abuse (see Mead, Beauchaine, & Shannon, 2010). Chronic stress decreases dendritic branching in the hippocampus (stress increases dendritic branching in the amygdala) which results in increased fear conditioning coupled with impaired fear extinction (Shin & Liberzon, 2010). The amygdala is involved in emotional learning, aversive conditioning, and responsiveness to emotions (most notably fear). The amygdala is not only important for understanding antisocial/externalizing behaviors but also internalizing conditions, such as anxiety disorders where a hyper-responsive amygdala makes individuals prone to feelings of fear, threat, and distress. Indeed, an over-reactive amygdala is associated with panic disorder, social phobias, specific phobias, generalized anxiety disorder, and posttraumatic stress disorder (Shin & Liberzon, 2010).

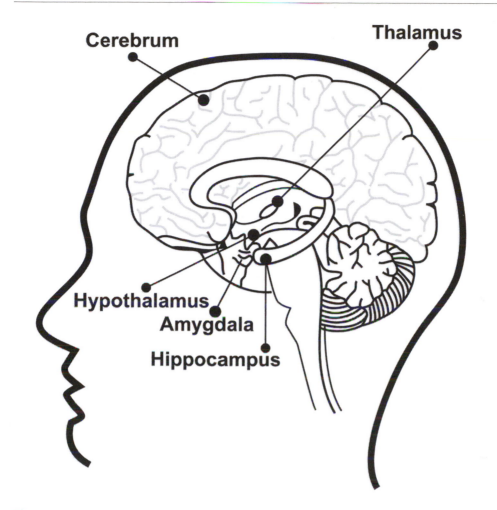

Figure 8.1 The limbic system

The septum is implicated in memory and is closely connected with the hippocampus, amygdala, and hypothalamus. The cingulate gyrus is involved in autonomic functions such as the regulation of heart rate, blood pressure, and processing of stimuli. The anterior cingulate cortex has connections with the amygdala, hippocampus, and hypothalamus and is importantly related to the processing of emotional information and the regulation of emotional responses. The anterior cingulate cortex has both a cognitive and an affective subdivision that are responsible for assessing situations for potential conflict and modulating anger for the maintenance of interpersonal relations (Bush, Luu, & Posner, 2000). The anterior cingulate cortex has been referred to as a "mediator" because it controls the effects of stress on the individual by mollifying the negative emotions projected from the amygdala (Tancredi, 2005).

The hypothalamus is involved in monitoring information from the autonomic nervous system, controlling the pituitary gland, and regulating the endocrine system. Another important role of the hypothalamus is to synthesize the hormone oxytocin, which is involved in mother–infant bonding and is believed to be an important hormonal catalyst for affiliative, prosocial behavior (Kosfeld, Heinrichs, Zak, Fischbacher, & Fehr, 2005). For instance, inhaling oxytocin has been found to increase social behavior (e.g., making eye contact, experiencing greater social interaction, experiencing enhanced feelings of trust) among persons with autism (Andari et al., 2010), a pervasive developmental disorder that although not characterized by antisocial behavior is characterized by asocial behavior. The hypothalamus' role in synthesizing oxytocin is additionally important because oxytocin has been shown to modulate the reactivity of the amygdala to both negative and positive stimuli (Domes et al., 2007; Petrovic, Kalisch, Singer, & Dolan, 2008). The thalamus is the relay station that communicates with cortical regions and thus relays information from the limbic system to be modulated frontally.

Other brain regions are peripherally but importantly related to the limbic system. For instance, the nucleus accumbens has connectivity to the amygdala and is believed to be a neural substrate for impulsive antisocial behavior because of its involvement in dopamine release. In a recent brain imaging study, Buckholtz and colleagues (2010) advanced that the nucleus accumbens produces increased levels of dopamine that in turn leads to a pathway of excessive use of limbic reward messages that are poorly inhibited frontally. Another important brain area that is implicated in the limbic-cortical substrate of antisocial behavior is the uncinate fasciculus, which are white matter tracts that connect the amygdala and orbitofrontal cortex. A recent study was the first to document uncinate fasciculus abnormalities in psychopathic offenders who had been convicted of violent crimes such as murder and rape. Specifically, psychopathic offenders had reduced structural integrity in the right uncinate fasciculus compared to controls matched by age and IQ (Craig et al., 2009).

Although the limbic system generally and the amygdala specifically are viewed as neural systems that undergird antisocial behavior, it is essential to remember that the limbic system is closely connected to frontal cortices. In this way, both neural systems in tandem produce liability for antisocial behavior. As noted by Blair, "the amygdala and OFC dysfunction cannot be attributed to dysfunction in only one of these systems that is propagated, because of their intimate connections to the other system" (2010, p. 79). To illustrate, a recent study found that multiple forms of empathy are associated with both left and right prefrontal activity (Light et al., 2009), suggesting that emotions are not solely a limbic function.

Amygdala Dysfunction, Fear Conditioning, and Psychopathy

Within the limbic system, the amygdala has emerged as one of the most important structures in terms of its implications for the development of antisocial behavior and crime (Blair, Mitchell, & Blair, 2005; DeLisi, Wright, Vaughn, & Beaver, 2009). The amygdala is principally responsible for fear induction where feelings of fear and anxiety are conditioned to negative stimuli such as antisocial behavior and, equally importantly, the negative consequences that stem from antisocial behavior. For individuals with healthy amygdala functioning and intact fear conditioning, caution and anticipatory fear serve to deter antisocial conduct. These physiological and psychological effects are powerful. According to Davis and Whalen, "A stimulus that predicts an aversive outcome will change neural transmission in the amygdala to produce the somatic, autonomic, and endocrine signs of fear, as well as increased attention to that stimulus" (2001, p. 13). But for those with amygdala dysfunction there is a fearlessness that bypasses the safeguards or deterrents to antisocial behavior and an attendant unresponsiveness to the punishments that spring from misbehavior. In this sense, fearlessness is a likely precondition for crime. Indeed, impaired fear conditioning has been shown in several antisocial groups including conduct disordered adolescent females (Fairchild, Stobbe, van Goozen, Calder, & Goodyer, 2010), psychopathic children (Blair, Colledge, Murray, & Mitchell, 2001; Jones, Laurens, Herba, Barker, & Viding, 2009), conduct disordered children (Marsh et al., 2008; Vloet, Konrad, Huebner, Herpertz, & Herpertz-Dahlmann, 2008), and conduct disordered adolescent males (Fairchild, van Goozen, Calder, Stollery, & Goodyer, 2009) .

Amygdala dysfunction is central to Blair's noteworthy recent theory of psychopathy. According to Blair and his colleagues (Blair, 1995, 1997, 2003, 2004, 2005, 2006, 2008a, 2008b; Blair et al., 2001, 2005), the inculcation of empathy is essential for effective socialization and empathy induction requires appropriate amygdalar responses to emotions like fear and sadness. In this way, a neural, emotional, and psychological connection is made between antisocial conduct, the infliction of harm on a victim, and the social consequences of the violation. When there is an impairment in recognizing the distress of a victim, then victimizing others comes somewhat easily. When there is appropriate socialization, then victimizing others is more difficult. Indeed, a recent study found that youths with severe conduct disorder exhibited reduced amygdala/frontal connectivity while watching images of pain being inflicted on another person (Decety, Michalska, Akitsuki, & Lahey, 2009). Still other research using data from a community—not a clinical or correctional—sample found that youths who scored higher on an inventory of callous and unemotional traits were more "fear-blind" based on difficulty labeling not only fearful faces but also fearful body poses and body language (Muñoz, 2009).

Recent research suggests that early life fear conditioning indeed has long-term negative consequences. Gao, Raine, Venables, Dawson, and Mednick (2010) studied the potential link between fear conditioning at age three and criminal behavior at age 23 using data from a large birth cohort of 1,795 children from Mauritius. Based on electrodermal responses, which is the ability of skin to conduct electricity after a stimulus, they found that those who were criminal offenders at age 23 failed to show fear conditioning at age three compared to those who were not criminal at age 23. It has long been recognized that fearlessness is a potent risk factor for externalizing and antisocial behaviors, and more recent neuroscientific studies are showing that a fearless disposition likely is the manifestation of neural dysfunction in the limbic system.

Perhaps nowhere are the negative effects of fearlessness more frighteningly instantiated than in the psychopath. The evidence from brain imaging research is compelling that significant structural and functional brain differences exist between psychopaths and non-psychopaths (for an overview, see Müller, 2010). These include bilateral volume reductions in the amygdala (Glenn, Raine, & Schug, 2009; Yang, Raine, Narr, Colletti, & Toga, 2009), reduced activity in multiple limbic structures (Kiehl et al., 2001) reduced volume in the hippocampus (Raine et al., 2004), volume increases in the striatum (Glenn, Raine, Yaralian, & Yang, 2010), and gray matter concentration differences in the right dorsal anterior cingulate and left posterior cingulate (Rijsdijsk et al., 2010). In a limbic system model of psychopathy, Kiehl (2006) noted that removal of the anterior temporal (i.e., limbic) lobe of antisocial patients results in reduced violence, increased social relationships, and greater empathy. Moreover, antisocial individuals who have undergone amygdalotomies demonstrate reductions in aggression and improvements in emotional control.

In addition to neural differences, it is understood that severe offenders often themselves have extensive victimization histories that suggest a truly vicious childhood (DeLisi, 2005). Households characterized by abuse, low parental investment, low parental bonding, and low paternal care can result in enduring psychophysiological deficits in stress response and fear conditioning (Patrick, Fowles, & Krueger, 2009). For instance, Gao, Raine, Chan, Venables, and Mednick (2010) found that early parenting trauma was associated with psychopathic personality 25 years later especially among children with low maternal care and high child abuse victimization. That early life environments affect brain functioning vis-à-vis psychopathic personality is chilling given the longitudinal stability of psychopathy. For example, Lynam et al. (2009) found no evidence of change in psychopathy across childhood and adolescence among boys in the Pittsburgh Youth Study.

Associations with Homicide

As discussed at the outset of this chapter, criminal events often reflect emotionally-laden interpersonal disputes, the culmination of which is homicide. A variety of scholars have utilized brain imagine methodologies (e.g., magnetic resonance imaging, positron emission tomography, functional magnetic resonance imaging, single photon emission computed tomography) to explore brain regions of interest that are hypothesized to be neural substrates for antisocial and violent behavior. In a brain imaging study of 41 murders and 41 age- and sex-matched controls, Raine, Buchsbaum, and LaCasse (1997) found numerous limbic system differences. Murderers had reduced left and increased right amygdala activity, reduced left and increased right activity in the hippocampus, and greater right activity in the thalamus compared to controls. Due to concern about handedness and brain laterality, they conducted additional analyses of left- and right-handed murderers and found that handedness did not account for the asymmetric limbic activity in addition to the reduced frontal activity. Recently, Yang et al. (2010) found gray matter volume reductions in the hippocampus and parahippocampal gyrus, which is involved in information processing for impulse control and emotional regulation, among homicide perpetrators who also have schizophrenia.

Limbic differences also differentiate the type of murderer. In another positron emission tomography study which measured glucose metabolism in areas of interest in the brain, Raine and colleagues (1998) compared cortical and limbic regions for predatory/instrumental murderers and affective/reactive murderers compared to controls. They found that affective murderers had higher right hemisphere limbic functioning and lower right hemisphere prefrontal/limbic ratios. This comports with the notion that impulsively violent offenders are unable to inhibit their emotional responses during heated confrontation. On the other hand, predatory murderers had cortical functioning that was intact and on par with controls while also having excessive right limbic activity. This is consistent with the idea that instrumentally violent people can victimize others due to impairments in the limbic system (e.g., callousness, lacking conscience).

It is important to recognize that the psychopathology demonstrated by homicide offenders is often itself suggestive of limbic dysfunction. For instance, in their study of 166 convicted sexual homicide offenders, Briken, Habermann, Berner, and Hill (2005) found that 30 percent of their sample had brain abnormalities and among these offenders half also presented with sadistic personality disorder which is characterized by the infliction of pain, humiliation, and suffering on victims for the gratification of the offender. By definition, the disorder implies the absence of empathic emotion and likely amygdala dysfunction.

Finally, an actual syndrome linking the limbic system to homicide offending has been advanced. Pontius (1997) proposed Limbic Psychotic Trigger Reaction which is characterized by motiveless, well-remembered, unplanned homicidal acts committed by an offender who was temporarily psychotic, autonomically aroused, and who displayed flat affect. Pontius documented 14 cases of Limbic Psychotic Trigger Reaction syndrome and suggested that the limbic system undergoes a seizure that is started or "kindled" by a very specific trigger that is associated with stressors in the individual's memory.

Limbic-Based Theories of Antisocial Behavior

An assortment of biological process and theoretical models that utilize the limbic system to explain antisocial conduct have been advanced. For example, the hypothalamic-pituitary-adrenal or HPA axis is the major neurological-endocrine response system to stress (e.g., the fight or flight syndrome) and it is intimately connected to the limbic system. In very stressful conditions requiring a fight or flight response, corticotrophin-releasing factor is released from the hypothalamus that in turn stimulates the release of adrenocorticotropin hormone from the pituitary gland. This in turn prompts the adrenal glands to release cortisol. Chronic and acute stress damages the HPA axis (stress is particularly detrimental to the hippocampus) and results in dysfunctional response to stressful conditions. In terms of a general behavioral theory, Gray's (1982) influential Behavioral Activation System (BAS) and Behavioral Inhibition System (BIS) theory implicates the dopaminergic system that innervates the limbic system and the hippocampus and septum, respectively. The BIS/BAS theory seeks to explain both behavioral restraint/inhibition and approach and has clear implications for both internalizing and externalizing conditions. Also at a general level, substance use and abuse reflects dopamine-driven activation in the "addiction" circuit of the brain that includes the amygdala, nucleus accumbens, striatum, and ventromedial prefrontal cortex (for a review, see Luciana, 2006).

In an influential work, Damasio (1994) developed the somatic marker model which suggests that emotional learning is guided by somatic or bodily feelings that are associated with positive and negative behaviors. For example, many individuals experience feeling of apprehension and fear that "mark" considerations of deviant conduct, and these negative feelings serve to deter it. This has clear implications for psychopathy (see Damasio, 2000). In a triple balance model of emotion, van Honk and Schutter (2005, 2006) suggest that three neurobiological processes involving balance or homeostasis at the subcortical or limbic area, subcortical-cortical communication, and cortical area are involved in emotional functioning that relates to the learning of reward and punishment. As a result of the imbalances between the limbic system and its allied connections in the frontal cortices, psychopathic persons are extremely reward motivated while non-responsive to punishment. This behavioral disposition in turn has negative effects on endocrine functioning, specifically an unbalanced ratio of cortisol (which encourages restraint) and testosterone (which encourages approach). According to van Honk and Schutter, psychopathy is a syndrome where the hypothalamic-pituitary-gonadal (HPG) axis is dominant over the hypothalamic-pituitary-adrenal (HPA) axis. Thus both the endocrine systems and the communication between limbic and frontal areas are compromised in psychopathic persons.

In their work on emotional regulation, Davidson and colleagues (Davidson, 2001, 2003; Davidson, Putnam, & Larson, 2000) describe the important interplay between limbic and cortical regions in the appropriate maintenance of affective style which is the ability to regulate negative emotion. According to his theory, the left prefrontal cortex is primarily involved in approach-related thoughts or the pursuit of appetitive goals while the right prefrontal cortex is primarily involved in withdrawal-related or inhibited behaviors. Both frontal regions are responding to negative emotions such as fear and uncertainty emanating from the amygdala. This neural circuit explains why antisocial persons are characterized by negative emotions/affect and the reaction to that negativity. According to Davidson, "Individuals who report greater dispositional negative affect and who show increased reactivity to stressful events are more likely to be those individuals who have difficulty regulating negative affect and specifically in modulating the intensity of negative affect once it has been achieved" (2001, p. 662). In sum, a diverse cast of theories have cited the importance of the limbic system or specific limbic structures as central to both general forms of behavior including antisocial and criminal forms.

Conclusion

Although recently a controversial notion, it is now uncontroversial to suggest that significant brain differences exist that differentiate violent and antisocial individuals from others as supported by a recent meta-analysis of 43 brain-imaging studies (Yang & Raine, 2009). Due to its integral roles in emotional learning and the interplay with the frontal cortex for behavioral regulation, the limbic system will likely figure prominently in the postgenomic era as scientists continue to investigate the genetic and neural underpinnings of behavior. Indeed this is already taking place. For example, catechol-O-methyl-transferase or COMT is an enzyme that regulates dopamine and other neurotransmitters in the brain. There is a common mutation in COMT, Val158Met or the Val allele, that causes a valine to methionine mutation that results in significantly less efficient enzyme activity. The COMT gene is expressed at high levels in the hippocampus and recent research found that the Val allele was associated with reduced memory retrieval and poorer coupling with the prefrontal regions (Bertolino et al., 2006). The same allele has also been shown to confer greater reactivity to fearful stimuli in the amygdala which contributes to anxiety disorders (Montag et al., 2008). While there has long been recognition about the role of the limbic system in antisocial behavior and other psychiatric conditions, contemporary research is articulating how the limbic system contributes to behavior at the genetic level.

There is no question that the amygdala will be the subject of particular focus due to its linkages to severe antisocial syndromes including psychopathy and psychiatric conditions including anxiety disorders. For example, recent research found that carriers of a common functional deletion in the α2b-adrenoreceptor gene (ADRA2B) manifest increased amygdala responses during periods of acute stress, but no genetic effects were found during periods of non-stress (Cousijn et al., 2010). The gene has been implicated in recurrent feelings of stress stemming from traumatic events and may serve as a candidate gene associated with anxiety disorders and related conditions.

Another important gene of interest is the low activity allele of the MAOA gene that is associated with neural systems that process threats and emotions such as anger, and the effects are particularly pronounced for males (Williams et al. 2009). The low activity allele has been shown to predict reduced limbic system reductions and hyperresponsive amygdala activity during emotional arousal using functional magnetic resonance imaging data (Meyer-Lindenberg et al., 2006). Further still, the low activity allele of MAOA has also been shown to predict gang membership, and once in gangs, the use of weapons during a fight (Beaver, DeLisi, Vaughn, &

Barnes, 2010) in addition to general criminal offending (Beaver, DeLisi, Vaughn, & Wright, 2010). In the twenty-first century, criminologists are able to specify the ways that the "visceral brain" and the risk polymorphisms that suffuse the limbic system work to manifest in criminal behavior and assorted antisocial acts.

References

Andari, E., Duhamel, J.-R., Zalla, T., Herbrecht, E., Leboyer, M., et al. (2010). Promoting social behavior with oxytocin in high-functioning autism spectrum disorders. *Proceedings of the National Academy of Sciences of the United States of America, 107,* 4389–4394.

Beaver, K. M., DeLisi, M., Vaughn, M. G., & Barnes, J. C. (2010). Monoamine oxidase A genotype is associated with gang membership and weapon use. *Comprehensive Psychiatry, 51,* 130–134.

Beaver, K. M., DeLisi, M., Vaughn, M. G., & Wright, J. P. (2010). The intersection of genes and neuropsychological deficits in the prediction of adolescent delinquency and low self-control. *International Journal of Offender Therapy and Comparative Criminology, 54,* 22–42.

Bertolino, A., Rubino, V., Sambataro, F., Blasi, G., Latorre, V., et al. (2006). Prefrontal-hippocampal coupling during memory processing is modulated by COMT Val159Met genotype. *Biological Psychiatry, 60,* 1250–1258.

Birbaumer, N., Veit, R., Lotze, M., Erb, M., Hermann, C., et al. (2005). Deficient fear conditioning in psychopathy. *Archives of General Psychiatry, 62,* 799–801.

Blair, R. J. R. (1995). A cognitive developmental approach to morality: Investigating the psychopath. *Cognition, 57,* 1–29.

Blair, R. J. R. (1997). Moral reasoning in the child with psychopathic tendencies. *Personality and Individual Differences, 22,* 731–739.

Blair, R. J. R. (2003). Neurobiological basis of psychopathy. *British Journal of Psychiatry, 182,* 5–7.

Blair, R. J. R. (2004). The roles of orbital frontal cortex in the modulation of antisocial behavior. *Brain and Cognition, 55,* 198–208.

Blair, R. J. R. (2005). Applying a cognitive neuroscience perspective to the disorder of psychopathy. *Development and Psychopathology, 17,* 865–891.

Blair, R. J. R. (2006). Subcortical brain systems in psychopathy: The amygdala and associated structures. In C. J. Patrick (Ed.), *Handbook of psychopathy* (pp. 296–312). New York: The Guilford Press.

Blair, R. J. R. (2008a). The amygdala and ventromedial prefrontal cortex: Functional contributions and dysfunction in psychopathy. *Philosophical Transactions of the Royal Society B, 363,* 2557–2565.

Blair, R. J. R. (2008b). The cognitive neuroscience of psychopathy and implications for judgments of responsibility. *Neuroethics, 1,* 149–157.

Blair, R. J. R. (2010). Neuroimaging of psychopathy and antisocial behavior: A targeted review. *Current Psychiatry Reports, 12,* 76–82.

Blair, R. J. R., Colledge, E., Murray, L., & Mitchell, D. G. (2001). A selective impairment in the processing of sad and fearful expressions in children with psychopathic tendencies. *Journal of Abnormal Child Psychology, 29,* 491–498.

Blair, J., Mitchell, D., & Blair, K. (2005). *The psychopath: Emotion and the brain.* Malden, MA: Blackwell.

Briken, P., Habermann, N., Berner, W., & Hill, A. (2005). The influence of brain abnormalities on psychosocial development, criminal history, and paraphilias in sexual murderers. *Journal of Forensic Sciences, 50,* 1204–1208.

Buckholtz, J. W., Treadway, M. T., Cowan, R. L., Woodward, N. D., Benning, S. D., et al. (2010). Mesolimbic dopamine reward system hypersensitivity in individuals with psychopathic traits. *Nature Neuroscience, 13,* 419–421.

Bush, G., Luu, P., & Posner, M. I. (2000). Cognitive and emotional influences in anterior cingulate cortex. *Trends in Cognitive Sciences, 4,* 215–222.

Clark, D. L., Boutros, N. N., & Mendez, M. F. (2008). *The brain and behavior: An introduction to behavioral neuroanatomy.* New York: Cambridge University Press.

Cousijn, H., Rijpkema, M., Qin, S., van Marle, H. J. F., Franke, B., et al. (2010). Acute stress modulates genotype effects on amygdala processing in humans. *Proceedings of the National Academy of Sciences of the United States of America, 107,* 9867–9872.

Craig, M. C., Catani, M., Deeley, Q., Latham, R., Daly, E., et al. (2009). Altered connections on the road to psychopathy. *Molecular Psychiatry, 14,* 946–953.

Damasio, A. R. (1994). *Descartes' error: Emotion, reason, and the human brain.* New York: Grosset/Putnam.

Damasio, A. R. (2000). The neural basis of sociopathy. *Archives of General Psychiatry, 57,* 128–129.

Davidson, R. J. (2001). Toward a biology of personality and emotion. *Annals of the New York Academy of Sciences, 935,* 191–207.

Davidson, R. J. (2003). Affective neuroscience and psychophysiology: Toward a synthesis. *Psychophysiology, 40,* 655–665.

Davidson, R. J., Putnam, K. M., & Larson, C. L. (2000). Dysfunction in the neural circuitry of emotion regulation: A possible prelude to violence. *Science, 289,* 591–594.

Davis, M., & Whalen, P. J. (2001). The amygdala: Vigilance and emotion. *Molecular Psychiatry, 6,* 13–34.

Decety, J., Michalska, K. J., Akitsuki, Y., & Lahey, B. B. (2009). Atypical empathic responses in adolescents with aggressive conduct disorder: A functional MRI investigation. *Biological Psychology, 80,* 203–211.

DeLisi, M. (2005). *Career criminals in society.* Thousand Oaks, CA: Sage.

DeLisi, M., Umphress, Z. R., & Vaughn, M. G. (2009). The criminology of the amygdala. *Criminal Justice and Behavior, 36,* 1241–1252.

DeLisi, M., Wright, J. P., Vaughn, M. G., & Beaver, K. M. (2009). Copernican criminology. *The Criminologist, 34,* 14–16.

Domes, G., Heinrichs, M., Gläscher, J., Büchel, C., Braus, D. F., et al. (2007). Oxytocin attenuates amygdala responses to emotional faces regardless of valence. *Biological Psychiatry, 62,* 1187–1190.

Fairchild, G., Stobbe, Y., van Goozen, S. H. M., Calder, A. J., & Goodyer, I. M. (2010). Facial expression recognition, fear conditioning, and startle modulation in female subjects with conduct disorder. *Biological Psychiatry, 68*, 272–279.

Fairchild, G., van Goozen, S. H., Calder, A. J., Stollery, S. J., & Goodyer, I. M. (2009). Deficits in facial expression recognition in male adolescents with early-onset or adolescence-onset conduct disorder. *Journal of Child Psychology and Psychiatry, 50*, 12–168.

Gao, Y., Raine, A., Chan, F., Venables, P. H., & Mednick, S. A. (2010). Early maternal and paternal bonding, childhood physical abuse and adult psychopathic personality. *Psychological Medicine, 40*, 1007–1016.

Gao, Y., Raine, A., Venables, P. H., Dawson, M. E., & Mednick, S. A. (2010). Association of poor childhood fear conditioning and adult crime. *American Journal of Psychiatry, 167*, 56–60.

George, D. T., Rawlings, R. R., Williams, W. A., Phillips, M. J., Fong, G., et al. (2004). A select group of perpetrators of domestic violence: Evidence of decreased metabolism I the right hypothalamus and reduced relationships between cortical/subcortical brain structures in positron emission tomography. *Psychiatry Research, 130*, 11–25.

Glenn, A. L., Raine, A., & Schug, R. A. (2009). The neural correlates of moral decision-making in psychopathy. *Molecular Psychiatry, 14*, 5–6.

Glenn, A. L., Raine, A., Yaralian, P. S., & Yang, Y. (2010). Increased volume of the striatum in psychopathic individuals. *Biological Psychiatry, 67*, 52–58.

Gordon, H. L., Baird, A. A., & End, A. (2004). Functional differences among those high and low on a trait measure of psychopathy. *Biological Psychiatry, 56*, 516–521.

Gray, J. A. (1982). *The neuropsychology of anxiety: An enquiry into the functions of the septo-hippocampal system*. New York: Oxford University Press.

Hariri, A. R., Bookheimer, S. Y., & Mazziotta, J. C. (2000). Modulating emotional responses: Effects of a neocortical network on the limbic system. *Neuroreport, 11*, 43–48.

Jones, A. P., Laurens, K. R., Herba, C. M., Barker, G. J., & Viding, E. (2009). Amygdala hypoactivity to fearful faces in boys with conduct problems and callous-unemotional traits. *American Journal of Psychiatry, 166*, 95–102.

Kiehl, K. A. (2006). A cognitive neuroscience perspective on psychopathy: Evidence for paralimbic system dysfunction. *Psychiatry Research, 142*, 107–128.

Kiehl, K. A., Smith, A. M., Hare, R. D., Mendrek, A., Forster, B. B., et al. (2001). Limbic abnormalities in affective processing by criminal psychopaths as revealed by functional magnetic resonance imaging. *Biological Psychiatry, 50*, 677–684.

Kosfeld, M., Heinrichs, M., Zak, P. J., Fischbacher, U., & Fehr, E. (2005). Oxytocin increases trust in humans. *Nature, 435*, 673–676.

Lee, T. M. C., Chan, S. C., & Raine, A. (2008). Strong limbic and weak frontal activation in aggressive stimuli in spouse abusers. *Molecular Psychiatry, 13*, 655–660.

Light, S. N., Coan, J. A., Zahn-Wexler, C., Frye, C., Goldsmith, H. H., et al. (2009). Empathy is associated with dynamic change in prefrontal brain electrical activity during positive emotion in children. *Child Development, 80,* 1210–1231.

Luciana, M. (2006). Cognitive neuroscience and the prefrontal cortex: Normative development and vulnerability to psychopathology. In D. Cicchetti & D. J. Cohen (Eds.), *Developmental psychopathology volume 2: Developmental neuroscience* (pp. 292–331). New York: John Wiley and Sons.

Lynam, D. R., Charnigo, R., Moffitt, T. E., Raine, A., Loeber, R., et al. (2009). The stability of psychopathy across adolescence. *Development and Psychopathology, 21,* 1133–1153.

MacLean, P. D. (1949). Psychosomatic disease and the visceral brain: Recent developments bearing on the Papez theory of emotion. *Psychosomatic Medicine, 11,* 338–353.

MacLean, P. D. (1955). The limbic system (visceral brain) and emotional behavior. *Archives of Neurology and Psychiatry, 73,* 130–134.

MacLean, P. D. (1990). *The triune brain in evolution: Role in paleocerebral functions.* New York: Plenum.

Marsh, A. A., Finger, E. C., Mitchell, D. G. V., Reid, M. E., Sims, C., et al. (2008). Reduced amygdala response to fearful expressions in children and adolescents with callous-unemotional traits and disruptive behavior disorders. *American Journal of Psychiatry, 165,* 712–720.

Mead, H. K., Beauchaine, T. P., & Shannon, K. E. (2010). Neurobiological adaptations to violence across development. *Development and Psychopathology, 22,* 1–22.

Meyer-Lindenberg, A., Buckholtz, J. W., Kolachana, B., Hariri, A. R., Pezawas, L., et al. (2006). Neural mechanisms of genetic risk for impulsivity and violence in humans. *Proceedings of the National Academy of Sciences of the United States of America, 103,* 6269–6274.

Montag, C., Buckholtz, J. W., Hartmann, P., Merz, M., Burk, C., et al. (2008). COMT genetic variation affects fear processing: Psychophysiological evidence. *Behavioral Neuroscience, 122,* 901–909.

Müller, J. L. (2010). Psychopathy: An approach to neuroscientific research in forensic psychiatry. *Behavioral Sciences and the Law, 28,* 129–147.

Muñoz, L. C. (2009). Callous-unemotional traits are related to combined deficits in recognizing afraid faces and body poses. *Journal of the American Academy of Child and Adolescent Psychiatry, 48,* 554–562.

Papez, J. W. (1937). A proposed mechanism of motion. *Archives of Neurology and Psychiatry, 38,* 725–743.

Patrick, C. J., Fowles, D. C., & Krueger, R. F. (2009). Triarchic conceptualization of psychopathy: Developmental origins or disinhibition, boldness, and meanness. *Development and Psychopathology, 21,* 913–938.

Petrovic, P., Kalisch, R., Singer, T., & Dolan, R. J. (2008). Oxytocin attenuates affective evaluations of conditioned faces and amygdala activity. *Journal of Neuroscience, 28,* 6607–6615.

Pontius, A. A. (1997). Homicide linked to moderate repetitive stresses kindling limbic seizures in 14 cases of limbic psychotic trigger reaction. *Aggression and Violent Behavior, 2,* 125–141.

Price, J. L., & Drevets, W. C. (2010). Neurocircuitry of mood disorders. *Neuropsychopharmacology, 35,* 192–216.

Raine, A., Buchsbaum, M., & LaCasse, L. (1997). Brain abnormalities in murderers indicated by positron emission tomography. *Biological Psychiatry, 42,* 495–508.

Raine, A., Ishikawa, S. S., Arce, E., Lencz, T., Knuth, K. H., et al. (2004). Hippocampal structural asymmetry in unsuccessful psychopaths. *Biological Psychiatry, 55,* 185–191.

Raine, A., Meloy, J. R., Bihrle, S., Stoddard, J., LaCasse, L., et al. (1998). Reduced prefrontal and increased subcortical brain functioning assessed using positron emission tomography in predatory and affective murderers. *Behavioral Sciences and the Law, 16,* 319–332.

Rijsdijsk, F. V., Viding, E., De Brito, S., Forgiarini, M., Mechelli, A., et al. (2010). Heritable variations in gray matter concentration as a potential endophenotype for psychopathic traits. *Archives of General Psychiatry, 67,* 406–413.

Schneider, F., Habel, U., Kessler, C., Posse, S., Grodd, W., et al. (2000). Functional imaging of conditioned aversive emotional responses in antisocial personality disorder. *Neuropsychobiology, 42,* 192–201.

Shin, L. M., & Liberzon, I. (2010). The neurocircuitry of fear, stress, and anxiety disorders. *Neuropsychopharmacology, 35,* 169–191.

Tancredi, L. (2005). *Hardwired behavior: What neuroscience reveals about morality.* New York: Cambridge University Press.

van Honk, J., & Schutter, D. J. L. G. (2005). Dynamic brain systems in quest for emotional homeostasis. *Behavioral and Brain Sciences, 28,* 220–221.

van Honk, J., & Schutter, D. J. L. G. (2006). Unmasking feigned sanity: A neurobiological model of emotion processing in primary psychopathy. *Cognitive Neuropsychiatry, 11,* 285–306.

Vloet, T. D., Konrad, K., Huebner, T., Herpertz, S., & Herpertz-Dahlmann, B. (2008). Structural and functional MRI findings in children and adolescents with antisocial behavior. *Behavioral Sciences and the Law, 26,* 99–111.

Williams, L. M., Gatt, J. M., Kuan, S. A., Dobson-Stone, C., Palmer, D. M., et al. (2009). A polymorphism of the MAOA gene is associated with emotional brain markers and personality traits on an antisocial index. *Neuropsychopharmacology, 34,* 1797–1809.

Yang, Y., & Raine, A. (2009). Prefrontal structural and functional brain imaging findings in antisocial, violent, and psychopathic individuals: A meta-analysis. *Psychiatry Research: Neuroimaging, 174,* 81–88.

Yang, Y., Raine, A., Han, C.-B., Schug, R. A., Toga, A. W., et al. (2010). Reduced hippocampal and parahippocampal volumes in murderers with schizophrenia. *Psychiatry Research: Neuroimaging, 182,* 9–13.

Yang, Y., Raine, A., Narr, K. L., Colletti, P., & Toga, A. W. (2009). Localizations of deformations within the amygdala in individuals with psychopathy. *Archives of General Psychiatry, 66,* 986–994.

Neurobiological Perspectives of Brain Vulnerability in Pathways to Violence over the Life Course

Denise Paquette Boots

Introduction

The idea that criminality and human violence may be linked to biosocial origins is a controversial one that has been argued since the inception of behavioral and social sciences. Since the first work highlighting the nature versus nurture debate was published by Francis Galton (1865), scientists have sought a more lucid understanding of how genetic links might explain human behavior (Plomin & Asbury, 2005). In recent years, the merging of criminological inquiries with disciplines such as neurology, public health, biology, epidemiology, and psychology has resulted in developmental, holistic perspectives that have decidedly moved away from strictly sociological or ecologically-based explanations regarding the genesis of criminogenic behaviors. Accordingly, an intriguing body of research has emerged that endorses an interdisciplinary, biosocial focus regarding the pathways leading to violence and aggression over the lifespan, especially with regard to early onset antisocial behaviors (Viding, 2004). A steady stream of works incorporating new and innovative methods and designs is reinvigorating the level of discourse on whether crime is a result of "nature versus nurture," or genetic versus environmental theories of antisocial behavior.

One of the main areas of this research focuses around the plasticity and resiliency of the brain and the link between neuropsychology, vulnerabilities, processes, and life outcomes. In the late 1970s, Dorothy Otnow Lewis and her colleagues began to present compelling evidence regarding this relationship, positing that neurological impairments, or vulnerabilities, within individuals' central nervous systems were associated with antisocial and violent behaviors. Specifically, genetics, neurological impairment, psychiatric illnesses, cognitive deficits and injuries, and child abuse and maltreatment were postulated to collectively combine to render people more intrinsically vulnerable (Lewis, Lovely et al., 1988). Lewis and her collaborators further suggested that violent acts were more likely to be committed by such individuals when they were exposed to intense psychological, environmental, and social stressors (Lewis, Pincus et al., 1988). As such, these vulnerable subjects had "cope[d] with brain dysfunction, cognitive limitations, severe psychopathology, and violent abusive households" (Lewis, Pincus et al., 1988, pp. 588–589) that stretched them beyond their limits and consequently led them to deviance. A myriad of subsequent studies have since examined these neurobiological factors and have contributed substantially to our understanding of violence pathways. These issues have crucial public policy implications with regards to prevention and intervention efforts to reduce violence and other negative life-course outcomes (Greenberg, 2006).

The newest iteration of genetic and biosocial theories offers viable rubrics to frame the system of human networks and social and biological processes, as it argues that heritable traits, brain structure, and neurological insults play a vital role in explaining deviance and the emergence of antisocial behaviors across developmental stages. A perusal of the neuropsychosocial literature reveals a multitude of works that offer robust support for a relationship between neuropsychological impairments and human violence. This rubric does not propose that biology and environment are independent of each other. Instead, this holistic approach to "aggression is based on the assumption that aggressive behavior is multi-determined and dynamic over the life span, and a product of a complex continuous interaction of the multiple psycho-biosocial changes" (Ramirez, 2003). Rather than disregard environmental factors, then, the latest theories regarding developmental vulnerability acknowledge the competing processes between the human experience within the environment and from biological regulation. Indeed, "the relationship between neurobiological and environmental processes is interactive, fluid, and cumulative in their ability to influence an individual's developmental progress and alter subsequent behavioral outcomes. Given the codependent relationship between these processes, brain function is now believed to be malleable via manipulations of the environment in ways that may decrease liability for psychopathology" (Fishbein & Tarter, 2009, p. 1205). The present chapter offers an overview of the contributions of a host of neuropsychological vulnerabilities, risk and protective factors, as well as brain plasticity and resilience, all subsumed under a biosocial framework, as robust predictors of antisocial and violent behaviors over the lifespan. First, a short review of brain structure, the central nervous system, and neuroimaging studies of the brain are offered for the reader.

Brain and Central Nervous System Structure, Deficits, and Risk Factors

To appreciate how neuropsychological vulnerabilities and brain plasticity may alter pathways to aggression and violence over the life-course, it is necessary to consider the development of the brain and nervous system as humans mature. The brain weighs approximately three pounds at full size and continues to change and produce new cells via "neurogenesis" throughout life (Gage, 2002). The central nervous system is comprised of nerve cells, called neurons, which communicate critical information about the functions of life, sensory impulses, and body reactions via chemical substances called neurotransmitters (Nevid, Rathus, & Greene, 2000). Neural pathways continue to change over the life-course. Each neurotransmitter has a unique chemical structure that fits a certain receptor site, or receiving neuron. Examples of neurotransmitters include dopamine, norepinephrine, acetylcholine, and serotonin.

Where the spinal cord meets the brain is called the hindbrain, consisting of the medulla, pons, and cerebellum, the latter of which helps control motor coordination, muscle tone, and balance. The medulla controls the vital functions of heart rate, respiration, sleep, and blood pressure; the pons also contributes to sleep, respiration, and attention. The midbrain area controls many auditory, visual, and motor functions. Finally, the forebrain center holds many critical areas such as the thalamus (which relays sensory information to higher areas through the cerebral cortex) and the hypothalamus (which regulates body temperature, body fluids, nutrient storage, motivation, emotions, and sexual activities). The larger limbic system is located in the forebrain and comprised of the thalamus, hypothalamus, septum, hippocampus, caudate nucleus, and amygdala (Golden, Jackson, Peterson-Rohne, & Gontkovsky, 1996). In coordination with the brain stem, the limbic system regulates vital health functions such as heartbeat, blood pressure, and sugar levels, as well as controlling complex emotional responses and nerve impulses throughout the skeletal system and in other internal organs. It also is responsible for libido, appetite, and sleep as well as the emotional state of the brain (Wright, Tibbetts, & Daigle, 2008). As part of the limbic system, the amygdala is the central organ related to the regulation of fear (Solms & Turnbull, 2002). The largest and most evolved region of the brain is the cerebral cortex, including the cerebrum, which distinguishes humans from other animals due to the unique size and learning center housed in the cerebrum (Wright et al., 2008). Together, these sensitive areas of the brain can be separated into four lobes of the cerebral cortex (or the surface of the brain with its ridges and valleys). These four lobes include the frontal, temporal, parietal, and occipital; only the occipital region is not linked with antisocial behaviors (see Vaske, Galyean, & Cullen, 2011 for a more detailed discussion of the Brodmann areas (or regions) of the brain that perform different functions). Connecting these lobes together is a thick fiber bundle called the corpus callosum. Although a small organ in relative size to others in the body, the brain governs all aspects of behavior, mood, cognition, and regulation of voluntary and involuntary functions and is extraordinarily complex.

Life-Course Development of the Brain and Neurological Risk Factors

Until quite recently, researchers believed that the bulk of growth and development in the human brain occurred within just the first few years of life. Brain development begins with the formation of the neural tubes in the third or fourth week of prenatal development (Levitt, 2003). While up to 95 percent of brain structure has formed by age six and most neurons have been developed in utero, the human brain continues to mature and change in functionality and internal configuration across the lifespan (Wright et al., 2008). Some of the newest studies on life-course development have shown that the human brain continues to change substantially through age 25, although the most rapid period of growth occurs in the first five years of life (Shonkoff & Marshall, 2000). Thus, childhood represents a time of critical neurocognitive maturation and development that is quite susceptible to environmental vulnerabilities that emerge during this period.

Prenatally, a fetus is impacted by the mother's emotional, physical, and environmental experiences, all of which in turn directly influence the health of the growing fetus across key periods of physiological, mental, and cognitive development. Nutrition, maternal depression, lead exposure, substance use, maternal stress, domestic violence, and smoking have all been studied extensively as they relate to poor outcomes for the offspring (e.g. Beaver, Sak, Vaske, & Nilsson, 2010; Cummings & Davies, 1994; Olds, 2007; Wills, Schreibman, Benson, & Vaccaro, 1994). Lou and colleagues (1994), for example, followed over 3,000 women throughout their pregnancies and found a significant positive relationship between maternal stress and smoking with small head circumference, low birth-weight, and premature birth of offspring. A higher level of maternal prenatal stress was also correlated with lower scores for children on the neonatal examinations, indicating a greater risk for vulnerability at the time of critical brain growth in these children. Other research has found that raised maternal cortisol levels in response to stress may be related to elevated postnatal aggression in children (Lewis, 2002). Importantly, chronic gestational stress is believed to cause sustained neural modifications and vulnerabilities that further mediate and reinforce long-term negative maternal behaviors (Meaney & Champagne, 2000). In this way, environmental adversity and maternal emotional stability combine to have a direct effect on child outcomes because "chronic stress increases anxiety and fearfulness, and thus decreases maternal responsivity, which in turn influences the stress reactivity in the offspring" (Parent et al., 2004, pp. 2–20). Both perinatal and prenatal factors have been shown to affect the temperaments of infants and a multitude of environmental influences may influence vulnerable youngsters if caretakers are stressed or otherwise compromised mentally or physically in providing basic nutrition, affection, and needs for their children (Farrington & Welsh, 2007).

At birth, environmental and social influences immediately impact the brain and its growth. Roughly 75 percent of the cerebrum grows postnatal, with certain areas continuing to grow and evolve (Shonkoff & Marshall, 2000). The brain is rapidly changing in the first two years of life as cells and synaptic connections explode in number. While many more of these synapses will be created than are used, early life experiences such as attachment, nurturing, parental interactions with the child, and various forms of deprivation and maltreatment will influence which synapses will be strengthened or dissolved from misuse (Singer, 1995). Some scholars have posited that there are more critical periods of development where brain vulnerability is especially salient to normal progression (Scarr, 1993). Strong, healthy attachment bonds with caretakers appear to be related to healthy cognitive outcomes for children, which is important in the early stages of life as the frontal lobes continue to develop through the second year. Kids possessing disorganized attachment patterns, or those youngsters whose mothers are depressed and dysfunctional in coping with stressors, were significantly more likely to express aggression at age seven (Lyons-Ruth, 1996) and in elementary school (Renken, Egelan, Marvinney, Mangelsdorf, & Sroufe, 1989). In turn, these children are at significantly greater risk for caretaker neglect and abuse, which is a predictor for both antisocial behaviors and mental health issues later in life (Cicchetti & Barnett, 1991).

Chronic, pervasive abuse has devastating effects on the brain and physical advancement during the critical stages of childhood and adolescence. "Such abuse, it seems, induces a cascade of molecular and neurobiological effects that irreversibly alter neural development" (Teicher, 2002). A convincing link between brain trauma and antisocial behaviors and psychological disorders has emerged in the past two decades (Raine, Lencz, Bihrle, LaCasse, & Colletti, 2000; Silver, Hales, & Yudofsky, 1997), especially when considering a number of non-prospective studies that have pointed directly at serious abuse like head injury as the major catalyst of neurological defects (see Sparling & Cohen, 1997). Studies examining the consequences of child abuse and victimization have also reported that maltreated individuals were at increased risk for such violent behaviors as dating/courtship violence (Dodge, Bates, & Pettit, 1990), physical abuse of their own children (Widom 1989a, 1989b), spousal and partner abuse (Rosenbaum & O'Leary, 1981), caretaker and sibling violence (Kratcoski, 1984), delinquency (Fagan, 2005), and adult criminality (DeGue & Widom, 2009) when compared to non-abused persons. Overall, severe, recurrent child abuse has been shown to be comparable in severity to accidental brain injuries. In one study, it was found that mental deficiencies were present in only 5 percent of children who suffered accidental injuries versus 45 percent of kids who were abused (Ewing-Cobbs et al., 1998). Central nervous system trauma, including prenatal distress, interpersonal violence, mental health problems, and accident-induced head injuries, has been frequently observed in violent juveniles when compared to non-violent controls (Lewis, Pincus, Feldman, Jackson, & Bard, 1986; Lewis, Pincus, et al., 1988; Moffitt, 1990b; Lewis & Shanok, 1979).

Individuals with biological weaknesses or vulnerabilities are at substantially greater risk for a pathological response to environmental stressors, and these outcomes vary depending on the frequency and severity of the individual risk factors impacting these persons. Gerald Patterson and his colleagues (1992) have described a cycle of coercive parenting whereby "interactions in which maladaptive and ineffective management strategies regarding preschool disobedience actually reinforce, perpetuate, and model aggressive behavior" (Twemlow & Bennett, 2008, p. 1164). These negative parent–child relationships create outcomes similar to disorganized attachment patterns. From a biosocial perspective, abusive and dysfunctional family environments foster neurochemical imbalances that stymie brain growth and handicap normal development at especially sensitive periods of growth. When combined with the presence of severe abuse, including brain trauma, these effects can be devastating to children in their developmental progression.

Cumulatively, these scholarly works suggest that existence of perinatal and pregnancy-related complications, as well as childhood-related abuse that leads to physical trauma or injury, are significant predictors of future violence over the life-course (Kandel & Mednick, 1991). The more systemic these environmental and social risks become, the greater the damage to the child long-term and there is less chance of resiliency to overcome these obstacles. Pincus (2000) argues that "the effect of even mild traumatic brain injury can be permanent and debilitating if there is a history of prior brain injuries. Abuse and neglect magnify the malign influence of traumatic brain injury through this mechanism" (p. 779).

Deficiencies and/or the overproduction of neurotransmitters and hormones have also been linked to multiple mental health problems such as mood, anxiety, sleep, eating, and schizophrenic disorders (McBurnett, Pfiffner, Capasso, Lahey, & Loeber, 1997; Zuckerman, 1994) and play a substantive role in neurological vulnerabilities. A number of studies have implicated imbalances of serotonin, cortisol, triiodothyroine, endocrine and other biochemicals with impulsivity, irritability, hostility, antisocial personality disorder, and persistent aggression (Anderson & Silver, 1999; Dolan, 1994; Virkkunen et al., 1994; World Health Organization, 1992). A large body of literature has also found a link between deviations in genetic structure, called polymorphisms, and the production of the neurotransmitters serotonin, norepinephrine, and dopamine which put individuals at increased risk for addiction (Fishbein, 1998). A host of physiological, neuropsychological, and neuroimaging studies suggest that brain dysfunction and vulnerability leads to risky behaviors and poor outcomes, including conduct disorder, problems with emotion regulation, impulsivity, sensation-seeking, and impaired judgment (Raine, 2002; Werner, 2000).

The ongoing longitudinal studies that are examining youngsters from conception through birth and then throughout the various stages of human development will help to tease out the unique roles that various forms of biological, neurochemical, and psychosocial deficits play in the genesis of violence and aggression. The proposed relationship between various structures in the brain and human violence is further supported by vast empirical evidence in the neuropsychological literature surrounding brain lesions, imaging technologies (e.g. Positron Emission Tomography or PET scans), electro-encephalogram (or EEG) scans, and other forms of neuropsychological testing. A concise synthesis of this literature is offered in the following section.

Brain Imaging Studies and Violence

Neuroimaging studies have emerged as one of the most significant and exciting advances in recent years in the study of brain disorders and abnormalities as they correlate with aggression and violence. Newer, more advanced technological tests are able to capture information on brain dysfunction and structural impairment that were not obvious on the comprehensive neuropsychological batteries commonly administered in the past (Filley et al., 2001). Mounting evidence has surfaced that connects dysfunction in the orbitofrontal regions of the brain with antisocial behaviors, regardless of whether individuals possess structural lesions or display more subtle impairments (Grafman et al., 1996). While this relationship between orbitofrontal impairment and aggression remains somewhat ambiguous, "one suggestion is that the antisocial personality disorder as well as other conditions such as borderline personality disorder, histrionic personality disorder, and dissociative identity disorder may result from brain dysfunction induced by childhood physical and sexual abuse" (Filley et al., 2001, p. 9).

Some of the first EEG studies focused on murderers to determine if brain abnormalities could be detected within these samples (Williams, 1969). One of the first studies found half of 105 killers did indeed have abnormal values (Hill & Pond, 1952). Numerous other studies have also found higher rates of abnormal EEGs in violent, aggressive, and homicidal populations (Mark & Ervin, 1970; Raine, 1993), with few exceptions (Miller, 1999). Raine and his colleagues have presented compelling evidence of a relationship between violence and brain vulnerabilities. In one early review of advanced neuroimaging research, for instance, Mills and Raine (1994) analyzed studies using Computed Tomography (CT), Magnetic Resonance Imaging (MRI), PET, and other advanced technologies. These studies largely sought to determine the extent of neurological damage in violent offenders when compared to non-violent persons. After reviewing the evidence at that time, Mills and Raine offered two possible explanations. First, the available data suggested that frontal lobe impairment was related to violent offending, whereas violent sexual offending was associated with temporal and frontal-temporal lobe damage, respectively. An opposing viewpoint was also offered that suggested that any form of anterior brain impairment (meaning frontal, temporal, or frontal-temporal) "may represent a general predisposition to offending, irrespective of the specific location of the dysfunction, and that the specific nature of the offense (e.g., violent, sexual, or violent and sexual) may be determined primarily by nonbiological factors, such as life history and personality" (Hawkins & Trobst, 2000, p. 154). Raine, Buchsbaum, and LaCasse (1997) also found significant metabolic decreases in the prefrontal and left subcortical regions of the brains of 41 murderers who pled not guilty by reason of insanity. Furthermore, the researchers found both reduced metabolism in the prefrontal and subcortical cortexes, as well as abnormal asymmetries of brain activity in the amygdala, thalamus, and medial temporal lobes of the homicidal group when compared to matched controls (Raine et al., 1997). Other scholars have similarly reported a significant association between aggressive behavior and the presence of lesions in the prefrontal cortex of brain-injured Vietnam veterans using CT imaging (Grafman et al., 1996).

Raine et al. (2001) considered the effects of childhood abuse as well in another study using functional MRI (fMRI) technology. The researchers compared four groups of subjects, including: (1) non-violent and unabused controls, (2) non-violent subjects who reported severe physical and sexual abuse prior to age 11, (3) violent, unabused participants, and (4) severely abused, seriously violent individuals. The fMRI results indicated that severely abused violent offenders had reduced functioning in the right temporal cortex. Moreover, the abused but non-violent persons showed lower left hemisphere activity and increased activity in the temporal lobes. These findings suggest right hemisphere dysfunction, a neurobiological risk factor, when combined with severe childhood abuse, a psychosocial risk factor, greatly increases the likelihood of serious violent behaviors.

Subsequent research supports these findings. For instance, another study of seven subjects with repetitive extreme violence were administered PET, neuropsychiatric, and neuropsychological tests, and then compared to nine control subjects who showed no evidence of organic brain dysfunction (Seidenwurm, Pounds, Globus, & Valk, 1997). Again, the PET scans indicated significant metabolic abnormalities in the temperolimbic areas of the violent subjects' brains. The authors argued that these results, at least in part, confirm previous studies that have found temporal lobe hypometabolism (Volkow & Tancredi, 1987) and limbic system abnormalities in capital murderers evaluated for psychiatric measures (Raine et al., 1994).

Another well-cited study presented by Blake and colleagues (1995) focused on 31 accused or convicted murderers who were referred to psychiatric and neurological testing. Compelling evidence of frontal lobe dysfunction was reported in 64.5 percent of those subjects examined neurologically, and all study participants were found to have some type of abnormalities from the neuropsychological examinations. Moreover, roughly two-thirds of the subjects were diagnosed with specific neurological problems, including mental retardation, epilepsy, traumatic brain injury, and fetal alcohol syndrome. The authors identified a triad of factors contributing to the genesis of violence in these individuals, including: (1) a high frequency of severe and chronic abuse, (2) brain dysfunction and damage, and (3) acutely paranoid thoughts and behaviors. Additively, these individual factors created a "matrix of violence" (p. 1646) that was far more influential than any factor would be singularly. The extended abuse, or "torture," of these brain-damaged subjects was posited to have created dissociative states that could be easily mistaken for partial seizures. This potent cocktail of pervasive abuse, brain damage and trauma, and severe mental illness/paranoia has been supported by the work of Lewis, Pincus, and their co-authors that have reported similar episodes of impulsive, random dyscontrol in violent offender groups (e.g., Lewis, Pincus, & Glaser, 1979; Lewis et al., 1986; Lewis, Pincus, et al., 1988; Pincus, 1996, 2000).

Other research has focused more on the propensity for violence within individuals diagnosed with complex partial seizures or temporal lobe epilepsy (Bear & Fedio, 1977; Mark & Ervin, 1970; Mendez, 1998). Impaired inhibitory systems or excited adjacent neurons may lead to excessive neural activity, called seizures, which may occur sporadically as the neurons discharge (Rosenhan & Seligman, 1995). While the vast majority of persons with epilepsy do not commit violence against others, a constellation of contributing factors emerge regarding why a relative few epileptic patients become violent. Mendez et al. (1993), for example, found that aggressive patients with temporal lobe epilepsy had significant differences across psychopathological and mental retardation measures. Other scientists have found similar significant relationships, but exclusively for temporal lobe epileptics (Volavka, Martell, & Convit, 1992) and juvenile homicide offenders (Lewis et al., 1985). Overall, research on epileptics has generally found acts of aggression as random acts, set off by physical and/or psychological stressors, rather than as premeditated and controlled aggressive acts around the seizure event (Lewis & Pincus, 1989).

However, a more consistent relationship has been established between epilepsy and a specified neurological condition known as "episodic dyscontrol." This form of impairment is associated with temporal lobe and limbic system damage, both of which serve as emotion regulators within the body. Indeed, "studies in animals and clinical reports have suggested that violent individuals suffer from intrinsic neurological deficits and that their violent acts may be the direct result of epileptic-type discharges of neurons in these sensitive brain regions. The term 'episodic dyscontrol' has been used to describe paroxyoval outbursts of violent behavior thought to occur in this manner" (Blake et al., 1995, p. 1641). First identified by Kaplan (1899) and Meninger (Meninger & Mayman, 1956), episodic dyscontrol is distinctly marked by recurrent acts of anger that vary in severity, intensity, and form, but which may appear without provocation.

In a critical analysis of more advanced neuroimaging tests, Brower and Price (2001) reviewed numerous studies ranging from 1987 through 2000 that used a host of methodological techniques to determine what differences, if any, appeared in the brains of antisocial, aggressive, and violent subjects. The authors reported strong evidence of frontal lobe abnormalities in violence pathways across these studies. A large number of studies have also shown significant brain differences between psychopathic and normal controls using a variety of neuroimaging methodologies (see, e.g., Beauregard, 2007; Pridemore, Chambers, & McArthur, 2005). While the present review offers just a few examples of this vast area of research and new research is being published in this field at a dramatic rate, these studies presented here clearly highlight the place of developmental perspectives in neuroimaging in studies on aggression. Some of the most promising research coming out of the neurosciences focuses on identification of specific brain regions and dysfunction, the role of gene and environmental factors in pathways to aggressive behaviors, and the development of emotion regulation, as discussed in the following section.

Brain Dysfunction, Neurogenetics, and Emotion Regulation

Clearly, "the relationship between the temporal lobes of the brain and violent and aggressive behavior has been recognized for many years" (Seidenwurm et al., 1997, p. 625). One of the seminal works that examined the influence of the temporal lobes on aggression was that of Kluver and Bucy (1939). After performing bilateral temporal lobectomies (removal of the amygdala and surrounding temporal cortex) on monkeys, the team observed that the primates exhibited less aggression, a reduction in emotional reactivity, and hypersexual responses. An abundance of later studies have further corroborated this proposed relationship between the temperolimbic areas and human violence. In particular, the amygdala's proximity to the temporal lobe has been linked to aggression (Krakowski, 1997).

Human frontal lobes are significantly larger than those of other animals and represent "the biggest and most obvious difference between the brains of humans and other primates" (Pincus, 2000, p. 782). The frontal area of the brain comprises one-third of the mass of the cerebral cortex and plays a vital role in regulating attention, decision-making, inhibitions, impulsivity, and goal executions (Laakso et al., 2001). This "directing and controlling source of the brain" (Hawkins & Trobst, 2000, p. 149) produces most of our crucial human-like behaviors such as planning, higher-order information processing, programming commands, initiating and demanding behaviors, and adaptation to our world. Recent studies have shown that damage to the orbitofrontal cortex has been linked with poor judgment, maladaptive behaviors, emotion regulation of inner drives, and an inability to anticipate poor outcomes (Schoenbaum, Chiba, & Gallagher, 1999; Tremblay & Schultz, 1999). Such impairments often lead individuals to commit impulsive and reckless acts with little regard for inevitable moral consequences (Martens, 2002).

When discussing the frontal lobes, this area includes the entire prefrontal region of the brain. These sensitive regions are constantly affected across the life-course and are subject to social, biological, and environmental factors that impact individuals. Case studies of frontal lobe damage and the link with antisocial outcomes date as far back as 1835, but perhaps the most famous case first widely-documented was that of Phineas Gage, a 25-year-old man who was seriously wounded in an explosion (Rosenhan & Seligman, 1995). Gage suffered severe head trauma when an iron bar over an inch in diameter was shot through the front of his skull from an explosion, damaging his frontal lobe. While he remained conscious through this ordeal, his post-accident personality was in stark contrast to his previous disposition. After the injury, he was prone to violent outbursts, impulsivity, profanity, and other antisocial behaviors, which led to complete social isolation and unemployment.

We now understand that this type of behavior is typical of severe frontal lobe trauma, with "prefrontal dysfunction theory suggest[ing] that damage or dysfunction to the frontal lobe of the brain may in part account for, or predispose [one] to, violent and aggressive behavior" (Raine & Liu, 1998, p. 107). Accordingly, frontal lobe syndrome is recognized as a distinct organic mental health disorder in the World Health Organization's *International Classification of Diseases*. "The principal manifestations of frontal lobe syndrome include impairment in self-control, foresight, creativity, and spontaneity, behaviorally observable 'as increased irritability, selfishness, restlessness, and lack of concern for others'" (Pallone & Hennessy, 2000, pp. 22–25). These individuals are commonly viewed as adversarial and predatory "because of their egocentricity, lack of empathy, lack of planning, and lack of the inability to anticipate the consequences of their behavior, they are also more likely to engage in behaviors that irritate or offend others" (Golden et al., 1996, p. 5). Not surprisingly, the "threshold" for aggressive and violent behaviors may be lower as a result of mood instability in these individuals (Hart & Jacobs, 1993). Lewis, Lovely and their colleagues (1988) further observed that these neuropsychological and neuroanatomical deficits contribute to the overall vulnerability of such individuals, thereby rendering them less resilient in coping with situations and stressors in a healthy or socially acceptable manner.

This categorization can easily be considered a precursor to antisocial behavior and fits into the classic mold of what is characteristically known as a psychopathic offender. Due to their neurological vulnerabilities and insults, individuals with frontal lobe damage are unable to regulate their emotional equilibrium and mood stability, which sometimes results in emotional responses that are drastically out of proportion to the stimulus (Devinski, Morrell, & Vogt, 1995). Although the origins of psychopathy (i.e. psychopathic personality disorder) is unsettled throughout the scientific community, a strong connection has been made between antisocial personality disorder and brain impairment and disorders. Traumatic brain injury (TBI) and dysfunction manifests commonly in frontal lobe functions, with these individuals having little control of their emotions or impulses and a lower threshold for aggressive behavior (Miller, 1990). Indeed, studies have indicated that individuals diagnosed with antisocial personality disorder exhibit similar behavioral features as those persons with acquired sociopathic traits via TBI which subsequently altered previously normal personalities (Tranel, 1994). Lykken (1995) has argued that antisocial persons may be born with irreversible defects of their central nervous system that render them incapable of learning from negative life events.

Some research supports these claims. Yuedall (1977), for instance, found that 91 percent of the psychopathological patients in Alberta, Canada, displayed dysfunction of the left side of the brain, whereas other criminal patients showed vulnerabilities in their right hemispheres. Raine et al. (2000) found that men with antisocial personality disorder had reduced autonomic activity combined with a significant reduction in the prefrontal gray matter of their brains. Miller (1987) has similarly found that more aggressive and impulsive psychopaths display less intelligence and have more frontal-lobe neuropsychological impairments. Still other researchers, however, have criticized the proposed relationship between antisocial or psychopathological behaviors and frontal lobe impairment. Kandel and Freed (1989) argued that this relationship was tenuous because of methodological and definitional issues, uncontrolled designs, and a lack of valid measures across studies. Still other scholars have argued that the tautological nature of the antisocial and psychopathological personality diagnoses rendered this research meaningless in explaining criminal behaviors.

Neurogenetic Links to Violence

Although the largest body of research on the relationship between the brain and violence concentrates on the frontal, temporal, and limbic regions of the brain, new and exciting collaborations within social neurobiology and other disciplines are integrating genetic and biosocial foci into studies regarding the etiology of aggressive behaviors. This has led to a surge of research over the past two decades focusing on the role of genetics in criminogenic outcomes using twin and adoption studies as well as nationally-representative samples (see, e.g., Beaver, DeLisi, Vaughn, &

Barnes, 2010; Beaver et al., 2007; Miles & Carey, 1997; Rutter, 2006). Heritability estimates range between 40 and 80 percent of the variance in antisocial phenotypes (Arsenault et al., 2003; Rhee & Waldman, 2002; Walsh, 2002). Phenotypes are measurable behavioral or neurobiological traits and result from interaction between the genotype (combination of genes transmitted from parents with recombinations or mutations that might occur during gestation) and the environment (Fishbein & Tarter, 2009). Environmental manipulations modify the expression of genes and, therefore, have a significant impact on behavior. As Fishbein and Tarter (2009) explain, "understanding this interactive process translates into the ability to redirect behavior by introducing particular experiences, directive training and opportunities that influence critical neurobiological functions" (p. 1207).

A number of studies measuring genetic polymorphisms have suggested that varying genetics alter the likelihood of engaging in aggressive or violent acts. For instance, Caspi and his colleagues (2002) reported that gene variants impacting the enzyme monoamine oxidase A (MAOA), which metabolizes catecholamine stimulants such as dopamine, serotonin, and norepinephrine (see Shih, 1991), were linked to elevated levels of aggression when individuals were victims of child abuse. In contrast, having normal genes suppressed the effects of child maltreatment. This finding is not surprising when considering the robust association found between low levels of MAOA and higher levels of dopamine and norepinephrine, which in turn are linked with impulsive forms of aggressive and violent behaviors (Rowe, 2002). Low activity MAOA has been connected to a host of poor life-course outcomes and criminogenic phenotypes, including psychopathological, antisocial, and cognitive problems (see, e.g., Caspi et al., 2002; Clark & Grunstein, 2000; Cohen et al., 2003; Haberstick et al., 2005; Kim-Cohen et al., 2006; Widom & Brzustowicz, 2006). A mutated version of the MAOA gene has also been linked within a large Dutch family by Brunner and colleagues (1993) to a host of violent behaviors, including impulsive aggression, attempted rape and arson. This research strongly supports the contention that there is a variable genetic component that influences the development of criminal behaviors and traits (Hamer & Copeland, 1998; Rowe, 2002; Wright & Beaver, 2005), especially with regard to vulnerabilities early in life via social experiences and childrearing (see, e.g., Newman et al., 2005). The MAOA genotype is more common in males, perhaps explaining some of the gender differences in offending (Wright et al., 2008).

The latest generation of genetic studies suggests a more complex interaction between human development, genes, and the environment (Beaver et al., 2007; Beaver, Sak, Vaske, & Nilsson, 2010; Miczek, Maxson, Fish, & Faccidomo, 2001; O'Connor, Reiss, McGuire, & Hetherington, 1998) that results in gene expression. As opposed to influencing behavior in a unidirectional manner, gene expression "may be both a cause and an effect of aggressive and other behaviors and experiences. Or to put it another way, even where genes are among the multiple determinants of violent behavior, they exert their effect only in interaction with other biological and many non-biological (psychological and social) variables" (Gilligan & Lee, 2004, p. 362). This research strongly supports the role of neuropsychological deficits and vulnerabilities as a critical risk factor in developmental pathways to crime and violence (Beaver, Vaughn, DeLisi, & Higgins, 2009; Farrington & Welsh, 2007; McGloin, Pratt, & Piquero, 2006; Moffitt, 1990a, 1993, 2006; Morgan & Lilienfeld, 2000). While it is beyond the scope of this chapter to provide the reader with a comprehensive review of this extant literature revolving around genetics and crime, a number of excellent texts have recently emerged to address this burgeoning specialty area within criminology (for examples see Beaver, 2009; Walsh & Beaver, 2008). Neurogenetics also plays a significant role in the development of advanced neurological skills and cognition in the PCF, as discussed below.

Emotion Regulation and Executive Cognitive Functioning

Higher-order executive cognitive functions (ECF) that regulate conscious and strategic thought, cognitive flexibility, attention, working memory, emotion-regulation, problem solving, temporal responses, planning, and goal-directed actions are largely focused in the PCF and have risen as key measures in intervention and treatment efforts for youth at-risk for aggression and behavioral problems (Riggs & Greenberg, 2004). Although the specific genetic polymorphisms that contribute to ECF deficits have not been identified yet, it is believed that these capacities are shaped by gene–environment interactions and that they work in concert with other regions of the brain in the PCF, anterior cingulated, and limbic system to regulate behavior and emotion (Fishbein & Tarter, 2009). The PCF plays a definitive role in the genesis of impulsive aggression and impulsivity (Blair, 2004; Siever, 2008; Berlin, Rolls, & Kischka, 2004) and the developmental of cortical self-control via mechanisms in the orbitofrontal cortex and lateral areas of the PCF (see Gansler et al., 2011). This inability to regulate emotion or behavior lays the groundwork for developmental perspectives on early onset and life-course persistent pathways to offending (Moffitt, 1993).

As Greenberg (2006) recently noted, the ethical and methodological considerations when studying child populations have limited investigations into the specific brain localization of neurocognitive defects; therefore, little data exists on youth under age 10. Exceptions include Cole et al. (1993), who studied preschoolers and found that neurocognitive issues were positively correlated with disruptive behaviors. Additionally, Olson and Hoza (1993) reported higher levels of impulsiveness in preschool-aged boys was associated with problem behaviors; girls also had low verbal skills in addition to impulsiveness.

A burgeoning number of studies have shown direct and moderating effects between reduced executive functioning and negative outcomes for children and adults alike (see Fishbein et al., 2006; Giancola, 2000; Klingberg et al., 2005). Briefly, Giancola and his colleagues have conducted several noteworthy studies examining the role of low ECF in predicting heightened aggression in youngsters. In one study (Giancola, Martin, Tarter, Pelham, & Moss, 1996a), the authors found antisocial behaviors were more likely in preadolescent boys with low ECF across mother and teacher reports; these effects were stronger for conduct-disordered youth with family histories of substance use. Similar results were reported in a related study examining reactive, or impulsive, aggression in the same sample of boys (Giancola, Moss, Martin, Kirisci, & Tarter, 1996b). Additional research replicates these findings, with Seguin et al. (1995) pointing to the specific importance of ECF scores as a predictor of physical aggression in preadolescent boys, even when controlling for low socioeconomic status. These effects have been replicated with adolescent females, which indicated a significant relationship between low ECF and disruptive, delinquent, and physically aggressive behaviors when controlling for drug use history, SES, and age (Giancola, Mezzich, & Tarter, 1998). A complementary study that added temperament and ADHD in the models found that conduct-disordered girls possessed lower ECF and more difficult temperaments when compared to controls, however ECF mediated this relationship between temperament and antisocial behaviors (Giancola & Mezzich, 1998).

Ford and her associates (2007) have suggested that African American youth with low ECF who also displayed externalizing disorders such as conduct disorder have lowered abilities to adapt and develop working plans when confronted with difficult scenarios. Robert Hare's (1984) work with incarcerated and antisocial personality disordered adults also shows reduced frontal lobe function in such individuals, with cognitive deficits correlated with higher psychopathy scores. Not surprisingly, then, poor ECF functioning has been reported across various samples, including conduct-disordered youngsters (Blume, Davis, & Schmaling, 1999) children with Attention-Deficit Hyperactivity Disorder (ADHD) (Barkley, 1997), as well as aggressive (Kandel & Freed, 1989) and substance abuse disordered subjects (Tarter et al., 2003).

While this empirical evidence displays a robust inverse link between ECF and violence, the question remains as to why it impacts human behavior in this manner. Giancola (1995) has opined that deficits in executive functioning compromise an individual's ability to respond in a healthy way to stressful or uncomfortable life situations. Thus,

> impaired self-monitoring, abstract reasoning, and attention skills may compromise the ability to correctly interpret potentially ambiguous social cues during interpersonal interactions, which may lead to misattributions in the perception of threat or hostility in conflict situations ... finally, compromised cognitive control over behavior may allow hostile cognitions and negative affective states to manifest as overt delinquency or physical aggression. (Giancola, 2000, p. 11-11)

To address the retrospective and methodological issues of the majority of studies that have investigated ECF, Riggs and Greenberg (2004) have stated that prospective, longitudinal research is critical to elucidating the complex interactions between the brain and the environment that contribute to neurological deficits in this area. Within biosocial investigations of aggression pathways, the plasticity and resilience of the human brain are a major focus, especially within the context of risk and protective factors that may influence outcomes at different stages of life.

Neural Plasticity and Resiliency

Biosocial theories and scholarly research offer an abundance of evidence regarding the plasticity and resiliency of the human brain. While this chapter cannot provide the reader a comprehensive review of this vast area of investigation, some background and highlights are offered here. In contrast to commonly held assumptions, this literature shows that the brain is not static, but rather is a dynamic organ that is able to change and adapt in circuitry, structure, and function (Kolb, Gibb, & Robinson, 2003). Additionally, brain development is not under strict maturational control across developmental stages. Instead, it grows along an extended developmental trajectory that begins at a cellular level just after conception and continues well into young adulthood. Therefore,

> the functional development of the brain is made possible by, in lay terms, the completion of the wiring diagram: the local and distal connections that are formed between and among areas by way of synapses and entire neural circuits. Nevertheless … the term *completion* may be inaccurate, because evidence is presented to suggest that such connections continue to be made and remade well into the lifespan. (Nelson, 2000, p. 215)

The dynamics of plasticity and resiliency within the human brain ranges from metabolic and chemical shifts to synaptic and cortex level changes, with a variety of social interventions and experiences across the lifespan dramatically impacting neurological developments (Buonomano & Merzenich, 1998; Goh & Park, 2009; Park & Reuter-Lorenz, 2009). Nelson (2000) describes the mechanisms of plasticity as including: (1) anatomical, (2) neurochemical, and (3) metabolic changes that occur at the neural level. Succinctly put, anatomical mechanisms of change refer to the process by which synapses (junctions) are modified and create new axons (a protoplasmic protrusion coming from a neuron that projects electrical impulses) or expanded dendrites surfaces (another type of projection from a nerve cell which generally receives signals). Neurochemical changes demonstrate plasticity via the adaption of new synaptic responses and the subsequent production and synthesis of related neurotransmitters. Metabolic plasticity is observed when cortical and subcortical metabolic production is altered due to neurological trauma or injury.

Thus, while plasticity is the most pronounced and accelerated in the childhood years, research has shown that substance use, malnutrition, heredity, exposure to environmental toxins, disease, and hormonal imbalances may all substantially influence brain structure and neurological processes throughout childhood and into adulthood (Andersen & Teicher, 2009; Chugani et al., 2001). These diverse life experiences each can kill neurons, alter structural networks in the brain, and facilitate the growth of new neural pathways as an adaptive response. Other works have suggested an additive negative impact on life-course outcomes for youth with brain dysfunction and central nervous system structural deficits, with behavioral, social, and intellectual failures that cascade across school, familial, and individual domains and which serve to further perpetuate aggressive reactions and impulsive violent responses to conflict (Lewis, 2002; Pincus, 2000). The brain and central nervous system appear to have varying abilities to rebound from such risks depending on what period over the lifespan these factors emerge, what areas of the brain are impacted, and in what combination risk factors and protective factors converge. For instance, although the deleterious effects of postnatal malnutrition can be reversed, intervention must occur within the first few years of life and be sustained with environmental and emotional support systems to be most effective and overcome early-life deficits (Pollitt & Gorman, 1994). Other factors appear to be more indirectly related to aggressive behaviors. While poverty may not be correlated as a stand-alone risk factor for violence, persons living in these conditions are at much greater risk for brain dysfunction, severe economic stressors, lack of a stable family environment, poor family attachments, more mental health issues, and victimization for child abuse and neglect (Loeber & Farrington, 2000; Loeber, Farrington, Stouthamer-Loeber, & Van Kammen, 1998), all of which contribute to neuropsychological vulnerabilities and aggression pathways.

Traumatic Stress and the Brain

As stated previously, there is a well-established association between child abuse and later violence, with resulting neurochemical and structural changes to the brain that may permanently alter function as a result of this form of chronic, pervasive stress. Traumatic stress is defined as "potentially harmful experiences eliciting feelings of helplessness, intense fear, or horror, with an associated alarm response" (Kolassa & Elbert, 2007, p. 321). This extreme exposure to ongoing, traumatic stress may therefore result in an acute release of stress hormones in the body (Elbert, Rockstroh, Kolassa, Schauer, & Neuner, 2006) and damage to the regulatory functions of hypothalamic-pituitary-adrenal (HPA) axis, which in turn may lead to the development of Post-Traumatic Stress Disorder (PTSD). The HPA plays a crucial role in mediating stress responses. Moreover, research has shown that early maternal deprivation in rats permanently altered the HPA axis into adulthood (Rots et al., 1995). Research has also shown an inverse relationship between high quality out-of-home child care and stress reactivity in children, with higher levels of HPA functioning (Dettling, Parker, Lane, Sebanc, & Gunnar, 2000).

Along these lines, studies have shown altered stress response systems and pathological changes in abused children where cerebral volumes were reduced by up to 7 percent in subjects with PTSD when compared to non-abused controls (De Bellis et al., 1999). Adults reporting PTSD symptoms and histories of trauma also had smaller hippocampal volumes and affected memory problems (Gilbertson et al., 2002). Preclinical and clinical findings show that exposure to traumatic stress results in neurological changes to the structure and functioning of the amygdala, hippocampus, and medial prefrontal cortex that impact memory, affective regulation, and memory (see Cicchetti, 2003 for a review; Shin, Rauch, & Pitman, 2006). Early life adversity and traumatic stress responses have been linked back to poor social, emotional, and cognitive competence in children (Gunnar, Tout, deHaan, Pierce, & Stansbury, 1997; Yates, 2007). In turn, failures across multiple domains subsequently put these children at increased risk of delinquency and further neurological insults (see Patterson et al., 1992).

Kolassa and Elbert (2007) offer an excellent timeline describing the building-block effect that occurs in the development of neural fear networks for individuals exposed to severe trauma such as war, genocide, abuse, or torture. They state that during traumatic events, unique perceptions and emotions are stored in the brain as memories. These memories form the nucleus of a fear network for the primary event and may include both "cold" or more neutral contextual memories, as well as "hot" memories that are sensory-perceptual and emotionally-laden in nature. Any additional traumatic events that occur after the time that this network is developed build upon this foundation such that new cold and hot memories become further integrated into the existing fear network until repetitive trauma responses synchronize the connections and eventually form a completed network. The long-term implications to the mental and physical health of PTSD and traumatic stress victims can be devastating and these effects may result in hippocampal atrophy, but it is not known how long it takes for permanent neuroplastic and degenerative effects to set in due to the lack of prospective studies (see Bonne et al., 2001).

Traumatic Brain Injury and Directions in Brain Resiliency Research

As discussed in previous sections, there is compelling evidence of a connection between TBI, antisocial behaviors, and mental health disorders that has been produced over the past two decades. TBI is the leading cause of death and serious disability for people under the age of 45, with males at two or three times the rate of females (Kraus & McArthur, 1996). The most frequent causes of head injury come from traffic injuries, sports events, work-related injuries, and violent assaults (Richardson, 1990), and frequently result in problems with cognitive functioning, although the pathology can be diffuse (Miller, 1999).

Although significant advances in neuroscience may bring a future reality when all regions of the brain can regenerate fully from brain insults at any stage of life, only the areas of the subventricular zone of the lateral ventricals connecting to the olfactory bulb and the dentate gyrus region of the hippocampus are known to have the ability to consistently regenerate neurons (see, e.g., Imayoshi et al., 2008; Pozniak & Pleasure, 2006). However, rapid developments over the past 40 years are offering intriguing insights into how damaged brains may spontaneously repair themselves well into adulthood. Toward this end, and as first postulated by Allen (1912) almost 100 years ago, "the persistence of neural stem cells and neurogenesis in the adult mammalian central nervous system (CNS) is now accepted" (Kernie & Parent, 2010, p. 267). Neurogenesis appears to be concentrated in the forebrain regions of mammals, including humans (Curtis et al., 2007). Scientists are currently attempting to unravel the mysteries of mammalian brain regeneration and stem cell survival and determine to what extent the brain is able to replace damaged or diseased cells after significant events such as TBI, stroke, neurodegenerative diseases, or brain seizures or traumatic brain injury (Kernie, Erwin, & Parada, 2001; Miles & Kernie, 2008). The treatment implications of such discoveries are enormous, as there are currently no regenerative therapies available for stroke patients despite the high level of mortality associated with this serious public health issue. Likewise, while the brain has demonstrated remarkable self-recovery abilities after non-severe TBI episodes, there remains little understanding of the mechanisms facilitating brain resilience, although injury-induced neurogenesis has been implicated as a possible explanation for TBI recovery (Chen et al., 2004; Kernie & Parent, 2010; Richardson, Sun, & Bullock, 2007). Indeed, "the enduring capacity for plasticity at the level of form and function is a central feature of the brain with processes related to cell proliferation, migration, differentiation, and death enabling both recovery from injury and untoward deviations following adversity" (Yates, 2007, p. 12).

Conclusion

As the present review clearly shows, "research into the causes of aggression and antisocial behaviors strongly supports the role of biological factors, in concert with well-known environmental and social influences, in these aberrant patterns of behavior" (Blake & Cantero, 2004, p. 7-2). While the fields of preventive intervention science, developmental criminology, neuropsychology, and neurogenetics have largely evolved in isolation from one another for many years, their integration and mutual understanding offers perhaps the best hope to unravel the secrets of the brain and the complex processes surrounding brain plasticity and resiliency that drive aggressive behaviors over the lifespan (Greenberg, 2006). Without question, these works have a tremendous potential to influence best practices for prevention, intervention, and treatment of youth with neuropsychological vulnerabilities and insults that may be predisposed to violent behaviors (Heide & Solomon, 2006).

While there is an abundance of research that spans across the biosocial and neurological sciences that focuses on the main correlates of violence, there is clearly much more to learn about the complexities surrounding the brain and how neuropsychological vulnerabilities contribute to aggression pathways over the life-course. This literature is vast and complex, spanning numerous disciplines and subareas of study. Based on the research to date, there is no singular "violence center" in the human brain. Instead, there appears to be a constellation of factors spanning from the genetic to the environmental that come together to impact brain health and resiliency. Further, having brain dysfunction in and of itself may not be enough to predict aggression without additional risk factors (Boots, 2008). In a sense, violence is proposed to originate from the earliest years of development as neurological vulnerabilities additively grow from environmental, genetic, and situational factors.

Although neuropsychological vulnerabilities and deficits have historically been ignored in the preventive intervention sciences (Riggs, Greenberg, Kusche, & Pentz,

2006), Riggs & Greenberg (2004) argue for the salience of these factors in future preventative efforts to reduce antisocial behaviors. Specifically, they postulate the benefits that neurobiological and neurocognitive factors may serve as moderators or mediators of aggressive and violent behaviors. Indeed, Raine (2002) has similarly argued that the preventive intervention programs may be the most effective means to target and reduce the likelihood of antisocial behaviors for youth with neurological vulnerabilities. With what has been learned regarding the interactive effects of environment on neurogenetics, especially with early intervention, there appears to be great promise in such holistic initiatives. "Research on vulnerability and protective factors suggests that tailored, targeted interventions will be the most effective when psychosocial manipulations are 'matched' to an individual's unique constellation of social psychological, and biological attributes, thereby reinforcing ore adaptive and normative phenotypes" (Fishbein et al., 2006, p. 47). Prospective, longitudinal, and developmentally-driven investigations offer the most promise for unraveling the complex interplay of how numerous risk factors such as environmental stressors, neurotoxicity, pre- and post-natal care, child abuse, head injuries, psychosocial factors, psychological and physical health disorders, and neurological dysfunction and disorders combine to create pathways toward violence in humans.

With the new knowledge that neurobiological inquiries revolving around brain plasticity and violence pathways will bring in the years to come, a number of salient public policy questions will need to be addressed that will dramatically impact how society approaches serious social problems such as maternal health, domestic violence, child exposure to toxins and violence, and child abuse, just to name a few. How is brain regeneration best facilitated for various diseases, injuries, and insults? What considerations should be made with regard to biocultural factors? How do genes and environment interact to determine the effectiveness of interventions once youngsters have been exposed to serious risk factors? What protective factors best insulate youth from neurological insults that put them at greatest risk for impulsive aggression and other forms of violence? How can we best utilize our ever-increasing understanding of the structure, resiliency, and plasticity of the brain to maximize public health initiatives and minimize youth violence trajectories over the lifespan? What are the legal and ethical considerations with regard to risk and child protection that may come from such research? These are critical issues that will have to be addressed as the field moves forward and societal standards evolve in parallel with technological and scientific advances.

References

Allen, E. (1912). The cessation of mitosis in the central nervous system of the albino rat. *Journal of Comparative Neurology, 22,* 547–568.

Andersen, S. L., & Teicher, M. H. (2009). Desperately drive and no brakes: Developmental stress exposure and subsequent risk for substance abuse. *Neuroscience and Biobehavioral Reviews, 33,* 516–524.

Anderson, K. E., & Silver, J. M. (1999). Neurological and medical diseases and violence. In K. Tardiff (Ed.), *Medical management of the violent patient* (pp. 87–124). New York: Marcel Dekker.

Arsenault, L., Moffitt, T. E., Caspi, A., Taylor, A., Rijsdijk, F. V., Jaffee, S. R., Ablow, J. C., & Measelle, J. R. (2003). Strong genetic effects on cross-situational antisocial behaviour among 5-year-old children according to mothers, teachers, examiner-observers, and twins' self-reports. *Journal of Child Psychology and Psychiatry, 44,* 832–848.

Barkley, R. A. (1997). Attention-deficit/hyperactivity disorder, self-regulation, and time: Toward a comprehensive theory. *Journal of Developmental and Behavioral Pediatrics, 18,* 271–279.

Bear, D. M., & Fedio, P. (1977). Quantitative analysis of interictal behavior in temporal lobe epilepsy. *Archives of Neurology, 34,* 454–467.

Beauregard, M. (2007). Mind does really matter: Evidence from neuroimaging studies of emotional self-regulation, psychotherapy, and placebo effect. *Progress in Neurobiology, 81,* 218–236.

Beaver, K. M. (2009). *Biosocial criminology: A primer.* Dubuque: Kendall Hunt Publishing.

Beaver, K. M., Delisi, M., Vaughn, M. G., & Barnes, J. C. (2010). Monoamine oxidase A genotype is associated with gang membership and weapon use. *Comprehensive Psychiatry, 51,* 130–134.

Beaver, K. M., Sak, A., Vaske, J., & Nilsson, J. (2010). Genetic risk, parent-child relations, and antisocial phenotypes in a sample of African-American males. *Psychiatric Research, 175,* 160–164.

Beaver, K., M., Vaughn, M. G., DeLisi, M., & Higgins, G. E. (2009). The biosocial correlates of neuropsychological deficits: Results from the National Longitudinal Study of Adolescent Health. *International Journal of Offender Therapy & Comparative Criminology, 54,* 878–894.

Beaver, K. M., Wright, J. P., DeLisi, M., Daigle, L. E., Swatt, M. L., & Gibson, C. L. (2007). Evidence of a gene x environment interactions in the creation of victimization: Results from a longitudinal sample of adolescents. *International Journal of Offender Therapy and Comparative Criminology, 51,* 620–645.

Berlin, H. A., Rolls, E. T., & Kischka, U. (2004). Impulsivity, time perception, emotion and reinforcement sensitivity in patients with orbitofrontal cortex lesions. *Brain, 127,* 1108–1126.

Blair, R. J. R. (2004). The role of orbital frontal cortex in the modulation of antisocial behavior. *Brain and Cognition, 55,* 198–208.

Blake, P., & Cantero, J. (2004). Differential assessent of neurological deficits in aggressive and violent behavior. In D. H. Fishbein (Ed.), *The Science, Treatment, and Prevention of Antisocial Behaviors* (Vol. 2, pp. 7-1, 7-21). Kingston, NJ: Civic Research Institute.

Blake, P. Y., Pincus, J. H., & Buckner, C. (1995). Neurologic abnormalities in murderers. *Neurology, 45,* 1641–1647.

Blume, A. W., Davis, J. M., & Schmaling, K. B. (1999). Neurocognitive dysfunction in dually-diagnosed patients: A potential roadblock to motivating behavior change. *Journal of Psychoactive Drugs, 31,* 111–115.

Boots, D. P. (2008). Neuropsychological perspectives of human violence, aggression, and homicide. In S. J. Evans (Ed.), *Public policy issue research trends* (pp. 21–66). New York: Nova Science Publishers.

Bonne, O., Brandes, D., Gilboa, A., Gomori, J. M., Shenton, M. E., Pitman, R. K., & Shalev, A. Y. (2001). Longitudinal MRI study of hippocampal volume in trauma survivors with PTSD. *American Journal of Psychiatry, 158,* 1248–1251.

Brower, M. C., & Price, B. H. (2001). Neuropsychiatry of frontal lobe dysfunction in violent and criminal behaviour: A critical review. *Journal of Neurology, Neurosurgery, and Psychiatry, 71*(6), 720–726.

Brunner, H. G., Nelen, M., Breakefield, X. O., Ropers, H. H., & van Oost, B. A. (1993). Abnormal behavior associated with a point mutation in the structural gene for monoamine oxidase A. *Science, 262,* 578–580.

Buonomano, D. V., & Merzenich, M. M. (1998). Cortical plasticity: From synapses to maps. *Annual Review of Neuroscience, 21,* 149–186.

Caspi, A., McClay, J., Moffitt, T. E., Mill, J., Martin, J., Craig, I. W., Taylor, A., & Poulton, R. (2002). Role of genotype in the cycle of violence in maltreated children. *Science, 297*(5582), 851–854.

Chen, J., Li, Y., Zhang, R., Katakowski, M., Gautam, S. C., Xu, Y., Lu, M., Zhang, Z., & Chopp, M. (2004). Combination therapy of stroke in rats with a nitric oxide donor and human bone marrow stromal cells enhances angiogenesis and neurogenesis. *Brain Research, 1005,* 21–28.

Chugani, H. T., Behen, M. E., Muzik, O., Juhasz, C., Nagy, F., & Chugani, D. C. (2001). Local brain functional activity following early deprivation: A study of post-institutionalized Romanian orphans. *NeuroImage, 14,* 1290–1301.

Cicchetti, D. (2003). Neuroendocrine functioning in maltreated children. In D. Cicchetti & E. F. Walker (Eds.), *Neurodevelopmental mechanisms in psychopathology* (pp. 345–365). New York: Cambridge University Press.

Cicchetti, D., & Barnett, D. (1991). Attachment organization in preschool aged maltreated children. *Development and Psychopathology, 3,* 397–411.

Clark, W. R., & Grunstein, M. (2000). *Are we hardwired? The role of genes in human behavior.* New York: Oxford University Press.

Cohen, I. L., Liu, X., Schutz, C., White, B. N., Jenkins, E. C., Brown, W. T., & Holden, J. J. A. (2003). Association of autism severity with a monoamine oxidase A functional polymorphism. *Clinical Genetics, 64,* 190–197.

Cole, P. M., Usher, B. A., & Cargo, A. P. (1993). Cognitive risk and its association with risk for disruptive behavior disorders in preschoolers. *Journal of Clinical Child Psychology, 22*, 154–164.

Cummings, E. M., & Davies, P. T. (1994). Maternal depression and child development. *Journal of Child Psychology and Psychiatry, 35*, 73–112.

Curtis, M. A., Kam, M., Nannmark, U., Anderson, M. F., Wikkelso, C., Holtas, S., van Roon-Mom, W. M., Bjork-Erikkson, T., Nordborg, C., Frisen, J., Dragunow, M., Faull, R. L., & Erikkson, P. S. (2007). Human neuroblasts migrate to the olfactory bulb via a lateral ventricular extension. *Science, 315*, 1243–1249.

De Bellis, M. D., Keshavan, M., Clark, D. B., Casey, B. J., Giedd, J., Boring, A. M., Frustaci, K., & Ryan, N. D. (1999). A. E. Bennett research award: Developmental traumatology, part II: Brain development. *Biological Psychiatry, 45*, 1271–1284.

DeGue, S., & Widom, C. S. (2009). Does out-of-home placement mediate the relationship between child maltreatment and adult criminality? *Child Maltreatment, 14*, 344–355.

Dettling, A. C., Parker, S., Lane, S., Sebanc, A. M., & Gunnar, M. R. (2000). Quality of care and temperament determine whether cortisol levels rise over the day for children in full-day childcare. *Psychoneuroendocrinology, 25*, 819–836.

Devinski, O., Morrell, M. J., & Vogt, B. A. (1995). Contributions of anterior cingulated cortex to behavior. *Brain, 118*, 279–306.

Dodge, K. A., Bates, J. E., & Pettit, G. S. (1990). Mechanisms in the cycle of violence. *Science, 250*, 1678–1682.

Dolan, M. (1994). Psychopathy: A neurobiological perspective. *British Journal of Psychiatry, 165*, 151–159.

Elbert, T., Rockstroh, B., Kolassa, I., Schauer, M., & Neuner, F. (2006). The influence of organized violence and terror on brain and mind: A co-constructive perspective. In P. Baltes, P. Reuter-Lorenz, & F. Rosler (Eds.), *Lifespan development and the brain: The perspective of biocultural co-constructionism* (pp. 326–349). Cambridge: Cambridge University Press.

Ewing-Cobbs, L., Kramer, L., Prasad, M., Canales, D. N., Louis, P. T., Fletcher, J. M., Vollero, H., Landry, S. H., & Cheung, K. (1998). Neuroimaging, physical, and developmental findings after inflicted and noninflicted traumatic brain injury in young children. *Pediatrics, 102*, 300–307.

Fagan, A. (2005). The relationship between adolescent physical abuse and criminal offending: Support for an enduring and generalized cycle of violence. *Journal of Family Violence, 20*, 279–290.

Farrington, D. P., & Welsh, B. C. (2007). *Saving children from a life of crime: Early risk factors and effective interventions.* New York: Oxford University Press.

Filley, C. M., Price, B. H., Nell, V., Antionette, T., Morgan, A. S., Bresnahan, J. F., Pincus, J. H., Gelbort, M. M., Weissberg, M., & Kelly, J. P. (2001). Toward an understanding of violence: Neurobehavioral aspects of unwarranted physical aggression: Aspen Neurobehavioral Conference Consensus Statement. *Neuropsychiatry, Neuropsychology, and Behavioral Neurology, 14*, 1–14.

Fishbein, D. (1998). Differential susceptibility to comorbid drug abuse and violence. *Journal of Drug Issues, 28*, 859–890.

Fishbein, D. H., Hyde, C., Eldreth, D., Pascall, M. J., Hubal, R., Das, A., Tarter, R., Ialongo, N., Hubbard, S., & Yung, B. (2006). Neurocognitive skills moderate urban male adolescents' responses to preventative intervention materials. *Drug and Alcohol Dependence, 82*, 47–60.

Fishbein, D., & Tarter, R. (2009). Infusing neuroscience into the study and prevention of drug misuse and co-occurring aggressive behavior. *Substance Use & Misuse, 44*, 1204–1235.

Ford, S., Farah, M. S., Shera, D. M., & Hurt, H. (2007). Neurocognitive correlates of problem behavior in environmentally at-risk adolescents. *Journal of Developmental & Behavioral Pediatrics, 28*, 376–385.

Gage, F. H. (2002). Neurogenesis in the adult brain. *Journal of Neuroscience, 22*, 612–613.

Galton, F. (1865). Heredity talent and character. *Macmillan's Magazine, 12*, 157–166, 318–327.

Gansler, D. A., Lee, A. K. W., Emerton, B. C., D'Amato, C., Bhadelia, R., Jerram, M., & Fulwiler, C. (2011). Prefrontal regional correlates of self-control in male psychiatric patients: Impulsivity facets and aggression. *Psychiatry Research: Neuroimaging, 191*, 16–23.

Giancola, P. (1995). Evidence for dorsolateral and orbital prefrontal cortical involvement in the expression of aggressive behavior. *Aggressive Behavior, 21*, 431–450.

Giancola, P. (2000). Neuropsychological functioning and antisocial behavior: Implications for etiology and prevention. In D. H. Fishbein (Ed.), *The science, treatment, and prevention of antisocial behaviors* (Vol. 1, pp. 11-1, 11-16). Kingston, NJ: Civic Research Institute.

Giancola, P., Martin, C., Tarter, R., Pelham, W., & Moss, H. (1996a). Executive cognitive functioning and aggressive behavior in preadolescent boys at high risk for substance abuse/dependence. *Journal of Studies on Alcohol, 57*, 352–359.

Giancola, P., & Mezzich, A. (1998). Executive cognitive functioning, temperament, and antisocial behavior in conduct disordered adolescent females. *Journal of Abnormal Psychology, 107*, 629–641.

Giancola, P., Mezzich, A., & Tarter, R. (1998). Disruptive, delinquent, and aggressive behavior in adolescent female substance abusers: Relation to executive cognitive functioning. *Journal of Studies on Alcohol, 59*, 560–567.

Giancola, P., Moss, H., Martin, C., Kirisci, L., & Tarter, R. (1996b). Executive cognitive functioning predicts reactive aggression in boys at high risk for substance dependence: A prospective study. *Alcoholism: Clinical and Experimental Research, 20*, 740–744.

Gilbertson, M. W., Shenton, M. E., Ciszewski, A., Kasai, K., Lasko, N. B., Orr, S. P., & Pitman, R. K. (2002). Smaller hippocampal volume predicts pathologic vulnerability to psychological trauma. *Nature Neuroscience, 5*, 1242–1247.

Gilligan, J., & Lee, B. (2004). The psychopharmaologic treatment of violent youth. *Annals of the New York Academy of Sciences, 1036*, 356–381.

Goh, J. O. & Park, D. C. (2009). Neuroplasticity and cognitive aging: The scaffolding theory of aging and cognition. *Restorative neurology and neuroscience, 27*, 391–403.

Golden, C. J., Jackson, M. L., Peterson-Rohne, A., & Gontkovsky, S. T. (1996). Neuropsychological correlates of violence and aggression: A review of the clinical literature. *Aggression and Violent Behavior, 1,* 3–25.

Grafman, J., Schwab, K., Warden, D., Pridgen, J., Brown, H. R., & Salazar, A. M. (1996). Frontal lobe injuries, violence, and aggression: A report of the Vietnam Head Injury Study. *Neurology, 46,* 1231–1238.

Greenberg, M. T. (2006). Promoting resilience in children and youth: Preventive interventions and their interface with neuroscience. *Annals of New York Academy of Sciences, 1094,* 139–150.

Gunnar, M. R., Tout, K., deHaan, M., Pierce, S., & Stansbury, K. (1997). Temperament, social competence, and adrenocortical activity in preschoolers. *Developmental Psychobiology, 31,* 65–85.

Haberstick, B. C., Lessem, J. M., Hopfer, C. J., Smolen, A., Ehringer, M. A., Timberlake, D., & Hewitt, J. K. (2005). Monoamine oxidase A (MAOA) and antisocial behaviors in the presence of childhood and adolescent treatment. *American Journal of Medical Genetics, 135B,* 59–64.

Hamer, D., & Copeland, P. (1998). *Living with our genes: Why they matter more than you think.* New York: Doubleday.

Hare, R. D. (1984). Performance of psychopaths on cognitive tasks related to frontal lobe function. *Journal of Abnormal Psychology, 93,* 133–140.

Hart, T., & Jacobs, H. (1993). Rehabilitation and management of behavioral disturbances following frontal lobe injury. *Journal of Head Trauma and Rehabilitation, 8*(1), 1–12.

Hawkins, K. A., & Trobst, K. K. (2000). Frontal lobe dysfunction and aggression: Conceptual issues and research findings. *Aggression and Violent Behavior, 5,* 147–157.

Heide, K. M., & Solomon, E. P. (2006). Biology, childhood trauma, and murder: Rethinking justice. *International Journal of Law and Psychiatry, 29,* 220–233.

Hill, D., & Pond, D. A. (1952). Reflections on 100 capital cases submitted to encephalography. *Journal of Mental Science, 98,* 23–43.

Imayoshi, I., Sakamoto, M., Ohtsuka, T., Takao, K., Miyakawa, T., Yamaguchi, M., Mori, K., Ikeda, T., Itohara, S., & Kageyama, R. (2008). Roles of continuous neurogenesis in the structural and functional integrity of the adult forebrain. *Nature Neuroscience, 11,* 1153–1161.

Kandel, E., & Freed, D. (1989). Frontal-lobe dysfunction and antisocial behavior: A review. *Journal of Clinical Psychology, 45,* 404–413.

Kandel, E., & Mednick, S. A. (1991). Perinatal complications predict violent offending. *Criminology, 29,* 519–529.

Kaplan, J. (1899). Kopftrauma und Psychosen. *Allgemeiner zeitschrift fur psychiatrie, 56,* 292–297.

Kernie, S. G., Erwin, T. M., & Parada, L. F. (2001). Brain remodeling due to neuronal and astrocytic proliferation after controlled cortical injury in mice. *Journal of Neuroscience Research, 66,* 317–326.

Kernie, S. G., & Parent, J. M. (2010). Forebrain neurogenesis after focal Ishemic and traumatic brain injury. *Neurobiology of Disease, 37,* 267–274.

Kim-Cohen, J., Caspi, A., Taylor, A., Williams, B., Newcombe, R., Craig, I. W., & Moffitt, T. E. (2006). MAOA, maltreatment, and gene-environment interaction predicting children's mental health: New evidence and a meta-analysis. *Molecular Psychiatry, 11*, 903–913.

Klingberg, T. E, Fernell, E., Olesen, J., Johnson, M., Gustafsson, P., Dahlstrom, K., Gillberg, C. G., Forssberg, H., & Westerberg, H. (2005). Computerized training of working memory in children with ADHD: A randomized, controlled trial. *Journal of the American Academy of Child & Adolescent Psychiatry, 44*, 177–186.

Kluver, H., & Bucy, P. C. (1939). Preliminary analysis of functions of the temporal lobes of monkeys. *Archives of Neurology and Psychiatry, 42*, 979–1000.

Kolassa, I., & Elbert, T. (2007). Structural and functional neuroplasticity in relation to traumatic stress. *Current Directions in Psychological Science, 16*, 321–325.

Kolb, B., Gibb, R., & Robinson, T. E. (2003). Brain plasticity and behavior. *Current Directions in Psychological Science, 12*, 1–5.

Krakowski, M. (1997). Neurologic and neuropsychologic correlates of violence. *Psychiatric Annals, 27*, 674–678.

Kratcoski, P. C. (1984). Perspectives on intrafamily violence. *Human Relations, 37*, 443–453.

Kraus, J. F., & McArthur, D. L. (1996). Epidemiological aspects of brain injury. *Neurologic Clinics, 14*, 435–450.

Laakso, M. P., Vaurio, O., Koivisto, E., Savolainen, L., Eronen, M., Eronen, H. J., Hakola, P., Repo, E., Soininen, H., & Tiihonen, J. (2001). Psychopathy and the posterior hippocampus. *Behavioural Brain Research, 118*, 187–193.

Levitt, P. (2003). Structural and functional maturation of the developing primate brain. *Journal of Pediatrics, 143*, S35–S45.

Lewis, D. O. (2002). Development of the symptom of violence. In M. Lewis (Ed.), *Child and adolescent psychiatry: A comprehensive textbook* (3rd ed., pp. 387–399). Philadelphia: Lippincott Williams & Wilkins.

Lewis, D. O., Lovely, R., Yeager, C., Ferguson, G., Friedman, M., Sloane, G., Friedman, H., & Pincus, J. H. (1988). Intrinsic and environmental characteristics of juvenile murderers. *Journal of the American Academy of Child and Adolescent Psychiatry, 27*, 582–587.

Lewis, D. O., Moy, E., Jackson, L. D., Aaronson, R., Restifo, N., Serra, S., & Simos, A. (1985). Biopsychosocial characteristics of children who later murder: A prospective study. *American Journal of Psychiatry, 142*, 1161–1167.

Lewis, D. O., & Pincus, J. H. (1989). Epilepsy and violence: Evidence for a neuropyschotic-aggressive syndrome. *Journal of Neuropsychiatry, 1*, 413–418.

Lewis, D. O., Pincus, J. H., Bard, B., Richardson, E., Feldman, M., Prichep, L. S., & Yeager, C. (1988). Neuropsychiatric, psychoeducational, and family characteristics of 14 juveniles condemned to death in the United States. *American Journal of Psychiatry, 145*, 584–589.

Lewis, D. O., Pincus, J. H., Feldman, M., Jackson, L., & Bard, B. (1986). Psychiatric, neurologic, and psychoeducational characteristics of 15 death row inmates in the United States. *American Journal of Psychiatry, 143*, 838–845.

Lewis, D. O., Pincus, J. H., & Glaser, G. H. (1979). Violent juvenile delinquents: Psychiatric, neurological, psychological, and abuse factors. *Journal of the American Academy of Psychiatry, 18*, 307–319.

Lewis, D. O., & Shanok, S. S. (1979). Perinatal difficulties, head, and face trauma and child abuse in the medical histories of seriously delinquent children. *American Journal of Psychiatry, 136*, 419–423.

Loeber, R., & Farrington, D. P. (2000). Young children who commit crime: Epidemiology, developmental origins, risk factors, early interventions, and policy implications. *Development and Psychopathology, 12*, 737–762.

Loeber, R., Farrington, D. P., Stouthamer-Loeber, M., & Van Kammen, W. B. (1998). *Antisocial behavior and mental health problems: Explanatory factors in childhood and adolescence*. Mahwah: Lawrence Erlbaum Associates.

Lou, H. C., Hansen, D., & Nordenfoft, M. (1994). Prenatal stressors of human life affect fetal brain development. *Developmental Medicine and Child Neurology, 36*, 826–832.

Lykken, D. (1995). *The antisocial personalities*. Hillsdale: Lawrence Erlbaum & Associates.

Lyons-Ruth, K. (1996). Attachment relationships among children with aggressive behavior problems: The role of disorganized early attachment patterns. *Journal of Consulting and Clinical Psychology, 64*, 64–73.

McBurnett, K., Pfiffner, L. J., Capasso, L., Lahey, B. B., & Loeber, R. (1997). Children's aggression and DSM-III-R symptoms predicted by parent psychopathology, parenting practices, cortisol, and SES. In A. Raine, P. A. Brennan, D. P. Farrington, and S. A. Mednick (Eds.), *Biosocial bases of violence* (NATO ASI Series, Series A: Life Sciences, Vol. 292, pp. 345–348). New York: Plenum.

McGloin, J. M., Pratt, T. C., & Piquero, A. R. (2006). A life-course analysis of the criminogenic effects of maternal cigarette smoking during pregnancy: A research note on the mediating impact of neuropsychological deficit. *Journal of Research in Crime and Delinquency, 43*, 412–426.

Mark, V. H., & Ervin, F. R. (1970). *Violence and the brain*. New York: Harper and Row.

Martens, W. H. J. (2002). Criminality and moral dysfunctions: Neurochemical, biochemical, and genetic dimensions. *International Journal of Offender Therapy and Comparative Criminology, 46*, 170–182.

Meaney, M. J., & Champagne, F. (2000). Latency to maternal behavior in high and low LG-ABN mothers/offspring. *Society for Neuroscience Abstracts, 26*, 2035.

Mendez, M. (1998). Postictal violence and epilepsy. *Psychosomatics, 39*, 478–480.

Mendez, M. F., Doss, R. C., & Taylor, J. L. (1993). Interictal violence in epilepsy: Relationship to behavior and seizure variables. *The Journal of Nervous and Mental Disease, 181*, 566–569.

Meninger, K. & Mayman, M. (1956). Episodic dyscontrol: A third order of stress adaptation. *Bulletin of the Meninger Clinic, 20*, 153–160.

Miczek, K. A., Maxson, S. C., Fish, E. W., & Faccidomo, S. (2001). Aggressive behavioral phenotypes in mice. *Behavioural Brain Research, 125*, 167–181.

Miles, D. K., & Kernie, S. G. (2008). Hypoxic–ischemic brain injury activates early hippocampal stem/progenitor cells to replace vulnerable neuroblasts. *Hippocampus, 18*, 793–806.

Miles, D. R., & Carey, G. (1997). Genetic and environmental architecture of human aggression. *Journal of Personality and Social Psychology, 72*, 207–217.

Miller, E. (1999). The neuropsychology of offending. *Psychology, Crime & Law, 5*, 297–318.

Miller, L. (1987). Neuropsychology of the aggressive psychopath: An integrative review. *Aggressive Behavior, 13*, 119–140.

Miller, L. (1990). Major syndromes of aggressive behavior following head injury: An introduction to evaluation and treatment. *Cognitive Rehabilitation, 7*, 91–96.

Mills, S., & Raine, A. (1994). Neuroimaging and aggression. In M. Hillbrand (Ed.), *The psychobiology of aggression* (pp. 145–158). Binghampton, NY: Haworth.

Moffitt, T. E. (1990a). The neuropsychology of juvenile delinquency: A critical review. In M. Tonry & N. Morris (Eds.), *Crime and justice: An annual review of research* (Vol. 12, pp. 99–169). Chicago: University of Chicago Press.

Moffitt, T. E. (1990b). Juvenile delinquency and Attention Deficit Disorder: Boys' developmental trajectories from age 3 to age 15. *Child Development, 61*, 893–910.

Moffitt, T. E. (1993). Adolescence-limited and life-course persistent antisocial behavior: A developmental taxonomy. *Psychological Review, 100*, 674–701.

Moffitt, T. E. (2005). The new look of behavioral genetics in developmental psychopathology: Gene-environment interplay in antisocial behaviors. *Psychological Bulletin, 131*, 533–554.

Moffitt, T. E. (2006). A review of research on the taxonomy of life-course persistent versus adolescence-limited antisocial behavior. In F. T. Cullen, J. P. Wright, & K. R. Blevins (Eds.), *Taking stock: The status of criminological theory: Advances in criminological theory* (Vol. 15, pp. 277–312). New Brunswick: Transaction.

Morgan, A. B., & Lilienfeld, S. O. (2000). A meta-analytic review of the relation between antisocial behavior and neuropsychological measures of executive function. *Clinical Psychology Review, 20*, 113–136.

Nelson, C. A. (2000). The neurological bases of early intervention. In J. P. Shonkoff and S. J. Meisels (Eds.), *Handbook of early childhood intervention* (pp. 204–227). New York: Cambridge University Press.

Nevid, J. S., Rathus, S. A., & Greene, B. (2000). *Abnormal psychology in a changing world* (4th ed.). Upper Saddle River: Prentice Hall.

Newman, T. K., Syagailo, Y. V., Barr, C. S., Wendland, J. R., Champoux, M., Graessle, M., Suomi, S. J., Higley, J. D., & Lesch, K. (2005). Monoamine oxidase A gene promoter variation and rearing experience influences aggression behavior in rhesus monkeys. *Biological Psychiatry, 57*, 167–172.

O'Connor, T. G., Reiss, D., McGuire, S., & Hetherington, E. M. (1998). Co-occurrence of depressive symptoms and antisocial behavior in adolescence: A common genetic liability. *Journal of Abnormal Psychology, 107*, 27–37.

Olds, D. L. (2007). Preventing crime with prenatal and infancy support of parents: The nurse-family partnership. *Victims and Offenders, 2*, 205–225.

Olson, S. L., & Hoza, B. (1993). Preschool developmental antecedents of conduct problems in children beginning school. *Journal of Clinical Child Psychology, 22*, 60–67.

Pallone, N. J., & Hennessy, J. J. (2000). Indifferent communication between social science and neuroscience: The case of "biological brain-proneness" for criminal aggression. In D. H. Fishbein (Ed.), *The science, treatment, and prevention of antisocial behaviors* (Vol. 1, pp. 21-1, 22-13). Kingston, NJ: Civic Research Institute.

Parent, C., Zhang, T., Champagne, D., Champagne, F., Caldji, C., & Meaney, M. (2004). Environmental influences on the development of individual differences in behavioral and endocrine responses to stress. In D. H. Fishbein (Ed.), *The science, treatment, and prevention of antisocial behaviors* (Vol. 2, pp. 2-1, 2-29). Kingston, NJ: Civic Research Institute.

Park, D. C., & Reuter-Lorenz, P. (2009). The adaptive brain: Aging and neurocognitive scaffolding. *Annual Review of Psychology, 60*, 173–196.

Patterson, G. R., Reid, J. B., & Dishion, T. J. (1992). *Antisocial boys.* Eugene, OR: Castalia.

Pincus, J. H. (1996). Violence: The scientific medical perspective. *Israel Journal of Medical Sciences, 32*, 511–514.

Pincus, J. H. (2000). Neurological evaluation of violent juveniles. *Child and Adolescent Psychiatric Clinics of North America, 9*, 777–792.

Plomin, R., & Asbury, K. (2005). Nature and nurture: Genetic and environmental influences on behavior. *The Annals of the American Academy of Political and Social Science, 600*, 86–98.

Pollitt, E., & Gorman, K. S. (1994). Nutritional deficiencies as developmental risk factors. In C. A. Nelson (Ed.), *Minnesota symposia on child psychology: Vol. 27. Threats to optimal development: Integrating biological, psychological, and social risk factors* (pp. 121–144). Hillsdale: Lawrence Erlbaum and Associates.

Pozniak, C. D., & Pleasure, S. J. (2006). Genetic control of hippocampal neurogenesis. *Genome Biology, 7*, 207.

Pridemore, S., Chambers, A., & McArthur, M. (2005). Neuroimaging in psychopathy. *Australian and New Zealand Journal of Psychiatry, 39*, 856–865.

Raine, A. (1993). *The psychopathology of crime: Criminal behavior as a clinical disorder.* San Diego: Academic Press.

Raine, A. (2002). Biosocial studies of antisocial and violent behavior in children and adults: A review. *Journal of Abnormal Child Psychology, 30*, 311–326.

Raine, A., Buchsbaum, M. S., & LaCasse, L. (1997). Brain abnormalities in murderers indicated by positron emission tomography. *Biological Psychiatry, 42*, 495–508.

Raine, A., Buchsbaum, M. S., Stanley, J., Lottenberg, S., Abel, L., & Stoddard, J. (1994). Selective reductions in metabolism in murderers. *Biological Psychiatry, 36*, 365–373.

Raine, A., Lencz, T., Birhle, S., LaCasse, L., & Coletti, P. (2000). Reduced prefrontal gray matter volume and reduced autonomic activity in antisocial personality disorder. *Archives of General Psychiatry, 57*, 119–127.

Raine, A., & Liu, J. (1998). Biological predispositions to violence and their implications for biosocial treatment and prevention. *Psychology, Crime & Law, 4*, 107–125.

Raine, A., Park, S., Lencz, T., Bihrle, S., LaCasse, L, Widom, C. S., Al-Dayeh, L., & Singh, M. (2001). Reduced right hemisphere activation in severely abused violent offenders during a working memory task: An fMRI study. *Aggressive Behavior, 27*, 111–129.

Ramirez, J. M. (2003). Hormones and aggression in childhood and adolescence. *Aggression and Violent Behavior, 8*, 621–644.

Renken, B., Egeland, B., Marvinney, D., Magelsdorf, S., & Sroufe, A. (1989). Early childhood antecedents of aggression and passive withdrawal in early elementary school. *Journal of Personality, 57*, 257–281.

Rhee, S., & Waldman, I. D. (2002). Genetic and environ- mental influences on antisocial behavior: A meta-analysis of twin and adoption studies. *Psychological Bulletin, 29*, 490–529.

Richardson, J. T. E. (1990). *Clinical and neuropsychological aspects of closed head injury.* London: Taylor & Francis.

Richardson, R. M., Sun, D., & Bullock, M. R. (2007). Neurogenesis after traumatic brain injury. *Neurosurgery Clinics of North America, 18*, 169–181.

Riggs, N. R., & Greenberg. M. T. (2004). The role of neurocognitive models I prevention research. In D. H. Fishbein (Ed.), *The science, treatment, and prevention of antisocial behaviors* (Vol. 2, pp. 8-1, 8-20). Kingston, NJ: Civic Research Institute.

Riggs, N. R., Greenberg, M. T., Kusche, C. A., & Pentz, M. A. (2006). The mediational role of neurocognition in the behavioral outcomes of a social-emotional prevention program in elementary school students: Effects of the PATHS curriculum. *Prevention Science, 7*, 91–102.

Rosenbaum, A., & O'Leary, K. D. (1981). Children: The unintended victims of marital violence. *American Journal of Orthopsychiatry, 51*, 692–699.

Rosenhan, D. L., & Seligman, M. E. (1995). *Abnormal psychology.* New York: WW Norton & Company.

Rots, N. Y., Workerl, J. O., Sutanto, W., Cools, A. R., Levine, S., de Kloet, E. R., & Oitzl, M. S. (1995). Maternal deprivation results in an enhanced pituitary-adrenal activity and an increased dopamine suspectibility at adulthood. *Society for Neuroscience Abstracts, 21*, 524.

Rowe, D. C. (2002). *Biology and crime.* Los Angeles: Roxbury.

Rutter, M. (2006). *Genes and behavior: Nature-nurture interplay explained.* Malden: Blackwell.

Scarr, S. (1993). Biological and cultural diversity: The legacy of Darwin for development. *Child Development, 64*, 1333–1353.

Schoenbaum, G., Chiba, A. A., & Gallagher, M. (1999). Neural encoding in orbitofrontal cortex and basolateral amygdala encode expected outcomes during learning. *Nature Neuroscience, 1*, 155–159.

Seguin, J., Pihl, R., Harden, P., Tremblay, R., & Boulerice, B. (1995). Cognitive and neuropsychological characteristics of physically aggressive boys. *Journal of Abnormal Psychology, 104*, 614–624.

Seidenwurm, D., Pounds, T. R., Globus, A., & Valk, P. E. (1997). Abnormal temporal lobe metabolism in violent subjects: Correlation of imaging and neuropsychiatric findings. *American Journal of Neuroradiology, 18,* 625–631.

Shanok, S., & Lewis, D. O. (1981). Medical histories of female delinquents. *Archives of General Psychiatry, 38,* 211–213.

Shih, J. C. (1991). Molecular basis of human MAO A and B in neurotransmitter metabolism and behavior. *Annual Review of Neuroscience, 22,* 197–217.

Shin, L. M., Rauch, S. L., & Pitman, R. K. (2006). Amygdala, medial prefrontal cortex, and hippocampal function in PTSD. *Annals of the New York Academy of Sciences, 1071,* 67–79.

Shonkoff, J. P., & Marshall, P. C. (2000). The biology of developmental vulnerability. In J. P. Shonkoff and S. J. Meisels (Eds.), *Handbook of early childhood intervention* (pp. 35–53). New York: Cambridge University Press.

Siever, L. J. (2008). Neurobiology of aggression and violence. *American Journal of Psychiatry, 165,* 429–442.

Silver, J. M., Hales, R. E., & Yudofsky, S. C. (1997). Neuropsychiatric aspects of traumatic brain injury. In S. C. Yudofsky & R. E. Hales (Eds.), *The American psychiatric press textbook of neuropsychiatry* (pp. 607–634). Washington, DC: American Psychiatric Press.

Singer, W. (1995). Development and plasticity of cortical processing architectures. *Science, 270,* 758–764.

Solms, M., & Turnbull, O. (2002). *The brain and the inner world.* New York: Other Press.

Sparling, Y. A., & Cohen, R. (1997). Neurobehavioral influences on propensity for juvenile violence. *Journal of Neuropsychiatry, 9,* 134–135.

Tarter, R. E., Kirisci, L., Mezzich, A., Cornelius, J. R., Pajer, K., Vanyukov, M., Gardner, W., Blackson, T., & Clark, D. (2003). Neurobehavioral disinhibition in childhood predicts early age of onset of substance use disorders. *American Journal of Psychiatry, 160,* 1078–1085.

Teicher, M. H. (March, 2002). Scars that won't heal: The neurobiology of child abuse. *Scientific American,* 68–75.

Tranel, D. (1994). "Acquired sociopathy:" The development of sociopathic behavior following focal brain damage. In D. C. Fowles, P. Sutker, & S. H. Goodman (Eds.), *Progress in Experimental, Personality, and Psychopathology Research* (pp. 285–311). New York: Springer.

Tremblay, L., & Schultz, W. (1999). Relative reward preference in primate orbitofrontal cortex. *Nature, 398,* 704–708.

Twemlow, S., & Bennett, T. (2008). Psychic plasticity, resilience, and reactions to media violence. *American Behavioral Scientist, 51,* 1155–1183.

Vaske, J., Galyean, K., & Cullen, F. T. (2011). Toward a biosocial theory of offender rehabilitation: Why does cognitive-behavioral therapy work? *Journal of Criminal Justice.* doi:10.1016/j.jcrimjus.2010.12.006.

Viding, E. (2004). On the nature and nurture of antisocial behavior and violence. *Annals of the New York Academy of Sciences, 1036,* 267–277.

Virkkunen, M., Rawlings, R., Tokola, R., Poland, R. E., Guidotti, A., Nemeroff, C., Bissette, G., Kalogeras, K., Karonen, S. L., & Linnoila, M. (1994). CSF biochemistries, glucose metabolism, and diurnal activity rhythms in alcoholic, violent offenders, fire setters, and healthy volunteers. *Archives of General Psychiatry, 51*, 20–27.

Volavka, J., Martell, D., & Convit, A. (1992). Psychobiology of the violent offender. *Journal of Forensic Science, 37*, 237–251.

Volkow, N. D., & Tancredi, L. R. (1987). Neural substrates of violent behavior: A preliminary study with positron emission tomography. *British Journal of Psychiatry, 151*, 668–673.

Walsh, A. (2002). *Biosocial criminology: Introduction and integration.* Cincinnati, OH: Anderson.

Walsh, A., & Beaver, K. M. (2008). *Biosocial criminology: New directions in theory and research.* New York: Routledge.

Werner, E. E. (2000). Protective factors and individual resilience. In J. P. Shonkoff and S. J. Meisels (Eds.), *Handbook of early childhood intervention* (pp. 115–132). New York: Cambridge University Press.

Widom, C. S. (1989a). The cycle of violence. *Science, 244*, 160–166.

Widom, C. S. (1989b). Does violence beget violence? A critical examination of the literature. *Psychological Bulletin, 106*, 3–28.

Widom, C. S., & Brzustowicz, L. M. (2006). MAOA and the "cycle of violence": childhood abuse and neglect, MAOA genotype, and risk for violent and antisocial behavior. *Biological Psychiatry, 60*, 684–689.

Williams, D. (1969). Neural factors related to habitual aggression: Consideration of differences between habitual aggressive and others who have committed crimes of violence. *Brain, 92*, 503–520.

Wills, T. A. Schreibman, D., Benson, G., & Vaccaro, D. (1994). Impact of parental substance use on adolescents: A test of a mediational model. *Journal of Pediatric Psychology, 19*, 537–555.

World Health Organization (1992). *ICD-10: The international statistical classification of diseases and related health problems.* Geneva: Author.

Wright, J. P., & Beaver, K. M. (2005). Do parents matter in creating self-control in their children? A genetically informed test of Gottfredson and Hirschi's theory of low self-control. *Criminology, 43*, 1169–1202.

Wright, J. P., Tibbetts, S. G., & Daigle, L. E. (2008). *Criminals in the making: Criminality across the life course.* Thousand Oaks: Sage Publications.

Yates, T. M. (2007). The developmental consequences of child emotional abuse: A neurodevelopmental perspective. *Journal of Emotional Abuse, 7*, 9–34.

Yuedall, L. T. (1977). Neuropsychological assessment of forensic disorders. *Canadian Mental Health, 25*, 7–18.

Zuckerman, M. (1994). *Behavioral expressions and biosocial bases of sensation seeking.* New York: Cambridge University Press.

The Neuroscientific Basis of
Situational Action Theory

Kyle Treiber

Knowledge about the neurological structures and functions which underlie human action has advanced rapidly in recent decades. This knowledge has not, however, been widely applied to theories of crime. One reason for this is that few theories accurately define crime and identify it as a type of action (and subsequently recognize that psychophysiology plays a significant role in action). Another is that most theories which do address action cognition focus on the content (e.g. opportunities, consequences) but not the processes through which that content is applied to action. Content, obviously, is of key importance, but it cannot be applied effectively to action unless the right processes are in place, and those processes will be governed by neurocognitive structures and functions. Criminological theories which do posit a process (e.g. rational choice) are typically uninformed, or ill-informed, about the psychophysiological mechanisms involved. My aim in this chapter is to look at one theory of crime – Situational Action Theory (SAT) – which tackles crime as a type of action and addresses the causal processes (mechanisms) which lead to crime (as well as their relevant content), and show how its framework is consistent with what we now know about the neuroscience of action decision making.

Neuroscientific work beginning in the late 1800s (e.g. Bianchi, 1922, Ferrier, 1875, Ferrier and Yeo, 1884, Franz, 1902, Hunter and Hall, 1941, Richter and Hines, 1938, Wundt, 1904) identified the frontal lobes as a brain region central to action, although there was still strong opposition to this supposition well into the 1900s (e.g. Campbell, 1905, Horsley and Schafer, 1888, Jackson, 1874, Loeb, 1901, Pavlov, 1941a, 1941b). More recently, the prefrontal cortex in particular has become associated with intentional, goal-directed action (Goldberg, 2001). Although there is still much that remains unknown about this area of the brain and the workings of its various subdivisions, what is known, as I aim to show, is consistent with the model of action decision making posited by SAT in its explanation of crime. Particular features of the SAT model which I will highlight include its emphasis on person–environment interactions as the source of action, its unique treatment of motivation and the perception of alternatives, and its dualistic model of action decision making.

Core Aims of Situational Action Theory

Situational Action Theory (SAT, see Wikström, 2004, 2005, 2006, 2007a, 2007b, 2009, 2010a, 2010b, Wikström and Treiber, 2007, 2009a, 2009b) was developed to address four major shortcomings in criminological theory: (1) the poor definition of crime (what criminological theories should explain); (2) the failure to differentiate between causes and correlates (to identify causal mechanisms); (3) the failure to integrate individual and environmental levels of explanation (to recognize and address their interactive nature); and (4) the failure to adequately explain development and change (how the factors which cause crime emerge, or "the causes of the causes"). Although it has not explicitly set out to create a framework informed by neuroscience, it has aimed to remain consistent with empirical evidence from multiple disciplines, and its focus on causal factors and the processes by which they influence action, as well as its attention to the interaction between individual and environmental factors, means that neurocognitive factors stand to be highlighted. Unlike other contemporary criminological theories (e.g. Gottfredson and Hirschi, 1990), SAT is open to exploring the role of such factors in its explanation of crime. This is particularly significant as SAT aims to present a general theory of crime (see Wikström, 2004, 2006, Wikström and Treiber, 2009a); if successful, it may consequently highlight the general role of neurocognitive structures and functions in acts of crime, which has implications for how we study the role of neurocognitive impairments and explain some developmental effects.

Crime as Moral Action

One of SAT's major contributions to criminological theory is its definition of crime – i.e. what is to be explained. SAT defines crime as a subcategory of moral action. Moral actions are those which follow or break moral rules, moral rules being rules about whether an action is right or wrong. Moral rules can be stipulated (and enforced) by different authorities (e.g. religious doctrine, political ideology, cultural dogma, etc.) and consequently may have a different bearing on different people's actions. Acts of crime represent a specific category of moral actions related to moral rules defined by law. Such rules apply to all people within a particular jurisdiction at a particular time and are subject to especially formal and stringent enforcement.

By identifying rule-breaking as the one characteristic all acts of crime (in all places, at all times) have in common, SAT clearly delineates what it is that criminological theories must explain. Because other criminological theories have struggled to pinpoint this common attribute, there has been widespread skepticism about the potential for developing a general theory of crime, leading to a somewhat piecemeal approach to explaining specific kinds of actions (such as violent crimes, hate crimes, sexual deviance, white collar crimes, terrorism, etc.). This has had a significant impact on the kinds of factors criminological theories have tended to focus upon, which has in turn affected its attention to neurocognitive elements. For example, theories which focus on violent crimes may highlight different elements of decision making – and therefore different parts of the brain – than theories which focus on instrumental crimes. For this reason, certain neurological factors have come to be seen as more or less important for different kinds of crime (e.g., serotonin activity has been linked to aggression, and hence violent crime – see Manuck et al., 2006, Miczek and Fish, 2006), while there is little general knowledge about the role of neurocognitive functions in acts of crime more generally. SAT does not propose to explain why people undertake certain kinds of action, but rather why they undertake such actions when those actions break a rule of law. For example, SAT does not propose to explain why a person shoots another person; in some cases the explanation is irrelevant to the explanation of crime, such as when a person shoots an enemy while at war, or someone by accident. The decision to act in these circumstances will differ from the decision to act which leads to shooting someone as an act of crime, as will some of the underlying neurocognitive processes.

There is increasing attention to and evidence supporting the centrality of morality to the explanation of crime (Antonaccio and Tittle, 2008, Wikström, 2010a, Wikström and Svensson, 2010). However, few criminological theories to date have explicitly addressed the role of morality, and those which have tipped their hats to it tend to rely on assumptions about what constitutes moral action (e.g. which actions are right or wrong). This is exemplified by the popular use of questions about religious affiliation as measures of individual morality. SAT makes no assertions as to whether certain actions are (or should be) right or wrong; although this is an important question, it is not one dealt with by the theory, nor one that needs to be. SAT is interested in why people break rules, not why those rules exist in the first place. Different rules of law will apply in different places at different times; SAT aims to explain acts which break any of those laws, regardless of whether doing so should or shouldn't be right or wrong.

Whether there are any universal human moral rules, and whether these are written into human biology through evolution is another important question facing social and behavioural scientists interested in the roots and nature of moral reasoning. The system appears to be designed like much of the rest of higher order human cognition: responsive to personal experiences, but equipped with built-in shortcuts or fallbacks to increase the efficiency of responses as required; hence there is compelling evidence for a core set of universal moral rules and also evidence of flexibility in moral reasoning, and the neurocognitive functions which underlie them (Bargh, 2006, Blasi, 1980, Borg et al., 2008, Brown, 1991, Casebeer, 2003, de Waal, 2006, Greene et al., 2004, Hauser, 2006, Izard, 1993, Moll et al., 2008,

Pinker, 2002, Ridley, 1996, Trivers, 1971, Wilson, 1993, Woodward and Allman, 2007, Wright, 1994).

SAT is able to exclusively address actions which break rules because it focuses on the *process* which leads people to break rules, rather than the *reasons* they break rules. People may commit the same action for many different reasons, and people may have the same reasons for committing the same action, yet some may and some may not do so. Reasons are not causes (Wikström, 2006). For example, one reason people may steal an iPod is because they can't afford to buy one. Not being able to afford an iPod, however, does not cause a person to steal one; many people who cannot afford an iPod do not steal one. Rather than causes, reasons represent *content* – factors which feed into the process that leads to crime. They play a role in motivation and attention but they do not, in themselves, explain why people break rules. According to SAT, people break rules because they perceive doing so as an alternative for action – i.e. an acceptable response to a particular motivation – and choose to pursue that alternative. The *causes* of crime are those factors which directly lead a person to perceive and choose crime as an alternative.

Those factors may be personal characteristics of the actor or features of the environment in which he/she is acting. The perception-choice process is the mechanism through which these factors interact, and that interaction determines whether or not an act of crime occurs. Although the process is always the same, the content (the personal and environmental factors) which characterizes it is not. Identifying what content results in acts of crime is another core aim of SAT detailed below.

Integrating Personal and Environmental Levels of Analysis

At the core of SAT is the argument that crime is the outcome of the interaction between crime-relevant personal characteristics of an actor (his/her crime *propensity*) and crime-relevant features of the setting in which he/she acts (his/her *exposure* to criminogenic settings).

$$P \times E \rightarrow C$$

Traditionally, criminological theories have focused on either personal characteristics and individual differences in crime involvement (explaining why some kinds of people are more likely to commit acts of crime – i.e. criminality, or crime propensity) (see, for example, Gottfredson and Hirschi, 1990, Moffitt, 1993) or environmental (e.g. neighborhood) effects and crime concentrations (explaining why crime is more likely to be committed in certain places – i.e. crime rates) (see, e.g., Brantingham and Brantingham, 1993, Kornhauser, 1978, Shaw and McKay,

1969). Few have addressed both levels of explanation, and even fewer (if any) have addressed the causal processes by which they lead to crime.[1]

To explain crime as an action requires attention to both. To think that personal characteristics or environmental features alone are enough to explain why actions take place overlooks the fundamental nature of action – that its function is to aide an organism in responding advantageously to its environment (Darwin, 1859) – and a fundamental feature of human action – the degree of personal agency which people are capable of exhibiting. That individual and environmental factors interact in causing crime is also consistent with the neurocognitive architecture which supports action decision making, as detailed below. Knowledge about this architecture alone should lead us to consider both personal and environmental characteristics in the explanation of crime.

At its most basic level, action refers to sequences of bodily movements under the guidance of an actor (Wikström, 2010b). The purpose of action is to provide a medium through which an organism can interact with its environment. To understand why an organism acts in a particular way in response to its environment, we need to know about the nature of the organism (for example, its capacity to sense its environment, and its capacity to act within that environment, i.e. its agency) and the environment (e.g. what opportunities, and obstacles, are present for action). It is impossible to explain action without taking both into account. It is also impossible to understand the role each plays in action without taking into account the structure and function of the brain. The brain – indeed, the entire nervous system – is the medium through which internal and external factors exert their influence on the action decision process.

While action is something of a whole brain activity which relies upon the workings of numerous cortical and subcortical structures, the prefrontal cortex plays the most explicit role, orchestrating the contribution of other brain regions (Goldberg, 2001, Stuss and Levine, 2002). Its core activities have been summarized as the "executive functions" (see, for example, Fuster, 1997, Goldberg, 2001, Moffitt and Henry, 1989, Stuss and Levine, 2002, Tranel et al., 1994). These "higher order" cognitive functions support goal-directed behavior by subserving the activation, evaluation, filtration, organization and integration of action-relevant information in order to identify and compare alternatives for action and predict their outcomes. They are often referred to as an aggregate, with little consideration given to their unified role, and studied in isolation (e.g. abstract reasoning, adaptive shifting, anticipation, attention, cognitive flexibility, concept formation, concentration,

---

1   Those which appear to address both levels – e.g. Gottfredson and Hirschi's self-control theory (Gottfredson and Hirschi, 1990), Cohen and Felson's routine activity theory (Cohen and Felson, 1979, Felson, 2002, 2006), Moffit's dual developmental taxonomy (Moffitt, 1993, 1997, 2003) and Sampson and Laub's age-graded theory of informal social control (Sampson and Laub, 1993, Laub and Sampson, 2003) – ultimately focus their explanation on one, discounting the other or failing to adequately develop its role (for further discussion see Wikström 2006, Wikström et al., 2010; Wikström and Treiber, 2009a). None, as yet, have provided a sufficient model for how they interact.

decision making, disengagement, inhibition, initiation, planning, sequencing, self-awareness and self-monitoring) (e.g. Ardilla et al., 2000, Hughes et al., 1994, Ishikawa and Raine, 2003, McEvoy et al., 1993, Miyake et al., 2000, Moffitt and Henry, 1989, Smith and Jonides, 1999, Tranel et al., 1994, Zelazo et al., 2003). This piecemeal approach has limited their theoretical and empirical applicability as well as their localization in specific brain structures (Miyake et al., 2000, Moffitt, 1990). Nonetheless, executive deficits are consistently linked to rule-breaking behavior (Dunn and Hughes, 2001, Giancola and Zeichner, 1994, Hughes and Dunn, 2000, Moffitt, 1990, Moffitt, 1993, Moffitt and Henry, 1989, Morgan and Lilienfeld, 2000, Raine, 2002, Seguin et al., 1999, Smith et al., 1992, Spellacy, 1977, Teichner and Golden, 2000, Toupin et al., 2000, White et al., 1994, Wikström and Treiber, 2007). A better understanding of precisely what these functions do, in isolation and as a whole, therefore, has the potential to advance our understanding of acts of crime, particularly the decision making process leading up to it.

Neuroscientific evidence suggests that, as a whole, the executive capabilities allow an actor to take control of his/her actions away from external factors and internalize it, bringing his/her knowledge and experience into play. They do so by facilitating the construction of *internal representations* of the circumstances surrounding an action decision. These representations reconstruct those circumstances to reflect perceived significance (rather than mere salience), relevant factors which are not accessible to the senses (e.g., social bonds, knowledge about hidden surveillance), and expectations for action (Bechara et al., 1997, Cohen and Servan-Schreiber, 1992, Fuster, 1997, Goldman-Rakic, 1987, Jonides et al., 1993, Zelazo et al., 2003). Psychophysiologically, an internal representation is comprised of a network of neural activation encompassing immediate sensory information (externally stimulated excitation) and galvanized experiential associations (internally stimulated excitation). Such representations may vary in detail (i.e. the type and quantity of information they represent) but they guide action by drawing attention to particularly relevant, situationally specific information.

Executive functions have been traditionally studied in relation to rational or deliberate action. More recently, as interest in the role of emotions in decision making has increased, researchers have drawn a distinction between these "cool" (analytical) executive functions and "hot" (affective) executive functions (Zelazo and Müller, 2002). Cool executive functions are those involved in managing information, including maintenance, elements of attention, categorization, planning and problem solving. Hot executive functions are those involved in valuing information, which play a key role in expectations, reinforcement and uncertainty. Both exhibit inhibitory capacities, and both provide means of representing action-relevant information internally.

The prefrontal cortex (encompassing Brodmann's areas 9–13, 24, 32–33 and 44–47) is the neurological seat of the executive functions (Goldberg, 2001). It is cleverly integrated with cortical and subcortical structures to pull together all the information necessary to construct internal representations and apply them to action. It is the apex of action information processing in the hierarchy of brain structures transmitting sensory and mnemonic action-relevant information. At the bottom of this hierarchy are the stimulus fields (each serving a different sense) through which external sensory information is collected and then transmitted to the brain along dedicated nerve pathways. This information travels directly to the appropriate primary sensory projection area, the frontline in information processing, where it is translated into the neurochemical language of neurons. This information is then conveyed to adjacent modality specific secondary association areas for interpretation, before it is finally transferred to tertiary, heteromodal association areas where it can be integrated with information from other sensory modalities. As the tertiary, heteromodal association cortex serving the primary motor cortex, the prefrontal cortex is the neurological centre for information pertaining to action (Goldberg, 2001).

The primary motor cortex is the primary sensory projection area for information about physical stimuli such as touch and movement (kinaesthesia or proprioception) (de Lafuente and Romo, 2002). The premotor and supplementary motor cortices (Brodmann's areas 4, 6 and 8, which together with the prefrontal cortex create the frontal lobe) serve as intermediate modality specific motor association areas which (in conjunction with the cerebellum) organize this information into motor sequences and (through the basal ganglia) stimulate intention and readiness to act (Goldberg, 2001). The prefrontal cortex receives this action specific information from the motor cortices as well as information from other association cortices regarding other sensory modalities.

In fact, the prefrontal cortex receives information from secondary association cortices for all sensory modalities (London et al., 2000). While impressive from the perspective of neurological architecture and evolution, this should not be surprising: actions are hugely diverse – from physical responses (running, shaking hands, closing one's eyes, etc.), to speech, to further information gathering (e.g. through listening, looking or touching), and so forth – as is the information relevant to them – from what someone has said, to something the actor has seen (an object or movement, etc.) or smelled or tasted, to something the actor has read, and so on. Very adaptable and efficient information processing capacities (and therefore structures) are required to deal effectively with this diversity of information and translate it into the appropriate kind of action.

The seemingly infinite varieties of action are one of the major factors which has hindered the study of crime as a type of action; to many criminologists it has appeared impossible to find a genuine commonality between all acts which qualify as crimes, as legality has the potential to be arbitrary (and to vary by time and place) (Gottfredson and Hirschi, 1990, Tittle, 1995, Wikström and Sampson, 2006, Wilson and Herrnstein, 1985). Because SAT identifies that commonality (rule-breaking) it is able to delimit what kinds of information (and information processing capacities) are particularly relevant to the explanation of crime – those which are relevant to the breaking of rules, e.g. information about rules, their reinforcement, and what may happen when rules are broken.

Below I will delve further in the neurophysiology of the prefrontal cortex and the specific neurocognitive capabilities behind the executive functions, as I look closer at the arguments of SAT. This overview provides the groundwork while demonstrating that the neurocognitive action guidance system is designed to support the integration of external and internal information, and to facilitate the interaction of a person with his/her environment by drawing upon information drawn from both. Action is not purely stimulus-response, driven either by external or internal motivators (e.g. provocations or drives), even in most animals (as evidenced by the repeal of pure behaviorism), and especially in animals with highly evolved prefrontal cortices – humans, of course, standing at the evolutionary apex (Coolidge and Wynn, 2001, Goldberg, 2001, Goldman-Rakic, 1987, Zelazo, 2005). The explanation of action is far more complex and there is much we can learn about human action by learning about the human brain.

The Perception-Choice Process

According to SAT, the interaction between a person and an environment takes the form of a perception-choice process by which the person, in response to a particular motivation, perceives alternatives for action and then chooses which alternative to pursue. This process is initiated by the actor's motivation toward a particular outcome – his/her goal-directed attention toward that outcome. Attention is directed toward a goal by a motivator, which may be a temptation (such as a lost wallet) or a provocation (such as an insult). Like action, motivation is the outcome of an interaction between an actor's personal characteristics and the features of a setting; in the case of temptations, external factors interact with a person's desires and belief that he/she can achieve them; in the case of provocations, external factors interact with a person's sensitivity (the negative affect he/she experiences) (Wikström, 2006, Wikström and Treiber, 2009a). Importantly, this implies that people will differ in their motivation to pursue certain outcomes in response to temptations or provocations, a fact that many criminological theories overlook or fail to address. Control theories in particular make gross assumptions about people's motivation to commit acts of crime, suggesting that most or even all people will desire their outcomes (and, one step further, see crime as an expedient means of obtaining those outcomes) (see, e.g., Gottfredson and Hirschi, 1990, Hirschi, 1969). As a consequence there is little attention to the concept of motivation in criminological theory and research.

However, there is a plethora of evidence that people exhibit different psychophysiological responses to the same stimuli; for criminologically relevant evidence see research with psychopaths (e.g., Fung et al., 2005, Patrick et al., 1994, Raine and Venables, 1988). However, one hardly needs to be invasive to see that people express different preferences and have different desires to pursue different outcomes. Some people are thrill-seekers, others crave tranquillity; some people have large appetites, others have no appetite at all; some people want attention, others want privacy. Neurotransmitters (particularly dopamine and serotonin) play a key role in many of these individual differences, as they activate and suppress different areas of the brain, modulating drives and appetites (Manuck et al., 2006, Miczek and Fish, 2006, Morgan and Lilienfeld, 2000, Rogers et al., 1999).

The significance of these differences for crime is that a situational factor may serve as a motivator for some people, but not for all people (e.g. not everyone who sees a CD wants to have it). So for some people, the reason they don't commit a crime (steal the CD) is because they don't desire its outcome. Another reason could be that they fail to perceive the factor in the first place (e.g. don't notice the CD is there). Attention and sensory perception (e.g. visual acuity) will play a role in these latter differences. In either case, what explains whether the person did or didn't commit the crime has nothing to do with the traditional "causes" of crime (e.g. self-control, social bonds, presence of a suitable target) and more to do with sensation, perception and personal preferences, and their neurocognitive scaffolding.

Once a person has perceived a motivator and been motivated by it, he/she must decide how to respond to it. The first step of this decision process is to identify alternatives for action. Many people will not see crime as an alternative because it won't cross their mind and/or they do not consider it a viable alternative because it breaks a moral rule.

Moral rules (both personal and applicable to the setting) act as a filter for viable action alternatives. If a moral rule asserts that an action is wrong under the present circumstances, that action may be eliminated as a possible alternative; whether it is eliminated, and how quickly, will depend on how strong the moral rule is (i.e. how right or wrong the actor believes it is) and how heavily it is enforced, either by deterrents in the setting or personal moral emotions (feelings of shame or guilt). If the rule is very strong it may be eliminated automatically (out of habit); if the rule is weak and other factors (e.g. motivators) exert opposing influences, the action may be considered as an alternative, but still eliminated after deliberation, depending on its level of enforcement; however, if the rule and its enforcement are both very weak it may be automatically selected (out of habit). Habitual and deliberate choices are discussed in detail below.

Although research into the neurobiology of morality is ongoing, what is known is consistent with these assertions. There appears to be no dedicated neurological centre for moral reasoning (Borg et al., 2008, Casebeer, 2003, Greene and Haidt, 2002, Woodward and Allman, 2007); rather, moral cognition draws upon a variety of brain regions involved in relevant action-related, and particularly affective, functions. The prefrontal cortex is one of these, especially its ventromedial region which is particularly implicated in dealing with information relating to emotions and reinforcement contingencies (e.g. expected outcomes; see further below) (Casebeer, 2003, Greene et al., 2001, 2004, Moll et al., 2002, 2008, Raine and Yang, 2006, Woodward and Allman, 2007). Findings certainly suggest that moral reasoning is a higher order cognitive function which draws upon information from cortical and subcortical areas involved in social cognition, emotion and judgment. Morality may therefore be considered more an issue of content than of unique cognitive processes.

Criminological theories have recognized and attempted to address the role of moral emotions such as shame and guilt in people's crime involvement. These are often included as part of the control calculus for why a person rationally chooses not to commit a crime. Few criminological theories have looked into the more intuitive, unconscious role of emotions and the fact they may exert their effects before rational calculus is initiated, or even required. Neurological evidence, which is reviewed below, shows that while emotions do serve to inform deliberate action decisions, and have a significant influence of the efficacy of those decisions, their predominant function may be to guide action less rationally and more spontaneously, quickly drawing attention to the preferred course of action, sweeping aside undesirable alternatives before valuable cognitive energy is wasted to write them off deliberately.[2]

The initial process of perceiving alternatives is critical for explaining why some people break rules and others don't (for example, when they may have the same *reasons* for doing so) but one which is almost always overlooked in criminological theories. Many theories (especially those in the control tradition) presume that the motivation to commit acts of crime is universal, while others focus only on people who are motivated (e.g. routine activity theory, see Cohen and Felson, 1979, Felson, 2002, 2006) but don't explain how that motivation originates; many criminological theories also presume that opportunities will be perceived, or begin their explanation from the point at which they are (e.g. control theories – see Gottfredson and Hirschi, 1990, Hirschi, 1969). Consequently, these theories focus their attention on the process of choice.

The Process of Choice

Once crime has been perceived as a possible response to a given motivation, an actor must then choose whether or not to pursue it. In criminology, choice is generally interpreted as a rational process involving conscious calculation of pros and cons, and many theories (again, control theories in particular) automatically attribute values and valences to certain kinds of factors. SAT, on the other hand, argues that the process of choice may be either habitual (automatic/intuitive) or deliberate (rational).

Habitual action has been principally ignored in criminological literature, although its implications for intervening in persistent patterns of crime involvement may be significant (Wikström and Treiber, 2009b). Habits are formed when a person learns through repeated exposure to a particular setting and circumstances to choose a particular action because it has certain predictable and desirable outcomes. This allows a person to respond efficiently to familiar situations, saving time and cognitive energy. In essence, habits are shortcuts for action informed by experience. Because most people routinely operate in a limited activity field, most of their day-to-day activities are facilitated by habits. SAT posits that when people act out of habit they perceive only that one alternative for action, and automatically choose

---

2   "It is highly adaptive for animals to be able to feel before they think" (Izard 1993: 73).

to carry it out. For example, a person could learn by experience that taking things from other people is an effective way of acquiring them; then when he/she wants an iPod and sees someone carrying one, he/she may automatically (habitually) decide to steal it, without considering other alternatives, such as buying one. A habit is broken when an actor becomes aware of other alternatives, at which point a more deliberate element enters the action decision process.

People make deliberate action choices when they perceive more than one alternative for action and must choose which they want to carry out. Deliberate choices involve the conscious consideration of information relevant to action, such as preferences, contingencies, intervening factors and expected outcomes (including consequences). Deliberation is therefore especially useful in unfamiliar or uncertain circumstances where many of these factors may be less well known (Wikström and Treiber, 2007, Wikström, 2010a). Deliberation is the *more* rational process of choice, although it is guided by emotion and preferential attention as much as calculating reason. It is also the only process through which controls may exert their effects; people do not exhibit self-control when they act out of habit (they see nothing to control), nor do they take into account deterrents.

Many action decisions will involve elements of both habit and deliberation. Deliberation requires time and cognitive effort; hence in time-limited circumstances deliberate elements of decision making may be curtailed and habitual elements heavily drawn upon. At the same time, deliberate elements may temporarily override habitual choices to allow for more conscious assessment before an actor falls back upon a habitual choice. However, although these processes are not mutually exclusive, certain kinds of crime may entail a more habitual or deliberate element, which may have implications for how they can be explained and potentially prevented (Wikström and Treiber, 2009b). Violent crimes, for example, may have a more habitual nature, while instrumental crimes may be more deliberate (Wikström and Treiber, 2009a).

A dualistic model of action decision making has been advocated in psychological theories for some time (see, for example, Gray, 1972, Witkin et al., 1977). Most recently, interest and evidence have endorsed a model featuring parallel associative/intuitive and rational/deliberate systems, which is supported by advancing knowledge about the structure and function of the prefrontal cortex and its major subdivisions (Kahneman, 2003, Sloman, 1996). The strength of such a system is that it strikes a balance between quick, efficient decision making and slower but more considered decision making, with the former drawing upon more "primitive" capacities upon which the latter builds (Moll et al., 2008). Working in parallel, these systems create an effective and efficient system for applying the right amount of information, and the right information, to action decisions ranging from everyday routines to singular predicaments.

According to this model, the associative/intuitive system supports faster, often unconscious decision making by drawing immediate associations between active information and readily accessible knowledge (often made accessible through an easily activated emotional element). This generates involuntary impressions which then influence action choices (for example, through "gut instincts" or preferences)

(Kahneman, 2003). These associations are learned through repeated interaction with a given set of circumstances and they provide an automatic system to guide action when those circumstances are routinely re-encountered without placing demands on the cognitive system. This system, clearly, supports what SAT (among other theories) refers to as habitual action.

The rational/deliberate system supports more conscious, reasoned decision making by organizing and evaluating relevant information to turn attention to information which is perceived as most significant to the actor, and the action, under the given circumstances. This provides a solution to action in unfamiliar or especially complex circumstances. However, because of the cognitive effort which must be expended, the use of this system will be limited to situations which require a more reasoned response; otherwise the simpler, more efficient associative/intuitive system will suffice (Kahneman, 2003). Hence, although most action will involve input from both systems, the majority of action may rely more on association/intuition than rational deliberation. As SAT has sought to highlight, this has important implications for explaining why those actions take place, and potentially preventing them from happening.

Moral action, like any other kind of action, has also been shown to be guided by two such complementary systems, and to be particularly informed by the associative/intuitive system (see, e.g., Casebeer, 2003, Greene et al., 2001, 2004, Izard, 1993, Moll et al., 2005). This is consistent with the argument proposed above that what differentiates moral reasoning from other kinds of reasoning is the content, not the process (or processes).

These two systems are dissociable not only psychologically, but neuroanatomically as well. Two major subdivisions of the prefrontal cortex, the ventromedial and dorsolateral prefrontal cortices, have been linked respectively to the associative/intuitive and rational/deliberate decision making systems. Although they serve distinct functions, these brain regions, and those functions, are interconnected. There is still much to learn about both regions, what they do and how they do it, but existing knowledge has allowed neuroscientists to draw the following conclusions.

The Ventromedial Prefrontal Cortex and Associative/Intuitive Action Decision Making

The ventromedial prefrontal cortex (VMPFC) is particularly implicated in facilitating the associative/intuitive system. The VMPFC is the most anterior region of the brain, lying just above the eye sockets, and encompasses several distinct prefrontal areas, including the orbitofrontal cortex (OFC; Brodmann's areas 11 and 12), the frontopolar and insular prefrontal cortices (Brodmann's areas 10 and 13,) and parts of the anterior cingulate cortex (ACC; lower Brodmann's area 24, areas 25 and 32) (Bechara, 2004, Bechara et al., 2000a, Dom et al., 2005, Dunn et al., 2006, Fuster,

1997, Goldman-Rakic, 1987, Rao et al., 1997). Together, these areas support aspects of decision making particularly linked to affect, including emotional perception, sensitivity to reward and punishment, and motivation, via their connections to the limbic system and related subcortical structures (Bechara, 2004, Bechara et al., 1994, 2000a, 2000b, Damasio, 1994, 1996, Fuster, 1997, London et al., 2000).

A core function of the VMPFC is mediating the activity of the amygdala, a limbic structure which plays a critical role in emotional reactions and memory. The VMPFC suppresses the amygdala via serotonergic pathways, dampening emotional reactions and clearing the way for more internally driven responses (Best et al., 2002). For example, serotonergic activity in the VMPFC has been linked to reduced aggression and increased prosocial behaviour in animals (Raleigh and Brammer, 1993) and humans (Linnoila et al., 1983, Siever et al., 1999). Serotonergic suppression of the amygdala is counteracted by dopaminergic activation. Dopamine is a critical neurochemical in the brain's reward circuit and frees the amygdala to respond to reinforcers, directing motivation and providing the VMPFC with affective information on stimuli's reinforcement characteristics, such as their association with positive or negative outcomes (Goldstein and Volkow, 2002, Rogers and Robbins, 2001, Volkow et al., 1993). An advanced function of the VMPFC is to then collate this information over repeated encounters with a stimulus into an affective valence – a *somatic marker* – which is automatically associated with that stimulus and activated when it is reencountered (Damasio, 1994, 1996). This creates an automatic expectation for action linked to that stimulus based on an actor's past experiences, which automatically and often unconsciously guides action without burdening the more deliberate decision making system.

This function of the VMPFC has been studied intensively by Antonio Damasio, Antoine Bechara and colleagues, and is summarized in their somatic marker hypothesis (Bechara et al., 1999, 2000b, 2005, Damasio, 1994, 1996, Damasio et al., 1990). Their observations of patients with VMPFC lesions led them to recognize that this area of the prefrontal cortex supported a dissociable, emotional element of action decision making which is integral to, but often overlooked in lieu of, more rational processes. The somatic marker hypothesis postulates that the VMPFC mediates action decision making by providing situationally relevant information about expected outcomes and reinforcement in the form of positive and negative valences (somatic markers) quantifying the emotional (and hence behavioral) significance of situational factors (Damasio, 1994, 1996, Overman et al., 2004).

Like other areas of the prefrontal cortex, the VMPFC receives projections from brain areas supporting all sensory modalities, through which it has access to information about the external setting (London et al., 2000). The VMPFC also receives projections from the amygdala and hypothalamus, through which it gains access to information about a person's somatic state. It is therefore perfectly situated to draw associations between the two (Damasio, 1994), linking emotional attributes (such as reinforcement characteristics) to a stimulus, establishing its motivational value (Kawasaki et al., 2001, London et al., 2000). The VMPFC not only creates somatic markers, it also reactivates them when a stimulus is reencountered (via interconnections with subcortical structures such as the amygdala, hypothalamus and various nuclei in the brainstem, which allow it to signal, or even recreate, an anticipated emotional state), and updates them whenever reinforcement characteristics change (Bechara et al., 2000a, 2000b, Damasio, 1994, 1996, Damasio et al., 1990).

These prefrontal functions are clearly capable of subserving a system of habitual action as described by SAT. When an actor encounters familiar circumstances (for example, sees something valuable, like money sticking out of someone's pocket), the VMPFC can draw immediate associations between that stimulus and expected outcomes (e.g., previous successful instances of pickpocketing), automatically directing motivation (toward the money) and advocating a particular habitual response (to steal it). These functions also support the breaking of habits when reinforcement contingencies change (for example, a person gets caught stealing and is punished). On the flip side, deficiencies in VMPFC functioning may lead to perseverative behavior which does not respond to changes in outcomes (e.g. punishment), a condition which is symptomatic of psychopathy and addiction. Indeed, many addictive substances impair VMPFC functioning, temporarily and often for an extended period of time, leading users to overvalue the effects and undervalue the consequences of their continued use (Bechara et al., 2001, 2002, London et al., 2000, Rogers and Robbins, 2001).

As psychologists and SAT argue, associative/intuitive decision making often works in tandem with rational/deliberate decision making, rather than entirely independently. The VMPFC paves the way for deliberate processes by inhibiting impulsive emotional responses, and provides important information about significance and expectations for action (Damasio, 1996). Although studies have evidenced an asymmetric dissociation between VMPFC functions and those associated with more deliberate decision making (e.g. working memory, described below) (Adinoff et al., 2003, Bechara, 2004, Bechara et al., 1998, Ernst et al., 2002), such that VMPFC functions depend upon functions associated with deliberation (e.g. maintenance and manipulation of information necessary to collate somatic markers) but not vice versa, there is also clear evidence that without input from the VMPFC, although deliberate decision making can take place, it is ineffectual (see, e.g., Eslinger and Damasio, 1985). This was one of the initial observations which led to further consideration of the VMPFC and its unique role in the decision making process.

Clear links have been drawn between VMPFC dysfunction, moral reasoning, and crime involvement. Research has shown that although patients with VMPFC lesions possess adequate social and moral knowledge, they are unable to apply that knowledge effectively to action (Bechara et al., 2000a, 2000b, Damasio et al., 1990, Eslinger and Damasio, 1985); hence they are able to state what they should do in a particular moral circumstance, but then choose to do something else. A similar behavioral pattern is seen in psychopathy; although some psychopaths are able to process affective information and understand the emotional implications of certain situations, they do not show the autonomic response which would indicate activation of relevant somatic markers (Dinn and Harris, 2000, Flor et al., 2002, Fung et al., 2005). Findings such as these suggest that the neurologic deficits which characterize psychopathy are not centered only on the subcortical structures, such as the amygdala, which control perception of emotion, but may also lie further up the perceptual hierarchy in the VMPFC (Bechara et al., 2000b, 2001, Birbaumer et al., 2005). Psychopaths may be an extreme example of why a purely rational/deliberate decision making system is not ideal; although psychopaths are often characterized as being cold and calculating (i.e. unemotional) they are clearly capable of making poor action choices. Affective, somatic information is particularly useful for guiding action, and has done so successfully in animals with less developed reasoning capacities for millions of years (Casebeer, 2003, Greene et al., 2004, Izard, 1993). Both systems have their advantages, and by working in tandem they exploit those advantages in a way designed to best serve each action decision.

By quantifying the stimulus-response relationship and allowing preferences (characterized by affective valences) to help determine action choices, the VMPFC allows an actor to take one step toward taking control of his/her actions away from the environment. The dorsolateral prefrontal cortex, which more explicitly supports rational/deliberate decision making, allows the actor to go one step further by organizing an internal representation – the unified executive function – to guide his/her action decision making. This allows him/her to consciously integrate external information with internal knowledge and tailor his/her action to suit him/herself and the circumstances he/she faces.

The Dorsolateral Prefrontal Cortex and Rational/Deliberate Action Decision Making

The dorsolateral prefrontal cortex (DLPFC; Brodmann's areas 9 and 46) is the evolutionary extension of the cortical architecture of the hippocampus, the brain's center for memory (Stuss and Levine, 2002). Consequently, its core functions revolve around active, or working, memory and the activation, organization, maintenance, manipulation and application of information to action. The dorsolateral prefrontal cortex is closely linked to the ventrolateral prefrontal cortex (VLPFC; Brodmann's areas 45 and 47), which is implicated in active retrieval of information from long-term storage (Petrides et al., 1993, Smith and Jonides, 1999), and together they make the creation of internal representations possible.

Working memory was first theorized by Baddeley and Hitch in 1974 and has since undergone a number of permutations (see Baddeley, 1992, 1996a, 1996b, 1998, 2000, 2001, Baddeley and Della Sala, 1996, Baddeley and Hitch, 1974); the basic model, however, has proven consistent with neuroscientific advances, down to the neurocellular level. Working memory is the "cognitive space" in which active information is evaluated, integrated and applied to a cognitive task, such as an action decision. This includes information from the person and the setting, from experience and the immediate senses, factual and emotional. The working memory model involves the maintenance of active information in specialized storage "units" (e.g. the visuospatial sketchpad and the phonological loop), which can be accounted for by information held in other cortices, such as the parietal cortex, that is activated and then kept active by the prefrontal cortex. This information is overseen and manipulated by a "central executive," which can be accounted for by the information processing capacities of the prefrontal cortex, such as those for selective attention, inhibition and integration (Adcock et al., 2000, Baddeley, 1996a, 1996b, Baddeley et al., 1991, Demetriou et al., 2002, Fuster, 1997, Jonides, 1995, Ribaupierre and Bailleux, 1994). In essence, the DLPFC functions as a neural traffic control unit, communicating with various parts of brain (neo- and subcortical) to ensure the right information is available as it is needed, and working memory represents the entire roadway network.

Neuroimaging studies support localization of working memory storage units in posterior brain regions, namely the parietal lobes, and the activities attributed to the central executive in the DL and VLPFC (Baddeley, 2000, Cohen et al., 1997, MacDonald et al., 2000, Prabhakaran et al., 2000, Smith and Jonides, 1997). Research at the neuronal level has evidenced the capacity of neurons in the DLPFC to retain visuospatial information, giving the DLPFC the capacity to retain a mental map of the visual field (Funahashi et al., 1989). This supports the proposition that the creation of an internal representation is the unifying executive function (Goldman-Rakic, 1987) (see also Bechara et al., 1997, Cohen and Servan-Schreiber, 1992, Daigneault et al., 1992, Fuster, 1997, Jonides et al., 1993, Zelazo et al., 2003). Further research at the neuronal level has also evidenced the capacity of DLPFC neurons to use information from multiple modalities (Ranier et al., 1998a, 1998b, Rao et al., 1997).

It is clear that this kind of information processing system could support rational/deliberate decision making. However, it has distinct limitations. One limitation is its capacity; only so many units of information can be kept active at one time. This is supported by cognitive and neurological evidence (Case et al., 1982, Kemps et al., 2000, Miles and Morgan, 1996, Miller et al., 1996, Ranier et al., 1998b, Towse and Hitch, 1995). Typically, adults can maintain five to nine units, although "clumping" strategies may compensate. Importantly, this capacity may vary considerably between people, with potential implications for their decision making.

Because working memory capacity is limited, people need to be able to identify the most pertinent, and eliminate superfluous, information. Hence the need for evaluative and comparative executive functions (many of which are supported by the VMPFC). Another dimension of working memory which varies between people is their processing efficiency – how quickly and effectively they can filter information. This is characterized by two key functions: speed of processing and control of processing (i.e. reducing interference) (Demetriou et al., 2002). While working memory capacity characterizes storage functions, processing efficiency is the domain of the central executive. It may compensate for deficits in working memory capacity; perhaps as a consequence, it has been more closely associated with behavioral impairments (Alderman, 1996, Baddeley and Della Sala, 1996). If a person cannot process information effectively, he/she may fail to consider important factors, or overvalue less important factors.

The rational/deliberate decision making system described by SAT is more consistent with this model than the pure rational choice model typically forwarded by criminological theories. SAT also provides a novel framework for understanding the role of executive functions (i.e. prefrontal activity) in acts of crime (see Wikström and Treiber, 2007). When a person has executive deficits, he/she may create and act upon a deficient internal representation. VMPFC deficits may be related to false expectations, disproportionate emotional reactions (exaggerated or insufficient), and the inability to learn from negative outcomes (perseverative behaviour). Such deficits have been linked to sociopathy and psychopathy (Bechara et al., 2000b, 2001, Birbaumer et al., 2005, Dinn and Harris, 2000, Lösel and Schmucker, 2004, van Honk et al., 2002) and social and moral behavioral impairments (Ackerly and Benton, 1948, Anderson et al., 1999, Bechara, 2004, Bechara et al., 1999, Price et al., 1990). Within the SAT framework this suggests that people with VMPFC deficits may be more sensitive to provocations, meaning they may be more prone to violence, which evidence from VMPFC lesion studies supports (Bechara, 2004, Bechara et al., 1999). DLPFC deficits may be related to acting upon faulty or incomplete information (the latter being linked with impulsivity), including the failure to fully consider moral implications (e.g. to take rules into account) and the potential consequences of one's actions. There has been considerable empirical research into these "cool" executive functions and their relationship to crime. A number of meta-analyses agree that the correlation between executive deficits and rule-breaking is consistent and robust (equivalent to a medium or large effect) (Morgan and Lilienfeld, 2000, Teichner and Golden, 2000, Toupin et al., 2000). Such deficits have been strongly linked to externalizing disorders and childhood behavioural problems, such as ADHD, CD and ODD, which are also linked to crime involvement (Moffitt, 1990, 1993, Moffitt and Henry, 1989, Raine, 2002, Toupin et al., 2000).

Executive deficits may be acquired in several ways. There is clearly a developmental element; people acquire executive capabilities at different rates, leading them to exhibit different decision making capacities at different ages. The general time frame for the development of executive capabilities is particularly drawn out – the prefrontal cortex is in fact the last area of the brain to fully mature (Bunge et al., 2002, Case, 1992, Case et al., 1982, Crone and van der Molen, 2004, Dempster and Corkill, 1999, Fuster, 1997, Goleman, 1995, Spear, 2000). This has particularly significant implications for understanding patterns of crime, such as the classic age-crime curve. The prefrontal cortex begins the final stage of its development during pre-adolescence and continues to mature into early adulthood. During this time the brain is particularly malleable to experience; neural pathways which are utilized become strengthened, while those which are neglected atrophy, such that how a person thinks and behaves has a lasting effect on the neural structure of his/her brain (Casey et al., 2000, Chugani et al., 1987, Giedd et al., 1999, Grotstein, 1994, Luna, 2004, Luna et al., 2001, Rakic et al., 1994, Sowell et al., 2001, White et al., 1994). Because how a person thinks and acts depends in part upon the settings he/she encounters, external influences may be especially significant during adolescence (e.g. parenting, see Landry et al., 2002), and neural development is experience-dependent (Blakemore and Choudhury, 2006, Greenough et al., 1987). Accordingly, evidence suggests that executive capabilities can be developed through practice and the right type of enrichment, which has important implications for prevention and intervention methods (Embry, 2005, Greenough et al., 1987, Riggs et al., 2006).

Prefrontal regions associated with inhibition are some of the very last to develop (Case et al., 1982, Casey et al., 2000, Chelune and Baer, 1986, Luciana et al., 2005). During adolescence the reward circuit, mediated by the limbic system, is wired into the prefrontal cortex to give it access to information of reinforcement contingencies and somatic states (Embry, 2005, Spear, 2000). During this process the limbic system is deprived of dopamine, impairing its ability to perceive and respond to outcomes and stimulate motivation. This may lead to a "reward deficiency syndrome" which has been linked to adolescent risk-taking and sensation-seeking (Bjork et al., 2004, Ernst et al., 2005, Spear, 2000).

These significant neurological changes during adolescence mean that executive capabilities are not fully realized until early adulthood. Working memory capacity expands steadily during adolescence and has been linked to age-related changes in cognitive functions such as attention and problem-solving (Demetriou et al., 2002, Gathercole, 1999, Kemps et al., 2000, Swanson, 1999, Towse et al., 1998). Processing efficiency also increases during adolescence (Demetriou et al., 2002, Kail and Salthouse, 1994) but may be more susceptible to environmental effects (Carmelli et al., 2002). This has interesting implications for enrichment interventions. Young people's proficiency in creating and using somatic markers likewise undergoes significant developmental effects during adolescence (Crone et al., 2005, 2006, Crone and van der Molen, 2004, Hooper et al., 2004, Overman et al., 2004) which may peak later than those associated with working memory. While these capacities are under development, adolescents' decision making abilities may be comprised. At the same time, however, they experience greater independence and personal agency. The fact that these two circumstances overlap may help to explain surges in crime involvement amongst adolescents.

Executive deficits do not only arise through developmental deficiencies. They may result from brain injury, and because they are involved in the acquisition as well as the application of information, injuries at a younger age, especially prior to adolescence, may have particularly detrimental effects on behavior (Ackerly and Benton, 1948, Anderson et al., 1999, Bechara, 2004, Bechara et al., 1999, Price et al., 1990). Executive deficits may also be temporary. Alcohol and many substances can suppress prefrontal functioning. Certain substances may target different parts of the brain (for example, cocaine and its derivatives have been shown to affect the VMPFC while cannabis and alcohol affect the DLPFC), leading to temporary (but also potentially prolonged or even permanent) specific executive deficits (Bechara et al., 2001, 2002, Brown and Tapert, 2004, Dao-Castellana et al., 1998, Goldstein et al., 2004, Goldstein and Volkow, 2002, Koob and Bloom, 1988, London et al., 2000, Nestler and Aghajanian, 1997, Porrino and Lyons, 2000, Rogers et al., 1999, Rogers and Robbins, 2001, Stein et al., 1997, Volkow and Fowler, 2000, Volkow et al., 1993, White, 2004). Extreme or prolonged stress (e.g. emotional duress) may also impair executive functioning. Prolonged exposure to stress-induced cortisol in the brain interferes with mnemonic functions and serotonergic activity in the hippocampus, a subcortical structure supporting memory functions, as well as the prefrontal cortex (Bremner, 1999, López et al., 1999).

All of these factors have implications for how we understand the role of executive functions in crime involvement. One testable implication of SAT is that these deficits will only be related to crime in circumstances where the actor perceives crime as an alternative – i.e. has weak personal moral rules – and many executive functions (especially "cool" executive functions related to the DLPFC) will only be related to crime when an actor makes a deliberate action choice (Wikström and Treiber, 2007). A related implication is that controls (internal self-control and external deterrence) will also only play a role in deliberate acts of crime, although this contention goes against the assertions of many control theories, which argue that controls play a central role in explaining all acts of crime (Wikström, 2010a, 2010b, Wikström and Treiber, 2009a). Only deliberate action choices, which draw upon the more complex information processing functions of the DLPFC, will deal with conflict between opposing motivations and alternatives, and therefore have something to control. However, as SAT and most other dualistic perspectives on action decision making agree, most action decisions involve elements of both habit and deliberation, hence what will vary between most such decisions is the degree to which controls are taken into account, as well as the degree to which certain executive functions will play a role (and therefore certain executive deficits may be relevant). Theories like Gottfredson and Hirschi's explore variation in control from the individual level, but their model is one-dimensional, ignoring the complementary role of environmental factors and failing to explode the model to consider various pathways to action. Both the role of controls and the role of specific executive functions linked to the VMPFC and DLPFC are being studied through the Peterborough Adolescent and Young Adult Development Study (PADS+), which is described briefly below.

The Causes of Crime

At the core of SAT is its argument that personal and environmental characteristics interact to cause crime. The causal process through which this occurs is the process of perception and choice described above. Hence the "causes of crime" are those factors (personal or environmental) which lead a person to perceive crime as an alternative and choose to commit it. SAT aims to identify these key factors, and posits the following.

Key personal characteristics are a person's morality (personal moral rules and relevant emotions) and ability to exercise self-control (to act in accordance with personal moral rules when tempted to act otherwise). Key environmental features include the moral context (the rules which apply to the setting, and their level of enforcement – i.e. deterrence) and motivators such as temptations and provocations. Personal morality and temptations and provocations mainly influence motivation (goal-directed attention) and the perception of alternatives, and therefore play a central role in habitual choices (whether or not one perceives a single uncontested alternative). Self-control and deterrence, as argued above, only play a role in deliberate action choices.

These factors can be seen as the most critical pieces of information which will inform and guide the decision to commit an act of crime. Morality is key because of the nature of crime as a form of rule-breaking. Whether or not a person takes moral rules into account in his/her decision to act depends on what rules he/she recognizes and the significance he/she attributes to them. The significance will be learned through experience and represented somatically by the VMPFC. The DLPFC will play a role in whether that information is activated and attended to, how it is interpreted under the given circumstances, and how it is applied to action. Motivators are key because they trigger expectations and initiate the perception process, readying a person for action. Self-control is key because it can help an actor deal with conflicting motivation to break rules in response to temptations or provocations by inhibiting impulsive responses, and follow moral rules consistent with personal moral beliefs through reasoned decision making. Deterrence is key because it guides moral action externally by countering people's motivation to break rules when their personal moral rules do not do so.

Together, SAT sees a person's morality and ability to exercise self-control as the key factors which determine his/her crime propensity – the extent to which he/she perceives crime as an alternative he/she then chooses to pursue when confronted with a criminogenic setting. The key features of a criminogenic setting are the presence of motivators and the absence of strong moral rules and enforcement (deterrence), which creates a moral context conducive to crime. This detail fleshes out the core argument of SAT that P x E → C (Wikström, 2009, 2010b, Wikström et al., 2010).

Conclusions

SAT argues that crimes are actions and should, therefore, be explained as such. Those actions are caused by the fact that people perceive crime as an alternative and choose to commit it. The process of perception determines whether or not the process of choice will be habitual (if the person perceives only one alternative for action) or deliberate (if the person perceives more than one alternative for action). Whether or not people perceive and choose crime as an alternative depends on their crime propensity and exposure to criminogenic settings (i.e. what kind of people they are and what kinds of settings they take part in). The key factors that determine a person's propensity and exposure are personal moral rules and emotions and the ability to exercise self-control; and motivators, the moral rules of the setting, and their enforcement (deterrence); respectively. People's crime involvement can be explained, via this model, as an outcome of an interaction between their crime propensity and their exposure to criminogenic settings. People's propensity and exposure are an outcome of wider social conditions and life events, *the causes of the causes* (this final argument is detailed elsewhere – see Wikström, 2005, 2006, 2009, Wikström and Sampson, 2003).

These arguments are consistent with neurological evidence concerning the nature of action decision making, especially the structure and function of the prefrontal cortex. Some are already being tested through the Peterborough Adolescent and Young Adult Development Study (PADS+; see Wikström et al., 2010, 2011a, 2011b; www.pads.ac.uk), an ongoing longitudinal study designed to test SAT within a random population of young people as they age from preadolescence into adulthood. There is still much that is not known about the neurobiology of action decision making, especially in regards to morality, which lies at the core of SAT. Further analysis of the neuropsychology of action decision making and its relation to criminal behavior will continue to shed light on this area of research. SAT aims to advance knowledge about crime involvement by incorporating insights from criminology as well as related sciences, including neuropsychology. It will continue to take into account findings from neuropsychological research to bolster its explanation of crime.

References

Ackerly, S. & Benton, A. (1948) Report of a case of bilateral frontal lobe defect. *Proceedings of the Association for Research in Nervous and Mental Disease*, 27, 479–504.

Adcock, R., Constable, R., Gore, J. & Goldman-Rakic, P. (2000) Functional neuroanatomy of executive processes involved in dual-task performance. *Proceedings of the National Academy of Sciences USA*, 97, 3567–3572.

Adinoff, P., Devous, M., Cooper, D., Best, S., Chandler, P. & Harris, T. (2003) Resting regional cerebral blood flow and gambling task performance in cocaine-dependent subjects and healthy comparison subjects. *American Journal of Psychiatry*, 160, 1892–1894.

Alderman, N. (1996) Central executive deficit and response to operant conditioning methods. *Neuropsychological Rehabilitation*, 6, 161–186.

Anderson, S., Bechara, A., Damasio, H., Tranel, D. & Damasio, A. (1999) Impairment of social and moral behavior related to early damage in human prefrontal cortex. *Nature Neuroscience*, 2, 1032–1037.

Antonaccio, O. & Tittle, C. (2008) Morality, self-control, and crime. *Criminology*, 46, 801–832.

Ardilla, A., Pineda, D. & Roselli, M. (2000) Correlation between intelligence test scores and executive function measures. *Archives of Clinical Neuropsychology*, 15, 31–36.

Baddeley, A. (1992) Working memory. *Science*, 255, 556–559.

Baddeley, A. (1996a) Exploring the central executive. *Quarterly Journal of Experimental Psychology*, 49A, 5–28.

Baddeley, A. (1996b) The fractionation of working memory. *Proceedings of the National Academy of Sciences USA,* 93, 13468–13472.

Baddeley, A. (1998) Recent developments in working memory. *Current Opinion in Neurobiology,* 8, 234–238.

Baddeley, A. (2000) The episodic buffer: a new component of working memory? *Trends in Cognitive Sciences,* 4, 417–423.

Baddeley, A. (2001) Is working memory still working? *American Psychologist,* 56, 849–864.

Baddeley, A., Bressi, S., Della Sala, S., Logie, R. & Spinnler, H. (1991) The decline of working memory in Alzheimer's disease. A longitudinal study. *Brain,* 114, 2521–2542.

Baddeley, A. & Della Sala, S. (1996) Working memory and executive control. *Philosophical Transactions of the Royal Society of London B: Biological Sciences,* 351, 1397–1403.

Baddeley, A. & Hitch, G. (1974) Working memory. *Psychology of Learning and Motivation,* 8, 47–90.

Bargh, J. (2006) What have we been priming all these years? On the development, mechanisms, and ecology of nonconscious social behaviour. *European Journal of Social Psychology,* 36, 147–168.

Bechara, A. (2004) The role of emotion in decision-making: evidence from neurological patients with orbitofrontal damage. *Brain and Cognition,* 55, 30–40.

Bechara, A., Damasio, A., Damasio, H. & Anderson, S. (1994) Insensitivity to future consequences following damage to human prefrontal cortex. *Cognition,* 50, 7–15.

Bechara, A., Damasio, H. & Damasio, A. (2000a) Emotion, decision making and the orbitofrontal cortex. *Cerebral Cortex,* 10, 295–307.

Bechara, A., Damasio, H., Damasio, A. & Lee, G. (1999) Different contributions of the human amygdala and ventromedial prefrontal cortex to decision-making. *Journal of Neuroscience,* 19, 5473–5481.

Bechara, A., Damasio, H., Tranel, D. & Anderson, S. (1998) Dissociation of working memory from decision making within the human prefrontal cortex. *Journal of Neuroscience,* 18, 428–437.

Bechara, A., Damasio, H., Tranel, D. & Damasio, A. (1997) Deciding advantageously before knowing the advantageous strategy. *Science,* 275, 1293–1295.

Bechara, A., Damasio, H., Tranel, D. & Damasio, A. (2005) The Iowa gambling task and the somatic marker hypothesis: some questions and answers. *Trends in Cognitive Sciences,* 9, 159–162.

Bechara, A., Dolan, S., Denburg, N., Hindes, A., Anderson, S. & Nathan, P. (2001) Decision-making deficits, linked to a dysfunctional ventromedial prefrontal cortex, revealed in alcohol and stimulant abusers. *Neuropsychologia,* 39, 376–389.

Bechara, A., Dolan, S. & Hindes, A. (2002) Decision-making and addiction (part II): myopia for the future or hypersensitivity to reward? *Neuropsychologia,* 40, 1690–1705.

Bechara, A., Tranel, D. & Damasio, H. (2000b) Characterization of the decision-making deficit of patients with ventromedial prefrontal cortex lesions. *Brain,* 123, 2189–2202.

Best, M., Williams, M. & Coccaro, E. (2002) Evidence for a dysfunctional prefrontal circuit in patients with an impulsive aggressive disorder. *Proceedings of the National Academy of Sciences USA*, 99, 8448–8453.

Bianchi, L. (1922) *The mechanism of the brain and the functions of the frontal lobes.* New York: William Wood & Company.

Birbaumer, N., Veit, R., Lotze, M., Erb, M., Hermann, C., Grodd, W. & Flor, H. (2005) Deficient fear conditioning in psychopathy: a functional magnetic resonance imaging study. *Archives of General Psychiatry*, 62, 799–805.

Bjork, J., Knutson, B., Fong, G., Caggiano, D., Bennett, S. & Hommer, D. (2004) Incentive-elicited brain activation in adolescents: similarities and differences from young adults. *Journal of Neuroscience*, 24, 1793–1802.

Blakemore, S. & Choudhury, S. (2006) Development of the adolescent brain: implications for executive function and social cognition. *Journal of Child Psychology and Psychiatry*, 47, 296–312.

Blasi, A. (1980) Bridging moral cognition and moral action: a critical review of the literature. *Psychological Bulletin*, 88, 1–45.

Borg, J. S., Lieberman, D. & Kiehl, K. A. (2008) Infection, incest, and iniquity: investigating the neural correlates of disgust and morality. *Journal of Cognitive Neuroscience*, 20, 1529–1546.

Brantingham, P. L. & Brantingham, P. J. (1993) Environment, routine, and situation: toward a pattern theory of crime. In Clarke, R. V. & Felson, M. (Eds.) *Routine activity and rational choice. Advances in Criminological Theory Vol. 9.* New Brunswick: Transaction Publishing.

Bremner, J. D. (1999) Does stress damage the brain? *Biological Psychiatry*, 45, 797–805.

Brown, D. E. (1991) *Human universals.* New York: McGraw-Hill.

Brown, S. & Tapert, S. (2004) Adolescence and the trajectory of alcohol use: basic to clinical studies. *Annals of the New York Academy of Sciences*, 1021, 234–244.

Bunge, S., Dudukovic, N., Thomason, M., Vaidya, C. & Gabrieli, J. (2002) Immature frontal lobe contributions to cognitive control in children: evidence from fMRI. *Neuron*, 33, 301–311.

Campbell, A. (1905) *Histological studies on the localisation of cerebral function.* Cambridge: Cambridge University Press.

Carmelli, D., Swan, G., Decarli, C. & Reed, T. (2002) Quantitative genetic modeling of regional brain volumes and cognitive performance in older male twins. *Biological Psychology*, 61, 139–155.

Case, P., Kurland, D. & Goldberg, J. (1982) Operational efficiency and the growth of short-term memory span. *Journal of Experimental and Child Psychology*, 33, 386–404.

Case, R. (1992) The role of frontal lobe maturation in cognitive and social development. *Brain and Cognition*, 20, 51–73.

Casebeer, W. D. (2003) Moral cognition and its neural constituents. *Nature Review Neuroscience*, 4, 840–846.

Casey, B., Giedd, J. & Thomas, K. (2000) Structural and functional brain development and its relation to cognitive development. *Biological Psychology*, 54, 241–257.

Chelune, G. & Baer, R. (1986) Developmental norms for the Wisconsin card sorting test. *Journal of Clinical and Experimental Neuropsychology*, 8, 219–228.

Chugani, H., Phelps, M. & Mazziotta, J. (1987) Positron emission tomography study of human brain functional development. *Annals of Neurology*, 22, 487–497.

Cohen, J., Perlstein, W., Braver, T., Nystrom, L., Noll, D., Jonides, J. & Smith, E. (1997) Temporal dynamics of brain activation during a working memory task. *Nature*, 386, 604–607.

Cohen, J. & Servan-Schreiber, D. (1992) Context, cortex and dopamine: a connectionist approach to behaviour and biology in schizophrenia. *Psychological Review*, 99, 45–77.

Cohen, L. E. & Felson, M. (1979) Social change and crime rate trends: A routine activity approach. *American Sociological Review*, 44, 588–608.

Coolidge, F. & Wynn, T. (2001) Executive functions of the frontal lobes and the evolutionary ascendency of *homo sapiens*. *Cambridge Archaeological Journal*, 11, 255–260.

Crone, E., Bunge, S., Latenstein, H. & van der Molen, M. (2005) Characterization of children's decision making: sensitivity to punishment frequency, not task complexity. *Child Neuropsychology*, 11, 245–263.

Crone, E., Donohue, S., Honomichl, R., Wendelken, C. & Bunge, S. (2006) Brain regions mediating flexible rule use during development. *Journal of Neuroscience*, 26, 11239–11247.

Crone, E. & van der Molen, M. (2004) Developmental changes in real life decision making: performance on a gambling task previously shown to depend on the ventromedial prefrontal cortex. *Developmental Neuropsychology*, 25, 251–279.

Daigneault, S., Braun, C. & Whitaker, H. (1992) An empirical test of two opposing theoretical models of prefrontal function. *Brain and Cognition*, 19, 48–71.

Damasio, A. (1994) *Descartes' error: emotion, reason and the human brain*. London: Vintage Books.

Damasio, A. (1996) The somatic marker hypothesis and the possible functions of the prefrontal cortex. *Philosophical Transactions of the Royal Society of London B: Biological Sciences*, 351, 1413–1420.

Damasio, A., Tranel, D. & Damasio, H. (1990) Individuals with sociopathic behavior caused by frontal damage fail to respond autonomically to social stimuli. *Behavioral Brain Research*, 41, 81–94.

Dao-Castellana, M., Samson, Y., Legault, F., Martinot, J., Aubin, H., Crouzel, C., Feldman, L., Barrucand, D., Rancurel, G., Feline, A. & Syrota, A. (1998) Frontal dysfunction in neurologically normal chronic alcoholic subjects: metabolic and neuropsychological findings. *Psychological Medicine*, 28, 1039–1048.

Darwin, C. (1859) *On the origin of species*. London: John Murray.

De Lafuente, V. & Romo, R. (2002) A hidden sensory function for motor cortex. *Neuron*, 36, 785–786.

De Waal, F. (2006) *Primates and philosophers: How morality evolved*. Woodstock: Princeton University Press.

Demetriou, A., Christou, C., Spanoudis, G. & Platsidou, M. (2002) The development of mental processing: efficiency, working memory, and thinking. *Monograms of the Society for Research in Child Development*, 67, 1–155.

Dempster, F. & Corkill, A. (1999) Individual differences in susceptibility to interference and general cognitive ability. *Acta Psychologica*, 101, 395–416.

Dinn, W. & Harris, C. (2000) Neurocognitive function in antisocial personality disorder. *Psychiatry Research*, 97, 173–190.

Dom, G., Sabbe, B., Hulstijn, W. & van den Brink, W. (2005) Substance use disorders and the orbitofrontal cortex: systematic review of behavioural decision-making and neuroimaging studies. *British Journal of Psychiatry*, 187, 209–220.

Dunn, B., Dalgleish, T. & Lawrence, A. (2006) The somatic marker hypothesis: a critical evaluation. *Neuroscience and Biobehavioral Review*, 30, 239–271.

Dunn, J. & Hughes, C. (2001) "I got some swords and you're dead" Violent fantasy, antisocial behavior, friendship and moral sensibility in young children. *Child Development*, 72, 491–505.

Embry, D. (2005) Simple gifts for teens: practical, powerful, proven tools for youth development and success. *Simple gifts*. Tucson: PAXIS Institute.

Ernst, M., Bolla, K., Mouratidis, M., Contoreggi, C., Matochik, J., Kurian, V., Cadet, J., Kimes, A. & London, E. (2002) Decision-making in a risk-taking task: a PET study. *Neuropsychopharmacology*, 26, 682–691.

Ernst, M., Nelson, E., Jazbec, S., McClure, E., Monk, C., Leibenluft, E., Blair, J. & Pine, D. (2005) Amygdala and nucleus accumbens in responses to receipt and omission of gains in adults and adolescents. *Neuroimage*, 25, 1279–1291.

Eslinger, P. & Damasio, A. (1985) Severe disturbance of higher cognition after bilateral frontal lobe ablation: patient EVR. *Neurology*, 35, 1731–1741.

Felson, M. (2002) *Crime and everyday life*. Thousand Oaks: SAGE Publications.

Felson, M. (2006) *Crime and human nature*. Thousand Oaks: SAGE Publications.

Ferrier, D. (1875) The Croonian Lecture: experiments on the brain of monkeys (second series). *Philosophical Transactions of the Royal Society of London*, 165, 433–488.

Ferrier, D. & Yeo, G. (1884) A record of experiments on the effects of lesion of different regions of the cerebral hemispheres. *Philosophical Transactions of the Royal Society of London*, 175, 479–564.

Flor, H., Birbaumer, N., Hermann, C., Ziegler, S. & Patrick, C. (2002) Aversive Pavlovian conditioning in psychopaths: peripheral and central correlates. *Psychophysiology*, 39, 505–518.

Franz, S. (1902) On the functions of the cerebrum I: The frontal lobes in relation to the production and retention of simple sensory-motor habits. *American Journal of Physiology*, 8, 1–22.

Funahashi, S., Bruce, C. & Goldman-Rakic, P. (1989) Mnemonic coding of visual space in the monkey's dorsolateral prefrontal cortex. *Journal of Neurophysiology*, 61, 331–349.

Fung, M., Raine, A., Loeber, R., Lynam, D., Steinhauer, S., Venables, P. & Stouthamer-Loeber, M. (2005) Reduced electrodermal activity in psychopathy-prone adolescents. *Journal of Abnormal Psychology*, 114, 187–196.

Fuster, J. (1997) *The prefrontal cortex: anatomy, physiology and neuropsychology of the frontal lobe*. Philadelphia: Lippincott-Raven.

Gathercole, S. (1999) Cognitive approaches to the development of short-term memory. *Trends in Cognitive Sciences*, 3, 410–419.

Giancola, P. & Zeichner, A. (1994) Neuropsychological performance on tests of frontal-lobe functioning and aggressive behavior in men. *Journal of Abnormal Psychology*, 103, 832–835.

Giedd, J., Blumenthal, J., Jeffries, N., Castellanos, F., Liu, H., Zijdenbos, A., Paus, T., Evans, A. & Rapoport, J. (1999) Brain development during childhood and adolescence: a longitudinal MRI study. *Nature Neuroscience*, 2, 861–863.

Goldberg, E. (2001) *The executive brain: frontal lobes and the civilized mind*. Oxford: Oxford University Press.

Goldman-Rakic, P. (1987) Circuitry of primate prefrontal cortex and regulation of behavior by representational memory. In Mountcastle, V., Plum, F. & Geiger, S. (Eds.) *Handbook of physiology: a critical, comprehensive presentation of physiological knowledge and concepts. Section 1: The nervous system, Volume V: Higher functions of the brain, Part 1*. Bethesda: American Psychological Society.

Goldstein, R., Leskovjan, A., Hoff, A., Hitzemann, R., Bashan, F., Khalsa, S., Wang, G., Fowler, J. & Volkow, N. (2004) Severity of neuropsychological impairment in cocaine and alcohol addiction: association with metabolism in the prefrontal cortex. *Neuropsychologia*, 42, 1447–1458.

Goldstein, R. & Volkow, N. (2002) Drug addiction and its underlying neurobiological basis: neuroimaging evidence for the involvement of the frontal cortex. *American Journal of Psychiatry*, 159, 1642–1652.

Goleman, D. (1995) *Emotional intelligence: why it can matter more than IQ*. London: Bloomsbury.

Gottfredson, M. & Hirschi, T. (1990) *A general theory of crime*. Stanford: Stanford University Press.

Gray, J. A. (1972) The psychophysiological basis of introversion-extraversion: a modification of Eysenck's theory. In Nebylitsyn, V. D. & Gray, J. A. (Eds.) *The biological bases of individual behaviour*. San Diego: Academic Press.

Greene, J. & Haidt, J. (2002) How (and where) does moral judgment work? *Trends in Cognitive Sciences*, 6, 517–523.

Greene, J. D., Nystrom, L. E., Engell, A. D., Darley, J. M. & Cohen, J. D. (2004) The neural bases of cognitive conflict and control in moral judgment. *Neuron*, 44, 389–400.

Greene, J. D., Sommerville, R. B., Nystrom, L. E., Darley, J. M. & Cohen, J. D. (2001) An fMRI investigation of emotional engagement in moral judgment. *Science*, 293, 2105–2108.

Greenough, W., Black, J. & Wallace, C. (1987) Experience and brain development. *Child Development*, 58, 539–559.

Grotstein, J. (1994) Foreword. In Schore, A. (Ed.) *Affect regulation and the origin of the self: the neurobiology of emotional development*. Hove: Lawrence Erlbaum Associates.

Hauser, M. D. (2006) *Moral minds: How nature designed out universal sense of right and wrong*. New York: HarperCollins.

Hirschi, T. (1969) *Causes of delinquency*. New Brunswick: Transaction Publishers.

Hooper, C., Luciana, M., Conklin, H. & Yarger, R. (2004) Adolescents' performance on the Iowa Gambling Task: implications for the development of decision making and ventromedial prefrontal cortex. *Developmental Psychology*, 40, 1148–1158.

Horsley, V. & Schafer, E. (1888) A record of experiments upon the functions of the cerebral cortex. *Philosophical Transactions of the Royal Society of London B: Biological Sciences*, 179, 1–45.

Hughes, C. & Dunn, J. (2000) Hedonism or empathy? Hard-to-manage children's moral awareness and links with cognitive and maternal characteristics. *British Journal of Developmental Psychology*, 18, 227–245.

Hughes, C., Russell, J. & Robbins, T. (1994) Evidence for executive dysfunction in autism. *Neuropsychologia*, 32, 477–492.

Hunter, W. & Hall, B. (1941) Double alternative behaviour of the white rat in a spatial maze. *Journal of Comparative and Physiological Psychology*, 32, 253–266.

Ishikawa, S. & Raine, A. (2003) Prefrontal deficits and antisocial behavior: a causal model. In Lahey, B., Moffitt, T. & Caspi, A. (Eds.) *The causes of conduct disorder and serious juvenile delinquency*. New York: Guilford Press.

Izard, C. E. (1993) Four systems for emotion activation: cognitive and noncognitive processes. *Psychological Review*, 100, 68–90.

Jackson, H. (1874) On the nature of the duality of the brain, *Medican Press and Circular*, 1. Reprinted in Head, H. (1915) Hughlings Jackson on aphasia and kindred affections of speech. *Brain*, 38(1–2), 1–22.

Jonides, J. (1995) Working memory and thinking. In Smith, E. & Osheron, D. (Eds.) *Thinking: an invitation to cognitive science*. 2nd ed. London: The MIT Press.

Jonides, J., Smith, E., Koeppe, R., Awh, E., Minoshima, S. & Mintun, M. (1993) Spatial working memory in humans as revealed by PET. *Nature*, 363, 623–625.

Kahneman, D. (2003) Maps of bounded rationality: a perspective on intuitive judgment and choice. In Frangsmyr, T. (Ed.) *Les Prix Nobel. The Noble Prizes 2002*. Stockholm: Nobel Foundation.

Kail, R. & Salthouse, T. (1994) Processing speed as a mental capacity. *Acta Psychologica*, 86, 199–225.

Kawasaki, H., Kaufman, O., Damasio, H., Damasio, A., Granner, M., Bakken, H., Hori, T., Howard, M. & Adolphs, R. (2001) Single-neuron responses to emotional visual stimuli recorded in human ventral prefrontal cortex. *Nature Neuroscience*, 4, 15–16.

Kemps, E., De Rammelaere, S. & Desmet, T. (2000) The development of working memory: exploring the complementarity of two models. *Journal of Experimental and Child Psychology*, 77, 89–109.

Koob, G. & Bloom, F. (1988) Cellular and molecular mechanisms of drug dependence. *Science*, 242, 715–723.

Kornhauser, R. R. (1978) *Social sources of delinquency*. Chicago: University of Chicago Press.

Landry, S., Miller-Loncar, C., Smith, K. & Swank, P. (2002) The role of early parenting in children's development of executive processes. *Developmental Neuropsychology*, 21, 15–41.

Laub, J. H. & Sampson, R. J. (2003) *Shared beginnings, divergent lives: Delinquent boys to age 70*. Cambridge, MA: Harvard University Press.

Linnoila, M., Virkkunen, M., Scheinin, M., Nuutila, A., Rimon, R. & Goodwin, F. (1983) Low cerebrospional fluid r-hydroxyindoleacetic acid concentration differentiates impulsive from nonimpulsive violent behavior. *Life Sciences*, 33, 2609–2614.

Loeb, J. (1901) *Comparative physiology of the brain and comparative psychology*. London: John Murray.

London, E., Ernst, M., Grant, S., Bonson, K. & Weinstein, A. (2000) Orbitofrontal cortex and human drug abuse: functional imaging. *Cerebral Cortex*, 10, 334–342.

López, J. F., Akil, H. & Watson, S. J. (1999) Neural circuits mediating stress. *Biological Psychiatry*, 46, 1461–1471.

Lösel, F. & Schmucker, M. (2004) Psychopathy, risk taking, and attention: a differentiated test of the somatic marker hypothesis. *Journal of Abnormal Psychology*, 113, 522–529.

Luciana, M., Conklin, H., Hooper, C. & Yarger, R. (2005) The development of nonverbal working memory and executive control processes in adolescents. *Child Development*, 76, 697–712.

Luna, B. (2004) Algebra and the adolescent brain. *Trends in Cognitive Sciences*, 8, 437–439.

Luna, B., Thulborn, K., Munoz, D., Merriam, E., Garver, K., Minshew, N., Keshavan, M., Genovese, C., Eddy, W. & Sweeney, J. (2001) Maturation of widely distributed brain function subserves cognitive development. *Neuroimage*, 13, 786–793.

MacDonald, A., Cohen, J., Stenger, V. & Carter, C. (2000) Dissociating the role of the dorsolateral prefrontal and anterior cingulate cortex in cognitive control. *Science*, 288, 1835–1838.

McEvoy, R., Rogers, S. & Pennington, B. (1993) Executive function and social communication deficits in young autistic children. *Journal of Child Psychology and Psychiatry and Allied Disciplines*, 34, 563–578.

Manuck, S., Kaplan, J. & Lotrich, F. (2006) Brain serotonin and aggressive disposition in humans and nonhuman primates. In Nelson, R. (Ed.) *Biology of aggression.* Oxford: Oxford University Press.

Miczek, K. & Fish, E. (2006) Monoamines, GABA, glutamate, and aggression. In Nelson, R. (Ed.) *Biology of aggression.* Oxford: Oxford University Press.

Miles, C. & Morgan, M. (1996) Developmental and individual differences in visual memory span. *Current Psychology*, 15, 53–68.

Miller, E., Erickson, C. & Desimone, R. (1996) Neural mechanisms of visual working memory in prefrontal cortex of the macaque. *Journal of Neuroscience*, 16, 5154–5167.

Miyake, A., Friedman, N., Emerson, M., Witzki, A., Howerter, A. & Wager, T. (2000) The unity and diversity of executive functions and their contributions to complex "frontal lobe" tasks: a latent variable analysis. *Cognitive Psychology, 41,* 49–100.

Moffitt, T. (1990) The neuropsychology of juvenile delinquency: a critical review. *Crime and Justice, 12,* 99–169.

Moffitt, T. (1993) Adolescence-limited and life-course-persistent antisocial behaviour: a developmental taxonomy. *Psychological Review, 100,* 674–701.

Moffitt, T. (1997) Adolescence-limited and life-course-persistent offending: a complementary pair of developmental theories. In Thornberry, T. (Ed.) *Developmental theories of crime and delinquency: advances in criminological theory, Volume 7.* London: Transaction.

Moffitt, T. (2003) Life-course persistent and adolescence-limited antisocial behavior: a 10-year research review and a research agenda. In Lahey, B., Moffitt, T. & Caspi, A. (Eds.) *Causes of conduct disorder and juvenile delinquency.* New York: Guildford Press.

Moffitt, T. & Henry, B. (1989) Neuropsychological assessment of executive functions in self-reported delinquents. *Development and Psychopathology, 1,* 105–118.

Moll, J., De Oliveira-Souza, R., Bramati, I. & Grafman, J. (2002) Functional networks in emotional moral and nonmoral social judgments. *Neuroimage, 16,* 696–703.

Moll, J., R, De Oliveira-Souza & Zahn, R. (2008) The neural basis of moral cognition: sentiments, concepts, and values. *Annals of the New York Academy of Sciences,* 1124, 161–180.

Moll, J., Zahn, R., De Oliveira-Souza, R., Krueger, F. & Grafman, J. (2005) Opinion: the neural basis of human moral cognition. *Nat Rev Neurosci, 6,* 799–809.

Morgan, A. & Lilienfeld, S. (2000) A meta-analytic review of the relation between antisocial behavior and neuropsychological measures of executive function. *Clinical Psychology Review, 20,* 113–136.

Nestler, E. & Aghajanian, G. (1997) Molecular and cellular basis of addiction. *Science, 278,* 58–63.

Overman, W., Frassrand, K., Ansel, S., Trawalter, S., Bies, B. & Redmond, A. (2004) Performance on the IOWA card task by adolescents and adults. *Neuropsychologia,* 42, 1838–1851.

Patrick, C., Cuthbert, B. & Lang, P. (1994) Emotion in the criminal psychopath: fear image processing. *Journal of Abnormal Psychology, 103,* 523–534.

Pavlov, I. (1941a) *Lectures on conditioned reflexes, Volume I: Twenty-five years of objective study of the higher nervous activity (behaviour) of animals.* London: Lawrence and Wishart.

Pavlov, I. (1941b) *Lectures on conditioned reflexes, Volume II: Conditioned reflexes and psychiatry.* London, Lawrence and Wishart.

Petrides, M., Alivisatos, B., Evans, A. & Meyer, E. (1993) Dissociation of human mid-dorsolateral from posterior dorsolateral frontal cortex in memory processing. *Proceedings of the National Academy of Sciences USA, 90,* 873–877.

Pinker, S. (2002) *The blank slate: the modern denial of human nature.* London: Penguin Books Ltd.

Porrino, L. & Lyons, D. (2000) Orbital and medial prefrontal cortex and psychostimulant abuse: studies in animal models. *Cerebral Cortex, 10,* 326–333.

Prabhakaran, V., Narayanan, K., Zhao, Z. & Gabrielli, J. (2000) Integration of diverse information in working memory in the frontal lobe. *Nature Neuroscience*, 3, 85–90.

Price, B., Daffner, K., Stowe, R. & Mesulam, M. (1990) The comportmental learning disabilities of early frontal lobe damage. *Brain*, 113, 1383–1393.

Raine, A. (2002) Annotation: the role of prefrontal deficits, low autonomic arousal, and early health factors in the development of antisocial and aggressive behavior in children. *Journal of Child Psychology Psychiatry*, 43, 417–434.

Raine, A. & Venables, P. (1988) Skin conductance responsivity in psychopaths to orienting, defensive, and consonant-vowel stimuli. *Journal of Psychophysiology*, 2, 221–225.

Raine, A. & Yang, Y. (2006) Neural foundations to moral reasoning and antisocial behavior. *Social Cognitive and Affective Neuroscience*, 1, 203–213.

Rakic, P., Bourgeois, J. & Goldman-Rakic, P. (1994) Synaptic development of the cerebral cortex: implications for learning, memory, and mental illness. *Progress in Brain Research*, 102, 227–243.

Raleigh, M. & Brammer, G. (1993) Individual differences in serotonin-2 receptors and social behavior in monkeys. *Society for Neuroscience Abstracts*, 19, 592.

Ranier, G., Assed, W. & Miller, E. (1998a) Memory fields of neurons in the primate prefrontal cortex. *Proceedings of the National Academy of Sciences USA*, 95, 15008–15013.

Ranier, G., Assed, W. & Miller, E. (1998b) Selective representation of relevant information by neurons in the primate prefrontal cortex. *Nature*, 393, 577–579.

Rao, S., Ranier, G. & Miller, E. (1997) Integration of what and where in the primate prefrontal cortex. *Science*, 276, 821–824.

Ribaupierre, A. & Bailleux, C. (1994) Developmental change in a spatial task of attentional capacity: an essay toward an integration of two working memory models. *International Journal of Behavioral Development*, 17, 5–35.

Richter, C. & Hines, M. (1938) Increased spontaneous activity produced in monkeys by brain lesions. *Brain*, 61, 1–16.

Ridley, M. (1996) *The origins of virtue*. St Edmunds: Viking.

Riggs, N., Jahromi, L., Razza, R., Dillworth-Bart, J. & Mueller, U. (2006) Executive function and the promotion of social-emotional competence. *Journal of Applied and Developmental Psychology*, 27, 300–309.

Rogers, R., Everitt, B., Baldacchino, A., Blackshaw, A., Swainson, R., Wynne, K., Baker, N., Hunter, J., Carthy, T., Booker, E., London, M., Deakin, J., Sahakian, B. & Robbins, T. (1999) Dissociable deficits in the decision-making cognition of chronic amphetamine abusers, opiate abusers, patients with focal damage to prefrontal cortex, and tryptophan-depleted normal volunteers: evidence for monoaminergic mechanisms. *Neuropsychopharmacology*, 20, 322–339.

Rogers, R. & Robbins, T. (2001) Investigating the neurocognitive deficits associated with chronic drug misuse. *Current Opinion in Neurobiology*, 11, 250–257.

Sampson, R. J. & Laub, J. H. (1993) *Crime in the making: Pathways and turning points through life*. Cambridge, MA: Harvard University Press.

Seguin, J., Boulerice, B., Harden, P., Tremblay, R. & Pihl, R. (1999) Executive functions and physical aggression after controlling for attention deficit hyperactivity disorder, general memory, and IQ. *Journal of Child Psychology and Psychiatry*, 40, 1197–1208.

Shaw, C. R. & McKay, H. D. (1969) *Juvenile delinquency and urban areas*. Chicago: University of Chicago Press.

Siever, L., Buchsbaum, M., New, A., Spiegel-Cohen, J., Wei, T., Hazlett, E., Sevin, E., Nunn, M. & Mitropoulou, V. (1999) d,l-fenfluramine response in impulsive personality disorder assessed with [18F]fluorodeoxyglucose positron emission tomography. *Neuropsychopharmacology*, 20, 413–423.

Sloman, S. (1996) The empirical case of two systems of reasoning. *Psychological Bulletin*, 119, 3–22.

Smith, E. & Jonides, J. (1997) Working memory: a view from neuroimaging. *Cognitive Psychology*, 33, 5–42.

Smith, E. & Jonides, J. (1999) Storage and executive processes in the frontal lobes. *Science*, 283, 1657–1661.

Smith, S., Arnett, P. & Newman, J. (1992) Neuropsychological differentiation of psychopathic and nonpsychopathic criminal offenders. *Journal of Personality and Individual Differences*, 13, 1233–1243.

Sowell, E., Delis, D., Stiles, J. & Jernigan, T. (2001) Improved memory functioning and frontal lobe maturation between childhood and adolescence: a structural MRI study. *Journal of the International Neuropsychological Society*, 7, 312–322.

Spear, L. (2000) The adolescent brain and age-related behavioral manifestations. *Neuroscience and Biobehavioral Reviews*, 24, 417–463.

Spellacy, F. (1977) Neuropsychological differences between violent and nonviolent adolescents. *Journal of Clinical Psychology*, 33, 966–969.

Stein, R., Strickland, T., Khalsa-Dennison, E. & Andre, K. (1997) Gender differences in neuropsychological test performance among cocaine abusers. *Archives of Clinical Neuropsychology*, 12, 410–411.

Stuss, D. & Levine, B. (2002) Adult clinical neuropsychology: lessons from studies of the frontal lobes. *Annual Review of Psychology*, 401–433.

Swanson, H. (1999) What develops in working memory? A life span perspective. *Developmental Psychology*, 35, 986–1000.

Teichner, G. & Golden, C. (2000) The relationship of neuropsychological impairment to conduct disorder in adolescence: a conceptual review. *Aggression and Violent Behavior*, 5, 509–528.

Tittle, C. (1995) *Control balance: toward a general theory of deviance*. Boulder: Westview Press.

Toupin, J., Dery, M., Pauze, R., Mercier, H. & Fortin, L. (2000) Cognitive and familial contributions to conduct disorder in children. *Journal of Child Psychology and Psychiatry*, 41, 333–344.

Towse, J. & Hitch, G. (1995) Is there a relationship between task demand and storage space in tests of working memory capacity? *Quarterly Journal of Experimental Psychology A*, 48, 108–124.

Towse, J., Hitch, G. & Hutton, U. (1998) A reevaluation of working memory capacity in children. *Journal of Memory and Language*, 39, 195–217.

Tranel, D., Anderson, S. & Benton, A. (1994) Development of the concept of "executive function" and its relationship to the frontal lobes. In Boller, F. & Spinnler, H. (Eds.) *Handbook of neuropsychology, Volume 9, Section 12: The frontal lobes.* Oxford: Elsevier.

Trivers, R. (1971) The evolution of reciprocal altruism. *Quarterly Review of Biology,* 46, 35–57.

Van Honk, J., Hermans, E., Putman, P., Montagne, B. & Schutter, D. (2002) Defective somatic markers in sub-clinical psychopathy. *Neuroreport,* 13, 1025–1027.

Volkow, N. & Fowler, J. (2000) Addiction, a disease of compulsion and drive: involvement of the orbitofrontal cortex. *Cerebral Cortex,* 10, 318–325.

Volkow, N., Fowler, J., Wang, G., Hitzemann, R., Logan, J., Schyler, D., Dewey, S. & Wolf, A. (1993) Decreased dopamine-(d)2 receptor availability is associated with reduced frontal metabolism in cocaine abusers. *Synapse,* 14, 169–177.

White, A. (2004) Substance use and the adolescent brain: an overview with a focus on alcohol. *Topics in Alcohol Research.*

White, J., Moffitt, T., Caspi, A., Bartusch, D., Needles, D. & Stouthamer-Loeber, M. (1994) Measuring impulsivity and examining its relationship to delinquency. *Journal of Abnormal Psychology,* 103, 192–205.

Wikström, P.-O. H. (2004) Crime as alternative: towards a cross-level situational action theory of crime causation. In McCord, J. (Ed.) *Beyond empiricism: institutions and intentions in the study of crime. Advances in Criminological Theory.* New Brunswick: Transaction.

Wikström, P.-O. H. (2005) The social origins of pathways in crime: towards a developmental ecological action theory of crime involvement and its changes. In Farrington, D. (Ed.) *Integrated developmental and life course theories of offending. Advances in criminological theory.* New Brunswick: Transaction.

Wikström, P.-O. H. (2006) Individuals, settings, and acts of crime: situational mechanisms and the explanation of crime. In Wikström, P. & Sampson, R. (Eds.) *The explanation of crime: context, mechanisms and development.* Cambridge: Cambridge University Press.

Wikström, P.-O. H. (2007a) In search of causes and explanations of crime. In King, R. & Wincup, E. (Eds.) *Doing research on crime and justice.* 2nd ed. Oxford: Oxford University Press.

Wikström, P.-O. H. (2007b) The social ecology of crime: the role of the environment in crime causation. In Schneider, H. (Ed.) *Internationales handbuch der kriminologie.* Berlin: de Gruyter.

Wikström, P.-O. H. (2009) Crime propensity, criminogenic exposure and crime involvement in early to mid adolescence. *Monatsschrift fur Kriminologie und Strafrechtsreform,* 92, 253–266.

Wikström, P.-O. H. (2010a) Explaining crime as moral actions. In Hitlin, S. & Vaisey, S. (Eds.) *Handbook of the sociology of morality.* London: Springer.

Wikström, P.-O. H. (2010b) Situational Action Theory. In Cullen, F. & Wilcox, P. (Eds.) *Encyclopedia of criminological theory.* London: SAGE Publications.

Wikström, P.-O. H. & Sampson, R. (2003) Social mechanisms of community: influences on crime and pathways in criminality. In Lahey, B., Moffitt, T. & Caspi, A. (Eds.) *The causes of conduct disorder and serious juvenile delinquency.* New York: Guilford Press.

Wikström, P.-O. H. & Sampson, R. (2006) Introduction. In Wikström, P. & Sampson, R. (Eds.) *The explanation of crime: context, mechanisms and development.* Cambridge: Cambridge University Press.

Wikström, P.-O. H. & Svensson, R. (2010) When does self-control matter? The interaction between morality and self-control in crime causation. *European Journal of Criminology, 7,* 395–410.

Wikström, P.-O. H. & Treiber, K. (2007) The role of self-control in crime causation: beyond Gottfredson and Hirschi's general theory of crime. *European Journal of Criminology, 4,* 237–264.

Wikström, P.-O. H. & Treiber, K. (2009a) Violence as situational action. *International Journal of Conflict and Violence, 3,* 75–96.

Wikström, P.-O. H. & Treiber, K. (2009b) What drives persistent offending? The neglected and unexplored role of the social environment. In Savage, J. (Ed.) *The development of persistent offending.* Oxford: Oxford University Press.

Wikström, P.-O. H., Ceccato, V., Hardie, B. & Treiber, K. (2010) Activity fields and the dynamics of crime. Advancing knowledge about the role of the environment in crime causation. *Journal of Quantitative Criminology, 26,* 55–87.

Wikström, P.-O. H., Oberwittler, D., Treiber, K. & Hardie, B. (2011a) *Breaking rules: The social and situational dynamics of young people's urban crime.* Oxford: Oxford University Press.

Wikström, P.-O. H., Treiber, K. & Hardie, B. (2011b) Examining the role of the environment in crime causation: small area community surveys and space-time budgets. In Gadd, D., Kerstedt, S. & Messner, S. F. (Eds.) *The SAGE handbook of criminological research methods.* London: SAGE Publications Ltd.

Wilson, J. (1993) The moral sense. *American Political Science Review, 87,* 1–11.

Wilson, J. Q. & Herrnstein, R. J. (1985) *Crime and human nature.* New York: Touchstone Books.

Witkin, H. A., Moore, C. A., Goodenough, D. R. & Cox, P. W. (1977) Field-dependent and field-independent cognitive styles and their educational implications. *Review of Educational Research, 47,* 1–64.

Woodward, J. & Allman, J. (2007) Moral intuition: its neural substrates and normative significance. *Journal of Physiology – Paris, 101,* 179–202.

Wright, R. (1994) *The moral animal.* London: Abacus.

Wundt, W. (1904) *Principles of physiological psychology.* London: Swan Sonnenschein & Co., LIM.

Zelazo, P. (2005) Executive function part four: brain growth and the development of executive function. AboutKidsHealth News.

Zelazo, P., Müller, U., Frye, D. & Marcovitch, S. (2003) The development of executive function in early childhood. *Monographs of the Society for Research in Child Development, 68.*

Zelazo, P. D. & Müller, U. (2002) Executive function in typical and atypical development. In Goswami, U. (Ed.) *Handbook of childhood cognitive development*. Oxford: Blackwell.

PART IV
ENVIRONMENTS AND CRIME

The Independence of Criminological "Predictor" Variables: A Good Deal of Concerns and Some Answers from Behavioral Genetic Research

H. Harrington Cleveland, Charles Beekman, and Yao Zheng

This chapter is organized around two expressions relevant to the quantitative investigation of the etiology of delinquent and criminal behavior. The first is a warning the first author remembers hearing from his Graduate Statistics Professor: "It is the lion you don't see that gets you." This expression has both theoretical and methodological implications. It suggests that perspectives and models that ignore alternative influences on their outcomes risk being undercut by the factors they ignore. In the case of environmentally-oriented theorists and researchers, this expression reminds us that genetically-influenced processes, because they are ignored by such researchers, threaten to undercut the validity of their research programs. This is a straightforward message, one that has been presented before. The version that we present herein emphasizes that not only are the outcomes (e.g. delinquency) that criminologists examine influenced by genetic variance, but so are the environmental and experiential factors which are often used to predict these outcomes. Ignoring these influences, which work through processes termed gene–environment correlations, presents a substantial risk to the validity of socio-criminological research.

The second saying, the relevance of which emerged as we wrote this chapter, is *"All models are wrong, but some are useful"* (Box & Draper, 1987). The importance of this quote, which is credited to the industrial statistician George E. P. Box, became clear as we reviewed different common and less common behavioral genetic designs. For each design, we set out its underlying logic, the type of gene–environment correlation it can be used to investigate, and its shortcomings. During this process, we became aware that it is important to address not only what different behavioral genetic models do well but also what behavioral genetic models generally fail to do. What they fail to do, as pointed out by proponents of developmental systems theory, is to capture the co-dependent processes through which traits (and people) develop. We argue that although the substance of this criticism rings true, it does not follow that the findings of behavioral genetic models are not useful (and actually not "wrong" on the analytic level on which they operate). In other words, behavioral genetic models might be *"wrong"* (if one believes their purpose is to explain the complex co-dependency of development) but useful. In fact, they are useful in an important way: they conclusively demonstrate that sociological conceptualizations and operationalizations of how environmental experiences affect outcomes are clearly wrong and likely not too useful.

Before making our argument that the sociological conceptualizations of environmental influences, which is the sine qua non of sociological criminology, are both incorrect and not very useful, we set out to explain the phenomena collectively known as gene–environment correlations. We define and provide criminological examples for the three types of GE-correlations. Considering the different types of gene–environment correlations and the variables that they affect leads us to propose a spectrum of genetically influenced selection that we hope can provide guidance for researchers when considering the degree to which their designs may be confounded by genetically influenced selective processes.

In addition to reviewing different commonly used behavioral genetic designs, such as univariate and multivariate ACE decompositions, we review the Children of twins design and the discordant twin control design, both of which have characteristics that can make them especially valuable to sociologically-oriented researchers.

Heritability

Perhaps the best place to start is with the concept of heritability. Heritability is indicated when variance in a phenotype (trait, behavior, etc.) can be attributed to differences in genetic inheritance. The more heritable a phenotype, the more individual differences in that phenotype are associated with genetic variance. The variance in phenotypes that is not accounted for by genetic factors is assigned to two types of environments: shared environments, those associated with household membership; and unshared environments, which are those that vary for siblings within the same households.

Heritability is most commonly studied using a naturally-occurring quasi-experimental design that involves comparing the phenotypic similarity of monozygotic (MZ) and dizygotic (DZ) twin pairs on a given phenotype. The power of the classic twin design lies in the known genetic similarities of monozygotic (MZ) and dizygotic (DZ) twins. MZ twins share all of their segregating genes, whereas DZ twins have (on average) 50 percent of their segregating genes in common. Therefore, if MZ twins are more alike than DZ twins for a given phenotype, this difference indicates heritability; with greater differences in MZ similarity relative to DZ similarity indicating greater heritability (Plomin, 1990). This model can be extended and further powered by the inclusion of other sets of siblings for which genetic similarity is known such as full siblings (50 percent), half siblings (25 percent), and genetically unrelated siblings (0 percent) (Neiderhiser, Reiss, & Hetherington, 2007).

An extensive body of findings generated by classic twin studies provides the foundation for the generally accepted conclusion that many, if not most, commonly studied individual characteristics are heritable (Boomsma, Busjahn, & Peltonen, 2002; Plomin, DeFries, McClearn, & Rutter, 1997). Of course, these heritability estimates range in magnitude across phenotypes. Over the last 20 years there has been an acceptance, albeit sometimes begrudging, across the social sciences that many outcomes, however complex, studied by psychology and sociology are significantly heritable. Despite this growing recognition little has been done to change the way in which behavioral science in some disciplines is carried out. In particular, criminology, dominated by sociology, has largely continued the use of biologically naïve designs. A possible rationale for this continued course may be that using such designs remains legitimate because although the targeted outcomes may be influenced by genetics they are influenced by environmental variance. Thus, it may be legitimate to consider associations between these outcomes and aspects of the environment that are contributing to their variance. We disagree. We propose that this position, because it ignores the fact that the purported environmental predictors as well as the outcomes themselves evince heritability, is not tenable.

The Lion Socio-Criminologists Don't See: Gene–Environment Correlations

The predator the criminologists apparently do not see is the heritability of environments and experiences. That environments can reflect genetic influences, via processes collectively known as gene–environment correlations, has been recognized for several decades by behavioral geneticists (Eaves, Last, Martin, & Jinks, 1977; Plomin, DeFries, & Loehlin, 1977). Gene–environment correlations (i.e. rGE) occur when genotypes are more (or less) likely to be exposed to certain environments. If a delinquent child is more likely to be exposed to an environment, such as exposure to peer delinquency, this may be due to a gene–environment correlation. Three types of gene–environment correlation have been proposed and should be considered when evaluating the vulnerability of research findings to genetic confounds: passive, active, and evocative (i.e. reactive) (Plomin et al., 1977).

Passive Gene–Environment Correlation

Passive rGE occur between the genetically-influenced characteristics of a child and the environment that they inherit from their biological parents. In the context of criminology, passive rGE is perhaps best understood by thinking about an antisocial parent, their child, and that child's rearing environment. In this scenario, genes that influence the development of antisocial behavior in a parent are passed on to their child, who is genetically predisposed to also develop antisocial behavior. The parent's antisocial behavior may also lead to a chaotic and dysfunctional rearing environment for their child. Thus, the genetic variance that is associated with parents' antisocial behavior drives the association between environmental context and child behavior by both affecting the environment in which a child is reared and predisposing the child toward delinquency, hence the correlation. Because of the potential for such processes to be at work one should pause before interpreting associations between family experiences and child outcomes within biological families as reflecting purely environmental cause (Rutter et al., 1997). It is important to note that chaotic and dysfunctional rearing environment produced by the parents' genetically influenced characteristics may further foster the development of antisocial behavior in their child. Thus, the existence of a passive gene–environment correlation does not assume that exposure to the genetically-influenced environment does not also play a causal role. However, in a typical biological family design there is no way to determine what portion of the association between the family environment and the child outcome is due to this passive rGE process and what portion is due to environmental cause.

Active Gene–Environment Correlation

The role that the child plays in each type of rGE is especially important. Passive rGE is so named because it considers the child to be a passive entity in creating the association between their genes and their rearing environment (Plomin et al., 1977). This passivity is in stark contrast to the role the child is thought to play in an active gene–environment correlation. Active rGE occurs when children with a certain genotype are systematically more (or less) likely to seek out (or select) and therefore be exposed to certain environments. Thus, individuals are an *active* force in selecting their environments (Rutter et al., 1997; Scarr & McCartney, 1983). For example, a child with a genetic propensity toward antisocial behavior may be more likely to seek out an antisocial peer network. Failure to consider this self-selection of environments can result in overestimating the importance of a specific environment because the same genetic factors may be responsible for both the child's antisocial behavior and their membership of a given peer group.

Evocative Gene–Environment Correlation

Evocative rGE is present when a genetically influenced trait systematically "evokes" a particular response from an environment. Evocative rGE is commonly thought to involve relationships and reactions to genetically influenced behavior by other people rather than a specific environment itself (Rutter et al., 1997). Thus, individuals' genetically influenced characteristics are the targets of others' selective processes. An example would be when a child's genetically influenced disruptive and antisocial behavior may evoke harsh reactions from parents or teachers (or rejection from prosocial peers). Like other rGE processes, the experiences linked to evocative rGE may further exacerbate the child's behavior leading to a cycle of maladaptive behavior.

Creating Risky Contexts for the Risk Prone

A recurring theme in the above descriptions of rGE types is that only part of the rGE story is about methodological confounds. Clearly these processes create links between individuals' genetically-influenced traits and their environments. However, these processes need to be also understood as part of the developmental processes leading to the expression of risk behaviors. As a group, rGE processes stack the deck against aggression prone children. First, passive-rGE processes make aggressive children systematically more likely to be reared in households defined by chaotic and inconsistent parenting. Second, active rGE will place aggressive children in contexts such as being exposed to aggressive peers, where they are more likely to express their risk-prone characteristics. Third, evocative rGE works to ensure that aggressive children are exposed to more hostile parenting, unstable friendships, and less supportive relationships with teachers.

It is important to note that social experiences do not have to be largely or substantially heritable to present problems for the validity of sociological findings purporting to document the influence of social experiences on outcomes, as the effect sizes of these experiential factors found in conventional criminological research tend to be modest. For example, Giordano et al. (2010), in an article appearing in the flagship journal *Criminology*, found a 0.06 association between romantic partner verbal conflict and ego delinquency. Given associations of such modest sizes it seems clear that any significant genetic influences on environments or experiences would be sufficient to create concern that such associations may not reflect the environmental causality they are purported to indicate.

Different Behavioral Genetic Designs and How They Can be Used to Address GE Correlations

Univariate ACE

One of the most common designs in the behavioral genetic tool kit is the classic univariate twin model. This model decomposes variance of a phenotype into the three basic components of behavioral genetic variance, additive genetic (A), shared environmental (C), and nonshared environmental (E) variance. Thus it is often referred to as an ACE model. Because it is the first model we present, we elaborate on some technical aspects of the modeling process more than for subsequent models. As noted above, the components in the univariate ACE model are modeled as independent of (aka orthogonal to) each other. Additive genetic influences make genetically related individuals similar to each other. For example, if MZ twins are more similar to each other than DZ twins, this indicates the presence of genetic influences. Shared environmental influences (or C) are those influences that are both shared (i.e. common, which is why C is used to abbreviate this component) between siblings in the same household and make them similar to each other (regardless of genetic relatedness). Nonshared (E) influences are those that make siblings different from each other. Also included in the E component is measurement error.

When describing C and E components it is somewhat useful to give examples of experiences that could theoretically contribute to each of these components. For example, the parenting style of parents, family structure, household income, degree of parental religiosity, and level of neighborhood affluence can all contribute to the shared environmental experiences of siblings reared within the same household. Examples of experiences that may contribute largely to E include different peer experiences and school experiences. It is important to note that although examples of such environmental experiences can help add substance to the technical definitions of shared and nonshared environmental influences, these examples can sometimes be misleading. Aspects of generally shared experiences, such as of parenting practices, can differ substantially between siblings, and aspects of school and peer experiences may be substantially similar for siblings. Thus, while it is sometimes useful to describe the types of experiences that may contribute to C and E, it is important to always stress that E influences are limited to those that make siblings different and C influences are those that are both shared by siblings in the same household and work to make siblings similar to each other. If this definition of C seems too restrictive, it is worth noting that such patterns of influence are theoretically consistent with family-based main effects. Thus, if household factors – such as parenting style or family structure – have the systematic effects that sociological theories propose they have, such household environment main effects should contribute to C.

In addition to these basic issues of what the components of the behavioral genetic models are and what causal processes should contribute to each, other aspects for the models are worth mentioning. First, the Standard ACE model assumes that there are no interactions between the model components. Not modeling interactions if they are present has important implications for the interpretation of A, C, and E. These implications will be elaborated on later in this chapter. Second, this basic model also assumes that there is no assortative mating. This assumption is often incorrect. However, assortative mating would increase the genetic relatedness of dizygotic pairs for the trait by which parents assort. Thus, models that do not take assortative mating into account underestimate heritability. In other words, that most behavior genetic models do not take assortative mating into account is not a reason to believe that heritability is overstated.

In practice, the measured outcome/phenotype is modeled as a manifest variable, with factor loadings on three components, A, C, and E, which are modeled as latent factors. The variance of each of these latent factors is set to 1.0. The factor loadings are set to be equal across twins, requiring that the influence of each of the three components on the same family member pairs to be the same. Because they share all of their genes, the correlation between additive genetic influences (A) of two twins in a pair is set to be 1 for monozygotic twins. Because they share half of their segregating genes on average, this association is set to 0.5 for dizygotic twins.

The correlation between shared (or common) environmental influences (C) is set to 1.0 for both MZ and DZ pairs. This 1.0 correlation between shared environments of twins within the same households is not a statement that twins share all aspects of their household experience – rather that only aspects of their experience that they do share by virtue of their being in the same household can contribute to the factor loading connecting the manifest variable and the latent C component. By definition, nonshared environmental influences (E) are not correlated.[1]

Univariate ACE models are useful for estimating the unique contributions of genetic, shared environmental, and nonshared environmental influences to any phenotype. When applied to experiences, such as parenting received by young children or adolescents, these models can address the assumption that variance in such experiences is driven primarily by parents, and thus would be largely explained by the C component. However, in the case that MZ twins share more similar parenting than do DZ twins, this pattern of associations suggests evocative or active gene–environment correlation, the former being more theoretically likely. Note that this design cannot distinguish between evocative or active gene–environment correlations. Determining or rather deciding which of these processes is the better candidate for contributing to heritability relies on which is more theoretically plausible for the phenotype being decomposed, as well as the strategy used to measure the phenotype. In the case of *experienced parenting*, evocative processes seem more likely. In contrast, a large heritability for adolescents' affiliations with

---

1   Note that sometimes one can also model non-additive genetic influence, or D, dominant effects. In this situation, the correlation between D of monozygotic twins are still set to be 1 but 0.25 for dizygotic twins and biological siblings, because the genetic similarities decrease on average among them when we also consider the interactions among genes themselves.

delinquent peers might indicate both active, via target adolescents selecting their friends based upon the target adolescents' genetically-influenced preferences, and evocative, through their friends selecting them based upon the target adolescents' genetically-influenced characteristics, gene–environment correlations.

Because measurement error contributes to nonshared environmental influence, E is nearly always necessary in the final model. In fact, in contrast to the C component, which is often relatively small or zero, E commonly accounts for substantial variance.

Perceptional rGE

Despite their simplicity, univariate designs have made substantial contributions to understanding the influence of genetics on environment and measures of the environment. One the most important domains in which this is true is the area of perceptual rGE, a process that directly affects the validity of behavioral science conclusions. The classic studies in this domain were performed by Rowe (1983) nearly 30 years ago. These studies used straightforward univariate ACE designs to show children's perceptions of parenting were influenced by genetics. Specifically, perceptions of parental warmth, but not parental control, were shown to be substantially influenced by genetic variance. Such findings suggest reports of children's perceptions of family environments, at least those that are more subjective, such as harsh parenting and quality of parent–child relationships, are of questionable utility. At minimum, it seems that multiple-respondent designs, such as those with child, parent, and teacher reports of child behaviors, should be used whenever possible.

Phenotypes such as the peers' delinquency phenotype discussed above would also be very susceptible to perception-based active rGE. Non-genetic analyses by Bauman and Ennett (1996) demonstrated the vulnerability of peer behavioral assessments to project processes. Given this general vulnerability, it would seem that whenever possible researchers should use the most direct measures of such phenotype. In the case of peer behaviors, reports by and of peers themselves would be preferable to reports of the target adolescents' perceptions of their peers.

Multivariate ACE

The basic ACE model can be easily extended to accommodate more than one manifest variable. In the bivariate case, a model extended in this way estimates A, C, and E influences that are common to both variables and those that uniquely influence each variable. Conventional applications of the bivariate model may investigate sources of influence on individuals' dispositions, such as sensation seeking and a criminological phenotype, such as non-violent delinquency. In this example, the results of a bivariate ACE would address the degree to which the link between these two variables is driven by their common genetic, shared environmental influences, and nonshared influences; as well as the sources of influence on unique variance of these phenotypes.

In a bivariate ACE model, two manifest variables have factor loadings to their common genetic, shared environmental influences and nonshared influences. The factor loadings from the same common latent variable are set to be equal, indicating that this influence is the same/driven by the same influence. In addition, each of the two manifest variables has factor loadings to their own unique genetic, shared environmental influences, and nonshared influences. One can easily extend this model to a tri-variate situation.

Applied to an rGE question, this design could be used to determine whether genetic or environmental factors drive the associations between family experiences, such as parental supervision, and person-level behaviors, such as delinquency. Results from such a multivariate model are relevant for the development of prevention programs. For example, finding that associations between delinquency and parenting behaviors are largely driven by genetic factors would suggest that family-based interventions targeting parental supervision of children may not be as effective in reducing delinquency as school-based programs.

The Cholesky Decomposition

One special application of the bivariate ACE model is the bivariate Cholesky decomposition, which estimates common genetic and environmental influences on two phenotypes, and specific components on one phenotype, in contrast to estimating common and specific components on both as is in the general bivariate ACE model. The phenotype with specific components is typically called the downstream variable. This model, or decomposition, is often applied to address the influences on two or more phenotypes, especially when the phenotypes can be ordered in a theoretically guided fashion whereby some are temporally or phenomenologically prior to other variables. When applied to the same variable measured over time, for example delinquency measured at age 8, 10, 12, 14, and 16, such a decomposition could address whether variance in delinquency across adolescent development is due to emerging genetic or environmental factors. For example, greater genetic influences on delinquency may emerge as adolescents hit puberty. To investigate rGE processes, this design could be used to decompose influences on affiliations with delinquent peers and individuals' own delinquency.

Adoption Designs

Another quasi-experimental research design that can be used to address gene–environment correlations is the adoption design. In this design, children who are adopted at birth are studied, along with their biological parents and adoptive parents. Examples of well-known adoption designs include the Colorado Adoption Project (CAP; Plomin & DeFries, 1983) and the Early Growth and Development

Study (EGDS; Leve et al., 2007). The power of this research design lies in the fact that the adoptive children are being raised by genetically unrelated adoptive parents. Associations between birth parents' and adoptive children's characteristics imply genetic influences and associations between adoptive parent or rearing environment and child characteristics imply environmental influences on the development of behavior.

The adoption design can also be leveraged to estimate the importance of certain gene–environment correlations. When children are raised in their biological parents' home, passive rGE may be in play and its effects on parent–child correlations cannot be distinguished from environmental cause. However, passive rGE is not present for adoptive children because adoptive parents do not contribute any *genetic* influence to the development of their adoptive child characteristics (Plomin et al., 1977). This facet of the adoption design allows for a direct test of the importance of passive rGE for a phenotype by comparing the variance in that phenotype in adoptive children and the variance of that phenotype in non-adopted children of the same birth parents. Differences in phenotypic variance for adopted and non-adopted children imply the operation of passive rGE (Plomin et al., 1977).

Adoption designs can also be used to test for the presence of evocative and active rGE (Leve et al., 2007; Plomin et al., 1977). Associations between birth parent characteristics and characteristics of the adopted children's environments suggest the operation of evocative rGE. This test relies on the associations between birth parents' phenotypes (e.g. criminal record, which is used as a proxy for the adopted child's genotype) and children's rearing environments being due to the children selecting or evoking the household experience.

Although adoption designs have proven to be very powerful in disentangling genetic and environmental effects and useful in attempting to parse out the different types of gene–environment correlation, they are not without limitations. Most adoption designs rely on the assumption that children are not selectively placed into adoptive environments and that there is sufficient variance in the range of adoptive environments into which children are placed (i.e. adoptive parents tend not to be drawn from the portion of the population involved in criminal activity). Some have argued that these issues are problematic enough to substantially degrade the value of adoption designs (see Stoolmiller, 1998; Turkheimer, 2000). However, others have concluded that although these concerns are not trivial, they do not outweigh the unique opportunities these designs present for genetically informative analyses (for an analyses and discussion see McGue, Keyes, Sharma, et al., 2007).

Children of Twins Design

One design that is gaining traction in the quantitative genetic literature is the children of twins design (COT; D'Onofrio et al., 2003). This design is uniquely suited to differentiate genetic and specific environmental factors involved in familial influences on a phenotype. The COT design models data from MZ and DZ twins along with their children (who have different rearing environments), who do not share households. By measuring multiple generations of participants for which genetic similarity is known, the COT design can estimate a direct environmental effect from parent phenotype to child phenotype by parsing out genetic and environmental influences that are shared by twins *and* their children. Because this design examines phenotype similarity between cousins (who vary from 0.25 to 0.125 in genetic relatedness depending on if their parents are monozygotic or dizygotic twins) net of shared environmental influences, it is able to estimate the influence of specific (i.e. measured) environmental effects, independent of passive rGE influences that can be shared by twins and siblings reared in the same household. This analytic advantage is a huge step forward in attempting to accurately assess the influence of specific environmental influences within the home. In fact, this design accomplishes what conventional sociological (i.e. biofamily) designs that examine presumptively causal associations between parents and their biological kids seek to accomplish. Moreover, because the children are raised in separate households by their parents (one of whom is a twin), rather than sharing a household with a co-twin, this design avoids issues that may be associated with a *"special twin environment"* and has no particular barriers preventing it from being population representative. Unfortunately, the use of this design has been limited by two factors. First, the design has relatively low power to estimate genetic effects due to comparing cousins that differ genetically by a relatively small amount; $rG = 0.25$ and 0.125. In contrast, the genetic correlations between conventional twin pairs are 1.0 and 0.5. As a result, the COT design requires a substantial sample size. Second, it is a difficult design for which to gather a sample, requiring the identification of older twins and complete data from both the twin generation and their children. Because of these two barriers, this design is not used as often as it should be.

Discordant Twin Control Designs

The emphasis of the most well-known behavioral genetic designs, such as ACE twin designs, is determining the relative contributions of the A, C, and E variance components to total variation. However, twin data can be used to address hypotheses regarding specific causal influences. An example of such an application of genetically-informative data is the discordant twin control design. This design can be used to examine whether presumptive causal factors can withstand family-level environmental and genetic third variable threats. The applicability of the design is limited to situations (i.e. causal presuppositions) in that both the proposed independent variable and dependent variable are free to differ across siblings or twins within the same family. It is best suited for situations in which a researcher might be (or *should be*) concerned about family-level environmental or genetic third-variable threats. Lynskey and colleagues (2003) applied this design to gateway drug theory, the core idea of which is that use of marijuana leads via a few proposed pathways to increased risk of hard drug use in the future. It is important that the proposed causal links operate through pathways that are essentially environmental cascades, including the pharmacological effects of marijuana use increase propensity of other drug use, marijuana use reduces the perceived risk of using other drugs and/or leads to greater opportunities to use other drugs. In many ways, gateway drug theory is a typical environmentally-focused behavioral science theory. On one hand, there is substantial support for the existence of data patterns consistent with the idea that marijuana increases the risk, including longitudinal data supporting the progression of use from marijuana to hard drugs over time. On the other hand, as admitted by its major proponents (Kandel & Jessor, 2002), it is difficult to address the considerable third variable threats that could alternatively contribute to the link between marijuana and hard drug use. Two domains in which these threats exist are family-based environmental influences and genetic influences. Among possible/plausible family influences that could contribute to both marijuana and hard drug use are family-levels of parenting practices, family structure, or poverty. It is similarly possible that genetically influenced characteristics, such as sensation seeking or a tendency to self-medicate, may link marijuana and hard drug use. Framed in the language of rGE, the initial use of marijuana would be considered vulnerable to active rGE processes.

It is important to emphasize that although it is easy to develop a list of possible third variable influences, it is difficult to effectively control for them. According to Gateway proponents Jessor and Kandel, who are not behavioral geneticists, the standard approach of statistically controlling for third variable threats is insufficient. Primary reasons for the problem of this approach include that it is unlikely that all potentially relevant third variables would be measured in a single study. In fact, most studies that pursue the statistical control strategy only use a handful of demographic variables as statistical controls, neglecting important aspects of both context and individual characteristics. Kandel and Jessor go on to call for the use of genetically informative designs; such as the discordant twin control design applied by Lynskey.

Reviewing the details and logic of this design as well as how Lynskey applied it to investigate the causal propositions at the core of gateway drug theory will help demonstrate the potential utility of this design for many criminological questions. The Lynskey study used 311 twin pairs, within each was a twin that reported marijuana use before their seventeenth birthday and one that did not. Lynsky and colleagues proposed that if such early marijuana use (before 17 years of age) created a causal cascade leading to later hard drug use, the early using twin in each household's pair should be at greater risk of subsequent hard drug use. However, if the gateway sequence is a product of environmental third variable influences associated with household membership then later hard drug use of twins reared within the same household should be similar despite the initial earlier discordance for marijuana use. This is because both twins in each pair – the early pot user and his or her twin – would be subject to identical household-level associated risk factors (in contrast to all environmental risk factors in the household – some of which could obviously differ across twins) for hard drug use. Thus, if such household-level influences are the primary influence connecting marijuana use to hard drug use then the initial use of marijuana by one twin (which in the context of a behavioral genetic model belongs to the unshared environment domain) will not create increased risk of later use by that twin. The investigation of genetic third variable influences on the proposed causal link between early marijuana use and later hard drug use leverages the different levels of relatedness between MZ and DZ pairs. In brief, if the progression from marijuana use to later hard drug use is due to an environmental cascade between early pot use and later hard drug use, then within-twin pair discordance will not only predict subsequent hard drug use discordance (thus overcoming family environmental third variable threats) across all twin pairs, it will do so to the same degree regardless of the level of genetic similarity of the twin pairs. In contrast, if genetically influenced endowments assemble the behavioral trajectory from marijuana use to hard drug use, then the different (and greater) risk of hard drug use among the early using twins within twin pairs will only be found among twin pairs who differ in genetic endowments (i.e. the dizygotic twin pairs). Among the MZ pairs, who are the same genetically, initial within-pair differences in marijuana use should not lead to systematic differences in later hard drug use.

Before leaving our discussion of the discordant twin control design several points should be made. First, despite the application of these quasi-experimental controls for household-level and genetic third variable influences, the Lynskey study found support for the nonshared environmental causal linkage between adolescent pot use and subsequent hard drug use. Second, the strong causal inference made possible by the quasi-experimental aspects of the discordant twin control design potentially comes at a cost to generalizability. This hit to generalizability comes most directly from the use of discordant twin pairs. By definition such pairs have one pair that has experienced the presumptive causal factor and one that does not. When applied to considering the causal impact of marijuana use, the design requires that 50 percent of the sample used marijuana. As critiques of Lynskey et al. explained (see Schier, Nelson, & Hoffman, 2003), this level of use far exceeds that of the general population and undercuts the generalizability of the findings. Although this concern may not be trivial, the threat created by requiring 50 percent of the sample to be affected by the presumptive causal factor will vary in degree across studies depending on the population frequency of the causal factor being investigated.

The second point is that the design, in its conventional form, requires dichotomous independent variables. To address this limitation, Cleveland and Wiebe (2008) extended the design to use continuous versions of the marijuana use independent variables. The use of continuous marijuana use variables has the effect of changing the model from one examining the degree of increased risk of hard drug use for the early "marijuana using" twin to predicting that whichever twin uses marijuana more frequently will be at greater risk for subsequent hard drug use. Thus, it is both a more general version of the early risk model operationalized by the discordant twin control design and allows the model to take differences in degree into account, which in the case of involvement in deviant behaviors – such as drug use or delinquency – would seem theoretically relevant.

Moreover, by not requiring discordant pairs, this difference score approach broadens the sampling strategy to include all available twins, not only those who were discordant for initial marijuana use. As a result, the analyses sample can be representative for the independent variable. In the case of Cleveland and Wiebe's (2008) analysis, they were able to use all Add Health same-sex twin pairs with valid marijuana and hard drug use data, providing a sample with similar levels of substance use to the full Add Health sample, which itself is representative of adolescents attending high schools in the United States.

Taken together the adoption design (Plomin et al., 1977), the children of twins design (D'Onofrio et al., 2003), the discordant twin control design (Lynskey et al., 2003), and the difference score version used by Cleveland and Wiebe (2008) present environmentally-oriented researchers with tools to consider their hypothesized causal processes while controlling for the substantial threats presented by gene–environment correlations.

The Spectrum of Selection: Differing Vulnerability to rGE Across Environments

Because rGE operates through selecting and modifying environments, rGE is not equally implicated in all measures of environments and experiences. Measures extracted from family, school and community, and peer environmental contexts (as well as selected experiences such as adolescent marijuana use) vary in level of susceptibility to rGE and the reason for that susceptibility.

Low to Moderate Levels of Selection: Community-Level Contexts

Starting at the less-affected end of the spectrum, community-level variables – depending on the level and characteristic being considered – would seem to have relatively low susceptibility to rGE, especially when adolescents are the targets of the research. For example, because adolescents' parents rather than adolescents' themselves select their residences, the socio-economic disadvantages associated with their neighborhoods are not a direct target of adolescents' own genetically influenced characteristics or endowments – thus ruling out the involvement of active or evocative rGE correlations.

Unlike active or evocative rGE operating through adolescents, passive rGE implicated via parents' genetically influenced traits contributing to their selection into neighborhoods may operate to create correlations between individuals and their neighborhoods. As alluded to above, the degree to which such passive rGE process might contribute to adolescent-context associations is potentially attenuated, however, by both the known (0.50) association between parents' and offspring genotypes (perhaps somewhat higher due to assortative mating for such traits as aggression) and the likely modest degree to which genotypes of parents contribute systematically to their selection of residences. Given the indirect processes through which such a passive rGE would have to operate, the overall magnitude of such effects is unlikely to be substantial. In other words, because parents are the actors, rather than adolescents themselves, the relevant selection processes may not be strong enough to create a strong rGE between adolescents' genotypes and their neighborhoods.

One specific exception to what may otherwise be low levels of selection into neighborhoods, might be the pathway associated with divorce and its heritability (McGue & Lykken, 1992). As the proportion of divorced and non-married households, while found in all neighborhoods, do peak in lower SES neighborhoods (and to the extent that this process is due to individual characteristics rather than social stratification and racial segregation processes), the heritability of divorce may cluster together families with adolescents biased toward present rather than future-oriented strategies. Such characteristics may interact with lower levels of parental supervision that can easily emerge in neighborhoods when high proportions of single-parent households cluster together in neighborhoods (see Cleveland, 2003).

Genetically-mediated associations between school contexts and adolescents, at least for variation between public schools, are likely limited by the same processes that potentially constrain the influence of rGE associations on the community level. Possible exceptions to such limitations are children who are placed in religious, special needs, magnet, and other specific school environments based upon family-level or individual-level characteristics with non-trivial heritability.

Although the potential for rGE operating on actual macro-contexts of individuals is relatively small, because they may be influenced by genetically-influenced aspects of individuals' personalities, the perceptions of neighborhood quality or safety may be substantially biased by genetic influences. Accordingly, it is very important to closely consider whether neighborhood is being measured objectively, such as via Census or Uniform Crime Reports, or being measured via the target individual's perceptions before concluding that rGE is not confounding study conclusions.

The Midpoint: Family Processes

The direct genetic link between parents and offspring presents an obvious and substantial confound for research investigating the influence of family experiences and relationships on child outcomes. Good examples of family-based rGE confounds are research questions investigating the influence of family structure, types of parenting, and birth order (see Rogers, Cleveland, Van den Ord, & Rowe, 2000). Regarding family structure, although there are many good reasons to believe that on average growing up within a single-parent household may present more risks of involvement in delinquent behaviors – these include dynamics in the home, such as less time available for parental supervision and less financial resources, as well as increased risk of residential instability – divorce itself has been found to have a substantial heritability (McGue & Lykken, 1992). This heritability creates the possibility that associations between family structures and risk behaviors, including delinquency, may be largely spurious – in some cases.

When such spuriousity may or may not apply to links between family structure and delinquency was examined by Cleveland, Wiebe, and Rowe (2005). This study applied a genetically informative design – using half- and full-sibling pairs in the Children of the National Longitudinal Study of Youth – to model genetic and environmental influences on mean differences in behavior problems among adolescents across intact and non-intact households. Specific findings included that the majority (81 to 94 percent across four different scales) of the mean-level differences in behavior problems between two-parent full sibling and mother-only half-sibling families were found to be due to genetic differences. In contrast, differences in shared environments across family types were the source of the majority (67 to 88 percent) of mean-level differences in behavior problems between two-parent full sibling and mother-only half-sibling families. These findings suggest that passive rGE is a primary contributor to the overlap between half-sibling one-parent family structure and the average level of behavior problems reported by adolescents within these families. In contrast, the primary contributor to elevated levels of behavior problems among adolescents from mother-only full-sibling households compared to those found in two-parent full-sibling households appear to be experiences and environments common to children in the same household – a finding completely consistent with socially-oriented theories of divorce. Thus, while divorce may be heritable (McGue & Lykken, 1992), these findings suggest that any genetic influences on divorce generally are not those that lead to any heightened level of behavior problems among mother-only full-sibling families.

These findings direct attention toward the processes that contribute to family formation, and the endowments of individuals involved. Specifically, mother-only full-sibling families require that mothers have children with the same partners, implying a threshold level of relationship stability that is at odds with giving birth to children by different fathers in quick succession. Of course, both mothers' and fathers' endowments might contribute to such processes. Characteristics similar to those that can contribute to adolescent problem behaviors, such as impulsivity and low concern for future consequences, may make potential biological mothers and biological fathers more likely to participate in unprotected sexual encounters. On the mother's side, willingness to have unprotected sex with a different male partner after already having one child with another male (who presumptively was never or is no longer living with the mother) or to have unprotected sex in short-term relationships, might indicate a lack of concern about paternal investment and relationship stability. On the father's side, willingness to participate in unprotected sex might reflect similar characteristics.

In contrast, the non-intact full sibling family formation might reflect different parental characteristics. At the minimum, such a formation suggests the biological parents were romantically paired for a long enough period to have two children together. Thus, having two children with the same father suggests a threshold level of stability.

Of course, the heritable parental characteristics that can undercut the formation and maintenance of stable parental relationships, such as impulsivity and aggression, can also directly influence parent–child relationships. Thus, associations between parent–child relationships and child behaviors may also be impacted by genetically-influenced spuriousity. In addition to the obvious passive rGE whereby parents' genes may first directly influence their own behaviors and parent–child relationships (via direct heritability) and second indirectly (via being passed down to their children) influence their children's behaviors, there is the additional reactive process whereby parent–child relationships are shaped by child behaviors. An excellent example of research documenting how genetic may influence this reactive process is the groundbreaking work of Ge and colleagues (1996). Using an adoption design with information on biological parents' drug and alcohol abuse and dependency use and antisocial personality disorder, adoptive children's antisocial and hostile behaviors, and adoptive mothers' and fathers' parenting, Ge and colleagues found not only that biological parents' disorders predicted children's antisocial/hostile behaviors, reflecting the basic heritability of these behaviors, but that these biological parents' disorders predicted the degree to which adoptive parents' expressed harsh/inconsistent and nurturant/involved parenting practices. Of course, reactive parenting is not a new concept. Citing the hugely important, but unfortunately often ignored, conclusion of Bell from 1966, Ge et al. remind us that "children are not simple passive recipients of environmental influence, their heritable characteristics can have substantial and systematic effects on the types of parenting they receive from their caregivers" (Bell, 1968; Bell & Chapman, 1986).

This genetically-influenced reactivity is not something that is contained inside the home. Cleveland and Crosnoe (2004) showed that variance in parents' knowing the parents of their children's friends is substantially influenced by genetic as well as shared environmental influences. This phenomenon, known as intergenerational closure among sociologists (Coleman, 1988) is thought to provide a conduit of social capital and promote prosocial outcomes among adolescents. Although many would expect to find that intergenerational closure is associated with common household variance (i.e. shared environmental variance), finding genetic influences on its variance would surprise many sociologically-oriented researchers. This finding reveals that genetic influences can draw upon the responsive nature of parents and parenting behaviors to extend their reach outside of the home. Genetic influences on parenting are an aspect of reactive rGE. In this case, it is plausible that parents' likelihood of knowing the parents of their adolescent children's friends would be affected by both their children's own behaviors and their choice of friends. First, adolescents' behaviors, such as degree of involvement in delinquency (Rowe; 1983; Rowe & Osgood, 1984) and involvement in school activities (Edelbrock, Rende, Plomin, & Thompson 1995; Plomin, 1983) are substantially influenced by genetics. Second, so are adolescents' patterns of peer affiliations (Cleveland, Wiebe, & Rowe 2005) (this point will be expanded upon below). Parents' ability to know the parents of their kids' friends would be affected by both of these processes. In the case of their adolescents' own delinquency, it may push adolescents away from their households, reducing parents' opportunities to meet their adolescent children's friends. If their friends are delinquents themselves, they would be more likely to come from disorganized and perhaps single-parent homes, which would on average decrease the availability of these friends' parents.

Thus, not only can biological parents' and their children's behaviors be correlated for passive rGE reasons, but also for evocative or reactive rGE reasons. This is not to argue that the directional arrow cannot extend from parents to children for environmental reasons. However, such parent to child environmental causation is only one of several processes that contribute to such parent–child associations. Unfortunately, with the data commonly relied upon by environmentally-oriented researchers, it is not possible to consider passive or evocative rGE influences on this association. Regardless of these limitations on the data, such associations are commonly interpreted as manifestations of parent-to-child influences.

The Far Point of Selection: Peers and Other Social Experiences

The far point on the spectrum of selection is defined by peers and social experiences themselves. It is arguable that peer experiences are the aspect of the environment that is most vulnerable to genetically-oriented selective influences. Not only do individuals actively select their peer affiliates from a broad range of possible associates provided by most school contexts, but potential peers do the same to them. There is substantial evidence that adolescents' peer group affiliations are influenced by genetic variance. Among these is the work by Cleveland, Wiebe, and Rowe (2005) that estimated that 64 percent of the variance in adolescents' exposure to friends who smoke and drink could be explained by genetic influences – whereas shared environmental influences were zero. This pattern of results provides strong evidence of active and/or evocative gene–environment correlations, and provides somewhat shocking evidence of the ineffectiveness of family-based environmental variance in influencing adolescents' exposure to peer substance use.

The Issue of Main Effects: Or, "All Models are Wrong, Some are Useful"

When considering results like those reported above, and other similar findings indicating strong genetic and low or null shared environmental influences, it is reasonable to wonder if such findings indicate that parenting is unimportant. If one only thinks of parenting in terms of main effects – which is how it is conventionally examined in both behavioral genetic and non-behavioral genetic models, then the answer would be *perhaps*. However, there is an important reason to think that parenting is important. To explain why parenting is important it is necessary to return to the issue of how behavioral genetic models apportion variance.

The basic behavioral genetic model, the univariate decomposition of twin data, divides total variance into orthogonal components of additive genetic, shared environmental, and unshared environmental variance. This "main effects" conceptualization is not theoretically consistent with transactional perspectives, such as developmental systems theory (Gottlieb, 1991, 1995), that emphasize the integrated and dependent nature of genetic and environmental influences. At the core of this co-active dependency is the idea that the actions and influences of genes and environments are not divisible, especially not into the orthogonal components of variance that are the product of behavioral genetic models. One extreme conclusion drawn from the discord between co-active nature of gene–environment interplay and the orthogonal main-effects operationalization of Behavioral Genetic models is that the result of the latter should be dismissed (see Gottlieb, 1991, 1995). Proponents of behavioral genetic modeling respond to this conclusion by emphasizing that behavioral genetic designs are not intended to capture the complexity of development that leads to human variance and that these designs are accurate divisions of variance on the level of data on which they operate (see Turkheimer, 2004). In brief, the models do what they are designed to do, which is to decompose total variance of phenotypes by the definitions of the three components of variance they model.

Rather than trying to resolve this debate here, a better tactic may be to focus on the particular fashion in which variance associated with interactions between genetics and environmental influences is assigned in behavioral genetic models, and what that means for the likelihood of substantial environmental main effects. Before taking the discussion to the level of the model, let us first consider a hypothetical example for two siblings growing up in the same family. In this example, the siblings are male full-siblings (as genetically related on average as two dizygotic twins). The parents are strict. Sibling One, Bill, is more sensation seeking than Sibling Two, Bob. The reason we use sensation seeking here is that it has obvious implications for risk behaviors and that it has been found to have a fairly strong genetic influence (see Zuckerman, 1983). Returning to the example of our siblings: Bob, the low sensation seeker, has few problems living under the rules of his parents; in fact, he finds the high degree of structure comforting, tends to stay at home, does his homework every night, does well in school, and participates in little or no drug use or delinquency. Bob goes on to college and has a successful career. In contrast, Bill, the sensation seeking sibling, is constantly running afoul of the family rules, has a conflictual relationship with his parents, rebels against them, spends more time with his similarly free-spirited friends, is exposed to opportunities for and models of drug use and delinquency – and partakes in both.

Of course, things don't have to work out the way they do in the above example. It is just an example, and a rather simplified and extreme one at that. But it provides a clear chance to consider how variance associated with genes and environments working together finds a home in behavioral genetic decompositions. So let us take this example into the conventional behavioral genetic decomposition and see what happens. Family influences are important influences on both siblings. However, only those influences that manifest systematically (i.e. make siblings in the same household the same) end up contributing to the shared environment component. In the example above, the siblings – in spite of being exposed to the same strict parenting style – end up being very different in terms of their delinquency. Thus, shared environmental influences will be found to be zero or near zero. The interaction between their similar exposure to strict parenting and their genetically influenced differences in sensation seeking, because it ends up leading the siblings to different delinquent and drug use outcomes based on their genetically influenced traits, ends up contributing to genetic influences component of the model. Note that for both siblings developing their non-delinquent (Bob) or delinquent (Bill) lives involved both genetically influenced characteristics and environmental experiences. However, because these genetically different siblings end up with genetically different phenotypic endpoints, the pattern of data created by Bill and Bob contributes to genetic influences only. Because interactions between these two influences follow genetic expectations (i.e. they make genetically identical siblings similar and genetically different siblings discordant) – based on the operationalizations of the model – this assignment is accurate. However, it also means that processes that are just as contributed to by environmental experiences as they are by genetic influences contribute to the genetic component. In contrast, unlike the other two components of the ACE model, only true main effects – those that have the same effect on siblings regardless of genetic predispositions – will contribute to the C component (see Turkheimer, 2004 for a full explication of these issues).

It is argued herein that the reasonable goal for statistical models is to be useful (rather than correct) and that not addressing gene–environment transactional processes is a shortcoming rather than tragic flaw that would justify dismissing behavioral genetic findings; and while this shortcoming reduces the scope and depth of questions answerable with conventional applications of behavioral genetic design, it does not discredit behavioral genetic findings. That being said, it may be important for environmentally-oriented behavioral scientists, such as the majority of criminologists, to consider that while behavioral genetic models strongly undercut the position that parenting has important and systematic main effects on most criminological outcomes, they do not rule out such environmental factors play important roles in gene–environment transactive or co-active processes. Thus, environmentally-oriented criminologists are presented with a choice: hold onto main effects conceptualizations of their independent variables, which are unlikely to reflect reality, or learn from the message of behavioral genetic findings (both intended and unintended) and embrace the perspective that environmental experiences are often associated with genetic variance (via gene–environment correlations) and act differently depending on genetics – this why C is so small. Holding onto old-fashioned ideas of environmental main effects is a losing battle.

Summary and Conclusions

This chapter has covered a lot of ground. We have argued that sociologically-based criminology has a problem: its independent variables are not independent. Instead, many of the most common criminological predictor variables are confounded with genetic influences. We used the concept of gene–environment correlations (rGE) as a lens through which to view these genetic confounds. This rGE framework explicates how genetic influences involve themselves in what would conventionally be thought of as "environmental processes." Because behavioral genetic findings cannot be separated from their methods, we have supplemented our discussion of different gene–environment processes with an explanation of different designs that can be used to investigate them. Some of these designs focus on the conventional behavioral genetic decomposition of variance; others provide powerful tools to examine the presumptive environmental causal processes underlying conventional theories of crime and delinquency. It is important that environmentally-oriented criminologists understand the former. Hopefully, they will consider using the latter. Because not all confounds are created equal, we set out a spectrum of selection that provides a thumbnail sketch of the threats genetic influences present across different domains of environmental experiences.

Finally, we briefly layout discrepancies between the co-active perspective of gene–environment transactions provided by developmental systems theory (see Gottlieb, 1991, 1995) and the operationalization of behavioral genetics models. Considering developmental systems theories arguments against the validity of behavioral genetic models reminds us of the importance of focusing on the pros and cons of how behavioral genetic models operationalize A, C, and E influences. Ironically, the ultimate victim of developmental systems perspective that genes and environment do not act alone, but rather co-act, may not be behavioral genetic models themselves, but sociological theories of environmental influence.

References

Bauman, K. E. and Ennett, S. T. (1996). On the importance of peer influence for adolescent drug use: Commonly neglected considerations. *Addiction, 91,* 185–198.

Bell, R. Q. (1968). A reinterpretation of the direction of effects in socialization. *Psychological Review, 75,* 81–95.

Bell, R. Q., & Chapman, M. (1986). Child effects in studies using experimental or brief longitudinal approaches to socialization. *Developmental Psychology, 22*(5), 595–603.

Boggess, N. L., & Hipp, R. J. (2010). Violent crime, residential instability and mobility: Does the relationship differ in minority neighborhood? *Journal of Quantitative Criminology, 26,* 351–370.

Boomsma, D., Busjahn, A., & Peltonen, L. (2002). Classical twin studies and beyond. *Nature, 3*, 872–882.

Box, E. P. & Draper, N. R. (1987). *Empirical model building and response surfaces.* New York: Wiley.

Capaldi, M. D., Kim, K. H., & Owen, D. L. (2008). Romantic partners' influence on men's likelihood of arrest in early adulthood. *Criminology, 46*, 267–299.

Cleveland, H. H. (2003). Disadvantaged neighborhoods and adolescent aggression: Behavioral genetic evidence of contextual effects. *Journal of Research on Adolescence, 13*, 211–238.

Cleveland, H. H., & Crosnoe, R. (2004). Individual variation and family-community ties: A behavioral genetic analysis of the intergenerational closure in the lives of adolescent boys and girls. *Journal of Adolescent Research, 19*, 174–191.

Cleveland, H. H., & Wiebe, R. (2008). Understanding the progression from adolescent marijuana use to young adult serious drug use: Gateway effect or developmental trajectory? *Development and Psychopathology, 20*, 615–632.

Cleveland, H. H., Wiebe, R., & Rowe, D. C. (2005). Genetic influences on associations with substance using peers. *Journal of Genetic Psychology, 166*, 153–169.

Coleman, J. (1988). Social capital and the creation of human capital. *American Journal of Sociology, 94*, 596–620.

D'Onofrio, B. M., Turkheimer, E. N., Eaves, L. J., Corey, L. A., Berg, K., Solaas, M. H., & Emery, R. E. (2003). The role of the Children of Twins design in elucidating casual relations between parent characteristics and child outcomes. *Journal of Child Psychology and Child Psychiatry, 44*(8), 1130–1144.

Eaves, L. J., Last, K. A., Martin, N. G. & Jinks, J. L. (1977). A progressive approach to non-additivity and genotype-environmental covariance in the analysis of human differences. *Brit. J. Math. Statist. Psychol, 30*, 1–42.

Edelbrock, C., Rende, R., Plomin, R., & Thompson, A. L. (1995). A twin study of competence and problem behavior in childhood and early adolescence. *Journal of Child Psychology and Psychiatry, 36*, 775–785.

Ge, X., Conger, R. D., Cadoret, R. J., Neiderhiser, J. M., Yates, W., Troughton, E., et al. (1996). The developmental interface between nature and nurture: A mutual influence model of child antisocial behavior and parent behaviors. *Developmental Psychology, 32*(4), 574–589.

Giordano, C. P., Lonardo, A. R., Manning, D. W., & Longmore, A. M. (2010). Adolescent romance and delinquency: A further exploration of Hirschi's "cold and brittle" relationships hypothesis. *Criminology, 48*, 919–946.

Gottlieb, G. (1991). Experiential canalization of behavioral development: Theory. *Developmental Psychology, 27*, 4–17.

Gottlieb, G. (1995). Some conceptual deficiencies in "developmental" behavioral genetics. *Human Development, 38*, 131–141.

Kandel, D. B. & Jessor, R. (2002). The gateway hypothesis revisited. In D. B. Kandel (ed.), *Stages and Pathways of Drug Involvement: Examining the Gateway Hypothesis* (pp. 365–372). New York: Cambridge University Press.

Leve, L. D., Neiderhiser, J. M., Ge, X., Scaramella, L. V., Conger, R. D., Reid, J. B., Shaw, D. S., & Reiss, D. (2007). The early growth and development study: A prospective adoption design. *Twin Research and Human Genetics, 10*(1), 84–95.

Lynskey, M. T., Heath, A. C., Bucholz, K. K., Slutske, W. S. , Madden, P. F., Nelson, E. C., Statham, D. J., & Martin, N. G. (2003). Escalation of drug use in early-onset cannabis users vs co-twin controls. *JAMA: Journal of the American Medical Association, 289,* 427–432.

McGue, M. & Lykken, D. T. (1992). Genetic influence on risk of divorce. *Psychol Sci, 3,* 368–373.

McGue, M., Keyes, M., Sharma, A., Elkins, I., Legrand, L., Johnson, W., & Iacono, W. G. (2007). The environments of adopted and non-adopted youth: Evidence on range restriction from the Sibling Interaction and Behavior Study (SIBS). *Behavior Genetics, 37,* 449–462.

Neiderhiser, J. M., Reiss, D., & Hetherington, E. M. (2007). The Nonshared Environment in Adolescent Development (NEAD) Project: A longitudinal family study of twins and siblings from adolescence to young adulthood. *Twin Research and Human Genetics, 10*(1), 74–83.

Plomin, R. (1983). Developmental behavioral genetics. *Child Development, 54,* 253–259.

Plomin, R. (1990). The role of inheritance in behavior. *Science, 248,* 183–188.

Plomin, R. & DeFries, J. C. (1983). The Colorado Adoption Project. *Child Development, 54*(2), 276–289.

Plomin, R., DeFries, J. C., & Loehlin, J. C. (1977). Genotype-environment interaction and correlation in the analysis of human behavior. *Psychological Bulletin, 84*(2), 309–322.

Plomin, R., DeFries, J. C., McClearn, G. E., & Rutter, M. (1997). *Behavior genetics* (3rd ed.). New York: Freeman.

Rogers, J. L., Cleveland, H. H., van den Ord, E. J. C. G., & Rowe, D. C. (2000). Do large families make low-IQ children, or do low-IQ parents make large families? *American Psychologist, 55,* 599–612.

Rowe, D. C. (1983). Biometrical genetic models of self-reported delinquent behavior: A twin study. *Behavior Genetics, 13,* 473–489.

Rowe, D. C., & Osgood, D. W. (1984). Heredity and sociological theories of delinquency: A reconsideration. *American Sociological Review, 49,* 526–540.

Rutter, M., Dunn, J., Plomin, R. Simonoff, E., Pickles, A., Maughan, B., Ormel, J., Meyer, J., & Eaves, L. (1997). Integrating nature and nurture: Implications of person-environment correlations and interactions for developmental psychopathology. *Development and Psychopathology, 9,* 335–364.

Scarr, S. & McCartney, K. (1983). How people make their own environments: A theory of genotype-environment effects. *Child Development, 54,* 424–435.

Schier, J. G., Nelson, L. S., & Hoffman, R. S. (2003). Letter to the editor. *JAMA: Journal of the American Medical Association, 290,* 329.

Stoolmiller, M. (1998). Correcting estimates of shared environmental variance for range restriction in adoption studies using a truncated multivariate normal model. *Behavior Genetics, 28*(6), 429–441.

Turkheimer, E. (2004). Spinach and ice cream: Why social science is so difficult. In DiLalla, L. F. (Ed.). *Behavior genetics principles: Perspectives in development, personality, and psychopathology*. Washington, DC: American Psychological Association.

Zuckerman, M. (1983). Biological bases of sensation seeking, impulsivity and anxiety. Hillsdale: Erlbaum.

Birth Complications and the Development of Criminality: A Biosocial Perspective

Stephen G. Tibbetts

Introduction

This chapter will explore the various issues and empirical findings that involve the risk factors and descriptions of a variety of birth and delivery complications, as well as their consequent implications on disposing individuals to criminality. As with most of the other developmental factors covered in this book, birth complications are often a result of, as well as a cause of, a complex combination of both physiological and environmental risk factors. Notably, the issue of birth/delivery complications in the area of developmental theory is an archetype or "poster-child" of biosocial criminology, in the sense that what happens just prior, during and soon after the actual birth, in terms of both physical and social/developmental factors, has an immense impact on the future of a child's risk for being disposed to crime in their future environment.

Perhaps one of the largest barriers for social scientists (such as criminologists and sociologists) examining such birth complications is that they were not trained to understand such medical problems, which often involve medical lingo that is, understandably, quite foreign to them given the lack of exposure to such early physiological factors in the traditional training of most criminologists toward only social-psychological concepts. Thus, this chapter will present an abbreviated primer regarding the description, risk factors, prognosis, and developmental effects of a variety of birth/delivery complications that are likely to predispose youths to future criminality.

Furthermore, studies have consistently shown that what happens just after and into the child's first years, in terms of household and other social factors, for youths with such birth complications has a huge impact on the long-term effects of such birth/delivery factors, particularly in terms of biosocial interactions. To clarify, it is the early physiological factors and complications at delivery that tend to interact with the environment and rearing aspects in infancy and toddler stages that have the most significant impact on predicting future criminality among children. So we will discuss this both prior to and at the end of our review of such various complications.

Given the limitations of the length of this chapter, it is impossible to cover all of the risk factors and issues of the various birth complications that may have an impact on this very early stage of life. Therefore, we will examine the most relevant and robust of these factors related to birth and delivery complications as identified by the extant scientific literature, especially to the extent that these complications interact with environmental or household risk factors in infancy/early development. Finally, we will examine some intervention programs that have been found to have some success in thwarting this disposition toward criminality by infants who experienced such delivery/birth complications.

Overview of Risk Factors in the Birth/Delivery Phase

There are literally hundreds (perhaps thousands) of factors that impact the perinatal phase of a person's life. These range widely from the pre-natal vitamins and supplements a female is medically advised to take even before a child is conceived, to every item a mother eats, drinks or snorts/shoots into her body while she is pregnant, to the multitude of things that can occur close to the delivery/labor stages. We will focus on the primary risk factors that actually affect the birth/delivery and early infancy phase, with the assumption and understanding that problems in the pre-natal stage almost always tend to result in problems in the delivery and/or post-delivery stage. To clarify, a mother who experiences problems in the pre-natal stage of pregnancy, is far more likely to experience complications in the birth/delivery phase, as well as the infancy or post-partum phase. So this chapter should be seen as an extension of prior work on pre-natal risk factors, especially in the sense of the birth/delivery complications interacting with various environmental factors, such as poverty and familial/developmental aspects of early infancy and toddlerhood.

Empirical studies and reviews of such studies have concluded that birth/delivery complications appear to have even more serious implications for future criminality of the infant than the various problems and risk factors of the earlier pre-natal stages. This is perhaps due to the vast amount of possible medical complications and acutely stressful nature the delivery process itself to the mother and infant (for reviews, see Raine, 1993; Raine et al., 1994; Piquero & Tibbetts, 1999; Arsenault, Tremblay, Boulerice, & Saucier, 2002; Raine, 2002; Beaver & Wright, 2005; Tibbetts, 2009). This noted emphasis on the relative importance of birth complications and criminality in children was noted many decades ago in the medical and psychological literature, yet has been largely neglected, with some exceptions, in criminological research and theory development. This emphasis on delivery/birth complications was displayed prominently in an early study by Pasamanick et al. in 1956 in the *American Journal of Psychiatry*, which was one of the first notable articles in the medical field linking such birthing experiences with future developmental disorders in the children (Pasamanick, Rodgers, & Lilienfield, 1956). Specifically, Pasamanick et al. (p. 613) reported that "The prenatal and paranatal records of children with behavior disorders ... show significantly more complications of pregnancy and delivery ... [t]hese associations are still present even when intellectual and environmental factors are controlled." Subsequent studies have found similar results in the association between delivery complications and behavioral problems in young children (Cocchi, Felici, Tonni, & Venanzi, 1984; Arsenault et al., 2002; Beaver & Wright, 2005; for a review, see Tibbetts, 2011), as well as supporting the higher risk of the birth/delivery phase than most of the earlier pre-natal risk factors.

As pointed out by Beaver and Wright (2005), there are a couple of leading theories for why such delivery complications impact the future criminality of infants due to their impact on the central and autonomic nervous system development and functioning. One theory places a focus on how such birth complications can clearly have a significant influence on the brain and, thus, the central nervous system functioning. Such detrimental impact is likely to impact the various inhibitory structures of the brain (e.g. prefrontal cortex), which would increase the likelihood that individuals would act on impulses from the other regions of the brain (e.g. amygdala) without the "brakes" that such inhibitory brain structures provide. Further, it is interesting that the more inhibitory structures of the brain, mostly contained in the frontal lobes, are typically the last to develop, and thus the most vulnerable to damage in the perinatal stages (Wright, Tibbetts, & Daigle, 2008), whereas some of the more emotional/impulsive structures of the brain are primarily located in the more embedded/developed structures of the limbic system (Beaver, 2009).

The other leading theory of the association of birth complications predicting future chronic offending involves an interaction between such complications with disadvantaged environments. Specifically, many of the more recent studies that have examined the link between birth complications and future behavioral problems have found that the link is highly dependent on environmental factors (for reviews of these findings, see Arsenault et al., 2002; Raine, 2002; Wright et al., 2008; Beaver, 2009; Tibbetts, 2011). To clarify, a consistent finding appears to be that either parental or household conditions appear to enhance the risks of children who have experienced birth complications. For example, Raine et al. found that birth complications when combined with early maternal rejection in infancy significantly predisposed such youth to violent crime later on in their teenage years (Raine, Brennan, & Mednick, 1994). Also, Piquero and Tibbetts (1999) found that an index of birth complications interacted with a weak family structure in early life to predict violent offending, but not for non-violent offending. Thus, it appears that the direct relationship between birth complications is often somewhat weak or moderate in terms of developing criminality, but there are highly consistent findings for the interaction between birth complications and environmental maladies in predicting early onset of offending (Tibbetts, 2009), as well as chronic, persistent violence among youth (for reviews, see Raine, 2002; Beaver, 2009).

Although some criminologists have recently begun to acknowledge and more closely devote research to birth complications and the effects they have on future criminality over the last few decades, such emphasis has only been devoted attention by a few select criminological scholars. It is very likely that the reason for the apprehension among the vast majority of criminologists in examining such complications is due to the fact that most of them have not been trained in or presented with the information to build an understanding of various birth complications. This chapter will review, in detail, some of the important birth complications, with an emphasis on the complications that have already been implicated by studies in influencing the development of criminality, as well as risk factors that have not yet been directly linked to future offending but are very likely to have a significant influence on such behavior.

Types of Birth Complications in Criminological Research

There exists a multitude of complications that can occur during pregnancy and delivery of an infant. Some of the more notable delivery complications that have been analyzed and/or implicated by recent criminological studies in terms of predicting future criminality include abruptio placentae, breech birth, Cesarean section births, eclampsia, fetal distress, meconium, placenta previa, prolapsed cord, anoxia, APGAR scores, and low birth-weight. In this section, we will review each of these complications, as well as review studies that have examined each. The reason for such lengthy discussion on each of these complications is due to the need across the criminological field to clearly understand the various types of birth complications that have been linked to future criminality by empirical studies.

Abruptio Placentae (Placental Abruption)

Abruptio placentae, also referred to as placental abruption, is a pregnancy complication in which the lining of the placenta has become separated from the mother's uterus, at some point between the halfway point (approximately 20th week) of pregnancy and birth (Denno, 1990). Such abruption is one of the most common causes of bleeding in late pregnancy, not to mention the risk to the development of the fetus/infant, as studies have shown (Usui et al., 2007). In fact, according to Denno (1990: 136), abruptio placentae "is one of the most serious accidents that can occur" in a pregnancy/delivery. Although the condition varies widely, from mild/partial detachment to complete detachment (which almost always results in the death of the infant), any form of such abruption is an extremely high risk factor for the infant(s).

It should be noted that placental abruption occurs in only approximately 1 percent of births worldwide, but when it does occur, it is extremely high-risk in terms of both the infant and mother's mortality. Of course this depends on the degree of the separation of the placental lining from the uterus of the mother. Furthermore, the heart rate of the developing infant has been linked to the degree or severity of such abruption (Usui et al., 2007).

In terms of the infant, such abruption will likely result in distress until the infant is delivered, and likely will include a premature birth. Even after such birth, the infant will likely have to be housed in an intensive care unit (ICU) due to problems regarding feeding, breathing, blood pressure, etc. (Usui et al., 2007). If such problems are not resolved, the long-term issues are likely brain damage, largely due to a lack of oxygen getting to the brain (see anoxia below). In terms of the mothers, women who experience such complications tend to have more hemorrhaging, lack of blood clotting, uterus not contracting properly after delivery, and (in severe cases) a case of shock among other vital organs, such as the pituitary, kidney, liver, etc.

There are a number of risk factors that have been identified to provide warning signs and perhaps catch this condition early on. Some of these risk factors include (see Flowers, Clark, & Westney, 1991; Denno, 1990): maternal hypertension (which is common in virtually half of all documented incidents); maternal trauma, such as falls, assaults, and driving accidents; maternal age (under 20 or older than 35); short umbilical cord; previous abruption; and heavy cocaine usage. It is important for medical professionals, as well as many others, to recognize these risk factors in terms of being able to provide an adequate intervention if so needed to address such placental abruption. After all, there are prescribed medical interventions, such as immediate delivery, blood replacement, etc., when such a condition is identified.

Although a number of studies have included abruptio placentae in examinations of the effects of birth/delivery complications and future criminality, virtually all of these studies have only included them as part of an index/scale measure. For example, Deborah Denno (1990) included abruptio placentae in her extensive study of a cohort of pregnant mothers and their infants from Philadelphia, but only as a single count in an index measure of 17 types of pregnancy/delivery complications. Other studies have followed this model as not examining such abruption separately, but only including it in an index or scale measure of birth/delivery complications (Piquero & Tibbetts, 1999). Thus, there are virtually no criminological studies that have specifically examined the effects of this serious birth complication in terms of predicting future criminality. But given the nature of this complication, as discussed above, this is the very type of birth complication that should be explored more closely in future research in terms of biosocial development and life-course models of offending.

Breech Birth (Breech Presentation)

Presentation refers to the "relation of the long axis of the fetus to the long axis of the mother" (Taylor, 1976: 188; see review in Denno, 1990: 128–131). The presentation can vary quite a bit, ranging from head first or vertex/occipital (which is typical and good), to partial face/skull presentation, to several types of being completely breeched, which is buttocks/pelvis or legs first, which is highest risk for complications (Taylor, 1976: 275; Denno, 1990: 129). Even within this category of breech, there are several categories: Footling Breech, in which feet/legs come out first; Frank Breech, in which the baby's bottom comes out first; or Complete Breech, in which the baby is crosslegged, with the knees and hips flexed. The majority of breech births are delivered via Cesarean section in the United States, which is consistent with using C-sections for high-risk deliveries (Vendittelli et al., 2008).

There are a number of risk factors that increase the probability of doctors calling for a C-section. Specifically, premature birth is one of the primary causes for such a delivery. Interestingly, about a quarter of fetuses are in breech position at close to 32 weeks of gestation, but only 3 percent of full-term infants that are delivered are in such a position because the increasing size of the fetus typically makes the body turn head-downward, which is likely due to the weight of the baby's head and its natural fit into the mother's pelvis (Vendittelli et al., 2008). It makes sense that pre-term deliveries are more likely to be breeched because they have not had the time to naturally turn downward. Other risk factors for such breech births include the mother having a prior Cesarean section pregnancy, higher or lower volume of amniotic fluid, or multifetal pregnancy, such as twins, triplets, or more fetuses (Krebs, 2005).

As with other birth complications, a breech birth is associated with high risk of anoxia, or lack of oxygen to the infant, as well as many other factors, such as squeezing the baby's torso through the pelvis before the head has gone through and further opened up the passage, that predispose the child to a higher likelihood of developing criminality. Although Denno (1990) included breech births in an index measure of birth complications that showed some significance in predicting future offending, it is impossible to make conclusions regarding this risk factor because it was only one item in a larger composite measure. However, it is likely that breech birth is a very likely factor for future research regarding biosocial effects on criminality, and it is advised that the varying degrees of breech, such as Frank Breech versus Complete Breech, be specifically analyzed.

Cesarean Section (i.e. C-section or Cesarean Birth)

Cesarean section birth is the method of delivery that involves an incision through the abdominal wall and the uterus in order to extract the fetus (Denno, 1990: 129–131). As mentioned above and below, Cesarean section birth almost always identifies as a risk factor, and is also associated with other risk factors in the sense that when other primary risk factors exist close to the delivery stage (e.g. prolapsed cord) doctors typically advise a C-section. However, to a very large extent, it is not the actual Cesarean birth that is the cause of risk, but rather a spurious, medically-advised event that occurs due to other causal factors of risk. To clarify, the fact that a mother has had a previous C-section is on virtually all measures of risk for mothers giving birth (Beaver & Wright, 2005; Denno, 1990; Taylor, 1976). But it is not the C-section itself that presents risk; on the contrary, a C-section is often performed to most successfully deal with high-risk deliveries due to other birth/

delivery complications. So although Cesarean section births should always be a "red-flag" regarding high-risk births, it should be seen as only an indicator, and not a cause, of future development in terms of criminality. Rather, it should be seen as a sign that other major issues were present, including many of the other birth complications covered in this chapter. This is likely one of the reasons why one recent study that controlled for many other birth complications found that Cesarean births did not have a significant effect on future propensities to low self-control (a consistent indicator of criminality) among such infants.

Fetal Distress

Fetal distress is a sort of "catch-all" category, in which various signs that women have just prior or during delivery tend to show that the fetus is not healthy. Due to the ambiguity of the concept, there are various definitions provided in the medical literature. It is difficult to specify what is meant by fetal distress, given the lack of precision of the term, but it could likely include any of the complications discussed elsewhere in this chapter, as well as: increased or decreased fetal heart rate (called tachycardia and bradycardia, respectively); meconium in the amniotic fluid; breathing problems by the fetus/infant; uterine rupture; and many other signs or problems. Given that this is a "catch-all" category, it is not surprising that not too many criminological studies have examined fetal distress. The one study that did include it as a single measure (Beaver & Wright, 2005) found no significant findings, probably because they also accounted for many of the other birth complications that would go into such a measure of fetal distress. Still, the concept of fetal distress should be further examined in future research on the development of infants, especially when combined with disadvantage environments, which the sole study that examined distress did not address.

Eclampsia

Varying degrees of seizures and coma present another risk factor in delivery, often referred to as eclampsia. As with other disorders, eclampsia has a wide range of degrees, ranging from tonic to clonic seizures, and the distinguishing characteristic is that such seizures did not occur before pregnancy. Although these seizures are of the mother, the biggest risk for the infant is regarding elevated blood pressure and successful delivery. Although not very common, one recent criminological study (Beaver & Wright, 2005) examined this risk factor in terms of being related to a key factor in the development of low self-control, but found no significant effect for eclampsia in predicting this personality trait of self-control that has been consistently related to criminality. Still, this factor should remain on the list of potential risk factors among birth complications being related to future offending until more studies can be performed to rule it out as an influence during the birth/delivery phase.

Meconium

Like it or not, fecal matter does matter, at least in terms of knowing a lot about what an infant has been exposed to in utero. Although not technically a birth complication, meconium refers to an infant's stool samples in their earliest day(s), which represents the most sterile form of sample that can be used to see what the child has ingested during the final stages in the womb (Jimenez et al., 2008). Such stool samples can be used to check a variety of substances or fluids that can give much insight into both the ingestion of substances by the mother, as well as nutrients that were present or lacking while in the womb. Earlier definitions of meconium referred to the mucus or bile expelled by a fetus during delivery (Denno, 1990), which was seen as a sign of fetal distress in terms of a severe irritant of the lungs. Relatedly, meconium is sometimes released into the amniotic fluid prior to or during birth (producing a distinctive brown color), but typically it is in the first stool produced by the infant after birth. Such meconium can be tested for drugs and alcohol, and thus, the local child protective offices can be notified for intervention services.

Although meconium is not exactly a birth complication, it is a very good indicator of future criminality by the infant in terms of determining what the infant ingested in the womb just prior to birth/delivery. Like a C-section (discussed above), meconium is not considered a causal factor for development of future offending behavior, but it is an indicator for determining which infants are at high risk for criminality. After all, if the meconium shows that the infant was recently exposed to drugs/alcohol or was highly deficient in receiving certain vitamins or nutrients, such a medical conclusion would throw up a "red-flag" on the potential need for intervention into the needs of such infants. Furthermore, such a finding would also likely require the local child protective agencies to intervene. Regardless, if the meconium shows deficiency in any areas for infants, they are likely to be predisposed to future offending unless measures are taken to adequately address the deficiencies or toxins that are in their bodies.

Only two notable studies have actually examined the influence of meconium on future criminality. The first was Denno (1990), which included meconium during labor, but it was only included as an item in a composite measure of birth complications, so it is impossible to make conclusions about meconium itself. A more recent study by Beaver and Wright (2005) included meconium as an independent measure, and found no significant direct support for this factor in predicting future low self-control propensities. However, no studies have examined the direct influence of meconium on future criminality, so future research should examine this birth factor.

Placenta Previa (Placenta Praevia)

Another major birth/pregnancy complication is placenta previa (or placenta praevia) in which the attachment of the placenta to the lower uterine wall covers—

either entirely or partially—the cervix, thereby blocking a clear birthing passage of the infant during delivery (Denno, 1990; Naeye, 1977). The primary risk of previa, especially with a vaginal delivery, is that it often requires trying to manipulate the head or a leg of the infant to try to go through the cervix. In this process, there is a high risk for separating the infant from the placenta and, thus, increasing the amount of bleeding as well as cutting off the blood and oxygen/nutrient supply to the infant.

There is no established cause of this complication, but it is believed to be associated with prior trauma or infections in the embryonic/fetal stages, particularly those involving some form of scarring (Weerasekera, 2000). As with other types of birth complications, the risk of damage from placenta previa matters by the degree to which it occurs. Specifically, there are at least four types identified by the medical literature, ranging from Type I or the placenta being low-lying but not infringing on the cervix, to Type IV, meaning that the placenta completely blocks the top of the cervix (Bhide & Thilaganathan, 2004).

According to Weerasekera (2000) some of the key risk factors of placenta previa involve mother's smoking or drug usage, mothers who are older than 35 or younger than 20, mothers with a large placenta from previous births or having twins, or mothers with scarring from previous deliveries (such as a previous D&C or Cesarean delivery). Although previa has traditionally been treated as a serious birth complication, modern medical research has allowed for relatively minor forms of previa, especially if diagnosed early on, to be treated and monitored with virtually no risk to the infant or mother. When acute and serious forms are discovered, such as at the delivery phase, previa tends to pose far more risk to the infant, and typically a Cesarean delivery is advised. Unfortunately, sometimes there are not adequate resources for a C-section, in which case every effort should be made that blood volume and plasma are readily available, in order to ensure healthy blood pressure and essential nutrients are provided. Furthermore, in such vaginal births, there are high risks for the fetus if the head cannot be moved down and positioned for delivery, which can result in the use of forceps, which is a notable risk factor for youths born using such devices (Denno, 1990). Studies have shown that mothers who experience placenta previa tend to have severe post-partum haemorrhage, sometimes requiring a total abdominal hysterectomy (Weerasekera, 2000). Thus, this birth complication is quite risky for both the infant and the mother.

As with abruptio placenta discussed above, similar types of risk for the infant (and the mother) are typically experienced by those who have placenta previa, in terms of loss of blood pressure, heart rate, etc. Perhaps most importantly, previa can lead to hypoxia/anoxia, and even seconds, let alone minutes, of such deprivation of oxygen in an infant can be detrimental. Such complications early in life are bound to have an impact on development and future criminality. Although some criminological studies have measured placenta previa, virtually all of these studies have included the existence of this complication in an index measure of birth complications (see Denno, 1990; Piquero & Tibbetts, 1999). Thus, it is difficult to say if previa has any association with future criminality, and it is advised that future research on placenta previa be conducted, because it appears to be a likely influence on the behavioral patterns of the children who experienced this birth complication.

Prolapsed Cord and Wrapped Cord

A prolapse of the umbilical cord is when membranes are ruptured due to the cord lying below or alongside the presenting part of the fetus (Denno, 1990: 132). Like the other birth complications examined above, there are various degrees of prolapse, varying from the cord being near the pelvis but can't be reached, to the extreme of the cord protruding outside the vagina. When the fetus moves down through the cervix in this situation, there is a lot of pressure on the cord, which tends to cut off blood supply, which can result in an acute state of lack of oxygen, nutrients, blood, etc. Like other birth complications, it tends to be associated with other delivery complications (e.g. rupture of the amniotic sac), and if it is not readily identified and dealt with it can lead to the death of the infant. However, if the prolapse is of a lesser degree or medical intervention prevents such tragedy, it is still likely that such prolapse will lead to other issues, such as anoxia, malpositions, issues regarding amniotic fluid, etc. (Denno, 1990; Taylor, 1976). Typically, a Cesarean section is performed due to the obvious complications involved with a vaginal pregnancy, but even then there are inherent risks.

Risk factors of mothers experiencing a prolapsed cord include many of the same of those of other birth complications, but some other notable risks are long umbilical cord, breech delivery, fetal malpresentation, and pelvic tumors (Decherney & Nathan, 2007). Past studies that have examined a prolapsed cord in predicting youth health and development have found that this birth complication is predictive of neurological disorders and mental retardation (for a review, see Taylor, 1976). More recent studies on prolapsed cord are somewhat consistent with this prior finding. Specifically, some studies have included the existence of prolapsed cord in indexes of the measure of birth complications (Denno, 1990; Piquero & Tibbetts, 1999). However, these more recent studies have implicated such index measures in the development of violent offending, so it is impossible to determine how much this one item contributed to the effect that the overall index had on future criminality. Thus, it is advised that future research be devoted to examining the sole affect of varying degrees of prolapsed cords on the development of future offending behavior.

Another similar type of birth complication is that of a wrapped umbilical cord, which includes both tight forms (even up to eight loops around the neck) and loose forms. However, a review of studies concluded that "In most cases, loose loops around the neck are not harmful to the infant. However, loops may become tight enough to constrict blood vessels and induce … hypoxia, premature separation of the placenta, fetal distress" (Denno, 1990: 133). In fact, Naeye (1977) claimed that a tight cord wrap in the neck region was one of the key causes of infant mortality. The risk factors involved in wrapped cords are very similar to those of prolapsed cords. However, virtually no studies have specifically examined the association between such wrapped cords and the development of criminality. One exception is Denno (1990), but this study included wrapped cords in an index measure with many other pregnancy and birth complications, so although the index measure in this study had some influence on development of criminality, no solid conclusions can be made directly regarding wrapped cords. Nevertheless, wrapped cords in birthing should be given far more attention in future criminological research, especially in the area of biosocial/developmental perspectives.

Low Birth-Weight (and Early Gestational Delivery)

Low birth-weight has been defined by virtually all medical professionals as being under 5.5 pounds (or the international equivalent) at the time of birth. It is obvious that infants that are under a healthy weight at the time of birth are likely at high risk of many developmental disorders, regardless of what caused such low weight at birth. It is also notable that this is one of the aspects of birth complications that has been studied directly along with interactional effects in the criminological literature.

Specifically, empirical studies have closely examined not only the effect of low birth weight, but also the interactional effects this factor has when combined with disadvantaged familial environments in which the child is raised. For example, Tibbetts and Piquero (1999) found in a cohort sample of close to 1,000 youth born in inner-city Philadelphia that the combination of low birth-weight and lower socio-economic class significantly predicted which youth would commit an offense at an early age (which is one of the strongest predictors of which individuals will become chronic, violent offenders in the future). Furthermore, the authors reported that the finding was only valid regarding males in their population, not females. Given that this study was based on only one sample from only one city, it remains to be seen how robust the findings of this study are, especially regarding the interactional effects with social/environmental factors. Also, McGloin and Pratt (2003) found that the interaction between low birth-weight and cognitive abilities was highly predictive of future delinquent behaviors. In addition, a recent study by Ratchford and Beaver (2009), using a sample from the National Survey of Children, showed that measures of birth complications and low birth-weight had significant effects on levels of self-control, which is one of the key personality traits that have been linked to delinquency.

So while studies appear to find a consistent association between low birth-weight and criminality, virtually no criminological studies have examined the effects of extremely low birth-weight, defined as under three pounds (or the international equivalent), on future criminality. It is likely that this group will be even more at high risk for engaging in offending behavior in their development, especially when coupled with familial/social variables. Thus, this remains a key area that future criminological research should explore.

Regarding early gestational deliveries, there is an association between race and social class with the average gestational age of infants at delivery. For example,

Denno (1990: 154) found that among her sample, the mean gestational age was approximately 38 weeks for Blacks and over 40 weeks for Whites in her sample. As she stated (154), "short gestational age has been linked to numerous prenatal and perinatal complications as well as adverse outcome for the fetus." Furthermore, preterm (premature) birth medically refers to the birth of a baby who is less than 37 weeks of gestational age. Before approximately 37 weeks, a baby has not entirely developed mature organs to allow normal postnatal development and/or survival. Thus, such infants are at much higher risk for both short- and long-term disabilities and complications (Steer, 2005). Virtually no criminological studies have examined the effects of delivery at pre-gestational age of delivery on future offending behavior. Like most other birth complications examined in this chapter, gestational age is a key area that future empirical studies on future criminality should examine. Furthermore, studies should also specifically examine infants who are born with extremely limited gestational age, such as those born at 35, or even fewer, weeks of gestational age.

Apgar Scores

When an infant is born, a series of diagnostic measures are taken, which largely comprise the infant's Apgar score. The Apgar is an acronym meaning: appearance, pulse, grimace, activity, respiration. This score/acronym was created by Dr. Virginia Apgar in 1952 and is a fast and efficient way to assess a newborn's health, as well as to simplify it so that it could be easily used by other medical staff at other hospitals. Put simply, a score of 7–10 is normal/good, 4–6 is low (infant at risk), and scores of 3 and below are very high risk. These scores are typically taken for each infant at 1 minute of life, 5 minutes, 10 minutes, and 20 minutes after birth.

Despite the Apgar score being used nearly universally in developed countries over the last few decades, there are very few studies of Apgar scores reported in the criminological literature. To date, perhaps the only study that has been done linking low scores on Apgar to future offending is that of Gibson and Tibbetts (1998). This study found that low 1-minute scores on the Apgar were associated with criminal offending, particularly when the mother smoked during pregnancy. Another recent study found that in a cohort study of approximately 177,000 male infants born throughout Sweden between 1973 and 1976, infants with low Apgar scores were significantly more likely to have a low IQ score later in life, specifically at age 16 (Odd, Rasmussen, Gunnell, Lewis, & Whitelaw, 2008). Although there have only been a couple of studies that have examined the predictive effects of Apgar scores on future offending, both of them have found significant findings, with the first implicating an interactional effect with behavior by the mother (namely, smoking tobacco during pregnancy), and the second implicating a possible interaction between Apgar scores at birth and later cognitive abilities. Thus, it appears that Apgar scores should be a key concept that criminologists should focus on in future research on biosocial development.

Anoxia

Anoxia is the medical term used to describe a fetus/infant not getting enough oxygen to the brain, which is obviously very critical in terms of the development in the fetal/embryonic stages. It should be noted that anoxia generally refers to a massive (even total) decrease in oxygen levels, whereas a more mild form of oxygen deficiency is referred to as hypoxia. Hypoxia will not be examined in this chapter, but it is very likely that any form of low oxygen levels, no matter how mild—such as those categorized as hypoxia—are still potential risk factors in terms of embryonic/fetal and infant development.

Regarding anoxia, as Denno (1990: 157) claimed, "lack of oxygen to the brain, is suggested as the primary correlate of prenatal brain damage." Although lack of oxygen to the brain can occur throughout pregnancy, it is likely that the time an infant/fetus is most vulnerable to anoxia is during delivery, due to the high level of shifting and movement of the fetus during the delivery. Denno also noted several birth or infant related factors that tend to increase the risk of anoxia/hypoxia, such as prolapsed umbilical cord, low birth-weight, pre-term deliveries, abruptio placentae, etc. There were other specific complications given by Denno, but it is likely that most of the many complications that can occur during pregnancy are likely to result in lack of oxygen to the brain of the fetus/infant.

To date there have been very few published criminological studies regarding the effects of anoxia on future offending by fetuses or infants that suffered from this perinatal disorder, and yet the small amount of research that has been done on anoxia is an obvious area for further study (Beaver & Wright, 2005). To illustrate, Beaver and Wright used a sample from the Early Childhood Longitudinal Study-Kindergarten Class of 1998–99, to predict which of various birth complications predicted low self-control (one of the strongest predictors of criminality). They found that anoxia was the only birth complication (out of seven) that had a consistent and significant, direct effect on such disposition after controlling for other factors. However, it is notable that other birth complications had a significant, rather inconsistent effect, such as premature (i.e. early gestational age), eclampsia, and meconium, on at least some measures of low self-control. Given these findings, although from one data set, it appears that birth complications, especially anoxia, are quite worthy of further study by criminologists in future research.

Other Various Birth Complications

There are many more birth/delivery complications that are warranted more attention that were not discussed previously, as pointed out by Denno (1990). Such conditions include: forceps marks at delivery; sinus rapture; use of oxytocic during labor; plurality of birth; diabetic mother; use of sedatives during delivery; venereal conditions of the mother (which is even more important in current times given the prevalence of HIV); neurological and psychiatric conditions of the mother; anesthetic shock during pregnancy; uterine bleeding during pregnancy;

and fetal death or premature birth of siblings. We did not have space in this chapter to explore these other notable birth complications, but all of them warrant far more attention by criminologists in future research. Like most of the primary birth complications we discussed at length in this chapter, future researchers are strongly encouraged to examine the *direct associations* these complications have on the long-term development of infants, as opposed to simply including them in an index or composite measure of birth complications. By directly measuring and estimating the effects of single complications on criminality, there will be less ambiguity regarding which types of birth disorders are actually driving some of the reported influences of such scale measures. Furthermore, it is strongly suggested that future research also examine the interactional or conditional effects these individual complications have when coupled with disadvantaged environments, such as low socio-economic status, single-headed households, disruptive/abusive home environment, etc.

Birth/Delivery Complications Interacting With Environmental Factors

According to a review by Raine (2002), a number of studies have shown that infants who suffer birth complications are significantly more likely to develop delinquency, conduct disorder, and violent tendencies in adulthood, especially violent acts that are impulsive (also see Arsenault et al., 2002; McGloin & Pratt, 2003). Raine (2002: 62) also pointed out the importance of not simply examining birth complications by themselves in predisposing antisocial and criminal behavior, but "may require the presence of negative environmental circumstance to trigger later adult crime and violence." More recent studies have supported this claim of a biosocial interaction between delivery complications and maladaptive environments (Wu, Ma, & Carter, 2004; Turner, Hartman, & Bishop, 2007; for a recent review, see Beaver, 2009).

There has also been a consistent finding of intimate personal violence (IPV), clearly an environmental factor, associated with various birth complications, such as low birth-weight (for a review, see Sharps, Laughon, & Giangrande, 2007). Other studies have provided strong support for the influence of IPV on both a variety of birth complications, as well as the strong association of IPV in perinatal stages with long-term disadvantaged household environments (for a review, see Tibbetts, 2011). Furthermore, studies have shown that infants having such birth complications, such as low birth-weight, actually increase the risk that such young children will be abused or neglected (Sidebotham & Hweon, 2006). This is likely to be a spurious effect from the pre-birth environment, but is also possibly due to some parents or caregivers being less patient (or even hostile) to infants who have such developmental disorders. A seemingly common paradox is that the population of infants who are most risk to suffer the various birth complications are often the most likely to also face the most adverse, maladaptive environments in their household/neighborhood (Tibbetts, 2011). Such coupling of both physiological and environmental problems obviously predisposes such infants to future criminality, a type of "double-whammy" in terms of risk factors. Even worse, given the nature of such biosocial interactive effects that tend to be non-linear or exponential (i.e. the total risk is far greater than the sum of the parts), rather than linear, it actually is more like a "triple-whammy" or worse, at least in terms of risk.

Intervention Programs

The good news is that there is a "light" at the end of the tunnel. Specifically, empirical evaluations have shown much promise with home-visitations by nurses to households of high-risk infants and toddlers, many of whom had some (or many) of the birth complications reviewed above (Olds, Henderson, & Robert, 1998). A comprehensive review of the positive aspects of such programs was recently reviewed by Olds (2007), and he provides some key insights on the type(s) of programming that can make a big difference in counteracting some of the negative effects of birth complications. Because the existence of perinatal factors such as birth complications cannot be reversed or taken back, obviously much of his review emphasizes the medical practitioners and others working with the families to attempt negating their detrimental impact, especially in terms of working toward a prosocial environment (as opposed to a maladaptive one) in the infants' households and rearing. Still, such programs and others (for reviews of such early intervention programs, see Beaver, 2009; Tibbetts, 2009, 2011) can certainly go a long way toward reducing the risk that such youth will go on to a life of crime. Specifically, a recent story in *Time* magazine (November 1, 2010: 41), citing research from the National Academy of Sciences, reported that for every dollar spent by public-health programs on prevention of central nervous system disorders and mental illness among young children (often associated with perinatal complications) is likely to be paid back as much as *28 times* over the course of a lifetime. Other researchers have promoted the cost-efficient nature of such early interventions in such high-risk youth (e.g., Wright et al., 2008; Beaver, 2009), but this figure was even higher than virtually all criminologists had estimated.

In addition to such recent success in such programs, there are several statistics that have been presented that reassure us that medical technology, not just in the United States, is developing to try to curb some of these birth complications. Specifically, *Time* magazine very recently reported, citing research from the World Health Organization, that the maternal mortality rate (which is very highly related to birth/delivery complications) has been reduced in Ethiopia from a 2000 rate of 750 mothers per 100,000 births to 470 in 2008, which is just one example "reflecting a global trend" (*Time*, December 6, 2010: 21). The article went on to say that "many nations have made progress toward reducing the number of women dying from complications during pregnancy and childbirth, in part by training more midwives and increasing female education" (*Time*, December 6, 2010: 21). However, the article also notes that the majority of the world's maternal deaths (and thus birth complications in general) occur in sub-Saharan Africa and South Asia. Although the research and theorizing in this chapter has been somewhat specific to the United States, it is quite likely that the implications of the research and extant literature discussed above regarding various birth complications and programs for intervening in such cases transcend this nation and apply to countries worldwide. Given the obvious comparison between Olds and his colleagues' evaluations of nurse-visitations to the noted training of midwives and other social workers in such places as Africa, this supports the proposition that such implications from modern criminological and medical research have been utilized on a grand scale.

Conclusion

In this chapter, we reviewed the vital importance of birth/delivery complications, and the profound impact they have on the future development of youth, especially in terms of criminality. A variety of birth complications were reviewed in detail, largely for the purpose of informing criminologists and other researchers who have not been typically trained to understand what these disorders are exactly, as well as the risk factors and related issues involved with each. This chapter also summarized some of the key studies that have implicated birth complications in the development of chronic offending among such youth, especially when compounded with disadvantaged environments in their early life. Finally, we discussed some promising intervention programs for such high-risk youth that have suffered from such delivery complications. Ultimately, a significant amount of recent research has been done in trying to understand the level of such birth complications in affecting the development of an individual, but the bottom-line is that far more research must be done to specify the direct, indirect, and interactive effects that these various complications have on future criminality.

References

Arsenault, L., Tremblay, R. E., Boulerice, B., & Saucier, J. F. (2002). Obstetrical complications and violent delinquency: Testing two developmental pathways. *Child Development, 73,* 496–508.

Beaver, K. M. (2009). *Biosocial Criminology: A Primer.* Dubuque: Kendall/Hunt.

Beaver, K. M., & Wright, J. (2005). Evaluating the effects of birth complications on low self-control in a sample of twins. *International of Offender Therapy and Comparative Criminology, 49(4),* 450–471.

Bhide, A., & Thilaganathan, B. (2004). Recent advances in the management of placenta previa. *Current Opinion Obstetrical Gynecology, 16(6),* 447–451.

Cocchi, R., Felici, M., Tonni, L., & Venanzi, G. (1984). Behavior troubles in nursery school children and their possible relationship to pregnancy or delivery difficulties. *Acta Psychiatrica Belgica, 84*, 173–179.

Decherney, Alan H., & Nathan, Lauren. (2007). *Obstetric and Gynecologic Diagnosis and Treatment*, 10th edition. New York: McGraw-Hill.

Denno, D. (1990). *Biology and Violence: From Birth to Adulthood*. Cambridge: Cambridge University Press.

Flowers, D., Clark, J. F., & Westney, L. S. (1991). Cocaine intoxication associated with abruption placentae. *Journal of the National Medical Association, 83(3)*, 230–232.

Gibson, C., & Tibbetts, S. (1998). Interaction between maternal cigarette smoking and Apgar scores in predicting offending. *Psychological Reports, 83*, 579–586.

Jimenez, E., Marin, M., Martin, R., Odriozola, J., Olivares, M., Xaus, J., Leonides, F., & Rodriguez, J. (2008). Is meconium from healthy newborns actually sterile? *Research in Microbiology, 159(3)*, 187–193.

Krebs, L. (2005). Breech at term: Early and late consequences of mode of delivery. *Danish Medical Bulletin, 52(4)*, 234–252.

McGloin, J. M., & Pratt, T. (2003). Cognitive ability and delinquent behavior among inner-city youth: A life-course analysis of main, mediating and interaction effects. *International Journal of Offender Therapy and Comparative Criminology, 47*, 253–271.

Naeye, R. L. (1977). Causes of perinatal mortality in the U.S. Collaborative Perinatal Project. *Journal of the American Medical Association, 238(3)*, 228–229.

Odd, D. Rasmussen, F., Gunnell, D., Lewis, G., & Whitelaw, A. (2008). A cohort study of low Apgar scores and cognitive outcomes. *Archives of Disease in Childhood: Fetal and Neonatal Education, 93*, 115–120.

Olds, D. L. (2007). Preventing crime with prenatal and infancy support of parents: The nurse-family partnership. *Victims & Offenders, 2*, 205–225.

Olds, D. L., Henderson, C. R., & Robert, C. (1998). Long-term effects of nurse home visitation on children's criminal and antisocial behavior. *Journal of the American Medical Association, 280*, 1238–1244.

Pasamanick, B., Rodgers, M. E., & Lilienfield, A. M. (1956). Pregnancy experience and development of behavior disorders in children. *American Journal of Psychiatry, 112*, 613–618.

Piquero, A., & Tibbetts, S. (1999). The impact of pre/perinatal disturbances and disadvantaged familial environment in predicting criminal offending. *Studies on Crime and Crime Prevention, 8*, 52–70.

Raine, A. (1993). *The Psychopathology of Crime: Criminal Behavior as a Clinical Disorder*. San Diego: Academic Press.

Raine, A. (2002). Biosocial studies of antisocial and violent behavior in children and adults: A review. *Journal of Abnormal Child Psychology, 30*, 311–326.

Raine, A., Brennan, P., & Mednick, S. A. (1994). Birth complications combined with early maternal rejection at age 1 year predispose to violent crime at age 18 years. *Archives of General Psychiatry, 51*, 984–988.

Ratchford, M., & Beaver, K. M. (2009). Neuropsychological deficits, low self-control, and delinquent involvement: Toward a biosocial explanation of delinquency. *Criminal Justice and Behavior, 36,* 147–162.

Sharps, P. W., Laughon, K., & Giangrande, S. K. (2007). Intimate partner violence and the childbearing year: Maternal and infant health consequences. *Trauma, Violence & Abuse, 8,* 105–116.

Sidebotham, P., & Hweon, J. (2006). Child maltreatment in the "children of the nineties": A cohort study of risk factors. *Child Abuse & Neglect, 30,* 497–522.

Steer, P. (2005). The epidemiology of preterm labor. *British Journal of Obstetrics and Gynaecology, 112,* 1–6.

Taylor, E. S. (1976). *Beck's Ostetrical Practice and Fetal Medicine* (10th ed.). Baltimore: Williams & Wilkins.

Tibbetts, S. G. (2009). Perinatal and developmental determinants of early onset of offending: A biosocial approach for explaining the two peaks of early antisocial behavior. In J. Savage (ed.), *The Development of Persistent Criminality.* New York: Oxford University Press, pp. 179–200.

Tibbetts, S. G. (2011). Prenatal and perinatal predictors of antisocial behavior: Review of research and interventions. In M. DeLisi & K. M. Beaver (eds.), *Criminological Theory: A Life-Course Approach.* Sudbury, MA: Jones & Bartlett, pp. 31–50.

Tibbetts, S. G., & Piquero, A. (1999). The influence of gender, low birth weight, and disadvantaged environment in predicting early onset of offending: A test of Moffitt's interactional hypothesis. *Criminology, 37,* 843–878.

Time. (November 1, 2010). Keeping young minds healthy. 40–50.

Time. (December 6, 2010). Maternal mortality in Ethiopia. 21.

Turner, M. G., Hartman, J. L., & Bishop, D. M. (2007). The effects of prenatal problems, family functioning, and neighborhood disadvantage in predicting life-course persistent offending. *Criminal Justice & Behavior, 34,* 1241–1261.

Usui, R., Matsubara, S., Ohkuchi, A., Watanabe, T., Izumi, A., & Suzuki, M. (2007). Fetal heart rate pattern reflecting the severity of placental abruption. *Archives of Gynecology and Obstetrics, 277(3),* 249–253.

Vendittelli, F., Riviere, O., Crenn-Hebert, C., Rozan, M., Maria, B., & Jacquetin, B. (2008). Is a breech presentation at term more frequent in women with a history of cesarean delivery? *American Journal of Obstetrics and Gynecology, 198(6),* 521–538.

Weerasekera, D. S. (2000). Placenta praevia and scarred uterus – an obstetrician's dilemma. *Journal of Obstetrics and Gynaecology, 20(5),* 484–485.

Wright, J. P., Tibbetts, S. G., & Daigle, L. (2008). *Criminals in the Making: Criminality Across the Life Course.* Thousand Oaks, CA: Sage.

Wu, S. S., Ma, C., & Carter, R. L. (2004). Risk factors for infant maltreatment: A population-based study. *Child Abuse & Neglect, 28,* 1253–1264.

Presaging Problem Behavior: The Mutuality of Child Temperament, Parenting, and Family Environments from Gestation to Age Three

Matt DeLisi and Michael G. Vaughn

The history of man for the nine months preceding his birth would, probably, be far more interesting and contain events of greater moment than all the three score and ten years that follow it.

Samuel Taylor Coleridge (1885, cited in DiPietro, Ghera, & Costigan, 2008)

Parenting sets in motion an avalanche of enduring effects that generalize throughout and beyond the family.

Gerald Patterson, Marion Forgatch, and David DeGarmo (2010)

Introduction

Historically considered to be competitors for explanatory prominence, today it is understood that individual-level traits and environmental contexts work together in complex ways to produce behavioral outcomes. In this way, biological variables and social variables are part of the same equation, or as Feldman (2008) elegantly stated, "At the moment of conception, and perhaps earlier, environment begins to impinge on the developing brain" (p. 235). The nature and nurture/individual and context dynamic is especially true for the study of antisocial behavior which encompasses an extraordinary swath of behavioral styles and life stages ranging from self-regulation and emotional expression during infancy through criminal behavior during adulthood. Perhaps nowhere is this dynamic more illustrative than the interrelationship between child temperament, parenting, and family environments during the first years of life. Whereas some temperamental profiles lend themselves to relatively easy and uneventful parenting interactions, others do not, and it is in these challenging family situations where the seeds of potentially lifelong problem behaviors are sown.

Here we review research on child temperamental profiles occurring from gestation to age three that likely presage problem behaviors because of their role in self-regulation deficits and the expression of negative emotionality. As suggested by prior researchers (e.g. Bowlby, 1969, 1988; Calkins & Keane, 2009; Kagan, 1994, 2003; Thomas & Chess, 1977), adverse temperamental styles in turn contribute to problematic parenting that serves to exacerbate the underlying dispositional liabilities. This leads to an ongoing snowball-like developmental process that places individuals at significant risk for future conduct problems.

Temperamental Profiles from Gestation to Age Three

It is commonly understood that gestation is an environment. Like all environments, positive inputs serve to enhance the human and social development and negative inputs serve to jeopardize the human and social development of those within a particular environment. And it is also true that each individual brings to every environmental context a unique temperamental profile, a profile that is moderated by or transcends that context. An intriguing literature examines the fetal development of infant temperament. DiPietro and her colleagues conducted a study of 31 fetuses at six gestational ages between 20 and 39 weeks and also gathered data on maternal reports of the infant's apparent temperament at ages three and again at six months. They found that fetal neurobehavior accounted for between 22 and 60 percent of variance in the prediction of temperament scores. More specifically, higher fetal heart rate was associated with lower emotional tone, lower activity level, and unpredictability. Even more fascinating, more active fetuses were more difficult, and had greater difficulty adapting as infants (DiPietro, Hodgson, Costigan, & Johnson, 1996). A similar profile is seen among "regulatory disordered infants" which is defined as being behaviorally difficult and demonstrating disturbances in sleep, feeding, state control, self-calming, and mood regulation (DeGangi, DiPietro, Greenspan, & Porges, 1991).

A related study examined the effects of maternal emotional activation during pregnancy on fetal response, and whether that fetal response had enduring predictive power on infant temperament at six weeks. Fetuses with greater intensity in their reaction to their mother watching a birth video, particularly the birth scene, demonstrated greater irritability during their six-week developmental pediatric exam (DiPietro et al., 2008). In a study of prenatal dopamine levels among mothers and the temperamental expression of their neonates in the first weeks of life, Field and colleagues (2008) found that low dopamine levels among women during pregnancy was associated with the expression of negative emotionality and low orienting skills among infants during the first two weeks of life. The neonates in the high dopamine group, on the other hand, had better overall autonomic stability and excitability.

Still another area of research has studied temperament among very preterm neonates. An advantage of this approach is the direct observation of children whose physiological maturity is comparable to fetuses. Klein, Gaspardo, Martinez, Grunau, and Linhares (2009) recently investigated 26 preterm infants to examine if neonatal biobehavioral reactivity and recovery from pain and distress was associated with temperament later in toddlerhood. They found that neonates with greater reactivity to stress and pain had greater negative affect and fear according to scores on mother's report. Early physiological responses among preterm infants measured in the first three hours of life have also been found to predict later illness severity during infancy (Saria, Rajani, Gould, Koller, & Penn, 2010).

Braungart-Rieker, Hill-Soderlund, and Karrass (2010) examined infant anger and fear reactivity among a sample of 143 mothers and infants who visited a laboratory at four, eight, 12, and again at 16 months. They found that maternal ratings of temperamental fear and anger (as measured by the Infant Behavior Questionnaire; Rothbart, 1981) predicted laboratory ratings of fear and anger, respectively. Moreover, infants characterized by reduced self-regulatory ability demonstrated greater anger reactivity across the study period. Others have found that infants who at four months are characterized as extreme in display of negative emotionality and motor arousal continue to display this profile at age four (Fox, Henderson, Rubin, Calkins, & Schmidt, 2001; also see Fox & Henderson, 1999). In related work, He et al. (2010) found that infants who were highly anger-prone had greater approach and less withdrawal behaviors with commensurate left frontal EEG asymmetry.

In a prospective study of children ages two and three, Earls and Jung (1987) found that two temperamental characteristics, low adaptability and high intensity of emotional expression, at age two accounted for 30 percent of variance in problem behaviors at age three. It is often the case that early emerging behavioral problems segue into more challenging conduct disorders. Drawing on data from a New Zealand birth cohort, Moffitt and Caspi (2001) found that boys and girls who ultimately became life-course-persistent offenders had temperaments characterized as difficult at age two and undercontrolled at age three. These future chronic offenders were also hyperactive, aggressive, and had an array of neuropsychological deficits. Ebstein and colleagues (1998) examined the role of the dopamine D4 reception (DRD4) and the serotonin transporter (5HTTLPR) in the determination of neonatal temperament. They found that polymorphisms in the DRD4 gene were associated with anger display, interest/attention to structured play, and activity level during a free play session. Significant temperament effects by 5HTTLPR genotype were found for fear response to a stranger and experience of positive emotionality during structured play. Infants with risk alleles for both polymorphisms demonstrated the lowest looking/attention during block play.

Schmidt, Fox, Perez-Edgar, and Hamer (2009) examined the linkages between temperament, frontal brain asymmetry, and polymorphisms in the DRD4 gene in an infant sample. They discovered that children who at nine months exhibited left frontal EEG asymmetry and who possessed the long allele for DRD4 (which is associated with approach-related behaviors such as novelty seeking) were more easily soothed at age 48 months. Infants at nine months with right frontal EEG asymmetry and the long allele of DRD4 demonstrated difficulties with sustained attention and focusing compared to carriers of the short allele. Other research has implicated additional polymorphisms in the dopaminergic system (e.g. DAT1, DRD2, DRD4, and COMT) that are significantly associated with differences in attention among infants age nine months (Holmboe et al., 2010). Still other research reported that behavioral inhibition measured as early as four months was associated with substance-abuse related problems in adolescence particularly when inhibited children were also high scoring on risk taking (Williams et al., 2010).

In utero and in the first moments of life, there are clear temperamental differences in terms of children's self-regulation and reactivity to environmental conditions. And theory and research have consistently documented a generally difficult temperamental style among infants and toddlers that broadly and consistently centers on three constructs. The first relates to *activity level* that is characterized by high-intensity approach behaviors. Variously known as extraversion or surgency, activity level manifests in impulsive, sensation-seeking behaviors. The second broad dimension of temperament centers on *negative emotionality* which is characterized by feelings of anger, fear, sadness, discomfort, and anxiety. Individuals with high levels of negative emotionality are more aversive or annoying, traits that are conducive for negative social interactions. The third global dimension is known as *self-control*, effortful control, or inhibitory control and it relates to the ability of an individual to regulate and modulate behavior in the face of impulses.

Parenting and Family Environments

A robust literature has documented the importance of parenting behaviors and the ways that positive parenting practices contribute to prosocial development, the ways that negative parenting practices contribute to antisocial development, and the ways that child temperamental traits interact with parenting practices to produce maladaptive outcomes (e.g., Barrett & Fleming, 2011; Bowlby, 1969; Derryberry & Rothbart, 1997; Kochanska, Friesenborg, Lange, & Martel, 2004; Moffitt & Caspi, 2001; Quay, Routh, & Shapiro, 1987; Thomas & Chess, 1977; van Ijzendoorn, Schuengel, & Bakermans-Kranenburg, 1999). For instance, positive emotionality is generally speaking a positive temperamental construct, but it is also associated with high levels of approach behaviors which can be maladaptive. But when children have high positive emotionality and effortful control in parental interactions, they have better self-regulation (Kochanska, Aksan, Penney, & Doobay, 2007). In isolation, specific temperamental facets such as hyperactivity and poor attention/orienting skills that are suggestive of neuropsychological deficits can give way to problem behaviors (Farrington & Welsh, 2007; Moffitt, 1990, 1993; Murray, Irving,

Farrington, Colman, & Bloxsom, 2010; White, Moffitt, Earls, Robins, & Silva, 1990), but when these deficits are amplified by low parental investment, low parental cognitive stimulation, low parental emotional attachment, maternal controlling behavior, and other problematic parenting behaviors, conduct problems are even more likely (Moffitt, 1993; Murray et al., 2010). Indeed, weak maternal monitoring, harsh discipline, inconsistent discipline, frequent changes in caregivers, and mother psychiatric problems coupled with difficult temperaments at age two give rise to lifelong conduct problems (Moffitt & Caspi, 2001).

An assortment of studies has demonstrated the ways that parents contribute to the regulatory and reactive problems of their children. The mechanism by which this happens mostly stems from poor recognition by the parent of the temperamental tendencies of their children and the ways in which parents can modify their home environments to be more in sync with their child's disposition. For example, research has found that children who at six months of age look at frustrating events, such as the removal of a toy, are more likely to be aggressive at age 2.5 years. Moreover, infants who shift attention away from frustrating events are less aggressive. Furthermore, when mothers did not help high reactive infants shift attention away from frustration, the child was more likely to be aggressive later (Crockenberg, Leerkes, & Barrig Jo, 2008).

Whereas most parents are able to weather the storm of challenging temperamental displays during early life (e.g., the terrible twos), others are not (Pierce et al., 2010). For example, Pauli-Pott and Beckmann (2007) found among a German sample of parents and their infants assessed prospectively from age four months to 30 months that infant negative emotionality and parental conflict were potent predictors of behavioral inhibition. Moreover, infants with temperaments characterized by frequent and pervasive negative emotionality developed more serious behavior problems when reared in homes characterized by parental conflict. Even if infants express high levels of anger, the negative emotionality is mitigated when they develop cooperative bonds with their parents (Kochanska, Aksan, & Carlson, 2005).

Hayden and her colleagues (2010) conducted a gene x environment interaction study that examined the brain-derived neurotrophic factor (BDNF) gene, parental depression, parental relationship discord, and negative emotionality among children age three. Specifically, a single nucleotide polymorphism produces a valine (val)-to-methionine (met) substitution at codon 66 of the BDNF gene that is associated with negative emotionality. Hayden and colleagues found that children with at least one BDNF met allele displayed higher levels of negative emotionality, but only when there was parental discord or parent history of depressive disorder. When these family dynamics or family depressive history was not present, the met allele was associated with very low expression of negative emotionality.

Others used molecular genetic association designs to examine the interplay of genes and environment on the development of self-control. Kochanska, Philibert, and Barry (2009) examined the polymorphism in the serotonin transporter gene (5HTTLPR) and its interaction with maternal attachment at age 15 months on self-regulation at 25, 38, and 52 months. Children at genetic risk (the short ss/sl allele of

5HTTLPR) who were insecurely attached had poor regulatory capacities, children at genetic risk but secure attachment had normal self-regulatory capacity. Still others examined neuroregulatory behaviors among neonates. Auerbach and her colleagues (2005) assessed 158 healthy male infants some of whom were at familial risk for ADHD based on paternal symptoms of the disorder. They found that children at risk for ADHD had state organization and regulation difficulties pertaining to irritability, state lability, and self-quieting ability. These neuroregulatory problems were also seen when children were accessed at age seven months. Importantly, parents with ADHD symptoms demonstrate the very impairments that contribute to suboptimal forms of parenting.

Based on data from the Early Childhood Longitudinal Study-Kindergarten Class 1998–1999, Beaver, Wright, and DeLisi (2007) found that neuropsychological deficits were associated with self-control in kindergarten and first grade, but so were a host of parenting behaviors. These included parental involvement and parental affection where higher levels resulted in greater child self-control, and parental withdrawal and physical punishment where higher levels resulted in reduced child self-control. Similarly, Leve, Kim, and Pears (2005) from the Oregon Social Learning Center reported that girls who were assessed as highly impulsive at age five were prone to externalizing behaviors at age 17. Highly impulsive girls were also subjected to harsher parental discipline and this moderation effect further increased problem behaviors. Drawing on data from the Minnesota Twin Family Study, Derringer, Krueger, Irons, and Iacono (2010) found that harsh discipline characterized by being hit in the face or hit with an object by parents was associated with multiple problem behaviors through age 25, including antisocial behavior, conduct disorder, alcohol use, and tobacco use.

Pediatric psychology researchers have found that infant persistence or how often the infant seeks parental attention and then continues to fuss when his or her mother is unresponsive has been linked to aggression at age two and conduct problems during the preschool years (Shaw, Bell, & Gilliom, 2000). Moreover, fussiness during infancy coupled with maternal responsiveness often leads to aversive mother–child interactions. In their longitudinal research, for example, Lahey and his colleagues (2008) found that infant fussiness during the first year of life predicted conduct problems through age 13.

When considering more pernicious constructs such as anger, aggression, and even psychopathy, the importance of parenting becomes even clearer in part because of the stability of these constructs over time. For example, Nagin and Tremblay (2001) found that kindergarten boys who are oppositional and hyperactive are about three-fold more likely than other children to be highly aggressive *in high school*. Using data from a high-risk Montreal, Canada sample, they also found that persistently aggressive kindergarteners often came from homes characterized by teenage mothers, family dissolution, and poverty. These boys also had low IQs, few prosocial skills, and attention difficulties, risk factors that would be enduringly predictive of aggression nearly a decade later.

Based on data from a sample of low-income boys and their families, Shaw, Lacourse, and Nagin (2004) found that chronic group comprising less than 7 percent of the sample of 284 boys demonstrated high levels of overt conduct problems, such as aggressive acts between ages two and 10. During this span, their use of aggression was several times that of other trajectories of children. Moreover, about 20 percent of the sample displayed chronic hyperactivity and attention problems between ages two and 10. And in a study of 10 Canadian cohorts including nearly 11,000 children followed over six years, Côté, Vaillancourt, LeBlanc, Nagin, and Tremblay (2006) found about 17 percent of children demonstrating high levels of aggression between the ages of two and 11. These youths were mostly males from impoverished families. Unlike their peers, they were unable to inhibit the use of force against others.

The stable and enduring course of psychopathic personality disorder ineluctably means that its earliest indicators can be seen in childhood, especially in the areas of temperament and psychophysiology. As Lynam (1996) observed, "tomorrow's antisocial adults are found among today's antisocial children" (p. 210). Longitudinal research indeed has demonstrated that early life temperamental features are associated with psychopathy in adulthood. Glenn, Raine, Venables, and Mednick (2007) reported that adults age 28 who scored higher on a self-report psychopathy scale also scored low on fearfulness, scored high on stimulation/sensation seeking, and scored low on inhibition at age three. The study is the first evidence of a prospective link between age three temperamental profiles and psychopathy in adulthood (25 years later). An association between fearlessness in infancy and antisocial conduct in later childhood was also shown among a sample of children from the National Longitudinal Survey of Youth (Colder, Lengua, Fite, Mott, & Bush, 2006).

Recently, Beaver, DeLisi, and Vaughn (2010) explored the biosocial etiology of psychopathic personality by examining prenatal exposure to cigarette smoke and family structure drawing on data from the National Institute of Child Health and Human Development Study of Early Child Care. They found that prenatal exposure to cigarette smoke was associated with higher scores on the Youth Psychopathic Traits Inventory during adolescence. Interestingly, the effects were only found among youths raised in a two-parent household. Other research has similarly implicated early childhood lead exposure as a predictor of psychopathic personality into adulthood, and the empirical relationship between childhood blood lead levels and adult psychopathy withstood competing effects of sex, race, mother's IQ, intellectual achievement, and quality of the home environment (Wright, Boisvert, & Vaske, 2009).

Finally, a related construct in the study of emerging temperamental precursors of psychopathic personality is the conscience. As noted by Kochanska (1997), the conscience is believed to emerge during toddlerhood as children internalize rules of conduct and empathic concern for others' distress. Fear also plays an important part in the development of the conscience. Children ages two to three who are more fearful tend to experience anxiety in response to wrongdoing. And when parents use subtle and gentle forms of discipline that plays on or exploits the child's inner discomfort, conscience development is fostered. Fearless children experience lower levels of inner discomfort to transgressions. As such, their anxiety and nascent guilt are less available for parents to utilize. Instead, positive and responsive parental bonds are used to cultivate the fearless child's positive motivation, which contributes to conscience development. Indeed, laboratory research of children observed at 25, 38, and 52 months found that toddlers with a strong history of understanding and internalizing parental rules, and who have empathy toward their parents, were more competent, were higher functioning, and had few conduct problems later in childhood (Kochanska, Keonig, Barry, Kim, & Yoon, 2010). In other words, if a temperament characterized by negativity and poor behavioral control is the raw material of conduct problems, problematic parenting is the cauldron that allows it to take form.

Conclusion

A host of explanatory models articulate that core temperamental and behavioral systems are underlain by specific neural substrates and/or specific neurotransmitter systems (e.g., Cicchetti & Tucker, 1994; Cloninger, 1987; Depue & Collins, 1999; Derringer, Krueger, Dick, Saccone, Grucza, et al., 2010; Ernst & Fudge, 2009; Hines, 2010; Tyrka et al., 2006; Vonderlin, Pahnke, & Pauen, 2008). These neural substrates are remarkably plastic during the crucial developmental phases in childhood and particularly in the first years of life. The developing brain is affected by an assortment of adverse and antisocial inputs from parents that in turn can inculcate in their children, ranging from drug use and exposure during gestation to abuse and neglect to parenting styles that poorly fit the repertoire of the child. Although the latter concept is less sinister than the others, parenting sets into motion an avalanche of processes, as the quotation at the beginning of this chapter suggests, that interact with and mold the temperamental characteristics of the young child. Almost like a recipe, a difficult child temperament coupled with parenting styles that are poorly suited to handle it often leads to problems.

Absent a comprehensive program to treat its symptoms, the course of poor self-regulation and the expression of negative emotionality in young children continues to deteriorate. The negative temperament and negative behavioral performance make for multiple adverse interactions in the family, in the school setting, in peer groups, and in broader social relations which sets the stage for behavioral disorders including Oppositional Defiant Disorder and Conduct Disorder (Barker, Oliver, & Maughan, 2010; Keenan et al., 2011). Indeed, children with Conduct Disorder during the preschool years are more than 20 times more likely than preschoolers without it to manifest the disorder in later childhood (Kim-Cohen et al., 2005). Moreover, longitudinal research has found that childhood conduct disorder predicts antisocial conduct in adulthood (Olino, Seely, & Lewinsohn, 2010). In a 24-year follow-up, Reef, Diamantopoulou, van Mears, Verhulst, and van der Ende (in press) found that children with temperamental profiles consistent with extreme externalizing behaviors were four to five times more likely to become adult offenders. And boys who consistently employ aggression against their siblings at age three are significantly likely to progress into bullying and other antisocial behaviors during the school years (Ensor, Marks, Jacobs, & Hughes, 2010), and these effects have been shown to be specific to boys whose mothers had low educational attainment.

What can be done to overcome these early child temperament and parenting dynamics risks that presage problem behaviors? Fortunately, the overwhelmingly design of prevention programs is to improve parenting behaviors (DeLisi & Vaughn, 2011). There are also novel approaches to modifying neurotransmitter systems that are involved in temperamental expression. For instance, Crockett, Clark, Hauser, and Robbins (2010) recently conducted a study where healthy volunteers were administered citalopram, which is a selective serotonin reuptake inhibitor, and compared to controls who received a placebo. They found that enhancing serotonin made individuals more likely to judge harmful actions as forbidden in cases where harms were emotionally salient and made subjects less likely to reject unfair offers. These effects were most pronounced among persons who scored high in trait empathy. Taken together, the results suggest that prosocial behavior can be promoted by enhancing harm aversion as it relates to moral judgment and behavior.

But as the study of criminal careers demonstrates (DeLisi, 2005), many children who display severe risk factors for conduct problems are not helped, nor do they participate in comprehensive prevention and related social programs. Their antisocial disposition metastasizes in a sense. Criminologists have referred to this as a coherence theory of concentrated personal disadvantage where antisocial behavior is viewed as an emergent property that drives additional antisocial conduct and its negative social consequences, and it has been empirically validated using data from the National Survey of Children (Wright, Beaver, & Gibson, 2010). The study of temperament is usually the province of personality psychologists, developmental psychologists, and neuroscientists. Criminologists can be added to that list, for the adult criminal who recurrently creates trouble because of his or her nasty disposition started somewhere.

References

Auerbach, J. G., Landau, R., Berger, A., Arbelle, S., Faroy, M., & Karplus, M. (2005). Neonatal behavior in infants at familial risk for ADHD. *Infant Behavior and Development, 28,* 220–224.

Barker, E. D., Oliver, B. R., & Maughan, B. (2010). Co-occurring problems of early onset persistent, childhood limited, and adolescent onset conduct problem youth. *Journal of Child Psychology and Psychiatry, 51,* 1217–1226.

Barrett, J., & Fleming, A. (2011). Annual research review: All mothers are not created equal: Neural and psychobiological perspectives on mothering and the importance of individual differences. *Journal of Child Psychology and Psychiatry, 52,* 368–397.

Beaver, K. M., DeLisi, M., & Vaughn, M. G. (2010). A biosocial interaction between prenatal exposure to cigarette smoke and family structure in the prediction of psychopathy in adolescence. *Psychiatric Quarterly, 81,* 325–334.

Beaver, K. M., Wright, J. P., & DeLisi, M. (2007). Self-control as an executive function: Reformulating Gottfredson and Hirschi's parental socialization thesis. *Criminal Justice and Behavior, 34,* 1345–1361.

Blandon, A. Y., Calkins, S. D., Keane, S. P., & O'Brien, M. (2010). Contributions of child's physiology and maternal behavior to children's trajectories of temperamental reactivity. *Developmental Psychology, 46,* 1089–1102.

Bowlby, J. (1969). *Attachment and loss: Volume 1. Attachment.* New York: Basic Books.

Bowlby, J. (1988). *A secure base.* New York: Basic Books.

Braungart-Rieker, J. M., Hill-Soderlund, A. L., & Karrass, J. (2010). Fear and anger reactivity trajectories from 4 to 16 months: The roles of temperament, regulation, and maternal sensitivity. *Developmental Psychology, 46,* 791–804.

Calkins, S. D., & Keane, S. P. (2009). Developmental origins of early antisocial behavior. *Development and Psychopathology, 21,* 1095–1109.

Cicchetti, D., & Tucker, D. (1994). Development and self-regulatory structures of the mind. *Development and Psychopathology, 6,* 533–549.

Cloninger, C. R. (1987). A systematic method for clinical description and classification of personality variants. *Archives of General Psychiatry, 44,* 573–588.

Colder, C. R., Lengua, L. J., Fite, P. J., Mott, J. A., & Bush, N. R. (2006). Temperament in context: Infant temperament moderates the relationship between perceived neighborhood quality and behavior problems. *Journal of Applied Developmental Psychology, 27,* 456–467.

Côté, S., Vaillancourt, T., LeBlanc, J. C., Nagin, D. S., & Tremblay, R. E. (2006). The development of physical aggression from toddlerhood to preadolescence: A nation-wide longitudinal study of Canadian children. *Journal of Abnormal Child Psychology, 34,* 69–82.

Crockenberg, S. C., Leerkes, E. M., & Barrig Jo, P. S. (2008). Predicting aggressive behavior in the third year from infant reactivity and regulation as moderated by maternal behavior. *Development and Psychopathology, 20,* 37–54.

Crockett, M. J., Clark, L., Hauser, M. D., & Robbins, T. W. (2010). Serotonin selectively influences moral judgment and behavior through effects on harm aversion. *Proceedings of the National Academy of Sciences of the United States of America, 107,* 17433–17438.

DeGangi, G. A., DiPietro, J. A., Greenspan, S. I., & Porges, S. W. (1991). Psychophysiological characteristics of the regulatory disordered infant. *Infant Behavior and Development, 14,* 37–50.

DeLisi, M. (2005). *Career criminals in society.* Thousand Oaks, CA: SAGE.

DeLisi, M., & Vaughn, M. G. (2011). The importance of neuropsychological deficits relating to self-control and temperament to the prevention of serious antisocial behavior. *International Journal of Child, Youth and Family Studies, 1&2,* 12–35.

Depue, R. A., & Collins, P. F. (1999). Neurobiology of the structure of personality: Dopamine, facilitation of incentive motivation, and extraversion. *Behavioral and Brain Sciences, 22,* 491–569.

Derringer, J., Krueger, R. F., Dick, D. M., Saccone, S., Grucza, R. A., Agrawal, A., Lin, P., Almasy, L., Edenberg, H. J., Foroud, T., Nurnberger, Jr., J. I., Hesselbrock, V. M., Kramer, J. R., Kuperman, S., Porjesz, B., Schuckit, M. A., Bierut, L. J., as part of the Gene Environment Association Studies (GENVA) Consortium. (2010). Predicting sensation seeking from dopamine genes: A candidate-system approach. *Psychological Science, 21*, 1282–1290.

Derringer, J., Krueger, R. F., Irons, D. E., & Iacono, W. G. (2010). Harsh discipline, childhood sexual assault, and MAOA genotype: An investigation of main and interactive effects on diverse clinical externalizing outcomes. *Behavior Genetics, 40*, 639–648.

Derryberry, D., & Rothbart, M. K. (1997). Reactive and effortful processes in the organization of temperament. *Development and Psychopathology, 9*, 633–652.

DiPietro, J. A., Ghera, M. M., & Costigan, K. A. (2008). Prenatal origins of temperamental reactivity. *Early Human Development, 84*, 569–575.

DiPietro, J. A., Hodgson, D. M., Costigan, K. A., & Johnson, T. R. B. (1996). Fetal antecedents of infant temperament. *Child Development, 67*, 2568–2583.

Earls, F., & Jung, K. G. (1987). Temperament and home environment characteristics as causal factors in the early development of childhood psychopathology. *Journal of the American Academy of Child and Adolescent Psychiatry, 26*, 491–498.

Ebstein, R. P., Levine, J., Geller, V., Auerbach, J., Gritsenko, I., & Belmaker, R. H. (1998). Dopamine D4 receptor and serotonin transporter promoter in the determination of neonatal temperament. *Molecular Psychiatry, 3*, 238–246.

Ensor, R., Marks, A., Jacobs, L., & Hughes, C. (2010). Trajectories of antisocial behavior towards siblings predict antisocial behavior towards peers. *Journal of Child Psychology and Psychiatry, 51*, 1208–1216.

Ernst, M., & Fudge, J. L. (2009). A developmental neurobiological model of motivated behavior: Anatomy, connectivity and ontogeny of the triadic nodes. *Neuroscience and Biobehavioral Reviews, 33*, 367–382.

Farrington, D. P., & Welsh, B. C. (2007). *Saving children from a life of crime: Early risk factors and effective interventions.* New York: Oxford University Press.

Feldman, R. (2008). The intrauterine environment, temperament, and development: Including the biological foundations of individual differences in the study of psychopathology and wellness. *Journal of the American Academy of Child and Adolescent Psychiatry, 47*, 233–235.

Field, T., Diego, M., Hernandez-Reif, M., Figueiredo, B., Deeds, O., Ascnecio, A., Schanberg, S., & Kuhn, C. (2008). Prenatal dopamine and neonatal behavior and biochemistry. *Infant Behavior and Development, 31*, 590–593.

Fox, N. A., & Henderson, H. A. (1999). Does infancy matter? Predicting social behavior from infant temperament. *Infant Behavior and Development, 22*, 445–455.

Fox, N. A., Henderson, H. A., Rubin, K. H., Calkins, S. D., & Schmidt, L. A. (2001). Continuity and discontinuity of behavioral inhibition and exuberance: Psychophysiological and behavioral influences across the first four years of life. *Child Development, 72*, 1–21.

Glenn, A. L., Raine, A., Venables, P. H., & Mednick, S. A. (2007). Early temperamental and psychophysiological precursors of adult psychopathic personality. *Journal of Abnormal Psychology, 116*, 508–518.

Hayden, E. P., Klein, D. N., Dougherty, L. R., Olino, T. M., Dyson, M. W., Durbin, C. E., Sheikh, H. I., & Singh, S. M. (2010). The role of brain-derived neurotrophic factor genotype, parent depression, and relationship discord in predicting early-emerging negative emotionality. *Psychological Science, 21*, 1678–1685.

He, J., Degnan, K. A., McDermott, J. M., Henderson, H. A., Hane, A. A., Xu, Q., & Fox, N. A. (2010). Anger and approach motivation in infancy: Relations to early childhood inhibitory control and behavior problems. *Infancy, 15*, 246–269.

Hines, M. (2010). Sex-related variation in human behavior and the brain. *Trends in Cognitive Sciences, 14*, 448–456.

Holmboe, K., Nemoda, Z., Fearon, R. M. P., Csibra, G., Sasvari-Szekely, M., & Johnson, M. H. (2010). Polymorphisms in dopamine system genes are associated with individual differences in attention in infancy. *Developmental Psychology, 46*, 404–416.

Kagan, J. (1994). *The nature of the child: Tenth anniversary edition.* New York: Basic Books.

Kagan, J. (2003). Biology, context, and developmental inquiry. *Annual Review of Psychology, 54*, 1–23.

Keenan, K., Boeldt, D., Chen, D., Coyne, C., Donaldd, R., Duax, J., Hart, K., Perrott, J., Strickland, J., Danis, B., Hill, C., Davis, S., Kampani, S., & Humphries, M. (2011). Predictive validity of DSM-IV oppositional defiant and conduct disorders in clinically referred preschoolers. *Journal of Child Psychology and Psychiatry, 52*, 47–55.

Kim-Cohen, J., Arsenault, L., Caspi, A., Tomas, M. P., Taylor, A., & Moffitt, T. E. (2005). Validity of DSM-IV conduct disorder in 4 ½ – 5 year old children: A longitudinal epidemiological study. *American Journal of Psychiatry, 162*, 1108–1117.

Klein, V. C., Gaspardo, C. M., Martinez, F. E., Grunau, R. E., & Linhares, M. B. M. (2009). Pain and distress reactivity and recovery as early predictors of temperament in toddlers born preterm. *Early Human Development, 85*, 569–576.

Kochanska, G. (1997). Multiple pathways to conscience for children with different temperaments: From toddlerhood to age 5. *Developmental Psychology, 33*, 228–240.

Kochanska, G., Aksan, N., & Carlson, J. J. (2005). Temperament, relationships, and young children's receptive cooperation with their parents. *Developmental Psychology, 41*, 648–660.

Kochanska, G., Aksan, N., Penney, S. J., & Doobay, A. F. (2007). Early positive emotionality as a heterogeneous trait: Implications for children's self-regulation. *Journal of Personality and Social Psychology, 93*, 1054–1066.

Kochanska, G., Friesenborg, A. E., Lange, L. A., & Martel, M. M. (2004). Parents' personality and infants' temperament as contributors to their emerging relationship. *Journal of Personality and Social Psychology, 86*, 744–759.

Kochanska, G., Koenig, J. L., Barry, R. A., Kim, S., & Yoon, J. E. (2010). Children's conscience during toddler and preschool years, moral self, and a competent, adaptive developmental trajectory. *Developmental Psychology, 46,* 1320–1332.

Kochanska, G., Philibert, R. A., & Barry, R. A. (2009). Interplay of genes and early mother-child relationship in the development of self-regulation from toddler to preschool age. *Journal of Child Psychology and Psychiatry, 50,* 1331–1338.

Lahey, B. B., Van Hulle, C. A., Keenan, K., Rathouz, P. J., D'Onofrio, B. M., Rodgers, J. L., & Waldman, I. D. (2008). Temperament and parenting during the first year of life predict future child conduct problems. *Journal of Abnormal Child Psychology, 36,* 1139–1158.

Leve, L. D., Kim, H. K., & Pears, K. C. (2005). Childhood temperament and family environment as predictors of internalizing and externalizing trajectories from ages 5 to 17. *Journal of Abnormal Child Psychology, 33,* 505–520.

Lynam, D. R. (1996). Early identification of chronic offenders: Who is the fledgling psychopath? *Psychological Bulletin, 120,* 209–234.

Moffitt, T. E. (1990). The neuropsychology of juvenile delinquency: A critical review. In M. Tonry & N. Morris (Eds.), *Crime and justice: An annual review of research* (vol. 12, pp. 99–169). Chicago: University of Chicago Press.

Moffitt, T. E. (1993). Adolescence-limited and life-course-persistent antisocial behavior: A developmental taxonomy. *Psychological Review, 100,* 674–701.

Moffitt, T. E., & Caspi, A. (2001). Childhood predictors differentiate life-course persistent and adolescence-limited antisocial pathways among males and females. *Development and Psychopathology, 13,* 355–375.

Murray, J., Irving, B., Farrington, D. P., Colman, I., & Bloxsom, C. A. J. (2010). Very early predictors of conduct problems and crime: Results from a national cohort study. *Journal of Child Psychology and Psychiatry, 51,* 1198–1207.

Nagin, D. S., & Tremblay, R. E. (2001). Parental and early childhood predictors of persistent physical aggression in boys from kindergarten to high school. *Archives of General Psychiatry, 58,* 389–394.

Olino, T. M., Seeley, J. R., & Lewinsohn, P. M. (2010). Conduct disorder and psychosocial outcomes at age 30: Early adult psychopathology as a potential mediator. *Journal of Abnormal Child Psychology, 38,* 1139–1149.

Patterson, G. R., Forgatch, M. S., & DeGarmo, D. S. (2010). Cascading effects following intervention. *Development and Psychopathology, 22,* 949–970.

Pauli-Pott, U., & Beckmann, D. (2007). On the association of interparental conflict with developing behavioral inhibition and behavior problems in early childhood. *Journal of Family Psychology, 21,* 529–532.

Pierce, T., Boivin, M., Frenette, É., Forget-Dubois, N., Dionne, G., & Tremblay, R. E. (2010). Maternal self-efficacy and hostile-reactive parenting from infancy to toddlerhood. *Infant Behavior and Development, 33,* 149–158.

Quay, H. C. (1987). The psychobiology of undersocialized aggressive conduct disorder: A theoretical perspective. *Development and Psychopathology, 5,* 165–180.

Quay, H. C., Routh, D. K., & Shapiro, S. K. (1987). Psychopathology of childhood: From description to validation. *Annual Review of Psychology, 38,* 491–532.

Reef, J., Diamantopoulou, S., van Meurs, I., Verhulst, F. C., & van der Ende, J. (in press). Developmental trajectories of child to adolescent externalizing behavior and adult DSM-IV disorder: Results of a 24-year longitudinal study. *Social Psychiatry and Epidemiology*. doi: 10.1007/s00127-010-0297-9.

Rothbart, M. K. (1981). The measurement of infant temperament. *Child Development, 52*, 569–578.

Saria, S., Rajani, A. K., Gould, J., Koller, D., & Penn, A. A. (2010). Integration of early physiological responses predicts later illness severity in preterm infants. *Science Translational Medicine, 2*, 48ra65.

Schmidt, L. A., Fox, N. A., Perez-Edgar, K., & Hamer, D. H. (2009). Linking gene, brain, and behavior: DRD4, frontal asymmetry, and temperament. *Psychological Science, 20*, 831–837.

Shaw, D. S., Bell, R. Q., & Gilliom, M. (2000). A truly early starter model of antisocial behavior revisited. *Clinical Child and Family Psychology Review, 3*, 155–172.

Shaw, D. S., Lacourse, E., & Nagin, D. S. (2004). Developmental trajectories of conduct problems and hyperactivity from ages 2 to 10. *Journal of Child Psychology and Psychiatry, 45*, 1–12.

Thomas, A., & Chess, S. (1977). *Temperament and development.* New York: Brunner/Mazel.

Tyrka, A. R., Mello, A. F., Mello, M. F., Gagne, G. G., Grover, K. E., Anderson, G. M., Price, L. H., & Carpenter, L. L. (2006). Temperament and hypothalamic-pituitary-adrenal axis function in healthy adults. *Psychoneuroendocrinology, 31*, 1036–1045.

van Ijzendoorn, M. H., Schuengel, C., & Bakermans-Kranenburg, M. J. (1999). Disorganized attachment in early childhood: Meta-analysis of precursors, concomitants, and sequelae. *Development and Psychopathology, 11*, 225–249.

Vonderlin, E., Pahnke, J., & Pauen, S. (2008). Infant temperament and information processing in a visual categorization task. *Infant Behavior and Development, 31*, 559–569.

White, J. L., Moffitt, T. E., Earls, F., Robins, L., & Silva, P. A. (1990). How early can we tell? Predictors of childhood conduct disorder and adolescent delinquency. *Criminology, 28*, 507–533.

Williams, L. R., Fox, N. A., Lejuez, C. W., Reynolds, E. K., Henderson, H. A., Perez-Edgar, K. E., Steinberg, L., & Pine, D. S. (2010). Early temperament, propensity for risk-taking and adolescent substance-related problems: A prospective multi-method investigation. *Addictive Behaviors, 35*, 1148–1151.

Wright, J. P., Beaver, K. M., & Gibson, C. L. (2010). Behavioral stability as an emergent process: Toward a coherence theory of concentrated personal disadvantage. *Journal of Youth and Adolescence, 39*, 1080–1096.

Wright, J. P., Boisvert, D., & Vaske, J. (2009). Blood lead levels in early childhood predict adulthood psychopathy. *Youth Violence and Juvenile Justice, 7*, 208–222.

Social Class and Criminal Behavior through a Biosocial Lens

Anthony Walsh and David G. Mueller

SES and Crime

The relationship between social class (socioeconomic status—SES), and criminal behavior has been central to sociological criminology since its inception. Theories such as anomie, social disorganization, differential association, Marxist-conflict, labeling, and rational choice theories, make logical claims that we should expect to see a negative class–crime relationship (Tittle, 1983; Walsh, 2011). Careless reasoning even led some criminologists to posit that social class *causes* crime; at least if it is conceptualized as the poverty–non-poverty dichotomy that Hirschi (1969:71) maintains constitutes the true class–crime relationship implicit in most theories. Of course, SES per se does not directly cause crime or anything else; it is only a convenient label conceptualized and measured in different ways to categorize people in order to compare them on outcomes across various domains of interest.

Most sociological theories of crime ignore the moral culpability of the flesh and blood creatures who commit crimes and to indict society for its own victimization. Everything and everybody, or so it seems, is responsible for crime except those who actually commit it. Poverty, or being on the bottom rung of the SES ladder, is the cause of crime most frequently nominated, and society is considered the cause of poverty. Robert Sampson (2000:711) notes the pervasiveness of the "poverty causes crime" mantra, writing that: "Everyone believes that 'poverty causes crime' it seems; in fact, I have heard many a senior sociologist express frustration as to why criminologists would waste time with theories outside the poverty paradigm. The reason we do ... is that the facts demand it." Schmalleger (2004:223) also notes that sociologists assume that the "root causes" of crime are poverty and various social injustices, but also notes that: "Some now argue the inverse of the 'root causes' argument, saying that poverty and what appear to be social injustices are produced by crime, rather than the other way around."

Mainstream sociology tends to assume that the advantages and disadvantages of childhood SES largely determine adult SES. This status ascription position views SES as socially "inherited" and it supposedly does not require any explanation beyond that. SES is included in almost all statistical models of criminal behavior as an independent variable, but we must come to terms with the fact that it is a dependent variable as well; i.e., "caused" as well as "causal." SES is shorthand for a composite of variables used to place individuals on a continuum based on their ability to legitimately secure valued resources. We rarely view SES as *caused* by these parts, only as *causing* these parts.

For instance, Rank, Yoon, and Hirschl (2003:6) list a number of things associated with the risk of poverty including giving birth out of wedlock, having large numbers of children at an early age, dropping out of school, divorce, and welfare dependence, and then turn these very private choices into problems of "structural failure." Structural failure has thus led to class position and class position to criminal behavior. Schwalbe et al. (2000:428) make plain that these thing are the result of sub-culturally channeled personal choices: "[T]hose who do well by the standards of the street acquire habits and create situations (drug addiction, lack of education, multiple dependents, criminal records) that are debilitating and risky, and diminish chances for mainstream success, even in the form of stable working-class employment." The view that this abstraction called "society" is responsible for one's conduct and position on the class ladder strips us of agency by refusing to grant us the dignity of personal responsibility.

Nevertheless, if class is the result of the failure of social institutions, and if class is a cause of crime, then criminal behavior must ultimately be blamed on these same institutional failures. After all, humans are designed to incorporate environmental information into the physical structures of their brains and genomes. But we cannot forget that people create their environments as much as their environments create them. Social ecologists of the Chicago school make much of the effects of neighborhoods on individuals' behavior, but never vice versa. Yet "neighborhood" is, after all, a macro mirror reflecting the combined micro images of all the individuals who live in it. As Wright, Boisvert, Dietrich, and Ris (2009:148) explain: "It should be expected that individuals with similar traits and abilities, who have made many of the same choices over their life-course, should tend to cluster together within economic and social spheres. In other words, a degree of homogeneity should exist within neighborhoods, within networks within those neighborhoods, and within families within those neighborhoods." Obviously, choices people make are often constrained by factors beyond their power to control. We cannot do anything about the genes or rearing environment our parents bequeathed to us, the fact that the factories have moved out of town, or that the people around us sell drugs and are not very nice. We can, however, decide to respond to the inevitable travails of life constructively or destructively within the limits of our abilities.

Blaming society for all human malevolence is a proposition losing its cachet, even among sociologically trained criminologists, as the evidence from the more advanced sciences is becoming too strong to ignore. The whole notion of criminal behavior as the result of "strained" individuals righteously hitting back at a society that has denied them opportunities to obtain status and resources legitimately is deservedly pooh-poohed by Vold, Bernard, and Snipes (1998:177): "It is not merely a matter of talented individuals confronted with inferior schools and discriminatory hiring practices. Rather, a good deal of research indicates that many delinquents and criminals are untalented individuals who cannot compete effectively in complex industrial societies." Of course, SES *is* related to the probability of criminal behavior, but the position taken in this chapter is that the same traits that put individuals at risk for lower SES also put them at risk for criminal behavior.

The importance of stratification for understanding social behavior (regardless of the mechanisms that lead to one's position within it) is noted by biosociologist Theodore Kemper (1994:47–48): "Perhaps the fundamental social structure of society is the system of stratification. It so bluntly determines individual conduct, belief, and value preferences, on the one hand, and sheer biological fate on the other ... that for many purposes it is ... the social structure par excellence worthy of close attention." Given this, one wonders about the lack of discussion about the origins of the mechanisms of stratification. There is rarely any discussion of the psychology of status or of the evolutionary processes underlying that psychology. But this is not too surprising, for as Kemper (1994:48) also points out: "If sociology and biology have not been on speaking terms in general, sociological distain for the biological reaches its apogee when it comes to social stratification."

Perhaps this is so because many sociologists are more concerned with the politics of advocacy and deriding Western societies for their sins than advancing the scientific status of their discipline. Any talk of biology conjures up the ghosts of Lombroso, social Darwinism, and other boo words such as "reductionism" and "determinism" for them. Sociologists fear that if they allow that biology has anything to do with status attainment it would mean that class position is predetermined and immutable. This view is derived from an understanding of biology to which many sociologists are not only hostile, but also "militantly and proudly ignorant" (Van den Berghe, 1990:177). Few are willing to rectify this matter, because as Cooper, Walsh, and Ellis' (2010) survey of 770 criminologists found, the modal number of biology classes taken by them was a fat zero while the modal number of sociology classes was 10.

However, there is a cadre of biosocial criminologists (as this volume attests) who are producing voluminous amounts of research integrating genetics, neurobiology, and evolutionary thinking into their work. One example of a theory that integrates these disciplines is Robert Agnew's (2005) *general* or *super traits* theory. Agnew, formerly a dyed-in-the-wool sociological criminologist, has showed a steady movement toward the biosocial perspective as the data began to demand it. In this theory Agnew identifies five *life domains*—personality, family, school, peers, and work— that interact and feedback on one another across the lifespan. He suggests that personality traits set individuals on a particular developmental trajectory that influence how other people in the various social domains react to them in evocative gene–environment correlation (rGE) fashion. The theory also shows how personality variables "condition" the effect of social variables on criminal behavior, which is an example of gene x environment interaction (GxE) (see Chapter 6 in this volume for a discussion of rGE and GxE).

The traits of *low self-control* and *irritability* are identified as the super traits, both of which are known to be underlain by low serotonergic functioning (Wright

& Beaver, 2005) and by prefrontal cortex deficits (Friedman et al., 2008). These phenotypic traits are composites of many endophenotypes such as sensation seeking, impulsivity, poor problem-solving skills, and low empathy. In terms of SES, Agnew states that "Individuals from low-SES families may be more likely to inherit these traits [or rather the alleles underlying them], as these traits may be more common among low-SES individuals" (2005:143). Low-SES individuals may not only be more likely to inherit irritability/low self-control (or more correctly, the polymorphisms underlying these traits), but are also more likely than higher SES individuals to suffer environmental insults such as prenatal exposure to toxic substances, birth complications, poor maternal health, and other environmental insults that effect the biological mechanisms associated with these traits (Walsh & Yun, 2011).

People with low self-control and irritable temperaments are likely to evoke negative responses from family members, school teachers, peers, and workmates that feedback and exacerbate those tendencies (the multiplier effect in evocative rGE). Agnew states that "biological factors have a direct affect on irritability/low self-control and an indirect affect on the other life domains through irritability/ low self-control" (2005:213). He also notes neuroscience evidence that the immaturity of adolescent behavior mirrors the immaturity of the adolescent brain, and that teens experience massive hormonal surges that facilitate aggression and competitiveness. Thus, says Agnew, neurohormonal changes during adolescence *temporarily* increase irritability/low self-control among adolescents who limit their offending to that period; for those who continue to offend, irritability and low self-control are *stable* characteristics.

In his earlier work in the anomie/strain tradition Agnew moved us away from the implicit Mertonian notion that strain impacted individuals in the same social class of origin in more or less similar ways. Agnew asserted that the presence of strain is less important than how one copes with it. The traits that differentiate people who cope poorly from those who cope well include: "temperament, intelligence, creativity, problem-solving skills, interpersonal skills, self-efficacy, and self-esteem. These traits affect the selection of coping strategies by influencing the individual's sensitivity to objective strains and the ability to engage in cognitive, emotional, and behavioral coping" (Agnew, 1992:71). These traits not only help to determine how one copes with strain, for obvious reasons they also help to determine the SES level one ultimately achieves.

The Biological Basis of Status Concerns

The primordial origins of social stratification, whatever the particular form it may take across time and cultures, lie in the psychology of individuals striving for respect, recognition, and status in group settings. As Loch, Galunic, and Schneider (2006:222) remark: "People crave general respect and recognition … in all cultures of the world. In other words, the *striving* for success is hard-wired." This basic feature of human nature is universal and "hard wired" because status leads to priority of access to resources and mating opportunities, the twin central concerns of all sexually reproducing animals. Of course, status can be and is valued for its own sake, and the criteria by which status is attained and conferred and the symbols that signify that its holders possess it are cultural. Nevertheless, the ultimate origin of social stratification is the fundamental trait of individual status striving. The fathers of sociology—Durkheim, Marx, and Weber—recognized that social life was at bottom the pursuit of social power as a way to acquire social status, but the lesson is lost on many of their offspring (Walsh, 2009). Given the importance of status to social animals, it follows that natural selection has designed multiple biological mechanisms relevant to its acquisition.

As already noted, status is a ubiquitous concern of all sexually reproducing animals that expend energy and resources obtaining mates in the face of sometimes brutal competition. High standing in the group relieves those who enjoy it of having to compete with others because status simultaneously draws females to those who have it and leads lower status males to defer. Testosterone (T), serotonin, and cortisol are the chemicals most related to striving status across animal species (Anestis, 2006; Archer, 2006). High T levels foster dominance and extraversion, low cortisol reflects low levels of stress, anxiety, and fear, and high serotonin fosters confidence and self-esteem. These substances operate within the context of an interacting soup of other neurotransmitters, hormones, and receptor and transporter molecules entailing complex feedback loops, with their secretion patterns influenced by the social context. That is, although basal levels of these substances are heritable, they rise and fall according to the organism's experiences. In established status hierarchies leaders best assert their leadership by a subtle mix of coercion and bonhomie. Henrich and Gil-White (2001) refer to this leadership style as *persuasive* because it relies on the leader's prestige and the freely conferred deference of followers.

In hierarchies characterized by chaos more aggressive strategies may be needed to maintain control and thus require a different leadership style that Henrich and Gil-White (2001) call a *dominance* style characterized by the use of force or the threat of force. A shift in leadership strategies requires a different mix of chemistry. For instance, a male who has a high T level and also has a hyperactive autonomic nervous system will encounter anxiety and fear when challenged, and this will elevate cortisol. One of the effects of cortisol is that it suppresses T, so the combination of anxiety and the loss of T-driven surgency may lead such a male to withdraw from future status competitions. Thus different genotypes rise to high rank depending on the social context.

Serotonergic mechanisms modulate cortisol and T responses in status competitions among primates (Anderson & Summers, 2007). When male vervet monkeys are administered exogenous serotonin they tend to attain high dominance status in the troop, and in naturalistic settings the highest ranking males have the highest levels of serotonin (Anestis, 2006). Low ranking males, typically low in serotonin, defer without much fuss to higher ranking males over access to females and other resources in established hierarchies. When the hierarchy is in flux, however, it is the low status males who become the most aggressive in seeking status. If a low status male is successful in improving his status, his serotonin level rises to levels commensurate with his new status, which again emphasizes the feedback nature of behavior-related chemistry and environmental events. The same relationship between serotonin and violence are consistently found among human males, as one would expect given the common fitness concerns among all primates. Indeed, the relationship between low serotonin and impulsive violence among humans has been called "perhaps the most reliable findings in the history of psychiatry" (Fishbein, 2001:15).

Given the bidirectional relationship between social status and neurohormonal mechanisms, we might hypothesize that natural selection has equipped us to adjust ourselves to the social statuses we find ourselves in within well-ordered groups ("Best not to challenge when the status hierarchy is solid and I have little chance to challenge successfully"). This is not social Darwinism asserting that the status quo exists because it is naturally ordained and therefore good (the naturalistic fallacy). These same mechanisms also equip those with little to lose with the necessary biological wherewithal to attempt to elevate their status by taking violent risks when social restraints are weak, as they are in our lowest SES neighborhoods (Anderson & Summers, 2007). Anderson points out that in the inner-city "there are always people looking around for a fight in order to increase their share of respect—or 'juice'" and that young men will risk their lives to gain status (1999:73).

There is a fair amount of evidence linking SES to serotonergic mechanisms. A study of the serotonin–status relationship subjected a sample of 270 black and white males and females to a neuro-pharmacological challenge that enabled researchers to measure serotonergic responsiveness (Matthews et al., 2000). Each person's SES, impulsiveness, and hostility were also measured. Serotonin responsivity was inversely related to SES and hostility-impulsiveness overall and across both races and sexes. In a multiple regression model, SES remained significantly related to serotonin after adjusting for a wide range of biological variables and for scores on the hostility-impulsiveness scales. It should be noted that the researchers hypothesized the causal direction to be low SES→low serotonin/high hostility-impulsiveness, not low serotonin→low SES/high hostility-impulsiveness, although there are arguments about causal direction. Of course, it does not have to be linear in either direction; it is most likely bidirectional as it is in other primate species.

Thus it is plausible to assert that the ultimate origins of social status in any society past or present lie in primate dominance struggles which afforded the winners priority of access to food, territory, and mates. These dominance struggles are not a matter of brute strength and aggression, but more a matter of coalition building in which favored members of the alliance share in the fruits of alpha's success at the expense of those not favored. Herein is also the origin of exploitation of one class (alpha's "ruling alliance") of another. But as Lopreato and Crippen (1999:225) point out, dominant males and their allies maintain social order in the group, and in exchange for this vital social role a certain amount of exploitation (expropriating more than their fair share of resources and mates) is tolerated by the exploited.

Social Structure and the Genome→Ability→Status Relationship

We wish to allay concerns that all this talk about status striving being hard-wired means that social class is fixed across generations by biological fiat and that social structure does not matter. Social structure matters immensely because it determines the extent to which genes matter for the attainment of social status; they may have a large impact on achieving social class level in some societies, but hardly at all in others. Sociologists Daniel Adkins and Guang Guo (2008) demonstrate this with a model of the shifting influence of the human genome on status attainment across different levels of societal development. Genes matter most in modern open societies in which legal equality is the norm, and hardly at all in societies characterized by social closure; that is, slave and caste societies. This is, of course, one of the fundamental principles of behavioral genetics: genes matter least in the most unequal and disadvantaged environments and their influence increases linearly as environments become more equal and advantaged. This is the central maddening irony facing egalitarians—the more equal the environment becomes the more people are differentiated by their genes.

Using data from the *Standard Cross-Cultural Sample of the Ethnographic Atlas* (SCCS), Adkins and Guo found that the influence of the genotype on status attainment describes a reverse J pattern across the expanse of human history. Hunter-gatherer societies lack surplus resources, so all individuals engage in subsistence activities, leaving little possibility for the emergence of elite classes to exploit others. There are, of course, differences in status among hunter-gathers, but these differences are a function of individual characteristics such as skilled hunter, fighter, strategist, speaker, leader, manipulator, and so forth. In such societies status assortment begins on a fairly level social playing field within each generation and thus the genome→ability relationship is strong since all members develop in almost identical environments. This also means that the ability→status relationship would also be strong since there is little likelihood of social closure thwarting that relationship.

With the advent of food surplus and storage in horticultural societies we see the beginning of social stratification systems and the weakening of the genome→ability and ability→status relationships. Inequality and social closure reached its zenith with the arrival of agrarian societies. The SCCS data shows that 96.8% of agrarian societies had class stratification and 52% had hereditary leadership, compared with 7.4% on both dimensions in hunter-gatherer societies. Agrarian societies are characterized by huge environmental inequalities between the elites and commoners, thus drastically reducing both the genome→ability relationship and the ability→status relationship.

The democratization of the polity marching in lockstep with the industrialization of the economy in the early nineteenth century reduced power and economic inequality in industrialized societies. Modern societies require a constant flow of millions of ambitious and capable individuals to fill positions vital to economic growth. The people who fill the most important positions demand compensation commensurate with their training and education. Thus the genome→ability relationship and the ability→status relationships become strong again, although not as strong as it was in hunter-gatherer societies since hierarchies had already established intergenerational privilege.

The decreasing income inequality observed during industrialization began to reverse in the 1970s due to economic globalization, and this trend casts "uncertainty on the direction of future changes of the strength of genetic influence on status outcomes" (Adkins & Guo, 2008:251). Between 1979 and 2004 real (after tax) income rose by 9% for the poorest fifth of Americans, 69% for the richest fifth, and 176% for the richest 1% (Sawhill & Morton, 2007). This trend reversal may work in two opposite directions vis-à-vis the genome–ability–status relationships. For genotypes that confer exceptionally high levels of the phenotypic traits necessary for success in the modern workforce, the genome→ability and ability→status relationships may increase in strength due to increased competition for desirable professional jobs while reducing the relationships for those not so well equipped.

Adkins and Guo (2008:252) see hope for sociology's future role in discussions of SES if only it can get over its dread of biology and require its students to learn some: "[W]e suggest that sociology may find a role in the oncoming synthesis of social and biological sciences in the very maxim that has described its reluctance. Structure matters—not only to social processes, but also to the actualization of genetic potential."

Status in a Meritocratic Society: The Role of Intelligence and Temperament

The status attainment model of SES avers that individual cognitive ability and motivation (talent + effort) largely determine adult SES in modern democratic societies, and that they do so regardless of childhood SES (Nielsen, 2006). Even if sociological criminologists accept the status attainment model, they tend to view the end result as unfair and criminogenic. For instance, Messner and Rosenfeld (2001:9; emphasis added) correctly point out that the competition for economic success *requires* inequality of outcomes because "winning and losing have meaning only when rewards are distributed unequally." They also claim that inequality in the United States is not an aberration of the American Dream but an expression of it. It is because inequality is a natural outcome of competition that: "High crime rates are intrinsic to American society ... at all social levels, *America is organized for crime.*" Although accepting the status attainment view, Sawhill and Morton (2007:4) also question the fairness of meritocracy when they write: "people are born with different genetic endowments and are raised in different families over which they have no control, raising fundamental questions about the fairness of even a perfectly functioning meritocracy."

The concept of fairness appeals to our moral sentiments because fairness is a process by which we expect to "make things right." We feel sorry for individuals burdened with environmental and genetic disabilities they did not create, and would like to make it right for them. But having sympathy for such individuals does not tell us how their position in life coheres with the moral issue of fairness. Fairness is a philosophical issue saturated with contradictory notions; we all praise it but differ as to when its promise is fulfilled. Conservatives tend to view fairness as an equal opportunity *process*—a non-discriminatory chance to play the game— which governments can guarantee via law; liberals tend to view fairness as equality of *outcome*—all are winners—which no power on earth can guarantee. If we enter a fair race, then the abilities we bring to it will determine the outcome, and the primary ability is intelligence.

Intelligence

When we discuss merit in terms of success in modern complex societies we are mostly talking about intelligence, the quintessential human trait. To discuss intelligence as a determinant of a person's social class is sociological heresy. Discussions of IQ in the sociological literature ignore decades of hard genetic and neuroscience evidence for the biological underpinnings of human variation in IQ. Lee Ellis' (1996:28) comment is apropos here: "Someday historians of social science will be astounded to find the word intelligence is usually not even mentioned in late-twentieth-century text books on social stratification." IQ tests were designed to be a class-neutral measure of aptitude that was supposed to turn schools into capacity-catching institutions by siphoning off the brightest children to provide an increasingly complex economic system with competent workers (Pinker, 2002). Whatever one's IQ score is, however, it is not an indicator of innate inferiority, moral value, or social worthiness, but rather an indicator of the probability of being able to master intellectually demanding tasks.

Sociologists claim that SES is the cause of IQ because of the correlation between parental SES and children's IQ, which is within the 0.30 to 0.40 range (Lubinski, 2004). But to say that parental SES causes offspring SES via the link between parental SES offspring IQ is a horse of a different color. If parental SES "caused" offspring SES the correlations between adults' IQs and their own SES would not be very different from the correlation between their IQ and their parents' SES; i.e., in the 0.30 to 0.40 range. However, correlations between offspring IQ and offspring attained SES are in the 0.50 to 0.70 range (Lubinski, 2004), thus offspring IQ is a considerably more powerful predictor of offspring adult SES than is parental SES.

For instance, a study examining 60 years of data from males born between 1925 and 1932 who had lived in poor high-crime neighborhoods in Boston when growing up found that parental SES was weakly but significantly related to offspring occupational status at age 25, but dwindled to non-significance at age 65. The only two variables significantly related to occupational success by age 65 were IQ and years of education. This study supports the behavior genetic "law" that states that as we age the effects of shared environment (in this case, childhood SES and all the baggage that comes with it) on phenotypic traits fade to insignificance while genes and non-shared environments become more salient (DiRago & Vaillant, 2007).

A longitudinal study of 4,298 British males found that individual meritocratic factors (IQ, motivation, and educational qualifications) that were assessed when subjects were 11 and 16 years old accounted for 48% of the variance in occupational status at age 33 (Bond & Saunders, 1999). All measured background variables (parental SES, type of housing, type of school, and parents' aspirations) combined accounted for only 8% of the variance. Another British longitudinal study (Nettle, 2003) followed a cohort of all children born in one week in 1958 to the age of 42. The primary finding of this study was that childhood intellectual ability is associated with class mobility in adulthood uniformly across all social classes of origin. An IQ difference of 24.1 points separated those who attained professional status from those in the unskilled class, regardless of the class of origin. Parental SES independently accounted for only 3% of the variation in attained social class. Nettle concluded that "intelligence is the strongest single factor causing class mobility in contemporary societies that has been identified" (2003:560).

An American behavior genetic study pitting the ascription thesis against the achievement thesis found strongly in favor of the latter (Nielsen 2006). The variables examined were verbal IQ (VIQ), grade-point average (GPA), and college plans (CPL). The heritability coefficients were VIQ = 0.536, GPA = 0.669, and CPL = 0.600; the shared environment coefficients were VIQ = 0.137, GPA = 0.002, and CPL = 0.030, and the non-shared environmental variances were VIQ = 0.327, GPA = 0.329, and CPL = 0.370. Shared environment is everything shared by siblings as they grew up, including parental SES as well as other factors sociologists employ to explain important life outcomes such as neighborhood and school characteristics, and ethnic status. The proportions of variance explained by SES of origin in VIQ, GPA, and CPL is miniscule compared with the proportions explained by genes and non-shared environment.

Numerous other studies (see Walsh, 2011, for a review) document the weak effect of parental SES on offspring SES in modern open societies. This weak effect is considered almost a truism outside of sociology: "The net impact of measured family background on economic success is easy to summarize: very little. This conclusion holds across different data sets with different model specifications and measurements and applies to both occupational status and earnings" (Kingston, 2006:121).

Temperament

Temperament is the second major determinant of attained social status. Chamorro-Premuzic and Furnham (2005:352) inform us that temperament and intelligence are "the two great pillars of differential psychology." They add that these two constructs are vital to predicting all kinds of life outcomes, including social class attainment. As we have seen, temperament and intelligence are identified by Agnew (1992) as important factors in determining prosocial versus antisocial responses to strain.

Temperament is defined as "individual differences in emotional, motor, and attentional reactivity [that are] biologically based and linked to an individual's genetic endowment" (Rothbart, 2007:207). The various components of temperament are highly heritable and exert their influence largely through the variation in autonomic nervous system arousal. People with temperamental difficulties find it tough to form social bonds and to compete successfully in life. Children with disinhibited temperaments evoke negative responses from parents, teachers, and peers (evocative rGE), and these children find acceptance only among peers with similar dispositions (active rGE) (reviewed in Sanson, Hemphill, & Smart, 2004). Differences in temperament make children differentially responsive to socialization, which is exacerbated by the fact that temperaments of parents and children are generally positively correlated. That is, children temperamentally unresponsive to socialization will have parents who are inconsistent disciplinarians, irritable, and unstable, rendering them unable or unwilling to cope constructively with their children, thereby saddling them with both a genetic and an environmental liability (Saudino, 2005).

Longitudinal studies typically find that children from low SES families are over-represented at the "problematic end of temperament dimensions, especially those relating to child difficulty" (Sanson et al., 2004:158). Caspi, Bem, and Elder's (1989) longitudinal study illustrates the heterogeneity of negative outcomes that can arise from a single temperamental dimension. This study identified males from middle-class families with or without a history of temper tantrums in childhood and traced them for 30 years investigating multiple areas of their lives. The majority of bad tempered boys ended up in lower status occupations than their fathers, had erratic work histories, and experienced more unemployment than other males with more placid temperaments and were more than twice as likely as other men to be divorced by age 40.

Temperament is the biological superstructure upon which personality, the relatively enduring, distinctive, integrated, and functional set of psychological traits, is built. The two major traits associated with occupational success (positively) and criminal behavior (negatively) are conscientiousness and agreeableness. Conscientiousness is the broad term applied to a number of subtraits that range from well-organized, disciplined, scrupulous, orderly, responsible, and reliable at one end of the continuum, and disorganized, careless, unreliable, irresponsible, and unscrupulous at the other (Lodi-Smith & Roberts, 2007). Conscientiousness is particularly important to success in the workforce and climbing the class ladder, and thus, if the class-based crime theories have merit, to criminal behavior. Behavior genetic studies of conscientiousness find a mean heritability of 0.49 (Bouchard et al., 2003).

Agreeableness is the tendency to be friendly, considerate, courteous, helpful, and cooperative with others. Agreeable persons tend to trust others, to compromise with them, to empathize with and aid them. This list of subtraits suggests a high degree of concern for prosocial conformity and social desirability. Disagreeable persons simply display the opposite characteristics—suspicion of others, unfriendly, uncooperative, unhelpful, and lacking in empathy—which all suggest a lack of concern for prosocial conformity and social desirability. A pooled heritability estimate of 0.48 for agreeableness is reported by Jang, McCrae, Angleitner, Riemann, and Livesley (1998). Conscientiousness and agreeableness are positively correlated but far from perfectly. A person can be conscientious at work but thoroughly disagreeable socially (think of the Machiavellian white-collar criminal), and one can be most agreeable socially but lackadaisical at work (think of the happy-go-lucky ritualist of Mertonian theory).

From a meta-analysis of personality and antisocial behavior, Miller and Lynam (2001:780) describe the personality of the typical criminal: "Individuals who commit crimes tend to be hostile, self-centered, spiteful, jealous, and indifferent to others (i.e., low in Agreeableness). They tend to lack ambition, motivation, and perseverance, have difficulty controlling their impulses, and hold nontraditional and unconventional values and beliefs (i.e., are low in Conscientiousness)." Miller and Lynam's (2001) meta-analysis comparing 29 prisoner/non-prisoner samples found a weighted mean effect size of -0.41 for agreeableness and antisocial behavior and -0.25 for conscientiousness and antisocial behavior. Another meta-analysis (Saulsman & Page, 2004) examining the relationship between the so-called big five personality traits and each of the behavioral disorders listed in the *Diagnostic and Statistical Manual of Mental Disorders* (DSM-IV) found mean effect sizes for antisocial personality disorder over 15 studies of -0.35 for agreeableness and -0.26 for conscientiousness.

Employers can be expected to favor high levels of conscientiousness in their employees and prospective employees, and they do. Conscientiousness is more important in high autonomy jobs than in low autonomy jobs because it "affects motivational states and stimulates goal setting and goal commitment" (Schmidt & Hunter, 2004:169). In an intergenerational study following subjects from early childhood to retirement, Judge and his colleagues (1999) found that conscientiousness measured in childhood predicted adult occupational status (r = 0.49) and income (r = 0.41) in adulthood. These correlations are only slightly less than the correlations between "general mental ability" (GMA) and the same variables (0.51 and 0.53, respectively). Schmidt and Hunter's (2004:170) analysis of GMA and personality variables in attaining occupational success concluded that "the burden of prediction is borne almost entirely by GMA and conscientiousness."

Why DNA is not SES Destiny

Social class is a macro phenotype far from the genotype; it is a complex composite of a large number of endophenotypes such as intelligence, conscientiousness, agreeableness, and ambition that are themselves the results of a maze of neurological, genetic, epigenetic, and environmental inputs. There are thus many processes on the journey from genotype to SES that militate against the hardening of social class into caste-like systems. Fixed caste-like classes do not naturally beget themselves; only very strong socio-cultural practices such as those present in agrarian cultures can maintain artificial social classes across the generations.

Although genetic endowment contributes immensely to an individual's SES, this does not mean that the offspring of these individuals will possess the same endowment. During the process of meiosis the chromosomes separate and the alleles are segregated into two different gametes (the *law of segregation*). Because traits conducive to SES attainment are quantitative, and thus polygenic, the genes coding for proteins underlying them will most likely reside on separate chromosomes or at distant loci of the same one. Thus the law of segregation assures that very few of them will be passed on to the next generation *in toto*. Then there is the law of independent assortment stating that allele pairs separate independently during the formation of gametes, meaning that traits (or rather the genes underlying them) are transmitted to offspring independently of one another. Segregation and independent assortment assure that whatever constellation of proteins that may have contributed to parental social class will be inherited piecemeal rather than intact, and the larger the number of alleles contributing to the SES phenotype the more likely this is.

The phenomenon of *regression to the mean* may reflect the effects of independent assortment and segregation. The genetic shuffling of meiosis assures a great deal of variability in the traits being passed from parents to offspring, but we know that typically bright parents give birth to bright children and that dull parents give birth to dull children. However, children born to high IQ parents are usually less bright than their parents, although they are brighter than average, and children of low IQ parents are usually brighter than their parents, although still below average. Sandra Scarr (1996) points out that parents in the professional classes have an average IQ of 120 and their children an average 115, and that unskilled worker parents have an average IQ of 90 and their children an average of 95; this is regression to the mean (of the population).

Regression to the mean is common for a number of polygenic traits and may operate in the following way: extremely bright and extremely dull parents are, respectively, the recipients of a larger than average number of IQ-enhancing or IQ-depressing alleles. Because parents pass on a random half of their genes, the odds are greatly against their offspring receiving the same large number of IQ-enhancing or IQ-depressing alleles. The larger the difference between mid-parent IQ and the population mean, the less the odds are, and thus the greater the offspring regression to the population mean. Rushton and Jensen (2005:263) liken this to rolling a pair of dice and having them come up two sixes (high IQ) or two ones (low IQ), and say that "the odds are on the next roll [the next generation], you will get some value that is not quite as high (or low)." The laws of genetics work against the hardening of populations into caste-like systems of social stratification: "regression mixes up the social classes, ensures social mobility, and favors meritocracy" (Eysenck & Kamin, 1981:64).

Another phenomenon that operates to prevent caste-like groups emerging for genetic reasons is the *Hardy-Weinberg equilibrium* (H-WE). The H-WE is a basic law of evolutionary genetics stating that allele frequencies in a mating population tend to remain stable. To give a hypothetical example: suppose there is an autosomal recessive allele (*a*) with a 1% frequency in the population coding for a protein that results in an average loss of 10 IQ points. If both parents are homozygous (*aa*) for the allele both are afflicted, as will be all of their offspring. This does not imply a cross-generational inheritance of social class (to the extent that IQ indexes SES); in fact, unaffected heterozygous (*aA*) parents will contribute more of this recessive trait to the next generation than will the affected homozygous parents. Here is why. If the probability of the recessive allele (*a*) in the population is 0.01 the probability of the dominant allele (*A*) is 0.99. If $p + q = 1$ then $(p + q)^2 = 1$ also. In binomial expansion: $(p + q)^2 = p^2 + 2pq + q^2 = 1$. Thus the allelic frequencies are: $a^2 + 2aA + A^2 = 100\%$ of all alleles at that locus. Given the 1% frequency of the *aa* allele and doing the math we have: $0.0001 + (2)(0.0099) + 0.9801 = 0.0001 + 0.0198 + 0.9801 = 1.0$.

Assuming random mating (which is never the case), the probability of the mating of two homozygous aa individuals certain to have affected offspring is (aa) (aa) = (0.0001)(0.0001) = 0.000001. The probability of two heterozygous individuals mating is (aA)(aA) = (0.0198)(0.0198) = .00039204. The laws of Mendelian genetics tell us that on average one-fourth of the offspring of heterozygote matings would be homozygous for the recessive allele; i.e., 0.00039204/4 = 0.00009801. Thus the number of affected offspring of unaffected heterozygotes will be on average 98 times (0.00009801/0.000001 = 98) greater than the number of affected offspring of homozygotes.

Decreased assortative mating is another process working against the hardening of social class by lessening intellectual differences between families. Assortative mating means that we tend to mate with partners who are similar to us. The strongest assortment is for race, religion, and ethnicity, followed by education level, attitudes, IQ, SES, height and weight, and personality traits (Hur, 2003).

Assortative mating requires assortative meeting, and the lessening institutional and financial constraints on opportunities to meet individuals from other classes will have the effect of mixing up the classes. The average correlation between American spouses for SES of 0.30 (Hur, 2003) is tiny compared to what it was 100 years ago when people rarely married outside their class (van Leeuwen & Maas, 2002). Looking at assortative mating across 55 countries, Smits (2003) found that in countries where access to higher education is most open, the strength of the relationship between spouses for SES diminishes; i.e., it becomes more random with respect to class of origin. Open societies in which individuals from diverse backgrounds are thrown together in educational, occupational, and recreational situations will reduce assortative mating and therefore add to the fluidity of social class.

The Perils of Lower-Class Childhood: How Experience Affects Our Biology

Just as our biology influences the environments we expose ourselves to, our environments influence our biology. The deprivation suffered by innocent children in truly horrendous family environments prevents them from realizing their potential for normal development. Children in these environments are subjected to more crowding, family and neighbor conflict and instability, ambient pollution, abuse and neglect, and numerous other stress-inducing problems than are the vast majority of children. Such stressors are endemic in many lower SES and inner-city environments in which children simply find themselves and have done nothing to create (Evans, Kim, Ting, Tesher, & Shannis, 2007). Relentless stress can alter neurobiological mechanisms in such a way as to put those who experience them at an elevated risk for all kinds of antisocial behavior.

Stress and Allostasis

Stress is a useful state of psychophysiological arousal because it focuses and energizes us to confront the stressor. The stress response is mediated by two separate but interrelated systems controlled by the hypothalamus: the autonomic nervous system (ANS) and the hypothalamic-pituitary-adrenal (HPA) axis. When an organism perceives a threat to its well-being the hypothalamus directs the ANS's sympathetic system to mobilize the body for vigorous action aided by pumping out the hormone epinephrine (adrenaline). When the organism perceives that the threat is over the ANS's parasympathetic system restores the body to homeostasis.

Adults who experienced average levels of childhood stress most likely possess brains calibrated to navigate life better than those who experienced a relatively stress-free childhood. While stress is functional, toxic and protracted stress damages vital brain areas responsible for memory storage and behavioral regulation such as the amygdala and hippocampus since both have high concentrations of receptors for cortisol, the stress hormone. Frequent activation of stress response mechanisms may lead to the dysregulation of these mechanisms, leading to a number of psychological, emotional, and behavioral problems (Gunnar & Quevedo, 2007).

The HPA axis is activated in situations that call for a prolonged rumination rather than the visceral immediacy of the ANS's preparation of the body for fight or flight (Gunnar & Quevedo, 2007). The HPA axis response begins with the hypothalamus feeding various chemical messages to the pituitary gland which leads to further chemical products that stimulate the adrenal glands to release the hormone cortisol. The brain is a major target for cortisol which, unlike epinephrine, is able to cross the blood/brain barrier (van Voorhees & Scarpa, 2004). Cortisol is the fuel that energizes our coping mechanisms by increasing vigilance and activity, and is therefore functional within the normal range. But frequent HPA axis arousal may lead to upward or downward dysregulation of arousal mechanisms. Upward dysregulation means the overproduction of cortisol, or *hypercortisolism*. Hypercortisolism leads to anxiety and depressive disorders and is most likely to be found in females who have been maltreated because females activate significantly more neural systems associated with emotional stress and with encoding it into long-term memory than males (van Voorhees & Scarpa, 2004).

Hypocortisolism, on the other hand, suggests an adaptive downward adjustment to chronic stress and leads to externalizing problems. It is adaptive because frequent stressful encounters habituate the organism to them, and as a consequence the organism does not react to further encounters as it had previously. Habituation means that both HPA axis and ANS response mechanisms have become blunted. Hypocortisolism has been linked to early onset of aggressive antisocial behavior (McBurnett, Lahey, Rathouz, & Loeber, 2000), to criminal behavior in general (Ellis, 2005), and is more likely to be found in maltreated males than in females (van Goozen, Fairchild, Snoek, & Harold, 2007). Blunted arousal means a low level of anxiety and fear, which is quite useful for those committing or contemplating a crime.

The development of hypocortisolism is an example of the process of allostasis — the achievement of physiological stability through change. Allostasis describes the body's attainment of balance by *altering* the acceptable range of physiological set-points in the face of extreme acute stress or chronic stress rather than returning them to their previous state as in homeostasis (Goldstein & Kopin, 2007). Frequent allostatic responses is termed allostatic load, which Goldstein and Kopin (2007) liken to having the heating and cooling systems running simultaneously, a situation guaranteed to hasten the wear-and-tear of both systems and eventual breakdown.

SES and Teratogenic Risk

There are numerous other factors associated with a lower SES background leading to outcomes that are risk factors for antisocial behavior, starting in the womb. During the early process of brain development, immature neurons must migrate from their birthplace to their eventual home guided by molecular messengers. The brain is most vulnerable to insults during the migratory phase of maturation because these molecular guides are susceptible to attacks by teratogenic chemicals, which may direct neurons to the wrong area or to self-destruct (Prayer et al., 2006). The most common teratogen is alcohol. When pregnant women drink they introduce their fetuses to neurotoxins that produce a number of neurological disorders, the most serious if which is fetal alcohol syndrome (FAS). FAS affects behavior via its effects on the frontal lobes, amygdala, hippocampus, hypothalamus, the serotonergic system, and the myelination process (Noble, Mayer-Proschel, & Miller, 2005).

The prevalence of fetal alcohol disorders (not all are full-blown FAS) in the United States is around 1% of live births (Manning & Hoyme, 2007). Because heavy drinking is most prevalent among low SES individuals (Casswell, Pledger,

& Hooper, 2003), FAS rates are higher in the lower classes. A review of numerous studies by the National Institute of Alcohol Abuse and Alcoholism (May & Gossage, 2008) found an average rate of FAS of about 0.26 per thousand for the middle class and one of about 3.4 per thousand for the lowest classes, which is about 13 times greater. Besides low IQ, other developmental deficits associated with FAS that are linked to high levels of antisocial and criminal behavior independent of FAS are hyperactivity, impulsiveness, poor social, emotional, and moral development (Jacobson & Jacobson, 2002).

Lead Exposure

Exposure to noxious substances outside the womb such as lead also has deleterious effects on children's brain, manifested most clearly in their IQs. The IQ decrement per one unit increase in µg/dl (micrograms per deciliter of blood) of lead is an average of 0.50 points (Koller, Brown, Spurfeon, & Levy, 2004). Low SES neighborhoods contain the oldest houses, and the main source of lead exposure today is lead paint dust in older houses.

An fMRI study found that brain grey matter was inversely correlated with mean childhood lead concentrations in mostly black young adults taken from the longitudinal Cincinnati Lead Study (Cecil et al., 2008). The mean childhood blood lead concentration of this sample was 13.3µg/dl, which is far in excess of the 2006 average of 1.5µg/dl for the general population (Bellinger, 2008). Although the grey matter lost to lead exposure was relatively small (about 1.2%), it was concentrated in the frontal lobes and the anterior cingulate cortex, which are vital behavior moderating areas responsible for executive functioning and mood regulation. Another sample from the same Cincinnati Lead Study examined the relationship between childhood blood lead and verified criminal arrests. The main finding of this study was that after adjusting for relevant covariates for every 5µg/dl lead increase there was an increase in the probability of arrest for a violent crime of about 50% (Wright et al., 2008).

Breastfeeding

Prolonged breastfeeding has many positive effects, and is probably the major environmental factor contributing to IQ level. This was demonstrated in a study of 13,889 Belarusian breastfeeding mothers, a random half of whom were given incentives that encouraged prolonged breastfeeding while the remaining half continued their usual maternity hospital and outpatient care. Their children were assessed six years later and the major finding was that the children breastfed for six months or more had a mean IQ almost six points higher than the control group children and received higher academic ratings from teachers (Kramer et al., 2008).

The experimental design allowed researchers to measure breastfeeding effects on IQ without any biasing confounds such as the positive relationship between mothers' IQs and the probability of prolonged breastfeeding.

Kramer and his colleagues could not determine if the breastfeeding–IQ relationship was due to the constituents of breast milk, mother/child interactions and the warm skin-to-skin contact experienced during breastfeeding, or both. Breastfeeding and tactile stimulation results in the release of oxytocin, a polypeptide known popularly as "the cuddle chemical," the proximate molecular mechanism of mother/infant bonding. Oxytocin released during breastfeeding reduces the mother's sensitivity to environmental stressors, which allows for greater sensitivity to the infant's needs. It has been repeatedly shown via skin conductance and cardiac-response measures that lactating mothers show significantly fewer stress responses to infant stimuli than non-lactating mothers, and show a significantly greater desire to pick up and cuddle their infants in response to all infant-presented stimuli (Hiller, 2004).

Unfortunately, the literature consistently shows a marked downward gradient in the rates of breastfeeding as IQ, income, education, and occupational status fall, and children of lower class women are thus more likely to be deprived of important evolutionarily experience-expected input (Glaser, 2000). A random sample of 10,519 mothers in California found that the odds of breastfeeding for the women in the highest income category was 3.65 times the odds of the women in the lowest income category (Heck, Braveman, Cubbin, Chavez, & Kelly, 2006).

Conclusion

We have examined the class–crime relationship through a biosocial lens. This lens allows us a magnification factor far more powerful than the direct "structural failure→low SES→crime" model favored by traditional criminology. No science advances without integrating insights from the more fundamental and advanced sciences into its own concepts, theories, and methods. We have sympathy for the sociological notion that society "prepares the stage for crime," but point out that crime is committed by flesh and blood human beings with brains, genes, hormones, and an evolutionary history. No biological or environmental factor (or even set of factors) is a necessary or sufficient cause of a person's socioeconomic status or criminal behavior. There are many pathways to these destinations just as there are to becoming ill. By integrating robust findings from the hard sciences, however, we gain far more insight into human behavior than we do by treating humans as if they are simply empty vessels into which society pours its prescriptions and proscriptions. It is interesting to see what Douglas Massey, ex-President of the American Sociological Association, has to say about the kind of biosocial analyses presented here (2004:22):

by understanding and modeling the interaction between social structure and allostasis, social scientists should be able to discredit explanations of racial differences in terms of pure heredity [of course, no scientists we are aware of view things in terms of "pure heredity"]. In an era when scientific understanding is advancing rapidly through interdisciplinary efforts, social scientists in general—and sociologists in particular—must abandon the hostility to biological science and incorporate its knowledge and understanding into their work.

Like Massey, we believe that social scientists have worried themselves silly over the supposed fixity and determinism of biology. This view is totally erroneous and can easily be rectified by learning something about human biology. Colin Badcock (2000:71) goes so far as to assert that our genes "positively guarantee" human freedom and agency. After all, our genes are *our* genes, constantly extracting information from the environment and manufacturing the proteins we need to navigate it, and thus enabling rather than constraining us. They are what make us uniquely ourselves and resistant to environmental influences which grate against our natures. Rather than viewing biology as a threat to criminology we should welcome it as an opportunity to collaborate with a very robust ally. The social and biological sciences need each other and belong together. As the history of the physical and natural sciences demonstrate, cross-fertilization of concepts, methods, and theories breeds hybrid vigor in their resulting offspring (Walsh, 1997).

References

Adkins, D. & G. Guo (2008). Societal development and the shifting influence of the genome on status attainment. *Research in Social Stratification and Mobility*, 26:235–255.

Agnew, R. (1992). Foundations for a general strain theory of crime and delinquency. *Criminology*, 30:47–87.

Agnew, R. (2005). *Why do criminals offend? A general theory of crime and delinquency.* Los Angeles: Roxbury.

Anderson, E. (1999). *Code of the street: Decency, violence, and the moral life of the inner city.* New York: W.W. Norton.

Anderson, W. & C. Summers (2007). Neuroendocrine mechanisms, stress coping strategies, and social dominance: Comparative lessons about leadership potential. *Annals of the American Academy of Political & Social Science*, 614:102–130.

Anestis, S. (2006). Testosterone in juvenile and adolescent chimpanzees (Pan troglodytes): Effects of dominance, rank, aggression, and behavioral style. *American Journal of Physical Anthropology*, 130:536–545.

Archer, J. (2006). Testosterone and human aggression: An analysis of the challenge hypothesis. *Neuroscience and Biobehavioral Reviews*, 30:319–345.

Badcock, C. (2000). *Evolutionary psychology: A critical introduction.* Cambridge: Polity Press.

Bellinger, D. (2008). Neurological and behavioral consequences of childhood lead exposure. *PLoS Medicine,* 5:690–692.

Bond, R. & P. Saunders (1999). Routes of success: Influences on the occupational attainment of young British males. *British Journal of Sociology,* 50:217–240.

Bouchard, T., N. Segal, A. Tellegen, M. McGue, M. Keyes, & R. Krueger (2003). Evidence for the construct validity and heritability of the Wilson-Patterson conservatism scale: A reared-apart twins study of social attitudes. *Personality and Individual Differences,* 34:959–969.

Caspi, A., D. Bem, & G. Elder (1989). Continuities and consequences of interaction styles across the lifecourse. *Journal of Personality,* 57:375–406.

Casswell, S., M. Pledger, & R. Hooper (2003). Socioeconomic status and drinking patterns in young adults. *Addiction,* 98:601–610.

Cecil, K., C. Brubaker, C. Adler, K. Dietrich, M. Altaye, J. Egelhoff, S. Wessel, I. Elangovan, R. Hornung, K. Jarvis, & B. Lanphear (2008). Decreased brain volume in adults with childhood lead exposure. *PLoS Medicine,* 5:742–750.

Chamorro-Premuzic, T. & A. Furnham (2005). Intellectual competence. *The Psychologist,* 18:352–354.

Cooper, J., A. Walsh, & L. Ellis (2010). Is criminology ripe for a paradigm shift? Evidence from a survey of American criminologists. *Journal of Criminal Justice Education,* 21:332–347.

DiRago, A. & G. Vaillant (2007). Resilience in inner city youth: Childhood predictors of occupational status across the lifespan. *Journal of Youth and Adolescence,* 36:61–70.

Ellis, L. (1996). A discipline in peril: Sociology's future hinges on curing its biophobia. *American Sociologist,* 27:21–41.

Ellis, L. (2005). A theory explaining biological correlates of criminality. *European Journal of Criminology,* 2:287–315.

Evans, G., P. Kim, A. Ting, H. Tesher, & D. Shannis (2007). Cumulative risk, maternal responsiveness, and allostatic load among young adolescents. *Developmental Psychology,* 43:341–351.

Eysenck, H. & L. Kamin (1981). *The intelligence controversy.* New York: John Wiley.

Fishbein, D. (2001). *Biobehavioral perspectives in criminology.* Belmont, CA: Wadsworth.

Friedman, N., A. Miyake, S. Young, J. DeFries, R. Corely, & J. Hewitt (2008). Individual differences in executive functions are almost entirely genetic in origin. *Journal of Experimental Psychology,* 137:201–225.

Glaser, D. (2000). Child abuse and neglect and the brain—A review. *Journal of Child Psychology and Psychiatry,* 41:97–116.

Goldstein, D. & I. Kopin (2007). Evolution of the concept of stress. *Stress,* 10:109–120.

Gunnar, M. & K. Quevedo (2007). The neurobiology of stress and development. *Annual Review of Psychology,* 58:145–173.

Heck, K., P. Braveman, C. Cubbin, G. Chavez, & J. Kelly (2006). Socioecomonic status and breastfeeding initiation among California mothers. *Public Health Reports*, 121:51–59.

Henrich, J. & F. Gil-White (2001). The evolution of prestige: Freely conferred deference as a mechanism enhancing the benefits of cultural transmission. *Evolution and Human Behavior*, 22:165–196.

Hiller, J. (2004). Speculations on the links between feelings, emotions and sexual behaviour: Are vasopressin and oxytocin involved? *Sexual and Relationship Therapy*, 19:1468–1479.

Hirschi, T. (1969). *The causes of delinquency*. Berkeley: University of California Press.

Hur, Y. (2003). Assortative mating for personality traits, educational level, religious affiliation, height, weight, and body mass index in parents of a Korean twin sample. *Twin Research*, 6:467–470.

Jacobson, J. & S. Jacobson (2002). Effects of prenatal alcohol exposure on child development. *Alcohol Research & Health*, 26:282–286.

Jang, K., R. McCrae, A. Angleitner, R. Riemann, & W. Livesley (1998). Heritability of facet-level traits in a cross-cultural twin sample: support for a hierarchical model of personality. *Journal of Personality and Social Psychology*, 74:1556–1565.

Judge, T., C. Higgins, C. Thoresen, & M. Barrick (1999). The big five personality traits, general mental ability, and career success across the life span. *Personnel Psychology*, 52:621–652.

Kemper, T. (1994). Social stratification, testosterone, and male sexuality. In L. Ellis (Ed.), *Social stratification and socioeconomic inequality, vol. 2: Reproductive and interpersonal aspects of dominance and status*, pp. 47–61. Westport, CT: Greenwood.

Kingston, P. (2006). How meritocratic is the United States? *Research in Social Stratification and Mobility*, 24:11–130.

Koller, K., T. Brown, A. Spurfeon, & L. Levy (2004). Recent developments in low-level lead exposure and intellectual impairment in children. *Environmental Health Perspectives*, 112:987–994.

Kramer, M., F. Aboud, E. Mironova, I. Vanilovich, R. Platt, L. Matush, S. Igumnov, E. Fombonne, N. Bogdanovich, T. Ducruet, J.P. Collet, B. Chalmers, E. Hodnett, S. Davidovsky, O. Skugarevsky, O. Trofimovich, L. Kozlova, S. Shapiro, for the Promotion of Breastfeeding Intervention Trial (PROBIT) Study Group (2008). Breastfeeding and child cognitive development: New evidence from a large randomized trial. *Archives of General Psychiatry*, 65:578–584.

Loch, C., D. Galunic, & S. Schneider (2006). Balancing cooperation and competition in human groups: The role of emotional algorithms and evolution. *Managerial and Decision Economics*, 27:217–233.

Lodi-Smith, J. & B. Roberts (2007). Social investment and personality: A meta-analytic analysis of the relationship of personality traits to investment in work, family, religion, and volunteerism. *Personality and Social Psychology Review*, 11:68–86.

Lopreato, J. & T. Crippen (1999). *Crisis in sociology: The need for Darwin*. New Brunswick, NJ: Transaction.

Lubinski, D. (2004). Introduction to the special section on cognitive abilities: 100 years after Spearman's (1904) "General intelligence," objectively determined and measured. *Journal of Personality and Social Psychology*, 86:96–111.

Manning, M. & H. Hoyme (2007). Fetal alcohol syndrome disorders: A practical clinical approach to diagnosis. *Neuroscience and Biobehavioral Review*, 31:230–238.

Massey, D. (2004). Segregation and stratification: A biosocial perspective. *Du Bois Review*, 1:7–25.

Matthews, K., J. Flory, M. Mulldoon, & S. Manuck (2000). Does socioeconomic status relate to serotonergic responsivity in humans? *Psychosomatic Medicine*, 62:231–237.

May, P. & P. Gossage (2008). Estimating the prevalence of fetal alcohol syndrome: A summary. National Institute of Alcohol Abuse and Alcoholism. National Institute of Health. Online at http://pubs.niaaa.nih.gov/publications/arh25-3/159-167.hm.

McBurnett, K., B. Lahey, P. Rathouz, & R. Loeber (2000). Low salivary cortisol and persistent aggression in boys referred for disruptive behavior. *Archives of General Psychiatry*, 57:38–43.

Messner, S. & R. Rosenfeld (2001). *Crime and the American dream*. 3rd ed. Belmont, CA: Wadsworth.

Miller, J. & D. Lynam (2001). Structural models of personality and their relation to antisocial behavior: A meta-analytic review. *Criminology*, 39:765–798.

Nettle, D. (2003). Intelligence and class mobility in the British population. *British Journal of Psychology*, 94:551–561.

Nielsen, F. (2006). Achievement and ascription in educational attainment: Genetic and environmental influences on adolescent schooling. *Social Forces*, 85:193–216.

Noble, M., M. Mayer-Proschel, & R. Miller (2005). The oligodendrocyte. In M. Rao & M. Jacobson (Eds.), *Developmental neurobiology*, pp. 151–196. New York: Kluwer/Plenum.

Pinker, S. (2002). *The blank slate: The modern denial of human nature*. New York: Viking.

Prayer, D., G. Kasprian, E. Krampl, B. Ulm, L. Witzani, L. Prayer, & P. Brugger (2006). MRI of normal fetal brain development. *European Journal of Radiology*, 57:199–216.

Rank, M., H. Yoon, & T. Hirschl (2003). American poverty as a structural failing: Evidence and arguments. *Journal of Sociology and Social Welfare*, 30:3–29.

Rothbart, M. (2007). Temperament, development, and personality. *Current Directions in Psychological Science*, 16:207–212.

Rushton, J. & A. Jensen (2005). Thirty years of research on race differences in cognitive ability. *Public Policy and Law*, 11:235–294.

Sampson, R. (2000). Whither the sociological study of crime. *Annual Review of Sociology*, 26:711–714.

Sanson, A., S. Hemphill, & D. Smart (2004). Connections between temperament and social development: A review. *Social Development*, 13:142–170.

Saudino, K. (2005). Behavioral genetics and child temperament. *Journal of Developmental and Behavioral Pediatrics*, 26:214–223.

Saulsman, L. & A. Page (2004). The five-factor model and personality disorder empirical literature: A meta-analytic review. *Clinical Psychology Review*, 23:1055–1085.

Sawhill, I. & J. Morton (2007). *Economic mobility: Is the American dream alive and well?* Washington, DC: The Economic Mobility Project/Pew Charity Trusts.

Scarr, S. (1996). How people make their own environments: Implications for parents and policy makers. *Psychology, Public Policy, and Law*, 2:204–228.

Schmalleger, F. (2004). *Criminology today*. Upper Saddle River, NJ: Prentice Hall.

Schmidt, F. & K. Hunter (2004). General mental ability in the world of work: Occupational attainment and job performance. *Journal of Personality and Social Psychology*, 86:162–173.

Schwalbe, M., S. Goodwin, D. Holden, D. Schrock, S. Thompson, & M. Wolkomer (2000). Generic processes in the reproduction of inequality: An interactionist analysis. *Social Forces*, 79:419–452.

Smits, J. (2003). Social closure among the higher educated: Trends in educational homogamy in 55 countries. *Social Science Research*, 32:251–277.

Tittle, C. (1983). Social class and criminal behavior: A critique of the theoretical foundation. *Social Forces*, 62:334–358.

Van den Berghe, P. (1990). Why most sociologists don't (and won't) think evolutionarily. *Sociological Forum*, 5:173–185.

van Goozen, S., G. Fairchild, H. Snoek, & G. Harold (2007). The evidence for a neurobiological model of childhood antisocial behavior. *Psychological Bulletin*, 133:149–182.

van Leeuwen, M. & I. Maas (2002). Partner choice and homogamy in the nineteenth century: Was there a sexual revolution in Europe? *Journal of Social History*, 36:101–123.

van Voorhees, E. & A. Scarpa (2004). The effects of child maltreatment on the hypothalamic-pituitary-adrenal axis. *Trauma, Violence, and Abuse*, 5:333–352.

Vold, G., T. Bernard, & J. Snipes (1998). *Theoretical criminology*. New York: Oxford University Press.

Walsh, A. (1997). Methodological individualism and vertical integration in the social sciences. *Behavior and Philosophy*, 25:121–136.

Walsh, A. (2009). *Biology and criminology: The biosocial synthesis*. New York: Routledge.

Walsh, A. (2011). *Crime and social class: A biosocial perspective*. New York: Routledge.

Walsh, A. & K. Beaver (2009). *Biosocial criminology: New directions in theory and research*. New York: Routledge.

Walsh, A. & I. Yun (2011). Developmental neurobiology from embryonic neuron migration to adolescent synaptic pruning: Relevance for antisocial behavior. In M. Delisi & K. Beaver (Eds.), *Criminological theory: A life-course approach*, pp. 69–84. Boston: Jones and Bartlett.

Wright, J. & K. Beaver (2005). Do parents matter in creating self-control in their children? A genetically informed test of Gottfredson and Hirschi's theory of low self-control. *Criminology*, 43:1169–1202.

Wright, J., D. Boisvert, K. Dietrich, & M. Ris (2009). The ghost in the machine and criminal behavior: Criminology for the 21st century. In A. Walsh & K. Beaver

(Eds.), *Biosocial criminology: New directions in theory and research*, pp. 73–89. New York: Routledge.

Wright, J., K. Dietrich, M. Ris, R. Hornung, S. Wessel, & B. Lanphear (2008). Association of prenatal and childhood blood lead concentrations with criminal arrests in early childhood. *PLoS Medicine*, 5:732–740.

PART V
EVOLUTIONARY
PSYCHOLOGY AND CRIME

Women's Avoidance of Rape:
An Evolutionary Psychological
Perspective[1]

William F. McKibbin and Todd K. Shackelford

Evolutionary Psychological Theory

This chapter reviews the topic of women's rape avoidance from a modern evolutionary psychological perspective (for an overview see, for example, Barkow, Cosmides, & Tooby, 1992; Buss 2004; Confer et al., 2010). An evolutionary psychological perspective is a powerful heuristic tool that can be used to generate novel and testable hypotheses across all domains of psychology. Evolutionary psychology rests on a number of key premises (Buss, 2004). The first premise states that natural selection is the only known process capable of producing complex functional systems such as the human brain. The complexity of human behavior can only be understood completely by taking into account human evolutionary history and natural selection.

The second premise of evolutionary psychology is that behavior depends on evolved psychological mechanisms. These are information-processing mechanisms housed in the brain that register and process specific information and generate as output specific behaviors, physiological activity, or input relayed to other psychological mechanisms. The third premise is that these evolved psychological mechanisms are functionally specialized to perform a specific task or to solve a specific adaptive problem. Adaptive problems are specific problems that recurrently affected reproductive success over evolutionary history. This third premise is often referred to as domain specificity. Finally, the premise of numerousness states that human brains consist of many specific evolved psychological mechanisms that work together to produce behavior. Together with other theoretical tools and heuristics provided by modern evolutionary theory, these premises are used to generate evolutionary theories of psychology and behavior.

---

1   Adapted from McKibbin, W.F. & Shackelford, T.K. (in press). Women's avoidance of rape. *Aggression and Violent Behavior*.

One such heuristic tool that informs evolutionary psychology is parental investment theory (Trivers, 1972). Parental investment theory consists of two premises. First, in sexually reproducing species, the sex that invests more in offspring (typically the female) will be more discriminating about mating. Second, the sex that invests less in offspring (typically the male) will be more intrasexually competitive for sexual access to the higher-investing sex. These premises have been supported in research with numerous species, including humans. Human females, like the females of most biparental species, invest more in offspring, whereas males invest more in mating effort. These sex differences are greatest in short-term mating contexts (Buss, 1994a, 1994b, 2004).

Misconceptions about Evolutionary Psychology

Some scholars believe that evolutionary psychological research is conducted to justify racism, sexism, or other undesirable "-isms." For example, Tang-Martinez (1997, p. 116) describes a common feminist view that evolutionary psychology is "inherently misogynistic and provides a justification for the oppression of women." More recently, however, the feminists to whom Tang-Martinez refers are committing what is known as the *naturalistic fallacy*: the error of deriving what *ought* to be from what *is*. This error can be demonstrated clearly with an example: no sensible person would argue that a scientist researching the causes of cancer is thereby justifying or promoting cancer. Yet, some people continue to argue that investigating rape from an evolutionary perspective justifies or legitimizes rape (e.g., Baron, 1985; Marshall & Barrett, 1990, cited in Thornhill & Palmer, 2000).

Related to the naturalistic fallacy is the false belief of *genetic determinism*: the idea that behavior is unalterable, programmed, or otherwise unchangeable. This argument has been debunked numerous times. Biologist John Maynard Smith noted that genetic determinism is "an incorrect idea that is largely irrelevant, because it is not held by anyone, or at least not by any competent evolutionary biologist" (1997, p. 524). No evolutionary psychologist would argue that because rape is produced by evolved mechanisms, it cannot be prevented or that we should simply accept its occurrence. The goal of evolutionary psychology, like the goal of any science, is to further our understanding of the phenomenon of interest, which in this case is rape. Researching rape from an evolutionary psychological perspective does not justify or promote this heinous act. Whether evolutionary psychological hypotheses about rape are correct, new perspectives often allow researchers to gain new insights into the target phenomenon. Gaining a greater understanding about why rape occurs is fundamental to decreasing its occurrence.

Finally, researchers using an evolutionary psychological perspective often frame hypotheses in terms of the costs and benefits to an organism of performing a particular behavior. These costs and benefits refer to the effects on reproductive success over evolutionary time, i.e., costs decreased the probability of successful reproduction, whereas benefits increased the probability of successful reproduction.

These terms are sometimes misconstrued as referring to a more general idea of perceived costs and benefits to the individual or to society. However, these terms carry no moral or ethical meaning, and are used only in terms of naturally-selected biological functioning.

Evolutionary Perspectives on Rape

Definitions of rape vary. It is typically defined, and will be defined in this chapter, as the use of force or threat of force to achieve sexual penile-vaginal penetration of a woman without her consent (Kilpatrick, Edmunds, & Seymour, 1992; Thornhill & Palmer, 2000). Rape appears to have been a recurrent adaptive problem across many species. Evolutionary theory predicts sexual coercion and rape are likely to occur in any species in which males are more aggressive, more eager to mate, more sexually assertive, and less discriminating in choosing a mate (Thornhill & Palmer, 2000). Examples of sexual coercion and rape can be found to occur in insects (Dunn, Crean, & Gilburn, 2002; Linder & Rice, 2005; Thornhill, 1980, 1981, 1987; Vahed, 2002), amphibians and reptiles (Olsson, 1995; Reyer, Frei, & Som, 1999; Shine, Langkilde, & Mason, 2003; Sztatecsny, Jehle, Burke, & Hödl, 2006), fish (Magurran, 2001; Plath, Parzefall, & Schlupp, 2003), birds (Gowaty & Buschhaus, 1998; McKinney, Derrickson, & Mineau, 1983; Pizzari & Birkhead, 2000), and primates (Robbins, 1999; Smuts & Smuts, 1993; Wrangham & Peterson, 1996), among others. Rape has been a recurrent adaptive problem for many species, including humans.

Rape is an unfortunate fact of life across human cultures (Broude & Greene, 1978; Rozée, 1993; Sanday, 1981). In American samples, estimates of the prevalence of rape are as high as 13% for women (Kilpatrick et al., 1992; Resnick, Kilpatrick, Dansky, Saunders, & Best, 1993). Rape is likely more common, however, because rapes often go unreported (Kilpatrick et al., 1992). Although other forms of rape occur (e.g., male-male rape), this chapter focuses on how women may behave to avoid being raped by a man.

Rape became a public and academic focus following the publication of Brownmiller's (1975) book, *Against our will: Men, women, and rape*. Brownmiller argued that rape is "a conscious process of intimidation by which *all men* keep *all women* in a state of fear" (p. 15, emphasis in original). Since then, feminist theories of rape have dominated the rape research literature. A prominent version of feminist theory contends that rape is the result of social traditions in which men have dominated political, economic, and other sources of power (Ellis, 1989). Feminist theorists inspired by Brownmiller often interpret rape as a method by which men maintain this power and dominance over women. Moreover, feminist theorists have argued explicitly that rape is not about sexual gratification and often seem more focused on making ideological, rather than scientific, statements about human psychology and behavior (Thornhill & Palmer, 2000). Recently, researchers have begun to examine rape and rape avoidance from an evolutionary psychological perspective.

Women's Defenses against Rape

Rape is a traumatic event that is likely to have been a recurrent problem for women over evolutionary history (Thornhill & Palmer, 2000). Rape often leads to many negative consequences for women and, therefore, women may have evolved psychological mechanisms designed to motivate rape avoidance behaviors. There are several reasons why rape is traumatic for women. These include disrupting a woman's parental care, causing a woman's partner to abandon her, and causing a woman serious physical injury or death (Thornhill & Palmer, 2000). Women are sometimes killed after being raped (Shackelford, 2002a, 2002b). Aside from death, perhaps the greatest cost to women who are raped is the circumvention of their mate choice (Wilson, Daly, & Scheib, 1997). This is because anything that circumvents women's choice in mating can severely jeopardize their reproductive success (Symons, 1979).

Researchers have speculated that a variety of female traits evolved to reduce the risks of being raped. Smuts (1992) argued that women form alliances with groups of men and other women for protection against would-be rapists. Similarly, Wilson and Mesnick (1997) proposed and found support for the *bodyguard hypothesis*: women's mate preferences for physically and socially dominant men may reflect anti-rape adaptation. Of course, women may form alliances or prefer dominant mates for reasons other than to avoid rape. Alliances offer protection from such dangers as assault or predation, and dominant mates may possess higher quality genes, for example. Finally, Davis and Gallup (2006) proposed the intriguing possibility that preeclampsia and spontaneous abortion may be adaptations that function to terminate pregnancies not in the woman's best reproductive interests, such as those resulting from rape. Relatively little empirical work has been conducted to identify specific psychological mechanisms that evolved to solve the recurrent problem of rape avoidance.

Thornhill and Thornhill (1990a, 1990b, 1990c, 1991) have demonstrated that the psychological pain that women experience after being raped may be produced by evolved mechanisms designed to focus women's attention on the circumstances of the rape, particularly the social cirumstances that resulted in the rape. Thornhill and Thornhill (1990a, 1990b, 1990c, 1991) argue that, like physical pain, psychological pain motivates individuals to attend to the circumstances that led to the pain and to avoid those circumstances in the future. Victims of rape who have more to lose in terms of future reproductive success will also experience more psychological pain relative to women with less to lose in terms of future reproductive success (Thornhill & Thornhill, 1983, 1990a; Thornhill & Palmer, 2000). For example, reproductive-aged women are hypothesized to experience more psychological pain due to the greater risk of conception. Thornhill and Thornhill (1990a) provided support for this hypothesis, documenting that reproductive-aged women are more traumatized by rape than are post-reproductive aged women or pre-reproductive aged girls.

The research conducted by Thornhill and Thornhill focuses on the after-effects of being raped and on the psychological pain that may motivate women to avoid the circumstances leading to the rape. Very little research, however, has been conducted to identify the specific behaviors women may deploy to avoid being raped. Scheppele and Bart (1983) conducted interviews of women who had been raped, or who had been attacked and successfully avoided being raped. Some of these women described "rules of rape avoidance" (p. 64) and how they followed them, e.g., "I would never be alone on the street" and "I would watch what I wear" (p. 65). These qualitative data provide preliminary evidence for rape-avoidance adaptations in women.

Petralia and Gallup (2002) examined whether a woman's capacity to resist rape varies across the ovulatory cycle. Women in the fertile phase of their ovulatory cycle showed an increase in handgrip strength, but only when presented with a sexual coercion scenario. Women not in their fertile phase did not show an increase in handgrip strength. Furthermore, women in all other conditions, including women in the fertile phase who were presented with the neutral control scenario, showed a *decrease* in hand strength post-test. This provides evidence for specialized mechanisms designed to motivate women to behave in ways that cause them to be less likely to be raped. Women who experience increased strength during their fertile phase would be better equipped to defend themselves from would-be rapists. The research by Petralia and Gallup provides evidence consistent with the hypothesis that women have evolved mechanisms that motivate rape avoidance behaviors.

Chavanne and Gallup (1998) investigated the performance of risky behaviors by women in the fertile phase of their ovulatory cycles. A sample of women were asked where they were in their ovulatory cycles, and to indicate whether they had performed a range of behaviors in the previous 24 hours. Behaviors were ranked by an independent sample of women in a previous study according to how likely performing the behaviors might result in a woman being sexually assaulted, with riskier behaviors given higher risk scores. Individuals' risky behavior was estimated by taking the summed composite score of all performed activities. Women in the fertile phase of their ovulatory cycle reported performing fewer behaviors representing a greater risk of being raped. There was no difference in the likelihood of performing low-risk behaviors between women in their fertile phase and women outside their fertile phase. This research has some methodological problems that prevent firm conclusions, however. First, the researchers used only one method (i.e., the forward-cycle method) to assess women's ovulatory status. Also, Chavanne and Gallup do not specify how the inventory of risky behaviors was developed, noting only that a preliminary sample of women rated the riskiness of the behaviors. In addition, the dependent variable may be confounded by diversity of activity. For example, a woman who performed 10 non-risky behaviors (each scored as a "1" on the riskiness scale) could receive the same score as a woman who performed two high-risk behaviors (each scored as a "5" on the riskiness scale; see Bröder and Hohmann, 2003, for discussion). Despite these methodological issues, this research documented a significant decrease in performance of risky behaviors by women in the fertile phase of their ovulatory cycle. This evidence is consistent with the hypothesized function of rape-avoidance mechanisms, particularly when women are fertile.

Chavanne and Gallup's (1998) study was replicated by Bröder and Hohmann (2003) using a within-subjects design. Twenty-six women who did not use oral contraceptives were tested weekly for four successive weeks. The results indicated that women in the fertile phase of their ovulatory cycle selectively inhibit behaviors that would expose them to a higher risk of being raped, despite performing *more* non-risky behaviors. These results provide a conceptual replication of the results reported by Chavanne and Gallup. Women perform fewer risky behaviors when they are fertile, while still demonstrating a higher overall activity level (Morris & Udry, 1970) and even while engaging in more consensual sex (Morris & Udry, 1982). This selective behavior indicates that women may have evolved specialized psychological mechanisms designed to motivate behaviors that decrease the risk of being raped. Although this study addressed many of the issues in the Chavanne and Gallup research, there is still no indication of how risky behaviors were identified. This study also used the somewhat problematic forward and reverse-cycle counting methods for identifying the fertile phase of the ovulatory cycle, both of which depend on the potentially unreliable self-reports of participants (Bröder & Hohmann, 2003).

A recent study by Garver-Apgar, Gangestad, and Simpson (2007) tested the hypothesis that women are more attuned to signs of a man's potential sexual coerciveness during the fertile phase and are more accurate at detecting sexually coercive men during the fertile phase. A sample of 169 normally-ovulating women watched short segments of videotaped interviews of men. The women were then asked to rate the men on several items that were summed to create an overall coerciveness rating. Average coerciveness ratings for each man were computed. Finally, women's ovulatory status was estimated using the reverse-cycle counting method. The results indicated that women in the fertile phase of their ovulatory cycle rated the men as more sexually coercive. This suggests that women at greater risk of conception may be more attuned to signs of male sexual coerciveness than women at lesser risk of conception. This may represent an evolved cognitive error management bias (see Haselton, Nettle, & Andrews, 2005, for an overview) toward identifying men as sexually coercive, which might serve to protect women from being raped. This research provides more evidence that women may have evolved psychological mechanisms that motivate behaviors that guard against men's sexual coercion and rape. Note, however, that the participants viewed videos of strangers. Studies demonstrate that women have a greater fear of stranger rape than of being raped by someone they know (Thornhill & Thornhill, 1990b), which suggests that stranger rape was the greater adaptive problem. This is despite modern patterns of rape, which indicate that women are more likely to be raped by someone they know (Kilpatrick et al., 1992; Resnick et al., 1993). These results may reflect the greater potential costs associated with stranger rape, such as a decreased likelihood of investment by the genetic father of resulting offspring. Would similar results be found by testing women's coerciveness ratings of acquaintances or other familiar men? Future research is needed to explore these effects in greater detail. For example, researchers might ask women to rate the coerciveness of familiar faces of classmates or celebrities.

In summary, several studies provide evidence that women may have mechanisms that motivate rape avoidance. Women may have mechanisms that motivate them to assess the risk of being raped (e.g., the riskiness of walking in a dark parking lot alone) or the likelihood that a particular man may be sexually coercive. However, these previous studies of rape avoidance assessed different behaviors that were selected for assessment without an explicit rationale, making it difficult to compare specific results across the studies. There exists a need for a standard instrument to assess women's specific rape avoidance behaviors that has been shown to be broad in scope and empirically sound (McKibbin et al., 2009). After presenting an argument for the need for a reliable, valid measure of rape avoidance, McKibbin et al. (2009) developed just such a measure.

Rape Avoidance Inventory

Beginning with act nomination procedures similar to those pioneered by Buss and Craik (1983), McKibbin et al. (2009) sought to first identify specific behaviors women may perform to avoid being raped. Using the acts nominated through women's self-reports, the researchers constructed an inventory to assess these behaviors. The Rape Avoidance Inventory (RAI) assesses performance of 69 behaviors, all specifically nominated by women as behaviors they performed to avoid being raped. Using principal components analysis, behaviors nominated by women were identified as belonging to one of four relatively independent components: Avoid Strange Men, Avoid Appearing Sexually Receptive, Avoid Being Alone, and Awareness of Surroundings/Defensive Preparedness.

The Avoid Strange Men component consists of behaviors which appear to motivate women to avoid unfamiliar men, and behaviors motivating women to avoid men who may represent a greater risk of being sexually coercive (e.g., "Avoid men who make me feel uncomfortable," "Avoid drunk men"). The Avoid Appearing Sexually Receptive component consists of behaviors that may diminish a woman's physical or sexual attractiveness to a potential rapist (e.g., "Avoid wearing sexy clothing," "Avoid making out with a man I have just met"). The Avoid Being Alone component consists of behaviors that appear to motivate a woman to stay around others (e.g., "When I go out, I stay with at least one other person that I know"). Finally, the Awareness of Surroundings/Defensive Preparedness component includes behaviors that appear to motivate a woman to be especially attentive to her surroundings (e.g., "Pay special attention to my surroundings"), as well as behaviors that enhance a woman's ability to thwart a would-be rapist (e.g., "Carry a knife").

These components map closely onto a taxonomy of four "guidelines" for female defense against rape derived independently by Judson (2002, p. 121) following a review of cross-species research addressing primarily non-humans. These four guidelines are: "avoid groups of idle males," "don't attract attention," "don't leave home alone," and "do carry weapons." The conceptual confuence of the current four components with those derived by Judson provides preliminary evidence for the construct validity of the RAI.

It could be argued that the RAI consists of a disproportionate number of items which relate to stranger rape rather than acquaintance rape. This is despite the fact that rapes are most often perpetrated by someone known to the victim (Greenfield, 1997). The items on the RAI were derived from behaviors nominated by women themselves, however. This, the authors suggest, indicates that while indeed less frequently occurring, stranger rape may elicit more fear in women. Items on the RAI may reflect the most relevant adaptive problems experienced by women over human evolutionary history (McKibbin et al., 2009).

Further analyses provided preliminary evidence of both the reliability and validity of the RAI. The full-scale and four component scales demonstrated high levels of internal reliability. Uniformly positive yet moderate correlations among scores on the total and component scales of the RAI provided additional evidence of the utility of the four-component nature of the RAI. These scores demonstrated that the four components were interrelated, yet still relatively distinct from one another. Finally, McKibbin et al. (2009) demonstrated a consistent pattern of negative correlations between RAI scores and interest in and pursuit of short-term sex (which places women at increased risk of rape). As predicted, items on the RAI (which represent decreased risk of sexual assault or rape) were negatively correlated with a measure consisting of behaviors which represent a greater risk of sexual assault or rape. These findings provided initial evidence for the convergent and descriminative validity of the RAI as an assessment of women's rape avoidace behaviors.

Individual Differences in Rape Avoidance

As the work reviewed previously has demonstrated, women appear to possess evolved psychological mechanisms associated with rape avoidance. This is because ancestral women who responded to increased rape-related risk (such as at the time of ovulation) with more rape avoidance behaviors may have been more reproductively successful than women who did not. It may be the case that there are a number of other individual differences in women which lead to differences in the deployment of rape-avoidance behaviors. Guided by an evolutionary perspective, McKibbin, Shackelford, Miner, Bates, and Liddle (2011) identified several such variables that may influence women's rape-related risk. Specifically, they predicted that individual differences in women's attractiveness, relationship status, number of family members living nearby, and age would covary with women's rape avoidance behaviors.

Cross-culturally, men more than women report a preference for physical attractiveness in a prospective romantic partner, because attractiveness in women more than in men is an indicator of fertility and expected future reproduction (e.g., Buss, 1989). Research suggests that would-be rapists also may prefer and target more attractive women, in order to maximize the probability of conception (Ghiglieri, 2000; Greenfield, 1997; Kilpatrick et al., 1992; McKibbin, Shackelford, Goetz, & Starratt, 2008; Thornhill & Palmer, 2000; Thornhill & Thornhill, 1983).

If women's psychology includes mechanisms that motivate rape avoidance behaviors, then more attractive women may be more motivated to perform rape avoidance behaviors, relative to less attractive women. Therefore, McKibbin et al. (2011) predicted that women's attractiveness will correlate positively with women's reports of the frequency with which they perform rape avoidance behaviors.

Mated women, as compared with unmated women, may incur additional costs associated with being raped (Thornhill, 1999; Thornhill & Palmer, 2000). Specifically, if a woman's regular partner interprets the rape as an infidelity, a mated woman risks losing her partner's support and resources for herself and her offspring (Thornhill & Palmer, 2000; Thornhill & Thornhill, 1992). Thornhill and Thornhill (1990a) documented that mated women report more psychological pain than did unmated women following rape. They suggested that the psychological pain experienced by mated women functions to focus women's attention on the costs or losses they have experienced such that women will find ways to avoid similar costly situations. Unmated women might be expected to experience greater costs associated with being raped, because the rape may produce offspring that would not benefit from the support and investment of a regular partner. Based on the findings of Thornhill and Thornhill, however, McKibbin et al. (2011) generated the following prediction. Because mated women may experience greater losses than unmated women as a result of a rape, women in a relationship will report higher frequencies of rape avoidance behaviors than women not in a relationship.

Over evolutionary history, individuals with psychological mechanisms that motivated reciprocal exchange of resources and support with close family members are likely to have been more successful than individuals without such mechanisms (Hamilton, 1964). Close genetic relatives also may incur costs if a female relative is raped, such as decline in inclusive fitness associated with her injury, inability to contribute to the family, or care for her own offspring. This helping may occur in multiple domains, and may include behaviors that decrease the risk of a female genetic relative being raped (e.g., parents discouraging their daughter from wearing revealing clothing or men accompanying their daughters or sisters at night). Indeed, research has demonstrated that family members do act in such ways. Figueredo et al. (2001) found that the presence of adult male kin living nearby decreased the likelihood of a female relative being raped, perhaps because would-be rapists fear retaliation by the rape victim's adult male kin. Individuals also may act in ways that more directly decrease the likelihood of a female relative being raped. Perilloux, Fleischmann, and Buss (2008) found that parents exerted more control over their daughters' behavior than their sons' behavior, particularly their mating behavior. Compared to how they interacted with their sons, parents were more likely to express upset in response to a daughter's risky sexual activity, to use curfews to control a daughter's behavior, and to exert control over a daughter's clothing choices, all of which may decrease a daughter's risk of being vulnerable to rape or being targeted for rape. Other close kin, such as siblings, also may act to prevent women from being raped. For example, brothers may accompany a sister outside at night. Because a woman's relatives may guard her directly or attempt to influence her rape-relevant behaviors, it was predicted that the number of women's family members living in close proximity will correlate positively with the frequency with which women perform rape avoidance behaviors (McKibbin et al., 2011).

Women's fertility—risk of conception per copulation—peaks in the early 20s and declines with age (Thornhill & Thornhill, 1983). Men have evolved preferences for fertile mates and, accordingly, men generally express a preference for younger mates (Buss, 1989). Would-be rapists also may target younger women, relative to older women. Indeed, younger women are over-represented in reported rapes and rapes unreported to authorities (Greenfield, 1997; Kilpatrick et al., 1992; Thornhill & Palmer, 2000; Thornhill & Thornhill, 1983). Because younger women are more likely to be raped, it was predicted that women's age would correlate negatively with the frequency with which women perform rape avoidance behaviors (McKibbin et al., 2011). In general, the results generated using women's self-reports of their rape avoidance behaviors supported the predictions such that the frequency with which women reported performing rape avoidance behaviors varied predictably with several individual differences among women.

The results of the correlational analyses provided support for the prediction that women's attractiveness would correlate positively with women's reports of the frequency with which they performed rape avoidance behaviors. A positive correlation was found between women's self-reported attractiveness and total rape avoidance behavior. Because attractive women may be preferentially targeted by rapists (McKibbin et al., 2008; Thornhill & Palmer, 2000), these women appeared to perform more rape avoidance behaviors relative to less attractive women. These findings provide preliminary evidence that more attractive women, relative to less attractive women, avoid situations in which they are alone and vulnerable. They also pay special attention to their surroundings and were more likely to carry defensive weapons such as mace.

Also as predicted, McKibbin et al. (2011) documented a positive correlation between relationship status and the frequency of women's rape avoidance behaviors. Women who reported being in a long-term committed relationship reported greater frequencies of total rape avoidance behaviors than women who did not report being in a committed, long-term relationship. This may be because mated women must manage the additional risk of losing their partner's investment. Specifically, mated women performed more behaviors in the Avoid Appearing Sexually Receptive and Awareness of Surroundings/Defensive Preparedness components of rape avoidance behaviors. Mated women performed more behaviors that downplayed their attractiveness and perceived sexual receptivity. They also paid extra attention to their surroundings and were more likely to carry defensive weapons. Because mated women bear additional potential costs associated with being raped (Thornhill, 1996; Thornhill & Palmer, 2000; Thornhill & Thornhill, 1990;

Wilson & Mesnick, 1997), they appear to perform more rape avoidance behavior relative to non-mated women.

McKibbin et al. (2011) also predicted that the number of women's family members living in close proximity would correlate positively with the frequency with which women performed rape avoidance behaviors. Women's reports of rape avoidance behaviors were indeed positively correlated with the number of male and female family members living close by. Individuals are able to manage their inclusive fitness interests by protecting genetic female relatives from being raped. This protection may often be indirect, with relatives encouraging women to behave in ways that diminish the risk of being raped. Examining the component scores for women's rape avoidance revealed two components in particular that seemed to drive this effect. Specifically, men and women encouraged behaviors in the Awareness of Surroundings/Defensive Preparedness component. Men also appeared to encourage behaviors from the Avoid Appearing Sexually Receptive component. Examining subsequent multiple regression analyses, McKibbin et al. (2011) demonstrated that the number of female family members living close by did not uniquely predict women's rape avoidance. Rather, it is the number of male family members living close by that predicted uniquely women's behaviors in the Awareness of Surroundings/Defensive Preparedness component. Although men and women appeared to actively encourage rape avoidance behaviors in their female close relatives, men in particular seemed to encourage their female family members to behave in ways to avoid rape.

McKibbin et al. (2011) did not find support for the prediction that women's age correlated negatively with the frequency with which women performed rape avoidance behaviors. Only one component, Avoid Appearing Sexually Receptive, correlated significantly with age, and this was in the opposite direction than was predicted. The researchers noted, however, that the current results were inconsistent with the preponderance of evidence linking rape and the age of the victim (Felson & Krohn, 1990; Greenfield, 1997; Kilpatrick et al., 1992; Perkins & Klaus, 1996; Perkins, Klaus, Bastian, & Cohen, 1996; Thornhill & Thornhill, 1983). The researchers also noted that approximately 80% of the participants in the study were under 30 years old, arguing that this restricted age range may have made it difficult to find the predicted relationship between rape avoidance behavior and age.

Limitations of RAI Research

The research highlighted above is based exclusively on data self-reported by women. Although the women may not accurately remember how often they performed each rape avoidance behavior, such data cannot be defensibly secured from other data sources. Because the researchers were interested in behaviors that women perform specifically for the purpose of avoiding rape, there is no compelling reason to believe that other parties, such as independent observers or a woman's close friends, would have the information and perspective to provide more accurate reports than the women themselves.

Women in long-term committed relationships scored higher on the RAI. These findings were interpreted to suggest that mated women perform more rape avoidance behaviors to avoid the additional potential costs for mated women associated with being raped. An alternative explanation for the difference between mated and unmated women may be that mated women are less likely to go to parties or clubs, or to perform mate-seeking behaviors such as flirting (McKibbin et al., 2011). Similarly, mated women may be less likely to be alone than are unmated women, simply by virtue of spending much of their time in their partner's presence. However, regression analyses reported by McKibbin et al. indicated that women in long-term committed relationships also reported a greater frequency of behaviors associated with awareness of the environment and preparedness. In addition, women who did not report being in a committed, long-term relationship may nevertheless be in another type of non-committed or short-term relationship. Their responses may be different than the responses provided by women who were not in any type of relationship. These findings cannot lead to a conclusive argument that mated women perform more rape avoidance behaviors. Subsequent studies should more carefully define relationship status and more carefully examine shifts in women's rape avoidance behavior associated with relationship status, perhaps by examining shifts in the performance frequency of individual behaviors rather than categories of overall rape avoidance behavior.

The participants in research utilizing the RAI (McKibbin et al., 2009, 2011) were limited to middle-class college students attending psychology courses at a single state university in Florida. Future studies should attempt to replicate these findings in other samples, particularly from other countries or cultures when possible, although some of the items in the RAI may not apply to non-Western cultures equally well.

Conclusions and Future Directions

Because of the severe costs associated with rape, it is likely that women have evolved psychological mechanisms that motivate rape avoidance behavior. However, because the risk of rape is not the same for every woman, these mechanisms may be sensitive to individual differences between women that influence their risk of being raped. A growing body of research suggests that this may be the case. Women do appear to possess evolved mechanisms that motivate rape avoidance behavior. Research also suggests that these evolved mechanisms are sensitive to individual differences in women and their environments.

Few researchers have studied women's strategies of rape avoidance, particularly from an evolutionary psychological perspective. Thankfully, this is changing as more researchers begin investigations in this area. With a greater understanding of the underlying psychological processes associated with women's rape avoidance, researchers and other professionals can better help women to avoid being raped. One such way for example, may be to design rape awareness or prevention programs that are informed by the empirical work presented here and in other studies.

The variables examined in this chapter do not represent an exhaustive list of the variables that may influence rape avoidance behavior. An evolutionary perspective can be used to identify other important variables for future study. For example, there may be a relationship between the number of dependent children a mated woman has and her performance of rape avoidance behaviors. A mated woman who has dependent children may perform more rape avoidance behaviors than a mated woman without dependent children because she risks losing her partner's support for herself as well as her offspring.

Previous studies have identified ovulatory shifts in women's behavior associated with increased risk of rape (Bröder & Hohmann, 2003; Chavanne & Gallup, 1998). Women might exhibit similar shifts in behaviors included in the RAI. If the RAI does in fact represent a valid measure of women's rape avoidance behavior, subsequent research should find that women show clear shifts in the behaviors indexed by the RAI when they are ovulating. Future research is needed to investigate whether these shifts do in fact occur.

Finally, women's self-reports of their rape avoidance behaviors may differ from the actual frequency with which they perform these behaviors. Or women may perform behaviors without consciously understanding why they do so. Future research might examine whether observer-reported (e.g., as reported by same-sex best friend) frequencies of these behaviors differ from women's self-reports. Furthermore, no research has assessed the effectiveness of these behaviors. Future research should assess whether women who more frequently perform these behaviors (or particular components of these behaviors) in fact are less likely to report being raped.

Evolutionary psychology is a powerful heuristic tool that allows researchers to consider rape in a new light. Researchers have hypothesized that women have evolved mechanisms that motivate behaviors to avoid being raped. A growing body of evidence supports this hypothesis (e.g., Bröder & Hohmann, 2003; Chavanne & Gallup, 1998; Petralia & Gallup, 2002). Researchers should continue to investigate the psychological mechanisms associated with women's rape avoidance behavior. Such information will not only inform scientific theory, but also may improve the lives of women around the world.

References

Barkow, J.H., Cosmides, L., & Tooby, J. (Eds.) (1992). *The adapted mind: Evolutionary psychology and the generation of culture.* New York: Oxford University Press.

Baron, L. (1985). Does rape contribute to reproductive success? Evaluations of sociobiological views of rape. *International Journal of Women's Studies, 8,* 266–277.

Bröder, A., & Hohmann, N. (2003). Variations in risk-taking behavior over the menstrual cycle: An improved replication. *Evolution and Human Behavior, 24,* 391–398.

Broude, G.J., & Greene, S.J. (1978). Cross-cultural codes on 20 sexual attitudes and practices. *Ethnology, 15,* 409–440.

Brownmiller, S. (1975). *Against our will: Men, women, and rape.* New York: Simon & Schuster.

Buss, D. M. (1989). Sex differences in human mate preferences: Evolutionary hypotheses tested in 37 cultures. *Behavioral and Brain Sciences, 12,* 1–49.

Buss, D.M. (1994a). The strategies of human mating. *American Scientist, 82,* 238–249.

Buss, D.M. (1994b). *The evolution of desire: Strategies of human mating.* New York: Basic Books.

Buss, D.M. (2004). *Evolutionary psychology: The new science of the mind* (2nd ed.). Boston: Allyn & Bacon.

Buss, D.M., & Craik, K.H. (1983). The act frequency approach to personality. *Psychological Review, 90,* 105–126.

Chavanne, T.J., & Gallup, G.G. (1998). Variation in risk taking behavior among female college students as a function of the menstrual cycle. *Evolution and Human Behavior, 19,* 27–32.

Confer, J.C., Easton, J.A., Fleischman, D.S., Goetz, C.D., Lewis, D.M.G., Perilloux, C., & Buss, D.M. (2010). Evolutionary psychology: Controversies, questions, prospects, and limitations. *American Psychologist, 65,* 110–126.

Davis, J.A., & Gallup, G.G. Jr. (2006). Preeclampsia and other pregnancy complications as an adaptive response to unfamiliar semen. In S.M. Platek & T.K. Shackelford (Eds.), *Female infidelity and paternal uncertainty* (pp. 191–204). New York: Cambridge University Press.

Dunn, D.W, Crean, C.S., & Gilburn, A.S. (2002). The effects of exposure to seaweed on willingness to mate, oviposition, and longevity in seaweed flies. *Ecological Entomology, 27,* 554–564.

Ellis, L. (1989). *Theories of rape: Inquiries into the causes of sexual aggression.* New York: Hemisphere Publishing Corporation.

Felson, R., & Krohn, M. (1990). Motives for rape. *Journal of Research in Crime and Delinquency, 27,* 222–242.

Figueredo, A.J., Corral-Verdugo, V. Frias-Armenta, M., Bachar, K.J., White, J., McNeill, P.L., Kirsner, B.R., del Pilar Castell-Ruiz, I. (2001). Blood, solidarity, status, and honor: The sexual balance of power and spousal abuse in Sonora, Mexico. *Evolution and Human Behavior, 22,* 293–328.

Garver-Apgar, C.E., Gangestad, S.W., & Simpson, J.A. (2007). Women's perceptions of men's sexual coerciveness change across the menstrual cycle. *Acta Psychologica Sinica, 39,* 536–540.

Ghiglieri, M.P. (2000). *The dark side of man.* New York: Perseus Books.

Gowaty, P.A., & Buschhaus, N. (1998). Ultimate causation of aggressive and forced copulation in birds: Female resistance, the CODE hypothesis, and social monogamy. *Integrative and Comparative Biology, 38,* 207–225.

Greenfield, L. (1997). *Sex offenses and offenders*. Washington, DC: Bureau of Justice Statistics, US Department of Justice.

Hamilton, W.D. (1964). The genetical evolution of social behavior. I and II. *Journal of Theoretical Biology, 7*, 1–52.

Haselton, M.G., Nettle, D., & Andrews, P.W. (2005). The evolution of cognitive bias. In D.M. Buss (Ed.), *The handbook of evolutionary psychology* (pp. 724–746). Hoboken, NJ: John Wiley & Sons.

Judson, O. (2002). *Dr. Tatiana's sex advice to all creation*. New York: Henry Holt & Company.

Kilpatrick, D., Edmunds, C., & Seymour, A. (1992). *Rape in America*. Arlington, VA: National Victim Center.

Linder, J.E., & Rice, W.R. (2005). Natural selection and genetic variation for female resistance to harm from males. *Journal of Evolutionary Biology, 18*, 568–575.

Magurran, A.E. (2001). Sexual conflict and evolution in Trinidadian guppies. *Genetica, 112–113*, 463–474.

Maynard Smith, J. (1997). Commentary. In P. Gowaty (Ed.), *Feminism and evolutionary biology* (p. 522). New York: Chapman & Hall.

McKibbin, W.F., & Shackelford, T.K. (in press). Women's avoidance of rape. *Aggression and Violent Behavior*.

McKibbin, W. F., Shackelford, T.K., Goetz, A.T., Bates, V.M. Starratt, V.G., & Miner, E.J. (2009). Development and Initial Psychometric Assessment of the Rape Avoidance Inventory. *Personality and Individual Differences, 39*, 336–340.

McKibbin, W.F., Shackelford, T.K., Goetz, A.T., & Starratt, V.G. (2008). Why do men rape? An evolutionary psychological perspective. *Review of General Psychology, 12*, 86–97.

McKibbin, W.F., Shackelford, T.K., Miner, E.J., Bates, V.M., & Liddle, J.R. (2011). Individual differences in women's rape avoidance behaviors. *Archives of Sexual Behavior, 40*, 343–349.

McKinney, F., Derrickson, S.R., & Mineau, P. (1983). Forced copulation in waterfowl. *Behavior, 86*, 250–294.

Morris, N.M., & Udry, J.R. (1970). Variations in pedometer activity during the menstrual cycle. *Sensory Processing, 2*, 90–98.

Morris, N.M., & Udry, J.R. (1982). Epidemiological patterns of sexual behavior in the menstrual cycle. In R. C. Friedman (Ed.), *Behavior and the menstrual cycle* (pp. 129–153). New York: Marcel Dekker.

Olsson, M. (1995). Forced copulation and costly female resistance behavior in the lake eyre dragon, *Ctenophorus maculosus*. *Herpetologica, 51*, 19–24.

Palmer, C.T. (1989). Is rape a cultural universal? A re-examination of the ethnographic evidence. *Ethnology, 28*, 1–16.

Perilloux, C., Fleischman, D.S., & Buss, D.M. (2008). The daughter-guarding hypothesis: Parental influence on, and emotional reactions to, offspring's mating behavior. *Evolutionary Psychology, 6*, 217–233.

Perkins, C., & Klaus, P. (1996). *Criminal victimization 1994. National crime victimization survey*. Bulletin, Bureau of Justice Statistics, U.S. Department of Justice.

Perkins, C., Klaus, P., Bastian, L., & Cohen, R. (1996). *Criminal victimization in the United States, 1993. National crime victimization survey report*. Bureau of Justice Statistics, U.S. Department of Justice.

Petralia, S.M. & Gallup, G.G. (2002). Effects of a sexual assault scenario on handgrip strength across the menstrual cycle. *Evolution and Human Behavior, 23*, 3–10.

Pizzari, T., & Birkhead, T.R. (2000). Female feral fowl eject sperm of subdominant males. *Nature, 405*, 787–789.

Plath, M., Parzefall, J., & Schlupp, I. (2003). The role of sexual harassment in cave and surface dwelling populations of the Atlantic molly, *Poecilia mexicana* (Poeciliidae, Teleostei). *Behavioral Ecology and Sociobiology, 54*, 303–309.

Resnick, H.S., Kilpatrick, D.G., Dansky, B.S., Saunders, B.E., & Best, C.L. (1993). Prevalence of civilian trauma and post-traumatic stress disorder in a representative national sample of women. *Journal of Consulting and Clinical Psychology, 61*, 984–991.

Reyer, H.-U., Frei, G., & Som, C. (1999). Cryptic female choice: Frogs reduce clutch size when amplexed by undesired males. *Proceedings of the Royal Society B: Biological Sciences, 266*, 2101.

Robbins, M.M. (1999). Male mating patterns in wild multimale mountain gorilla groups. *Animal Behaviour, 57*, 1013–1020.

Rozée, P.D. (1993). Forbidden or forgiven? Rape in cross-cultural perspective. *Psychology of Women Quarterly, 17*, 499–514.

Sanday, P.R. (1981). The socio-cultural context of rape: A cross-cultural study. *Journal of Social Issues, 37*, 5–27.

Scheppele, K.L., & Bart, P.B. (1983). Through women's eyes: Defining danger in the wake of sexual assault. *Journal of Social Issues, 39*, 63–81.

Shackelford, T.K. (2002a). Are young women the special targets of rape-murder? *Aggressive Behavior, 28*, 224–232.

Shackelford, T.K. (2002b). Risk of multiple-offender rape-murder varies with female age. *Journal of Criminal Justice, 30*, 135–141.

Shine, R., Langkilde, T., & Mason, R.T. (2003). Cryptic forcible insemination: Male snakes exploit female physiology, anatomy, and behavior to obtain coercive matings. *American Naturalist, 162*, 653–667.

Smuts, B.B. (1992). Male aggression against women. *Human Nature, 6*, 1–32.

Smuts, B.B., & Smuts, R.W. (1993). Male aggression and sexual coercion of females in nonhuman primates and other mammals: Evidence and theoretical implications. *Advances in the Study of Behavior, 22*, 1–63.

Symons, D. (1979). *The evolution of human sexuality*. New York: Oxford University Press.

Sztatecsny, M. Jehle, R., Burke, T., & Hödl, W. (2006). Female polyandry under male harassment: The case of the common toad (*Bufo bufo*). *Journal of Zoology, 270*, 517.

Tang-Martinez, Z. (1997). The curious courtship of sociobiology and feminism: A case of irreconcilable differences. In P. Gowaty (Ed.), *Feminism and evolutionary biology* (pp. 116–150). New York: Chapman & Hall.

Thornhill, N. (1996). Psychological adaptation to sexual coercion in victims and offenders. In D.M. Buss & N. Malamuth (Eds.), *Sex, power, conflict* (pp. 90–104). New York: Oxford University Press.

Thornhill, N., & Thornhill, R. (1990a). Evolutionary analysis of psychological pain of rape victims I: The effects of victim's age and marital status. *Ethology and Sociobiology, 11*, 155–176.

Thornhill, N., & Thornhill, R. (1990b). Evolutionary analysis of psychological pain following rape II: The effects of stranger, friend, and family member offenders. *Ethology and Sociobiology, 11*, 177–193.

Thornhill, N., & Thornhill, R. (1990c). Evolutionary analysis of psychological pain following rape victims III: The effects of force and violence. *Aggressive Behavior, 16*, 297–320.

Thornhill, N., & Thornhill, R. (1991). An evolutionary analysis of psychological pain following rape IV: The effect of the nature of the sexual act. *Journal of Comparative Psychology, 105*, 243–252.

Thornhill, R. (1980). Rape in *Panorpa* scorpionflies and a general rape hypothesis. *Animal Behavior, 28*, 52–59.

Thornhill, R. (1981). *Panorpa* (Mecoptera: Panorpidea) scorpionflies: Systems for understanding resource-defense polygyny and alternative male reproductive efforts. *Annual Review of Ecology and Systematics, 12*, 355–386.

Thornhill, R. (1987). The relative importance of intra- and interspecific competition in scorpionfly mating systems. *American Naturalist, 130*, 711–729.

Thornhill, R. (1999). The biology of human rape. *Jurimetrics Journal, 39*, 137–147.

Thornhill, R., & Palmer, C.P. (2000). *A natural history of rape.* Cambridge, MA: The MIT Press.

Thornhill, R. & Thornhill, N. (1983). Human rape: An evolutionary analysis. *Ethology and Sociobiology, 4*, 137–173.

Thornhill, R., & Thornhill, N. (1992). The evolutionary psychology of men's coercive sexuality. *Behavioral and Brain Sciences, 15*, 363–375.

Trivers, R.L. (1972). Parental investment and sexual selection. In B. Campbell (Ed.), *Sexual selection and the descent of man: 1871–1971* (pp. 136–179). Chicago: Aldine.

Vahed, K. (2002). Coercive copulation in the Alpine Bushcricket *Anonconotus alpinus* Yersin (Tettigoniidae: Tettigoniinae: Platycleidini), *Ethology, 108*, 1065–1075.

Wilson, M., Daly, M., & Scheib, J. (1997). Femicide: an evolutionary psychological perspective. In P.A. Gowaty (Ed.), *Feminism and evolutionary biology: Boundaries, intersections, and frontiers* (pp. 431–465). New York: Chapman & Hall.

Wilson, M., & Mesnick, S.L. (1997). An empirical test of the bodyguard hypothesis. In P.A. Gowaty (Ed.), *Feminism and evolutionary biology* (pp. 505–511). New York: Chapman & Hall.

Wrangham, R., & Peterson, D. (1996). *Demonic males: Apes and the origins of human violence.* New York: Houghton Mifflin.

The Search for Human Rape and Anti-Rape Adaptations: Ten Years after *A Natural History of Rape*

Ryan M. Ellsworth and Craig T. Palmer

> *[T]he question whether rape is an adaptation or a by-product cannot yet be definitively answered.*
>
> (Thornhill and Palmer, 2000, p. 85)

> *Social action is most likely to succeed if it is based on a realistic appraisal of the human condition.*
>
> (Symons, 1979, p. 66)

Introduction

Although the book *A Natural History of Rape* (Thornhill and Palmer, 2000, hereafter referred to as ANHR) was widely asserted to proclaim that human rape is an adaptation (e.g., see contributions in Travis, 2003), the first epigraph above demonstrates that it actually explicitly stated that existing evidence was *not* sufficient to warrant that conclusion. This chapter examines some of the research performed in the decade since the publication of ANHR to determine if a different conclusion is now warranted. It finds that there is still insufficient evidence to warrant the conclusion that male rape-specific adaptations exist in our species. However, it also concludes that continued research to further test a number of hypotheses is warranted. In regard to the evidence of anti-rape adaptations in women, Thornhill and Palmer found the evidence of adaptation more convincing, but still emphasized that "more research is needed to demonstrate" such adaptations (2000, p. 96). Recent research on potential female anti-rape adaptations will also be discussed.

The structure of the chapter will involve, first, introducing some important concepts of evolutionary biology in order to orient the reader unfamiliar with evolutionary theory. Next, we review the potential human male rape-specific adaptations listed in ANHR. Following this we summarize the research performed since ANHR related to each hypothesis, followed in some instances with suggestions for future research. After summarizing this body of evidence, we turn to potential human female anti-rape adaptations, and review the recent evidence bearing on these hypotheses. Finally, in the conclusion, we discuss the implications of evolutionary analyses of human rape, and briefly address the ongoing debate surrounding the motivation of rapists.

At the outset, we feel obliged to reiterate a point repeatedly emphasized throughout ANHR: the question of whether or not rape-specific adaptations exist in our species in no way implies that rape is inevitable, acceptable or should be treated as anything other than a horrible crime to be prevented and punished. To think otherwise is to commit the naturalistic fallacy: the erroneous conclusion that what is "natural" is therefore "good" or justifiable (see Thornhill and Palmer, 2000, pp. 5–6, 84, 107–111, 117, 119–122, 124, 148, 150, 179–180). By avoiding the naturalistic fallacy, readers can be in a position to evaluate how increased knowledge generated by studies of whether or not human rape involves rape-specific adaptations can help with the urgent practical task of decreasing the frequency of rape.

This chapter will be restricted to only studies that explicitly address the issue of rape-specific adaptations in humans. It should be remembered, however, that the vast majority of research on human rape continues to take place without any explicit reference to evolutionary theory. Many of the findings of such research may be relevant to the issue of rape-specific adaptations although not undertaken with an evolutionary approach in mind.

Key Concepts in Evolutionary Biology

Before reviewing hypotheses and evidence of human rape adaptations, it will be helpful to define some terms central to evolutionary biology (see chapter 1 in Thornhill and Palmer, 2000 for a detailed discussion of evolutionary biological theory). *Natural selection* refers to the non-random differential reproduction of individuals. Selection is non-random because it is "differential reproduction of individuals by consequence of their differences in phenotypic design" (Thornhill and Palmer, 2000, p. 6). The process of natural selection leads to two basic categories of traits: adaptations and by-products. *Adaptations* are traits (morphological structures, physiological [including psychological] mechanisms, and behaviors) that are present in individual organisms because they were favored by natural selection in ancestral generations. The *function* of an adaptation is the effect of the trait on ancestral survival and reproduction that led to its proliferation in descendant generations. *By-products* are traits that exist despite the fact that they themselves were not favored by natural selection. By-products have no evolved function, but were indirectly perpetuated through the process of selection. If a male rape-specific adaptation is identified, this means that men possess the trait because it contributed to the reproductive success of ancestral males with the trait specifically for its function in the context of rape. A female anti-rape adaptation is one in which the trait contributed to the reproductive success of ancestral females specifically in the context of preventing or coping with rape. If rape is a by-product, then it is the outcome of the interaction of evolved traits that were not selected for the specific function of rape. Stated differently, if rape is a by-product, then it is an incidental outcome of the evolutionary process, in the sense that human males do not possess traits that were selected *because* they led ancestral males to rape.

Adaptation is a "special and onerous concept that should be used only where it is really necessary" (Williams, 1966, p. 4). As Thornhill (1990, p. 32) puts it, "[r]ecognition of an adaptation involves identification of a feature of an organism that is too complexly organized to be due to chance"; that is, adaptations show evidence of the direct action of natural selection (a non-random, non-chance process) in their design. Random, fortuitous effects of a trait on reproduction are not grounds for claiming to have identified it as an adaptation. Rather, adaptation is reflected in the specificity, precision, efficiency, and economy with which the trait appears designed to perform some function (see Burian, 1983; Gangestad, 2008; Williams, 1966). As G.C. Williams argues, "an effect should not be called a function unless it is clearly produced by design" (Williams, 1966, p. vii). The analysis of functional design is at the heart of the evolutionary biological approach. To quote Pittendrigh (1958, p. 395), "[t]he study of adaptation is not an optional preoccupation with fascinating fragments of natural history, it is the core of biological study."

Now that we have described the criteria by which adaptations are identified, mention should be made of criteria that are inappropriate. Measures of heritability of a trait do not shed light on the evolutionary history of a trait. Heritability is a measure of the phenotypic variance in a trait that is due to correlated genetic variance across a specified population of individuals within a specified environmental context (Daly and Wilson, 1983, pp. 33–34). Heritability is not a property of an individual trait, but rather a property of a population of traits. Measures of heritability depend on the environmental context in which the trait is expressed, and thus any particular trait may show high or low heritability in differing environments (see Hoffman and Merilä, 1999; Pigliucci, 2001, pp. 11–12). Neither high nor low measures of heritability can validly distinguish a trait as an adaptation or by-product (Symons, 1992, p. 141). Applied to the topic of rape, this means that heritable differences between rapists and non-rapists need not be discovered to identify rape-specific adaptations. Measures of current reproductive success associated with traits are also not often useful in identifying adaptations, and this is especially true in the case of humans (Symons, 1992; Thornhill, 1990; Williams, 1966). Adaptations are traits that were favored by selection operating on ancestral generations in ancestral environments, and as such, they may or may not currently confer the reproductive advantage on their bearers that led to their evolution. Environmental novelty may disrupt the link between the evolved function of an adaptation and reproductive success. Applied to rape, this means that contemporary reproductive consequences are virtually irrelevant to the identification of a trait as a rape-specific adaptation.

Hypothesized Human Rape and Anti-Rape Adaptations

The question of whether human rape is an adaptation or by-product dates back at least to 1979 when Donald Symons concluded his research on the question by stating "I do not believe that available data are even close to sufficient to warrant the conclusion that rape itself is a facultative adaptation in the human male" (1979, p. 284). While concurring that existing evidence was not conclusive, Thornhill and Palmer (2000, pp. 65–66) listed the following hypothesized human rape-specific adaptations and stated that, "[o]ne, or more, or none of the following potential adaptations may exist."

1. Psychological mechanisms that help males evaluate the vulnerability of potential rape victims.
2. Psychological mechanisms that motivate men who lack sexual access to females (or who lack sufficient resources) to rape.
3. Psychological mechanisms that cause males to evaluate sexual attractiveness (as indicated by age) differently for rape victims than for consensual partners.
4. Psychological and/or other physiological mechanisms that result in differences between the sperm counts of ejaculates produced during rape and those of ejaculates produced during consensual copulation.
5. Psychological mechanisms that produce differences between the sexual arousal of males caused by depictions of rape and that caused by depictions of consensual mating.
6. Psychological or other mechanisms that motivate males to engage in rape under conditions of sperm competition.

It is important to remember that it is possible that no rape-specific adaptations exist in our species. It is also possible that there may be some adaptations designed for some types of rape, while other adaptations are designed for other types of rapes, and still other types of rape may not involve any rape-specific adaptations. For example, "Rape by men with high status and abundant resources may arise from a combination of impunity and the hypothetical adaptation pertaining to evaluation of a victim's vulnerability. If so, their raping must result from adaptations other than that suggested by the second hypothesis listed above; however, the proposed adaptation might still account for the raping behavior of males who lack resources" (Thornhill and Palmer, 2000, p. 68).

We now examine the evidence for each of the hypotheses listed in ANHR.

Evidence on Human Male Rape-Specific Adaptation

1. Psychological mechanisms that help males evaluate the vulnerability of potential rape victims.

Thornhill and Palmer state that the key to confirming this hypothesis is demonstrating "a psychological mechanism in men functionally specialized to evaluate the vulnerability of females to rape, as opposed to a broader mechanism designed to calculate the benefits and costs of other social transgressions (e.g., theft, murder)" (2000, p. 66). They conclude that although rape is frequent in war, when women are particularly vulnerable, "the current evidence on this type of focused rape adaptation is not sufficient to support the rape-specific-adaptation hypothesis ... [because] Theft too is rampant during war" (ibid.). Thus, "these patterns may be attributable to a cost-benefit-evaluation mechanism that is not specific to rape" (ibid.).

Research since ANHR has continued to document the high frequency of warfare related rape (see Gottschall, 2004), but they have not demonstrated rape-specific adaptations. For example, in Gottschall's (2004) review of theories of wartime rape, he concludes that the "biosocial theory" (which takes evolutionary history into account) is the most promising framework for understanding rape during war. However, Gottschall does not address the evidence bearing on the adaptation/by-product question of wartime rape.

We suggest that there may be ways to investigate empirically the question of whether or not rape during wartime is a result of a specialized cost-benefit algorithm designed specifically for producing rape behavior. For example, future research in the laboratory might prime male subjects with ecologically valid cues of intergroup aggression or coalitionary violence, followed by presentation of two scenarios associated with low-cost (small or no chance of punishment) sexual access to a female; the two scenarios differing only in the dimension of coercion versus female consent. If there is indeed male design for rape in the context of coalitionary violence, then only men primed with the cues to war should show sexual arousal (as measured phallometrically, for instance) in response to the scenario depicting rape.

In male subjects otherwise not demonstrating a deviant arousal to coercive sex, such results would constitute support for a rape-specific adaptation for motivating rape in wartime contexts, which would have been associated ancestrally with a cost-benefit ratio that made rape adaptive.

2. Psychological mechanisms that motivate men who lack sexual access to females (or who lack sufficient resources) to rape.

Although Thornhill and Palmer cite various sets of data indicating that "men of lower socioeconomic status are overrepresented among rapists" (2000, p. 67), they state that there are "a number of types of evidence that prevent the general pattern of rapists as socially disfranchised males from establishing the predicted mechanism." They conclude by saying that "[t]he mixed evidence with regard to the existence of a psychological adaptation connecting reduced sexual access to females or reduced resource holding with propensity to rape calls for further research to explore this candidate for a rape adaptation" (p. 70).

Recent research confirms that while the mate deprivation hypothesis may account for some rapes, it clearly is not responsible for others as some rapists apparently have "sex with more women than do men in general" (Ellis, Widmayer, and Palmer, 2009, p. 454). Elaborating how the mate deprivation hypothesis might account for some rapes, Lalumiére, Harris, Quinsey, and Rice (2005, p. 184) propose a "life-course model of antisociality and sexual coercion." In this model, one course involves competitive disadvantage for status and resources caused by neurodevelopmental impairment or poor developmental environments. According to Lalumiére et al. (2005), this disadvantage in social competition leads men to perceive a low likelihood of achieving social and mating success by conventional routes, prompting the use of antisocial tactics, including rape. They suggest that for this course, rape may be part of a conditional strategy cued by low embodied capital.

Thus, we might expect to find that the mate deprivation hypothesis applies only to a subset of rapists, namely, neurodevelopmentally impaired antisocial males. Support for this particular application of the mate deprivation hypothesis comes from Krill, Lake, and Platek (2006), who present evidence that their sample of convicted rapists had greater facial asymmetry, which possibly reflects developmental perturbations, rendering these men psychologically or socially disadvantaged in resource and mate acquisition.

While Lalumiére et al. (2005) point out a close link between antisociality and sexual coercion, and suggest that rape may be a conditional strategy employed by antisocial men, this need not mean that antisocial men possess a rape-specific adaptation. A link between antisociality and rape is not convincing evidence for rape-specific adaptation in antisocial men for two reasons. First, the positive relationship between sexual coercion and antisociality presents the possibility that this association may arise as a by-product of high mating effort found to be characteristic of antisocial individuals. Several studies have demonstrated a link between antisociality and high mating effort; that is, the pursuit of low-cost sexual access to a large number of sexual partners (see studies cited in Lalumiére et al., 2005, esp. p. 70). A by-product explanation is consistent with findings that some sexually coercive men often have high numbers of consensual sexual experiences (Lalumiére, Chalmers, Quinsey, and Seto, 1996; Ellis et al., 2009). Second, antisociality is associated with engagement in other delinquent and criminal behavior. Taken together, these two correlates of antisociality suggest that a parsimonious explanation of the relationship between antisociality and rape is lower inhibition against engaging in self-serving behavior, coupled with a greater motivation to achieve sexual access to a variety of females. The hostility, aggressiveness, impulsiveness, and lack of empathy, among other personality traits characteristic of antisocial individuals, compose a psychology that, instead of being specific to rape, would seem to facilitate the perpetration of crime in general.

3. Psychological mechanisms that cause males to evaluate sexual attractiveness (as indicated by age) differently for rape victims than for consensual partners.

Although Thornhill and Palmer conclude that "young adult females are vastly overrepresented … in the population of rape victims" (2000, p. 73), this does not demonstrate a rape-specific adaptation in victim selection that would "maximize the reproductive benefits of rape" (p. 70).

What is needed to support this hypothesis is evidence that males have a different appearance preference when evaluating potential rape victims as compared to evaluating willing sexual partners. For example, Gottschall and Gottschall (2003, p. 9) address the possibility of a mechanism enabling males who rape to target fecund/ovulating women, but emphasize the lack of evidence for such a rape-specific mechanism.

4. Psychological and/or other physiological mechanisms that result in differences between the sperm counts of ejaculates produced during rape and those of ejaculates produced during consensual copulation.

Thornhill and Palmer (2000, p. 74) report that no research had been done on this topic, but propose that "perhaps evidence could be gathered from studies in which subjects would masturbate to audio and video depictions of rapes and or consensual acts." If males possess adaptations to facultatively adjust semen parameters optimal for fertilization during rape, we should expect differences between the ejaculates produced in response to rape stimuli and those produced in response to consensual sex stimuli.

Gottschall and Gottschall (2003) mention that such a mechanism might be partially responsible for the apparently higher pregnancy rates from rape than from consensual sex. However, they concluded that: "It cannot be ruled out that some other property of the rapist's ejaculate could account for higher rape-pregnancy rates, but it is not the most parsimonious explanation" (Gottschall and Gottschall 2003, p. 9). At least one other study is compatible with the hypothesized capacity for adaptive changes in semen parameters of rapists. A study of married men in India found that those men who reported forcing sex on their wives, compared to men who did not report such behavior, were 2.6 times more likely to cause an unintended pregnancy (Martin et al., 1999). Of course this study does not demonstrate that the higher pregnancy rate is due to adaptive changes in the ejaculates of rapists.

5. Psychological mechanisms that produce differences between the sexual arousal of males caused by depictions of rape and that caused by depictions of consensual mating.

Although we do not know of any research that has been done to test the specific hypotheses put forth by Thornhill and Palmer, studies comparing other aspects of the sexual arousal patterns of rapists and non-rapists have continued. Most of these use phallometric measurements, which remain controversial (see Clegg and Fremouw, 2009; Lalumiére, Quinsey, Harris, Rice, and Trautrimas, 2003; Lalumiére and Rice, 2007; Looman and Marshall, 2005; Marshall, 2006; Marshall and Fernandez, 2000; Marshall and Fernandez, 2003). Lalumiére et al. (2005, p. 117), argue that phallometric studies using "optimal" procedures have found that about 60% of rapists show *"equal or greater"* arousal to rape stimuli than to stimuli of consensual sex, while around 10% of non-rapists show this pattern (see also Lalumiére et al., 2003). But, as pointed out by Clegg and Fremouw (2009), none of the studies have demonstrated significantly greater arousal to rape stimuli than consensual stimuli; only that rapists do not seem to discriminate between forced and unforced sex, at least with respect to their sexual arousal as measured phallometrically. As it stands, then, there is no phallometric evidence that definitively demonstrates that rapists in general *prefer* physically coercive sex to consensual sex.

Interestingly, Camilleri (2008), in a phallometric study comparing partner rapists (see hypothesis #6), non-partner rapists, and non-offenders found that partner rapists were significantly lower than non-partner rapists, and no different from non-rapists in their rape index scores (a measure of arousal to coercive sex relative to consensual sex). In other words, partner rapists in this study, as a group, did not show the deviant arousal patterns shown by the non-partner rapist group. While replication of these findings is certainly needed, these results suggest that partner and non-partner rape may have important causal differences.

More importantly for the question of adaptation is the fact that it is not clear whether any arousal differences between rapists and non-rapists are an effect or a cause of their previous raping experience. Thus, these studies have not demonstrated the role of any rape-specific adaptations in the cause of rape.

6. Psychological or other mechanisms that motivate males to engage in rape under conditions of sperm competition.

Thornhill and Palmer (2000, p. 77) emphasize that although legal recognition of marital rape as a crime is only relatively recent, "a rape is still a rape, regardless of the victim's relationship to the perpetrator." (For recent reviews of research on marital rape from non-evolutionary perspectives, see Bennice and Resnick, 2003; Bergen, 2004.) Thornhill and Palmer (2000) proposed that "Raping an unwilling pair-bonded mate may be a male tactic of sperm competition" and cite a number of sources of supporting evidence such as sexual jealousy being associated with marital rape (see pp. 77–78).

The logic of partner rape as a sperm competition tactic is as follows: when female infidelity cannot be prevented, one straightforward method to combat cuckoldry is to place an ejaculate into a female mate immediately upon detection of actual or potential extra-pair mating. In doing so, a male places his sperm in competition with any rival sperm inhabiting the female tract (Parker, 1984; Goetz and Shackelford, 2006; Shackelford, 2003), thereby increasing his chances of paternity of any resulting offspring. However, if a female can benefit from receiving genes for her offspring from an extra-pair male, it may not be in her best reproductive interest to risk fertilization by her primary mate (Gallup and Burch, 2006, 2004). Hence selection is expected to have favored those males who were able to overcome female resistance to mate after extra-pair copulation. A primary mechanism by which males are motivated to engage in partner rape may be sexual jealousy.

Several studies (in addition to those cited by Thornhill and Palmer 2000) provide tentative support for the argument that sexual jealousy in response to infidelity or perceived threat of infidelity may be a major precipitating cause of marital rape. Although not mentioned in ANHR, Shields and Hanneke (1983) found that victims of marital rape were more likely to have reported extra-marital sex than women who did not experience marital rape. In their examination of case files of a sample of convicted partner rapists, Camilleri and Quinsey (2009a) found that 72.7% had experienced cuckoldry risk events prior to the rape of their partner. Moreover, partner rapists experienced significantly more cuckoldry risk events than offenders of non-sexual partner assault prior to committing their offenses. In a study of sexual coercion in intimate relationships, Goetz and Shackelford (2006) found that men's reported use of sexual coercion was positively correlated with their perceptions of their partner's infidelities. Likewise, women's reports of their partner's use of sexual coercion also correlated positively with their own reports of infidelity.

Thornhill and Palmer (2000, p. 77) suggested that sexual unreceptivity to a mate may be a cue suggestive of infidelity: "Because men associate sexual unwillingness and resistance in their long-term mates with infidelity." Indeed, studies have confirmed that a sudden refusal of sex by a partner is rated as highly diagnostic of sexual infidelity (Schützwohl, 2005; Shackelford and Buss, 1997). In a study by Basile (2002) of 120 women who experienced sexual coercion in marriage, 34% reported forced copulation after their husband "begged and pleaded," indicating an explicit refusal for sex by the women. Understanding why a female might be reluctant to have sex shortly after sexual infidelity leads to consideration of another line of evidence in the evolutionary analysis of partner rape, the sexually selected phenotypes of human females.

Recent research on cycle-related changes in human females may generate new predictions to test in regard to partner rape. Several studies have demonstrated that women exhibit shifts in their psychology and behavior across the ovulatory cycle, manifesting what Gangestad and Thornhill (2008, p. 991) refer to as "dual sexuality." There exists a marked distinction between female preferences for male traits and features during the fertile phase compared to those during the non-fertile period of the ovulatory cycle. When in the fertile phase, women prefer a number of male traits thought to be indicators of genetic quality (see Table 1 in Gangestad and Thornhill, 2008, p. 993).

What is interesting about these cycle shifts in preferences is that they are exhibited more strongly by women with partners generally, and most strongly by women paired with asymmetric men specifically (see Thornhill and Gangestad, 2008, pp. 247–250). Jones and colleagues (2005) found that women in the fertile phase reported feeling less committed to their partner compared to non-fertile phases. In a series of studies, Gangestad et al. (2002; 2005) found that women in relationships reported greater attraction to extra-pair men when in the fertile phase, while there was no significant difference in attraction to primary partners across the cycle. These effects are mediated by a male partner's sexual attractiveness (Haselton and Gangestad, 2006; Pillsworth and Haselton, 2006).

The specificity and contexts of these shifts in preferences and behaviors has led Thornhill and Gangestad to argue that, "[g]enerally speaking, the primary context in which estrous preference shifts have been maintained by selection in human evolutionary history is the potential to obtain genetic benefits through EPC [extra-pair copulations]" (2008, p. 242). The research cited above strongly suggests that female sexual infidelity did pose a significant adaptive problem to ancestral human males, and partner rape might have been favored by selection as a counter-adaptation to the risk of cuckoldry.

Although there is still insufficient evidence for partner rape-specific adaptations, future research on this possibility is warranted in light of the existing evidence.

Evidence for Human Female Anti-Rape Adaptations

Thornhill and Palmer (2000) also discussed the evidence for several potential anti-rape adaptations in human females. These all involved adaptations involving degrees and types of psychological (or mental) pain experienced by rape victims. The specific predictions involved the age and marital status of victims, as well as the type of sexual behavior that occurred:

1. *Age.* "Young women (i.e., females of reproductive age) are predicted to suffer greater psychological distress from rape than girls (non-reproductive-age females) or older women (of non-reproductive age)" (p. 89).
2. *Marital status.* Married women would suffer greater psychological distress than unmarried women (p. 92).
3. *Type of sexual behavior.* The psychological distress of victims should be greater following assaults that include penile-vaginal intercourse, ejaculation in the victim's reproductive tract, and repeated intercourse (p. 93).

Thornhill and Palmer (2000, p. 96) emphasize that "[w]e realize that psychological pain is a complex and multifaceted mental state that may include a wide diversity of negative feelings—even so-called somatic (bodily) pain." They then conclude that "the findings on the pain of rape victims indicate that women have a special-purpose psychological adaptation that processes information about events that, over human evolutionary history, would have resulted in reduced reproductive success. However, more research is needed to demonstrate the specificity of such information processing in cases of rape relative to other crimes against women" (ibid.).

Thornhill and Palmer (2000) go on to list some of the predictions that could be tested in the future. In regard to age they state that: "It may be possible to derive predictions from the psychological-pain hypothesis about the mix of the various negative emotions (anxiety, fear, sadness, anger, guilt, shame) expressed by reproductive-age women versus other age categories of victims as time elapses after the rape and in different settings (e.g., pair-bonded or not)" (p. 95). In regard to marital status, they write: "Future research on psychological pain associated with rape would be facilitated if it were possible to distinguish between unmarried rape victims with boyfriends and those without boyfriends. Unmarried victims with investing boyfriends may respond more like married victims, since in both cases cuckoldry is possible in the event of rape" (p. 95). Thus, "victims paired to investing males are predicted to emphasize their resistance when recounting rapes to their partners, especially in the absence of physical evidence or force ... reproductive-age victims may show more fear of strange men and unfamiliar social settings after rape than victims in other age categories, and the fear may be specific to circumstances related to the potential of the occurrence of rape" (pp. 95–96). And finally, in regard to the sex of the victim, they add that "we predict a significant sex difference in factors related to psychological pain after rape" (p. 96).

Unfortunately, instead of following Thornhill and Palmer's call for new and better research on this crucially important topic, the interest in this topic has been focused primarily on searching for flaws in the original data cited in ANHR (McCahill, Meyer, and Fischman, 1979) and its interpretation by Thornhill and Thornhill (1990a, 1990b, 1990c, 1991) (see Coyne, 2003; Coyne and Berry, 2000; Vandermassen, 2010). We know of no recent evidence on psychological pain of rape victims related to the variables of age, marital status, and type of behavior, and we strongly encourage future research on these areas.

There has, however, been important and intriguing research done since ANHR on other potential forms of anti-rape adaptations. These focus on the possibility of mechanisms evolved to avoid certain environments when rape might be more likely and to respond to attempted rapes in certain ways. A particularly intriguing aspect to this research is the hypothesis that these mechanisms may be linked to the woman's ovulation cycle. While rape always carries potential costs, rape during a woman's fertile phase of the ovulatory cycle is especially costly because, in addition to social, psychological, and physical costs, a resulting pregnancy circumvents female sire choice—a principal component of female reproductive success—and negates those estrous adaptations for securing superior genes for offspring (see Roberts and Little, 2008 for discussion of genes and human mate preferences).

If rape is potentially most costly at the time when pregnancy is most likely, adult females are expected to evince traits most strongly suggestive of design to prevent or avoid rape at the fertile phase of the cycle. To date, a handful of studies have reported results consistent with the expectations of fertile phase anti-rape adaptations.

In a test of the hypothesis that women's ability to resist sexual assault increases at the time in the ovulatory cycle when rape carries the greatest costs, Petralia and Gallup (2002) found that women in the fertile phase who read a passage describing sexual assault showed a significant increase in handgrip strength from pre- to post-reading tests. We suggest that future research examine other possible changes in females related to the ability to physically deter and prevent forced sex.

In a test of the hypothesis that women in the fertile phase of the cycle should be especially attuned to the risks of sexual coercion, Bröder and Hohmann (2003) investigated women's activities across the ovulatory cycle. Replicating the results of Chavanne and Gallup (1998), Bröder and Hohmann found that women reduce their engagement in activities that pose a high risk of sexual coercion. Along the same line of reasoning, Garver-Apgar, Gangestad, and Simpson (2007) found that fertile-phase women viewing taped interviews of males rated them as more coercive than did non-fertile women. Additionally, the coerciveness rating of fertile women was better predicted by a man's average coercive rating than by these same men's rating by non-fertile subjects. Because fertility status did not have significant effects on ratings of three other traits—kindness, commitment, and faithfulness— Garver-Apgar et al. state that the effects on ratings of coerciveness "suggest that women may possess specially designed perceptual counter-strategies that guard against male sexual coercion" (2007, p. 536). A recent study by Navarrete, Fessler, Fleischman, and Geyer (2009) examining the effects of cycle phase on intergroup biases found that white women in the fertile phase exhibited higher levels of racial bias against black men, as indicated by a composite of five measures of race bias. The authors suggest that their results are consistent with the "coercion avoidance perspective," and suggest that socially transmitted negative racial stereotypes might be responsible for the increase in racial bias shown by fertile females (Navarrete et al., 2009, p. 664).

Findings such as those of the above studies on behavioral shifts across the cycle raise some interesting questions in light of recent developments in our understanding of other cycle-related changes in female psychology and behavior. As noted previously, there is considerable evidence in support of the idea that women possess estrous adaptations designed for procuring good genes for offspring (see references above). In addition to engaging in more mate-seeking activities, Gangestad, Thornhill, and Garver-Apgar (2010) found that partnered women in the fertile phase, compared to when these same women are in non-fertile phases report greater willingness to take advantage of sexual opportunities, and a greater willingness to engage in sex with unfamiliar men. These behavioral and psychological shifts toward sexual opportunism are difficult to reconcile with the rape avoidance hypothesis, as such dispositions would seem to place females at greater risk of sexual coercion when the costs of coercion are highest. These seemingly incompatible findings call attention to the need for more detailed study of the relationship between mate-seeking estrus adaptations and anti-rape features of the female phenotype, especially how women might balance the costs of rape with the ancestral benefits of securing superior genes at peak fertility.

Davis and Gallup (2006) have suggested that preeclampsia (the failure to achieve the second trophoblastic implantation phase following fertilization) may be a female adaptation to terminate maternal investment in response to unfamiliar semen; familiarity of semen, they hypothesize, being an index of the likelihood of future paternal investment in a woman's offspring. Rape by a stranger or uncommitted acquaintance may be a situation in which it would be adaptive for a female to terminate a resulting conception. However, Davis and Gallup also identify two other contexts of unfamiliar semen: dishonest male mating strategies (feigned commitment to achieve sexual access), and during the early phase of courtship, when the strength of the pair-bond is still undetermined. The fact that it may be in females' interest to terminate maternal investment in multiple circumstances in which male paternal investment is unlikely to be forthcoming weakens an argument that preeclampsia is a rape-specific adaptation.

Inconsistent with the hypothesis that female rape adaptations should be most apparent during times of high fertility in the cycle, Fessler (2003) argues that, despite claims that rape is less frequent during the periovulatory period, there is in fact no evidence that this is so (as mentioned above, Gottschall and Gottschall (2003) present data showing that pregnancy rates are higher for rape than consensual sex). Lack of evidence that rape is less likely at time of high fertility, as Fessler (2003, pp. 141–142) explains, might be a result of female anti-rape adaptations ceasing to function adaptively in evolutionarily novel modern environments, owing to, for example, increased access to privacy, and abundant and readily available mind-altering substances such as alcohol. It is important to re-emphasize here that adaptations need not be currently functioning *adaptively*—that is, currently contributing to survival or reproductive success—in order to be identified as such (see, e.g., Symons, 1990; Williams, 1966).

Conclusion

Understanding human behavior is greatly facilitated by knowledge of *what* we evolved to do (evolved functions), *how* we accomplished these things (proximate causation), and *why* we evolved to do so (natural history, or ultimate causation). Careful evolutionary analyses can provide answers to these questions—about rape just as much as any other human phenomenon, say, adherence to political ideology. After all, Darwinism is not a paradigm that is only selectively applicable to a few aspects of human nature; it applies to *all* of them.

We conclude by discussing what the eventual answers to the question of whether or not humans have adaptations designed for the context of rape will, and will not, tell us about human rape. First, we return once again to the need to avoid the naturalistic fallacy and emphasize that the answers will *not* imply that rape is acceptable or justifiable in any way. Second, answering the *evolutionary* (i.e., ultimate) level question of whether or not humans have adaptations specifically designed for the context of rape does not *directly* specify the *proximate* motivations that are necessary and sufficient for a rape to occur, and whose identification are thus the key to preventing the occurrence of this horrible crime. However, research designed to determine the presence or absence of adaptations designed for the context of rape can indirectly help identify the proximate causes of rape.

The first, and most obvious, reason why identifying the presence or absence of rape adaptations can help identify the proximate causes of rape is that the testing of evolutionary level explanations is often done by testing the specific conditions leading up to, and following, an act of rape. This is clearly demonstrated by the examples discussed in this chapter. The testing of hypotheses about adaptation, that is, hypotheses about functional design, yields evidence of the nature of the selective pressures that led to the trait's evolution (Thornhill, 1990). Understanding of these historical selective pressures provide us with insight, or at least testable hypotheses about the specific input the adaptation has evolved to respond to (the proximate causes).

The second reason why identifying the presence or absence of adaptations can help identify the proximate causes of rape is our contention that basing the study of these proximate conditions on the established scientific theoretical framework of evolutionary biology is more likely to generate accurate knowledge that can be used to prevent rape than the alternative of basing this study on an ideological position and evaluating the results of the study on its compatibility with the ideological position. This point is particularly important because so much of the controversy over ANHR was based on political ideology instead of scientific evidence. This was most clearly seen in the responses to ANHR's challenging of the claim that rape was a crime motivated not by sexual desire, but by a desire for such things as control, dominance, and power (see pp. 124–140). (For a recent advocation of the dominance/power/control explanation of rape, see Cowan (2009).)

Thornhill and Palmer's challenge to the "not sex" argument was met with a wide variety of counter-arguments, ranging the entire spectrum of possibility from repeated assertions of the "not sex" explanation of rape with even greater conviction, to the denial that such an argument was ever put forth (see Palmer and Thornhill, 2003a, pp. 252–255, 2003b, pp. 22–24). While such mutually contradictory responses could not be based on actual evidence, they are both consistent with a desire to defend feminist ideology from being seen as supporting a highly flawed argument. One defense was to argue that the argument was not flawed and embrace it as part of feminist ideology, the other defense was to admit the argument was flawed but detach it from feminist ideology.

A more subtle role of ideology can also be seen in a recent critique of the argument about the motivation of rapists put forth in ANHR. In contrast to the "not sex" explanation, ANHR stated that although a rapist *may* be motivated by any of a "countless number" of possible motivations, sexual desire was both a necessary and sufficient motivation for a rape to occur:

But have social scientists really demonstrated that any rapist is not at least partially motivated by sexual desire? Indeed, could any rape really take place without any sexual motivation on behalf of the rapist? Isn't sexual arousal of the rapist the one common factor in all rapes? ... Further, would a rapist have to have any of the possible non-sexual motivations in order to commit a rape? Isn't it possible for a male's sole motivation for committing a rape to be a desire for sexual gratification? (Thornhill and Palmer, 2000, pp. 131–132)

ANHR also argued that a major factor obscuring these seemingly obvious points is a failure to distinguish between the goals that motivate a behavior and the tactics used to accomplish those goals. In the case of rape, this means distinguishing between the goal of sex and the coercive, violent, or other tactics (e.g., drugs) used to accomplish it. To clarify this point, Thornhill and Palmer pointed out that prostitution includes both the giving of money and a sexual act, but this doesn't imply that a man is necessarily motivated to go to a prostitute out of an altruistic desire to give money to a woman, or even out of a desire to give money to a woman to have sex. Although a man might have a countless number of motivations for visiting a prostitute, sex is a necessary and sufficient motivation for doing so, and may often be the only motivation involved.

In a paper with the explicit goal of making evolutionary biological explanations of rape "congenial to feminist perspectives," Vandermassen (2010) has challenged this argument by asserting: "At the very least, the use of violence *implies* a motivation for the use of violence." By this logic, a man's use of a prostitute is indeed always motivated by an altruistic desire to give away his money, and a person breaking into a bakery to steal a loaf of bread can always be safely assumed to be motivated by a desire to break into buildings. Such an argument might be humorous if it didn't have such dire practical consequences, given that reducing the desire of people to break into buildings is unlikely to be an effective way of dealing with the theft of food by starving people, and efforts to reduce the altruistic desire of men to give their money away is unlikely to reduce prostitution. We suggest that the argument put forth by Vandermassen would never be made on the basis of logic and evidence, but only because it "accommodates feminist views" and is "congenial to feminist perspectives" (Vandermassen, 2010). This demonstrates why it is crucial that theory should be accepted not on the basis of ideology, but solely on the grounds that it accommodates evidence and is congenial to the further production of accurate knowledge.

The research reviewed in this chapter represents real advances in our scientific understanding of human nature, while expositions of the social science and feminist arguments on the motivations for rape that ignore the scientific evidence represents little more, if anything more, than the repetition of 40-year-old stagnant ideology (see Cowan, 2009; Griffen, 1971). To revisit the epigraph at the beginning of this chapter, "Social action is most likely to succeed if it is based on a realistic appraisal of the human condition" (Symons, 1979, p. 66). A realistic appraisal requires an accurate scientific understanding. If we are to succeed in efforts to eradicate rape, we must base these efforts on a realistic appraisal of rape. Adherence to ideological dogma and the rejection of knowledge because it is inconsistent with ideology is a choice that scholars are free to make. In the making of decisions, however, and in the unskeptical acceptance of the influence of unsupported ideological doctrine, it must be kept in mind that such choices risk jeopardizing our efforts at prevention of this terrible crime (see also Palmer, 1988, pp. 525–526).

Acknowledgments

The authors thank Troy Gardner and Karla Carter for their assistance in the preparation of this chapter. We also thank Randy Thornhill for thoughtful feedback on earlier drafts, and Erin Wood for helpful comments that improved the clarity of our arguments. Any and all remaining flaws or shortcomings are our own.

References

Basile, K.C. (2002). Prevalence of wife rape and other intimate partner sexual coercion in a nationally representative sample of women. *Violence and Victims, 17*(5), 511–524.

Bennice, J.A., and Resnick, P.A. (2003). Marital rape: history, research, and practice. *Trauma, Violence, and Abuse, 4*, 228–246.

Bergen, R.K. (2004). Studying wife rape: reflections on the past, present, and future. *Violence against Women, 10*, 1407–1416.

Bröder, A., and Hohmann, N. (2003). Variations in risk-taking behavior over the menstrual cycle: an improved replication. *Evolution and Human Behavior, 24*, 391–398.

Burian, R.M. (1983). Adaptation. In M. Grene (ed.), *Dimensions of Darwinism* (pp. 287–314). New York: Cambridge University Press.

Camilleri, J.A. (2008). *The psychology of partner sexual coercion*. Unpublished Doctoral thesis, Queens University, Ontario, Canada.

Camilleri, J.A., and Quinsey, V.L. (2009a). Testing the cuckoldry risk hypothesis of partner sexual coercion in community and forensic samples. *Evolutionary Psychology, 7*, 164–178.

Camilleri, J.A., and Quinsey, V.L. (2009b). Individual differences in the propensity for partner sexual coercion. *Sexual Abuse: A Journal of Research and Treatment, 22*, 111–129.

Chavanne, T.J., and Gallup, G.G. (1998). Variation in risk taking behavior among female college students as a function of the menstrual cycle. *Evolution and Human Behavior, 19*, 27–32.

Clegg, C., and Fremouw, W. (2009). Phallometric assessment of rapists: a critical review of the research. *Aggression and Violent Behavior, 14*, 115–125.

Cowan, G. (2009). The causes of rape: antisociality and reproductive strategies. *Sex Roles, 61,* 136–139.

Coyne, J.A. (2003). Of vice and men: a case study in evolutionary psychology. In C.B. Travis (ed.), *Evolution, Gender, and Rape* (pp. 171–189). Cambridge, MA: The MIT Press.

Coyne, J.A., and Berry, A. (2000). Rape as an adaptation: is this contentious hypothesis advocacy, not science? *Nature, 404,* 121–122.

Daly, M., and Wilson, M. (1983). *Sex, Evolution, and Behavior,* 2nd ed. Belmont, CA: Wadsworth Publishing Co.

Davis, J.A., and Gallup, G.G. (2006). Preeclampsia and other pregnancy related complications as an adaptive response to unfamiliar semen. In S. Platek and T. Shackelford (eds.), *Female Infidelity and Paternal Uncertainty: Evolutionary Perspectives on Male Anti-Cuckoldry Tactics* (pp. 191–204). Cambridge, MA: Cambridge University Press.

Ellis, L., Widmayer, A., and Palmer, C.T. (2009). Rapists continuing to have sex with victims following the initial assault: evidence for evolved strategies. *International Journal of Offender Therapy and Comparative Criminology, 53,* 454–463.

Fessler, D.M.T. (2003). Rape is not less frequent during the ovulatory phase of the menstrual cycle. *Sexualities, Evolution, and Gender, 5,* 127–147.

Gallup, G.G., and Burch, R.L. (2004). Semen displacement as a sperm competition strategy in humans. *Evolutionary psychology, 2,* 12–23.

Gallup, G.G., and Burch, R.L. (2006). The semen-displacement hypothesis: semen hydraulics and the intra-pair copulation proclivity model of female infidelity. In S.M. Platek and T.K. Shackelford (eds.), *Female Infidelity and Paternal Uncertainty: Evolutionary Perspectives on Male Anti-Cuckoldry Tactics* (pp. 129–140). New York: Cambridge University Press.

Gangestad, S.W. (2008). Biological adaptation and human behavior. In C. Crawford and D.L. Krebs (eds.), *Foundations of Evolutionary Psychology* (pp. 153–172). New York: Lawrence Erlbaum Associates.

Gangestad, S.W. and Thornhill, R. (2008). Human oestrus. *Proceedings of the Royal Society of London B, 275,* 991–1000.

Gangestad, S.W., Thornhill, R., and Garver, C. (2002). Changes in women's sexual interests and their partners mate retention tactics across the menstrual cycle: evidence for shifting conflicts of interest. *Proceedings of the Royal Society of London B, 269,* 975–982.

Gangestad, S.W., Thornhill, R., and Garver-Apgar, C. (2005). Women's sexual interests across the ovulatory cycle depend on primary partner fluctuating asymmetry. *Proceedings of the Royal Society of London B, 272,* 2023–2027.

Gangestad, S.W., Thornhill, R., and Garver-Apgar, C.E. (2010). Fertility in the cycle predicts women's sexual interest in sexual opportunism. *Evolution and Human Behavior, 31,* 400–411.

Garver-Apgar, C.E., Gangestad, S.W., and Simpson, J.A. (2007). Women's perceptions of men's sexual coerciveness change across the menstrual cycle. *Acta Psychologica Sinica, 39,* 536–540.

Goetz, A.T., and Shackelford, T.K. (2006). Sexual coercion and forced in-pair copulation as sperm competition tactics in humans. *Human Nature, 17,* 265–282.

Gottschall, J. (2004). Explaining wartime rape. *Journal of Sex Research, 41,* 129–136.

Gottschall, J.A., and Gottschall, T.A. (2003). Are per-incident rape pregnancy rates higher than per-incident consensual pregnancy rates? *Human Nature, 14,* 1–20.

Griffen, S. (1971). Rape: the all-American crime. *Ramparts, 10,* 26–36.

Haselton, M.G., and Gangestad, S.W. (2006). Conditional expression of women's desires and male mate retention efforts across the ovulatory cycle. *Hormones and Behavior, 49,* 509–518.

Hoffman, A.A., and Merilä, J. (1999). Heritable variation and evolution under favourable and unfavorable conditions. *Trends in Ecology and Evolution, 14,* 96–101.

Jones, B.C., Little, A.C., Boothroyd, L., DeBruine, L.M., Feinberg, D.R., Law Smith, M.J., Cornwell, R.E., Moore, F.R., and Perrett, D.I. (2005). Commitment to relationships and preferences for femininity and apparent health in faces are strongest on days of the menstrual cycle when progesterone level is high. *Hormones and Behavior, 48,* 283–290.

Krill, A.L., Lake, T.M., and Platek, S.M. (2006, June). *Do "good genes" predict forced copulation? A test of whether facial symmetry is related to sexual battery.* Poster presented at the meeting of the Human Behavior and Evolution Society, Philadelphia, PA.

Lalumiére, M.L., Chalmers, L.J., Quinsey, V.L., and Seto, M.C. (1996). A test of the mate deprivation hypothesis of sexual coercion. *Ethology and Sociobiology, 17,* 299–318.

Lalumiére, M.L., Harris, G.T., Quinsey, V.L., and Rice, M.E. (2005). *The causes of rape: understanding individual differences in male propensity for sexual aggression.* Washington, DC: American Psychological Association.

Lalumiére, M.L., Quinsey, V.L., Harris, G.T., Rice, M.E., and Trautrimas, C. (2003). Are rapists differentially aroused by coercive sex in phallometric assessments? *Annals of the New York Academy of Sciences, 989,* 211–224.

Lalumiére, M.L., and Rice, M.E. (2007). The validity of phallometric assessment with rapists: comments on Looman and Marshall (2005). *Sexual Abuse: A Journal of Research and Treatment, 19,* 61–68.

Looman, J., and Marshall, W.L. (2005). Sexual arousal in rapists. *Criminal Justice and Behavior, 32,* 367–389.

Marshall, W.L. (2006). Clinical and research limitations in the use of phallometric testing with sexual offenders. *Sexual Offender Treatment, 1,* 1–31.

Marshall, W.L., and Fernandez, Y.M. (2000). Phallometric testing with sexual offenders: limits to its value. *Clinical Psychology Review, 20,* 807–822.

Marshall, W.L., and Fernandez, Y.M. (2003). Sexual preferences: are they useful in the assessment and treatment of sexual offenders? *Aggression and Violent Behavior, 8,* 131–143.

Martin, S.L., Kilgallen, B., Tsui, A.O., Maitra, K., Singh, K.K., and Kupper, L.L. (1999). Sexual behaviors and reproductive health outcomes: associations with wife abuse in India. *Journal of the American Medical Association, 282,* 1967–1972.

McCahill, T.W., Meyer, L.C., and Fischman, A.M. (1979). *The aftemath of rape.* Lexington, MA: Lexington Books.

Navarrete, C.D., Fessler, D.M.T., Fleischman, D.S., and Geyer, J. (2009). Race bias tracks conception risk across the menstrual cycle. *Psychological Science, 20,* 661–665.

Palmer, C.T. (1988). Twelve reasons why rape is not sexually motivated: a skeptical examination. *Journal of Sex Research, 25,* 512–530.

Palmer, C.T., and Thornhill, R. (2003a). Straw men and fairy tales: evaluating reactions to "A Natural History of Rape." *Journal of Sex Research, 40,* 249–255.

Palmer, C.T., and Thornhill, R. (2003b). Posse of good citizens bring outlaw evolutionists to justice. *Evolutionary Psychology, 1,* 10–27.

Parker, G.A. (1984). Sperm competition and the evolution of animal mating strategies. In R.L. Smith (ed.), *Sperm Competition and the Evolution of Animal Mating Systems* (pp. 2–61). Orlando, FL: Academic Press.

Petralia, S.M., and Gallup, G.G. (2002). Effects of a sexual assault scenario on handgrip strength across the menstrual cycle. *Evolution and Human Behavior, 23,* 3–10.

Pigliucci, M. (2001). *Phenotypic Plasticity: Beyond Nature and Nurture.* Baltimore, MD: The Johns Hopkins University Press.

Pillsworth, E.G., and Haselton, M.G. (2006). Male sexual attractiveness predicts differential ovulatory shifts in female extra-pair attraction and male mate retention. *Evolution and Human Behavior, 27,* 247–258.

Pittendrigh, C.S. (1958). Adaptation, natural selection, and behavior. In A. Roe and G.G. Simpson (eds.), *Behavior and Evolution* (pp. 390–416). New Haven, CT: Yale University Press.

Roberts, S.G., and Little, A.C. (2008). Good genes, complementary genes and human mate preferences. *Genetica, 132,* 309–321.

Shackelford, T.K. (2003). Preventing, correcting and anticipating female infidelity. *Evolution and Cognition, 9,* 90–96.

Shackelford, T.K., and Buss, D.M. (1997). Cues to infidelity. *Personality and Social Psychology Bulletin, 23,* 1034–1045.

Schützwohl, A. (2005). Sex differences in jealousy: the processing of cues to infidelity. *Evolution and Human Behavior, 26,* 288–299.

Shields, N.M., and Hanneke, C.R. (1983). Attribution processes in violent relationships: perceptions of violent husbands and their wives. *Journal of Applied Social Psychology, 13,* 515–527.

Symons, D. (1979). *The Evolution of Human Sexuality.* New York: Oxford University Press.

Symons, D. (1990). Adaptiveness and adaptation. *Ethology and Sociobiology, 11,* 427–444.

Symons, D. (1992). On the use and misuse of Darwinism in the study of human behavior. In J. H. Barkow, L. Cosmides, and J. Tooby (eds.), *The Adapted Mind: Evolutionary Psychology and the Generation of Culture* (pp. 137–159). New York: Oxford University Press.

Thornhill, N., and Thornhill, R. (1990a). Evolutionary analysis of psychological pain of rape victims I: the effects of victims' age and marital status. *Ethology and Sociobiology*, *11*, 155–176.

Thornhill, N., and Thornhill, R. (1990b). Evolutionary analysis of psychological pain following rape II: the effects of stranger, friend and family member offenders. *Ethology and Sociobiology*, *11*, 177–193.

Thornhill, N., and Thornhill, R. (1990c). Evolutionary analysis of psychological pain following rape III: the effects of force and violence. *Aggressive Behavior*, *16*, 297–320.

Thornhill, N., and Thornhill, R. (1991). An evolutionary analysis of psychological pain following rape IV: the effect of the nature of the sex act. *Journal of Comparative Psychology*, *105*, 243–252.

Thornhill, R. (1990). The study of adaptation. In M. Beckoff and D. Jamieson (eds.), *Interpretation and Explanation in the Study of Animal Behavior, Vol. 2* (pp. 31–62). Colorado: West View Press.

Thornhill, R., and Gangestad, S.W. (2008). *The Evolutionary Biology of Human Female Sexuality*. New York: Oxford University Press.

Thornhill, R., and Palmer, C.T. (2000). *A Natural History of Rape: Biological Bases of Sexual Coercion*. Cambridge, MA: The MIT Press.

Travis, C.B. (2003). *Evolution, Gender, and Rape*. Cambridge, MA: The MIT Press.

Vandermassen, G. (2010). Evolution and rape: a feminist Darwinian perspective. *Sex roles*. DOI 10.1007/s11199-010-9895-y.

Williams, G.C. (1966). *Adaptation and Natural Selection: A Critique of Some Current Evolutionary Thought*. Princeton, NJ: Princeton University Press.

The Nature and Utility of
Low Self-Control

Richard P. Wiebe

Self-control is an encompassing concept, "central to most forms of virtuous behavior" which "can be regarded fairly as the primary or master virtue" (Baumeister & Exline, 2000, p. 29). In a broad sense, it is "control of the self by the self" (Muraven & Baumeister, 2000, p. 247) with which an organism "alters or overrides its own responses or acts contrary to its preferences and impulses" (Baumeister & Exline, 2000, p. 30). It has also been conceptualized as the ability to delay gratification (Kreuger, Caspi, Moffitt, White, & Stouthamer-Loeber, 1996). It is sometimes split into two components, "effortful control," meaning control over emotional processes (Kochanska, Murray, & Harlan, 2000), and "explicit processing" (MacDonald, 2008) or "executive control" (Henry, von Hippel, & Baynes, 2009), meaning control over cognitive processes. In any formulation, self-control lies at the heart of what it is to be human: our ability to exercise free will, to make decisions, and, if things break our way, to control our destinies.

We take self-control for granted. Even the least-controlled human doesn't pursue all of his or her desires like a dog chases a squirrel. When we find ourselves unable to control our desires, we say we have an addiction, or are possessed, or have suffered a great deal of stress—we say that we are controlled by forces that undermine our humanity. We also understand, or at least are informed from a very early age, that self-control will bring us what we want and that low self-control will get us into trouble.

But if self-control is so good, why are so many of us deficient in it? If, as the criminologists note, low self-control is strongly associated with crime and high self-control with success, why hasn't low self-control been eliminated from our repertoire? Low self-control, at least according to moralists, police, and parents, should handicap us in the way that not being able to use language or walk would handicap us. As humans, we are bipedal language users, and, in the absence of injury or disease, only a very few of us cannot walk upright, or speak or sign. But many of us commit crimes, cheat on tests, steal from work, gamble, drink or smoke too much, and engage in other activities associated with low self-control.

This chapter applies a biosocial approach, rooted mainly in evolutionary psychology and bolstered by findings from the brain sciences, to the question of why low self-control endures, as well as why self-control evolved in the first place. Evolutionary psychology is especially useful for examining the origins and utility of the elements of shared human nature (Tooby & Cosmides, 1990), and can also help us understand why variations remain in traits and abilities, such as our individual levels of self-control, that, in some lights, should have become fixed in the species. This chapter discusses the nature and origins of self-control, and concludes that low self-control, which basically involves allowing our emotions to make decisions for us without much input from the thinking, reasoning part of our brains, can be beneficial under certain circumstances, at least from a Darwinian perspective.

In the first part, the concept of self-control is reviewed from the perspective of criminology. Low self-control is a persistent negative correlate of crime and delinquency, and low self-control behaviors are aimed at satisfying desires.

The chapter then addresses the question: if low self-control behaviors can satisfy desires, why did high self-control develop? It examines the concept of synergy and its relationship to society, concluding that high self-control evolved in order to facilitate synergy, then looks at some of our adaptations related to social behavior. It places self-control at the apex of a hierarchy that rests on a foundation of emotions, both primary and social, and proceeds upwards through the moral sense. The chapter then discusses the development of the brain structures underlying self-control, noting that the brains of adolescents, especially those who go through puberty earlier than average, almost inevitably produce emotion-driven behavior.

The final sections use the life-history perspective to investigate the first question: if self-control is so good for us, why is it so often absent? The chapter presents crime as an epiphenomenon of a mating effort strategy (Rowe, 1996), and discusses various instances in which mating effort might be a successful strategy as well as ways to minimize its prevalence.

Self-Control in Criminology

Across academic disciplines, the definition of self-control varies. In criminology, "self-control" most often means the complex intrapersonal trait first described by Gottfredson and Hirschi in *A General Theory of Crime* (1990), claimed by the authors as, "for all intents and purposes, *the* individual level cause of crime" (p. 232, emphasis in original). Two decades after its introduction, the *General Theory* has become one of the best-known theories of crime causation, with over 3,700 scholarly cites to the 1990 book alone as of late 2010 (http://scholar.google.com/). Under this theory, crime occurs at the intersection of low self-control and criminal opportunity, when individuals "vulnerable to the temptations of the moment" (Gottfredson & Hirschi, 1990, p. 87) encounter those temptations, and, failing to exercise sufficient self-control, act upon them. Criminal opportunities represent suitable or attractive targets—a person to be robbed, an enemy to be ambushed, a bicycle to be liberated from its chains—that are not guarded well enough to prevent the crime (Felson & Boba, 2010), while self-control itself is "the tendency to avoid acts whose long-term costs exceed their short-term benefits" (Hirschi & Gottfredson, 2001, p. 82). Thus, persons with low self-control tend to disregard, or fail to perceive, the future consequences of their actions, while remaining focused on immediate and selfish gratification.

In deriving their version of self-control, Gottfredson and Hirschi looked not to the psychological research but to the characteristics of crimes themselves. They observed that crimes are generally exciting, immediately gratifying, easy to accomplish, and require little skill or planning, and that they yield few or meager long-term benefits and result in pain or discomfort for their victims (Gottfredson & Hirschi, 1990, pp. 89–90). From this picture of crime, they inferred the psychology of the offender: selfish and impulsive, focused on the future, looking for the easy way out (Hirschi & Gottfredson, 2001). These traits, which the authors noted "tend to come together in the same people" (Gottfredson & Hirschi, 1990, p. 91), correlate reliably not only with crime and delinquency (Pratt & Cullen, 2000) but with other dangerous, imprudent, and selfish acts like gambling, drinking, drug use, sexual promiscuity, and accidents, a phenomenon called "criminal and deviant versatility" (see generally Hirschi & Gottfredson, 1994). Because acts evincing low self-control impair an individual's future and often harm other people, the lower the level of self-control, the lower the chance of winning social approval and achieving conventional success and the greater the chance of ending up in prison or on skid row. It appears self-evident that high self-control is much better, for the individual and for society, than low self-control.

At least this is true where the interests of individuals and society coincide. But, as numerous criminologists have pointed out, society is not always concerned with maximizing the success of its marginal members, who tend to be those most likely to engage in crime—at least street crimes, as opposed to white-collar, corporate, or organized crime. Therefore, the interests of large groups of individuals may often deviate from the interests of society. For example, strain theory (Merton, 1938; see also Cloward & Ohlin, 1960) posits that mainstream society blocks opportunities for conventional success among persons in the lower classes, requiring them to "innovate" if they want to escape their fate. Much of this innovation involves crime. Other criminological theories also root crime in the structure of society. According to Cohen (1955), for example, members of the lower class become frustrated when they are unable to acquire status through conventional means, while, according to Miller (1955), the values and concerns of lower-class "street culture," such as the need to appear tough and to avoid kowtowing to authority figures, are more likely than mainstream values to lead to crime (see Walsh & Ellis, 2007, chapter 4). Thus, in lower-class communities, many of the behaviors associated with success— that lead to the acquisition of status, resources, and mating opportunities—are the products of low, not high, self-control.

What this means is that low self-control is not necessarily a bad thing, at least from the point of view of the individual. After all, at their base, crime and other behaviors stemming from low self-control are intended to satisfy desires or remove irritations (Gottfredson & Hirschi, 1990), just like many or most prosocial behaviors. In some instances, where opportunities for satisfying one's needs and desires in a prosocial manner are scarce, low self-control behaviors might provide an individual's best options (Wiebe, 2004). However, from the point of view of society, low-self-control behaviors are inherently destabilizing, since they undermine prosocial relations with other individuals and undercut future prospects, even when they achieve their desired results.

Synergy and Society

If crime can pay, at least in the short term, why would high self-control have developed in the first place? The answer lies in the nature and structure of society. Society exists because humans can benefit by collective action (Ridley, 1996; Wright, 2000). Cooperation allows us:

1. to be safer than we can be alone;
2. to spread this risk of failure or catastrophe, as through insurance;
3. to achieve efficiency through specialization and the division of labor;
4. to accomplish what we cannot do on our own; and
5. to let others know they can count on us in future, in both reciprocal interpersonal relationships and conflicts with other groups.

Successful cooperation creates more resources than could have been accumulated by pooling the products of individuals working alone, resulting in *synergy*, where the whole is greater than the sum of the parts. Provided the end product is distributed fairly, synergy benefits each individual as well as the group as a whole (Ridley, 1996). An individual with sufficient self-control is well-equipped to cooperate with others and follow social rules, and thereby to take advantage of synergy.

Cooperation doesn't always result in synergy. Despite our best efforts at working together, we sometimes fail to accomplish our goals, and in some instances, would have been better off alone. Further, under some conditions, such as those in a society that is hopelessly corrupt, under siege, or in violent transition, cooperation is impractical or impossible. But in a well-functioning society, the most important human actions are *inter*actions (Wiebe, 2009).

For our species in general, it is better to cooperate than to go it alone. However, not every individual sees it that way. Cooperation brings the temptation to cheat, either partially (doing a little less than your share but reaping the entire benefit) or wholly, either covertly (e.g., fraud) or overtly (e.g., armed robbery) (Raine, 1993). Cooperation also requires patience because, in many instances demanding cooperation, the payoff is not immediate, engendering the temptation to take a shortcut to the fulfillment of desires; this failure to delay gratification evinces low self-control (Hirschi & Gottfredson, 2001). Serious cheating, where someone else's person or property is violated for no good reason, is generally considered to be criminal. Whether technically guilty of a crime, the individual who violates legitimate rights of others violates their trust as well as the trust of society in general, and undermines synergy. Declaring an act to be criminal represents society's acknowledgment of the importance of preventing acts that undermine synergy.

Synergy is not only good for society, it is society's reason for being (Ridley, 1996; Wright, 2000). In synergistic interactions, the total resources available to everyone actually increase. By contrast, in criminal interactions, the total resources decrease, because, in almost all cases, the victim loses more—economically, psychologically, temporally—than the criminal gains, a phenomenon called the *magnitude gap* (Baumeister, 1997). A society in which people primarily preyed on each other would soon consume itself, because each interaction would drain the total pool of resources a little more until nothing's left. A society without self-control would not long endure.

Instantiating Sociality: Social Emotions, the Moral Sense, and Self-Control

At this point, it should be clear that humans can benefit from social interactions and the division of labor, whether they live in societies divided between hunters and gatherers or encounter the myriad niches provided by a modern complex society. Under a Darwinian perspective, it is also clear that individuals will be able to take advantage of the potential for synergy provided by human society if they are naturally amenable to social interactions; in other words, if they have psychological characteristics and behavioral tendencies that facilitate sociality, cooperation, and delayed gratification and can make meaningful individual contributions to the whole within the context of the division of labor. Collectively, these traits, characteristics, behaviors, and abilities constitute *sociality*. From Darwin onward, evolutionary thinkers have traced the evolution of sociality, from Hamilton's (1964) work on kin selection—sacrificing one's self or resources on behalf of genetic relatives—through Trivers's (1971) discussion of reciprocal altruism, essentially mutual back-scratching, to more comprehensive treatments by Axelrod (1984), Alexander (1987), Hrdy (1999), Sanderson (2001) and others, who have begun to catalogue the array of human adaptations that facilitate sociality and synergy.

Self-control would appear to be one of the most useful competencies for humans who live with other humans, and thus an essential component of sociality. Self-control allows us to act in our self-interest without unnecessarily impeding the legitimate rights of others and thereby attracting their wrath and stimulating their desire for justice. In other words, self-control, among its other laudable consequences, allows us to satisfy ourselves without committing crimes, which can be viewed in the Darwinian perspective as acts "intended to exploit people belonging to one's own social group in ways that reduce their fitness" (Rowe, 2002, p. 4).

Despite the correlation of low self-control with crime, there is nothing inherent in self-control in its basic sense—control of the self by the self—that requires it to be used prosocially. Both history and current events teem with examples of slavery, family violence, and other forms of personal exploitation; systemic political corruption; greedy and venal corporate behavior; powerful organized crime; and brutally effective despotism, effectuated by individuals whose behaviors embody effective future planning and the ability to resist momentary temptation in the service of future power and economic rewards. These acts clearly are intended to reduce the fitness of others who ostensibly lie within their social group. Further, studies of psychopaths, individuals who can relentlessly exploit others without remorse, reveal that many of them have reasonably high self-control (Patrick, 1994; see Bakan, 2004; Wiebe, 2003). Why, then, does self-control generally function as a virtue, producing a consistently negative correlation with crime and other selfish behaviors?

Part of the answer may simply be that high self-control crimes are less often detected, given the ability of their perpetrators to account for risks and plan for the future. However, this does not appear to be the whole answer. While high self-control crimes exist, at any age offending, or acts that would constitute criminal offenses if committed by an adult, correlates with low self-control (see Tremblay et al., 1999).

Another approach involves placing self-control atop a hierarchy of phenomena that includes, from the bottom up, emotions, both primary and social, and the moral sense. We share primary emotions and motives, such as hunger, lust, fear, and anger, with even asocial mammals, but social emotions such as love, empathy, guilt, and shame are relevant only in the context of other individuals or society in general (Mealey, 1995). By making us feel uncomfortable when we have harmed another individual or happy when we have facilitated the happiness of someone close to us, they help prevent antisocial behavior and encourage prosocial behavior (Mealey, 1995; Stuewig & Tangney, 2007), although they may also motivate antisocial behavior, by, for example, causing us to feel jealous or humiliated (Baumeister, Smart, & Boden, 1996; Kagan, 1998). The most basic of the social emotions likely stemmed from the necessity for mammalian mothers to bond with, and sacrifice for, their offspring (Hrdy, 1999).

Emotions are Signals

As Nesse and Ellsworth (2009) note, emotions in general are adaptations that help an organism recognize and react to "the adaptive challenges of a given situation" (p. 130), signals to the organism that, in the words of Willy Loman's wife, attention must be paid (Miller, 1951, p. 58; see Frank, 1988). Adaptive challenges represent the problems individuals must solve to achieve survival and reproductive success. Emotions relating to survival we share with other mammalian species, both social

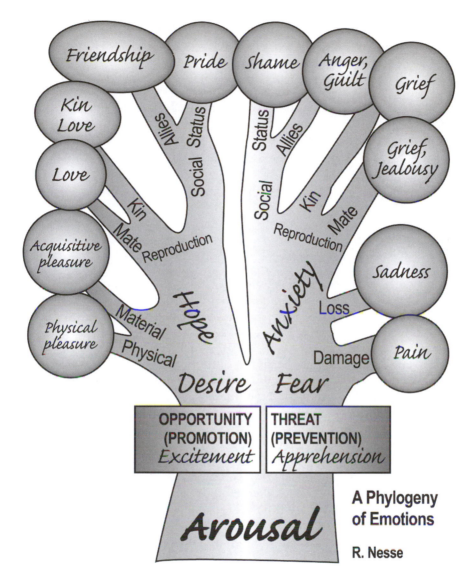

Figure 17.1 A possible phylogeny of emotions
Source: from Nesse & Ellsworth, 2009, p. 131.

and asocial: fear is fear, regardless of species, and the ability to recognize situations in which to flee, fight, or freeze and to execute an appropriate behavior benefits any endangered individual. With regard to reproductive fitness, however, the world that must be negotiated by social species becomes complicated. Buss (1991) provides a list of "reproductive problems" for us, like other social species (see Flack & de Waal, 2000), to solve: successful intrasexual competition, mate selection, successful conception, mate retention, reciprocal dyadic alliance formation, coalition-building and maintenance, parental care and socialization, and extra-parental kin investment (Buss, 1991, p. 465). One might add the problem of acquiring power and status within one's group and passing them on to descendants (Betzig, 1993). Each problem carries a host of complexities (Buss, 1991).

Like other emotions, social emotions cue us to two broad categories of situations: those that pose threats, requiring avoidance or prevention, and those that provide opportunities, inviting acquisition or approach (Nesse & Ellsworth, 2009; see Figure 17.1). These correspond to the "behavioral inhibition system" (BIS; Fowles, 1993) and the "behavioral approach system" (BAS; Gray, 1991), respectively. Avoidance emotions are said to have negative valence, while approach emotions have positive valence.

The Moral Sense

The social world of humans is extremely complex; our emotions reflect this complexity. However, for full participation in human society, social emotions are insufficient. When we feel guilty, what should we do about it, to maximize our future prospects and maintain or enhance our social relationships? A purely emotional reaction should be supplemented by both finely-tuned decision rules that provide a guide for appropriate behavior, once the social emotions are engaged, and by conscious control over our cognitions, emotions, and behaviors, so that we may successfully navigate the social landscape. The first set of phenomena—the internal guide to behavior—has been deemed the moral sense or conscience, and the second is the familiar self-control.

Darwin used the phrase "moral sense" in his second book about natural selection, *The Descent of Man* (1871/1981), in the following well-known passage: "[A]ny animal whatever, endowed with well marked social instincts, the parental and filial affections being here included, would inevitably acquire a moral sense or conscience, as soon as its intellectual power had become as well developed, or nearly as well developed, as in man" (pp. 68–69). In this passage, he explicitly ties the moral sense to the social emotions, asserting that the moral sense, when combined with sufficient cognitive abilities, inexorably rises out of the social emotions ("well marked social instincts"). Like emotions, the moral sense underlies consciousness, influencing decision-making, as illustrated by the four reasons Darwin gives for assuming that a moral sense would naturally develop among social creatures:

> [F]irstly, the social instincts lead an animal to take pleasure in the society of its fellows, to feel a certain amount of sympathy with them, and to perform various services for them. The services may be of a definite and evidently instinctive nature; or there may be only a wish and readiness, as with most of the higher social animals, to aid their fellows in certain general ways. But these feelings and services are by no means extended to all the individuals of the same species, only to those of the same association. *Secondly*, as soon as the

mental faculties had become highly developed, images of all past actions and motives would be incessantly passing through the brain of each individual; and that feeling of dissatisfaction which invariably results, as we shall hereafter see, from any unsatisfied instinct, would arise, as often as it was perceived that the enduring and always present social instinct had yielded to some other instinct, at the time stronger, but neither enduring in its nature, nor leaving behind it a very vivid impression. It is clear that many instinctive desires, such as that of hunger, are in their nature of short duration; and after being satisfied are not readily or vividly recalled. *Thirdly,* after the power of language had been acquired and the wishes of the members of the same community could be distinctly expressed, the common opinion how each member ought to act for the public good, would naturally become to a large extent the guide to action. But the social instincts would still give the impulse to act for the good of the community, this impulse being strengthened, directed, and sometimes even deflected, by public opinion, the power of which rests, as we shall presently see, on instinctive sympathy. *Lastly,* habit in the individual would ultimately play a very important part in guiding the conduct of each member; for the social instincts and impulses, like all other instincts, would be greatly strengthened by habit, as would obedience to the wishes and judgment of the community. (pp. 69–70)

Taken in order, the first assumption posits a sense of affiliation and the desire to aid one's associates (see Baumeister & Leary, 1995); the second, the importance and persistence of the need to satisfy social needs even when primary needs, such as hunger, are satisfied; the third, the desire to follow one's conscience, even in the face of contrary public opinion; and the fourth, a feedback loop between social instincts (social emotions) and behavior, so that the influence of social emotions on behavior increases as they are obeyed, which in turn strengthens the emotions themselves. Together, these assumptions paint a picture of the moral sense as a guide to social behavior, a roadmap through the social landscape, with social emotions as the moving force. But who's driving?

Driving is the job of self-control. Knowing what one should do is not the same as doing it, and the mark of our humanity, or at least of our sentience, is our belief that we control our behaviors by modulating or overriding our emotional impulses. Without emotions to signal to us what is meaningful, meaningful behavior is basically impossible (Damasio, 1994) but without self-control, we might as well not be human.

This tripartite scheme is similar to Freud's division of the psyche into the id (innate emotions and motives), ego (self-control), and superego (the moral sense), except that the id is thought to contain only selfishness and must be tamed—the wild beast of the brain (Hall, 1954). The self-control theory of Gottfredson and Hirschi reflects this view of the id, emphasizing the naturalness of crime but not the naturalness of affiliation.

One recent attempt to describe the moral sense was undertaken by Wilson (1993), who identified four components: sympathy (empathy plus a judgment that a person did not deserve the hurt or loss they suffered), duty, fairness, and self-control. Consistent with Darwin's ideas, each of these is based on social emotions but fine-tuned by culture and experience: notions of who deserves sympathy, or what the duties of a citizen or a son or daughter are, or who has been treated unjustly, or what level of self-control is required in various social situations, vary widely by context and culture. Though it also allows for culturally idiosyncratic content, the present model contrasts with Wilson's view of the moral sense by placing self-control on a different psychological plane: the plane of consciousness and free will.

Self-control may develop even in the absence of social emotions and an intact moral sense. An example is provided by so-called successful psychopaths (Widom, 1977). A psychopath might lack empathy, a conscience, a sense of remorse, and any regard for the rights and feelings of another person, but might still be able to modulate his or her behavior in order to satisfy relevant emotional needs in both the present and the future (Wiebe, 2009). As an example of a psychopath with high self-control, Lykken (1995) nominated the test pilot Chuck Yeager, a fearless individual with little or no need for human society, while Walsh and Wu (2008) suggested the Victorian adventurer Richard Francis Burton. Besides input from social emotions, the conscience develops in response to contingent learning, both operant and classical conditioning, in this way implicitly informing the individual of what is "right" (pleasurable) and "wrong" (painful). Even among children who lack fear and therefore are difficult to classically condition to avoid painful stimuli, praise and reward can help them learn, at a preconscious level, socially-desirable behavior (Kochanska, 1997).

Self-Control, Emotions, and Behavior

Social emotions can be negative. Jealousy, envy, and the ability to hold a grudge, like love and empathy, attain relevance only in a social context, and these negative social emotions can easily lead to violence and other forms of harmful behavior. Yet, we commit only a small fraction of the harmful acts that can, or imagine we can (Kagan, 1998). For society to function, the moral sense—the ability to appreciate right and wrong—becomes a "necessary feature for a species with a frontal lobe so large it permits a person to harbor resentment, envy, jealousy, and hostility for a long time after acute anger has passed" (Kagan, 1998, p. 193). And self-control becomes a necessary faculty for anyone who wishes to act in accordance with his or her moral sense, and not be overwhelmed by negative emotions, as well as for anyone who wishes to participate effectively in mutually-beneficial social interactions (MacDonald, 2008).

Self-control, then, should affect emotional states as well as behavior. In a study of Dutch teens, Finkenauer, Engels, & Baumeister (2005) found that self-control, defined as the conscious effort "to override and inhibit socially unacceptable and undesirable impulses and to alter and regulate one's behavior, thoughts, and emotions" (pp. 58–59), not only helped prevent delinquency but also depressive mood and stress, in models that controlled for parenting style as well. There was no ceiling effect. Instead, self-control was a "seemingly unmixed blessing" (p. 67).

MacDonald (2008) has analyzed the function and evolutionary history of "effortful control" over automatic mental processes, both cognitive and emotional, and has reviewed research indicating that the brain systems that control emotional processing differ from the mechanisms of cognitive control, which are generally called the executive function. This is consistent with the criminological view of self-control: Gottfredson and Hirschi (1990) separate the constructs of self-control and intelligence (see also Rowe, 1996), and implicitly acknowledge the role of emotional processing when they associate self-control with individual differences in the ability to defend oneself against the "temptations of the moment" (p. 87), which are emotional responses to environmental stimuli. Thus, self-control, like the moral sense, evolved because of "evolutionary pressure for cooperation" (MacDonald, 2008, p. 1024).

Whether called self-control, effortful control, explicit processing, or ability to delay gratification, self-control involves consciousness and free will, emanating from the prefrontal cortex (PFC) (Beaver, Wright, & DeLisi, 2007). It is responsible for modulating implicit processing taking place below the level of consciousness, including emotional systems, classical and operant conditioning, and other forms of implicit learning (MacDonald, 2008). With self-control, an individual can respond to novel situations in a way that enhances fitness, rather than simply following the dictates of evolved systems that learned what they learned in evolutionary time, i.e., across generations (MacDonald, 2008), in the same way that the moral sense responds to cultural contingencies and is not locked into hard and fast decision rules prescribed by genetic codes.

The Development of Self-Control: The Adolescent Gap

Self-control may be useful, but humans do not enter the world fully-equipped. As Gottfredson and Hirschi (1990) surmised, much of the task of parenting is to help offspring learn to delay gratification and consider the consequences of their actions. Although, as Tremblay and colleagues (1999) have noted, behaviors evincing low self-control peak at two years of age and decline thereafter, more serious offenses reach their peak in late adolescence, property crimes slightly earlier than violent crimes, a phenomenon called the *age-crime curve* (Gottfredson & Hirschi, 1990; Tittle & Grasmick, 1997; Walsh, 2009). Taken together, these findings indicate, first, that absolute levels of self-control tend to increase over time, and second, that there is something different about adolescence.

Synthesizing behavioral and brain development research, Casey, Jones, and Hare (2008) have provided a "biologically plausible model" (p. 111) to explain the jump in crime and other activity indicating low self-control during the teen years; using much of the same research, Walsh (2009) has proposed basically the same model.

Instead of thinking of self-control as a unitary phenomenon, or as a multifactorial construct à la Gottfredson and Hirschi, it can be useful to model self-control as the result of the interaction of two components, roughly corresponding to the BAS (behavioral approach system) and the BIS (behavioral inhibition system). Self-control declines with *either* increased strength of the BAS or decreased effectiveness of the BIS. As Casey and colleagues note, behavioral research reveals that, although the ability to inhibit impulses increase linearly with age, the tendency to take risks is greater in adolescence than in both childhood and adulthood.

The BAS and BIS are associated with different brain systems. While impulse control is localized in the PFC, risk-seeking is associated with limbic system structures, specifically the amygdala and the nucleus accumbens (Galvan, Hare, Voss, Glover, & Casey, 2007). The limbic system is a collection of subcortical brain structures responsible for, among other things, emotional processing (LeDoux, 1996).

Brain studies echo the findings from behavioral studies. To understand the age-crime curve, the important finding is that the PFC, implicated in impulse control, matures linearly, while the relevant parts of the limbic system, implicated in risk-seeking, show a great leap forward in early adolescence, and remain relatively hypertrophied, relative to the PFC, into early adulthood (Casey et al., 2008). Thus, the average adolescent has a gap between the emotional engine of their behavior and their ability to put on the brakes (see Figure 17.2). Moreover, there is evidence that the absolute amount of inhibitory neurotransmitters available to the brain decreases in adolescence (reviewed in Walsh, 2009), weakening the BIS and increasing the chances for risky behaviors.

Self-control does not develop easily, especially among the adolescents faced with brand new emotions, at intensities that never seem to let up. It has been likened to a muscle which can become stronger with repeated exercise but is easily depleted in the short term (Muraven, Baumeister, & Tice, 1999; see Gailliot et al., 2007). The social world continually presents teens with emotionally-challenging situations that threaten to exhaust whatever self-control they have developed (see Vohs et al., 2008). The problem is not with their cognitive capacity or moral sense: adolescents, in general, can understand the risks of their behaviors when they are away from temptation; that is, when they are not faced with immediate emotional demands (Reyna & Farley, 2006).

Because the augmentation of the BAS relates to the onset of puberty (Walsh, 2009), the gap between the strength of the engine (the BAS) and the effectiveness of the brakes and steering (the BIS) is greatest for adolescents entering puberty earlier than average. Therefore, we would expect to find more persistent, and earlier, offending among this group, and, indeed, early puberty is a characteristic of what Terrie Moffitt (1993) has called "life-course persistent" offenders who, according to one study, make up only 7% of offenders but who account for 50% of crime and delinquency (Henry, Caspi, Moffitt, & Silva, 1996). Life-course persistent offenders start offending earlier and desist later than most offenders (Moffitt, 1993).

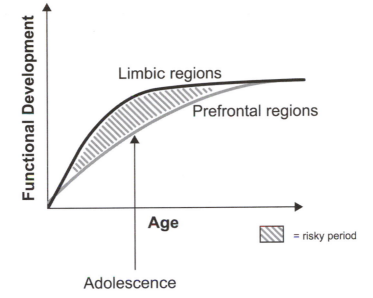

Figure 17.2 The traditional explanation of adolescent behavior has been that it is due to the protracted development of the prefrontal cortex. Our model takes into consideration the development of the prefrontal cortex together with subcortical limbic regions (e.g., nucleus accumbens and amygdala) that have been implicated in risky choices and emotional reactivity

Source: from Casey et al., 2008, p. 116.

How does this view of low self-control as the interaction between BAS and BIS compare with the criminological version? Not surprisingly, given its multifaceted nature, Gottfredson and Hirschi's construct comprises elements of both the BAS and the BIS, with a bit of the moral sense thrown in. A list of the components of low self-control that fairly reflects the *General Theory* and improves the ability of traditional measures to predict delinquency contains the following: impulsivity, risk-seeking, low frustration tolerance, shortsightedness, selfishness, a lack of diligence, and the tendency to neutralize guilt for one's wrongdoing (Wiebe, 2006). Of these, risk-seeking emanates from the BAS; impulsivity and low frustration tolerance represent the inability of the BIS to adequately control the BAS; shortsightedness — the tendency to value the present at the expense of the future — appears to be a cognitive component of impulsivity, or perhaps a rationalization for not working to develop self-control; a lack of diligence indicates a failure of the BIS to guard against distraction, frustration, and fatigue; the tendency to neutralize one's guilt, an unconscious process (Sykes & Matza, 1957), represents a failure of self-control over the moral sense — the inability or unwillingness to apply the standards contained within the moral sense to one's own actions; and selfishness might represent a basic deficiency in the social emotions or a higher-order corruption of the moral sense, perhaps corresponding to Mealey's (1995) primary and secondary sociopathy, respectively.

Selfishness is oddly underemphasized by Gottfredson and Hirschi. They do state that "people with low self-control tend to be self-centered, indifferent, or insensitive to the needs and feelings of others" (Gottfredson & Hirschi, 1990, p. 87) but their summary descriptions of low self-control only imply selfishness. The construct of psychopathy provides a better-developed description of the self-centered personality, although it overlaps with low self-control as well (Wiebe, 2003).

Why Low Self-Control? Crime as an Epiphenomenon of Mating Effort

Many commentators have noted that self-control and other moral virtues are essential to the success of a complex society (e.g., Kagan, 1998; Ridley, 1996; Wilson, 1993; Wright, 1994). Such virtues, implying some degree of conscious and willful control, supplement the work of the social emotions: the emotions that bind us to other human beings, that help us unconsciously evaluate our actions and those of other persons. However, arguments tracing the evolution of self-control to its adaptive value for an intensely social species would seem to be undermined by the observation that low self-control is so widespread and crime and similar behaviors so common, especially among adolescents, whose brains seem, in Walsh's (2009) term, "designed" to be ruled by emotions. Another look at the function of emotions can help address the conundrum: emotions tell us what is important. They alert us to objects of our desires and impediments to our success, and suggest, and often impel, appropriate approach or avoidance behaviors. And as classical and control theories remind us, crime and other low self-control behaviors are attempts to fill desires and remove irritations. In some instances, low self-control behaviors seem to the individual as the only behaviors available to address their needs (Caldwell, Wiebe, & Cleveland, 2006).

This is certainly how it appears to children, who come into this world with no concept of delayed gratification. They arrive equipped with both primary and social emotions, which begin to motivate behavior immediately (Eliot, 1999), and learn to control their emotional reactions with their parents' or other caregiver's assistance. Famously, Gottfredson and Hirschi (1990) trace the failure to develop self-control to insufficient parenting, with relative differences appearing early in life. While this perspective does not account for the shared genes that can affect both parent and child behaviors, resulting in ineffective parenting and delinquency, it does acknowledge that self-control is hard work: hard for parents to exercise; hard to inculcate in their children, especially among children with inherent traits, like "low intelligence, high activity level, physical strength, and adventuresomeness," that render them more difficult to socialize (p. 96); and hard for children to implement. According to the *General Theory* (after Patterson, 1982), good parenting requires affection, monitoring, the ability to recognize behavior requiring correction, and the willingness and ability to correct it. This is not always easy.

Adaptive Strategies: Low Self-Control and Mating Effort

Even effective parents face new challenges during adolescence, as illustrated by the age-crime curve and the research on brain development. The road to high self-control is neither smooth nor inexorable. Walsh's (2009) paper on the emotionally-driven behavior of adolescents is entitled "Crazy by design," which leads to the question: why would the adolescent brain be designed this way? A life-history perspective can help answer this question, by identifying different approaches to solving adaptive problems and applying them to different stages of life. An overall approach to solving adaptive problems is called an *adaptive strategy*, "an organized set of behaviors designed to maximize reproductive success over the life span" (Rowe, 1996, p. 269). It is important to recognize that the "organizing" takes place mainly at an unconscious level (emotions, cognitive and perceptual biases, etc.) and that the "designer" is Darwin's impersonal engine of natural selection (Kanazawa & Still, 2000).

Adaptive strategies can be placed on a continuum from mating effort and low parental investment to parenting effort and high parental investment. At the mating effort end, the individual allocates personal resources—economic, psychological, temporal—to the competition for mating opportunities, in the absence of, or at the expense of, existing mates and offspring. At the parenting effort end, the individual's resources go to existing mates and offspring (Rowe, 1996). The individual inclined toward mating effort might buy a fancy car, perhaps with a big loan s/he cannot repay, to impress potential mates, while the individual inclined toward parenting effort might put the money in the college fund. At the mating effort end, risky and aggressive behavior can have large payoffs, especially for males, since reproduction is in the future, there's nothing to lose now, and successfully negotiating risks and winning intrasexual competitions advertises good genes. Further, a male can successfully reproduce despite minimal contributions to the child and mother. In contrast, once the individual has something to protect, taking unnecessary risks can impair the prospects of existing offspring and undermine existing relationships. In other words, mating effort focuses on the here and now, and on the individual at the expense of others, while parenting effort focuses on the future, and on preserving and strengthening personal relationships and social bonds (see Hirschi, 1969).

Rowe (1996), following Rushton (1985) and Harpending and Draper (1988), outlined a theory that explicitly ties mating effort to crime. A close examination of low self-control, in the criminological sense, can make this connection clear. Whether conceived of as a general tendency to value the present over the future and the self over the other, or as a collection of traits like impulsivity, sensation- and risk-seeking, and the tendency to give up when the going gets tough and to take the easy way out, the psychological characteristics that facilitate crime also lead to short-term, unstable sexual relationships and indifferent or ineffective parenting, both indicative of mating effort. As reproduction pre-dates crime (Rowe, 1996), crime can fairly be thought of as an epiphenomenon—an unintended by-product— of an adaptive strategy rooted in mating effort.

Mating Effort and Adolescence

Since both mating effort and parenting effort are viable strategies, both remain in the human behavioral repertoire (Rowe, 1996), especially among adolescents (Kanazawa & Still, 2000). Young people have less to lose, and more to gain, from risky and shortsighted behavior than older people. Thus, they have less incentive to consider the future consequences of their actions, and must constantly be reminded to do so by parents, teachers, DARE officers, and other well-intentioned elders. Figure 17.3 below, based on a figure from Kanazawa and Still (2000), represents hypothesized risk and reward curves superimposed over the age-crime curve. As the risks of low self-control behavior—mating effort—increase over time, crime becomes decreasingly likely. The potential rewards of risky behavior, especially in competitions with younger men, are likely to decrease with age as well: winning a fight with a young man at age 50 may not be as impressive to potential mates as it would have at age 25.

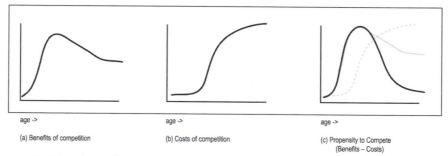

| age -> | age -> | age -> |

(a) Benefits of competition (b) Costs of competition (c) Propensity to Compete (Benefits – Costs)

Figure 17.3 Mating effort and age

Source: modified from Kanazawa & Still, 2000, p. 441.

When Else Does Mating Effort Pay?

It is not only among teens, compared with children and adults, that mating effort is often more attractive than parenting effort. Among other groups that may benefit from mating effort, or who may believe that parenting effort is pointless, are males, as opposed to females; children raised by indifferent or harsh parents; children with heritable biases for low self-control; individuals in unstable environments; individuals who perceive their environments as unstable; habitual criminals; individuals with low status; and individuals who live in a society that values mating effort and undervalues parenting effort. These groups overlap. Among them, an adaptive strategy rooted in mating effort and instituted through low self-control, while not endorsed by society, remains, for individuals for whom high self-control does not come easily, a viable alternative to parenting effort.

One caveat: the following discussion is not intended to imply that these factors *determine* adaptive strategy, which is a complicated outcome of a variety of predictors (Ellis, Figueredo, Brumbach, & Schlomer, 2009). It is intended only to set forth a variety of circumstances in which a mating effort strategy *can* succeed, from the standpoint of reproductive fitness, as a reminder that, first, low self-control is not likely to disappear from the face of the earth; and, second, low self-control is not necessarily pathological, indicating the failure of some system or developmental process to work properly (Wakefield, 1992).

Sex Differences

As noted above, aggression and risk-taking—emotional behavior unchecked by self-control—pay off better for males than females in terms of status and mating opportunities (Kanazawa & Still, 2000). Differences also emerge on the risk side. Women, on average, risk more than males by taking physical risks because even a female at the extreme mating effort end of the spectrum, to successfully reproduce, needs many more resources over a greater period of time than a male. Mostly, she needs an intact and healthy body (Campbell, 1999). According to Campbell, females are therefore, on average, naturally more averse to physically-threatening situations than males. This is reflected in crime rates, which diverge widely between the sexes for violent crimes like robbery but converge as the crime gets less violent. Females commit less than 10% of all robberies but nearly 40% of all embezzlement, fraud, and simple larceny (Campbell, 2009). Campbell (2009) also notes that, across cultures, male and female crime rates tend to rise and fall together, suggesting that the broad causes of crimes are identical across the sexes.

Mating effort may benefit females, and female crime rates rise, when they compete with each other for the few good available males (Campbell, 1995). If men are unavailable for long-term parenting, then competition centers on the quality of the genes, especially the genes that help win intrasexual competitions and survive risky behavior. A woman may choose single motherhood as the best option available (see Harpending & Draper, 1988).

An Adaptive Response to Poor Parenting

The very act of effortful (rather than neglectful) parenting signals to the child that the future is worth preparing for. On the other hand, neglectful parenting signals that the parents do not consider their children's future a worthwhile place in which to invest resources. In this case, the children perceive that they are basically on their own, with no good reason to delay gratification. Although children come into the world with the potential to develop both selfish and social behaviors, selfishness is the default (Brannigan, 1997). The effects of neglect can manifest physically as well as psychologically and behaviorally: Tottenham and colleagues (2010) found enlarged limbic structures, poor emotional control, and increased anxiety among adopted children who had been in orphanages for long periods.

Heritable Biases

Gottfredson and Hirschi's position that parenting is the most important determinant of self-control may be too simple, in large part because most of the studies showing parenting effects fail to control for genetic factors (Beaver et al., 2009). For children inheriting certain traits, mating effort may turn out to be the more viable alternative because parenting effort, without extraordinarily attentive parents, would be too difficult to develop. Mating effort often seems to be an "alternative" strategy as opposed to a "conditional" strategy, influenced by genetic predispositions more strongly than by environmental factors (Rowe, Vazsonyi, & Figueredo, 1997; see also Bailey, Kirk, Zhu, Dunner, & Martin, 2000; Moffitt, Caspi, Belsky, & Silva, 1992; Rowe, 2002). Heritable factors relating to mating effort and antisociality might be traits, such as low IQ or low conscientiousness, that leave an individual at a competitive disadvantage (Rowe, 1994), or could be perceptual, emotional, or cognitive biases directly related to a preference for immediate gratification and sexual variety. Modern behavioral science has identified some of the specific genes, as well as the functions of those genes, that appear connected to crime and mating effort, but still has a long way to go (Beaver, 2009).

Absence of Legitimate Opportunities for Conventional Success

Children may respond to harsh extrafamilial environments as they respond to harsh or neglectful parenting. Criminologists have long believed that harsh environments engender crime, because people in them perceive no realistic chance at conventional success and take whatever avenues are available to satisfying their needs (e.g., Merton, 1938). Parenting effort and delayed gratification work only when the future is worth waiting for and resources placed into parenting effort would not be better placed elsewhere (Daly & Wilson, 1988). In harsh environments, even children who are not genetically biased toward low self-control may become aggressive in order to compete. As expected under this model, the heritability of aggression is smaller in disadvantaged neighborhoods (Cleveland, 2003).

At the extreme, a failed state, such as postwar Iraq, may provide virtually no opportunities to obtain resources or settle disputes within the law within the context of a stable, well-functioning society. In this case, ordinary citizens must be prepared to take advantage of any opportunity they encounter.

Future Uncertainty

Although objective factors like neglectful parenting and harsh environments can bias individuals toward low self-control, these factors are filtered through the individual's perceptions. Thus, it may be important to separate an individual's perceptions of the value of developing self-control from an objective assessment of that value. Research has shown that *perceptions* of an uncertain future predict both delinquency and school problems, even after controlling for demographic, family, and socioeconomic variables (Caldwell et al., 2006).

Life-Course Persistent Offenders

Life-course persistent offenders face two kinds of problems. When they decide to desist from crime, society gives them few opportunities to succeed, and, even with opportunity, many lack the skills and abilities to take advantage. They are burdened with a criminal record, little or no job history, few marketable skills, social patterns honed in prison, weak or absent support from friends and family, unresolved mental health and addiction issues, and marginal social status (Petersilia, 2003), as well as the neuropsychological deficits and internalized personal histories that led them into the life in the first place. Emotional reactions that helped them survive prison—get angry quickly and decisively—serve them poorly in the workplace and elsewhere in the outside world, and they have missed years of opportunity to develop self-control. Though aging ex-convicts may no longer benefit from low self-control and mating effort behaviors, they face a future that may never reward them no matter how much self-control they exhibit. Desisting from crime in your 30s or 40s, when your cohort has established careers and families, as well as adult-appropriate levels of self-control, doesn't leave you on easy street.

Low Status

People age out of adolescence, yet low self-control can endure. This may be because of the adaptive value of impulsive, unpredictable behavior, what Miller (1997) called a "protean" strategy, for low-status individuals, especially males (Palmer, McGown, & Kerby, 1997). As numerous criminologists and sociologists have pointed out, it is in the interests of the "haves" that the "have-nots" not stir up too much trouble. If everyone demonstrated high self-control and fully accepted social rules, then the people least able, for reasons of racial or ethnic discrimination, economic or social status, political affiliation, personal history, or traits and abilities, to compete in the marketplace and achieve conventional success would simply accept their fate and go about their business meekly, creating the efficient society Huxley envisioned in his dystopic *Brave New World* (1932/1969). Therefore, impulsivity, risk-taking, and unpredictability may benefit those who would otherwise be permanently consigned to a life without hope, giving them mating opportunities and at least the illusion of potential economic success. Of course, these traits tend to, whatever the context, reduce conventional success, reinforcing a lifestyle based on short-term rewards.

Mating Effort Society

Finally, entire societies may reflect and reward mating effort. Harpending and Draper (1988) contrasted the !Kung, a southwest African desert people, with the Mundurucu, from the Amazon. When the studies were conducted, the !Kung lived in a harsh but predictable environment where contributions of both parents were necessary for offspring to survive. People lived as nuclear families, male–female relations were "cordial and egalitarian" (p. 297), and children were cared for intensely through puberty. There was no viable niche for antisocial or mating effort behavior, as an individual attempting crime or extra-pair copulation "would be readily detected and ostracized" (p. 297). The Mundurucu lived differently. Their environment was richer in resources, so they didn't have to work as hard to feed, clothe, and shelter themselves. Further, as hunters, the men's contributions to the total caloric intake of their village were dwarfed by the women's contributions from gathering, and they tended to use the meat they did procure to trade for sex rather than to provision their own children. Instead of living together as mutually-dependent families, which requires trust and fair dealing, men and women lived separately, the women with children in small huts and the men together in one large bunkhouse. Overall, male reproductive effort centered on male–male competition and mating effort, while females had little use for males, whose most important role seemed to be to protect them from other men.

Preventing Low Self-Control

Mealey (1997) considered certain human conditions "ethical pathologies" — bad for society while not necessarily causing distress to their hosts. The clearest example is psychopathy, whose "sufferers" do not necessarily feel that there's anything wrong with them. Low self-control may be, at least in some cases, another ethical pathology, particularly from a Darwinian perspective. Because low self-control is a natural state and can be useful when immediate gratification is more rewarding than gratification postponed and when you're on your own, mating effort and antisocial behavior may be dampened in a well-functioning society but will reappear under various circumstances. Some of these circumstances are intractable. Males, especially young and low-status males, will remain more tempted by physical risks than females. Other genetic risk factors besides the Y chromosome will also remain in the gene pool. While genetic engineering is a real possibility for the near future, one would hope that social engineers or nervous parents do not systematically seek and destroy all of our genes for sensation seeking, novelty, emotional coldness, resistance to authority, and other relevant predilections. In appropriate environments, under appropriate self-control, each has a valuable niche in human society.

Other circumstances are theoretically preventable but unlikely to be tampered with. Perhaps the most pervasive is the cycle of low self-control that occurs when parents with low self-control rear children who share their genes, likely including genes that make a child more challenging to discipline (Lykken, 1995). This cycle is compounded by child effects—difficult children become difficult teens, taxing their parents' capacities even further (Beaver & Wright, 2007; Huh, Tristan, Wade, & Stice, 2006; Wilson & Herrnstein, 1985). Difficult children can be successfully socialized, but through extraordinary effort, while easy children may do well under conditions of neglect. However, we are likely to see neither wholesale child-trading between parents with high and low self-control nor widespread collective child-rearing.

Other circumstances can be altered. Because self-control increases from adolescence to young adulthood, and education and other forms of social capital is more easily accumulated by a young person without children, delaying the age at first childbirth shows promise (Rutter, Giller, & Hagell, 1998). While we are not likely to impose parental licensure (Lykken, 2000) or put birth control chemicals in the water and require a prescription for the antidote (Scarr, 2000), teen parenthood remains a viable target for intervention. Similar programs—e.g., education, substance abuse prevention and recovery, gang prevention—are aimed at increasing the ability of young people to participate in and benefit from the wider synergistic society.

Ultimately, the problem of low self-control is about social justice. Perhaps the biggest challenges are to provide legitimate opportunities for conventional success to all members of society, as criminologists have been saying for decades (Walsh & Ellis, 2007), and to help people believe in these opportunities. Where people are desperate and hopeless, they offend (or otherwise give up on their future). Where men feel useless, they offend. When people drop out of school, when they believe that the future is going to be worse than the present, when they are persistently discriminated against and denied opportunities afforded other members of society, they offend. Even if nearly everyone had a legitimate chance to succeed, they would not necessarily take advantage. For the message to affect behavior, the emotional brain must be convinced.

References

Alexander, R. D. (1987). *The biology of moral systems*. New York: Aldine de Gruyter.

Axelrod, R. (1984). *The evolution of cooperation*. New York: Basic Books.

Bailey, J. M., Kirk, K. M., Zhu, G., Dunner, M. P., & Martin, N. G. (2000). Do individual differences in sociosexuality represent genetic or environmentally contingent strategies? Evidence from the Australian Twin Registry. *Journal of Personality and Social Psychology, 78*, 537–545.

Bakan, J. (2004). *The corporation: The pathological pursuit of profit and power*. New York: Free Press.

Baumeister, R. F. (1997). *Evil: Inside human violence and cruelty*. New York: W. H. Freeman.

Baumeister, R. F., & Exline, J. J. (2000). Self-control, morality, and human strength. *Journal of Social and Clinical Psychology, 19*, 29–42.

Baumeister, R. F., & Leary, M. R. (1995). The need to belong: Desire for interpersonal attachments as a fundamental human motivation. *Psychological Bulletin, 117*, 497–529.

Baumeister, R. F., Smart, L., & Boden, Joseph M. (1996). Relation of threatened egoism to violence and aggression: The dark side of high self-esteem. *Psychological Review, 103*, 5–33.

Beaver, K. M. (2009). Molecular genetics and crime. In A. Walsh & K. M. Beaver (Eds.), *Biosocial criminology: New directions in theory and research* (pp. 50–72). New York: Routledge.

Beaver, K. M., Shutt, J. E., Boutwell, B. B., Ratchford, M., Roberts, K., & Barnes, J. C. (2009). Genetic and environmental influences on levels of self-control and delinquent peer affiliation: Results from a longitudinal sample of adolescent twins. *Criminal Justice and Behavior, 36*, 41–69.

Beaver, K. M., & Wright, J. P. (2007). A child effects explanation for the association between family risk and antisocial lifestyle. *Journal of Adolescent Research, 22*, 640–664.

Beaver, K. M., Wright, J. P., & DeLisi, M. (2007). Self-control as an executive function: Reformulating Gottfredson and Hirschi's parental socialization thesis. *Criminal Justice and Behavior, 34*, 1345–1361.

Betzig, L. (1993). Sex, succession, and stratification in the first six civilizations: How powerful men reproduced, passed power on to their sons, and used power to defend their wealth, women, and children. In L. Ellis (Ed.), *Social stratification and socioeconomic inequality: Volume I: A comparative biosocial analysis* (pp. 37–74). Westport, CT: Praeger.

Brannigan, A. (1997). Self control, social control and evolutionary psychology: Toward an integrated perspective on crime. *Canadian Journal of Criminology, 39*, 403–431.

Buss, D. M. (1991). Evolutionary personality psychology. *Annual Review of Psychology, 42*, 459–491.

Caldwell, R. M., Wiebe, R. P., & Cleveland, H. H. (2006). The influence of future certainty and contextual factors on delinquent behavior and school adjustment among African American adolescents. *Journal of Youth and Adolescence, 35,* 587–598.

Campbell, A. (1995). A few good men: Evolutionary psychology and female adolescent aggression. *Ethology & Sociobiology, 16,* 99–123.

Campbell, A. (1999). Staying alive: Evolution, culture, and women's intrasexual aggression. *Behavioral and Brain Sciences, 22,* 203–252.

Campbell, A. (2009). Gender and crime: An evolutionary perspective. In A. Walsh & K. M. Beaver (Eds.), *Biosocial criminology: New directions in theory and research* (pp. 117–136). New York: Routledge.

Casey, B. J., Jones, R. M., & Hare, T. A. (2008). The adolescent brain. *Annals of the New York Academy of Sciences, 1124,* 111–126.

Cleveland, H. H. (2003). Disadvantaged neighborhoods and adolescent aggression: Behavioral genetic evidence of contextual effects. *Journal of Research on Adolescence, 13,* 211–238.

Cloward, R., & Ohlin, L. (1960). *Delinquency and opportunity.* New York: Free Press.

Cohen, A. (1955). *Delinquent boys.* New York: Free Press.

Daly, M., & Wilson, M. (1988). *Homicide.* Hawthorne, NY: Aldine De Gruyter.

Damasio, A. R. (1994). *Descartes' error: Emotion, reason, and the human brain.* New York: G. P. Putnam's Sons.

Darwin, C. (1871/1981). *The descent of man, and selection in relation to sex.* Princeton: Princeton University Press.

Eliot, L. (1999). *What's going on in there? How the brain and mind develop in the first five years of life.* New York: Bantam.

Ellis, B. J., Figueredo, A. J., Brumbach, B. H., & Schlomer, G. L. (2009). Fundamental dimensions of environmental risk: The impact of harsh versus unpredictable environments on the evolution and development of life history strategies. *Human Nature, 20,* 204–268.

Felson, M., & Boba, R. (2010). *Crime in everyday life (4th ed.).* Thousand Oaks, CA: Sage.

Finkenauer, C., Engles, R. C. M. E., & Baumeister, R. F. (2005). Parenting behaviour and adolescent behavioural and emotional problems: The role of self-control. *International Journal of Behavioral Development, 29,* 58–69.

Flack, J. C., & de Waal, F. B. M. (2000). "Any animal whatever": Darwinian building blocks of morality in monkeys and apes. *Journal of Consciousness Studies, 7,* 1–29.

Fowles, D. C. (1993). Electrodermal activity and antisocial behavior: Empirical findings and theoretical issues. In J.-C. Roy, W. Bouscein, D. C. Fowles, & J. H. Gruzelier (Eds.), *Progress in electrodermal research* (pp. 223–237). New York: Plenum.

Frank, R. H. (1988). *Passions within reason: The strategic role of the emotions.* New York: W. W. Norton.

Gailloit, M. T., Baumeister, R. F., DeWall, C. N., Maner, J. K., Plant, E. A., Tucem Duabbe N, B. L. E., & Schmeichel, B. J. (2007). Self-control relies on glucose as a limited energy source: Willpower is more than a metaphor. *Journal of Personality and Social Psychology, 92,* 325–336.

Galvan, A., Hare, T., Voss, H., Glover, G., & Casey, B. J. (2007). Risk-taking and the adolescent brain: Who is at risk? *Developmental Science, 10,* F8–F14.

Gottfredson, M. R., & Hirschi, T. (1990). *A general theory of crime.* Stanford, CA: Stanford University Press.

Gottfredson, M. R., & Hirschi, T. (2003). Self-control and opportunity. In C. L. Britt & M. R. Gottfredson (Eds.), *Control Theories of Crime and Delinquency (Advances in Criminological Theory, Volume 12)* (pp. 5–19). New Brunswick, NJ: Transaction.

Gray, J. A. (1991). The neuropsychology of temperament. In J. Strelau & A. Angleitner (Eds.), *Explorations in temperament: International perspectives on theory and measurement* (pp. 105–128). New York: Plenum.

Hall, C. S. (1954). *A primer of Freudian psychology.* New York: New American Library.

Hamilton, W. D. (1964). The genetical evolution of social behavior. *Journal of Theoretical Biology, 7,* 1–52.

Harpending, H., & Draper, P. (1988). Antisocial behavior and the other side of cultural evolution. In T. E. Moffitt & S. A. Mednick (Eds.), *Biological contributions to crime causation* (pp. 293–307). Boston: Martinus Nijhoff.

Henry, B., Caspi, A., Moffitt, T. E., & Silva, P. (1996). Temperamental and familial predictors of violent and nonviolent criminal convictions: Age 3 to age 18. *Developmental Psychology, 32,* 614–623.

Henry, J. D., von Hippel, W., & Baynes, K. (2009). Social inappropriateness, executive control, and aging. *Psychology and Aging, 24,* 239–244.

Hirschi, T. (1969). *Causes of delinquency.* Berkeley, CA: University of California Press.

Hirschi, T., & Gottfredson, M. (2001). Self-control theory. In R. Paternoster & R. Bachman (Eds.), *Explaining criminals and crime* (pp. 81–96). Los Angeles: Roxbury.

Hirschi, T., & Gottfredson, M. R. (1994). The generality of deviance. In T. Hirschi & M. R. Gottfredson (Eds.), *The generality of deviance* (pp. 1–22). Boston: Transaction Press.

Hrdy, S. B. (1999). *Mother nature: Maternal instincts and how they shape the human species.* New York: Ballentine.

Huh, D., Tristan, J., Wade, E., & Stice, E. (2006). Does problem behavior elicit poor parenting? A prospective study of adolescent girls. *Journal of Adolescent Research, 21,* 185–204.

Huxley, A. (1932/1969). *Brave new world.* Baltimore: Penguin.

Kagan, J. (1998). *Three seductive ideas.* Cambridge, MA: Harvard University Press.

Kanazawa, S., & Still, M. C. (2000). Why men commit crimes (and why they desist). *Sociological Theory, 18,* 434–447.

Kochanska, G. (1997). Multiple pathways to conscience for children with different temperaments: From toddlerhood to age 5. *Developmental Psychology, 33,* 228–240.

Kochanska, G., Murray, K. T., & Harlan, E. T. (2000). Effortful control in early childhood: Continuity and change, antecedents, and implications for social development. *Developmental Psychology, 36,* 220–232.

Kornhauser, R. R. (1978). *Social sources of delinquency: An appraisal of analytical models.* Chicago: University of Chicago Press.

Krueger, R. F., Caspi, A., Moffitt, T. E., White, J., & Stouthamer-Loeber, M. (1996). Delay of gratification, psychopathology, and personality: Is low self-control specific to externalizing problems? *Journal of Personality, 64,* 107–129.

LeDoux, J. (1996). *The emotional brain: The mysterious underpinnings of emotional life.* New York: Simon & Schuster.

Lykken, D. T. (1995). *The antisocial personalities.* Hillsdale, NJ: Lawrence Erlbaum Associates.

Lykken, D. T. (2000). The causes and costs of crime and a controversial cure. *Journal of Personality, 68,* 559–605.

MacDonald, K. B. (2008). Effortful control, explicit processing, and the regulation of human evolved predispositions. *Psychological Review, 115*(4), 1012–1031.

Mealey, L. (1995). The sociobiology of sociopathy: An integrated evolutionary model. *Behavioral and Brain Sciences, 18,* 523–599.

Mealey, L. (1997). Heritability, theory of mind, and the nature of normality. *Behavioral and Brain Sciences, 20,* 527–532.

Merton, R. (1938). Social structure and "anomie." *American Sociological Review, 3,* 672–682.

Miller, A. (1951). *Death of a salesman.* New York: Bantam.

Miller, G. F. (1997). Protean primates: The evolution of adaptive unpredictability in competition and courtship. In A. Whiten & R. W. Byrne (Eds.), *Machiavellian intelligence II: Extensions and evaluation* (pp. 312–340). Cambridge: Cambridge University Press.

Miller, W. (1955). Lower-class culture as a generating milieu of gang delinquency. *Journal of Social Issues, 14,* 5–19.

Moffitt, T. E. (1993). Adolescence-limited and life-course-persistent antisocial behavior: A developmental taxonomy. *Psychological Review, 100,* 674–701.

Moffitt, T. E., Caspi, A., Belsky, J., & Silva, P. A. (1992). Child experience and the onset of menarche: A test of a sociobiological model. *Child Development, 63,* 47–58.

Muraven, M., & Baumeister, R. F. (2000). Self-regulation and depletion of limited resources: Does self-control resemble a muscle? *Psychological Bulletin, 126,* 247–259.

Muraven, M., Baumeister, R. F., & Tice, D. M. (1999). Longitudinal improvement of self-regulation through practice: Building self-control strength through repeated exercise. *Journal of Social Psychology, 139,* 446–457.

Nesse, R. M., & Ellsworth, P. C. (2009). Evolution, emotions, and emotional disorders. *American Psychologist, 64,* 129–139.

Palmer, J., McGown, W., & Kerby, D. (1997). *The adaptive significance of "dysfunctional" impulsivity.* Unpublished manuscript, Northeast Louisiana University.

Patrick, C. J. (1994). Emotion and psychopathy: Startling new insights. *Psychophysiology, 31,* 319–330.

Patterson, G. R. (1982). *A social learning approach, volume 3: Coercive family process.* Eugene, OR: Castilia.

Petersilia, J. (2003). *When prisoners come home: Parole and prisoner reentry*. New York: Oxford University Press.

Pratt, T., & Cullen, F. T. (2000). The empirical status of Gottfredson and Hirschi's General Theory of Crime: A meta-analysis. *Criminology, 38*, 931–964.

Raine, A. (1993). *The psychopathology of crime*. San Diego, CA: Academic Press.

Reyna, V. F., & Farley, F. (2006). Risk and rationality in adolescent decision making: Implications for theory, practice, and public policy. *Psychological Science in the Public Interest, 7*, 1–44.

Ridley, M. (1996). *The origins of virtue*. New York: Viking.

Rowe, D. C. (1994). *The limits of family influence: Genes, experience, and behavior*. New York: The Guilford Press.

Rowe, D. C. (1996). An adaptive strategy theory of crime and delinquency. In J. D. Hawkins (Ed.), *Delinquency and crime: Current theories* (pp. 268–314). Cambridge: Cambridge University Press.

Rowe, D. C. (2002). *Biology and crime*. Los Angeles: Roxbury.

Rowe, D. C., Vazsonyi, A. T., & Figueredo, A. J. (1997). Mating effort in adolescence: Conditional or alternative strategy. *Personality and Individual Differences, 23*, 105–115.

Rushton, J. P. (1985). Differential K theory: The sociobiology of individual and group differences. *Personality and Individual Differences, 6*, 441–452.

Rutter, M., Giller, H., & Hagell, A. (1998). *Antisocial behavior in young people*. Cambridge: Cambridge University Press.

Sanderson, S. K. (2001). *The evolution of human sociality: A Darwinian conflict perspective*. Lanham, MD: Rowman & Littlefield.

Scarr, S. (2000). Toward voluntary parenthood. *Journal of Personality, 68*, 615–623.

Stuewig, J., & Tangney, J. P. (2007). Shame and guilt in antisocial and risky behaviors. In J. L. Tracy, R. W. Robins, & J. P. Tangney (Eds.), *The self-conscious emotions: Theory and research* (pp. 371–388). New York: Guilford.

Sykes, G. M., & Matza, D. (1957). Techniques of neutralization: A theory of delinquency. *American Sociological Review, 22*, 664–670.

Tittle, C. R., & Grasmick, H. G. (1997). Criminal behavior and age: A test of three provocative hypotheses. *Journal of Criminal Law and Criminology, 88*, 309–342.

Tooby, J., & Cosmides, L. (1990). On the universality of human nature and the uniqueness of the individual: The role of genetics and adaptation. *Journal of Personality, 58*, 17–67.

Tottenham, N., Hare, T. A., Quinn, B. T., McCarry, T. W., Nurse, M., Gilhooly, T., Millner, A., Galvan, A., Davidson, M. C., Eigsti, I.-M., Thomas, K. M., Freed, P. J., Booma, E. S., Gunnar, M. R., Altemus, M., Aronson, J., & Casey, B. J. (2010). Prolonged institutional rearing is associated with a typically large amygdala volume and difficulties in emotion regulation. *Developmental Science, 13*, 46–61.

Tremblay, R. E., Japel, C., Perusse, D., McDuff, P., Boivin, M., Zoccolillo, M., & Montplaisir, J. (1999). The search for the age of "onset" of physical aggression: Rousseau and Bandua revisited. *Criminal Behaviour and Mental Health, 9*, 8–23.

Trivers, R. L. (1971). The evolution of reciprocal altruism. *The Quarterly Review of Biology, 46*, 35–57.

Vohs, K. D., Schmeichel, B. J., Nelson, N. M., Baumeister, R. F., Twenge, J. M., & Tice, D. M. (2008). Making choices impairs subsequent self-control: A limited-resource account of decision making, self-regulation, and active initiative. *Journal of Personality and Social Psychology, 94*, 883–898.

Wakefield, J. C. (1992). The concept of mental disorder: On the boundary between biological facts and social values. *American Psychologist, 47*, 373–388.

Walsh, A. (2009). Crazy by design: A biosocial approach to the age-crime curve. In A. Walsh & K. M. Beaver (Eds.), *Biosocial criminology: New directions in theory and research* (pp. 154–175). New York: Routledge.

Walsh, A., & Ellis, L. (2007). *Criminology: An interdisciplinary approach.* Thousand Oaks, CA: Sage.

Walsh, A., & Wu, H.-H. (2008). Differentiating antisocial personality disorder, psychopathy, and sociopathy: Evolutionary, genetic, neurological, and sociological considerations. *Journal of Criminal Justice Studies*, 135–152.

Widom, C. S. (1977). A methodology for studying noninstitutionalized psychopaths. *Journal of Consulting and Clinical Psychology, 45*, 674–683.

Wiebe, R. P. (2003). Reconciling psychopathy and low self-control. *Justice Quarterly, 20*, 297–336.

Wiebe, R. P. (2004). Expanding the model of human nature underlying the General Theory of Crime: Implications for the constructs of self-control and opportunity. *Australian and New Zealand Journal of Criminology, 37*, 65–84.

Wiebe, R. P. (2006). Using an expanded measure of self-control to predict delinquency. *Psychology, Crime, & Law, 12*, 519–536.

Wiebe, R. P. (2009). Psychopathy. In A. Walsh & K. M. Beaver (Eds.), *Biosocial criminology: New directions in theory and research* (pp. 225–242). New York: Routledge.

Wilson, J. Q. (1993). *The moral sense.* New York: Free Press.

Wilson, J. Q., & Herrnstein, R. J. (1985). *Crime and human nature.* New York: Simon & Schuster.

Wright, R. (1994). *The moral animal: The new science of evolutionary psychology.* New York: Pantheon.

Wright, R. (2000). *Nonzero: The logic of human destiny.* New York: Pantheon.

PART VI
IMPLICATIONS OF
BIOSOCIAL RESEARCH

18

Biosocial Treatment and Prevention Strategies

Michael G. Vaughn and Ralph Groom

Introduction

Successful prevention and intervention of various forms of criminal and antisocial behavior requires greater progress in understanding and elaborating the biosocial roots of effecting change. Although much has been learned about what is effective in treating offenders, relatively little is known about what processes and mechanisms are key drivers of change. While effects can be empirically measured, we don't always know what the key ingredients are. In other words, how does a treatment like cognitive behavioral therapy or mentoring an at-risk youth get "under-the-skin"? Why not ignore this issue and just continue to test the effects of various intervention schemes? While experimental evidence regarding the "real world" effectiveness of interventions is critically important, comprehending the underlying biosocial interplay at work is important for at least two reasons. First, knowledge gained about these causal processes can enhance the specificity and efficiency of interventions and thereby reduce costs and wasting of resources. Second, intervention tests can in turn be used to inform etiologic research on causes within the context of the experimental design. Despite being pursued separately, causal and treatment research are intertwined.

This chapter provides an overview of the biosocial underpinnings of commonly employed treatments for offenders including those touted as being effective. We also consider important issues as it pertains to pursuing prevention and intervention strategies within a biosocial framework. One such important issue is the role of co-occurring conditions, which are often part and parcel of antisocial behavior syndromes. A number of important concepts necessary for future intervention work are also discussed. The guiding thesis of this chapter is that all interventions are biosocial in nature. Although certainly some may involve greater efforts on the environmental or the biological side of the coin, it is difficult to have one without the other. We should also mention up front that we cannot cover all of the possible prevention and intervention programs that exist and that our approach in this chapter focuses on interventions affecting the individual and not macro level policies and community level interventions to reduce crime. While we believe these interventions are also biosocial in nature, relative to individual treatments, there are very few that have been adequately tested.

Causal Relationships and Preventative Strategies

Causal factors that have implications for prevention methodologies involve both nature and nurture. Nurturing aspects involving such parenting factors as low parental involvement during childhood help contribute to the persistence of antisocial behaviors, and, thus, have been shown over time to be associated with antisocial behavior in adulthood (Hiatt and Dishion, 2008). Also, previous research on children that had been abused or neglected before 12 years of age, indicates that approximately 20 percent were given diagnosis of antisocial personality disorder 20 years later (Hiatt and Dishion, 2008). Preventative treatments for criminal offending will need to take into account a rich mix of biosocial factors such as socio-economic deprivation, antisocial parents/siblings, poor parental supervision and harsh child-rearing techniques, low intelligence, impulsivity, impaired decision-making, and delinquent peers.

Further complicating the design of prevention plans is that there appear to be different types of offenders with different factors being more salient. For example, Moffitt (1993) theorized that conduct problems for the adolescent-limited offender group are largely caused by peer influences. Peer relationships play a crucial role in maintaining and amplifying antisocial behaviors from adolescence into adulthood (Lahey, 2008). Moffitt (1993) also theorized that conduct problems among the life-course persistent youth are mainly caused by early neurodevelopmental deficits. Do these deficits occur naturally, are they nurtured, or both?

Behavior-genetic studies have provided heritability estimates of childhood aggression and adult crime. An important study conducted by Rhee and Waldman (2002), via a meta-analytic review of twin and adoption studies, found that genetic influences accounted for 41 percent of the variation in antisocial behavior. Strong evidence suggests that a causal link to conduct problems is genetic. Genes exert their influence on such behaviors through complex interplays with the environments they share (Lahey, 2008). These gene–environment interplays can be divided into three types of correlations: passive gene–environment, evocative gene–environment and active gene–environment correlations. Passive gene–environment correlation pertains to children who also have parents with mental health/antisocial problems. Evocative gene–environment correlation is associated with the child's genetically influenced behavior changing the social environment, which, in turn, influences their conduct problems. Active gene–environment correlation occurs when the child's selection of environments is influenced by genes, such as forming social bonds with delinquent peers (Lahey, 2008). Understanding the principles of these forms of gene–environment interplay will be a key to designing effective biosocial treatments in the future.

Biosocial Underpinnings of Common Interventions

Neural Substrates and Neuropsychological Processes

Key factors in the design of common interventions involve several neural substrates and neuropsychological processes. For example, motor and sensory functions mature earliest in the brain. Research has shown that the hippocampus is fully developed by two years of age, but the prefrontal cortex (PFC) region continues to develop in adolescence. The PFC is the last region of the brain to fully mature. It plays a crucial role in higher cognitive abilities and is important for regulating bad behavioral choices in favor of good ones that are more goal-directed (Casey, Jones, and Hare, 2008).

Another key area of the brain that has important implications for offending is the amygdala (DeLisi, Umphress, and Vaughn, 2009). The amygdala increases in volume under chronic stress. This region of the brain monitors fear/threats, and thus, because of the increase in volume under chronic stress, it aids in the survival of the individual by facilitating greater awareness of threatening information in their environment. Although some stress is needed for normal physiological responses and functions that mobilize the body to respond to survival, too much stress can invoke severe repercussions when comingled with environmental influences. Stress plays an important role in aggression problems for children and adolescence. The brain is sensitive to stress during both early childhood and old age, because it undergoes important changes during these periods. Stress triggers the hypothalamus-pituitary-adrenal (HPA) axis, which then produces glucocorticoids by the adrenals. Receptors for these steroids are varied throughout the brain, but their importance is in regulating gene expression.

Studies on children whose mothers experienced psychological stress suggest that there are prolonged neurodevelopmental effects. Maternal stress has been associated with increased basal HPA axis activity in their offspring at different ages (six months, five years and 10 years). Disturbances during childhood development and behavior have been correlated with maternal stress and depression during pregnancy (Lupien, McEwen, Gunnar, and Heim, 2009). During adolescence, there is heightened activity of the HPA axis, thus producing increased levels of glucocorticoids (Lupien et al., 2009), and, in turn, producing greater cortical dopamine levels, which help initiate an individual's risk-taking behavior (Casey et al., 2008).

Therapeutic Intervention Strategies

Persistent and serious antisocial behaviors place youth at greater risk for imprisonment, family disruption, economic insecurity, and drug dependence (Moffitt, 1993; Farrington, 1990). However, the social sciences have had a long and arduous road in convincing policy-makers about the importance and reliability of intervention treatments for such behavior. In a study that proved to be a damning indictment among criminologists and politicians against rehabilitation programs, Robert Martinson (1974) stated, "With few and isolated exceptions, the rehabilitation efforts that have been reported so far have had no appreciable effect on recidivism." Martinson went further suggesting that no treatment measure—counseling, skill development, or psychotherapy—reliably "worked" to diminish further criminal activity. It is thought that the Martinson's findings had a strong effect on bringing forth a punitive era in corrections where less funding for rehabilitation was the norm (Cullen, 2002).

Since Martinson's research, more reliable measurements have been created to analyze preexisting research. Meta-analysis is one such approach. Meta-analysis takes stock of existing research literature by providing a systematic and quantitative summary. The key contribution of meta-analysis is the effect size statistic, which measures the magnitude of the effect of a particular treatment on a particular outcome such as delinquent behavior. In a meta-analytic study focusing solely on recidivism in analyzing the effects of rehabilitation among juvenile delinquents, findings for intervention programs based on cognitive components were moderate to highly effective in reducing recidivism (Izzo and Ross, 1990). In another study that reviewed over 25 meta-analytic studies of treatments for children and youth with conduct problems, five treatment types were discovered to promote a diminishing effect on recidivism: cognitive behavioral therapy (CBT), family therapy, multimodal therapy, group therapy and pharmacotherapy (Litschge, Vaughn, and McCrea, 2010). Of these modes of treatment, multimodal and CBT interventions appeared to possess the highest success rate for treating problems associated with antisocial behavior (Losel and Beelmann, 2003; Kendall, 1993; Cullen, 2002).

CBT therapists believe that individuals perceive and rationalize the world through their cognitive structures or thoughts (Kendall, 1993). Some common CBT interventions include: cognitive appraisal, anger management, self-control training, problem-solving training, social support approaches and psychoeducation (Heyman and Smith Slep, 2007). Contemporary CBT has moved beyond the child–client interaction and toward incorporating strategies that involve parents, peers, and school personnel (Kendall, 1993). Teacher behavior therapy, token economies, group contingency therapy, peer management therapy, and self-management therapy all have demonstrated large effects on disruptive behaviors among youth in public education establishments (Litschge et al., 2010). These protocols are strongly rooted in behaviorist principles, which of course involve a physiologic response (biological) to an external stimulus (environmental).

Many rehabilitation programs in correctional institutions are based on medical/disease models of intervention that view criminal behavior as symptomatic of some underlying psychopathological condition requiring a "cure" through some form of "therapy" (Izzo and Ross, 1990). Punishment and deterrence oriented interventions don't seem to fare well under close empirical scrutiny. Results from several systematic reviews of the research suggests that such deterrence-oriented interventions, such as "scared straight," "boot camp," etc. do nothing but possibly increase recidivism rates (Cullen, 2002). There is no evidence that exists for the effectiveness of such programs.

Research has found that aggressive children pay attention to more aggressive environmental cues, have limited problem-solving skills, and place more emphasis on controlling the victim of the aggression (Kendall, 1993). Four effective treatment characteristics have been identified for these behaviors: interventions based on social learning or behavioral principles, structured rather than nondirective treatment, interventions that build human capital in offenders, and treatments that are multimodal (Cullen, 2002). Group interventions for high-risk youth have been found to increase, rather than decrease, delinquent behavior because of the iatrogenic effect of the intervention (Heyman and Smith Slep, 2007). The iatrogenic effect is when an intervention designed to help actually does more harm than good. This is not so surprising when you think about it. After all, learning principles would predict that placing high risk youth together would increase, rather than decrease, risk.

One of the most current and seemingly successful psychosocial interventions for the assessment and rehabilitation of adult offenders is the risk-need-responsivity (RNR) model (Thibaut et al., 2010; Hanson, Bourgon, Helmus, and Hodgson, 2009; Bonta and Andrews, 2007). The three core principles are determining the offender's risk to re-offend, assessing criminogenic needs of the offender and targeting them in treatment (i.e. substance abuse which leads to more crime, etc.), responding with CBT, and tailoring the intervention to the offender's skill set (learning, motivation, abilities, and strengths) (Bonta and Andrews, 2007). RNR that adheres to these core principles have had a 15–35 percent success rate, which is comparable to common medical interventions such as chemotherapy for breast cancer or bypass surgery for cardiac events (Bonta and Andrews, 2007, p. 12).

Psychosocial and Psychopharmacology Intervention Strategies

Violence and aggression can also be reduced through psychopharmacological agents, both during the short and long terms. Psychopharmacological agents that decrease aggression include: neuroleptics, stimulants, anti-hypertension agents, Lithium, anti-convulsants and Benzodiazepines. Neuroleptics, Lithium and anti-convulsants yield the most evidence to support their use in controlling episodic violence. Benzodiazepines, when given doses to sedate, also reduce aggression acutely (Kruesi, 2007).

Previous research has revealed that IQ is the most commonly assessed and biologically relevant trait among sexual offenders (Blanchard, Cantor, and Robichaud, 2006). Sexual offenders typically have an IQ in the low 90s, versus the population mean of 100. This score is labeled as "average intelligence" (Blanchard et al., 2006). There also exists an association between pedophilia and childhood head injuries, as well as child molestation and left-handedness (Blanchard et al., 2006). However, these findings alone do not indicate any certain causal relationship for having pedophilia or committing sexual offenses. Biosocial components for sexual offenders need further investigation, as evidence is mounting that there may be a neurodevelopment explanation that is tied to sexual offenders, especially pedophiles.

Interventions that combine both psychosocial and psychopharmacological treatments for sex offenders have provided mixed results (Thibaut et al., 2010; Hanson et al., 2009; Bourget and Bradford, 2008; Briken and Kafka, 2007). However, their combined use has not been well integrated into the CBT model (Briken and Kafka, 2007). Surgical castration, at times, has given positive results for diminishing recidivism rates for sexual offenders, however, the intrusiveness of this procedure comes with ethical considerations (Thibaut et al., 2010). Currently, more commonly used procedures to reduce recidivism among sexual criminals combine RNR therapy with psychopharmacological agents (Thibaut et al., 2010; Hanson et al., 2009). Some of the more common pharmacological treatments include medroxyprogesterone acetate (MPA), cyproterone acetate (CPA), luteinizing hormone-releasing hormone (LHRH) agonists, and some serotonin reuptake inhibitors (SSRI) (Bourget and Bradford, 2008, p. 135). (MPA accelerates testosterone metabolism, thus reducing testosterone production in the testes. CPA acts by blocking the effects of testosterone and dihydrotestosterone. LHRH agonists have been referred to as pharmacological "castration," because they decrease testosterone and dihydrotestosterone release through the medicines inhibitory effects on gonadotropin secretion. SSRIs increase serotonin production, thus causing erectile difficulties, reduced orgasm/ejaculatory capacity, and reduced sexual interest (Bourget & Bradford, 2008).) While the pharmacological evidence suggests some positive results for decreased recidivism rates among sexual offenders, there are numerous side effects associated with the use of androgen deprivation treatments, therefore, physician monitoring and risk assessment must be made prior to prescribing such chemical agents (Giltay & Gooren, 2009).

For psychopathic individuals, treatment has yielded mixed and, at times, inconclusive results (Salekin, Worley, and Grimes, 2010). While CBT is the optimal approach for most psychopaths, RNR tailored specifically to the individual patient (Bonta and Andrews, 2007) that is then combined with the administration of anti-aggression agents (Kruesi, 2007), as noted above, may produce prolonged results for diminishing recidivism rates among psychopathic-like individuals, but more research is still needed to make such conclusions much more valid and reliable (Salekin et al., 2010).

Attending to Comorbid Conditions

Criminal and antisocial behavior is typically part of an externalizing spectrum that also includes the misuse of psychoactive substances such as alcohol, cannabis, cocaine, and heroin (Krueger et al., 2002). Thus, criminal behavior is intertwined, or, in psychiatric parlance, is *comorbid* with alcohol and drug abuse. Reliable data has established that alcohol and drug use is present in the majority of violent crimes both in the United States and Europe. Alcohol abuse has consistently been shown to be associated with crime. For example, data from the Arrestee Drug Abuse Monitoring (typically referred to as ADAM) program which collects biomarker data on drugs in the body of persons arrested found that the rate of testing positive across 35 cities ranges between 40 and 80 percent.

A 2004 survey by the Bureau of Justice Statistics (BJS) indicated that approximately 33 percent of inmates committed their offense while under the influence of drugs and over half were using drugs in the past month prior to their offense. A sizable proportion of offenders report that they committed their offense in order to obtain money for drugs (17 percent of state inmates and 18 percent of federal inmates). The most common drugs of abuse were marijuana and cocaine/crack. Examining trends in this data reveals stability over time.

So, if offenders are likely to be alcohol and drug abusers what is the rate in the general population? Our best data available to answer this question comes from the National Epidemiological Survey of Alcohol and Related Conditions (NESARC), a nationally representative study of over 40,000 persons in the United States. NESARC data reveals that the prevalence of these disorders in the general population was about 2 percent in 2002. This substantial difference underscores the magnitude of co-occurring addiction issues among criminal offenders. Other studies using this data set have found a strong connection between such criminal victimization, bullying, and substance dependence (Vaughn et al., 2010a and 2010b).

Studies of youthful offenders also indicate the close relationship between substance abuse and delinquency. In a study of statewide population of youthful offenders, Vaughn and colleagues (2007) found that high rates of past drug abuse and property and violent offending tended to cluster together. In other words, youth who were more delinquent were also more reported greater use of alcohol and illicit substances. Seminal research by Linda Teplin and associates (2002) has shown in a randomly selected sample of nearly 2,000 detained youth in Chicago (Cook County) that approximately half of males and females had a diagnosable substance use disorder.

Interventions for Alcohol and Drug Abuse and Dependence

Given the close ties between substance abuse and crime, it seems that alcohol and drug treatment could possibly reduce both. Numerous treatments for alcohol and drug dependence have been tested in randomized clinical trials. These types of designs represent the "gold standard" for evaluating the effects of a treatment because there was random assignment of like individuals to a treatment condition and a non-treated or alternative treatment group termed the control condition. Despite the fact that accrued studies have generally not used criminal behavior as an outcome variable (rather outcomes were reductions in substance abuse), these studies do permit strong inferences to be made regarding the substance-abuse–crime connection.

As we have previously argued almost all treatments are biosocial in nature—certainly some are more explicitly so. The addiction field in particular has developed a number of evidence-based treatments that are clearly predicated on biosocial principles. This is largely because the addiction field considers addictive disorders diseases of the brain that are also sculpted by genetic vulnerability and environmental experiences. Treatments can be usefully organized as motivational, behavioral, and pharmacotherapy. First, motivational treatment, a popular technique, is a neurocognitive process yet is highly sensitive to context. Motivational interviewing was developed for drinking problems and popularized by the work of William Miller, a professor of psychology and psychiatry of the University of New Mexico. Numerous randomized clinical trials have supported the benefits of this approach (Miller and Rollnick, 2002). Motivational interviewing is goal centered and highly structured toward guiding clients toward commitment. It is a cost effective treatment that is usually executed in one to four treatment sessions.

The second area of treatment involves behavior-based treatments. Rooted in elemental physiological principles of stimulus-response and reinforcement of the organism toward new rewards (in place of the abused substance), behavioral interventions can be quite useful. According to Carroll and Rounsaville (2006), these treatments can be used to target impulse-control problems. Impulse management is critical to effectively dealing with the drive toward using psychoactive substances that typically involve craving. It is possible that behavior-based treatments for substance use disorders also simultaneously target many of the same mechanisms involved in criminal offending such as stealing or even anger or threat control possibly modulating aggression or reactive violence.

The third area involves pharmacotherapy. There are a growing number of medications being tested to combat substance dependence. Essentially, these medications work by functioning as *antagonists* and *agonists* in the brain. Antagonists bind to receptor sites and block the pleasurable effects of a given substance. Thus, there is no reward or "high" provided by taking the substance. In contrast, agonists bind to the receptor site and stimulate the site. Three medications are in use for the pharmacotherapy of alcohol dependence: Naltrexone, Acamprosate, and Topiramate. Naltrexone is an antagonist that blocks the rewarding effects of alcohol and therefore presumably increases abstinence and risk for relapse. The medication Acamprosate helps persons achieve sobriety by reducing the excitation of neurons and resulting stress during alcohol withdrawal and in turn increases the need to return to the pleasurable effects of alcohol consumption. Topiramate reduces the rewarding effects of alcohol by decreasing the release of dopamine. Numerous randomized clinical trials have revealed that these medications, when combined with psychosocial treatment, can have important benefits. We are not aware of any FDA approved drugs for central nervous system stimulants such as cocaine and methamphetamine, but clinical trials are under way.

Attention Deficit and Hyperactivity Disorder (ADHD)

ADHD interferes with optimal functioning that includes decision-making, sustaining attention, planning, self-monitoring, and behavioral inhibition. One of the causal factors in ADHD is impaired dopamine function, which partly explains its treatment by stimulants that increase dopamine release and the co-occurrence of ADHD and substance abuse (Volkow and Swanson, 2008). The estimated worldwide prevalence of ADHD is approximately 5 percent, but about 10 percent for males (Polanczyk, Silva de Lima, Horta, Biederman, and Rohde, 2007). However, there is considerable variation around this figure due to global differences in measurement and diagnosis. ADHD commonly co-occurs with conduct problems. The relevance of ADHD as a co-occurring condition to crime and antisocial behavior is clear in that many offenders are known to have had ADHD symptoms. Treatments for ADHD are clearly biosocial in nature involving mainly medications and behavioral training. However, a recent systematic review of 26 cognitive-based studies revealed that many of these show promise in alleviating ADHD symptoms (Toplak, Connors, Shuster, Knezevic, & Parks, 2008). A stronger evidence base exists for medications (established decades ago) and behavioral training (primarily parent and school based). Daughton and Kratochvil (2009) recently have identified a number of advantages and disadvantages in using these medications. Some of the advantages identified include safety, rapid effects, and overall a high response rate with strong effects. On the down side, the effects tend to be short lived with the need to be taken two or three times per day and this hampers adherence. In addition, these medications have the potential to impede normal growth rates in adolescents.

One popular and well supported form of behavioral training is parenting training, which involves therapists and parents working together to execute a behavior plan explicitly designed to modify the behavior of the child or adolescent in the home. Specific behaviors are targeted with easiest behaviors changed first. When this type of plan is used school teachers typically send reports home. Built on social learning theory the underlying principle of this type of behavior management approach is reinforcement.

Future of Biosocial Interventions

There are four areas of intervention research that we would like to highlight that may be important for future prevention and treatment strategies for criminal offenders and antisocial persons in general. These areas are neurodisinhibition, emotional processing, and the construct of resilience.

Neurodisinhibition

A newer form of behavioral intervention is cognitive remediation treatment. This type of therapy attempts to target and train components of executive function as if it were a muscle. One type of computer game or simulation that can be used aims at reducing impulsive acts within the context of the game and therefore rewards are linked to the exercise of self-control. These types of "brain train" treatment strategies are gaining traction by purportedly increasing an individual's ability for self-regulation. Research on cognitive remediation treatments is still in their infancy and early results are limited. However, they are plausible and are well-rooted in scientific principles and deserve to be tested. However, important questions remain to be answered such as under what condition are they effective? For who? And perhaps more importantly how long do these effects last? Despite these concerns these treatment have great potential to be used with offenders who tend to be impulsive and possess deficits in key executive functions.

Emotional Processing

There has been a spate of research in the past 10 years on the importance of callous and unemotional (CU) traits in relation to serious forms of delinquency and externalizing behavior (Frick and White, 2008). Callous unemotional traits reflect a lack of guilt or uncaring for harmful behaviors. Although co-occurring distress and mood disorders are not uncommon among antisocial persons, those displaying CU traits are less prone to these clinical manifestations (Frick and White, 2008). CU traits are a major part of historical and contemporary conceptualizations of psychopathy or psychopathic personality (Frick and White, 2008). CU traits appear to be relatively stable over the life-course. CU traits are correlated with aggression and misbehavior, and they may have distinct etiology or causal underpinnings perhaps involving amgdala hypoarousal or other morphological and functional impairment in this region of the brain (Blair, Mitchell, and Blair, 2005). It would appear that developing empirically supported treatments for CU deficits would be an important leap forward in reducing criminal and antisocial behavior. The type of intervention necessary would involve skill building in empathy development. Optimally, this would take place early in the life-course in order to prevent the deleterious consequence of the full bloom of CU traits.

Resilience is a Biosocial Process

The idea that some people are able to turn their lives around despite repeated exposures to harmful events and situations in their lives has resulted in the popularization of resilience. Resilience is a dynamic process encompassing positive adaptation in the context of significant adversity (Luthar, 1997; Rolf and Johnson, 1999). Advances in the usefulness of this construct remain because resilience is a process that is difficult to study. It certainly requires longitudinal designs and an exposed sample and the ability to control for characteristics that are plausibly related to a resilient outcome. In our view, resilience is a biosocial process that involves the interplay between heritable and cognitive factors on the one hand and psychosocial effects on the other. Very little research has accrued that has included genetic and even neurological components. This is important to include in order to better specify what environmental mechanisms are really important in helping to bring about resilient outcomes.

In a landmark study, Caspi and colleagues (2002) identified an interaction between childhood maltreatment and the MAOA gene based on a sample of Caucasian males selected from the Dunedin (New Zealand) Multidisciplinary Health and Development Study. Although 12 percent of the sample had been maltreated during childhood, males with the low-functioning allele of the MAOA gene who were abused accounted for 44 percent of violent convictions in the cohort. However, what was most important about this study was that children who had been abused but had the high-activity allele of the MAOA gene were buffered from the criminogenic effects of childhood maltreatment. Although some controversy remains regarding the replication of this study, it does point to the interactive nature of genes that are involved with key centers of neural transmission and environmental adversity. Interventions could be developed that provide a type of behavioral "immunization" to help those who are particularly sensitive to environmental adversity. Studying the effects of interventions within a behavior genetic design could yield important insight on how to increase the resilience capacity of individuals who are prone to misbehavior.

Conclusion

There are a number of useful interventions that can be employed to prevent and treat aggression and violence in juveniles and adults. Most of these interventions explicitly involve systematic modification of thought and behavior via a social interaction or to a lesser extent pharmacological delivery system. The long-term durability of these interventions is an open question. Although the effects from these various interventions are mostly beneficial, the magnitude of the effects is not large, does not work for everyone, and the active ingredients are not fully elucidated. These effects however are clearly biosocial in nature involving brain, behavior, and social input. In order to develop effective strategies targeting the reduction of aggression and violent crime, a better understanding of the biosocial processes underpinning these designs for change is necessary.

References

Bonta, J., & Andrews, D. A. (2007). *Risk-need-responsivity model for offender assessment and rehabilitation* (User Report 2007-06). Ottawa: Public Safety Canada.

Blair, J., Mitchell, D., & Blair, K. (2005). *The psychopath: Emotion and the brain.* Oxford: Blackwell Press.

Blanchard, R., Cantor, J. M., & Robichaud, L. K. (2006). Biological factors in the development of sexual deviance and aggression in males. In H. E. Barbaree & W. L. Marshall (Eds.), *The juvenile sex offender* (2nd ed., pp. 77–104). New York: Guilford Press.

Bourget, D., & Bradford, J. M. (2008). Evidential basis for the assessment and treatment of sex offenders. *Brief Treatment and Crisis Intervention, 8,* 130–146.

Briken, P., & Kafka, M. P. (2007). Pharmacological treatments for paraphilic patients and sexual offenders. *Current Opinion in Psychiatry, 20,* 609–613.

Carroll, K. M., & Rounsaville, B. J. (2006). Behavioral therapies: The glass would be half full if only we had a glass. Miller, W. & Carroll, K. M. (Eds.). *Rethinking substance abuse: What the science shows, and what we should do about it* (pp. 223–239). New York: Guilford Press.

Casey, B. J., Jones, R. M., & Hare, T. A. (2008). The adolescent brain. *Annals of the New York Academy of Sciences, 1124,* 111–126.

Caspi, A., McClay, J., Moffitt, T. E., Mill, J., Martin, J., Craig, I. W., & Poulton, R. (2002). Role of genotype in the cycle of violence in maltreated children. *Science, 297,* 851–854.

Cullen, F. T. (2002). Rehabilitation and treatment programs. In J. Q. Wilson & J. Petersilia (Eds.), *Crime: Public policies for crime control* (pp. 253–289). Richmond, CA: ICS Press.

Daughton, J. M. & Kratochvil, C. J. (2009). Review of ADHD pharmacotherapies: Advantages, disadvantages, and clinical pearls. *Journal of the American Academy of Child & Adolescent Psychiatry, 48,* 240–248.

DeLisi, M., Umphress, Z. R., & Vaughn, M. G. (2009). The criminology of the amygdala. *Criminal Justice and Behavior, 36,* 1231–1242.

Farrington, D. P. (1990). Implications of criminal career research for the prevention of offending. *Journal of Adolescence, 13,* 93–113.

Frick, P. J. & White, S. F. (2008). Research review: The importance of callous-unemotional traits for developmental models of aggressive and antisocial behavior. *Journal of Child Psychology and Psychiatry, 49,* 359–375.

Giltay, E. J., & Gooren, L. J. (2009). Potential side effects of androgen deprivation treatment in sex offenders. *Journal of the American Academy of Psychiatry and the Law, 37,* 53–58.

Gould, M. S., Greenberg, T., Velting, D. M., & Shaffer, D. (2003). Youth suicide risk and preventative interventions: A review of the past 10 years. *Journal of the American Academy of Child and Adolescent Psychiatry, 42,* 386–405.

Hanson, R. K., Bourgon, G., Helmus, L., & Hodgson, S. (2009). A meta-analysis of the effectiveness of treatment for sexual offenders: Risk, need, and responsivity. *Criminal Justice and Behavior, 36,* 865–891.

Heyman, R. E., & Smith Slep, A. M. (2007). Therapeutic treatment approaches to violent behavior. In D. J. Flannery, A. T. Vazsonyi, & I. D. Waldman (Eds.), *The Cambridge handbook of violent behavior and aggression* (pp. 602–617). New York: Cambridge University Press.

Hiatt, K. D., & Dishion, T. J. (2008). Antisocial personality development. In T. P. Beauchaine & S. Hinshaw (Eds.), *Child and adolescent psychopathology* (pp. 370–404). Hoboken, NJ: John Wiley & Sons, Inc.

Inzlicht, M., & Gutsell, J. N. (2007). Running on empty: Neural signals for self-control failure. *Psychological Science, 18*, 933–937.

Izzo, R. L., & Ross, R. R. (1990). Meta-analysis of rehabilitation programs for juvenile delinquents: A brief report. *Criminal Justice and Behavior, 17*, 134–142.

Kendall, P. C. (1993). Cognitive-behavioral therapies with youth: Guiding theory, current status, and emerging developments. *Journal of Consulting and Clinical Psychology, 61*, 235–247.

Krueger, R. F., Hicks, B. M., Patrick, C. J., Carlson, S. R., Iacono, W. G., & McGue, M. (2002). Etiologic connections among substance dependence, antisocial behavior, and personality: Modeling the externalizing spectrum. *Journal of Abnormal Psychology, 111*, 411–424.

Kruesi, M. J. (2007). Psychopharmacology of Violence. In D. J. Flannery, A. T. Vazsonyi, & I. D. Waldman (Eds.), *The Cambridge handbook of violent behavior and aggression* (pp. 618–635). New York: Cambridge University Press.

Lahey, B. B. (2008). Oppositional Defiant Disorder, Conduct Disorder and juvenile delinquency. In T. P. Beauchaine & S. Hinshaw (Eds.), *Child and adolescent psychopathology* (pp. 335–369). Hoboken, NJ: John Wiley & Sons, Inc.

Litschge, C. M., Vaughn, M. G., & McCrea, C. (2010). The empirical status of treatments for children and youth with conduct problems: An overview of meta-analytic studies. *Research on Social Work Practice, 20*, 21–35.

Losel, F., & Beelmann, A. (2003). Effects of child skills training in preventing antisocial behavior: A systematic review of randomized evaluations. *Annals of the American Academy of Political and Social Science, 587*, 84–109.

Lupien, S. J., McEwen, B. S., Gunnar, M. R., & Christine Heim. (2009). Effects of stress throughout the lifespan on the brain, behavior and cognition. *Nature Reviews Neuroscience, 10*, 434–445.

Luthar, S. S. (1997). Sociodemographic disadvantage and psychosocial adjustment: Perspectives from developmental psychopathology. In S. S. Luthar, J. A. Burack, D. Cicchetti, & J. R. Weisz (Eds.). *Developmental psychopathology: Perspectives on adjustment, risk, and disorder* (pp. 459–485). New York: Cambridge University Press.

Martinson, Robert (1974). What works?—questions and answers about prison reform. *The Public Interest, 35*, 22–54.

Miller, W. R., & Rollnick, S. (2002). *Motivational interviewing: Preparing people for change* (2nd ed.). New York: The Guilford Press.

Moffitt, T. E. (1993). Adolescence-limited and life-course-persistent antisocial behavior: A developmental taxonomy. *Psychological Review, 100*, 674–701.

Patterson, G. R. (1974). Interventions for boys with conduct problems: Multiple settings, treatments, and criteria. *Journal of Consulting and Clinical Psychology, 42*, 471–481.

Polanczyk, G., Silva de Lima, M., Horta, B. L., Biederman, J., & Rohde, L. A. (2007). The worldwide prevalence of ADHD: A systematic review and metaregression analysis. *The American Journal of Psychiatry, 164*, 942–948.

Rhee, S. H. & Waldman, I. D. (2002). Genetic and environmental influences on antisocial behavior: A meta-analysis of twin and adoption studies. *Psychological Bulletin, 128*, 490–529.

Rolf, J. E. & Johnson, J. L. (1999). Opening doors to resilience intervention for prevention research. In M. D. Glantz & J. L. Johnson (Eds.), *Resilience and development: Positive life adaptions. Longitudinal research in the social and behavioral sciences* (pp. 229–249). New York: Kluwer.

Salekin, R. T., Worley, C., & Grimes, R. D. (2010). Treatment of psychopathy: A review and brief introduction to the Mental Model Approach for psychopathy. *Behavioral Sciences and the Law, 28*, 235–266.

Teplin, L. A., Abram, K. M., McClelland, G. M., Dulcan, M. K., & Mericle, A. A. (2002). Psychiatric disorders in youth in juvenile detention. *Archives of General Psychiatry, 59*, 1133–1143.

Thibaut, F., Barra, F. D. L., Gordon, H., Cosyns, P., Bradford, J. M., & WFSBP Task Force on Sexual Disorders (2010). The World Federation of Societies of Biological Psychiatry (WFSBP) Guidelines for the biological treatment of paraphilias. *The World Journal of Biological Psychiatry, 11*, 604–655.

Toplak, M. E., Connors, L., Shuster, J., Knezevic, B., & Parks, S. (2008). Review of cognitive, cognitive-behavioral, and neural-based interventions for attention-deficit/hyperactivity disorder (ADHD). *Clinical Psychology Review, 28*, 801–823.

Vaughn, M. G., Freedenthal, S., Jenson, J. M., & Howard, M. O. (2007). Psychiatric symptoms and substance use among juvenile offenders: A latent Profile investigation. *Criminal Justice and Behavior, 34*, 1296–1312.

Vaughn, M. G., Fu, Q., Bender, K., DeLisi, M., Beaver, K. M., Perron, B. E., & Howard, M. O. (2010a). Bullying in the United States: Findings from the national epidemiologic survey on alcohol and related conditions. *Psychiatric Quarterly, 81*, 183–195.

Vaughn, M. G., Fu, J., DeLisi, M., Beaver, K. M., Perron, B. E., & Howard, M. O. (2010b). Criminal victimization and comorbid substance use and psychiatric disorders in the United States: Results from the NESARC. *Annals of Epidemiology, 20*, 281–288.

Volkow, N. D. & Swanson, J. M. (2008). Does childhood treatment of ADHD with stimulant medication affect substance abuse in adulthood? *The American Journal of Psychiatry, 165*, 553–555.

19

From Petri Dish to Public Policy: A Discussion of the Implications of Biosocial Research in the Criminal Justice Arena

Joseph Rukus and Chris L. Gibson

In 1994, Stephen Mobley was sentenced for a murder he committed at a Domino's Pizza in Oakwood, GA. The case would have been unmemorable except for the novel defense brought about by his legal team which, for the first time in modern-era jurisprudence, argued that their client's genetic makeup should mitigate his culpability for the crime (Levitt and Manson, 2007). The defense was unsuccessful, but this fact did not stop defense attorneys from attempting to use it with over 200 American and 20 British cases having some sort of genetic argument over the last five years (Feresin, 2009). These cases have all met the same fate as Mobley, but that changed with two rulings in 2009. The first was an Italian case where a court knocked four years off defendant Abdelmalek Bayout's 12-year murder sentence on the basis of test results showing he possessed five genetic polymorphisms indicative of violent behavior (Feresin, 2009). The second was in Tennessee where evidence provided by the defense indicated that a genotype linked to low levels of monoamine oxidase (MAO-A) expression might have been partially responsible for Bradley Waldroup's 2006 violent killing spree, which heavily influenced the jurors' decision to convict him of manslaughter instead of capital murder (Bradley-Haggerty, 2010). With the floodgates now open, it is only a matter of time before defense attorneys around the globe, citing the Bayout and Waldroup cases as precedents, press for similar reductions for their clients.

Interestingly, in the 15 years since Mobley, the criminological academic community has been relatively silent as to the role genetic research should play in the judicial process. Even those who conduct biosocial research limit their discussion of the broader implications their findings pose for society-at-large. Absent of clear and meaningful guidance from academics, practitioners are frequently forced to make it up as they go.

This is not to say that a degree of caution by criminologists is unwarranted when it comes to the role of genetic research informing issues in the criminal justice system, but this is not an excuse for the large absence of criminologists from the discussion regarding if and how genetic research should affect policy. Our hope in writing this chapter is to better explore these issues and lay the groundwork for criminologists to take their rightful place at the policy table. Criminologists know a great deal about the dynamics of antisocial behavior, delinquency, and criminal behavior, and this knowledge is something needed when debating society's response and reaction to questions raised by biosocial research. They have the ability to offer a unique insight into what the evidence does and does not suggest and how the evidence should be interpreted by society.

First, we begin this chapter with a discussion of the state of biosocial research. Specifically, we start with a brief historical perspective on eugenics and recount some negative implications that arose from early research linking biology to human behavior. Second, we examine recent advances and assess what research tells us about the link between genetics, delinquency and criminal behavior.

Third, we explore a more modern example of responding to ethical issues raised by genetic research by taking a glimpse into organ transplant science where those involved with conducting research have also taken an active role in shaping its implications. Importantly, we go into this discussion well aware that the issue over the proper role of researchers is centuries old (Mrydal, 1944). Our goal is not to reignite a debate that will remain unsettled, but instead to explore actual examples of differing levels of researcher involvement in approaching ethical issues. Fourth, we introduce and summarize recommendations for criminal justice made by medical researchers on the Nuffield Council on Bioethics regarding genetics and behavior. Fifth, we explore the current ethical infrastructure by describing standards which have been put in place by the hard sciences and DNA practitioners, then suggest that incorporating the approach often used by anthropologists, which is based on the premise of doing no harm, might make these standards more effective.

Sixth, following this discussion, we shift our focus to biosocial criminology. We look at the challenges faced by researchers and postulate how these obstacles may be partially responsible for the field's tepid response to policy implications. In so doing, we examine articles written by biosocial scholars. Our analysis shows that the discussion sections of many of those published in criminological journals fail to examine or discuss the broader impact of the research findings. The end result is that only cautious statements often appear in academic forums on if and how we should apply research findings on genetics and criminal behavior in the real world and the ethical questions that may arise.

Finally, we conclude with a discussion of the questions criminologists should discuss. We argue at least three areas are important in this discussion; harm, the role of the researcher, and informed consent. Based on the research presented in this chapter, we offer the beginnings of an evolving framework that our field may want to consider when addressing these issues. Acknowledging that the issues put forth in this chapter are controversial and that many researchers would prefer to eschew situations that "ruffle feathers," we do believe that criminologists should at the least be involved in discussions of what conclusions can and cannot be drawn from their research and most importantly when it has the potential to do harm.

A Brief History of Eugenics

Before embarking upon a description of a brief history of eugenics, it is important to provide a preface to our discussion. Beaver (2009, p. 15) stated that criminologists who are in opposition to biosocial research will often recall the unimaginable harms to humanity that occurred during the past century when eugenics researchers, such as those described in the pages to follow, encouraged involuntary sterilization to prohibit reproduction of those who were deemed genetically deficient. Importantly, our goal of this review is not to recall these atrocities for this purpose. We believe without a doubt that modern biosocial research has the potential to advance knowledge of criminality, and it has already. It also provides useful information that will shape intervention and prevention efforts in progressive and humane ways that sociological studies alone can not provide.

Our intention is to recall these atrocities for two reasons. First, history is open to repeat itself if forgotten. Second, we use this historical review for comparative purposes for describing where the majority of biosocial criminologists, geneticists, and biologists now stand with respect to the myths of the link between biology and crime.

Emergence of Eugenics

Darwin's (1871) seminal work on evolution in the Galapagos Islands became interpreted in a popular positivistic view in European political culture that evolutionary theory could be generalized to man, ultimately defining a social hierarchy based on genetic superiority. White, English, middle-class citizens were at the top of the evolutionary pyramid while other races, including those of Irish descent and those of English working class strata, were given a label of being genetically inferior. These ideas were pursued empirically by the eugenics movement founded by Galton in 1883 (www.eugenicsarchive.org), i.e., a so-called scientific movement that dealt with the improvement of hereditary qualities of a race or breed.

Many eugenicists promoted an ideology of Social Darwinism. Social Darwinism, defined by Gould (1996, p. 368) is "a general term for any evolutionary argument about the biological basis of human differences, but the initial meaning referred to a specific theory of class stratification within industrial societies, particularly to the idea that a permanently poor underclass consisting of genetically inferior people had precipitated down into their inevitable fate."

Darwin, of course, never endorsed these ideas. Rather, his science was interpreted wrongly and endorsed by the prevailing opinion in late nineteenth-century England to justify the construction of social classifications that resulted in some groups of people being labeled as biologically and genetically inferior. Eugenics landed on American shores in the early twentieth century. A large majority of American eugenicists pursued the segregation of people they deemed as being not fit for breeding by using sterilization and racial segregation methods. Such classifications were justified using mental or intelligence testing (Cold Spring Harbor Laboratory, 2011).

Intelligence emerged as a concept that was of great interest to scientists, eugenicists and politicians alike; many endorsing an ideology that ascribed the attribute to a hereditable process under the cloak of Social Darwinism. The objective of intelligence testing was to express numerically differences among persons in their ability to perform a variety of mental operations.

The concept of intelligence was of particular interest to Sir Francis Galton, a cousin of Charles Darwin, who coined the term eugenics and was generally credited with the title "founder of psychometrics" (Rust and Golombok, 1999, p. 5). Among his array of accomplishments, one of which included the development of analytic techniques for psychometrics, Galton established an anthropometric laboratory at South Kensington in 1880. Data produced in his laboratory were used to develop crude intelligence tests.

However, scholars other than Galton contributed to research on intelligence testing. In the late nineteenth century, Cattell and Gilbert continued the study and measurement of intelligence. But, it was not until the twentieth century that intelligence testing was taken out of the lab and applied to societal problems.

In the early twentieth century, Alfred Binet began to play a vital role in early intelligence testing. Unlike others before him, Binet took intelligence testing out of the laboratory and applied it to the persisting problem of retardation of children in the Paris Schools with the goal of identifying those with learning difficulties so that good intentioned interventions could be implemented. Binet created one of the first well known intelligence tests and before his death he published three versions of the instrument (Gould, 1996, pp. 178–184).

In America, Binet's test was translated and popularized by H.H. Goddard of the New Jersey training school for the feeble-minded at Vineland. Unlike the well intentioned Binet, Goddard used this instrument to label people as "morons," claimed that it measured a single entity, and largely attributed variability of this entity across people to heredity factors (Gould, 1996, pp. 188–194). Although Goddard introduced the Binet scale in America, Lewis Terman, a Stanford University professor, probably played the largest role in its widespread popularity in the United States. Similar to Goddard, Terman was a hereditarian who used intelligence testing to justify the eradication of people with low intelligence (Gould, 1996, pp. 204–212). Unlike Binet, many scholars in the United States supported that intelligence was a fixed, inborn, real entity. Group intelligence testing in America entered widespread use following World War I, and the credibility of intelligence testing would eventually be seriously questioned due to horrific uses of testing to justify policies that caused great physical and emotional damage to humanity.

Many of the primary uses of intelligence testing, although viewed by some as valid and reliable methods to establish individual differences in mental functioning, were to sort people into groups with the goal of institutionalizing those with less than normal intelligence and prohibit them from reproducing. Historically, many atrocious ideologies and practices existed supporting the control of those perceived to have low intelligence. Most of these ideas and practices, at least in America, came after the emergence of intelligence testing and the inception of psychometrics as scientific justifications to support a political and social agenda of control.

For instance, Goddard used the Binet intelligence scale to justify the prohibition of mating between what he called feeble-minded people or people with subnormal mental ages (as cited in Gould, 1996, p. 193):

> If both parents are feeble-minded all the children will be feeble-minded. It is obvious that such matings should not be allowed. It is perfectly clear that no feeble-minded person should ever be allowed to marry or to become a parent. It is obvious that if this rule is to be carried out the intelligent part of society must enforce it.

Goddard also proposed several solutions upon identification of feeble-minded people. Particularly, he recommended that something must be done to restrict marriage of feeble-minded people stating, "to this end there are two proposals: the first is colonization, the second is sterilization" (as cited in Gould, 1996, p. 194). Goddard's use of Binet's tests had dire consequences for immigrants who were returned home and for people who were forced into mental institutions and sometimes sterilized.

One of the most documented historical cases is the notorious *Buck* v. *Bell* ruling where the United States Supreme Court supported sterilization of humans— salpingectomy for women and vasectomy for men. In 1927, Oliver Wendell Holmes Jr. announced the Supreme Court's decision to uphold the Virginia sterilization law. The case involved a mother and daughter housed at the State Colony for Epileptics and Feeble Minded. Carrie Buck, the daughter, had been diagnosed in childhood as feeble-minded, scored a nine on the Stanford-Binet; whereas, her mother, then 52 years of age, scored a seven. At the time, such scores indicated mental ages that represented subnormal mental incompetence. Carrie Buck was the first person to be sterilized under Virginia's Eugenical Sterilization Act of 1924. In one of the most alarming and significant statements of last century, Holmes wrote (as cited in Gould, 1996, p. 365):

> We have seen more than once that the public welfare may call upon the best citizens for their lives. It would be strange if it could not call upon those who already sap the strength of the state for these lesser sacrifices ... Three generations of imbeciles are enough.

As of February 1980, the *Washington Post* printed that over 7,500 people were sterilized in Virginia alone. Most of these procedures were conducted in mental health institutions. Sterilizations were performed on white men and women. Specifically, both children and adults identified as feeble-minded through testing and possessing behavioral tendencies to engage in petty crime and disciplinary problems were sterilized (see Gould, 1996, p. 365). The impact of the *Buck* v. *Bell* decision was felt throughout the United States. By the early 1930s, 30 states had adopted similar eugenics laws. Some estimates indicate that from 1907 onward approximately 60,000 people were sterilized involuntarily, with California and Virginia having the most sterilizations per state (www.healthsystem.virginia.edu).

Similar incidents as those described above were quite prevalent across the world into the mid twentieth century. Eventually, the misuse of the science of psychometrics to justify intelligence testing as a way to select people for inhumane intervention resulted in a negative stigmatization of its study within the scientific and academic communities. Psychometrics became so unpopular that teaching it was de-emphasized or abandoned in psychology and education courses throughout the world (see Rust and Golombok, 1999, p. 6).

What do we Currently Know about the State of Biosocial Research on Genetics in Criminology?

The eugenics era and the late nineteenth and early twentieth-century biological investigations of criminality are largely responsible for shaping many criminologists' and sociologists' knowledge of biosocial research, their fear of its policy implications, and the resistance to the fact that biology plays an important role in understanding criminality. The dated knowledge that many have relied on to inform their opinion about the role of biology in understanding criminality is mostly wrong, especially given what is currently known about the intersection between biology and environment. In this section we very briefly summarize the state of biosocial research on criminality; a more extensive review is provided elsewhere (see Beaver, 2009). Second, we describe how this evidence debunks several myths about the link between biology and crime that has been rampant across the disciplines of sociology and criminology for decades. Third, we hope to set up the argument that simply explaining how current biosocial research debunks common myths is not enough. Our argument ultimately calls for biosocial criminologists to be more active in discussing the ethics of conducting biosocial research and to become more involved in policy discussions.

Results from behavioral genetics studies emerging in the last several decades confirm that biology plays an important role in understanding a large range of human characteristics, several of which are related to criminality and offending behaviors such as self-control, oppositional defiant disorder (ODD), attention deficit hyperactivity disorder (ADHD), and having delinquent friends to name a few. These studies are most commonly conducted using samples of monozygotic twin pairs, dizygotic twin pairs, and other sibling pairs that vary in their degree of genetic similarity. From the thousands of studies that have been published, we now know that most human traits have genetic and environmental components. For example, meta-analytic studies on antisocial behaviors conclude that genetics is responsible for approximately 50 percent of the variance in antisocial behavior with environments typically responsible for the remaining variance (Mason and Frick, 1994; Miles and Carey, 1997; Rhee and Waldman, 2002). Further, some research indicates that the genetic contributions to antisocial outcomes can vary depending on developmental period. To this end, genetic influences tend to be larger during adolescence and adulthood compared to childhood when kids are under more environmental controls (see Beaver, 2009). Other behavioral genetics studies now show that heritability can account for variance in the stability of behaviors over time (Beaver et al., 2010). In sum, these findings have been observed across historical periods, different data sets, various measures of criminality and correlates, and in different countries.

A particularly important contribution from behavioral genetics studies is the strong support they have garnered for environmental influences (shared and non-shared environments) on criminality and antisocial behavior. Unlike many studies by criminologists and sociologists that do not take into account biology, behavioral genetics studies control for heritability and still find that environmental influences are very important. On the other hand, most environmental-based sociological studies are typically unable to account for genetic influences, rendering the effects that are observed for environmental variables artificially inflated due to specification bias. To further complicate, most sociological-based studies on antisocial behavior and criminality are typically incapable of teasing apart shared and non-shared environmental influences due to the fact that siblings from the same household are hardly ever observed and appropriately modeled. From behavioral genetics studies we know that non-shared environments appear to be more important than shared environments in explaining variance in criminality and antisocial behaviors (see Beaver, 2009).

Nonetheless, behavioral genetics studies have encountered criticisms that in some ways challenge their ability to influence practice and policy. There is a trade-off in conducting behavioral genetics studies over more traditional sociological and criminological based studies. Through the methodological design and modeling of data, behavioral genetics research is able to tease apart genetic, shared, and non-shared environmental contributions to the variance in behavioral phenotypes, but these studies typically cannot inform us as to what specific genes and environmental variables are most important for explaining behavioral outcomes. It is likely that a number of genes are contributing to the understanding of behavior and they do so in combination with a variety of environments including, but not limited to, family, school, peers, and neighborhoods. This leads to the next criticism of behavioral genetics studies—they do not tell us how genes interact with environments to predict criminality. Finally, the third criticism of behavioral genetics research centers on how genetic influences on behaviors may be artificially biased upward because identical twins systematically share similar environments in comparison to fraternal twins thus inflating the genetic contributions. Although this argument has been made time and time again, conclusive evidence has not been presented that confirms this criticism. In sum, while behavioral genetics studies on criminality have been instrumental in concluding that both genetics and environments matter, specific policy implications from these studies are questionable and should be approached with much caution.

Within the last decade, biosocial researchers have begun to kick down the roadblocks inherent to behavioral genetics research by actually observing and measuring genes. Driven by the coding of the human genome, biosocial criminologists, geneticists, and biologists now incorporate data collection on molecular genetics into studies on human traits and behaviors. Arguably, this development transcends most advances in the social sciences in the last century.

With this advancement, many limitations of behavioral genetics can now be addressed. First, once hidden under the cloak of heritability estimates, scientists are now measuring and estimating the influences of actual genes, which are often referred to as genetic polymorphisms that vary across people in the population. Second, interactions between specific gene variants and specific environments can now be statistically modeled. This allows for empirical investigations of what most geneticists and biosocial researchers have believed for a long time—nature and nurture interact in complex ways to create behaviors and traits.

Studies assessing how measured genetic polymorphisms interact with specific environments show much promise for informing policy, prevention, and intervention efforts. First, biosocial researchers are quickly reaching an agreement that genes alone do not have important influences on traits and behaviors, but when coupled with criminogenic environments, genes are turned on to increase the probability of criminality and other related behaviors. For instance, studies show that a functional genetic polymorphism conferring low levels of (MAO-A) expression (aka the "warrior gene") is linked to violence when coupled with severe maltreatment during childhood (Caspi et al., 2002). Other genetic polymorphisms linked to neurotransmission (dopamine, sertonin, etc.) have been found to behave in a similar fashion when coupled with a variety of environmental variables (see Beaver, 2009).

We caution readers that this science is still developing and changing rapidly every day. For instance, within the last year biosocial researchers have found that genes thought to put children at risk for criminality when coupled with particular environments may indicate plasticity as opposed to only risk (Belsky and Beaver, 2010). This means that kids who have a specific variant of a gene—often referred to as "risk alleles"—are not only more at risk for bad behavioral outcomes when experiencing criminogenic environments, but these kids seem to do better than other kids without the specific gene variant when less exposed to the criminogenic environment. In sum, what we thought might be a genetic risk for a person can actually be a genetic benefit.

Without going into details of specific studies, genes, and findings, our goal has been to summarize advances in biosocial criminology. We believe that biosocial criminology has come a long way from its early years of eugenics and the early criminological studies compiled by Lombroso and others. And, by coming such a long way we have learned several lessons that can help to debunk some myths about research on biology and crime.

Beaver (2009) nicely summarizes several of the myths about biosocial criminology, and we briefly list some of these below. First, it has been argued that biological explanations for crime are deterministic and evil. Biosocial research doesn't argue, but actually shows that biological explanations for criminality are not deterministic. The statistical models used for biosocial research are based on probabilities, which by definition is counter to the term determinism. Further, biosocial criminologists collectively agree that genes and environments both matter and that genes interact with environments to decrease or increase the probability of a trait or behavior. Genes cannot be deterministic because their expression is contingent upon environment. Second, another myth is that biology is immutable and consequently efforts to prevent and intervene are impossible. This is simply wrong. Since research shows that genes are responsive to environmental stimuli a focus on environmental intervention is possible. Third, many have challenged and even dismissed the link between biology and crime because criminal behaviors are defined by laws that are socially constructed and subject to change over time, yet biology is constant. This is the farthest from being the truth. The effects of genes can and do change over the life course depending on the environment experienced. Further, human brain research suggests that the brain is still developing into adulthood; therefore, still changing. For a further explanation of these myths and others we refer readers to Raine (1993) and Beaver (2009).

Organ Transplants: Scientists in the Forefront

Even though biosocial researchers reject policies stemming from eugenics, the concerns raised by the eugenics era including those stemming from criminologists like Lombroso are real, and criminologists should play an active role to make sure that history does not repeat itself by being at the forefront of the ethical debate. Rose (2000) argues that in the decades following Lombroso, the discourse of neurological determinism changed from eugenics to a focus on public health with the goal being the provisioning of treatment to individuals deemed at risk. While this shift has led to protocols far gentler than sterilization of those deemed defective, Rose notes that practices of preventative detention, e.g. three strike laws, have already been put in place for individuals viewed as unredeemable. He feels it is only a matter of time before the use of such forced sequestering is broadened to ensnare an ever widening class of people believed to be unresponsive to treatment.

Such outcomes, however, are in no way destiny. For example, organ transplant technology provides an example of where researcher concerns about the ethical implications of their work has shaped the way research findings can possibly enhance public welfare. From the beginning, with the first kidney transplant in

1954, doctors have worked not only to develop safe procedures but have also been leading the ethical discussion of how the technology should be applied. As transplants started to become more frequent in the 1970s, a central computer-based matching system for donated organs was developed (UNOS, 2011). As it grew even further in the 1980s, scientists sought and received federal regulation of the organ donation process. The legislation, known as the National Organ Transplant Act of 1983, essentially codified what had been a system of voluntary best-practices into the legal code. It established a "national system through the use of computers and in accordance with established medical criteria [based on need], to match organs and individuals" (42 USC 6a II H § 274 b 2 A ii). A non-profit entity (42 USC 6a II H § 273 b 1 A ii) run by a board of directors composed of members of the transplant medical community and effected members of the general public (42 USC 6a II H § 274 b 1 K) was put in charge of the system. After hearing testimony from Dr H. Barry Jacobs detailing his plans to import foreign nationals for the purpose of organ harvesting (Rubenstein, 2007), legislators, in consultation with physicians, elected to prohibit the sale of transplant organs (42 USC 6a II H § 274 e). Eventually, this act would give rise to the United Network of Organ Sharing (UNOS) which today keeps a waitlist and distributes organs to patients (Graham, 2008).

Further clarification was added in 2000 through rules put forth by the Department of Health and Human Services after significant input from the organ transplant community. The rules stated the board of the Organ Transplant and Procurement Network, UNOS, should consist of a minimum of 50 percent transplant surgeons and physicians and 25 percent transplant candidates, transplant recipients, organ donors, and family members (42 CFR 121 § 121.3). Additionally, they reaffirmed the need-based, as opposed to market-based, distribution system by declaring transplant recipient decisions "shall be based on sound medical judgment" (42 CFR § 121.8 a 1) with the objective of achieving "the best use of donated organs" (42 CFR § 121.8 a 2) and be made in a way that "reduce inequities resulting from socioeconomic status" (42 CFR §121.4 a 3).

Now this is not to say the world of organ transplantation is without controversy. A study by a Bush administration panel again looked at the possibility of establishing a market where people could buy and sell organs, arguing that markets provided a "morally neutral mechanism for setting the value" of organs (Rubenstein, 2007). The proposal, which received virtually no support from the organ donation community, went nowhere. Currently, there is a great deal of discussion about the ethical updating that might be required in light of new technology making it possible for living donors to donate organs to people they designate (Troug, 2005). However, whenever such issues arise, the field debates them and then works with appropriate bodies to codify policy. The result is a system of transplantation which is universally lauded for its equity and is rigorously defended against challenges to its fairness (Segal and Bonnie, 2005; Zink, Wertlieb, Catalano, and Marwin, 2005).

Unlike much of criminology, those doing organ transplant research have taken a proactive approach to both raising and addressing ethical concerns that arise from their research. They have taken the lead to shape policy in a way that is consistent with the ethical stance of the discipline, and we believe criminologists can learn from them. Left to their own devices, some policy-makers could very well create policies that are unintentionally and perhaps even intentionally detrimental to the public welfare. But if criminologists follow examples from organ donation researchers, they have an opportunity to address the implications of their research and shape how their research is put to use in society.

Nuffield Council on Bioethics

In addition to the policy work being done by the transplant community, we would be remiss to not mention the efforts of the Nuffield Council on Bioethics (2002) in the United Kingdom. Comprised almost entirely of academics and practitioners in medically related fields, the council's aim was to proactively address the new set of issues being raised by emerging biomedical research. While not addressing an American audience, the group laid out a framework on how they felt was the best way to address ethical concerns. Included in their outline was recognition that genes (or a combination of genes) were not the sole determinant of behavior. Thus, they felt policy-makers should exercise great caution before considering coercive schemes based on genetic studies. In addition, they advocated for public health officials to build defenses, in the form of regulatory bodies, to assure treatment regimens were not developed for problems that did not exist, such as medications to fix traits that did not fall outside the normal range of human behavior. Other issues raised by the committee regarding concerns about research linking genetics to behavior included changing and selecting traits, discrimination and stigma, whether the science is robust, and general misuses of information.

Despite the fact there were no criminologists on the advisory council, they felt the issues raised by biosocial research in regards to crime were sufficiently serious to warrant a full chapter of their final report. The area in which they were most specific was in the predictive use of genetic information. They firmly believed that using genetic data to craft interventions to deal with delinquency that had not yet occurred was inappropriate. Quoting from the report:

> We take the view that while the reduction of antisocial behaviour and crime are important goals, any attempt to predict the behaviour of an individual who has not exhibited antisocial behaviour, and to intervene accordingly, poses a significant threat to civil liberties and should be treated with great caution. The use of predictive genetic tests to anticipate antisocial behaviour for the purposes of preventive action in the case of individuals who have not already exhibited such behaviour raises ethical questions about balancing the interests of individuals against those of society. (p. 171)

The council was much more vague on the role biosocial research should play in attributing responsibility and sentencing. On responsibility, they believed that most genetic variants should "not be considered an excuse for legal purposes" although they acknowledge future scientific discovery might be cause "for a reexamination of the legal implications" (pp. 165–166). In regards to sentencing, the council was of the opinion "criminal law should be receptive to whatever valid psychiatric or behavioural evidence is available" but that "the weight accorded to such information would be determined by a judge" (p. 168). Interestingly, they foresaw a time when biosocial research would become more advanced and would spark a substantial debate in these areas. Prophetically, they stated:

> Exchanges between genetics and the criminal law are at present not very productive given the uncertain nature of the evidence. This is likely to change. We recommend that the criminal justice system should be open to new insights from disciplines that it has not necessarily considered in the past. The regular exchange of ideas in this area between researchers in behavioural genetics, criminologists and lawyers could be an effective means of ensuring that legal concepts of responsibility are assessed against current evidence from the behavioural and medical sciences. (p. 168)

A decade later, we believe this time has come and that a discussion needs to be started among biosocial criminologists to discuss the concerns raised by the Nuffield Council on Bioethics.

DNA, Science, and Ethics

If criminologists are going to take a proactive path, they must first be aware of what ethical standards currently exist and how these standards might apply to the research they are conducting. The obvious starting point of such an enquiry is the hard sciences since this is where DNA research originated. Surprisingly, there appears to be little in the way of formal guidelines for American scientists. What standards do exist are found in the Health Insurance Portability and Accountability Act (HIPAA) (P.L. 104-191) and are designed to protect privacy. In addition, a recent law, the Genetic Information Non-Discrimination Act of 2008 (GINA) (P.L. 110-233) mandates that DNA data may not be used for the purpose of health insurance or employment discrimination. Interestingly, GINA does not protect against discrimination by life, disability, and long-term care insurance companies (University of Florida IRB personal communication, 2010). However, the review of protocols and their ethical implications, by and large, are left to Institutional Review Boards (IRB) which examine research proposals on a case-by-case basis. While IRB review has gotten consistently more rigorous over time, the lack of consistency inherent in a process administered by hundreds of geographically separated independent review panels is disconcerting. As many researchers will attest, it is often possible to get a study which one IRB has rejected approved through another. Consequently, such a system cannot completely insure against ethical abuses (Emanuel et al., 2006). That said, criminologists doing genetic research, perhaps using GINA as a model, may want to put in place field-appropriate protections against the use of their data for discriminatory purposes.

Federal Bureau of Investigation

A second important set of ethical practices which must be explored are those currently being used by criminal justice practitioners. Unlike hard scientists who are primarily concerned with protecting privacy, law enforcement's top priority is identification. Therefore, a completely different approach is required; one which protects against misidentification while at the same time respecting civil liberties. The discussion of a way to balance these sometimes competing interests started in the 1980s but did not begin in earnest until the 1990s when the use of DNA became more widespread among law enforcement (Presley, 1999). In the first major report to address the issue, governmental officials made clear they were in uncharted ethical territory and were uncertain of where scientific advances would eventually lead. At one point it was even suggested that all newborns be genetically tested (see Figure 19.1). While the report outlined a variety of different ways to approach the dilemmas created by advances in DNA technology, it made no firm recommendations on how to proceed forward (Office of Technology Assessment, 1990).

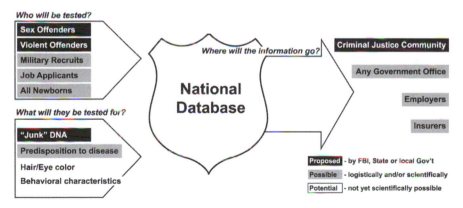

Figure 19.1 Report graphic entitled "How a DNA database could be created and used"

Source: Office of Technology Assessment, 1990, p. 130.

Instead, ethical guidelines have been developed in a hodge-podge fashion through a variety of mechanisms. Due to the varied nature of the standards that do exist, we limit our focus here to those of the FBI. For the most part, current FBI standards address two areas. The first is laboratory handling of DNA evidence. DNA, if not properly processed, can easily become contaminated (Petrovich, 1989). Thus, a set of scientifically validated protocols are essential for accurate interpretation of DNA data. Federal handling guidelines are outlined in a document entitled Quality Assurance Standards for Forensic DNA Testing Laboratories. The protocols listed are quite comprehensive and cover minimum staff qualifications, laboratory procedures, auditing, and the use of new DNA technologies (FBI, 2009). In addition, FBI laboratory technicians, like all FBI employees, are given ethics training as part of their orientation to the agency (personal communication, 2010).

The second area involves who should be required to submit their DNA into federal databases. This decision was made by Congress in legislation which states that DNA samples can be collected from "individuals who are arrested, facing charges, or convicted or from non-United States individuals under the authority of the United States" or probationers/parolees convicted of certain offenses (42 USC § 14135a 1 A). As of 2009, the FBI reported having 6.7 million individual DNA profiles and hoped to expand its collection rate to 1.2 million profiles a year by 2012 (Moore, 2009). Another act details procedures for expunging DNA records; a complicated process only made available to individuals who are not convicted of a charge or who have had their convictions overturned (42 USC § d 1 A). Curiously, this legislation is moot as to the purposes for which offender DNA data may be used.

Here again, it could be argued that law enforcement experience is of minimal relevance to a majority of criminologists. Academics working with secondary data have little input over whom DNA is collected from and the conditions under which samples are collected and analyzed. We feel this opinion is short-sighted. Without appropriate controls, the analysis of DNA data collected from vulnerable populations—the groups we, as criminologists, tend to focus many of our studies on—could be used for a multitude of purposes which some might consider questionable. If organizations collecting the data do not impose restrictions on the unethical use of data, the criminological community should have its own standards to assure against abuse.

Anthropology

Interestingly, the ethics discussion that probably most directly deals with the challenges of the academic criminologist is the one taking place in anthropology. While the archaeological discourse focuses largely on primary data collection, the "subjects" of many studies are dead and thus, like some criminal populations, lack the ability to give informed consent and have no say in how the data are used (Holm, 2001). Also similar is the fact that research findings can have broad ethical implications well beyond the research question of a particular study

(Kaestle and Horsburgh, 2002). These concerns have been addressed through the American Anthropological Association's (AAA) Code of Ethics (1998) which states a practitioner's primary responsibility is "To avoid harm or wrong, understanding that the development of knowledge can lead to change which may be positive or negative for the people or animals worked with or studied." Moreover, the code encourages researchers to maintain a dialogue with representatives of the population being studied (or the population itself if possible) to ensure it is kept informed of the potential impact of any findings. While, admittedly, the AAA only addresses DNA indirectly, anthropologists' academic journals have been more explicit with Kaestle and Horsburgh (2002, p. 108) stating in regard to DNA research: "It is necessary to have full knowledge of perceived potential hazards and the explicit recognition of many different stakeholders to move ahead with ethically sound scientifically based historical research."

It is our belief that anthropologists' concern for the impact of their research should serve as the foundation of an ethical code for working with DNA. Anthropologists are actively working to mitigate the potential risks emanating from DNA research. We believe criminologists should become involved in similar discussions.

Ethical Protocols in Criminology

Before making recommendations, it is prudent to first examine the protocols in place for criminological biosocial research. Present safeguards address two areas of the research process, use of data and informed consent of study participants. To our knowledge, at present the National Longitudinal Study of Health (Add Health) Project which was housed at the University of North Carolina's Carolina Population Center and now archived at the Interuniversity Consortium of Political and Social Science at the University of Michigan is the only ongoing study collecting genetic information at the molecular level that makes data available to the criminological community for secondary analysis. As such, we believe it is the best example of what is currently occurring in the field.

First on the issue of access, Add Health requires researchers to go through an involved application process. Although some data is available publicly, they have made permission to use sensitive data for criminological research an intentionally cumbersome process designed to assure data is accessed in a secure manner by serious academics.

The second area where safeguards are focused is on participants. Procedures used to collect Add Health data are minimally invasive involving only a buccal cell swabbing for saliva collection and a prick with a lancet for blood collection. Participants may opt to have any excess DNA placed into storage or to have it destroyed following the completion of the study. In line with restrictions placed on researchers, individuals providing DNA are assured all possible steps will be taken to protect their privacy as part of the informed consent process. In a refreshing statement of candor, however, they are warned that complete protection of their genetic data is impossible. Perhaps, the only real area of concern is the portion of the informed consent process dealing with benefits to society, as the statement is a little vague as to how research may be used. But overall, a strong set of safety and informed consent protocols have been developed which provide substantial protections for study participants (Add Health, 2009).

It appears researchers have done a good job of rising to the challenges posed by molecular genetics research when they are collecting data on humans. However, there is one troubling area these safeguards fail to address; the analysis of DNA data collected without informed consent. While university IRBs would never approve protocols involving involuntary DNA collection, recall the FBI collects data in this manner from individuals arrested for criminal activities. It may be only a matter of time before criminologists are solicited by the federal government to analyze this database. Less than a century after Nazi scientists performed unspeakable atrocities against humans in the name of science, we find ourselves once again confronted with a situation where people must involuntarily provide biological data to government officials that may ultimately lead to results that prove personally harmful. This is not to say government DNA collection procedures in any way resemble the reprehensible methods of the Nazi era and that, at times, DNA evidence cannot be helpful to defendants. However, the issue does create a dilemma as to whether academics can ethically analyze genetic data that were collected involuntarily (Cohen, 1990).

One would think such prospects would raise concern among IRBs. After all, the primary mission of IRBs is to protect the privacy and welfare of human subjects. Furthermore, IRBs have established a strict set of protocols that must be followed when collecting data from vulnerable populations, one of which is incarcerated individuals. These enhanced procedures are designed to assure that potential study participants are able to voluntarily consent to being a research subject (Levin Penslar, 1993).

Yet, it appears as if the analysis of involuntarily obtained genetic data would be perfectly permissible under current IRB protocols. Based on discussions with an IRB prisoner-research representative at a research university, researchers wishing to analyze data from the federal database could do so provided anonymity was preserved. It was also pointed out that many of those in the database would no longer be incarcerated at the time of analysis thus making them ineligible for the protections granted incarcerated populations. Moreover, this mixture of incarcerated and non-incarcerated individuals in the database would offer a further layer of protection making such an analysis even more ethically sound.

This position can lead to a structure that allows academics to circumvent informed consent. As long as some other entity does the data collection and the data are de-identified, some protections that have been decades in the making may no longer apply. The sensitive nature of conducting genetic research requires protocols that are even more stringent than those currently in place, not less. Consequently, we propose that IRBs not be regarded as the final arbiter of ethical behavior and that criminologists develop a code that goes above and beyond current IRB protocols to assure biosocial research, especially collection of genetic information, respects personal liberties.

Are Implications of Findings from Biosocial Criminological Research Being Discussed?

Criminologists are in a unique position to guide this discussion. We not only have the analytical wherewithal to discover relationships linked to delinquent behavior but also have a vibrant academic platform through which we are able to disseminate our findings. Additionally, the mainstream media normally thinks highly of our insights. In this section, we examine how effectively we are using the forums provided to us. And in the process raise the very important questions of what responsibilities do biosocial criminologists have in ensuring their research does not ultimately lead to draconian policy reactions.

Peer-Reviewed Journal Articles

Our first focus is on articles being published in the realm of biosocial criminology and specifically if and how implications are being addressed by authors in discussion sections of these articles. We constructed a sample of all articles referenced under the search terms[1] "biosocial," "DNA," "genes," "gene-environmental interaction," "heritability," or "twins" in one of the top 10 criminology journals (as measured by either five-year impact factor or citation frequency) published in the last 10 years (see Appendix A for full list of journals included). Those that included an empirical study of a biological trait interacting with a social variable were sequentially numbered (n=106). Thirty articles from this pool of articles were selected using a random sample generator. The discussion/conclusion sections of selected articles were then read by researchers to determine whether policy recommendations were discussed and how the research should be applied. Articles concluding that further interventions should be developed without defining what those interventions might possibly be were coded as not having made a policy recommendation.

Only 30 percent of the articles (nine out of 30) made a specific policy recommendation. For instance, Beaver et al.'s (2010) study of a link between language and self-control recommends:

> Overlooking the potential power that language deficits have on low self-control is particularly problematic because unrecognized language

---

1   Search terms were placed into each respective journal's search tool as provided through its online library interface.

> impairments cannot be targeted by intervention programs. When language-
> impaired children do not receive assistance for these deficits, their behavior
> can become even worse. (p. 960)

In sum, no discernable pattern was observed with articles making or not making
recommendations being spread evenly across all journals. Criminologists, at least
when publishing in the criminology and criminal justice journals, tend to take a
very conservative approach to how their work should be applied. While a degree of
caution is admirable, the negative policy implications that can potentially emanate
from researchers not advising how findings from their research should be used
is concerning. Even if criminologists do address these issues in their published
papers, we still realize practitioners and policy-makers have minds and agendas of
their own that can lead to various interpretations of the research findings.

The Media

Researchers have tended to be more policy oriented in the popular media. Although
many studies on the interplay between genes and environment are not picked up,
an article by Beaver et al. (2010)[2] linking the MAO-A gene to gang membership
recently received extensive coverage including write ups in the online version of
Time (Kingsbury, 2009), postings on the ABC (Callaway, 2009) and MSNBC (2009)
websites, and most recently, on National Geographic Television. The original study
concluded that males who possess a low MAO-A activity allele are more likely to
join a gang and once in are more likely to use weapons in fights. The absence of
a policy relevant discussion in the article was likely due to a multitude of factors,
some of which were likely beyond the control of the authors, but when given an
opportunity to discuss his work with *Time*, Beaver emphatically stated:

> money would be better spent not hunting for gene-based drugs ... but [on]
> expanding and improving neighborhood-based intervention programs, such
> as early childhood education and after-school activities. (Kingsbury, 2009,
> online)

He went on to elaborate to the ABC reporter that "It doesn't mean everyone with
this particular allele is going to be violent and is going to join a gang" (Callaway,
2009). Despite Beaver's emphasis on the nature/nurture nexus, the point was lost
in shorter pieces where Beaver wasn't interviewed. For example, a five-sentence
story that ran on the UPI (2009) wire made no reference to Beaver's comments
about the mitigating role played by environment, only mentioning that a link had
been found between a warrior gene and the propensity for gang activity. Thus, as

---

2   The media responded to the article in 2009 due to the fact *Comprehensive Psychiatry*
     posted the article online prior to its formal publication in 2010.

politicians know, care must be taken to control the message whenever possible. The fact authors rarely include (or aren't allowed to include) real world policy implications in their publications leaves such interpretations to the media which, in many instances, may miss the nuanced findings of many academic studies and reach policy conclusion that fail to take all information into account.

While it is easy to bash the media for lack of clarity on the issue, researchers share some of the blame too. Even though they appear to have many policy ideas in the abstract—at least in the popular press—their reaction to the use of a defendant's DNA profile as the basis to shorten a prison sentence by an Italian judge (the first example of bringing modern-era genetic theory into practice) was anything but authoritative. For instance, in a *London Times* (Ahuja, 2009) article on the ruling, researcher Terrie Moffitt, although making a number of suggestions, did not directly address the policy issues raised in the case. She stated she would not be drawn into the discussion she believed was "legal rather than scientific" (p. 9). We sympathize with academics like Moffitt because taking a firm public position on policy implications can easily turn into a no-win situation. However, when researchers' results are disseminated into the public realm and are being used in practice to make real life decisions they should discuss if and how findings from their research should be used and what the specific limitations are when applying findings to any specific case.

Next Steps: Considering Ethical Standards

The challenges involved with doing biosocial research are indeed daunting, especially when it involves primary data collection efforts to collect genetic information at the molecular level. Despite challenges, we believe biosocial criminology is here to stay and will reshape what we know about antisocial and violent behaviors for decades to come. It is no more possible to return to pre-biosocial times than it would be to go back to days of the typewriter. We believe it is time for the field to have discussions about the most ethical ways of collecting data and reporting research. Criminology and criminal justice biosocial research has come of age and it now needs ethical guidelines that reflect its grown-up status. Importantly, such guidelines can serve to quell the outcry from those in the discipline and society who fear the outcomes of biosocial research.

While the goal of this chapter is not to create an entire code of ethics for biosocial criminology, we would like to propose the beginnings of an outline to be considered by biosocial researchers. Based on the information we have presented, we believe three areas can be addressed. In the sections below, we put forth three areas that include doing no harm, the role of the researcher, and informed consent. We believe these areas can be included in the initial conversations and we suggest how these items might be best approached.

1. Do No Harm

Modern medicine is built on Hippocrates' (approx 400 BC [2004]) premise that a physician's first responsibility is to never do harm. Even though a substantial amount of anthropology DNA research involves deceased populations, the discipline found the potential of such research to injure the living was great enough that it incorporated this notion into its Code of Ethics (American Anthropological Association, 1998). We feel that criminologists can do the same.

Regardless of the many good intentions that are among us who conduct biosocial research and the safeguards that are in place, biosocial research still has the potential to do harm if interpreted by practitioners and politicians in ways that we did not originally intend. We as researchers may contend that a gene X environment interaction explanation of violent and other offending behaviors is still a call for prevention and enrichment programs that are social and developmentally based, yet the same results could easily be interpreted and used by others to justify the involuntary removal of individuals with specific gene variants associated with risk from environments deemed unsuitable. Thus, we have an obligation to state what is appropriate and inappropriate use of our research. We should also be active in educating the public on the misuses of biological based research on human behavior in the past while proactively trying to assure that history doesn't repeat itself. If academic journals are unwilling to allow these statements of opinion, researchers should seek out more popular mediums where the title "professor" all but guarantees a forum. We are not saying such activities are an assurance that research will not be misused. However, it does provide a mechanism for researchers to have an active role in the policy discussions; something we assert is vital.

2. Redefining the Role of the Researcher

Closely related to the obligation of minimizing harm is a redefinition of the role of a researcher. It is unfair to advocate for researchers to become more active in the policy arena without acknowledging the fact the academic infrastructure rarely rewards such activities. Tenure and promotion decisions are normally based on scholarly publications, not work for general public consumption. At the very least, editors of academic journals should request that policy related implications be discussed in more detail. Perhaps this could be done in an appropriately labeled subsection (we favor the term "Implications for Practice") of the conclusion/ discussion sections of articles.

We believe a better approach would be for research institutions to include efforts that take academic research from theory to practice in tenure/promotion decisions. Peer-reviewed research is important, but to place such a high value on this forum has the intended consequence of imprisoning researchers inside the Ivory Tower. When the moral and policy implications of research are so vast, we argue such a situation is untenable.

3. Informed Consent

The final area we would like to see ethics discussed is informed consent. Here we urge academics to take a strong stand to never make use of data collected without the informed consent of participants. The fact that such information can be obtained legally and that such an analysis could secure IRB approval is, we believe, irrelevant. We again point out that research done in German concentration camps would have met the same standards had an IRB process been in existence at that time. While data are now only being taken from the incarcerated, a population many feel has no right to object, this could be the beginning of a process that has the potential to snowball. A scenario where forceful data collection could be expanded to a substantially larger group of individuals is not inconceivable. We strongly believe criminologists should be the first line of defense against such an outcome and urge them to adopt a set of informed consent protocols that go beyond current legal and IRB safeguards. As transplant physicians have been able to use their active involvement in the research process to thwart efforts to create a market for organs, we feel stringent informed consent protocols give criminologists a valuable opportunity to protect individual liberties.

Conclusion

In writing this chapter, our goal has been to bring to the forefront the ethical complexities involved with the criminological pursuit of biosocial research. Biosocial researchers, including the authors of the current chapter, have probably been so involved in defending their right to this type of research, it is unlikely that they get to devote lengthy periods of time to seriously think about where biosocial research will ultimately lead society. We have written this chapter with the hope of changing that dynamic. While we would not be so presumptuous to assume our thoughts are the last words on the subject, we hope this chapter serves as impetus to start a dialogue. Biosocial research shows amazing promise to advance knowledge and prevent crime, but also, as has been shown in the past, has a great potential for abuse. A code of ethics would go a long way to reducing the possibility of the later outcome. Our hope is that this work serves as a first step in that process.

References

Add Health (2009). *Add Health Wave IV data collection: Wave IV data documentation.* Chapel Hill, NC: University of North Carolina.

Ahuja, Anjana (2009, November 17). The get out of jail free gene: The sentence of one killer in Italy has been reduced as he possesses a "violent gene". Could

DNA profiles be used as a defense in criminal courts in the future? *Times*, Section T2, pp. 8–9.

American Anthropological Association (1998, June). Code of ethics, retrieved from www.aaanet.org/committees/ethics/ethcode.htm.

Beaver, K. (2009). *Biosocial criminology: A primer*. Dubuque, IA: Kendal Hunt.

Beaver, K., DeLisi, M., Vaughn, M., & Barnes, J. (2010). Monoamine oxidase: A genotype is associated with gang membership and weapon use. *Comprehensive Psychiatry*, 51, 130–134.

Beaver, K., DeLisi, M., Vaughn, M., Wright, J., & Boutwell, B. (2008). The relationship between self-control and language: Evidence of a shared etiological pathway. *Criminology*, 46, 939–964.

Beaver, K., Gibson, C., Turner, M., DeLisi, M., Vaughn, M., & Holand, A. (2009) Stability of delinquent peer associations: A biosocial test of Warr's sticky-friends hypothesis. *Crime and Delinquency*, published online, 1-21.

Belsky, J. & Beaver, K. (2010). Cumulative-genetic plasticity, parenting and adolscent self-regulation. *Journal of Child Psychiatry and Psychology*. Online first.

Bradley Haggerty, B. (Producer) (2010, July 1). Can genes make you murder [Audio Podcast]. *Morning edition*, retrieved from www.npr.org/templates/story/story.php?storyId=128043329.

Caspi, A., McClay, J., Moffitt, T., Mill, J., Martin, J., Craig, I., Taylor, A., & Poulton, R. (2002). Evidence that the cycle of violence in maltreated children depends on genotype. *Science*, 297, 851–854.

Callaway, E. (2009, June 21). Gangsta gene identified in US teens. ABC News, retrieved from http://abcnews.go.com/Technology/story?id=7884397&page=1.

Cohen, B. (1990). The ethics of using medical data from Nazi experiments. *Journal of Halacha and Contemporary Society*, 19, 103–126.

Cold Spring Harbor Laboratory (2011). Eugenics archive, retrieved from www.eugenicsarchive.org/eugenics.

Darwin, Charles. (1871). *The descent of man*. London: John Murray.

Emanuel, E., Lemmons, T., & Elliott, C. (2006). Should society allow ethics boards to be run as for-profit enterprises? *PLOS Medicine*, 3, 941–944.

Federal Bureau of Investigation (2009). *Quality assurance standards for forensic DNA testing laboratories*. Washington, DC: Federal Bureau of Investigation.

Feresin, E. (2009). Lighter sentence for murderer with bad genes. *Nature*, retrieved from www.nature.com/news/2009/091030/full/news.2009.1050.html?s=news_rss.

Gould, S.J. (1996). *The mismeasure of man*. New York: W.W. Norton and Company, Inc.

Graham, W. (2008, May–June). The "Yin and Yang" of UNOS. *UNOS Update*, 4–5.

Hippocrates (2004). *Of the epidemics* (Francis Adams, Trans). Whitefish, MT: Kessinger Publishing.

Holm, S. (2001). The privacy of Tutankhamen—utilizing the genetic information in stored tissue samples. *Theoretical Medicine and Bioethics*, 22, 437–449.

Kaestle, F. & Horsburgh, K. (2002). Ancient DNA in anthropology: Applications and ethics. *Yearbook of Physical Anthropology*, 45, 92–130.

Kingsbury, K. (2009, June 10). Which kids join gangs? A genetic explanation. *Time*, retrieved from www.time.com/time/health/article/0,8599,1903703.

Levin Penslar, R. (1993). Office for Human Research Protections: IRB Guidebook, retrieved from www.hhs.gov/ohrp/irb/irb_guidebook.htm.

Levitt, M. & Manson, N. (2007). My genes made me do it? The implications of behavioural genetics for responsibility and blame. *Health Care Analysis*, 15, 33–40.

Mason, D.A. & Frick, P.J. (1994). The heritability of antisocial behavior: A meta analysis of twin and adoption studies. *Journal of Psychopathology and Behavioral Assessment*, 16, 301–323.

Miles, D.R. & Carey, G. (1997). Genetic and environmental architecture of human aggression. *Journal of Personality and Social Psychology*, 72, 207–217.

Moore, S. (2009, April 18). FBI and states vastly expand DNA database. *New York Times*, p. A1.

Mrydal, G. (1944). *An American dilemma: The Negro problem and modern democracy*. New York: Harper Brothers.

MSNBC (2009, June 5). Boys with warrior gene likely to join gang: Aggressive trait also linked to violence, weapon use, new study finds. MSNBC, retrieved from www.msnbc.msn.com/id/31128684/ns/health-kids_and_parenting.

Nuffield Council on Bioethics (2002). *Genetics and human behaviour: The ethical context*. London: Nuffield Council on Bioethics.

Office of Technology Assessment (1990). *Genetic witness: Forensic uses of DNA tests*. Washington, DC: US Government Printing Office.

Petrovich, S. (1989). DNA typing: A rush to judgment. *Georgia Law Review*, 24, 669–704.

Presley, L. (1999, September). The evolution of quality standards for forensic DNA analysis in the United States. *Profiles in DNA*, 10–11.

Raine, A. (1993). *The psychopathology of crime: Criminal behavior as a clinical disorder*. San Diego, CA: Academic Press.

Rhee, S.H. & Waldman, I.D. (2002). Genetic and environmental influences on antisocial behavior: A meta-analysis of twin and adoption studies. *Psychological Bulletin*, 128, 490–529.

Rose, N. (2000). The biology of culpability: Pathological identity and crime control in a biological culture. *Theoretical Criminology*, 14, 5–34.

Rubenstein, A. (2007). *On the body and transplantation: Philosophical and legal context*. Washington, DC: President's Council on Bioethics, unpublished work.

Rust, J. & Golombok, S. (1999). *Modern psychometrics: The science of psychological assessment* (2nd ed.). New York: Routledge.

Segal, G. & Bonnie, R. (2005). Reflections on fairness of unos allocation policies. *American Journal of Bioethics*, 5, 28–29.

Solomon, S. (2009, April 19). FBI and states vastly expand DNA databases. *New York Times*, p. A1.

Troug, R. (2005). The ethics of organ donation by living donors. *New England Journal of Medicine*, 353, 444–446.

United Network for Organ Sharing (UNOS) (2011). History. Retrieved from www.unos.org/donation/index.php?topic=history.

UPI (2009, June 5). Warrior gene linked to weapon use. UPI, retrieved from www.upi.com/Science_News/2009/06/05/Warrior-gene-linked-to-weapon-use/UPI-72041244231042.

Zink, S., Wertlieb, S., Catalano, J., & Marwin, V. (2005). Examining the potential exploitation of UNOs policies. *American Journal of Bioethics*, 5, 6–15.

Appendix A

Journals included in sample:
Aggression and Violent Behavior
British Journal of Crime and Delinquency
Crime and Delinquency
Crime and Justice
Criminal Justice and Behavior
Criminology
Journal of Criminal Law and Criminology
Journal of Interpersonal Violence
Journal of Quantitative Criminology
Journal of Research in Crime and Delinquency
Justice Quarterly
Sexual Abuse
Theoretical Criminology

Index